# BARRON'S

# SAT* SUBJECT TEST

# U.S. HISTORY

**Kenneth R. Senter, B.A., M.S.**

Oak Ridge High School
Oak Ridge, Tennessee

# BARRON'S

*SAT is a registered trademark of the College Board, which was not involved in the production of, and does not endorse this product.

## ABOUT THE AUTHOR

Kenneth Senter has been a high school teacher for over twenty years and presently teaches AP U.S. history and AP world history courses to sophomores and juniors at Oak Ridge High School in Oak Ridge, Tennessee. He has been both an AP reader and a teacher-training consultant for the College Board. He is now a coach for the ORHS academic quiz bowl team that recently won three regional championships in a row. He is also the founder and vice president of the WTC Steel Foundation, a non-profit organization dedicated to using education to address the root causes of international terrorism.

## ACKNOWLEDGMENTS

The author wishes to thank Bob O'Sullivan and Kristen Girardi for their patient and supportive guidance in bettering this test preparation manual, along with their team of evaluators, copy editors, artists, and marketing staff. Also, the ORHS Social Studies Department Coordinator emeritus, Cassandra Osborne, deserves thanks for urging the project on and for leading by example. ORHS librarians Henri Zolyniak and Sarah Hamilton never failed to provide reliable source material, and the history students in my classes never ceased to challenge me to learn more and to teach more. Finally, my wife, Sarah, and my three children have endured much and encouraged me the most. I am ever grateful.

*All inquiries should be addressed to:*
Barron's Educational Series, Inc.
250 Wireless Boulevard
Hauppauge, New York 11788
**www.barronseduc.com**

ISBN: 978-0-7641-4604-6 (Book)
ISBN: 978-1-4380-7060-5 (Book/CD-ROM Package)

Library of Congress Control Number: 2012930886

PRINTED IN THE UNITED STATES OF AMERICA

9 8 7 6 5 4 3 2

**10%**
**POST-CONSUMER WASTE**
Paper contains a minimum of 10% post-consumer waste (PCW). Paper used in this book was derived from certified, sustainable forestlands.

# Contents

# Preface

Congratulations! You have purchased this book because you want to achieve the best possible score you can on the SAT Subject Test in U.S History. This book presents you with the top twenty items you need to know from each era of history in order to do well on this exam. Barron's has done the work for you in selecting the most important material to review and presenting it to you in easily digestible, bite-sized chunks.

Whether you have only a couple of weeks to study for the exam or a couple of months, this book will provide you with a study plan that is best for you. The contents of this book have been carefully selected and organized in order to provide you with the most comprehensive and effective study guide currently available.

This book has everything you need to score higher on the SAT Subject Test in U.S. History! Read the Introduction and familiarize yourself with the test format, content, and question types so there are no surprises on test day. A Diagnostic Test is provided so you can pinpoint your weaknesses, further maximizing the efficiency of your study time. Reinforce what you have learned by taking the mini quizzes that appear after every five content chapters. Three additional practice tests are included to give you more test-taking practice and further insight into what you still need to review.

You will find that when you use this book to its fullest potential, you will have discovered the most fine-tuned study materials available to maximize your score on the SAT Subject Test in U.S. History.

# CHAPTER 1

# Welcome to the SAT Subject Test in U.S. History

*Do what you can, with what you have, where you are.*

—Theodore Roosevelt

President Roosevelt offered good advice for your situation as you face taking the SAT Subject Test in U.S. History. You've picked up this book because you face a momentous challenge. You must show college entrance and scholarship officials how much U.S. history you know in only one hour by taking a difficult multiple-choice test with ninety to ninety-five questions. The timed nature of this exam means you will have to answer each question in an average time of as little as thirty-eight seconds! Plus, you might not have taken a U.S. history course in over a year. This book is the solution to help you succeed on this difficult exam.

## Test Registration

The key to doing "what you can, with what you have" in this challenge is time. The test is offered monthly from October to January and once in both May and June. Visit the College Board website to see the dates when the exam is administered. You will need to determine how long you have to study before your scheduled exam. Whether you have six months or only two weeks to prepare for the test, this book is designed to make the most of your review efforts. Be honest with yourself about how much time you will devote to studying for this exam, and then pick the test date that will allow you that amount of time.

---

### Where to Register for the SAT Subject Tests

- Visit *www.collegeboard.com*
- Call toll-free domestic: 1-866-756-7346; foreign: 212-713-7789
- See your guidance counselor
- Write to: The College Board SAT Program
  P.O. Box 025505,
  Miami, FL 33102

---

To register, visit the College Board's website, call their toll-free number, or see your guidance counselor. You can also write to the College Board SAT program for information on how to register.

# How to Use This Book

Within this book you'll find several tools that will help you review the history of the United States. You will also find valuable information on the format of the test so that you will be prepared and confident on test day. The time you have available to prepare for the exam will determine how you use these tools. Following this chapter you will find a Diagnostic Test to help you determine where you are now. If you have limited time before the actual test, focus your study by taking this diagnostic test and reading the answer explanation for each question, even the ones you answered correctly. The Diagnostic Test will reveal the aspects of U.S. history that you will need to review the most. The simplest and quickest way to locate this material is to look up key words from the questions you missed in the book's index. After reviewing this material, take another practice exam to see how much you have improved and to determine what areas you might still need to review. Last, read "The Big Pictures" that are located at the end of each chapter. This approach is recommended if you have come across this book with only a week or two to prepare before taking the test.

If you have a few weeks or a month to prepare for the exam, start by taking the Diagnostic Test and reading the answer explanations for each question. Next, note that each chapter in this book contains a timeline and a section entitled "The Top 20 Things to Know." These items have been carefully selected to represent the mainstream people, events, and ideas that are the most significant in U.S. history. Take the time to read and study these items from each chapter to give you a basic review of the critical content covered on the SAT subject test. Drill yourself by taking the mini quizzes that appear between every five chapters. Take the remaining practice exams, each time reading the answer explanations for every question. You will see your score climb with each practice test you take, and by then you will have done nearly all you can with what time you have before the actual exam. Just before you take the actual test, read "The Big Picture" from each chapter to provide the analytical overview you will need to work quickly and efficiently in the one hour you will have to prove yourself.

If you are fortunate enough to have several months to prepare for the exam, and especially if you haven't taken a good survey course in U.S. history recently or at all, you are encouraged to read this book alongside a reliable college-level U.S. history textbook. The Diagnostic Test might even prove discouraging in this case, so you can save it for use as a regular practice exam later. Take several practice exams after reading as much of this book as possible in the time you have to prepare. Use the answer explanations to understand why you missed each question you got wrong. Look up items you missed in your history textbook and continue to review them in greater depth. Your history textbook will contain a narrative account of U.S. history that is beyond the scope of a review text, and it will be your best bet for understanding any particular information that continues to elude you after exhausting this book. An error journal can also be of use after taking each practice exam. Find out why you got each wrong answer, and then write down in a notebook the key fact, or facts, you need to remember. Of course, you may find that many of your wrong answers occurred because you misread a question while hurrying to answer it in thirty-eight seconds! This problem is normal on a timed exam and will diminish as you continue reviewing and practicing.

You can, of course, combine these approaches using the tools provided in this book to tailor a review strategy that is best for you. You are strongly encouraged to actively combine the content review in this book with the taking of and reflection on at least two practice tests.

---

### Three Approaches for Three Review Paces

**One or Two Weeks to Prepare**
- ✔ Take the Diagnostic Test.
- ✔ Read all the answer explanations.
- ✔ Use the results of the Diagnostic Test to pinpoint the material you most need to review.
- ✔ Find the material you need to review by looking up the key topics in the index.
- ✔ Review this material.
- ✔ Take one of the practice tests at the end of the book to see how much you improved and what areas you may still need to review.
- ✔ Last, read "The Big Picture" located at the end of each chapter.

**One Month to Prepare**
- ✔ Take the Diagnostic Test.
- ✔ Read all the answer explanations.
- ✔ Read and study all Timelines and "The Top 20 Things to Know."
- ✔ Take each Mini Quiz.
- ✔ Take the remaining practice exams and read all the answer explanations.
- ✔ Before taking the actual test, brush up by reading "The Big Picture" at the end of each chapter.

**Several Months to Prepare**
- ✔ Read this book along with a reliable college-level U.S. history textbook.
- ✔ Save the Diagnostic Test to be used as one of your regular practice exams.
- ✔ After reading as much of this book as possible, take the practice exams.
- ✔ Use the answer explanations to understand why you missed each question you answered incorrectly.
- ✔ Look up the items you missed in your history textbook and continue to review them in greater depth.
- ✔ Keep an error journal of your results of each practice exam. Include in the journal key facts you need to remember.

# Introduction to the Test

Colleges that require or recommend that you take SAT subject tests use the scores to make admissions and sometimes placement decisions. You are often asked to take three tests, and the U.S. history test is a good indicator of your mastery of material in a typical humanities course. You may take the SAT subject test in U.S. History more than once to improve your score, but this book is designed to give you a strong possibility of success on the first try. If you do very well, your score on this test could make a difference in your admission process or allow you to skip an introductory survey course in U.S. history.

Two key points about the SAT Subject Test in U.S. History are that the questions increase in difficulty as the test progresses from beginning to end, and that the test is designed to discourage random guessing. Both of these points have strategy implications that are discussed later in this chapter, but you should be aware of them from the beginning. Not all questions are as difficult as they might seem, and many in the beginning deserve only a fraction of the thirty-eight seconds you have per question. As for guessing, the test is scored in such a way that random guessing is a bad idea. You are awarded one point for each correct answer but penalized a quarter point for each wrong answer. Answers left blank neither gain nor lose points.

Again, you must have a strategy for dealing with various questions under these circumstances, and that strategy is discussed below. Your goal in working with this book is to know what you will face going into the test and preparing accordingly so you will be in control of the test and achieve your maximum potential. Your goal on the test is to score as high up on the 800-point scale as possible. The College Board will convert your raw score to a traditional 800-point scale based on the difficulty level of the particular test you take. The difficulty of any given SAT subject test is determined by comparing it to previous tests and by reflecting on the performance of all students who took those tests. All of these factors and more are taken into account as the scoring scale is set. Great care is taken to make the SAT Subject Test in U.S. History a fair assessment of your mastery of the history of the United States.

## Types of History on the Exam

A handy acrostic using the word *spice* will help you remember what types of history "spice up" the U.S. history covered on the exam. Social, political (including domestic and foreign policy), intellectual (including art), cultural (including religion), and economic history are covered on the test. These types of history are apportioned among the ninety to ninety-five questions on the test according to the table below. All of these topics incorporate broad social science concepts, generalizations, and approaches common to any history or social studies course.

**TIP**

Make only educated guesses! You are penalized for random guessing by having a quarter of a point deducted for each wrong answer.

**TIP**

**Types of History**
- **S**ocial history
- **P**olitical history
- **I**ntellectual history
- **C**ultural history
- **E**conomic history

| Type of History | Approximate Percentage of Test Coverage |
|---|---|
| Social history | 20–24% |
| Political history (with domestic and foreign policy) | 44–52% |
| Intellectual history (with art) | 6–8% |
| Cultural history (with religion) | 6–8% |
| Economic history | 13–17% |

## Types of Questions on the Exam

The questions on the SAT subject test are of several types as well as varying levels of difficulty. The simplest questions require you merely to recall basic facts and to be familiar with several terms and concepts fundamental to the study of U.S. history. You will therefore have to be readily familiar with many important aspects of U.S. history that are contained in the content reviews and practice tests in this book. With the more difficult questions, you will be asked to analyze and interpret lists of information; visuals like graphs, charts, paintings, political cartoons, photographs, and maps; as well as quotes from historical figures, documents, or literature. The most difficult types of questions require you to relate concepts and ideas to data supplied in the question and to evaluate that data for a particular interpretive purpose. You will have to judge what evidence supplied in the question is logically consistent with the concept being tested. You will often have to compare and contrast answer choices according to certain criteria when more than one answer seems to be correct. The only way to excel at answering questions of this type correctly is to review the content of this book thoroughly and to practice, practice, practice. The numbers in the box below correspond to questions from the Diagnostic Test that represent these styles of questioning.

| Type | Description of Task | Diagnostic Test Example |
|---|---|---|
| 1 | Recall facts, terms, ideas, and generalizations | Question 9 |
| 2 | Analyze or interpret information | Question 32 |
| 3 | Relate concepts to given data | Question 44 |
| 4 | Evaluate data for a specified purpose | Question 54 |
| Turn to the Diagnostic Test now to review these examples. | | |

One other organizational component of the SAT Subject Test in U.S. History should be mentioned. Three periods of the history of the United States receive coverage on the test according to the chart below.

| **Periods Covered** | |
|---|---|
| Pre-Columbian history to 1789 (the U.S. Constitution was ratified) | 20% |
| 1790 to 1898 (the Spanish-American War launched imperialism) | 40% |
| 1899 to the present (updated with each new edition of this book) | 40% |

The SAT subject test is created by college professors and high school teachers with the goal of reflecting what is actually taught in U.S. history survey courses. There is no one textbook to which the exam is tied, and the College Board uses surveys to gather information about what college professors are actually teaching. Because the results of these surveys are confidential proprietary information, there is no way to guess what will actually be covered on any given test. The parameters above are set by the College Board, so within these guidelines your best hope of being prepared is to review all of U.S. history according to the proportions above. Trends in the emphasis of history courses change; a comprehensive review is the only way to become adequately prepared.

## Multiple-Choice Strategies

Finally, before taking the Diagnostic Test, a look at strategies for successfully navigating through the topics, different difficulty levels, and different types of questions is in order. There are also general test-taking principles for taking the SAT Subject Test in U.S. History as there are for any rigorous college entrance exam. Because this exam consists only of multiple-choice questions, you will have to become proficient at answering sophisticated analytical questions as well as recalling information. You will not have an opportunity to balance your score on the multiple-choice section with your writing talent on essays.

Strategies for answering multiple-choice questions vary with the difficulty of the questions. Identification-level questions can be answered quickly and easily if you know the key data point or points, but you should still read all of the answer choices to be sure of your answer. However, most questions on the SAT Subject Test in U.S. History require more than factual recall. You will also have to demonstrate skill in recognizing categories of information, analyzing data, evaluating fine differences, understanding generalizations, and synthesizing various ideas into a larger whole. Just being aware of the use of these sophisticated social studies thinking skills on the test will make them less of a shock.

The College Board and its affiliates carefully increase the difficulty of questions by altering the options given as answer choices. They even have a special name for the wrong answers: *distracters*. Unsuspecting students will fall prey to distracters consisting of common misconceptions about U.S. history, statements that are true but irrelevant to the question at hand, statements that are either too broad or too narrow for a given question, or answers that merely sound plausible.

Furthermore, you can be rolling along answering questions rapidly and be caught by the infamous "EXCEPT" questions. The exam will have this word or a word like "NOT" in boldface print; you will have to consciously break yourself from the habit of looking for the correct answer and instead select the answer choice that is wrong. If you hurry through these questions, your instincts will simply seize on choice A, which will usually be true and correct. You have then missed the question out of habit, and it will be because you failed to read all of the answer choices.

Your fundamental strategy, therefore, is to read each question thoroughly *and* all of the answer choices knowing that each word in a question on a test of this sophistication was chosen extremely carefully and field tested. The authors of the test use words with specific, precise meanings, and the words mean exactly what the authors intend. You must unlock those meanings and pay close attention to what the question is asking. You have to choose the answer that fulfills all, not just some, of the requirements of the phrase in the question stem. Many possible answers are specifically designed to distract you by giving you that little "Aha!" feeling when your mind grabs information you recognize as being associated with the question stem. You might miss the question by not reading the rest of the distracters and therefore not finding the correct answer that will fully satisfy the logic of the question stem.

The matter of guessing deserves special attention on a test like the SAT Subject Test in U.S. History. With the scoring system described earlier in the chapter taking off a quarter of a point for every wrong answer, random guessing is dangerous. Anything but educated guesses are ill-advised. An educated guess on a multiple-choice test occurs only after you have eliminated entirely implausible options that you immediately recognized as incorrect. Because the questions on the SAT subject test give five possible answers, you will then be down to three or four. You must then intelligently consider information you do know about the era in history being discussed in the question.

As you try to eliminate other wrong answers, reflect on the political, economic, and social conditions within the era to rule out one or two more distracters.

No points will be taken off for skipped questions. Just be sure that you leave those numbers blank on your answer sheet! The easiest way to ruin your hope of success is to turn in an answer sheet filled with correct answers slightly shifted from their correct spaces on the answer sheet. Also, don't skip more than five or six questions, maximum. Do not allow the fear of guessing wrong to make you leave many of the ninety to ninety-five questions blank. Besides, with thorough review and practice using this book, you should be making confident answers with the need for only a few educated guesses!

**TIP**

Be on the lookout! Watch out for questions with "EXCEPT" or "NOT" in boldface. You must find the wrong answer choice to get the right answer.

**TIP**

Guess on a question only if you can narrow the five answer choices down to three, or preferably two, possible answers. If you cannot make this educated guess, leave the question blank.

# Test-Taking Strategies

There are several principles to follow that are not specific to the SAT Subject Test in U.S. History but nonetheless apply. You have already read about the need to read the stem of each question carefully and also to read each answer choice. Having taken two or more timed practice tests you should be able to pace yourself and, as you watch the clock, know what progress you should make as the hour advances. Here are other tips to keep in mind as you take this type of test:

1. Use your test booklet for writing notes or making marks at questions you skip. Your answer sheet must be kept neat and free from stray marks.

2. Check every so often to make sure you are putting your answers in the right spot on your answer sheet in order to avoid the fatal misalignment error.

3. Watch the clock in the room or your own wristwatch (cell phones will not be allowed even for timekeeping).

4. Pace yourself steadily. Remember that the harder questions begin somewhere midway through the test and will require more time than recall questions.

5. Never worry about the sequence of the letters you bubble on your answer sheet. Tests can have several of the same letter in a row, and no pattern is ever allowed to exist in the correct answers.

6. Once you have answered the last question in your first attempt, check the time and go back to attempt to answer questions you skipped.

7. Remember to make only educated guesses.

8. When you are certain of the questions you intend to leave blank, if any, check the answers you put down for the other questions.

9. Be careful about changing answers. Unless you are certain a previous answer is wrong, leave your first answer. People often change correct answers to incorrect answers. If you do change an answer, erase the old one completely.

10. Relax and congratulate yourself when the time is up. You can be proud that you have done what you could, with what you had, where you were.

# Final Advice

Regardless of how long you will study before you take the SAT Subject Test in U.S. History, the night before the exam will eventually come. You must spend the next twelve hours carefully in order to perform your best the next day. Yes, a last review is a good idea. Take one more practice test and review the answer explanations, or quickly read through all "The Big Pictures" at the end of each chapter. If you start early in the afternoon, maybe you can do both of these steps. However, you must stop this final review and be sure to sleep seven to eight hours in order to have a clear head during the test. After sleeping, the next most important step is a good breakfast. Do not try to take a test of this magnitude on an empty stomach even if you normally skip breakfast before school. Your breakfast should include protein to last the long haul as well as plenty of fluids to keep yourself hydrated.

Much of the effort you've spent reviewing U.S. history with this book can go to waste if you don't take care of your basic physical needs of rest, food, and fluids. The College Board allows you to take a snack to the testing site, and a bottle of water is also a good idea. Some hard peppermint candy can perk you up in the middle of the test as long as you unwrap the candy before testing begins. Arrive twenty to thirty minutes early at the testing site so you don't add to the stress of test day by getting lost or arriving at the last minute. There is nothing wrong with having this book with you to fill that time with a last look at history if it will help you feel like you have given this challenge all your effort. Then put this book away, relax, and listen carefully to all of the test proctor's instructions.

President Theodore Roosevelt had one more bit of advice that applies to you before you begin the Diagnostic Test and your subsequent review. He said, "Far and away the best prize that life has to offer is the chance to work hard at work worth doing." Reviewing for the SAT Subject Test in U.S. History will be hard work. Like the many other tasks you've taken on to prepare for the next stage of your education and life, this task is worth doing.

# Answer Sheet

## DIAGNOSTIC TEST

1 Ⓐ Ⓑ Ⓒ Ⓓ Ⓔ  24 Ⓐ Ⓑ Ⓒ Ⓓ Ⓔ  47 Ⓐ Ⓑ Ⓒ Ⓓ Ⓔ  70 Ⓐ Ⓑ Ⓒ Ⓓ Ⓔ
2 Ⓐ Ⓑ Ⓒ Ⓓ Ⓔ  25 Ⓐ Ⓑ Ⓒ Ⓓ Ⓔ  48 Ⓐ Ⓑ Ⓒ Ⓓ Ⓔ  71 Ⓐ Ⓑ Ⓒ Ⓓ Ⓔ
3 Ⓐ Ⓑ Ⓒ Ⓓ Ⓔ  26 Ⓐ Ⓑ Ⓒ Ⓓ Ⓔ  49 Ⓐ Ⓑ Ⓒ Ⓓ Ⓔ  72 Ⓐ Ⓑ Ⓒ Ⓓ Ⓔ
4 Ⓐ Ⓑ Ⓒ Ⓓ Ⓔ  27 Ⓐ Ⓑ Ⓒ Ⓓ Ⓔ  50 Ⓐ Ⓑ Ⓒ Ⓓ Ⓔ  73 Ⓐ Ⓑ Ⓒ Ⓓ Ⓔ
5 Ⓐ Ⓑ Ⓒ Ⓓ Ⓔ  28 Ⓐ Ⓑ Ⓒ Ⓓ Ⓔ  51 Ⓐ Ⓑ Ⓒ Ⓓ Ⓔ  74 Ⓐ Ⓑ Ⓒ Ⓓ Ⓔ
6 Ⓐ Ⓑ Ⓒ Ⓓ Ⓔ  29 Ⓐ Ⓑ Ⓒ Ⓓ Ⓔ  52 Ⓐ Ⓑ Ⓒ Ⓓ Ⓔ  75 Ⓐ Ⓑ Ⓒ Ⓓ Ⓔ
7 Ⓐ Ⓑ Ⓒ Ⓓ Ⓔ  30 Ⓐ Ⓑ Ⓒ Ⓓ Ⓔ  53 Ⓐ Ⓑ Ⓒ Ⓓ Ⓔ  76 Ⓐ Ⓑ Ⓒ Ⓓ Ⓔ
8 Ⓐ Ⓑ Ⓒ Ⓓ Ⓔ  31 Ⓐ Ⓑ Ⓒ Ⓓ Ⓔ  54 Ⓐ Ⓑ Ⓒ Ⓓ Ⓔ  77 Ⓐ Ⓑ Ⓒ Ⓓ Ⓔ
9 Ⓐ Ⓑ Ⓒ Ⓓ Ⓔ  32 Ⓐ Ⓑ Ⓒ Ⓓ Ⓔ  55 Ⓐ Ⓑ Ⓒ Ⓓ Ⓔ  78 Ⓐ Ⓑ Ⓒ Ⓓ Ⓔ
10 Ⓐ Ⓑ Ⓒ Ⓓ Ⓔ  33 Ⓐ Ⓑ Ⓒ Ⓓ Ⓔ  56 Ⓐ Ⓑ Ⓒ Ⓓ Ⓔ  79 Ⓐ Ⓑ Ⓒ Ⓓ Ⓔ
11 Ⓐ Ⓑ Ⓒ Ⓓ Ⓔ  34 Ⓐ Ⓑ Ⓒ Ⓓ Ⓔ  57 Ⓐ Ⓑ Ⓒ Ⓓ Ⓔ  80 Ⓐ Ⓑ Ⓒ Ⓓ Ⓔ
12 Ⓐ Ⓑ Ⓒ Ⓓ Ⓔ  35 Ⓐ Ⓑ Ⓒ Ⓓ Ⓔ  58 Ⓐ Ⓑ Ⓒ Ⓓ Ⓔ  81 Ⓐ Ⓑ Ⓒ Ⓓ Ⓔ
13 Ⓐ Ⓑ Ⓒ Ⓓ Ⓔ  36 Ⓐ Ⓑ Ⓒ Ⓓ Ⓔ  59 Ⓐ Ⓑ Ⓒ Ⓓ Ⓔ  82 Ⓐ Ⓑ Ⓒ Ⓓ Ⓔ
14 Ⓐ Ⓑ Ⓒ Ⓓ Ⓔ  37 Ⓐ Ⓑ Ⓒ Ⓓ Ⓔ  60 Ⓐ Ⓑ Ⓒ Ⓓ Ⓔ  83 Ⓐ Ⓑ Ⓒ Ⓓ Ⓔ
15 Ⓐ Ⓑ Ⓒ Ⓓ Ⓔ  38 Ⓐ Ⓑ Ⓒ Ⓓ Ⓔ  61 Ⓐ Ⓑ Ⓒ Ⓓ Ⓔ  84 Ⓐ Ⓑ Ⓒ Ⓓ Ⓔ
16 Ⓐ Ⓑ Ⓒ Ⓓ Ⓔ  39 Ⓐ Ⓑ Ⓒ Ⓓ Ⓔ  62 Ⓐ Ⓑ Ⓒ Ⓓ Ⓔ  85 Ⓐ Ⓑ Ⓒ Ⓓ Ⓔ
17 Ⓐ Ⓑ Ⓒ Ⓓ Ⓔ  40 Ⓐ Ⓑ Ⓒ Ⓓ Ⓔ  63 Ⓐ Ⓑ Ⓒ Ⓓ Ⓔ  86 Ⓐ Ⓑ Ⓒ Ⓓ Ⓔ
18 Ⓐ Ⓑ Ⓒ Ⓓ Ⓔ  41 Ⓐ Ⓑ Ⓒ Ⓓ Ⓔ  64 Ⓐ Ⓑ Ⓒ Ⓓ Ⓔ  87 Ⓐ Ⓑ Ⓒ Ⓓ Ⓔ
19 Ⓐ Ⓑ Ⓒ Ⓓ Ⓔ  42 Ⓐ Ⓑ Ⓒ Ⓓ Ⓔ  65 Ⓐ Ⓑ Ⓒ Ⓓ Ⓔ  88 Ⓐ Ⓑ Ⓒ Ⓓ Ⓔ
20 Ⓐ Ⓑ Ⓒ Ⓓ Ⓔ  43 Ⓐ Ⓑ Ⓒ Ⓓ Ⓔ  66 Ⓐ Ⓑ Ⓒ Ⓓ Ⓔ  89 Ⓐ Ⓑ Ⓒ Ⓓ Ⓔ
21 Ⓐ Ⓑ Ⓒ Ⓓ Ⓔ  44 Ⓐ Ⓑ Ⓒ Ⓓ Ⓔ  67 Ⓐ Ⓑ Ⓒ Ⓓ Ⓔ  90 Ⓐ Ⓑ Ⓒ Ⓓ Ⓔ
22 Ⓐ Ⓑ Ⓒ Ⓓ Ⓔ  45 Ⓐ Ⓑ Ⓒ Ⓓ Ⓔ  68 Ⓐ Ⓑ Ⓒ Ⓓ Ⓔ
23 Ⓐ Ⓑ Ⓒ Ⓓ Ⓔ  46 Ⓐ Ⓑ Ⓒ Ⓓ Ⓔ  69 Ⓐ Ⓑ Ⓒ Ⓓ Ⓔ

# Diagnostic Test

**Directions:** Each of the questions or incomplete statements below is followed by five suggested answers or completions. Select the one that is best in each case and then fill in the corresponding circle on the answer sheet. You can cut the answer sheet along the dotted line to make recording your answers easier.

1. Indentured servitude in colonial America

   (A) provided African slaves a chance to earn their freedom.
   (B) contributed only small amounts of laborers to the colonial workforce.
   (C) prevented laborers from ever rising from a status of servitude.
   (D) took hold only in New England.
   (E) allowed laborers to work their way to freedom within four to seven years.

2. "America is not composed, as in Europe, of great lords who possess everything and of a herd of people who have nothing."

   The statement above reveals the absence in eighteenth-century America of

   (A) property rights.
   (B) an aristocracy.
   (C) social mobility.
   (D) religious freedom.
   (E) a means of taxing the rich.

3. As the first Democrat, Andrew Jackson campaigned on behalf of

   (A) women and minorities.
   (B) banks and other large corporations.
   (C) states' rights in defiance of central authority.
   (D) the common man.
   (E) New England merchants.

4. Factory workers in the late nineteenth century in America

   (A) had no access to labor unions to improve their working conditions.
   (B) were largely foreign-born immigrants.
   (C) were exclusively male.
   (D) received wages superior to those of any other workers.
   (E) were highly respected because of their contribution to industrialization.

5. The United States entered World War I for all of the following reasons EXCEPT to

   (A) repel German aggression in Europe.
   (B) protect American shipments of goods to U.S. allies.
   (C) acquire German holdings in Africa for American use.
   (D) ward off a German-Mexican alliance.
   (E) punish Germany for unrestricted submarine warfare.

6. "Women's fashions have always fluctuated. . . . But during and after the war the skirt disappeared altogether to be replaced by a sort of tunic barely reaching the knee. Hampering petticoats were discarded, the corset was abandoned as a needless impediment to free movement."

   The statement above is most likely referring to ladies' fashion from what era?

   (A) The Early National period
   (B) Post-Civil War pioneer era
   (C) The 1920s
   (D) The Great Depression
   (E) The 1950s

7. Select the pair of twentieth-century decades famous for consumerism and materialism.

   (A) 1910s and 1920s
   (B) 1930s and 1940s
   (C) 1970s and 1980s
   (D) 1920s and 1950s
   (E) 1960s and 1990s

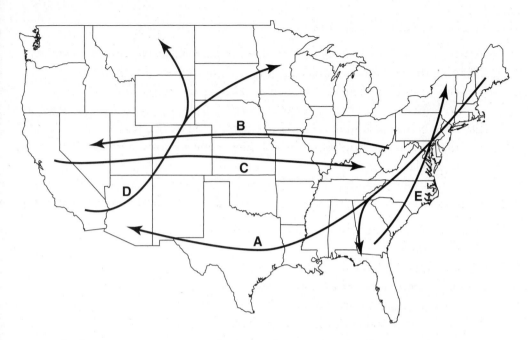

8. Which migratory arrow on the map above correctly illustrates the predominant migration pattern of U.S. citizens within America from 1950 to1980?
   (A) A
   (B) B
   (C) C
   (D) D
   (E) E

9. Which 1950s Supreme Court decision overturned the 1896 *Plessy v. Ferguson* ruling that said separate but equal educational facilities for blacks and whites were constitutional?

   (A) *NAACP v. Alabama*
   (B) *Bartkus v. Board of Education of Chicago, Illinois*
   (C) *Boynton v. Board of Education of Richmond, Virginia*
   (D) *Brown v. Board of Education of Topeka, Kansas*
   (E) *Engel v. Vitale*

10. The stated purpose of the United States in fighting Operation Desert Storm against Iraq in 1991 was to

   (A) drive Iraqi forces out of neighboring Kuwait.
   (B) secure access to oil from U.S. allies in the Middle East.
   (C) reach a settlement in the Arab-Israeli conflict.
   (D) enforce a no-fly zone in northern and southern Iraq.
   (E) remove the dictator Saddam Hussein from power in Iraq.

11. The British colonial policy of mercantilism mandated that

    (A) the American colonists were to develop basic industries in the colonies.
    (B) only the Parliament could tax colonists, not colonial legislatures.
    (C) countries like Spain and France were to be allowed to trade with colonists.
    (D) only New England colonies could participate in shipping.
    (E) the Parliament would use the colonial economy for the good of England.

12. Participants in the first Great Awakening in the 1730s and 1740s advocated a

    (A) return to Catholicism because most American colonists were Protestant.
    (B) strengthening of established churches.
    (C) ban on open-air preaching by traveling ministers.
    (D) more democratic style of church government.
    (E) strengthening of ties with the Church of England.

13. Opportunities for women expanded between 1800 and 1850 to include all of the following EXCEPT

    (A) access to higher education.
    (B) the right to vote.
    (C) ownership of land apart from that of fathers and husbands.
    (D) marriage choices based on affection.
    (E) access to basic manufacturing jobs.

14. Which change stated below occurred in the post-Civil War era?

    (A) The Supreme Court achieved status as an equal branch of the federal government.
    (B) Political party rivalries calmed during the Era of Good Feelings.
    (C) Businesses in several industries consolidated into large corporations.
    (D) American Indians were pacified east of the Mississippi River.
    (E) Universal white manhood suffrage was achieved.

15. The first attempt by states to regulate large corporations was

    (A) directed toward railroad companies.
    (B) designed to bolster labor unions.
    (C) aimed at the lumber industry.
    (D) accomplished through the establishment of workmen's compensation laws.
    (E) derived from the inspection of meat-packing plants.

16. What caused the surge of nativism from 1890 to 1910?

    (A) The sharp increase in the number of English and Germans fleeing trouble in Europe who then migrated to eastern cities looking for jobs
    (B) The lack of jobs resulting from a return to an agrarian economy
    (C) The perception that the immigrants arriving during this period would be incapable of assimilating into American society
    (D) The rise of the Know-Nothing American Party and the resulting instability in the American political system
    (E) The passage of the Quota Act limiting access for certain immigrants

17. All of the following statements about the experiences of African-American soldiers fighting for the United States in World War I are true EXCEPT that

    (A) many Europeans received the African-Americans warmly as liberators.
    (B) African-Americans fought in segregated units as they had in the Civil War.
    (C) an African-American became the most highly decorated American soldier.
    (D) returning to the discrimination back home proved especially difficult.
    (E) an African-American invented the mask that saved many from gas attacks.

18. The Jazz Age of the 1920s was named for the popularity of jazz music, but which other form of entertainment reached wide popularity in this era?

    (A) Television
    (B) Motion pictures
    (C) Amateur soccer leagues
    (D) Professional football
    (E) Running and jogging for exercise

19. Which statement best describes the relationship between Theodore Roosevelt's Square Deal and Franklin Roosevelt's New Deal?

    (A) The New Deal was merely a continuation of the Square Deal.
    (B) The Square Deal lay the foundation of Progressive Reform upon which the New Deal dramatically expanded.
    (C) The Square Deal and the New Deal were planned together by the Roosevelts as a long-term strategy to alter the role of the federal government.
    (D) The Square Deal and the New Deal were opposite strategies for using the power of the federal government because Theodore was a Republican and Franklin was a Democrat.
    (E) There was no connection between the policies of the Square Deal and those of the New Deal.

20. In which era did American voters participate the most in national elections?

    (A) The Era of Good Feelings (1810–1824)
    (B) The Civil War era (1854–1865)
    (C) The Gilded Age (1866–1900)
    (D) The Roaring Twenties (1920s)
    (E) The Stormy Sixties (1960s)

21. Which decisions in the legislative branch have been the most contentious between the major political parties in the modern U.S. Congress?

    (A) Environmental policy issues and initiatives
    (B) Civil rights legislation at home and human rights initiatives abroad
    (C) Foreign policy initiatives involving the European Union and Asian Tigers
    (D) Congressional leadership positions and committee posts
    (E) Foreign policy problems in the wake of the collapse of the Soviet Union

22. What benefited the American Indian cultures the most prior to 1890?

    (A) Climate change brought on by white settlement
    (B) The acquisition of firearms
    (C) Federal legislation offering assimilation of individuals as opposed to tribes
    (D) The introduction of written forms of native languages
    (E) The reintroduction of the horse to North America by Europeans

23. Why did the Articles of Confederation not endure as a framework for the American government?

    (A) Significant limitations on the central government made it too weak to hold the states together.
    (B) The haste with which the document was written caused too many errors to emerge in the design of the government.
    (C) The ratification process was deemed flawed once it was completed so the government never won the confidence of the people.
    (D) Americans rejected the document because it was crafted during the crisis of the Revolutionary War.
    (E) Contentious issues between the North and the South undermined the friendship the document required for the government to work.

24. The purchase of the Louisiana Territory from France

    (A) was made possible when Spain defended itself against Napoleon's attacks.
    (B) originated in the unconstitutional actions of strict constructionist Thomas Jefferson.
    (C) extended the United States to the Pacific Ocean through Oregon.
    (D) fulfilled President Jefferson's dream to acquire new sources of natural resources to fuel the industrial revolution in America.
    (E) was met with universal praise from the American people because it doubled the size of the country.

25. Transcendentalists believed in which of the following principles?

    (A) The acquisition of wealth for all classes should be obtained through the sharing of the nation's resources.
    (B) People should strictly adhere to traditional religious values.
    (C) Individuals should follow the dictates of their own consciences after contemplation of many sources of wisdom, including nature.
    (D) Every man was given a calling by God that he was supposed to pursue with all his might to bring glory to the Creator.
    (E) Mankind had only human wisdom to rely on for societal improvement because the Creator had merely wound up the universe like a clock.

26. Provisions of the Open Door Notes distributed by Secretary of State John Hay included all of the following EXCEPT

    (A) every imperialist nation receiving the note because of its interest in China would be assured a sphere of influence there.
    (B) the United States would be assured a sphere of influence even though it was behind European nations and Japan in developing trade with China.
    (C) no sphere nation would be permitted to build a railroad in China to facilitate trade with the interior.
    (D) China would be allowed to set its own tariff rates.
    (E) China would charge all of the sphere nations the same tariff rates.

27. In which decades of American history was the Ku Klux Klan most influential?

    (A) 1850s and 1870s
    (B) 1870s and 1920s
    (C) 1880s and 1910s
    (D) 1890s and 1950s
    (E) 1930s and 1960s

28. The Great Depression was caused mostly by which of the following trends?

    (A) The departure from the use of precious metal in American coins
    (B) The rapid collapse of American productivity after the end of World War I
    (C) The crippling effects on the economy of the rise of the labor movement
    (D) The unchecked investment schemes of an era of unregulated banking
    (E) The transition from an agrarian to an industrialized economy

29. In what way did the United States support the Allies fighting World War II before the attack on Pearl Harbor led to direct involvement?

    (A) Sending supplies by ships that were guarded by American naval vessels
    (B) Requiring American pilots to fight in the Royal Air Force disguised as British airmen
    (C) Sending all first-generation male immigrants of fighting age from Allied nations back to face conscription at home
    (D) Repealing the congressional legislation drafted by the Nye Commission after World War I in preparation for full-scale mobilization of the economy
    (E) Enacting a draft and training a large force of combatants in all branches of the American military

30. The graduated income tax was suggested by the Populists and enacted by the Progressives in order to

    (A) shift the tax burden to the wealthiest Americans after an era of a growing gap between the rich and the poor.
    (B) prevent the wealthiest Americans from passing down too much of their wealth to their descendants and creating a permanent aristocracy.
    (C) create political power for the middle and lower classes.
    (D) provide incentives to middle-class Americans to invest in stocks.
    (E) harness the economic power of the industrialists to the war effort as the future allies of the United States struggled in World War I.

31. At which point were the United States and the Soviet Union closest to the brink of an exchange of thermonuclear weapons?

    (A) During the immediate aftermath of World War II
    (B) During the Berlin Crisis and airlift
    (C) During the Korean War when General MacArthur was in charge
    (D) During the U-2 spy plane incident
    (E) During the Cuban Missile Crisis

32. Of these American Indian cultures in existence at the time of the arrival of Europeans in the New World, which had the most advanced civilization?

    (A) The Huron of the Great Lakes region
    (B) The Navajo of the Southwest
    (C) The Iroquois of what would become New York
    (D) The Cherokee of the Appalachian region
    (E) The Aztecs of Mexico

33. What prevented the Jamestown colony from failing as had all previous attempts at English colonization of the New World?

    (A) The arrival of second sons of the gentry due to primogeniture laws
    (B) The establishment of tobacco cultivation for export
    (C) The discovery of gold in nearby streams
    (D) The formation of the Virginia House of Burgesses for self-government
    (E) The departure of Lord de la Warr, whose tyrannical rule stifled growth

34. A chief success of the Congress established by the Articles of Confederation was the establishing of

    (A) a fair system of taxing the states for revenue to run the central government.
    (B) a clearly defined separation of the government into three branches.
    (C) the system to make new states out of territories given up by the first states.
    (D) the national economic system with a currency and regulation of trade.
    (E) a way to balance the power of states that satisfied large and small states.

35. As the last prominent Federalist in the central government, Supreme Court Chief Justice John Marshall used his influence to

    (A) expand the power of the executive branch of the federal government.
    (B) reduce the prestige of the Supreme Court in favor of lower courts.
    (C) establish English Common Law as the basis for all American laws.
    (D) expand the power of the federal government at the expense of the states.
    (E) destroy some private companies by using the new powers of taxation.

36. Which principle listed below best summarizes the notion of Manifest Destiny?

    (A) American Indian cultures must necessarily give way to white civilization.
    (B) The people of each territory should be able to decide for themselves to be a slave or free state by a vote upon application for statehood.
    (C) The frontier will provide a constant safety valve for oppressed classes and thus preserve democracy.
    (D) A diversified national economy must supplant a strictly agrarian economy.
    (E) American civilization is uniquely designed to spread political and religious freedom and thus deserves to expand.

37. "The words were still in the mouth of the scout, when the leader of the party, whose approaching footsteps had caught the vigilant ear of the Indian, came openly into view. A beaten path, such as those made by the periodical passage of the deer, wound through a little glen . . . and struck the river at the point where the white man and his red companions had posted themselves."

    This passage is most likely from the writings of which American author?

    (A) Edgar Allan Poe
    (B) James Fenimore Cooper
    (C) Mark Twain
    (D) Herman Melville
    (E) Washington Irving

38. Which statement best expresses why the Confederacy failed to win its independence in the Civil War?

    (A) New York City failed to secede and ally with the Confederacy despite its stated desire to do so after the Battle of Gettysburg.
    (B) The Confederate invasions of the North failed to capture the federal capital at Washington, D.C.
    (C) The war dragged on beyond the capacity of the southern economy to sustain it since the South was unable to ship cotton to the United Kingdom.
    (D) Former slaves and free African-Americans fought the South with a vengeance once they were permitted to join the Union Army.
    (E) The Confederate Army could not prevent northerners from mounting widespread insurgencies in southern cities.

39. "The contrast between the palace of the millionaire and the cottage of the laborer with us to-day measures the change which has come with civilization."

    The quotation above is most likely from what nineteenth-century writing?

    (A) *A Century of Dishonor* by Helen Hunt Jackson
    (B) *The Impending Crisis of the South* by Hinton R. Helper
    (C) "Civil Disobedience" by Henry David Thoreau
    (D) "The Gospel of Wealth" by Andrew Carnegie
    (E) *The Significance of the Frontier in American History* by Frederick J. Turner

40. What was the main difference between the roles of women in the workforce after World War I and after World War II?

   (A) After World War I women largely left the workforce but after World War II they stayed in large numbers.
   (B) Women were more respected for their work after World War I than after World War II.
   (C) After World War I women still could not vote until they proved themselves again by helping on the home front during World War II.
   (D) Women were allowed to serve in combat roles in the military after World War II, whereas combat was still considered unladylike after World War I.
   (E) More women than men entered college to pursue professions after World War II, whereas after World War I few women entered college.

41. Which of the following was true of the home front during World War II?

   (A) A revolution occurred in race relations during the war years.
   (B) The entire economy was mobilized for the war effort because of the severity and global scale of the war.
   (C) Consumers could purchase more goods than ever before because of the lucrative nature of emergency war work.
   (D) Americans embraced German and Japanese immigrants because they obviously valued American society over that of their homelands.
   (E) A giant boost was given to science and math education because of the superior sophistication of the technology of America's Soviet allies.

42. How did French colonization differ from either English or Spanish colonization in the New World?

   (A) New France consisted of Roman Catholic colonists, whereas England and Spain planted only Protestant colonies.
   (B) New France contained far more colonists than the English colonies because France claimed all of Canada and the Ohio River Valley.
   (C) France permitted religious dissenters to settle in New France, whereas Spain permitted only those who were loyal to the Pope to go.
   (D) New France's economy was more diversified than that of the English colonies.
   (E) New France's economy was almost entirely based on the fur trade with American Indians unlike the agricultural English or Spanish colonies.

43. Which event finally sealed the possession of Florida for the United States?

    (A) The British acquired Florida from the French after the French and Indian War and thus made it a colony that changed hands in the Treaty of Paris.

    (B) The United States conquered Florida during the War for Independence because the Spanish sided with the British.

    (C) Andrew Jackson's forces defeated the Seminole tribe of American Indians and forced them to sign a treaty turning Florida over to the United States.

    (D) John Quincy Adams negotiated a treaty called the Adams-Onis Treaty in which Spain agreed to sell Florida to the United States.

    (E) When Spain was under Napoleon's control he forced the Spanish to sell Florida to the United States along with his offer of the Louisiana Purchase.

44. Which principle stated below best represents the view of equality embodied in the American Revolution?

    (A) Once freed from British control all Americans should share middle-class status.

    (B) All males, regardless of race or creed, should have free access to economic and political opportunity.

    (C) Unnatural restraints should be removed to allow Americans to advance as far as possible according to each man's talent and energy.

    (D) American males, once freed, would then work to bring African-Americans and women up out of subservient roles.

    (E) All men are created equal, so slavery should be abolished.

45. In what episode did President Andrew Jackson challenge a decision of the Supreme Court?

    (A) In the Bank War over the constitutionality of the Bank of the United States

    (B) In the debate over Jackson's overuse of the veto power of the president

    (C) In the Nullification Crisis over the issue of the secession of South Carolina

    (D) In the aftermath of the Indian Removal Act leading to the Trail of Tears

    (E) In the controversy surrounding the first national nominating convention

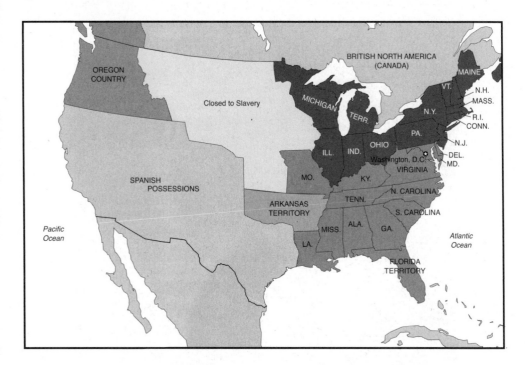

46. The map above illustrates what episode of American history prior to the Civil War?

    (A) The Adams-Onis Treaty
    (B) The Missouri Compromise
    (C) The Mexican Cession
    (D) The Compromise of 1850
    (E) The Kansas-Nebraska Act

47. In what way was the Populist Party unprepared for lasting national success?

    (A) The Populists barred women from leadership positions in their party.
    (B) The Populists were largely lacking in education and political experience.
    (C) The Populists' ideas failed to attract charismatic leaders.
    (D) The Populists failed to recognize the significance of the national currency.
    (E) The Populists were immigrant factory workers in an age of nativism.

48. "Combinations in industry are the result of an imperative economic law which cannot be repealed by political legislation. The effort at prohibiting all combination has substantially failed. The way out lies, not in attempting to prevent such combinations, but in completely controlling them in the interest of the public welfare."

    The quotation above is most likely a statement of which philosophy?

    (A) The ideology of William Jennings Bryan in the "Cross of Gold" speech
    (B) The antitrust policy of Woodrow Wilson's New Freedom
    (C) The good trust/bad trust stance of Theodore Roosevelt's New Nationalism
    (D) The socialist rhetoric of Eugene V. Debs
    (E) The organized labor goals of Samuel Gompers

Courtesy of Culver Pictures

49. The political cartoon above is suggesting that

   (A) the United States needs to incorporate overseas possessions into a new image of itself as a world power.
   (B) imperialism has caused the United States to grow too large and must be reversed.
   (C) William McKinley does not deserve the presidency.
   (D) Americans have grown obese and must participate in a physical fitness crusade.
   (E) the best years of the American experiment have come and gone.

50. The response to the New Immigration of the first decade of the twentieth century was

   (A) to embrace the new type of European immigrants as refreshingly different.
   (B) for the centers of America's largest cities to be revitalized.
   (C) deportation of all illegal immigrants.
   (D) an immediate assimilation of southeastern Europeans as Americans.
   (E) nativist laws designed to restrict immigration of "undesirable" ethnicities.

51. With which nation or region did Franklin D. Roosevelt's first major foreign policy initiative seek a new approach in contrast to Theodore Roosevelt's policy stance there?

    (A) East Asia
    (B) Africa
    (C) Canada
    (D) Latin America
    (E) Europe

52. Under which president's administration did the new policy of containment of the spread of communism give rise to the Cold War?

    (A) Woodrow Wilson
    (B) Franklin Roosevelt
    (C) Harry Truman
    (D) Dwight Eisenhower
    (E) John Kennedy

53. What was John Locke's most significant contribution to the formation of the United States of America?

    (A) Locke theorized that America was a "blank slate" and encouraged political experimentation to shun imperfect English traditions.
    (B) Locke provided philosophical justification for armed revolution in his theories surrounding the Social Contract.
    (C) Locke, as a radical political theorist, wrote the first draft of the Articles of Confederation.
    (D) Locke migrated to America and volunteered to fight in the Continental Army.
    (E) Locke was the strongest European proponent of capitalist economics.

54. "I might write to you at large about the religious liberty which is enjoyed in this province in the most extensive manner. . . . Christians of every denomination, as they choose their own ministers, so they also make provision for them . . ."

    This excerpt from a letter describes the tendency of colonial Americans to

    (A) respond to the preaching of traveling evangelists in revivals.
    (B) reject the notion of established churches.
    (C) mistrust growing religious diversity.
    (D) celebrate the Parson's Cause.
    (E) embrace traditional forms of church government.

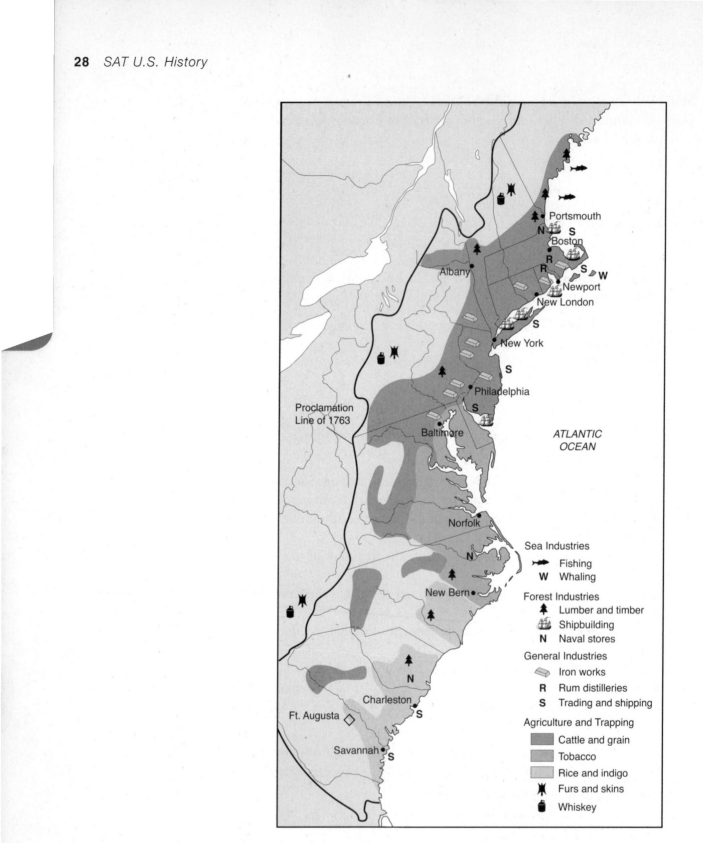

55. The map above illustrates which region in colonial America that had the least diversified economy?

(A) New England
(B) The middle colonies
(C) The Chesapeake region
(D) The frontier
(E) The Deep South

56. What prompted President James Monroe to issue the Monroe Doctrine?

    (A) Increasing encroachments on American territories by England and Russia
    (B) Resurgence of Spanish power in the New World
    (C) Migration to America by the Chinese during the gold rush
    (D) Migration to America by the Irish during the potato famine
    (E) Growing sectionalism of the North, South, and West

57. Which initiative was most impacted by Protestant Christianity during the early nineteenth century?

    (A) The move to stop imperialism known as isolationism
    (B) The rapid development of new communication technologies
    (C) The flourishing of the philosophical aspects of deism
    (D) The temperance movement
    (E) The parochial school movement

58. Which American president actively pursued American military forays into Latin America while denying European countries the same right to establish spheres of influence there?

    (A) James Monroe
    (B) Abraham Lincoln
    (C) William McKinley
    (D) Theodore Roosevelt
    (E) Harry Truman

59. Which New Deal measures were considered unconstitutional by the Supreme Court?

    (A) The Civilian Conservation Corps and the Tennessee Valley Authority
    (B) The Federal Emergency Relief Act and the Wagner Act
    (C) Social Security and the Federal Deposit Insurance Corporation
    (D) Works Progress Administration and the Public Works Administration
    (E) The Agricultural Adjustment Act and the National Recovery Administration

60. Why were Americans willing to support the Marshall Plan's expenditures of billions of dollars even after the massive expenditures for World War II?

    (A) The American economy was so strong that the amount spent was trivial.
    (B) Few Americans realized the extent of the Marshall Plan's expenditures.
    (C) Most Americans agreed that communism was a significant threat to peace.
    (D) Most Americans agreed that Europe should become dependent on the United States.
    (E) Recipient countries paid back the debts once they restored their economies.

61. What series of events first prompted African-Americans in large numbers to migrate away from the South where they had experienced slavery?

    (A) The enacting of "black codes" that led to the rule of Jim Crow
    (B) Educational opportunities offered by northern religious reformers
    (C) The passage of the Thirteenth, Fourteenth, and Fifteenth Amendments to the Constitution
    (D) The end of sharecropping as a viable economic arrangement after 1900
    (E) The need for workers in northern factories during the world wars

62. Ethnic diversity was greatest in what region of colonial America?

    (A) New England
    (B) The middle colonies
    (C) The Chesapeake region
    (D) The frontier
    (E) The Deep South

63. Which of the principles below was most strongly associated with Puritanism in colonial New England?

    (A) Each church member had to be able to confess to an actual conversion experience in which God's grace was the key to salvation.
    (B) Study of the Bible was less important than following one's inner light.
    (C) Reason was superior to faith in determining truth.
    (D) The best life was one of relaxed contemplation of "higher laws."
    (E) America was made up of so many different denominations and faiths that the key to societal peace was toleration for belief or nonbelief.

64. What was Benjamin Franklin's most important role in the founding of the United States of America?

    (A) As a printer publishing all the atrocities of the king and Parliament
    (B) As the chief author of the Declaration of Independence
    (C) As the inventor of many practical devices bettering American's lives
    (D) As the wise sage guiding the Constitutional Convention in Philadelphia
    (E) As a skillful negotiator in the diplomatic service during the Revolution

65. How did the United States manage to win the War of 1812?

    (A) Through a brilliant invasion of Canada centered on Montreal
    (B) By a stunning victory at New Orleans led by Andrew Jackson
    (C) By outlasting British resolve because England was at war in Europe
    (D) By invading England along with its ally, Napoleon Bonaparte
    (E) By forcing the war to spread to Europe and Asia

66. All of the following reforms inspired by the second Great Awakening were successful in the nineteenth century EXCEPT the

    (A) abolition of slavery.
    (B) prohibition of the manufacture, sale, and distribution of alcohol.
    (C) expansion of public schooling in the common school movement.
    (D) awareness that the mentally ill should not be treated as animals.
    (E) westward migration of converts to Mormonism.

67. What accounted for the dramatic growth of the slave population of the South prior to the Civil War?

    (A) The legalization of the African slave trade again
    (B) The extensive smuggling of Africans into slavery despite laws against it
    (C) Natural reproduction through improved treatment and medical care
    (D) The ending of the regular mass deaths associated with slave rebellions
    (E) The increased demand for slaves to fill the mines and factories of the South

68. Why did anti-Chinese sentiment develop among many Americans and lead to the Chinese Exclusion Act, the first federal law to limit immigration?

    (A) Chinese students excelled beyond native-born children in public schools.
    (B) Chinese people on the west coast were suspected of espionage in World War II.
    (C) Chinese people insisted on living in separate neighborhoods in American cities.
    (D) Chinese businesses were successful and their neighbors became jealous.
    (E) Chinese people refused to learn English and thus refused to assimilate.

69. What explains the increase in membership in labor unions despite the Great Depression of the 1930s?

    (A) Long lines of unemployed workers stood outside of all American factories.
    (B) The number of strikes in major industries tripled during the decade.
    (C) The violence associated with early labor demonstrations never returned.
    (D) The Supreme Court of the 1920s had been sympathetic to labor issues.
    (E) The Congress passed the first supportive legislation in over twenty years.

70. Which of the following best describes the outcome of the Korean War?

    (A) After advances by both sides the line between North and South Korea remained essentially where it began before the conflict.
    (B) The Chinese and the Soviets provided enough support to finally win North Korea its independence from South Korea.
    (C) North Korea advanced down the peninsula leaving South Korea only a tiny fraction of its original territory before ending the war with a treaty.
    (D) North Korea drove out the United States and its allies and united the peninsula as one communist state with two provinces divided at the thirty-eighth parallel.
    (E) American and UN forces invaded China and nearly ignited what would have become World War III.

71. Identify the correct era and explanation of the largest increase of the American birthrate during the twentieth century.

    (A) The 1920s due to the sexual revolution of the Jazz Age
    (B) The 1930s due to the focus on home life during the Great Depression
    (C) The 1940s due to the high casualties of World War II
    (D) The 1950s due to the restored confidence of Americans after the war
    (E) The 1960s due to the era of free love in the hippie lifestyle

72. Which ethnic group first penetrated the Appalachian frontier in large numbers during the colonial era?

    (A) The English
    (B) The Scots-Irish
    (C) The Swedish
    (D) The Dutch
    (E) The Spanish

73. Which of the following was a significant reason that many Americans opposed ratification of the U.S. Constitution in 1788 and 1789?

    (A) The lack of a resolution to the conflict between large and small states
    (B) The provisions in the powers of the legislative branch for a powerful central bank designed to regulate the economy
    (C) The absence of any specific wording to protect the rights of individuals from the abuses exhibited by the British government before the Revolution
    (D) The possibility of the slave-owning states exerting greater power in the House of Representatives by inflating their population by counting slaves
    (E) The removing of the judicial branch from any direct accountability to the will of the people

74. Which of the following issues caused the first serious sectional conflict of the period prior to the Civil War?

   (A) The sudden increase in the population of California due to the gold rush
   (B) The argument over where to locate the first transcontinental railroad
   (C) The animosity of the South for the North's protective tariffs
   (D) The surprising desire of Missouri to enter the Union as a slave state
   (E) The accusation that the Mexican War was intended to expand slavery

75. Which individual or group proposed the most punitive plan for the former Confederate states of the South during the Reconstruction era?

   (A) Poor whites who resented the power of the old slaveholding class
   (B) President Abraham Lincoln
   (C) The Union Army generals in charge of the five military districts
   (D) President Andrew Johnson
   (E) The Republican majorities in charge of both houses of Congress

76. Which action of the federal government in the nineteenth century was most representative of the concept of laissez-faire?

   (A) The issuing of land grants to encourage railroad construction
   (B) The support of high protective tariffs
   (C) The Homestead Act's encouragement of western settlement
   (D) The regulation of business with antitrust legislation
   (E) The amending of the U.S. Constitution during Reconstruction

77. Which one of the following labor organizations resorted to the most militant techniques to pursue its goals?

   (A) The National Labor Union
   (B) The Knights of Labor
   (C) The Socialist Party
   (D) The Industrial Workers of the World
   (E) The American Federation of Labor

78. Which event below was the last major violent encounter between the U.S. military and American Indians resisting federal authority?

   (A) The Battle of Wounded Knee
   (B) The Nez Perce War
   (C) The Battle of Little Big Horn
   (D) The Sioux Rebellion
   (E) The Blackhawk War

79. Samuel Gompers described the Clayton Antitrust Act as "labor's Magna Carta" because

    (A) Woodrow Wilson backed the legislation as the first Democrat in the presidency since Grover Cleveland who had opposed striking unions.
    (B) the law was the first federal legislation supporting collective bargaining, the bedrock principle behind labor unions.
    (C) the law was the first federal legislation to take on the monopolies established by big business combinations.
    (D) the law established the right of laborers to petition their government for redress of their grievances against management.
    (E) the federal government finally made a commitment to end the corruption of the Gilded Age.

80. Why was the Harlem Renaissance of the 1920s significant to the wider American culture?

    (A) The movement represented the first revitalization of an inner-city neighborhood that had fallen into decline in the wake of urbanization.
    (B) African-Americans and Jewish Americans found peace from social discrimination by living together in a mixed neighborhood.
    (C) African-Americans achieved wealth in an urban setting for the first time because of the concentration of merchants in one location.
    (D) African-American culture was accepted in a major urban center because Harlem poets, artists, and musicians also appealed to white audiences.
    (E) The first university instruction available to African-Americans was established by Columbia University.

81. What cornerstone of President Jimmy Carter's administration did he also encourage the United Nations to adopt as a major policy goal while he was still in office?

    (A) Intervening in the Arab-Israeli conflict in the Middle East
    (B) Monitoring the proliferation of nuclear weapons
    (C) Urging wealthy countries to help feed the people of developing countries
    (D) Constructing low-cost housing for impoverished peoples around the world
    (E) Monitoring human rights violations by governments around the world

82. What event prompted President Lyndon Johnson to ask for the support of Congress for escalation of the Vietnam War?

    (A) An invasion of South Vietnam by North Vietnam after a failed referendum to unite Vietnam under one government
    (B) The discovery of the influence of the Soviet Union in spreading communism to North Vietnam
    (C) An alleged attack by North Vietnamese forces on American naval vessels
    (D) The exposure of a conspiracy within South Vietnam to mount an insurgency by a group known as the Vietcong
    (E) The assassination of the American-backed South Vietnamese leader

83. Which aspect of American government was originally problematic but solved by an amendment to the U.S. Constitution?

    (A) The division of the federal government into three branches designed to wield checks and balances to keep the nation from extremes
    (B) The manner in which the president and vice president were elected
    (C) The federal system's providing for shared power between the central government and the states without providing for the rise of sectionalism
    (D) The interaction of political parties among the three branches of government and within each branch of the government
    (E) The controversy between states with large populations and those with small populations

84. All of the following aspects of the federal government during the early National Period were the result of Alexander Hamilton's plans EXCEPT the

    (A) ban on non-native-born Americans' being president.
    (B) interpretation of the elastic clause of the U.S. Constitution that expanded the power of the central government.
    (C) creation of a Bank of the United States modeled after the Bank of England.
    (D) assumption of state debts by the federal government and the system for funding the consequently higher national debt.
    (E) use of the national currency to regulate the economy by either expanding or contracting the amount of money in circulation.

85. The Populist Party pressed the government to adopt which policy?

    (A) The return to the gold standard to prevent inflation of the currency
    (B) The use of federal funding to subsidize cheaper rates for shipping crude oil
    (C) The opening of the country's borders to provide cheap labor on farms
    (D) The extensive use of silver in American coins in order to create inflation
    (E) The use of the strike to achieve higher wages for migrant farmworkers

86. The style of journalism known as muckraking was best exemplified in

    (A) war correspondent Stephen Crane's book, *The Red Badge of Courage.*
    (B) the abolitionist novel *Uncle Tom's Cabin* by Harriet Beecher Stowe.
    (C) the satirical writings of Samuel Clemens or Mark Twain.
    (D) the photography of Ansel Adams and Matthew Brady.
    (E) the photography of Jacob Riis and Lewis Hine.

87. Which statement below best describes the impact of World War I on the American economy?

    (A) The fact that American allies failed to pay back the loans they received crippled the economy for the next decade.
    (B) The war in Europe gave a tremendous boost to American farmers then trapped them in overproduction.
    (C) A baby boom and the rise of suburbia after the war led to a decade of rampant consumerism.
    (D) The American economy finally industrialized for the first time during the war because of the need for manufactured war munitions.
    (E) Large business combinations called trusts were assembled for the first time in order to finance the war effort of the Allied powers.

88. What was the unintended consequence of the decision of Winston Churchill and Franklin D. Roosevelt at the Atlantic Conference to push for unconditional surrender of the Axis powers?

    (A) The Axis powers resolved to fight to the death to avoid this humiliation.
    (B) The Axis powers formalized their alliance in the face of this threat.
    (C) Hitler sent the German army into the Balkans in order to refrain from attacking the Soviet Union directly.
    (D) The Allied powers who were fighting before the entry of the United States into World War II were divided because some still wanted appeasement.
    (E) Stalin withheld support for the Allied cause because he feared a similar policy would soon be directed toward his totalitarian rule.

89. What trend began during the cultural transformation of the 1960s?

    (A) The move of the American majority population into cities
    (B) The rise of Hollywood as the capital of the film industry
    (C) The infusion of British influences into American rock 'n' roll music
    (D) The popularity of channels on television dedicated to music videos
    (E) The "Just Say No" campaign against rampant drug use among youth

90. What technological advance was the most responsible for the advent of the Information Age?

    (A) The creation of vast telephone networks coast to coast in the United States
    (B) The laying of the transatlantic cable
    (C) The development of satellite communications
    (D) The formation of the World Wide Web through the Internet
    (E) The development of personal computers

# Answer Key
## DIAGNOSTIC TEST

| | | | | | | | |
|---|---|---|---|---|---|---|---|
| 1. | E | 24. | B | 47. | B | 70. | A |
| 2. | B | 25. | C | 48. | C | 71. | D |
| 3. | D | 26. | C | 49. | A | 72. | B |
| 4. | B | 27. | B | 50. | E | 73. | C |
| 5. | C | 28. | D | 51. | D | 74. | D |
| 6. | C | 29. | A | 52. | C | 75. | E |
| 7. | D | 30. | A | 53. | B | 76. | C |
| 8. | A | 31. | E | 54. | B | 77. | D |
| 9. | D | 32. | E | 55. | C | 78. | A |
| 10. | A | 33. | B | 56. | A | 79. | B |
| 11. | E | 34. | C | 57. | D | 80. | D |
| 12. | D | 35. | D | 58. | D | 81. | E |
| 13. | B | 36. | E | 59. | E | 82. | C |
| 14. | C | 37. | B | 60. | C | 83. | B |
| 15. | A | 38. | C | 61. | E | 84. | A |
| 16. | C | 39. | D | 62. | B | 85. | D |
| 17. | C | 40. | A | 63. | A | 86. | E |
| 18. | B | 41. | B | 64. | E | 87. | B |
| 19. | B | 42. | E | 65. | C | 88. | A |
| 20. | C | 43. | D | 66. | B | 89. | C |
| 21. | D | 44. | C | 67. | C | 90. | D |
| 22. | E | 45. | D | 68. | D | | |
| 23. | A | 46. | B | 69. | E | | |

# Test Analysis

**Step 1: Count the number of correct answers.**

Enter the total here: _____

**Step 2: Count the number of incorrect answers.**

Enter the total here: _____

**Step 3: Multiply the number of incorrect answers by .250**

Enter the product here: _____

**Step 4: Subtract the results obtained in Step 3 from the total obtained in Step 1.**

Enter the total here: _____

**Step 5: Round the number obtained in Step 4 to the nearest whole number.**

Raw Score = _____

## Scaled Score Conversion Table

| Raw Score | Scaled Score | Raw Score | Scaled Score | Raw Score | Scaled Score |
|-----------|--------------|-----------|--------------|-----------|--------------|
| 90–79 | 800 | 46–45 | 600 | 8–7 | 400 |
| 78 | 790 | 44–43 | 590 | 6–5 | 390 |
| 77–76 | 780 | 42–41 | 580 | 4–3 | 380 |
| 75 | 770 | 40 | 570 | 2–1 | 370 |
| 74 | 760 | 39–38 | 560 | 0 – –1 | 360 |
| 73–72 | 750 | 37–36 | 550 | –2 – –3 | 350 |
| 71 | 740 | 35–34 | 540 | –4 | 340 |
| 70–69 | 730 | 33–32 | 530 | –5 – –6 | 330 |
| 68 | 720 | 31–30 | 520 | –7 | 320 |
| 67–66 | 710 | 29–28 | 510 | –8 – –9 | 310 |
| 65–64 | 700 | 27 | 500 | –10 | 300 |
| 63 | 690 | 26–25 | 490 | –11 – –12 | 290 |
| 62–61 | 680 | 24–23 | 480 | –13 | 280 |
| 60–59 | 670 | 22–21 | 470 | –14 – –15 | 270 |
| 58–57 | 660 | 20–19 | 460 | –16 – –17 | 260 |
| 56–55 | 650 | 18–17 | 450 | –18 – –19 | 250 |
| 54–53 | 640 | 16–15 | 440 | –20 | 240 |
| 52–51 | 630 | 14–13 | 430 | –21 – –22 | 230 |
| 50–49 | 620 | 12–11 | 420 | | |
| 48–47 | 610 | 10–9 | 410 | | |

# Answer Explanations

1. **E**  Indentured servitude was especially widespread in the Chesapeake region and was the chief source of laborers who worked four to seven years. Although some never survived their servitude, others achieved wealth and rose to prominence.

2. **B**  The phrase *great lords* refers to a landed aristocracy. All the other choices existed in colonial America to one degree or another.

3. **D**  Andrew Jackson was famous as the president of the common man. He was directly or indirectly opposed to advancing the other choices.

4. **B**  All of the other choices are untrue, and the era of industrialization and immigration coincided in a favorable relationship for the American economy.

5. **C**  All of the other choices were true to a degree, and the United States disavowed any desire to acquire territory as a result of involvement in World War I.

6. **C**  Climbing hemlines came and went, but they were first higher than the knee and the undergarments mentioned fell out of fashion in the 1920s during the Jazz Age.

7. **D**  Both the 1920s and the 1950s were postwar periods of affluence and relief was expressed in notable fixation on consumer spending and the display of wealth, or certainly of comfort.

8. **A**  The arrow labeled "A" identifies the origin and direction of the migration to the Sun Belt during the time period in question.

9. **D**  The case named in answer D overturned *Plessy v. Ferguson.* The other cases are fictitious or not related to ending segregation.

10. **A**  Although the other choices were related directly or indirectly, and some were desirable, answer A was what prompted the first Bush administration to act militarily in Iraq.

11. **E**  Although the other choices would show economic self-rule and contribute to self-development, England held the mercantilist view of the colonies as economic tools to shape English economic growth, not colonial self-sufficiency.

12. **D**  All of the choices are the exact opposite of the spirit of the first Great Awakening except for the rise of democracy in church government.

13. **B**  These advances for women all occurred prior to 1850 except the right to vote (suffrage), which did not come until the Nineteenth Amendment was ratified in time for the 1920 presidential election.

14. **C**  All of these events occurred prior to the Civil War except for large-scale business consolidation.

15. **A**  Because railroads were the first large corporations in the nineteenth century it made sense for them to be the first targets of reform legislation.

16. **C**   The other choices are either false or they are a result of nativism, not a cause. The New Immigration that occurred in this time period came from southern and eastern Europe and had trouble blending with the original northern and western European stock.

17. **C**   All of the choices are true of the experiences of African-Americans in World War I except that Alvin York, a white man from Tennessee, became the most decorated American soldier.

18. **B**   Nothing in the 1920s compared to the nearly universal appeal of motion pictures in the era when the first talkie movie came out. The national popularity of television, soccer, professional football, and a running craze all came decades later.

19. **B**   Only this assertion is entirely true. Theodore launched Progressive Reform on the national scene, but Franklin's New Deal expanded its influence beyond anything the Square Deal attempted.

20. **C**   Despite the tempestuous time periods surrounding it in the question and the era of one-party rule expressed in the idea of the Era of Good Feelings, the Gilded Age saw voter turnouts for national elections that dwarfed those of the other eras.

21. **D**   Although each of these issues can cause disagreement to a degree between the parties, common ground can be found on all of them except committee roles and leadership positions that have almost always sparked contentious acrimony as the two major parties jockey for power.

22. **E**   Every one of the choices except climate change affected some segment of American Indian cultures, but the reintroduction of the horse to North America by the Spanish affected almost all tribes to a degree and radically altered the hunting, living, and strategic activities of many tribes.

23. **A**   All of the other choices contain only shades of truth and other disqualifying phrases. Answer A states the key problem directly.

24. **B** The Louisiana Purchase was criticized by Federalists after Napoleon's victory over Spain made it possible to acquire land that doubled the size of the country. The new territory did not extend beyond Oregon to the ocean, however, and Jefferson wanted its land to prevent industrialization, not to supply it. The only correct answer is that Jefferson loosely interpreted the U.S. Constitution to expand the power of the president enough to make the purchase treaty with France.

25. **C**   Erroneous, deistical, and Puritanical ideas are suggested to distract from the correct answer, which is an echo of Ralph Waldo Emerson's views on self-reliance.

26. **C**   All of the choices were a part of the American policy except answer C. The subsequent Russo-Japanese War was fought over railroad right-of-ways that both nations fully expected to receive.

27. **B**  The Ku Klux Klan had its greatest influence as a result of Reconstruction, when it was formed, and the conformist and nativist era of the Roaring Twenties.

28. **D**  This answer was a part of the chain of events causing the Great Depression, whereas the rest are either falsely stated or out of the time period leading up to it.

29. **A**  Only this answer was a true policy that directly supported the Allies. FDR remained technically neutral but took steps ever closer to war, including a peacetime draft, but the buildup of American military strength did not at first impact the war effort. FDR prepared for war despite the Neutrality Acts that remained on the books.

30. **A**  A graduated income tax increased the rate of taxation as individuals' income increased, a move the Populists wanted to ease economic disparities. The estate and capital gains taxes hinted at in the other answers were not directly tied to the income tax nor the income tax to political power.

31. **E**  Although all of these events were tense moments during the Cold War, the Cuban Missile Crisis came the closest because the showdown involved the unstable Fidel Castro being held in check by the insecure Nikita Khrushchev.

32. **E**  Despite the barbarity of their religious practices, the Aztecs did organize their large population around religion, and their society employed sophisticated agricultural techniques, conducted organized warfare on a large scale, and built monolithic structures. None of the other cultures matched these achievements traditionally associated with the definition of civilization.

33. **B**  Second sons of the gentry had arrived from the beginning, and the arrival of Lord de la Warr, not his departure, was a boon. He organized the colony to produce tobacco for export in 1614, five years before the House of Burgesses was required to keep order in the now-thriving colony. Virginians never discovered gold.

34. **C**  The government designed by the Articles of Confederation accomplished none of these tasks except resolving the land issues, which was quite an accomplishment among land-hungry states and citizens who now had to pay the Congress for the land.

35. **D**  All the other choices are opposites of Marshall's agenda or twists on his activities. Several of his landmark cases specifically enlarged the power of the federal government as a whole, not just in the executive branch, which he sometimes sought to curtail.

36. **E**  Although all of the answers are major issues created by or connected to expansion west, only answer E is the specific connotation of the meaning of Manifest Destiny.

37. **B**  The passage is a classic example of Cooper's genre taken from *The Last of the Mohicans*, one of his Leatherstocking Tales, and should be recognizable as such by anyone with passing familiarity with the works of these major American authors.

38. **C**   All of the answers were problems for the Confederate government except answer E, which is a fabrication. The fatal flaw of the Confederacy, however, was that its economy was largely based on the cash crop of the cotton kingdom. With exports cut off by the Union blockade, attrition set in and whatever military advantages the South possessed at the beginning of the war evaporated.

39. **D**   The only one of these famous writings that dealt specifically with millionaires was Andrew Carnegie's essay, "The Gospel of Wealth."

40. **A**   Answer E is the only one of the other choices with any truth to it, but the number of women attending college did not exceed that of men until much later and then not as a result of World War II. Although women were largely expected to give up their jobs to men returning from World War I, two-income families became much more common after World War II.

41. **B**   World War II required a complete mobilization of the American economy to supply the resources needed by America and her allies to win the war. The other choices are false, as in answer D, or happened after the war.

42. **E**   All or part of the other choices are untrue, whereas answer E expresses the true nature of an empire based largely on the fur trade.

43. **D**   Florida was founded by the Spanish, taken by the English in the French and Indian War, given back to the Spanish by the United States for aid during the Revolutionary War, and finally purchased by the United States from Spain with the Adams-Onis Treaty as the Spanish Empire fell into decline. Thus answers A and C hint at stages of the acquisition of Florida, whereas answers B and E are fabrications. Answer B is the exact opposite of what happened.

44. **C**   Despite revolutionary rhetoric, the only concept of equality held by the majority of Americans at the time was expressed in answer C. The expansion of the concept of equality in the direction of the other answers would come with time and much struggle and not exactly as indicated in some of the selections. The leap that slavery should be abolished was an ideal held by a small minority of citizens of the new country.

45. **D**   Although all of these events were controversies directly or indirectly involving Andrew Jackson, his dispute with John Marshall and the Supreme Court occurred over the fate of the American Indians as a result of the Indian Removal Act of 1830 that led to the Trail of Tears, a series of evacuations of the Cherokee and other tribes from 1835 to 1838.

46. **B**   The limit of American expansion indicated in the map as well as the shaded areas demarking slave states and free states along with the 36°30' line clearly show the map to be of the United States as a result of the Missouri Compromise.

47. **B**   All of the other answers are exactly the opposite of the nature of the Populists and Populism. The Populist Revolt that led to the rise of the Populist Party was initiated by farming interests like the Grange and the Farmers' Alliances. This movement set in motion the transformation of agriculture into a business requiring highly knowledgeable and skilled workers, but in its origins repre-

sented a constituency in American society largely separated from the halls of both education and political power back in the East.

48. **C** Bryan, Wilson, and Debs opposed all trusts on principle, and Gompers did not speak in terms of the government's regulating industry as much as industry and labor negotiating fair terms for mutual advancement. Theodore Roosevelt's express purpose in regulating trusts was to separate the good from the bad and to bust the bad for the good of the people. Those trusts he deemed good he left alone, but not without watchdog agencies monitoring them.

49. **A** While McKinley is portrayed as undersized in this cartoon, he and the subject of imperialism are treated positively as a step toward national greatness. The image was made during a time in American history when being overweight was a sign of wealth.

50. **E** Although nativists would have liked to deport all illegal immigrants (and most legal ones) in the wake of the New Immigration, no system existed capable of doing so. The only hope of those opposed to the process was to slow it down at the gates, which the immigration quota system of the 1920s tried to do. The positive answers mentioned about immigration did not occur until later.

51. **D** FDR's Good Neighbor Policy was a step toward a new relationship with Latin America before the events surrounding World War II became all consuming.

52. **C** Although all subsequent twentieth-century presidents had to respond in some way to the policy, containment originated with Harry S. Truman.

53. **B** All other choices twist the truth about Locke or attempt to associate him with the exploits of others. Locke's theories about the Social Contract indicated that it could be broken by a tyrant who then forfeited his subjects' obedience.

54. **B** Although answer A was true of American religious experience, the quote specifically refers to answer B; the other choices are erroneous.

55. **C** Even the people on the frontier who were primarily subsistence-level farmers traded whiskey and furs back East, whereas the plantation economy of the Chesapeake Region focused entirely on the production of cash crops. Even though the Deep South cultivated cash crops, they diversified to a degree by shipping timber and naval stores.

56. **A** Russia was colonizing Alaska and even the coast of California, and England was poised to take advantage of Spanish holdings as Spain's empire weakened, not strengthened. The other choices occurred after President Monroe's time in office.

57. **D** Although the parochial school movement of Roman Catholicism in America was a reaction to Protestant influence in public schools, the temperance movement was a direct-reform initiative inspired by new interpretations of scripture by Protestants associated with the second Great Awakening. The other answers were either contrary to Protestant doctrine or indifferent to it.

58. **D** The policy described is the direct application of the Roosevelt Corollary to the Monroe Doctrine, and Theodore Roosevelt employed his Big Stick policy to enforce it.

59. **E** Although nearly all of these policies caused conservatives pause, the Agricultural Adjustment Act and the National Recovery Administration were directly challenged in court cases leading to FDR's scheme to pack the court.

60. **C** The Marshall Plan was Truman's initiative to rebuild countries in Europe in order to help them but also to prevent the spread of communism through his policy of containment. Most Americans came to understand the global goals of the Soviets and other communists and to support the containment policy. None of the other answers are completely true.

61. **E** African-Americans, remarkably, did not leave the South in large numbers until the incentive of work in factories for the war effort became available. A "great migration" occurred even between the world wars that only accelerated after World War II began in Europe.

62. **B** New York and New Jersey were particularly ethnically diverse, and even Pennsylvania absorbed the immigration of non-English colonists like Germans.

63. **A** Only answer A expresses Puritan doctrinal beliefs. The other answers are those of Quakers, Enlightenment philosophers, deists, and the typical American religious position resulting from pluralism.

64. **E** All of the answers represent truths or half-truths about Franklin's incredible life, but during the founding of the country his singular contribution was his skillful manipulation of the French whose contributions to the war effort proved invaluable. Although Franklin had made himself rich as a printer, he did so by printing royal publications earlier in life as well as other projects like his famous almanac. By the time of the American Revolution, Franklin had sold his printing business.

65. **C** Although all of the other events would have been helpful, they were beyond the capacity of the fledgling United States except Jackson's victory at New Orleans that occurred after the Treaty of Ghent had already ended the war. The treaty was negotiated as a sort of draw without the exchange of any territory but still marked an accomplishment for the young country. Great Britain realized that Napoleon was a serious threat and had to concentrate on him the most.

66. **B** The temperance movement attempted to advance this reform along with the others that were successful in the nineteenth century, but prohibition did not succeed until the twentieth century, and then only temporarily.

67. **C** Only answer C occurred markedly enough to increase the population of slaves significantly, although some of the other answers did occur.

68. **D** All of the answers are part of the reality or mythology of the Chinese immigrant experience except for answer B, which happened to Japanese immigrants. The Chinese Exclusion Act, however, occurred after the gold rush. The construction of the first transcontinental railroad had secured a place for Chinese

workers in California and after they developed control of local industries with the intention of staying permanently. Their living in separate neighborhoods was a common practice among all immigrant groups in American cities.

69. **E**   Only answer E is completely true or would help increase the membership of labor unions. The legislative milestones referenced are the Wagner Act and the much earlier Clayton Antitrust Act.

70. **A**   Answer A is the one that occurred even though all of the other answers were possibilities associated with the Korean War.

71. **D**   Answer D is the best reference to the famous baby boom beginning in 1946 and running throughout the 1950s.

72. **B**   A few Spaniards and an occasional Englishman made forays into Appalachia, but the Scots-Irish were the first group to actively settle there as the pioneers.

73. **C**   All of the other answers were resolved before ratification or did not arise until later, but the fear of the loss of individual rights prompted some states to insist on the addition of what became the Bill of Rights before they would ratify the Constitution.

74. **D**   Missouri requested to enter the Union as a slave state in 1819, prior to all of the other events.

75. **E**   The Radical Republicans in Congress were called such partly because they blamed the Democrats of the South for the Civil War and sought to punish the former Confederacy by radically altering the social, political, and economic fabric of the relationship between whites and African-Americans. This motive is not to say that many Radical Republicans sincerely wanted to elevate the condition of African-Americans in the South. The two presidents listed both proposed more lenient plans for Reconstruction, and the generals enforced policy, not formed it.

76. **C**   All of these acts of government were the commonly cited violations of a strict hands-off policy implied by the concept of laissez-faire that have caused some historians to suggest that laissez-faire never really existed. The Homestead Act, however, was the only one with no strings attached. The government did actually give out free land in order to settle the West, and what the people made of this bounty was left entirely to their own devices.

77. **D**   Although violence occurred in association with or coincidentally with several labor organizations, the Industrial Workers of the World was the most radical and purposefully resorted to murder and sabotage to pursue its ends.

78. **A**   The Battle of Wounded Knee was more of a massacre than a battle, but it was the result of the last American Indian uprising in American history. The year was 1890, the same year the frontier was closed, and these two events together signified that the troubled period of the settlement of the West was done.

79. **B**  Samuel Gompers made his famous comment for the reason stated in answer B. The other answers hint at pieces of legislation or contextual clues to mislead.

80. **D**  All the other choices have shades of truth, but the Harlem Renaissance was such a milestone in American culture not just because of the new vibrancy of celebrating African-American culture but because white urban audiences appreciated jazz, Langston Hughes poetry, and other examples of a cultural flourishing that went mainstream. The concentration and interplay of artists and thinkers spilled over, in other words, to impact all of American culture.

81. **E**  The advocacy of President Carter with the United Nations marked a major turning point in diplomatic history as the United Nations took on the difficult task of bringing those guilty of crimes against humanity to heel. The process is not always successful, but this role is a positive opportunity for the United Nations to change the world. The other answers revolve around Carter's personal initiatives after the presidency, were goals established by others, or were not pursued by the United Nations during Carter's presidency.

82. **C**  The other answers are either real events or hints from real events, but what provoked an American military response was the Gulf of Tonkin Incident described in answer C that prompted the Congress to pass the Gulf of Tonkin Resolution through which the entire American response to the Vietnam War was organized. Only later did it come out that the attack was provoked by American espionage conducted during military maneuvers off the coast of North Vietnam.

83. **B** The difficulties encountered in some early presidential elections were solved by the provisions of the Twelfth Amendment. The three branches of government were not a problem but a solution to a problem. The issues in answer C regarding sectionalism within a federal system were never solved by an amendment but by the Civil War. Answer D can be problematic even today, and no constitutional amendment has yet been proposed with a remedy; the Founding Fathers did not mention political parties in any of the provisions of the U.S. Constitution. Answer E was solved not by an amendment but by the Great Compromise over representation in the legislative branch.

84. **A**  All of the other answers were Hamiltonian schemes, but answer A was not because it could have prevented Hamilton from being president, as he was born on one of the islands of the British West Indies.

85. **D**  The other answers were issues that were largely opposite of the Populist agenda, whereas the free coinage of silver to create inflation was the cornerstone Populists believed would save the American farmer. Farmers were usually in debt and sought inflationary policies to make their debts easier to pay off with cheaper dollars.

86. **E**  Jacob Riis and Lewis Hine were photographic journalists who famously chronicled the lives of the immigrant poor and child laborers, respectively. These social issues were key targets of muckraking investigatory reporting.

87. **B**   Many of these answers were impacts on the American economy associated with other wars, and answer A twists the amazing truth that the American economy boomed after World War I despite the failure of almost all of America's allies to repay their loans. The economy boomed, that is, except for farmers who were no longer feeding American allies in Europe and suddenly experienced a drop in prices that put them in the Great Depression a decade early.

88. **A**   Unconditional surrender was set as a goal in this first significant meeting of FDR and Churchill and reiterated in almost every subsequent conference. An unintended result was that the Axis powers fought all the harder realizing that they were essentially in a fight to the death. The Axis powers had already formalized the Rome/Berlin/Tokyo Alliance, and Hitler invaded the Balkans for other strategic reasons before eventually invading the Soviet Union. By the time of the Atlantic Conference the policy of appeasement had already been understood to be foolish and dangerous. Finally, whatever Stalin might have been thinking about the future, he supported the Allied cause as an act of self-preservation under the encroachment of the Axis powers.

89. **C**   All of the other answers occurred before or after the 1960s in which the year 1964 marked the arrival of the Beatles on an American tour. The influence of these and other British artists left an impact on American rock music for much longer.

90. **D**   Although all of these events were instrumental in launching the Information Age to one degree or another, the Information Age is embodied in the World Wide Web. Some debate exists as to what the Information Age is, but the phenomenal access to instant information via the Internet relies on all the other items mentioned except the transatlantic cable that was replaced by satellites. The impact of this availability of information is an order of magnitude higher than that of any other previous medium except for perhaps the invention of writing.

# Motives and Methods of European Exploration

*Following the light of the sun, we left the Old World.*
—Christopher Columbus, 1492

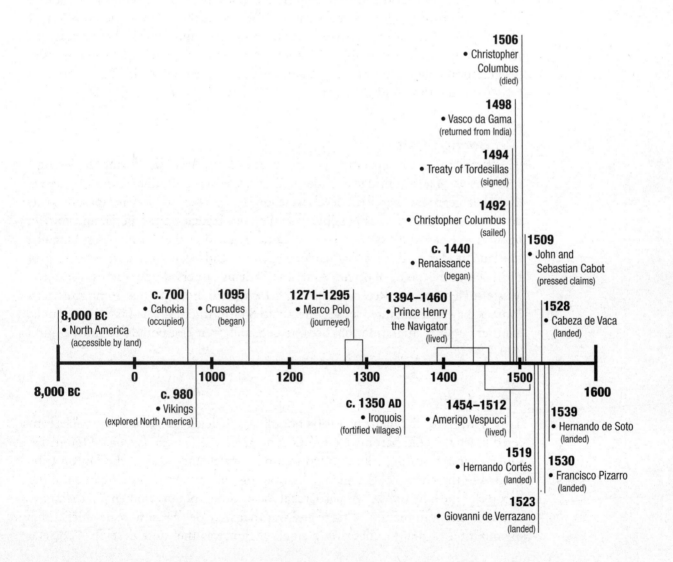

# Top 20 Things to Know

## 1 North America

The United States is the centerpiece of a vast continent containing nearly every type of biome. When the American Indians arrived North America contained seemingly endless forests and the Great Plains. The oldest mountains, the Appalachians, are in the east. The younger and much larger Rocky Mountains in the west are part of a chain that runs from Canada all the way down the length of South America. The Great Lakes and the Grand Canyon are scars telling of the impact of tremendous geological forces over time. Two large rivers, the Missouri in the west and the Ohio in the east, join with many other lesser tributaries to form the Mississippi River that drains into the Gulf of Mexico at New Orleans. Severe climates of North America range from the arctic stretches of unbroken ice to the arid southwest deserts that contain Death Valley, the hottest, lowest, and driest place on the continent. Conveniently poised to cradle early colonial settlements on the Atlantic Ocean is a large coastal plain that permitted river transportation 100 miles inland before reaching the first impassable waterfalls. The American Indians adapted well to almost every geographical region after crossing a land bridge that existed at the Bering Strait as recently as ten thousand years ago.

## 2 Bering Strait

This stretch of ocean separating North America from Asia was, during the Ice Age, the location of a land bridge as wide as Alaska. Glaciers and other forms of ice were of such large extent that ocean levels were lowered. As recently as ten thousand years ago human migration was possible over the land bridge from Siberia, and human beings came across likely in pursuit of game. Even after the Bering Sea submerged the land bridge as the Ice Age ended, Eskimos and Aleuts made the crossing in boats. From this point of origin, American Indians dispersed down across the entire Western Hemisphere. Recent archeological evidence indicates that some American Indians may have migrated by sea directly to South America. The Hawaiian Islands, another target of migration that became U.S. soil, were not populated until around 300 A.D.

## 3 Iroquois

This word is not the name of a tribe but of a confederacy of six separate tribes centered in what would become New York. The Mohawk, Seneca, Cayuga, Onondaga, Oneida, and Tuscarora tribes united in a military alliance against the Huron tribe located in the Great Lakes region. The Iroquois called themselves a name meaning "people of the long house." A matriarchal society, the Iroquois women ran their government except in matters of trade and war that were delegated to male chiefs. This organization of many tribes over a single region was the most developed societal structure of any in North America at the time of the arrival of European colonists. Emerging victorious over the Huron in their ancestral struggle, the Iroquois proved to be useful allies to the British in the colonial wars of the eighteenth century.

# 4 Vikings

Vikings were the traveling warriors of Scandinavian peoples whose cultures originated in what are now Denmark, southern Sweden, and Norway. Most of these Norsemen were farmers, but their Germanic religion predisposed them to seek adventure and to engage in violent acts with impunity. By the year 700 A.D., Viking craftsmen had perfected their most important weapon, their ships. Made entirely of oak, the Viking ships were expertly designed vessels with which to raid coastlines even across the Atlantic Ocean. The ships were constructed in such a way as to be seaworthy in the open ocean in all weathers but also with shallow enough drafts to permit following rivers far upstream. Greenland was settled by Erik the Red in the late tenth century. Documents called *The Icelandic Sagas* recount that Erik's son, Leif Eriksson, explored lands even farther west that in their descriptions are similar to the east coast of Canada. This reported discovery of the Americas five hundred years before Columbus was held in doubt until archeological evidence found in the 1960s proved that Vikings had in fact been the first Europeans to set foot in North America in what is today Newfoundland. These settlements were not permanent, however, and retreated from pressure from tribes that lived inland that the Vikings called Skraelings. Columbus called them Indians.

# 5 Cahokia

Cahokia is today merely an archeological site and a series of 120 sacred mounds. Beginning around 700 A.D., however, it housed a thriving culture based on the cultivation of maize (corn) in fertile river bottoms in what is today Illinois. Cahokians built the largest city north of Mexico before European colonization. The 30,000–40,000 inhabitants disappeared without a trace and without a linguistic or traceable ethnic legacy. A part of the Mississippian culture, Cahokia was a trade center with connections over nearly all of North America until the civilization growing there collapsed around 1300 A.D. due to disease, deforestation, dispersal, or all three. All was not peaceful in Cahokia as evidenced by a two-mile-long stockade that encircled the main city. The mounds were sometimes made in the shape of living creatures, and to this feat the inhabitants of Cahokia added the construction of large earthen pyramids that were likely the tombs of important leaders. The historical significance of Cahokia is that it provided tantalizing evidence of the potential of the original settlers of North America to produce a lasting civilization, but just as important is that they failed (or chose not to keep trying). No other North American Indians approached the level of advancement exhibited at Cahokia prior to the arrival of European colonizers.

# 6 Reciprocity

The key to all of the good and bad interactions between Europeans and American Indians as well as that among various American Indian tribes was reciprocity. The common value system shared by North American Indian tribes was based on reciprocity of gifts and favors but also of sleights and injuries. Indian chiefs often obtained their position by giving superior gifts to others within their tribes. Attacks or other injuries between individuals, though, could also bring about repayment by families, clans, and even whole tribes. Far from the noble savage ideal established by Rousseau and by James Fenimore Cooper, American Indians routinely made war on each other. Most of what is today the state of Kentucky was uninhabited because it served as a hunting ground and as a site for intertribal wars. When Europeans arrived they exploited the reciprocity system by trading goods and trinkets unusual to American Indians for property rights, when no such concept existed in native cultures. The worst misfortune of the reciprocity system after the arrival of Europeans occurred when ruthless individuals from both sides drew their larger cultures into inevitable wars based on a never-ending series of reprisals for atrocities.

# 7 Crusades

With the cry, "Deus volt" (God wills it!), Pope Urban II in 1095 launched the first military campaigns to take back Palestine from whom medieval Europeans considered infidels: the Muslims. The eight or more campaigns were called Crusades, and the crusaders met with some success. As the eleventh, twelfth, and thirteenth centuries unfolded, though, it became clear they would not achieve lasting control of what they considered the Holy Land. The bearing the Crusades have on the history of the United States is that these excursions stimulated the first travel and trade Europeans experienced since the collapse of the Roman Empire. Crusaders encountered silks, spices, perfumes, glass, jewels, and other goods long absent from European trade. These luxury items were sought after in earnest by royalty, aristocrats, and newly rich townsmen alike. The rebirth of world trade originated from this clash over access to the scenes of the life of Christ and his apostles. Renewed trade laid the foundation for the Renaissance that in turn provided the means and the motives for early exploration. Europeans sought a water route to India and China to skirt the dominance of Muslims in the Middle East.

# 8 Marco Polo

Born into a prominent Venetian merchant family, Marco Polo at seventeen accompanied his father on the most famous journey of any European along the Silk Road through Mongolia to China. Motivated by the tales and trade items of returning Crusaders, Polo left in 1271 and did not return until twenty-four years later in 1295. Kublai Khan, a great Mongol ruler, received Marco Polo into his court. Upon his return to Venice, Polo dictated a book, *Discourse Concerning Various Experiences.* This book became a bestseller and, whether fact or fiction, a basis for maps and travel guides as overland trade with China was restored. Europe became a market hungry for Asian goods and vice versa. The curiosity inspired by Marco Polo propelled several European city-states and nations to scramble for access to the Far East along various routes.

# 9 Renaissance

The invention of the printing press by 1440 and the rise of international commerce created both a keen interest in learning and the means to more readily spread ideas. Italian scholars rediscovered many ancient Roman works of law and literature, as well as art. The flowering of scholarship and individualistic and humanistic endeavor became known as the Renaissance, or the "rebirth." The Renaissance effectively ended the medieval period of European history along with the rise of nations. Renewed trade and curiosity like that earlier exhibited by Marco Polo became commonplace. Individuals, city-states, and nations vied for prominence in wealth and in artistic achievement, and ultimately in feats of navigation and exploration. As the ideas of the Renaissance spread north, the desire for reform of the Catholic Church would eventually lead to the Protestant Reformation. These two intellectual and cultural movements led to a transformation of Western civilization and to the founding of colonies in the New World by several European countries.

# 10 Amerigo Vespucci

Born in 1454 in Florence, Vespucci was an embodiment of the Renaissance. In the employ of the powerful Medici family of Florence, Vespucci traveled to Spain, then Portugal, and on to what he was the first to realize was a New World, not the coast of Asia. In a total of three voyages he explored the coast of South America including the mouth of the Amazon River. While doing so, he was the first modern person to conceive of a way to calculate longitude and was thus able to fairly accurately determine how far west he had sailed. While sailing as a navigator for Spain, Portugal, and the Medicis, Vespucci produced many descriptive letters regarding both physical and human geography. These letters were a popular tool to acquaint Europeans with the wonders of the New World. Vespucci contracted malaria on his third voyage and died in Spain in 1512, but a German scholar familiar with his letters drew up a famous map using Vespucci's Christian name as the basis for the word *America*. Soon maps were using the word to describe both North and South America, and the names stuck.

# 11 Prince Henry the Navigator

Born the third son of the king of Portugal in 1394, the life of Prince Henry was timed to take full advantage of the Renaissance as it reached his country. While never sailing himself, Henry founded a school to advance knowledge of navigation, cartography (map making), and shipbuilding. His shipbuilders developed a new, faster craft known as a caravel that made long voyages beyond the Mediterranean practicable. He sponsored over forty separate voyages sent to explore the coast of Africa with two goals in mind, to break the superstitious ignorance that caused sea captains to fear falling off the earth and to dominate the spice trade with India. Before his death in 1460, Portuguese captains were out front and well on their way to accomplishing this mission.

# 12 Vasco da Gama

Following on the heels of the discovery of the Cape of Good Hope by Bartholomew Dias, Vasco da Gama's voyage pushed around the African continent and sailed all the way to India and back to Portugal by 1498. He brought back shiploads of spices. His accomplishments won him the favor of the Crown and won for Portugal trading posts on both coasts of Africa and in the Indian Ocean. On a second voyage to India he cut the time of the journey in half and thus established regular trade with the Spice Islands and India itself. By his death he was named Viceroy of India, where he died in 1524. The exploits of Portuguese traders inspired Spanish exploration.

# 13 Christopher Columbus

Few men in history are as praised and hated as Christopher Columbus. The dark interpretation of his career places blame for disease, war, famine, and enslavement of the first settlers of the Western Hemisphere on his shoulders. On the other hand, no one has had more places in the United States named after him with the possible exception of George Washington. Genoese by birth, he applied to the king of Portugal for sponsorship of a voyage west to reach the Far East. Rebuffed there, Columbus found patrons in the new sovereigns of Spain: Ferdinand and Isabella. Columbus had conceived his idea of a westward voyage from extensive reading, and through determination finished successfully not one but four voyages to the Western Hemisphere. Part of the knowledge recovered by this Renaissance hero was that many ancients knew the earth was round. While Columbus did not prove this fact to the skeptical and superstitious, those who did circumnavigate the globe certainly followed in his wake. A better promoter and explorer than administrator, Columbus fell out of favor with the Spanish Crown over reported mismanagement of Hispaniola, the seat of his government. His explorations opened up the Caribbean Sea and Central America to colonization by the Spanish, thus launching the Spanish Empire. He died in 1506 in Spain still trying to recover his prestige and privileges.

# 14 Treaty of Tordesillas

After Europe had time to digest what Columbus had done in 1492, a dispute quickly arose between Portugal and Spain. The notoriously corrupt Pope, Alexander VI, was born in Spain, and he issued two bulls (decrees) that allowed Spain to possess any new lands discovered that did not already belong to a Christian nation. A line was drawn, or imagined, that circled the globe and thus divided land targeted for imperial acquisition between the two disputing Christian nations. When more became known of just how much land these decrees gave to Spain, the king of Portugal negotiated a treaty with Ferdinand and Isabella. In 1494, the Treaty of

Tordesillas was signed with the Pope's sanction to extend the boundary line west, thus giving Portugal access to what is today Brazil. The questionable nature of the pre-Reformation sway the Pope held over international affairs was heightened by the fact that nations like England, France, and the Netherlands were banned from the New World. Such actions added to the jealousy among the nations of Christendom and spurred their rivalry to include even piracy against fellow Christians.

## 15 Hernando Cortés

The archetype of all conquistadors, Cortés led the expedition to explore Mexico for Spain. In 1519, he landed and quickly subdued two Indian tribes unable to withstand the attack by armored infantry and cavalrymen with long lances and firearms, including cannons. The Spanish and their Indian allies reduced the influence of a growing Aztec Empire. Cortés held cordial talks with Montezuma at the Aztec capital city of Tenochtitlán. Over time, however, relations broke down. Montezuma was killed by his own people, and the Spanish crushed a general revolt after hard fighting. The actions of Cortés and his soldiers destroyed the Aztec Empire and ended their brutal rituals of human sacrifice and cannibalism opening the way for Spanish settlement and the transfer of mounds of gold and silver treasures. Francisco Pizarro repeated the process with the Inca civilization of Peru beginning in 1530.

## 16 Francisco Pizarro

Although Cortés could be just as ruthless, Francisco Pizarro retains the legacy of the most brutal acts against the civilized American Indians of South America. He arrived in 1530, fortuitously just after a civil war between two brothers fighting to become the Inca, the ruler of the natives of Peru. Pizarro's small force surrounded the winner of this struggle while he was still recovering from wounds received during the war. Pizarro took Atahualpa captive and held him for an immense ransom in gold and silver. When the Incas supplied the precious metals, Atahualpa was killed anyway. Pizarro quickly conquered the rest of Peru and ruled it with an iron fist until he was assassinated by his own men in 1541.

## 17 Cabeza de Vaca

Despite a less than glorious name (it means "head of a cow"), this Spanish explorer was one of four survivors of an expedition of nearly three hundred men sent to explore Florida in 1528. Abandoned by their ships and assailed by American Indians and disease, the expedition set out across the Gulf of Mexico on rafts. Coming ashore in Texas, only eighty survivors set off overland looking for a Spanish outpost. After eight years Cabeza de Vaca and three others completed this nightmarish yet wonderful trek as the first Europeans to see the Southwest. Their reports of bison herds and gold drew further Spanish expansion into what became New Mexico. Cabeza de Vaca served as a provincial governor until he too was deposed.

## 18 Hernando de Soto

He was the first Spaniard to successfully explore Florida but did not stop there. Hernando de Soto landed with six hundred men in 1539 and surveyed virtually the entire Southeast. He discovered the Mississippi River but died in 1542 of a fever. The survivors of his expedition explored for another year before floating down the Mississippi River back to Spanish civilization.

## 19 John and Sebastian Cabot

This father-son team of Venetians worked for the English Crown (the father-son team of Henry VII and Henry VIII). The father secured the commission to explore for England but died before the journey began. Sebastian carried on in 1509 and claimed the fishing beds off the coast of Canada for his employer. The Cabots are therefore responsible for the first English toehold in the New World.

## 20 Giovanni de Verrazano

Since other European monarchs indulged in the hiring of Italian explorers, Francis I sent the Florentine Verrazano to claim land for France. Verrazano steered his ship in 1523 toward the modern-day Carolinas, then up the coast to as far north as Nova Scotia. French interest in further exploration and colonization as well as claim to Canada were spurred by Verrazano's report back to the king. Verrazano has the distinction of being the only North American explorer known to have been killed and eaten by American Indians. His demise came in 1528. For his troubles, a modern suspension bridge was named after him in New York Harbor.

## The Big Picture

1. The stage set for U.S. history on the continent of North America was a sparsely populated scene of great variety, vast distances, and virtually untapped natural resources.

2. The first settlers of North America came from Asia via the land bridge and dispersed after the Ice Age over the entire Western Hemisphere establishing varied cultures but no lasting civilizations save those in Central and South America.

3. The combined impact of the rise of nations, the return of trade, and the rebirth of learning in the Renaissance made Europeans curious, courageous, and competitive enough to launch voyages of discovery and to found colonies to exploit the New World's riches.

4. Beginning with the voyage of Christopher Columbus, Spanish explorers and colonizers established the largest empire since the Roman Empire by pursuing service to God, personal glory, and wealth in the form of shiploads of silver and gold.

5. The nations of Portugal, England, France, and the Netherlands were jealous of the immediately lucrative nature of Spain's achievements and hired their own Italian navigators in order to lay claim to lands in the New World before it was too late.

# Spanish, French, and Dutch Colonization

# CHAPTER 3

*Thereupon the gold on the shields and on all the devices was taken. . .
and the Spaniards made the gold into bricks.*
—Bernardino de Sahagún in the Florentine Codex, 1547

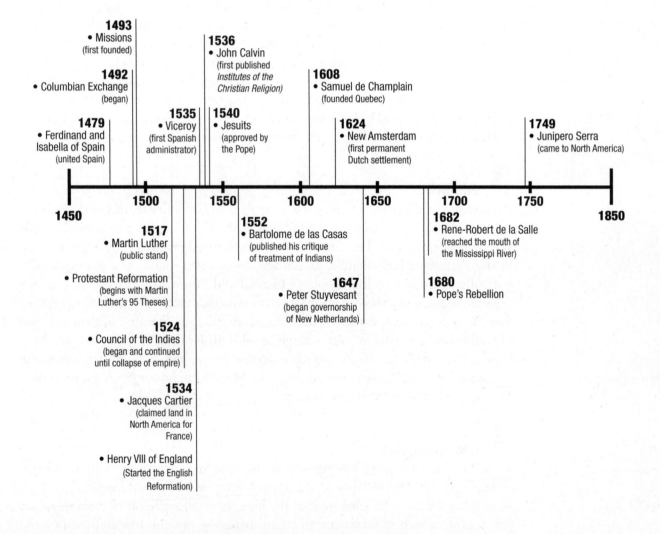

**1493**
• Missions
(first founded)

**1492**
• Columbian Exchange
(began)

**1479**
• Ferdinand and
Isabella of Spain
(united Spain)

**1535**
• Viceroy
(first Spanish
administrator)

**1536**
• John Calvin
(first published
*Institutes of the
Christian Religion*)

**1540**
• Jesuits
(approved by
the Pope)

**1608**
• Samuel de Champlain
(founded Quebec)

**1624**
• New Amsterdam
(first permanent
Dutch settlement)

**1749**
• Junipero Serra
(came to North America)

1450    1500    1550    1600    1650    1700    1750    1850

**1517**
• Martin Luther
(public stand)

• Protestant Reformation
(begins with Martin
Luther's 95 Theses)

**1524**
• Council of the Indies
(began and continued
until collapse of empire)

**1534**
• Jacques Cartier
(claimed land in
North America for
France)

• Henry VIII of England
(Started the English
Reformation)

**1552**
• Bartolome de las Casas
(published his critique
of treatment of Indians)

**1647**
• Peter Stuyvesant
(began governorship
of New Netherlands)

**1682**
• Rene-Robert de la Salle
(reached the mouth of
the Mississippi River)

**1680**
• Pope's Rebellion

# Top 20 Things to Know

## 1 Ferdinand and Isabella of Spain

Ferdinand of Aragon and Isabella of Castille united the Spanish nation when their marriage ended the rivalry of their kingdoms. They also united the forces of Spain to drive out the Moors, Muslims who had taken over the Iberian Peninsula centuries before. They became the patrons of Christopher Columbus and launched the Spanish Empire upon hearing of his discoveries of a supposed water route to Asia. They established management precedents that capitalized on the treasures discovered in the New World but also served as a model for other European nations to attempt similar exploits.

## 2 Missions

Missions were the chief method of Spanish colonization through peaceful interaction with American Indians. A friar or priest founded each mission as a self-sufficient farming village and converted the locals, or at least convinced them to work peacefully and to attend the Catholic mass. A church was erected as a town center, as well as a place of worship. This structure was surrounded by a wall behind which cooperative Indians could seek shelter when hostile tribes like the Apache and Comanche marauded through. Many clergymen, especially Jesuits, sought to educate the American Indians who thereby were more easily assimilated into the combined culture that made up the bulk of the population.

## 3 Jesuits

Representing the highest ideals of scholarly Roman Catholicism, this religious order was founded by Ignatius Loyola and became the chief instrument of the Catholic Counter-Reformation. The Counter-Reformation sought to win back ground lost to the Protestant Reformation in Europe. Jesuits also made up a strong contingent of missionaries to the people of Central and South America. As their efforts expanded, Jesuit priests entered into North America, especially the Southwest. As their de facto control of areas of the Spanish Empire rose because of their superior education and zeal, the Spanish Crown recalled all Jesuits from the New World to prevent them from gaining too much independence. The Jesuits still left a legacy of commitment to education in the universities founded in honor of Loyola or Francis Xavier, another noted Jesuit missionary.

## 4 Encomiendas

These licenses were privileges granted by the Spanish Crown as a method of organizing American Indian labor in the Spanish Empire but also of keeping purebred Spanish colonists, or Creoles, loyal to the king. Each encomienda allowed its bearer first a salary, which could be cut off for misbehavior, but also title to the labor and tribute of the American Indians in a given area. American Indians were used in mining operations but also in farming and ranching, that is, until their numbers dwindled due to disease and the hardships of the labor. Then the importation of African slaves was used both in the Spanish Empire and in Brazil to replace the American Indians who lacked resistance to disease.

## 5 Pope's Rebellion

A Pueblo medicine man named Pope (po-pay) organized resistance to Spanish rule after being whipped at the Santa Fe mission. Pope crafted an alliance between the Zuni and Hopi tribes of the Pueblo who were persecuted by the Spanish for continuing native religious practices after their supposed conversion to Catholicism. In 1680 a widespread, coordinated attack by over 17,000 Pueblo Indians swept across the Rio Grande River Valley killing most of the friars and hundreds of Spanish men, women, and children. The Pueblo Revolt was a clear sign of continued animosity toward the Spanish invaders and for a time achieved independence for the American Indians of New Mexico. Spanish military forces returned, however, and again subjugated them.

## 6 Council of the Indies

This advisory body in the Spanish government answered only to the Crown in shaping policies for every aspect of religious and secular life in the Spanish Empire in the New World. This agency collected meticulous records, dispensed information, dispatched imperial civil and military employees, and oversaw even the activities of the Roman Catholic clergy in the Americas. No other European imperial power could match the efficiency of the Council of the Indies although all tried, and despite corruption and the great distance involved the agency maintained firm control of the empire for around three hundred years. When revolutions removed the Council in the nineteenth century, however, the new societies suffered from having never experienced the autonomy enjoyed by other European colonists.

## 7 Viceroy

Just beneath the Crown in the power structure of the Spanish Empire sat this representative position sent to govern first two divisions in the New World and then four as the empire grew in size and population. Handpicked, loyal men were placed in these positions and were periodically rotated or removed to prevent allegiances being formed that would rival the honor due the Crown. Each viceroy served as the head of the civil government but also as the commander in chief of Spanish military forces in his region. The Spanish position of viceroy served as a model for other European nations that sought stricter control over their colonies.

## 8 Columbian Exchange

The contact initiated by Columbus and the launch of the Spanish Empire was the first encounter of the civilizations and peoples of the New World who until then had developed in complete isolation. Animals and plants of the Old and New Worlds were transferred as well as precious metals and diseases. Europeans brought to the New World peoples food and draft animals, fruit trees, grains, olives, grapes, sugarcane, honeybees, new vegetables, and the coffee bean. Important crops discovered in the New World included potatoes, tomatoes, squash, peppers, maize (corn), peanuts, vanilla beans, pineapples, and new strains of tobacco. Although the economies of all the nations of the world have been positively impacted by this exchange, the diseases Europeans and Africans had exchanged for centuries proved devastating to American Indian populations who lacked immunity and died by the millions of smallpox, influenza, diphtheria, and typhus.

## 9 Bartolome de las Casas

This Dominican friar, priest, and scholar worked tirelessly through the sixteenth century traveling back and forth between Spain and the New World decrying the plight of the American Indians. He actively lobbied the Spanish Crown for reforms of the treatment of American Indians in the military campaigns of Spanish conquest and in the encomienda system of Spanish colonization. He went so far as to attempt what might have been the first utopian community in the Western Hemisphere based on principles of fairer treatment of and cooperation with willing American Indians. His efforts at reform largely failed, as did his utopian dream, but his writings revealed that some Europeans questioned the policies of empire. Unfortunately, as African slavery began in the New World, some of its advocates used the writings of las Casas to justify subjugation of Africans as a means of helping American Indians.

## 10 Junipero Serra

This Franciscan friar, priest, and scholar lived in the latter part of the Spanish Empire during the eighteenth century and followed the mainstream Spanish and Roman Catholic policies of expansion of both civil and religious authority using the mission system. Serra was personally responsible for the founding of nine missions in what would become California, including San Diego, and is thus responsible for spreading civilization to this important region. His methods, however, showed that the Spanish maintained a policy of harsh treatment of resistant American Indians that could then be considered part of the reason for the collapse of the Spanish Empire.

## 11 Protestant Reformation

Several centuries of dissatisfaction with the doctrine and practice of the Roman Catholic Church climaxed in the early sixteenth century with the writings of the priest and scholar Martin Luther. Luther's emphasis on the biblical doctrines of grace transformed European, and thus American, Christianity either directly or by inspiring the Catholic Counter-Reformation. Catholics launched the Inquisition and the Society of Jesus, or Jesuits, to protect Catholic doctrine and territory. Protestantism spread to other parts of Europe and established churches independent from Rome. Continued church reform launched careers of men like John Calvin and John Knox and movements like Puritanism in England. Many colonists went to America seeking freedom to pursue doctrine and practices more in keeping with their interpretation of the Bible. Protestants held the key doctrine of each person's having an individual calling and the Christian duty to work diligently at that calling for the glory of God. The ideas of Protestantism, including this work ethic, became seminal attributes of American society through the influence of Dutch, English, Swedish, German, and French Huguenot colonists.

## 12 Martin Luther

The German priest and scholar who defied Rome and launched the Protestant Reformation by contesting certain teachings of the Roman Catholic Church beginning in 1517. Luther was a Renaissance scholar who translated the Bible into German and thus with his own actions embodied the connection between the Renaissance and the Reformation, both of which were critical to the upheaval in Europe that led to not only the exploration and colonization of the New World but also the peopling of what would become the United States. As a result of these two transforming movements in European history, the people of the United States originated through the sometimes contradictory impulses of reform and liberty of conscience.

## 13 John Calvin

This Frenchman began as a priest but joined the Protestant cause as a legal scholar and minister in Geneva, Switzerland. His *Institutes of the Christian Religion* became the most thorough and systematic statement of Protestant doctrine. His emphasis on the sovereignty of God in salvation and over all of life influenced the formation of the Presbyterian and Congregational churches through the English Reformation. Calvin's student, John Knox, formed the Scottish Presbyterian Church brought to the shores of America by Scots-Irish immigrants. The Puritans were also Calvinist in doctrine and were the founders in the English colonies of what would become Congregational churches in New England.

## 14 Henry VIII of England

This Tudor king of England cited scriptural and national security reasons to justify his divorce from Catherine of Aragon, the daughter of Ferdinand and Isabella of Spain, and his marriage to Anne Boleyn. Since the Roman Catholic Church opposed his actions, Henry launched the English Reformation. Although other Protestant reformers would come later in English history with more sincerely spiritual motives, Henry did sever ties with Rome and permit the Bible to be printed in English legally for the first time. His next important action was to die and guide succession to the English throne with his last will and testament. His sickly son, Edward, came first, but upon his death Henry's daughters Mary and then Elizabeth held the throne. These two English monarchs were responsible for lasting war between Spain and England that led to the great clash in 1588 at which the Spanish Armada was defeated.

## 15 Jacques Cartier

This first French explorer of Canada worked with and learned from Giovanni de Verrazano, the Italian first hired by France to explore the New World. Cartier made a total of three voyages and is responsible for naming Canada. In 1534 he sailed as far as 1,000 miles into the interior up the St. Lawrence River and brought back rumors of an immensely rich region similar to the fabled cities of gold that motivated so much of Spanish exploration. The rumors had the same effect on the French until they realized the gold of New France wasn't precious metal but fur. Samuel de Champlain followed in Cartier's wake and founded Quebec in 1608.

## 16 Northwest Passage

With war between Spain and England as well as the dangers of the lengthy route around the southern tip of South America, all European nations that founded colonies in North America sought this nonexistent route to Asia. Believing that a water route around what would become Canada lay somewhere just around the next bend, explorers were dispatched from up and down the Atlantic seaboard in the quest for it. The desperation to find the Northwest Passage revealed the zeal the competitive nations possessed to claim a shorter route to trade with China and India that had stimulated exploration and led to the discovery of the Western Hemisphere in the first place.

## 17 Samuel de Champlain

One of the searchers for the fabled Northwest Passage was this ship captain and cartographer from France. Champlain explored as far south as Cape Cod, but he concentrated his search up the St. Lawrence River and as far west as the shore of two of the Great Lakes. He therefore shaped the birth of New France as he founded the settlements that would become both Quebec and Montreal. After solidifying a French alliance with the Huron Indians against their foe, the Iroquois, he lived out his days as the governor of Montreal.

## 18 Rene-Robert de la Salle

This French explorer followed up on Champlain's journeys to discover more of the extent of the Great Lakes, and he followed up on the journey of Marquette and Joliet to prove their theory that the Mississippi River did indeed flow into the Gulf of Mexico. After claiming the mouth of the Mississippi River for France and naming the delta region Louisiana for the French king, la Salle returned to France and was granted power to found a colony there. Upon his return trip, however, he was unable to find the mouth of the Mississippi from the Gulf and was killed in a mutiny by his crew. The combined efforts of Champlain, la Salle, and thousands of French fur trappers, however, lay claim to the largest territory in North America for any European nation. The problem came in keeping it.

## 19 New Amsterdam

This Dutch colony in North America began on Manhattan Island by 1624 when Peter Minuit purchased the best harbor on the Atlantic seaboard from local American Indians with a few trading goods. The Dutch also proved to be competent fur traders and excellent merchants who created a fleet of ships to rival that of England, the main maritime power. As Dutch colonists settled farther onto the coastal plain up various rivers, the wider Dutch holdings became the colony of New Netherland. The Dutch were responsible for founding the most ethnically diverse colony in the settlement of New Amsterdam that, fittingly, became the site of the trade and cultural capital of the world, New York City.

## 20 Peter Stuyvesant

This governor of New Netherland was the last hope of Holland and the Dutch East India Company to hold on to their investments. While competent as both a civil and military leader, the challenges of being surrounded by New France, rising English colonies, and hostile American Indians proved too great. His efforts to defend Dutch interests and territory served to keep the French at bay long enough for England to establish viable colonies that could protect themselves. For his trouble the English ultimately assailed and absorbed the colony in 1664 after the Dutch were weakened by a year of war with American Indians. The English renamed New Amsterdam the city of New York, and the colony of New York became one of the original thirteen English North American colonies. Most of the Dutch colonists and their diverse neighbors within their colony were allowed to remain and to retain their property, thus further enriching the diverse colonial population of what would become the United States.

## The Big Picture

1. The Spanish shifted their emphasis from conquering to colonizing and established an efficient bureaucracy to manage their far-flung New World empire by subjugating both American Indians and African slaves.

2. Spanish colonization focused on the mission system of spreading Roman Catholicism along with political and economic control, and the resulting exchange of culture and goods enriched both the Old and New Worlds but also spread deadly diseases among American Indians.

3. The Protestant Reformation stimulated great change in European society far beyond its religious roots and motivated religious dissenters to seek opportunities in the New World for freedom of worship according to the dictates of their consciences.

4. France established a vast New World empire based on fur trading that stretched from the St. Lawrence River in Canada, around the Great Lakes, and down the Mississippi River to the Gulf of Mexico, and became the main competitor with England for control of North America.

5. The Dutch were the other great strain of Europeans to establish a colony in North America at New Amsterdam, and the ethnic and linguistic diversity for which New York City is known today was already evident in this colonial forerunner before it was absorbed by the English.

# English Colonization

*We . . . for the glory of God, and advancement of the Christian faith, and honor of our King and country . . . in the presence of God and one another, covenant and combine ourselves together into a civil body politic. . . .*
—The Mayflower Compact, 1620

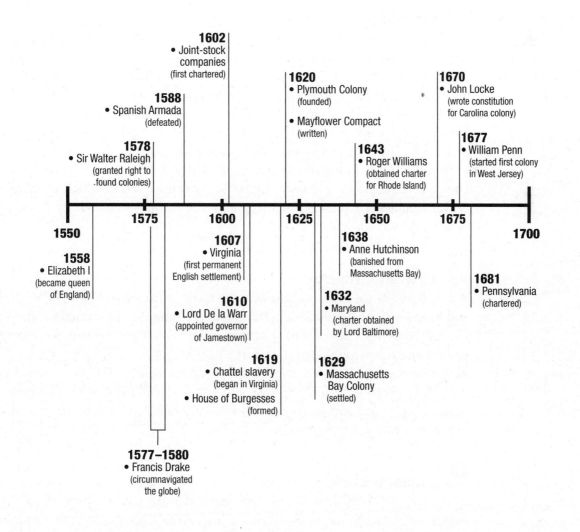

**1602**
• Joint-stock companies
(first chartered)

**1620**
• Plymouth Colony
(founded)

• Mayflower Compact
(written)

**1670**
• John Locke
(wrote constitution
for Carolina colony)

**1588**
• Spanish Armada
(defeated)

**1643**
• Roger Williams
(obtained charter
for Rhode Island)

**1677**
• William Penn
(started first colony
in West Jersey)

**1578**
• Sir Walter Raleigh
(granted right to
found colonies)

**1550**  **1575**  **1600**  **1625**  **1650**  **1675**  **1700**

**1558**
• Elizabeth I
(became queen
of England)

**1607**
• Virginia
(first permanent
English settlement)

**1638**
• Anne Hutchinson
(banished from
Massachusetts Bay)

**1681**
• Pennsylvania
(chartered)

**1610**
• Lord De la Warr
(appointed governor
of Jamestown)

**1632**
• Maryland
(charter obtained
by Lord Baltimore)

**1619**
• Chattel slavery
(began in Virginia)
• House of Burgesses
(formed)

**1629**
• Massachusetts
Bay Colony
(settled)

**1577–1580**
• Francis Drake
(circumnavigated
the globe)

# Top 20 Things to Know

## 1 Elizabeth I

The daughter of Henry VIII and Anne Boleyn, this monarch of England was more responsible than any other for positioning her country to take advantage of New World discoveries. When she became queen in 1558, England was reeling from battles between Anglican Church leaders and those wanting more church reform like the Puritans. Elizabeth ended strife over religion long enough to unify the country and strengthen the military, especially the navy. Her refusal to marry kept a foreign monarch from meddling in English affairs, but the rebuffed Philip II of Spain initiated a war as a result. Elizabeth lived to see England win the war and died in 1603 only a few years from seeing a permanent English settlement in the New World.

## 2 Francis Drake

A pirate who wound up the most celebrated sea captain of his day, Drake sought revenge for damages done by the Spanish to his merchant fleet. In a daring voyage beginning in 1577, Drake sailed his *Golden Hind* down the Atlantic coast of the Spanish Empire and plundered every port he could. When he arrived at the southern tip of the Western Hemisphere, he decided to sail on into the Pacific Ocean. He kept plundering Spanish ports up the Pacific coast and then boldly circumnavigated the globe. He arrived in 1580 with a ship laden with Spanish gold and spices acquired in the actual West Indies that Columbus had been looking for in the first place. His voyage inspired other profit-seeking ventures, and he was knighted by Elizabeth I for his troubles. He proved instrumental in the ensuing naval war by defeating the Spanish Armada in 1588.

## 3 Sir Walter Raleigh

A true Renaissance man, Raleigh won the favor of Elizabeth I by fighting the Irish and Spanish and by establishing colonies in Virginia that he named for the Virgin Queen. Although his colonizing efforts ultimately failed, he and Sir Humphrey Gilbert and others published *Discourse Concerning Western Planting*, the book that explained the rationale for English colonization. While Elizabeth lived, Raleigh defended the realm from the Spanish and was rewarded for it. After Elizabeth died, Raleigh kept on attacking the Spanish and was beheaded for it by James I, the first of the Stuart kings of England.

## 4 Primogeniture

This caveat of English common law stated that all the property of an English nobleman had to be passed down to the firstborn son, and only to that son. While the measure stabilized land holdings and thus the politics of England, second and third (or more) sons of the gentry were left with little to do and no land with which to build their own estates. If a career in the church or the military did not appeal to them, these landless aristocrats were all dressed up and educated but bored. The answer for thousands came in making a go of life in colonial America where land was ultimately available aplenty. A life of ease made the rigors of carving civilization out of a wilderness beyond the capacity of some, and their refusal to do manual labor was almost the ruination of Jamestown.

## 5 Joint-stock Companies

These economic arrangements were the forerunners of modern corporations. Drake's voyage around the globe and eleven English colonies were backed by advertising a share in the profits if citizens of England purchased stock in the companies. A broad spectrum of English society thus took interest in the New World and minimized the risk to any one planter or group of planters. The incredible profits of Drake's voyage inspired wider investment. English colonies were private ventures that governed themselves and made several risky decisions based more on the search for profit than for the well-being of colonists. The autonomy of the original companies, however, established key political and economic precedents.

## 6 Spanish Armada

The ill-fated invasion fleet of Spain set out for England in 1588. As the more than one hundred Spanish ships crowded into the English Channel, Sir Francis Drake attacked from behind. Several decrepit English ships were set afire and driven by the wind into the mass of Spanish ships that could only escape by sailing up and around Scotland. When they entered the North Sea, a storm destroyed even more ships. With this tremendous victory, apparently believed to be assisted by God, the English began their longtime supremacy of the seas. Greater capacity to extend and defend its shipping led to great zeal in England's colonization.

## 7 Virginia

The first colony of the original thirteen began abysmally at an ill-chosen site and with ill-chosen goals. After the deaths of several thousand colonists to disease, starvation, and American Indian attacks, the first permanent settlement of Jamestown had grown from a small settlement and a fort to a colony with towns. Key colonial precedents occurred in 1619 when John Rolfe cultivated a viable strain of hybrid tobacco and established a firm foundation for a colonial economy in cash-crop agriculture and when property owners demanded more secure justice and protection by forming a colonial government, the House of Burgesses. Although Virginia would go on to be the birthplace of presidents and famous generals, it also was the birthplace of African slavery in English America. The Virginia Company eventually went bankrupt and the colony was salvaged by becoming a royal colony with a royal governor, William Berkeley, in 1642.

## 8 Lord De la Warr

This new governor and captain of Virginia arrived with three ships filled with new colonists and supplies at Jamestown in 1610 just as the colony was on the brink of collapse. His energetic and militaristic rule galvanized the colony and set it back on the road to viability. Lord De la Warr used his own fortune to buttress Virginia and established the key turning point in giving Virginia Company land to Virginians as their own private property. Thus the lack of incentive to follow company orders was transformed into the seeds of the American dream and of the economic system of capitalism. On a return trip to England, Lord De la Warr's ship was blown off course into the mouth of a river that was subsequently named the Delaware.

## 9 House of Burgesses

The first representative assembly in the Western Hemisphere was established in 1619 in Virginia to protect the property and other rights of Englishmen that the colonists of Jamestown and its environs had come to expect. Villages in Virginia were known as burgs, and the representatives elected from each burg were called burgesses. The establishment of the House of Burgesses proved an assertion later made by Thomas Jefferson in the Declaration of Independence that the powers of legislation are incapable of annihilation. Without firm guidance or protection from England, Virginians had no one else to turn to besides themselves. Even when England did send a royal governor, William Berkeley wisely agreed to share power with an existing colonial legislature. These steps were crucial precedents for the American Revolution.

## 10 Indentured Servitude

Impoverished Londoners and other English men and women displaced by the population boom and failed wool market also looked for opportunity in America like their aristocratic counterparts fleeing primogeniture. These colonists, however, were too poor to afford the trip to Virginia and thus answered advertisements in London newspapers to take ship on a free voyage in return for four to seven years of service to whoever had paid their passage. The terms of the agreement were written in a contract that was subsequently torn in such a fashion as to leave a pattern of indentations in the two halves, hence the term *indentured*. When the halves were put back together they were proof of the identity of the servant and the obligation of the master to provide the means for the new freeman to establish himself as a yeoman farmer. Indentured servants often did not survive the period of their service, and even when they did, stingy masters sometimes refused to supply the land, tools, mules, seeds, and so on, needed.

## 11 Chattel Slavery

Although the original African slaves brought to Virginia were treated more like indentured servants, the legal status of African-Americans soon became that of chattels. The word in English law came out of the medieval period, meaning "property," and was closely akin to cattle. Chattel slavery placed African slaves on a par with buildings or livestock and removed all human rights except those granted by the mercy or whim of masters. Abject cruelty toward slaves was later made illegal by the House of Burgesses, but chattel slaves and their descendants were reduced to this status with few exceptions until after the Civil War.

## 12 Plymouth Colony

A short-lived but symbolically important colony was founded in 1620 at Cape Cod, in what would become Massachusetts, by Separatists and other more secularly minded colonists. Blown off course, the one hundred survivors of the ocean passage drafted the Mayflower Compact to increase their obligation to stand together in the wilderness they saw ashore. Half the original settlers were lost, but Plymouth Colony survived to contribute a vivid legacy of integrity and faith before they were eventually absorbed by their much larger neighbor, the Massachusetts Bay Colony. William Bradford, the long-term governor of Plymouth Colony, recorded their history in a work he called *Of Plymouth Plantation.*

## 13 Mayflower Compact

The key legacy of Plymouth Colony lay in this document, which is considered the first written constitution of the English-speaking world. In a few paragraphs the forty-one signers of the document pledged before God and those present to form a government, a "civil body politic," with just laws and bound the signers to obedience and mutual support. Other colonies soon sought the protection of a tangible social contract once they found themselves 3,000 miles away from the more nebulous legal precedents that made up the intangible English constitution, or common law.

## 14 Massachusetts Bay Colony

After some preliminary settlements were made in 1624, the Massachusetts Bay Company founded a Puritan colony in 1629. After that point more and more Puritans came to America until their passage became known as the Great Migration. Fleeing persecution for their religious beliefs, whole communities of Puritans came to settle Boston, Salem, and other towns and villages. Families and church congregations arrived intact and soon acquired a level of development and a lifespan significantly beyond that of the English colonists to the south. Harvard University was founded by Puritans seeking more educated ministers in 1636. Puritan colonies, which included the expansions of Massachusetts Bay named Connecticut and New Hampshire, adopted a colonial legislature like Virginia's House of Burgesses but called it a General Court.

## 15 Anne Hutchinson

This Bostonian began to teach doctrines the Puritans believed to be heretical in her home with several men, even ministers, in attendance. This practice incurred the ire of the Puritan authorities who put her on trial for heresy. Hutchinson held an antinomian view of Christianity more similar to Quakerism than to the Christianity of her Puritan neighbors. She stressed the importance of God's grace as all Protestants did, but departed from the need to manifest that grace through obedience to God's law. She taught that each person could receive divine revelation. In a Puritan colony these heretical doctrines took on the flavor of sedition and contempt, especially when she refused to stop teaching them. She was thus banished from Massachusetts Bay and lived in Rhode Island, then New York. Hutchinson was a pioneer in American religious liberty in a colony that had sacrificed everything to acquire it for themselves with no thought of extending it to others.

## 16 Roger Williams

Another pioneer of religious liberty, Williams was a Puritan minister whose dispute with the Puritan authorities was more about civil government being in the hands of church authorities than along doctrinal lines. He is thus also among the first in centuries of European practice to advocate the separation of church and state. The Anglican Church was the established church in Virginia, and the Congregational Church was established in Massachusetts Bay, but Williams was banished because he did not think church and civil government should be one and the same or even closely related. He lived among American Indians outside of Massachusetts and ultimately founded a new colony, Rhode Island, in 1636. Here complete religious liberty became a part of the legacy of colonial American society, and Roger Williams became the father of what would be called Baptist churches in America.

## 17 Maryland

George Calvert, Lord Baltimore, sought to found a colony along the Potomac River north of Virginia as a refuge for Roman Catholics also facing persecution from the Anglican Church. Maryland became the chief outpost of Catholicism in the English colonies, but later Lord Baltimore had to step down from being the proprietor because of the influx of Protestants from Virginia. An Act of Toleration was passed in 1649, however, that permitted all Trinitarian Christians freedom of worship. The port city bearing the original proprietor's name eventually turned Maryland into a thriving shipping center.

## 18 John Locke

The central figure of English political philosophy at the time of the founding of the American colonies was John Locke. Building on the ideas of Thomas Hobbes about the Social Contract, Locke theorized that governments were instituted among men for the preservation of life, liberty, and property and that they should employ a balance of powers. Beyond the fact that nearly all of the Founding Fathers were students of Locke's writings, Locke's contribution to U.S. history included the constitution he wrote for the Carolina Colony as secretary to one of its eight proprietors. This document, called the Fundamental Constitution for Carolina, set new standards for utopian planning when it was drafted in 1669. Locke tried to codify distribution of land and easy citizenship standards to encourage settlement of the colony but also wrote in firm religious freedom.

## 19  William Penn

Perhaps the only man to take part in the founding of three of the original thirteen colonies, William Penn was instrumental in the formation of East and West Jersey as well as his own Pennsylvania, from which Delaware sprang. Having been converted to Quakerism, or the Society of Friends, Penn lobbied the English government for this sect of antinomian Christianity. The king owed Penn's family money, and the debt was discharged by the grant of Pennsylvania, or "Penn's woods." William Penn proved to be an enlightened law giver who drafted several versions of a constitution for Pennsylvania as circumstances changed over his lifetime. He sowed humanitarian, even libertarian, principles into the society of his colony and made peaceful relations with the Indians. He was such a visionary as to be the first person to propose the British colonies be placed under one government, but although that idea was ahead of its time, his ideas of government for the people were not. Because of a thriving economy Penn's colony thrived and embodied nearly all of the other "American" legacies.

## 20  Pennsylvania

The most "American" colony of all the thirteen colonies, Pennsylvania had a diverse society and what would be the largest colonial city, Philadelphia. As one of the Middle Colonies, Pennsylvania was perfectly located to also possess a diversified economy consisting of grain farming, basic manufacturing, and shipping. The border between the Penn family holdings and the colony of Maryland was surveyed and became known as the Mason-Dixon Line, the symbolic border between North and South. As the Quaker refuge, peace lasted with American Indians in Pennsylvania the longest time of any English colony, but western expansion eventually led to armed clashes. When settlers sought aid, the pacifist Quaker government refused. In the Glorious Revolution, the Quakers again refused to support an armed conflict, this time with the very king who had granted their charter, James II. For these breaches of the social contract the Penn family lost control of its own colony, but vast tracts of land remained their private property.

## *The Big Picture*

1. Even though English colonization began with disorganization and failure, English society had several distinct qualities that ultimately formed colonies with greater societal vitality than those of the Spanish, Dutch, or French.

2. Every English colony followed roughly the pattern experienced in the founding of Jamestown including a point of near disaster followed by a long climb toward a feasible economy and stable self-government.

3. Each English colony contributed significant legacies to what would become the society of the United States, and some colonies, like Pennsylvania, early on experienced a culture fashioned of all of the positive colonial legacies.

4. A chronic labor shortage in the colonies led to two extremes to secure enough manpower; indentured servitude allowed poor English men and women to come to America and work their way to freedom, whereas chattel slavery permitted the purchase of African slaves as laborers for life who were considered personal property.

5. After the defeat of the Spanish Armada in 1588 and the establishment of viable colonies in the New World starting in 1607, England began to eclipse Spain as the nation with the potential to launch a world empire.

# Colonial "American" Society

*He is an American who, leaving behind him all his ancient prejudices and manners, receives new ones from the new mode of life he has embraced, the new government he obeys, and the new rank he holds.*

—Jean de Crèvecoeur, c. 1770

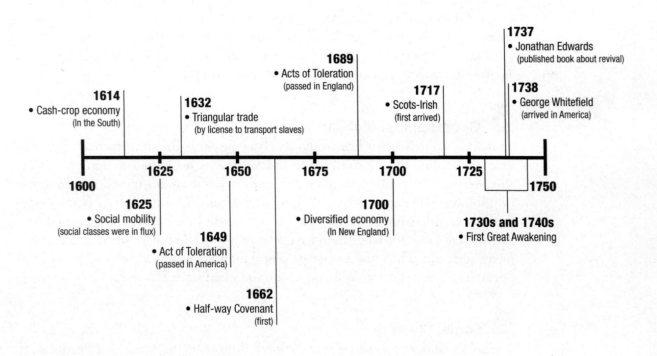

# Top 20 Things to Know

## 1 Proprietors

These dignitaries were fortunate people indeed! Most consisted of friends of the king of England or those who had done exceptional service to their monarch. All of them were granted large tracts of land in colonial America for their trouble. Families like the Penns and the Calverts were given personal possession of Pennsylvania and Maryland, respectively, and looked upon themselves as social reformers creating sanctuaries for religious minorities like Quakers and Roman Catholics. The eight proprietors of the Carolina Colony had assisted the king in the Restoration and were given land consisting of modern North and South Carolina and Tennessee. Proprietors established governments for their colonies and tried to attract colonists. They collectively represented a powerful tradition of private property rights in America, and simultaneously, how little the British monarchy valued the wilderness the British Empire had acquired in North America.

## 2 Coastal Plain

This important geographical feature contributed profoundly to the success of the original thirteen colonies. Extending from the fall line in the foothills of the Appalachian Mountains out to the Atlantic Ocean, the Coastal Plain contained fertile soil and was crisscrossed with rivers that served as highways. Settlement went upriver as far as boats could travel and then widened out from there.

## 3 Geographical Mobility

In marked contrast with British subjects back in Great Britain, American colonists enjoyed freedom of movement westward toward an uncharted wilderness. Indentured servants who completed their terms of service invariably moved west in search of unclaimed land upon which they could establish subsistence-level farms. Some servants even left before their contracts expired and either went west or fled to a town where a chronic labor shortage led employers to hire them without asking too many questions. The impact of geographical mobility was an expanding level of opportunity for American colonists to climb the social ladder.

## 4 Social Mobility

The social ladder in America was far more fluid than the structured organism of British society. Geographical mobility and unusual shrewdness, pluck, or diligence permitted individuals to advance their station in life usually beyond that of their parents, sometimes considerably. America thus proved to be a land of opportunity. Mishaps or mismanagement could just as easily reverse fortunes, though, and colonists could slip down the ladder because there was a steady stream of new climbers.

# 5 Demographics

The study of population is important to trace throughout American history. The colonial period was one of rapid growth with the population of British America doubling every twenty-five years and easily outstripping French and Spanish growth in the region. The ethnic blend of peoples arriving in colonial America is one of the most important facets of American society although 60 percent of colonists were English. Population study also tracks the distribution of the ages in society, and colonial America was young. Society also consisted of more males than females. Americans were almost an entirely rural people as well.

# 6 Capital

As crucial for the growth of American society as were new colonists, sources of investment funds were necessary to support everyone from proprietors (who were often already wealthy) to new entrepreneurs to craftsmen (of which there were few) to freed indentured servants. Banks in London and joint-stock companies provided the necessary capital to establish American economic networks until the banking industry could be begun in the few American cities that existed.

# 7 Diversified Economy

This economy existed in the Middle Colonies and in New England, more out of necessity than by choice. Geographical constraints prevented the establishment of a cash-crop economy that was the easy route to riches. While northerners did raise food crops and livestock, most were involved with harvesting furs, lumber, and other resources. On the coast sailors sought fish and whales or became merchant shippers (Yankee traders). Although little manufacturing was begun in colonial America, a diversified economy existed that permitted flexibility in responding to market trends like the fashion of wearing beaver hats (until the beaver were gone, then New Englanders produced rum).

# 8 Cash-crop Economy

This type of economy existed to a degree in the Middle Colonies with grain production, but the Southern Colonies were largely dedicated to it. Climate and soil as well as the long growing season permitted the cultivation of tobacco, sugar, indigo, and even rice. Since profits were impressive at first, landowners used up the soil and expanded chattel slavery. The weakness of the cash-crop economy came when the climate did not cooperate as in periods of drought, hurricanes, or other storms that destroyed whole crops. Little flexibility existed, and planters were at the mercy of market prices for their goods. All in all, the northern economy produced more capital over time and laid the foundation for the Industrial Revolution there but also for the victory of the Union over the Confederacy in the Civil War, a conflict stemming largely from the inability of the South to diversify.

# 9 Triangular Trade

The shrewd merchants of New England discovered a way to capitalize on the ready supply of lumber in their forests by building ships with which they plied the seas for profit. Goods were shipped up and down the Atlantic seaboard, but more importantly across the Atlantic. Raw materials filled the hulls of ships leaving Boston, New York, and Baltimore that were sold either in England or bartered for slaves in Africa. Africans were brought back to the British colonies of the Caribbean where molasses was picked up and taken back to Boston to be made into rum. Favorable trade winds facilitated the transit both toward England and away from Africa. Profits from shipping built northern cities. Southerners were at the mercy of their northern brethren not only for charges to ship goods to Europe but also the prices on their manufactured and luxury items ordered for return.

# 10 Soil Depletion

Crops like tobacco and corn stripped nitrogen from the soil and did nothing to replace it. As soil lost its fertility, planters and small farmers had to clear more land to the west. This process pushed settlement upriver across the Coastal Plain and caused recurrent problems with American Indian tribes in almost every colony. Soil depletion remained a crucial agricultural problem until crops like alfalfa were sown for hay and clover was sown in pastures. Alfalfa and clover are legumes, like beans and peas, which fix nitrogen in the soil and thus increase and preserve soil fertility. Modern fertilizers also expanded agricultural production of nonlegume crops but with other costs.

# 11 Franchise

A critical trend in colonial American history was the extension of the franchise, or the right to vote. While primogeniture and enclosure laws served to limit land ownership, which was the prerequisite to voting rights in England, land ownership became the norm in America. Access to property came simply by moving west with a little capital or through land grants given to former indentured servants. Therefore, a larger percentage of males became voters in American society compared to English society. Both the literal and figurative definitions of democracy were thus expanded as the first steps in a long series of stages until all adults would possess the right to vote.

# 12 Anglican Church

Otherwise known as the Church of England, the Anglican Church was founded under dubious circumstances by Henry VIII but with far-reaching implications including true spiritual reform. England moved toward Protestantism in the English Reformation, and thus produced the Puritans and the Protestant work ethic. Colonists were either sworn to be loyal Anglicans, as in Virginia, or were intent on becoming either more reformed, as in Massachusetts, or more dedicated to Roman Catholicism, as in Maryland. The Church of England was thus an established church run by the government that could not be ignored. Both religious orthodoxy and religious dissent were profound influences in colonial American society. For various reasons, however, the control of the Anglican Church eroded throughout the colonial period. Loyal Anglicans who later became independent Americans through the American Revolution changed the name of the Anglican Church in America to the Episcopal Church, a name that emphasized rule in the church by bishops.

## 13 High Church Versus Low Church

These distinctions refer to liturgy, or style of worship, rather than to social class, but the two were often intertwined. The Anglican Church was a High Church with a ritualized worship not unlike Roman Catholicism. Puritans and later evangelicals emphasized a simpler worship focused more on preaching and singing than on ceremonies. With time, most churches in colonial America reflected the simpler, more democratic society by producing more egalitarian practices.

## 14 Acts of Toleration

As time went on in the wake of the English Reformation and the English Civil War, Acts of Toleration were passed in both England and in colonies like Maryland where Protestants moved to take up residence and grew in numbers beyond the Roman Catholics who founded the colony. Certain minimum shared doctrinal positions, like that of the Trinity, were established as cultural norms. Thus, religious toleration broadened the diversity in other doctrinal matters and church practices, and served to lessen religious strife. The toleration of diversity, however, undermined the support for established churches. American society thus began the road for complete religious liberty that was known in the colonial period in only a minority of the colonies like Rhode Island and Pennsylvania.

## 15 Half-way Covenant

This compromise in the doctrine of the Congregational, or Puritan, churches ultimately led to the downfall of the Puritan movement in America. As fewer people devoted themselves to religion in prosperous New England, fewer could claim an actual conversion experience. Church membership, so important in Puritan colonial societies, was a prerequisite for holding political office and even for voting. The Half-way Covenant allowed people who desired church membership but lacked credible professions of faith in Christ for salvation to join the church anyway. Over time, the churches became populated with and even led by unbelievers. Unitarianism, a religious movement that rejected the doctrine of the Trinity and thus the deity of Christ, arose out of the resulting doctrinal confusion.

## 16 Scots-Irish

Less a crossbreed (although intermarriage did happen), this important ethnic distinction speaks of a journey. Presbyterian Scots fled persecution before the Acts of Toleration to Ireland and took up residence there. When persecution followed them to Ireland, many migrated to the American colonies where they found welcome in especially Carolina, New Jersey, and Pennsylvania. Fiercely independent minded and with no love of their Anglican persecutors, Scots-Irish Presbyterians were among the first white settlers of the Appalachian Mountains and beyond. They proved to be ardent revolutionaries and the ethnic origin of men like Patrick Henry and Andrew Jackson.

## 17 Germans

The other large ethnic transfer into American society was from Germany. As German kings sat on the English throne (the Hanoverian Georges), and because English was a Germanic language, German immigrants had little trouble assimilating into American colonies. Western Pennsylvania became a center of German settlement where the colonists were known as the Pennsylvania Dutch, a distortion of *Deutsch*.

## 18 First Great Awakening

Certain ministers noticed the declining devotion to God and to the Church among their parishioners who were, after all, required to come to church by law. These ministers prayed for and preached about a revival of the Christian religion as an act of God through the Holy Spirit. Beginning in Massachusetts, widespread conversions among first church members gathered force until revival fervor spread throughout the colonies. Missionary activity also increased among Indians, and a greater attention toward spiritual matters and church attendance became pervasive through the decades of the 1730s and 1740s after which the revival died down. Public morals were lastingly impacted, however, and the shared experience of the First Great Awakening was the first unifying event in the history of colonial America. Americans for the first time contemplated themselves as Americans rather than Virginians, Marylanders, New Yorkers, and so on. This newfound unity and identity was instrumental as a forerunner of the movement toward independence.

## 19 Jonathan Edwards

This preacher from Northampton, Massachusetts, was one of the most scholarly men ever produced in America. His book on his unusual experiences at the beginning of the First Great Awakening spread the movement both in America and in England where it was published. His famous sermon, "Sinners in the Hands of an Angry God," dramatically impacted his congregation and fostered ardent repentance. Despite the emotional response to his preaching, Edwards stressed the rationality of faith but also reconciled philosophy and mysticism as true expressions of religion along with doctrinal purity. After a doctrinal dispute led to his dismissal from his Northampton church, he turned to missionary work among Indians and to writing. He ended his life as president of Princeton University.

# 20 George Whitefield

Whitefield was the other famous preacher of the First Great Awakening. An evangelical and Calvinist Anglican, he traveled from England to preach throughout the American colonies and was widely known because of his booming, eloquent voice. What Jonathan Edwards helped begin, George Whitefield spread both in America's most urban setting, Philadelphia, and in remote, open-air settings. Less interested in the role of the church in preserving sound doctrine, Whitefield remained a popular itinerant preacher well into the latter part of the eighteenth century.

## *The Big Picture*

1. A tremendous store of natural resources, vast geographical space, and advantageous climatic conditions were unlocked as wellsprings of American prosperity during the colonial period.

2. A wider selection of society in America gained access to social, economic, and political opportunity than back in England despite the typically poor origins of most American colonists.

3. Two distinct types of economies developed in the North and the South with the more diversified northern economy both benefiting from and surpassing the potential of the southern agrarian economy.

4. Overall the combined capacities of the two colonial economies slowly became an integral component of the wider economy of the British Empire, a fact that would eventually lead to two wars between the colonies and their mother country, then lasting peace.

5. Colonial American society was a religious society with growing religious diversity and rising and falling doctrinal purity, thus becoming a testing ground for pioneering experiments in religious liberty.

# Mercantilism and Colonial Wars

*Half the continent had changed hands at the scratch of a pen.*
—Francis Parkman, historian, 1884

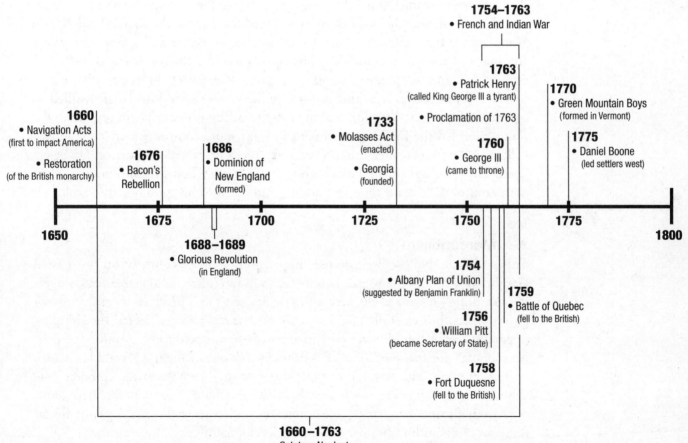

**1754–1763**
• French and Indian War

**1763**
• Patrick Henry
(called King George III a tyrant)

• Proclamation of 1763

**1770**
• Green Mountain Boys
(formed in Vermont)

**1660**
• Navigation Acts
(first to impact America)

• Restoration
(of the British monarchy)

**1733**
• Molasses Act
(enacted)

• Georgia
(founded)

**1760**
• George III
(came to throne)

**1775**
• Daniel Boone
(led settlers west)

**1676**
• Bacon's
Rebellion

**1686**
• Dominion of
New England
(formed)

1650    1675    1700    1725    1750    1775    1800

**1688–1689**
• Glorious Revolution
(in England)

**1754**
• Albany Plan of Union
(suggested by Benjamin Franklin)

**1759**
• Battle of Quebec
(fell to the British)

**1756**
• William Pitt
(became Secretary of State)

**1758**
• Fort Duquesne
(fell to the British)

**1660–1763**
• Salutary Neglect

# Top 20 Things to Know

## 1 Restoration

After the successful Puritan Revolution that prompted the English Civil War, the Protectorate was established under the rule of Oliver Cromwell, the lord protector of England. This former general of the New Model "Roundhead" army moved toward dictatorship, as a viable parliamentary government proved unworkable among religious and political strife. After Cromwell's death, the remaining members of Parliament asked the exiled son of the executed Charles I to ascend to the throne as Charles II. This event occurred in 1660, and the Restoration of the monarchy had profound implications for colonial America. For the duration of his reign and that of his successor, James II, the British Crown sought more stringent control over its New World holdings.

## 2 Salutary Neglect

The phrase *salutary neglect* refers to the attitude of the British government toward the American colonies from the founding of Jamestown through the Restoration and again from the Glorious Revolution until the end of the French and Indian War. During these periods, private joint-stock companies and a few proprietors administered their own colonies as business ventures, refuges for religious dissenters, or both. In the vacuum created by a lack of direction from the mother country, crucial precedents regarding self-government were established that instilled in colonists a fervent desire to protect their rights as Englishmen. Therefore, when the Restoration led the British government to exert more control, American colonists balked. After the new measures proved unenforceable, the second period of neglect lasted until the end of the French and Indian War. When England attempted to exert control the second time around, the American Revolution was the result.

## 3 Mercantilism

This economic philosophy asserted that nations were in competition for a fixed amount of wealth in the world. Economic rivals were thus natural enemies competing for limited resources like access to raw materials and precious metals. Imperial governments thus carefully guarded economic secrets and monitored the shipping of goods. The British Crown and Parliament were assumed to be running the British economy for the good of all Englishmen, and they sought a favorable balance of trade not only with rival nations but also with their own American colonies. The colonists were to provide raw materials and to purchase their manufactured goods only from British merchants. Over time, the colonists in British America found these restraints stifling to their economic development.

## 4 Navigation Acts

The Navigation Acts were passed soon after Charles II sought a new colonial policy of control. Certain goods called enumerated commodities were to be shipped only by British merchants so that no other European powers would profit from their sale. The goal of this mercantilist policy was to raise revenue for the Crown and to keep British gold in British hands. Even such a prosperous traffic as the triangular trade operated as a virtual smuggling ring by leaving England out of the triangle. American colonists realized the laws were unenforceable over the vast stretches of the Atlantic Ocean and developed sophisticated techniques to avoid compliance.

## 5 Dominion of New England

This scheme was the most overt effort on the part of Britain to run its colonies as the Spanish had with tight bureaucratic control. Concocted by the unpopular and domineering James II, this measure erased existing colonial boundaries and governments to establish Edmund Andros as a viceroy over New England. Having cherished their freedoms enjoyed through the period of salutary neglect, Puritans and other American colonists chafed under this insult until it was ended by the Glorious Revolution.

## 6 Glorious Revolution

Knowing that the Puritans had removed the wily Charles I by force, the British people rejected the authoritarian and nearly absolutist rule of James II in favor of his daughter, Mary, and her husband, William of Orange. Mary had the royal lineage, and William had an army. This overthrow did not include the execution of the king as did the Puritan Revolution, but both occasions served as precursors to the American Revolution.

## 7 Georgia

The last of the thirteen colonies that would become the United States, Georgia was founded in 1733 by James Oglethorpe as a reform of British debtor prisons. Georgia's particular type of colonist bound for what amounted to a penal colony was considered expendable. Georgia served, therefore, as a buffer colony between the southern extremity of British America and Spanish Florida. The colony was also meant to serve the British Empire as an alternate source of silk, but the unfortunate choice of the wrong type of mulberry tree ruined the enterprise.

## 8 Bacon's Rebellion

Nathaniel Bacon was a Virginia planter and member of the colonial government who became frustrated in 1676 by Governor Berkeley's refusal to help colonists on the frontier who faced atrocities from Indians. Bacon gathered a force of former indentured servants who attacked both the Indians and eventually Jamestown itself.

The first capital of the colony of Virginia was thus burned as Governor Berkeley fled. Bacon's Rebellion fell apart after Nathaniel Bacon died suddenly of disease. This early example of frustration with British mismanagement foreshadowed an American willingness to resort to violence during extreme conflict with British authority.

# 9 French and Indian War

This war was the climax of several eighteenth-century military conflicts among the mercantilist nations of Great Britain, France, and Spain. Begun in 1754 by George Washington during exploration of the no-man's land between colonial France and Britain, the war soon spread to Europe where it was known as the Seven Years' War. The British government eventually fielded a superior army and with its Iroquois allies defeated France and her Huron allies. In the Treaty of Paris of 1763 France was thus largely deprived of its New World empire, and Canada and the Ohio River Valley became British soil. Parliament made an attempt to pass the costs of the war onto the American colonists who were granted peace on their frontiers. The enforcement of new taxation laws was a primary cause of the American Revolution.

# 10 Albany Plan of Union

Fearing Indian attacks and a French invasion of New England or New York, Benjamin Franklin proposed this first attempt at a central government for the colonies in order to better coordinate defense. Representatives met and listened to Franklin's proposal of a unified government for all of the British colonies except Georgia and Nova Scotia. A strong aversion to executive authority in America and a mistrust of the motives of the plan in England made it unpopular with both the colonies and the Crown. The idea was more easily resurrected in the American Revolution, however, when Franklin could even reuse his promotional political cartoon depicting a severed snake with the caption, "Join, or die."

# 11 Fort Duquesne

The flash-point region where the French and Indian War began irritated the British because it contained forts like Fort Duquesne. George Washington ran into the fort and was repulsed only later to lead British general Edward Braddock back for a second attack. Braddock foolishly mounted a frontal assault against the fort and lost his army and his life as a result. After William Pitt gave the British people the resolve and the resources to win, Fort Duquesne was taken and renamed Fort Pitt. The outpost held the conjunction of three rivers for the British and later became the city of Pittsburgh. The episodes surrounding the campaigns to take Fort Duquesne revealed important differences between British regular troops and those soldiers who were American colonists.

## 12 Battle of Quebec

This battle in 1759 proved to be the climax of the French and Indian War and one of the most glorious victories of British military action. British general Wolfe determined that Quebec was the key to victory over French Canada and discovered a way to assault the fortress from behind. When French general Montcalm decided to come out and meet the army blocking his escape on the Plains of Abraham, Wolfe's disciplined troops inflicted over twice as many casualties as they received and won the battle. Both commanders were mortally wounded, however, as were the hopes of the French government to continue the war. The French surrendered Canada by 1760 because the fortress captured in the Battle of Quebec had guarded their supply line.

## 13 William Pitt

This industrious and honest British statesman continued what Elizabeth I and Oliver Cromwell had set in motion: the formation of the British Empire. From the cream of the British aristocracy, Pitt handled the money for the British military until his outspoken criticism of Crown policy led to his rise as secretary of state and then prime minister. William Pitt focused British attention on North America and rallied support against the French. His resolve turned around British fortunes in the French and Indian War, but victory eventually proved to be too expensive for Great Britain to bear.

## 14 Molasses Act

This act of Parliament proved to be only one of the measures motivated by mercantilism that grew odious to American colonists. Just as American shippers began to amass capital in the sugar trade, Great Britain insisted that American colonial merchants sell their sugar supply only to Britain. This step hampered the colonists' desire to sell to the highest bidder and inspired intense smuggling efforts.

## 15 George III

This third Hanoverian king of England came to power at the climax of the French and Indian War in 1760, one hundred years after the Restoration. He, like Charles II, supported efforts to exert firmer control over the colonies in America. His manner was more autocratic than even most Englishmen in Great Britain preferred, but to American colonists he became the symbol of arbitrary and abusive power. His bouts of mental illness did not help the situation, and George III was the king from whom Americans rebelled.

## 16 Proclamation of 1763

Despite the fact that Great Britain left a standing army in America, George III declared he did not intend to use it to protect colonists from Indian attacks west of the Appalachian Mountains. Pontiac's Rebellion made this gesture appear negligent especially because the American colonists who fought in the French and Indian War had done so largely to secure access to the lush soil of the Ohio River Valley. The king now said they could not have their prize. In fact, settlers who had already moved west of the crest of the Appalachians were supposed to return. As most of these were Scots-Irish Presbyterians, they were not about to return into the bosom of their Anglican mother country. Defiance of the Proclamation of 1763 stirred an attitude of defiance of British authority as well as expanded the horizons of colonists hungry for land.

## 17 Land Fever

After the French and Indian War was over, the burgeoning population of British America sought to push west to relieve growing tensions in the Coastal Plain. As soil depletion and population growth served to worsen these tensions, continued immigration and the collapse of indentured servitude made settlers eager to acquire land at all costs. Those living on the frontier experienced American Indian attacks and other harsh conditions, but in an agrarian society land was the one commodity none could do without.

## 18 Daniel Boone

A veteran of the French and Indian War and many years as a long hunter in the American wilderness, Daniel Boone came to personify the origins of westward migration. He is said to have discovered the Cumberland Gap in his explorations and to have led a party of settlers through it into Kentucky by 1769. He was a man of many trades who rose from obscurity to lead a frontier militia and to positions in colonial government. When down on his luck he simply moved west. He so embodied this notion, which came to be a national trend, that he was the inspiration for James Fenimore Cooper's series of novels known as the Leatherstocking Tales, a romanticized version of a trailblazer's life that had little basis in truth.

## 19 Green Mountain Boys

This militia group was a classic example of frontiersmen and land speculators dissatisfied with eastern authority as they sought freedom and property in the west. In this case, Ethan Allen and others organized a resistance to the authority of New York in what would become the state of Vermont. Although considered outlaws by the British government in Albany, the Green Mountain Boys proved to be an effective militia force in the American Revolution, after which Vermont became a state.

# 20 Patrick Henry

Another hero of frontier elements, this time in Virginia, was Patrick Henry. Henry started out as an innkeeper but became a lawyer and a fiery orator in the Virginia House of Burgesses. He first spoke against the king of England publicly in the Parson's Cause, a measure attempting to buttress an increasingly unpopular established church. As a Presbyterian, Henry viewed the king's unfair support of Anglican ministers as a violation of his compact binding him to look out for the interests of his subjects. He would later go on to deliver the famous, "Give me liberty, or give me death!" speech that ignited revolutionary support in Virginia and other colonies. Although an unswerving American patriot, he did not fancy the excessive centralization of power he perceived in the Constitutional Convention of 1787. He died within a decade of the ratification of the U.S. Constitution.

# *The Big Picture*

1. As British political and economic philosophies continued to evolve, each change had lasting impact on the relationship between the mother country and her American colonies.

2. Strife arose when the British government twice attempted to exert stronger control over colonial America after many decades of inattention and lax enforcement.

3. After participating in three colonial wars on the side of the British, American colonists began to form a more independent identity and the beginnings of American societal and national unity.

4. Acts of Parliament and the attitude of several monarchs alienated Englishmen in the colonies who felt their rights were being abused or at least neglected as mercantilism and latent absolutism festered.

5. Several actual rebellions erupted that conveyed American colonists' willingness to resort to violence to seek redress of grievances, usually led by those on the frontier dissatisfied with the more conservative, loyalist eastern powers.

# Mini Quiz

1. The largest organization of North American Indians in existence upon the arrival of European explorers and colonizers was the

   (A) Huron tribe located around the Great Lakes.
   (B) settlement of Cahokia in what would become Illinois.
   (C) Anasazi cultures in the Southwest.
   (D) Iroquois Nation in what would become New York.
   (E) Powhatan Confederacy of the Chesapeake region.

2. The most severe military conflict among European powers as colonization commenced existed between which two European countries?

   (A) England and France
   (B) England and Spain
   (C) Spain and Portugal
   (D) Spain and France
   (E) The Netherlands and France

3. What qualities made New Spain unique among European colonies in the New World?

   (A) The presence of Roman Catholicism
   (B) The existence of a representative assembly
   (C) The monarch's strict bureaucratic control
   (D) Strong military presence
   (E) Peaceful relations with American Indians

4. The Europeans who first explored the length of the Mississippi River claimed it for which country?

   (A) England
   (B) France
   (C) The Netherlands
   (D) Portugal
   (E) Spain

5. The strength of joint-stock companies lay in which fact?

   (A) Large amounts of capital could be invested in risky enterprises with less individual risk.
   (B) Citizens of many European nations could pool their resources to fund joint ventures.
   (C) The genetic strengths of many strains of livestock could make stronger offspring.
   (D) Colonists did not have to worry about making a profit from their activities.
   (E) The English government was the chief source of funding for colonial companies.

6. Which document represented the first attempt at a written constitution in English history?

   (A) The Fundamental Constitution of Carolina
   (B) *Leviathan* by Thomas Hobbes
   (C) John Locke's Social Contract
   (D) The Magna Carta
   (E) The Mayflower Compact

7. The primary goal of the Massachusetts Bay Colony was to establish what?

   (A) A refuge for all the victims of religious persecution in England
   (B) A thriving colony based on shipping and harvesting fish and whales
   (C) A commonwealth with laws derived from Puritan doctrine
   (D) An agrarian society producing cash crops for market in Europe
   (E) A manufacturing center with basic industries and small farms

8. Most colonists to England's New World colonies arrived in America as

   (A) religious dissenters.
   (B) criminals and debtors released from prison.
   (C) second sons of the aristocracy fleeing primogeniture laws.
   (D) military conscripts.
   (E) indentured servants.

9. The English colony possessing the societal components most resembling modern American society was which colony?

   (A) Virginia
   (B) Pennsylvania
   (C) Plymouth
   (D) Georgia
   (E) Maryland

10. Most leaders in English colonies in America by 1750 came to be defined by which characteristics?

    (A) Wealth as a result of the American Dream
    (B) Distaste for organized religion
    (C) Aristocratic birth traced back to England
    (D) Competency and shrewdness proven in new challenges
    (E) Disregard for English cultural tastes

11. Religion in eighteenth-century colonial America more and more followed which trend?

    (A) The expansion of established churches to every colony
    (B) The complete religious toleration of all levels of belief or unbelief
    (C) A growing measure of democracy in church government
    (D) The increased respect for traditional doctrines of the Protestant Reformation
    (E) The insistence on having educated ministers who favored the Enlightenment

12. Mercantilism as an economic philosophy dictated that the

    (A) English government control the economy rather than market forces.
    (B) American colonists implement a balanced industrial and agrarian economy.
    (C) American colonists maintain a favorable balance of trade with the English people.
    (D) American colonists expand trade relations with all other European powers.
    (E) English economy focus mainly on providing resources to expand colonial holdings.

13. The French and Indian War

    (A) began in America but became a predominantly European conflict.
    (B) saw the English and the French ally against a coalition of American Indian tribes.
    (C) inspired the first successful central government for the American colonies.
    (D) was fought mostly by a professional English army shipped to America for the war.
    (E) settled the question as to which European power would control the Ohio River Valley.

14. After the French and Indian War relations between colonists and American Indians

    (A) generally improved.
    (B) settled into an uneasy truce.
    (C) escalated because of expansion of settlement west.
    (D) experienced peaceful cultural exchanges for the first time.
    (E) were ignored by the British government.

15. The conflicts that arose between the American colonies and the mother country occurred because of what new factors after 1760?

    (A) The ascendancy to the throne of England by a weak monarch
    (B) The crippling war debt resulting from England's ongoing resolve to beat the French
    (C) The invasion of England for the first time by a French army that demanded terms
    (D) The growing disunity among the thirteen American colonies because of English manipulation
    (E) The growing desire on the part of most American colonists to return to English traditions

# Answer Explanations

1. **D**  Both the Cahokia and Anasazi civilizations had disappeared before European arrival, and of the three other choices, the Iroquois Nation was the largest.

2. **B**  All of these European nations were in conflict through the era of exploration and colonization, but the conflict between England and Spain prior to the defeat of the Spanish Armada in 1588 was a protracted war conducted over vast distances.

3. **C**  Although both Spain and France were Catholic nations, only England had a colonial representative assembly. No colonies enjoyed entirely peaceful relations with American Indians and thus all had strong military presence throughout their colonial experience. Of all the colonies Spain achieved the most direct control by exerting the monarch's will through the Council of the Indies and the position of viceroys.

4. **B**  Although Spanish explorer Hernando de Soto first discovered the Mississippi River, several French explorers eventually traversed its length and claimed the Mississippi Valley for France.

5. **A**  Joint-stock companies were created by England and not open to broad European investment. They had nothing to do with livestock but did collect money from numerous investors and thereby kept any one investor from facing complete ruin. Colonists most assuredly were urged to make profits for these private, not government, ventures.

6. **E**  Although the Magna Carta and other documents codified various rights of Englishmen, no attempt to form a government by writing down principles existed until the Mayflower Compact.

7. **C**  Massachusetts Bay Colony was formed by Puritans for Puritans and predominantly for religious, not economic reasons.

8. **E**  Although all of these types of individuals settled in the New World, the chronic labor shortage and surplus population of England dictated that most American colonists arrived by 1700 as indentured servants.

9. **B**  All colonies sowed key legacies into the American tradition, but early on Pennsylvania possessed all the attributes of the other colonies in one colony that closely resembled modern American society.

10. **D**  Not all leaders in America were wealthy or high born, but most all were respected and thus elected because they exhibited competence. Most maintained some type of Christian profession in organized churces and most sought to be more, not less, like Englishmen back in England.

11. **C**   The vagaries of the First Great Awakening undermined established churches and traditional doctrines and opened American Christianity to more democratic and less educated leadership. The heightened fervor of religious sentiment did not translate into widespread religious toleration.

12. **A**   All other choices are either directly or indirectly the opposite of mercantilist doctrine.

13. **E**   The French and Indian War began in and was largely fought in America by an army consisting of equal portions of colonists and regulars. England and her American Indian allies fought against France and the Huron Indians. Although the Albany Plan of Union was an attempt at a central government, it was unsuccessful.

14. **C**   As a result of the winning of the Ohio River Valley from France, English colonists pushed westward and Pontiac's Rebellion resulted.

15. **B**   William Pitt's resolve to pay for a victory led to the alienation through legislation enacted by Parliament and to taxation without representation for the American colonists.

# The American Revolution and the War for Independence

# CHAPTER 7

*I know not what course others may take, but as for me,
give me liberty or give me death!*

—Patrick Henry's speech before the Virginia Assembly, 1775

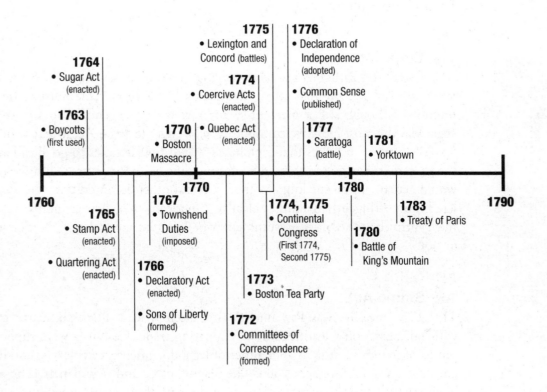

**1764**
• Sugar Act (enacted)

**1763**
• Boycotts (first used)

**1775**
• Lexington and Concord (battles)

**1774**
• Coercive Acts (enacted)

**1776**
• Declaration of Independence (adopted)

• Common Sense (published)

**1770**
• Boston Massacre

• Quebec Act (enacted)

**1777**
• Saratoga (battle)

**1781**
• Yorktown

1760

**1765**
• Stamp Act (enacted)

• Quartering Act (enacted)

**1767**
• Townshend Duties (imposed)

1770

**1766**
• Declaratory Act (enacted)

• Sons of Liberty (formed)

**1773**
• Boston Tea Party

**1772**
• Committees of Correspondence (formed)

**1774, 1775**
• Continental Congress (First 1774, Second 1775)

1780

**1780**
• Battle of King's Mountain

**1783**
• Treaty of Paris

1790

# Top 20 Things to Know

## 1 Quebec Act

Despite the severity of the more well-known acts of Parliament like the two that follow, some historians believe the 1774 Quebec Act was the most odious to American colonists. The measure certainly found its way into the Declaration of Independence, on the heels of the First Great Awakening. The concessions made to the Roman Catholic French colonists still living in Canada were disturbing to the largely Protestant Americans. Parliament granted toleration to the Catholics in return for which the French gave up the right of local self-rule in exchange for a centralized local council answerable directly to the British government, something akin to the Council of the Indies in the Spanish Empire. Trial by a jury was also abolished in civil cases. Apart from these political and religious scruples, the dramatic enlarging of Canada down to the Ohio River again arbitrarily kept Americans from the luscious land they had fought for in the French and Indian War. The Second Continental Congress made the charge in the Declaration of Independence that the Quebec Act was merely a trial run for what England had in mind for her British subjects in America.

## 2 Sugar Act

As early as 1764 Parliament set about trying to wring money from the colonies, and the Sugar Act was the first attempt to pass a law with the sole purpose of raising revenue. Although still a mercantile, indirect tax on an enumerated commodity, sugar was the most lucrative commodity. Cleverly, the Sugar Act lowered the duties (taxes) on sugar in hopes that merchants would find it easier to go ahead and pay the tax rather than go to the trouble of smuggling, with the hopes that more revenue would actually reach the king's coffers. Certain other commodities were also regulated more stringently making it clear to Americans that their economy was under the control of the British government whether that control was to their benefit or not.

## 3 Stamp Act

This 1765 measure was Parliament's first attempt at a direct tax, a tax charged with no mercantilist justification of regulating trade. Colonists were supposed to purchase stamps to affix to all manner of legal documents, certificates, and licenses and to even humbler paper goods like playing cards and newspapers. The novelty of a direct tax and the pervasive extent of the proposed taxation met with universal opposition in America and prompted the cry, "No taxation without representation!" Resistance to the Stamp Act led to violent protests but also to the Stamp Act Congress, the first attempt since the Albany Plan of Union to gather colonial representatives and to air grievances. As a result of the opposition, Parliament did the worst possible thing if it intended to keep order—it backed down. No stamps were ever actually sold. Parliament did pass the Declaratory Act, though, which stated that it had the right to tax the colonists however it saw fit. Such a statement sounded like a petulant whimper to the colonists who soon sensed a chance for freedom.

## 4 Sons of Liberty

This secret society was just one example of the revolutionary organizations that spontaneously formed to rally colonists to resist British authority. The Sons of Liberty led the resistance to the Stamp Act by committing acts of arson and vandalism in Boston, but chapters of the organization existed in almost every town. Prominent citizens led the meetings and planned the protests that were carried out by a cross-section of American society. In Boston, the Sons of Liberty also perpetrated the most infamous act of vandalism, the Boston Tea Party.

## 5 Committees of Correspondence

Originating in Boston under the auspices of Samuel Adams of the Sons of Liberty, this revolutionary network collected evidence of British abuses and circulated them widely over all of Massachusetts. Boycotts and other forms of resistance were coordinated through this type of communication including the publication of newspaper accounts and editorials. Newspapers became daily publications and more and more regularly used words like *independence* as a result of Adams's spreading the ideas of James Otis and other revolutionary thinkers. Ultimately, Committees of Correspondence were established across the thirteen colonies as the American Revolution reached its climax in the War for Independence.

## 6 Declaratory Act

More of a whimper than a roar from the British lion, the Declaratory Act was passed by Parliament after it repealed the Stamp Act. The law boldly proclaimed that Parliament retained the right to tax the colonies, "in all cases whatsoever," but this pronouncement merely stirred the debate of actual versus virtual representation for the colonies in Parliament. Plus, coming after the stiff resistance in the Stamp Act Crisis, the Declaratory Act strongly resembled an exasperated parent lashing out verbally at a child who was no longer listening, and whatever respect for the British government that remained after the Stamp Act dissipated among those beginning the push for independence.

## 7 Townshend Duties

Charles Townshend was the latest in a series of ministers King George III went through trying to find a solution to the alienation created by legislation. Townshend's answer was to raise revenue by taxing particular commodities that colonists would have to buy from Britain because they couldn't produce them for themselves. He picked glass, lead, paper, paint, and tea. Nonimportation agreements, or boycotts, were so successful in shutting down the consumption of these goods among the colonies that most of the taxes were repealed. The lack of consumption was costing the British economy more than the taxes were bringing in for the government. Still, Parliament kept one tax in place as another reminder of their authority. The commodity chosen was tea, and Americans' love affair with coffee dates back to their decision to sidestep this token of direct taxation without actual representation.

## 8 Quartering Act

Speaking of direct taxation, the Quartering Act was the most creative example hatched in Parliament schemes to raise both money and to exert colonial control. Colonists were saddled with the duty to house and feed soldiers, the clearest manifestation of British desire to pass on the costs of protecting the American colonies with a standing army to those being protected. The installing of military personnel in private homes, however, was also a means of surveillance as the British government attempted to ferret out revolutionary leaders or to observe their movements and the schedule of their meetings.

## 9 Boycotts

These organized forms of resistance included nonimportation and nonconsumption agreements aided and abetted by the Committees of Correspondence. All Americans could contribute to the struggle by going without luxuries and even some items considered necessities. This method highlighted the true importance of the American colonies to the British economy as well as delineated between loyalists and patriots. One of the items boycotted was textiles, and American patriots were clearly discernible by their wearing of rougher, simpler clothes made at home, or homespun.

## 10 Boston Massacre

The tension created by British actions and American reactions had to break out in serious violence somewhere, and Boston was the most likely spot. A handful of soldiers were assailed there by a mob hurling projectiles at them; scared for their lives, the soldiers fired into the crowd. Thus began the auspicious decade of the 1770s. Five people received mortal wounds, and the army only averted a larger massacre by withdrawing from the city, another fateful concession. While John Adams sought to prove American fairness by getting the soldiers acquitted, his cousin Sam Adams and silversmith Paul Revere turned the event into a propaganda bonanza. Revere's engraving of the incident did not reveal the mob's provocation but portrayed British regimentation of cold-blooded killing.

## 11 Boston Tea Party

In 1773, the first of many planned shipments of tea by the East India Company arrived in Boston. The company had recently been given a monopoly on the trade through the Tea Act. Colonists refused to pay the import tax left by the Townshend

Duties, and the ship captain refused to leave until it was paid. Samuel Adams led a meeting where it was determined that the tea should be destroyed, and men disguised as Mohawk Indians worked all night to dump the £10,000 worth of tea in the harbor. This act of vandalism prompted Parliament to punish Boston with the Coercive Acts.

# 12 Coercive Acts

The Coercive Acts, known in America as the Intolerable Acts, were a series of laws passed in 1774 designed to shut down revolutionary actions in Boston as a result of the 1773 Boston Tea Party. The port was closed and martial law was enacted giving Thomas Gage control. General Gage used his power to take over public buildings and to otherwise enforce the Quartering Act and the punitive measures of the Coercive Acts. As news of these events spread, other colonies sent supplies for the relief of Boston, a step that further united the colonies in opposition to British oppression.

# 13 Lexington and Concord

Such a tense situation could not last long without the outbreak of serious violence. American militiamen gathered weapons and prepared to defend their rights. By 1775, Gage determined to confiscate the weapons rumored to be at Concord, Massachusetts. Warned by Paul Revere and others that the British were coming, groups of minutemen gathered to await developments. After skirmishes in Concord, around four thousand American militiamen gathered at various points to assail the British troops marching back to Lexington. Of the seven hundred British soldiers making the expedition, 273 were killed, wounded, or missing at the day's end. When compared to the ninety-three American casualties, these running skirmishes encouraged the colonists and convinced the British that more repressive measures were necessary.

# 14 Continental Congress

After a largely unsuccessful first attempt at organizing a central government in 1774, a Second Continental Congress convened in Philadelphia in 1775 in the wake of the first armed conflicts. Those known as the Founding Fathers gathered as representatives of their respective colonies. John Hancock ultimately rose as the president of the congress, and George Washington, a representative from Virginia, was asked to take command of a Continental Army. The Second Continental Congress was the legislative body that, after some prompting, eventually issued the Declaration of Independence, the Articles of Confederation, the dollar as a currency, and otherwise led the colonies through the Revolutionary War.

# 15 Common Sense

The Second Continental Congress was prompted to action by the popularity of this eloquent propaganda pamphlet written by Thomas Paine. Rather than writing a scholarly treatise of political philosophy as John Adams and others had done,

Paine appealed to the common masses quoting only the Bible as a source (although Paine himself rejected Christianity). The compelling themes of the piece were that kings by their nature were evil and that an island like Britain should not rule over a continent like North America. The essay went through many printings and served to drum up support for the eventual move toward independence by the Congress.

# 16 Declaration of Independence

This document placed in writing the values derived from the American colonial experience and the Enlightenment theories emanating from Europe in contradistinction to the arbitrary and oppressive acts of King George III and Parliament. Drafted by a committee consisting of Thomas Jefferson, John Adams, Benjamin Franklin, and others, it was adopted by the Second Continental Congress in the summer of 1776 after the Revolutionary War was under way with the Battle of Bunker Hill. As a sophisticated form of propaganda, the Declaration moved enough of the colonial population to support the war to make independence a reality. As a statement of the American ideals of equality and freedom that included, "life, liberty, and the pursuit of happiness," this birth certificate of the United States of America established goals that have stimulated the pursuit of human rights around the globe.

# 17 Saratoga

This most significant battle in the north occurred in 1777 when British general Burgoyne attempted a convergence of three British armies in New York. The planned assembling of an overwhelming force was thwarted, though, by heroic American assaults on the British columns coming from the north and the west and the foolish diversion into Philadelphia by the army coming from the south. Thus Burgoyne met superior numbers under the command of Horatio Gates and wound up surrendering his whole force. The news of Saratoga encouraged the American people but also the French who forged a formal military alliance by 1778 following the surprise victory. The French nation provided money, men, and a navy in revenge for the loss of their North American holdings in the French and Indian War.

# 18 The Battle of King's Mountain

This battle proved to be the most significant on the frontier when elements of the British Army under Cornwallis were surprised by a contingent of frontiersmen who had crossed the Appalachian Mountains. Taking up defensive positions on the ridge, the surrounded British were picked off by sharpshooting militiamen until the survivors surrendered. This battle discouraged Cornwallis from any further attempt to take North Carolina and ultimately to abandon his southern campaign. The Continental Congress was encouraged by this good news after reports of British atrocities had come from the region. Cornwallis eventually made his way back to Virginia and defeat.

# 19 Yorktown

George Washington's army besieged that of Cornwallis in 1781 at Yorktown, Virginia, when the British general tried to evacuate his army by sea. The French fleet under Admiral De Grasse drove away the British transports, and Cornwallis was left to the mercy of American and French cannon. The siege lasted from August into October when Cornwallis surrendered. His army was the last major British army in the field, and peace negotiations were begun after a few smaller operations bottled up the remaining British forces.

# 20 Treaty of Paris

To the astonishment of the world the United States had held on through eight years of battles against the superior British military. Negotiations in Paris ended the war in 1783 and recognized American independence. The boundaries of the new country were set from the Atlantic Ocean to the Mississippi River and from Canada to Florida. This territory was larger than the Americans had even dreamed and finally secured for them access to westward expansion in the Ohio River Valley and beyond.

## *The Big Picture*

1. The British government changed its administrative policies for a second time in a way that was perceived by American colonists to be unfairly restraining their prosperity without granting representation in Parliament.

2. A gradual increase in American resistance to British authority was organized by revolutionary leaders in response to repeated increases in taxes and restrictions on the American economy and on the personal liberty of colonists.

3. As tensions mounted, so did preparations on both sides for armed conflict resulting in outbreaks of both mob violence and actual military clashes.

4. The American Revolution consisted of numerous ideas regarding justice and political philosophy that resulted from a history of societal change throughout the colonial period.

5. The War for Independence was the military climax to the American Revolution and proved to be a protracted struggle among several nations resulting from ongoing mercantilist competition and latent animosity from earlier wars of empire.

# The Critical Period and the Formation of American Values

*All sober inquiries after truth, ancient and modern, pagan and Christian,
have declared that the happiness of man, as well as his dignity,
consists in virtue.*

—John Adams, *Thoughts on Governments. . .,* 1776

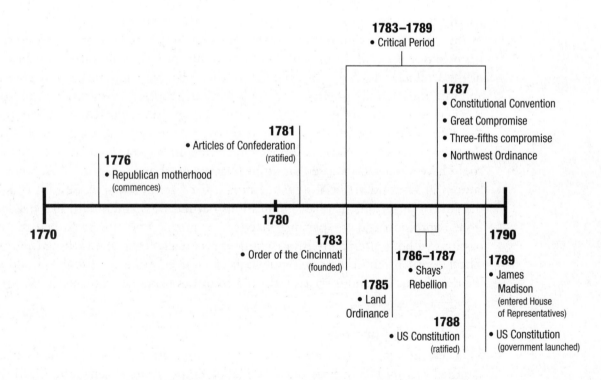

**1783–1789**
• Critical Period

**1787**
• Constitutional Convention
• Great Compromise
• Three-fifths compromise
• Northwest Ordinance

**1781**
• Articles of Confederation
(ratified)

**1776**
• Republican motherhood
(commences)

**1770**

**1780**

**1783**
• Order of the Cincinnati
(founded)

**1785**
• Land
Ordinance

**1786–1787**
• Shays'
Rebellion

**1788**
• US Constitution
(ratified)

**1790**

**1789**
• James
Madison
(entered House
of Representatives)

• US Constitution
(government launched)

# Top 20 Things to Know

## 1 Republic

The form of government chosen by the founders of the United States was that of a republic. Most of the men prominent in the formation of the country were scholars familiar with republican precedents from the classical world and saw the United States as the new manifestation of political wisdom and self-government, hence the return to classical architectural styles for public buildings. The United States was technically not a democracy but a democratic republic. Power was vested in the people who were supposed to vote for representatives who then made and enforced laws. The "ruler" of a republic was designed to be the law that represented the will of the people and to which all the people, including the representatives, were subject as a part of a social contract. These provisions were thought to make a republic the least likely form of government to degenerate into either mob rule or tyranny. The Founding Fathers understood such a system to have hope of success only when the citizenry was moral and responsible.

## 2 American Dream

Because of both geographical and social mobility, most Americans could expect to rise above the station in life to which their parents were born. While this definition of the American Dream has met with some debate in recent years, this condition has held true up until the present day. Some of the greatest Americans in the history of the United States have thus risen from total obscurity, ignorance, and poverty, and thus the existence of classes of people without property or education were from the beginning not the norm. Importantly, though, individuals had to combine these opportunities with diligence and shrewdness in order to make good. Even those from the higher classes, especially in families that had just attained that status, could have a generation arise that slipped backward, though, because there were no laws as in England artificially maintaining a fixed set of social classes. Of course, the American Dream also had implications beyond class and wealth like freedom from oppression and the personal freedom to pursue one's interests, beliefs, and passions without interference from a king or eventually from an established church. The average citizen in the new republic lived a longer, more comfortable, healthier life than his or her counterpart in the old countries from whence Americans came.

## 3 Yeoman Farmers

This class of people made up the bulk of the population for at least the first one hundred years of U.S. history once the Declaration of Independence and the Treaty of Paris established the country. Cheap, or free, land-led native-born Americans and immigrants alike pushed west to secure enough property to subsist as farmers with hopes of making small profits from cash crops in the future. The combination of land fever and the notion of the American Dream were powerful forces that set off large-scale migration and enough confidence in the opportunity for many farmers to go into debt to establish their holdings. The enterprising nature of the venture along with all the hard work necessary for the clearing of land and the establishment of agriculture led Thomas Jefferson to venerate this simple stock of rural Americans as the key citizens of the new republic.

## 4 Critical Period

From the ratification of the Articles of Confederation to the ratification of the U.S. Constitution was a time of great peril for the fledgling country. The vagaries of the Revolutionary War were such as to make the formation of a viable central government impossible. When the war ended in 1783, the government found itself unequal to the task of keeping the newly united states working together for the good of all. Enough time transpired without an internal or external disaster, however, for leaders to go back to the drawing board and come up with a more lasting form of government that has been the basis of American stability and prosperity ever since.

## 5 Articles of Confederation

Written by the same committee that wrote the Declaration of Independence, this document called into being a "league of friendship" among the thirteen states. Because of certain weaknesses in this first draft of a government, the centralized government and national unity were unraveling by the war's end. A lack of a system of taxation, poor interstate economic controls, and the absence of a sound national currency or even an executive branch in the government all doomed the Articles of Confederation to failure. Certain successes, however, allowed the country to survive the critical period. The Congress got all the states to give their western land claims to the central government as a source of income from land sales. The view that the articles needed revision led to the Annapolis Convention; the realization that a total revision was necessary led to the Constitutional Convention.

## 6 Order of the Cincinnati

Named after an ancient Roman hero, Cincinnatus, this attempt at a secret society of Revolutionary War officers ran counter to the societal and political trends that set the American Revolution in motion. Some within the Order flirted with the notion of establishing themselves as a landed aristocracy for their service in the war. They even contemplated making George Washington King George I of America. George Washington himself squashed this idea, although the Order remained. His deterrence of this movement staved off the formation of a noble class and allowed America to live up to its revolutionary and republican rhetoric.

## 7 Land and Northwest Ordinances

These measures for organization of western lands were the most successful outcomes of the government under the Articles of Confederation. Congress appropriated the lands of the Ohio River Valley extending up to the Great Lakes, the territory known as the Old Northwest, and called for it to be surveyed and sold. To this day the orderly survey lines on this flat topography are visible from the air in the forms of a grid of crisscrossed roads dividing the land into sections called townships. The ordinances also established two crucial precedents in American life. One square of each township's land was sold with the proceeds going to support education, a mainstay of republican life. The other precedent was that Congress under the Articles of Confederation banned slavery from the entire territory. Abraham Lincoln would later point to this step as a turning point in the slavery question for the whole nation.

## 8 Penitentiary

As the word implies, these prisons were established as places for criminals to be penitent. The system of solitary confinement with only the Bible as reading material bespoke the optimism inherent in American society as a result of the successful American Revolution. Republics, it was thought, had the power and the duty to improve the lives of all citizens, even criminals. Although solitary confinement is considered a more stringent form of punishment today, in the eighteenth century it was merciful and hopeful. The European propensity for capital punishment lampooned in *A Tale of Two Cities* by Charles Dickens as late as the nineteenth century was largely done away with in the United States. Fewer and fewer crimes were eligible for executions, and a higher percentage of the American population resided in penitentiaries. The reform of the criminal justice system was just the beginning of a long series of reform movements that tried, and try, to work out the principles of the American Revolution and the First and Second Great Awakenings in American life.

## 9 Republican Motherhood

Societal reform started at home. Whereas American women would wrestle with second-class citizen status well into the twentieth century, a new perspective on the role of women was a result of revolutionary principles. Since a republic would only survive with a moral, responsible citizenry actively placing the common good over individual desires, American mothers were looked upon as sacred instruments in nurturing the future. This status also implied greater importance of children than had ever been contemplated by the masses. The outworking of the American Dream implied that any mother could be raising a great statesman, inventor, general, or artist.

## 10 Tariffs

A long history of taxing imported goods has seen the rising and falling of tariffs, or customs duties, throughout U.S. history. The need for tariffs arose from the history of the American colonies as sources of raw materials and agricultural products. When the United States sought to increase its domestic manufacturing, tariffs leveled the playing field by making imported manufactured goods more expensive, thus allowing domestic manufacturers to compete. Tariffs became most popular with northerners whose diversified economies permitted the first widespread pursuit of manufacturing. Under the Articles of Confederation, states in the United States charged tariffs on other states. As time passed, the tariff became a disputed issue between the North, which wanted a strong protective tariff, and the South, which disliked tariffs because they offended their customers and made their own manufactured goods more expensive even if purchased from the northern manufacturers on this side of the Atlantic.

## 11 Shays's Rebellion

In 1786 the state legislature of Massachusetts refused to issue a paper currency or to provide other relief for farmers struggling under mounting debts. Mob violence erupted that eventually coalesced into an armed rebellion under former Revolutionary War captain Daniel Shays. Shays's men numbered over 1,200, and their campaign lasted into 1787 when they nearly captured the federal arsenal at Springfield, Massachusetts. State militia forces put down the rebellion and captured Shays who was ultimately pardoned. The state legislature made it easier for farmers to seek relief in the courts, lowered taxes, and enacted policies that prevented destitution of farmers in debt trouble. The episode coincided with the onset of the Constitutional Convention and served as an impetus for strengthening the central government.

## 12 Constitutional Convention

This meeting in Philadelphia in 1787 is the direct or indirect basis for the rest of American history. A fortunate collection of brilliant minds like those of James Madison, Benjamin Franklin, and Alexander Hamilton were assembled under the leadership of George Washington. These men knit together the strands of political philosophy spun by the Enlightenment and by the practical experience most of the representatives had in their home states. Noble and ignoble compromises were reached to maintain unity. A system of checks and balances was put in place to distribute power in the federal government over three branches—executive, legislative, and judiciary. Debates lasted from May to December when the process of ratification began. By June of 1788 the ninth state ratified the U.S. Constitution making it the supreme law of the land.

## 13 James Madison

A young understudy of Thomas Jefferson was writing drafts for the Virginia state constitution while Jefferson was writing the draft of the Declaration of Independence. From there, Madison had a hand in nearly all of the processes discussed above for Virginia as the new state made its transition from the first colony to one of the most populous of the United States. He is considered the Father of the U.S. Constitution because he drafted the Virginia Plan, the winning side in most matters, as well as the Bill of Rights. He contributed to the influential Federalist Papers discussed in Chapter 9, but later split with the Federalist Party over policy issues. He served as both secretary of state (under Jefferson) and president through some of the most important formative years, including those of the War of 1812. Madison, then, could be said to have seen Virginia and the United States through two wars for independence and through the critical period. Madison's notes on the proceedings of the Constitutional Convention are the largest portion of history's knowledge of that gathering because the Convention's deliberations were kept secret.

## 14 U.S. Constitution

Whereas other documents could claim status as the birth certificate of the United States, this document ranked as the crowning achievement of the American Revolution. The Preamble bespoke the very nature of a republic with its opening words, "We the People. . . ." Few other documents have altered world history more than this one, which established a stable government and pulled the new country back from the abyss of dissolution. Debates raged as to its actual motives, but the governmental instructions therein have served to guide the American people through numerous crises and through the vagaries of changing societal values. The U.S. Constitution contains within it the method whereby it can be amended, a process resorted to relatively few times in history. That fact alone attests to the powerful insights into human nature and political science with which the United States was blessed at this crucial juncture.

## 15 New Jersey Plan

Espoused by William Patterson of New Jersey, this plan is otherwise known as the small-state plan in that it represented the interests of the less populous states. Patterson believed the Articles of Confederation could be revised by fixing the more glaring errors of a lack of a power vested in Congress to tax or to regulate commerce. He proposed an executive be elected, but would not have provided the president with a veto. In short, the small states were suspicious of their larger sister states and of a strong central government. In all matters of representation, the New Jersey Plan called for equal representation for each state as had been done through the Articles of Confederation that gave each state one vote in Congress regardless of state size.

## 16 Virginia Plan

Drafted by James Madison but presented by another, this proposal favored an entirely new government over a revised Articles of Confederation. The outline of what would eventually become the U.S. Constitution was clearly recognizable in this plan although several provisions would be revised. All in all, however, the small states recognized that the policies proposed in the Virginia Plan would benefit large states like Virginia and New York the most.

## 17 Enumerated Powers

Each article of the U.S. Constitution dealing with a branch of the government lists, or enumerates, several key powers or duties for the specific branches. Sometimes these powers overlap with those of other branches and with state law; others are reserved just to a particular branch or to the federal government as a whole. For example, the U.S. Constitution took away any ability of a state to have a separate foreign policy and directly assigned the administration of foreign policy to the executive branch with the consent of the Senate, which had to ratify all treaties that might be negotiated by a president or his appointees. The extent to which the Constitution limits these powers to those expressly stated in the document, or expands them to those implied by the document, is one of the problematic aspects of constitutional law and thus part of the origin of America's two-party political system.

# 18 Checks and Balances

All three branches of the federal government were given by the U.S. Constitution the power to hold other branches in check as each branch sought to fulfill its duties listed in its enumerated powers. The balance would be created by both support and opposition among the branches. For example, the Supreme Court is staffed through nominations of the executive branch that must be accepted by the legislative branch before becoming legitimate. The Supreme Court can, in turn, advise the other branches on the legality of their activities. The clearest mechanisms to balance the branches are the president's veto power over laws passed by the legislative branch and the ability of Congress to override presidential vetoes. As James Madison explained in Federalist No. 51, "If men were angels, no government would be necessary. If angels were to govern men, neither external nor internal controls on government would be necessary." The checks and balances inherent in the U.S. Constitution, although sometimes ignored, have always proven to be necessary in the end.

# 19 The Great Compromise

Championed at the Constitutional Convention by Roger Sherman of Connecticut, this agreement was the crucial compromise that saved the union. The argument was over proportional versus equal representation in the Congress. Sherman suggested that the U.S. Senate consist of two senators from each state, thereby ensuring equal representation in this body responsible for war and peace. The House of Representatives would consist of representatives from the states based on the population within each state being assured at least one congressman regardless of size. With this hurdle out of the way, the Convention could move toward final drafting and ratification.

# 20 Three-fifths Compromise

Most of the southern slaveholding states were plagued by a handicap in smaller populations due to the rural nature of their society created by their cash-crop economy. When the Great Compromise was adopted these states proposed the counting of their slaves for representation in the House of Representatives. The North reduced the impact of this hypocritical provision by allowing only the counting of three-fifths of the southern states' slaves. Although this agreement permitted unity, it also indirectly sanctioned slavery.

## *The Big Picture*

1. Once the American people won independence from Great Britain, the cultural trends of the colonial period were manifested in a new, optimistic outlook and the formation of an entirely unique society.

2. Every aspect of American life was tinged with this new optimism from social class mobility to romantic love, and every American expected his or her life to be better than that of the previous generation.

3. The difficulty to maintain national unity under the Articles of Confederation led to a revision of the American government that increased the power of the federal government while allowing the states to retain some autonomy.

4. The U.S. Constitution was the result of the development of both theoretical and practical political philosophy over many centuries of history in Western civilization.

5. The government under the new constitution divided power into three branches and provided ways for the three branches, the large and small states, and the northern and southern states to compromise in order to pull the country through the critical period.

# The Federalist Age

*Real liberty is neither found in despotism or the extremes of democracy, but in moderate governments."*

—Alexander Hamilton, 1787

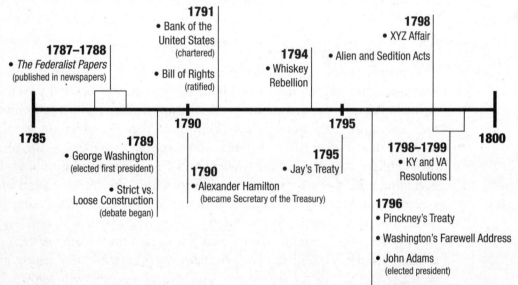

**1787–1788**
• *The Federalist Papers* (published in newspapers)

**1791**
• Bank of the United States (chartered)
• Bill of Rights (ratified)

**1794**
• Whiskey Rebellion

**1798**
• XYZ Affair
• Alien and Sedition Acts

1785

1790

1795

1800

**1789**
• George Washington (elected first president)
• Strict vs. Loose Construction (debate began)

**1790**
• Alexander Hamilton (became Secretary of the Treasury)

**1795**
• Jay's Treaty

**1798–1799**
• KY and VA Resolutions

**1796**
• Pinckney's Treaty
• Washington's Farewell Address
• John Adams (elected president)
• Treaty of Greenville

# Top 20 Things to Know

## 1 Federalist Party

The leaders who formed this first political party in American history were originally merely nationalists, or those who wanted a stronger central government to keep the United States united. Through the process of ratification of the U.S. Constitution it became apparent that they had banking and commercial interests and the desire to establish the credit of the government on a sound footing. Alexander Hamilton and John Adams masterminded the formation of their party, but even James Madison helped long enough to see the Constitution ratified. George Washington aligned himself in almost all matters with the Federalist Party, but his status as the Indispensible Man kept him somewhat above political party wrangling, which he despised. The Federalists were pro-British in foreign policy and fought to establish the Bank of the United States. Their stance on interpretation of the Constitution was loose construction, and they sought to increase the power of the federal government.

## 2 Anti-Federalist Party

The first reactionary political coalition as evidenced by its name, the Anti-Federalists formed around the genius of Thomas Jefferson. His beloved yeoman farmers, or the bulk of the population of the South and the West, rallied to him in an eventual government takeover by 1800. Until then they grumbled under the Federalist yoke, that is, they endured policies that were strict on the paying of debts and the establishment of a sound currency. Anti-Federalists wanted to hold the central government in check by using strict construction, the interpretation of the U.S. Constitution denying there were many implied powers and focusing mainly on the enumerated powers. To Hamilton's philosophy that if it doesn't say we can't, we can, the Anti-Federalists replied that if it doesn't say we can, we can't do it. The debate over the Bank of the United States was the first major testing ground for these principles, and for a time the Anti-Federalists (otherwise known by then as the Jeffersonian Republicans) gave ground. In foreign policy, they were pro-French, especially after the French Revolution. As to the economic future of the United States, Jefferson and his party hoped the country would remain agrarian and rural.

## 3 George Washington

The Indispensible Man was called such because of his status as the heroic champion of freedom coupled with civility and wisdom cultivated in him as the son of one of the first families of Virginia. Less a brilliant military or political strategist than a fine judge of the capacities of other men, Washington promoted the career of Alexander Hamilton as well as those of Thomas Jefferson and James Madison. His presence on the battlefield or in the Constitutional Convention created confidence and clarity. As president he despised party politics but endured them as necessary evils. He established isolationism as the foreign policy stance of the young nation, and he knew that everything he did as the first president, especially because he was elected unanimously by the Electoral College, would set crucial precedents. For example, his choosing to retire from politics after two terms as president was followed by all presidents facing that question until Franklin Roosevelt. Then the Constitution was amended to codify Washington's wisdom. He was the perfect example of a selfless leader of a republic who sacrificed his own desires for the good of the country, but he was also human and a product of his times. He owned slaves and even spirited them away in Philadelphia in the bottom of the presidential residence, but he did release all his slaves upon his death.

# 4 Alexander Hamilton

A chief adviser to Washington during the Revolutionary War and as secretary of the Treasury in the first presidential administration, Hamilton had more brains but fewer endearing qualities. He was of the elitist wing of the Federalist Party he masterminded and held little faith in the goodness of yeoman farmers or any other sort of common men. Therefore, he envisioned a strong federal government that would harness the energies of the republic with both incentives and harsh punishment for rebellion. His long-term vision for the United States actually came to pass. He did everything in his power to lay the foundation for commercial and industrial strength to match the agricultural potential of the new country. He would also eventually reveal state secrets to the British, and he is the first noted American politician to openly commit adultery. This mixed persona of financial genius and unscrupulous morals met a fitting end. Provisions were specifically added to the U.S. Constitution to allow him to become president even though he was not a native-born citizen, but he died in a foolish duel over party politics. He has forever remained a historical figure both honored and despised.

# 5 Federalist Papers

First written as anonymous editorials in New York newspapers, these expository essays became a crucial insight into the two great minds that both drafted the Constitution and put it into effect. James Madison and Alexander Hamilton, then, were the principal authors along with future Chief Justice of the Supreme Court John Jay. The editorials were designed to persuade New Yorkers to support ratification of the U.S. Constitution, but their lasting importance comes from the political science principles they examined. Madison's lament that government would not be necessary if all men were angels comes from Federalist No. 51, and his justification for the choice of a republic as the form of government is in Federalist No. 10. The editorials achieved their purpose but now help constitutional scholars and lawyers understand the words as well as the intentions of the Founding Fathers.

# 6 Bill of Rights

The greatest early contribution of the Anti-Federalist Party to the formation of the American government was their hesitancy to support the ratification of the U.S.

Constitution without first demanding protections of individual and states' rights. This push took the form by 1791 of ten amendments to the Constitution, nine of which specifically protected American citizens from being abused by their government in the ways Britain abused the American colonists. The Tenth Amendment reserves to the states those powers not given to the central government, thereby forming a federal government. The Bill of Rights became a cherished American heritage and the proving ground for individual and societal liberties through many varied events and interpretations, and they remain so today.

# 7 National Debt

The American government found itself in deep debt after surviving the War for Independence. Direct loans from foreign governments like France as well as the sale of war bonds to Americans and to people abroad were critical to the war effort. Recognizing that similar, if not worse, crises could arise in the future, Alexander Hamilton set about funding the debt as secretary of the Treasury. He realized that if the United States defaulted on these loans, no other credit would ever be extended to the government. Hamilton also proposed that bearing this burden together would make the states pull together. While this phenomenon may have been true in the early national period, the existence of a national debt henceforth was a divisive issue, especially as the national debt increased. Thomas Jefferson, in particular, abhorred the idea of passing one generation's expenses onto the next, or the next several.

# 8 Assumption

In keeping with his notion that the national debt would be a "cement of union," Hamilton wanted to assume, or take on, the debts of states that any might have acquired in paying for the war. This figure was substantial at $25 million. Critics of the idea either said this was too much to add or came from states, like Virginia, that had already paid off their war debts and considered federal assistance unfair. Assumption revealed to just what extent Hamilton was willing to go to forge national unity.

# 9 Funding at Par

Even more controversial than assumption was the notion of funding at par. This Hamiltonian brainchild sought not just states to be loyal supporters of the federal government but rich citizens who had speculated in war bonds. Through the ups and downs of the Revolutionary War, individual citizens who had purchased bonds feared they would amount to nothing. Those uncertain of ever receiving money back from their investment in independence willingly sold the bonds to wealthy buyers offering at least some cash. With independence secure, the popular notion was that the speculators had taken advantage of citizens of the new republic. Hamilton, however, wanted to reward them for their loyalty (and shrewdness) and to make them likely to buy bonds again if the government needed funding. Only through compromise could such seeming favoritism be permitted in a democratic republic, and this component of Hamilton's Financial Program (along with the Bank of the United States) were what the Federalists received for agreeing to let the South have the national capital at Washington, D.C.

# 10 Bank of the United States

Hamilton used implied powers granted to Congress by the "elastic clause" to propose the Bank of the United States (BUS). The U.S. Constitution said Congress could have powers besides those stated if they were "necessary and proper" in carrying out duties that were stated. Hamilton wanted a BUS in order to negotiate financial arrangements and to issue a currency, both of which were stated powers. He designed the bank to allow private investment in it as well as government funding to attach the prosperity of the country to the prosperity of individuals. When the Anti-Federalists compromised regarding the location of the national capital, Hamilton's loose construction of the elastic clause allowed him, with assumption and funding at par, to establish the economic underpinnings of a sound government and a national currency. Political wrangling over Hamilton's Financial Program gave rise to the two-party system, and the first BUS and its successors were controversial until another model was selected in the twentieth century.

# 11 Strict Versus Loose Construction

The two views of government derived from two methods of interpreting the U.S. Constitution were at the crux of the two-party system. Federalists favored loose construction because it used the elastic clause to increase the powers of the central government. Anti-Federalists favored a more limited government and used strict construction to claim that the central government should not cast about for more powers to add to those stated directly. Most presidents, Congresses, and even justices on the Supreme Court, found it difficult to adhere to either principle completely in the workings of government, but the balance between the two interpretations maintained moderation until the balance was removed. Most office holders since the twentieth century have been loose constructionists.

# 12 Whiskey Rebellion

Another component of Hamilton's financial program was an excise tax on whiskey. Whiskey was in prevalent use as a derivative of corn that could be more easily transported to market than grain. Whiskey was used as a currency in the West, a fact that sidestepped Hamilton's new national currency. In 1794, blustering Pennsylvanian farmers were warned by Washington to desist or be considered an insurrection. Nearly 15,000 militia soldiers, accompanied by Washington and Hamilton, convinced the rebels to disperse without firing a shot. Only two of the leaders were tried for treason, and Washington pardoned them. The central government proved that it was going to defend the U.S. Constitution and enforce the laws, thereby establishing stability and securing another source of revenue to help fund the national debt and the government.

## 13 Treaty of Greenville

Where two army expeditions had failed, General Anthony Wayne and 2,500 troops sent by Washington to the Great Lakes Region finally delivered a decisive defeat to American Indians harassing pioneers on the frontier. The battle in 1795 was called the Battle of Fallen Timbers because it was fought in Ohio over ground where a tornado had passed previously. Twelve American Indian tribes signed the peace treaty that ceded much of the territory that would become the State of Ohio as well as the cities of Detroit and Chicago. The fact that the Indians had been supplied liquor and guns by the British highlighted the tense relationship between the United States and Canada before Jay's Treaty was signed.

## 14 Jay's Treaty

Although all three of the major treaties of Washington's administration evidenced the new ability of the United States to control its own territory, Jay's Treaty, negotiated by John Jay in 1794, was the most significant. The British defied the Treaty of Paris of 1783 by keeping garrisons of soldiers on American soil. From these locations the British kept up a trade with American Indians that disturbed the peace on the frontier. The treaty also garnered trade concessions with the British for the rising maritime interests of the United States to have room to grow. In return, the American government pledged to see to it that British banks were compensated for the nearly $2.5 million in prewar debts American colonists still owed but refused to pay.

## 15 Pinckney's Treaty

The hesitancy of Spain to let the United States have free access to New Orleans with right of deposit for the storage of goods before shipping backfired. Thomas Pinckney discovered in 1795 that Spanish Florida was weakening and exacted from the Spanish not only access to New Orleans, which was so critical to the settlement of the Mississippi River Valley, but also the river itself. Rather than being merely the border between Spanish territory and the United States, the river was open to free navigation along its entire length. Thus in relations with American Indians and with foreign nations with interests in North America, the Washington administration asserted the rights of the new nation in its own neighborhood.

## 16 Washington's Farewell Address

As he departed into private life at last, Washington had published in newspapers an editorial that has gone down in history as his Farewell Address. While never delivered as a speech in his lifetime, his last important precedents were codified in this document. He explained why he was not pursuing a third term, warned against the factionalism of the party system and the sectionalism it would breed, urged the continuation of sound financial policy, and intoned isolationist foreign policy views with the admonition to avoid permanent alliances. None of this advice has been permanently followed by the country, but when not followed bad consequences have arisen that steer the nation back toward the wisdom of the father of his country who was "first in war, first in peace, and first in the hearts of his countrymen."

## 17 John Adams

Nearly any man would have difficulty standing next to George Washington and being remembered, but Adams always lived in the shadow of Washington, Franklin, and even Jefferson. Although he was instrumental in guiding the principles of independence to fruition, his presidency marked the decline of the Federalist Party despite the firm stance for both war and peace Adams took to save the country. The Alien and Sedition Acts sullied his reputation. When faced with the possibility of war with France or Great Britain or both, Adams oversaw the construction of the first Navy frigates while at the same time negotiating a peace with both nations that saved America from being destroyed in its infancy. He preserved some Federalist voice in government for years to come by placing John Marshall on the Supreme Court.

## 18 XYZ Affair

Most Americans wanted a war with France after hearing of the diplomatic debacle known as the XYZ Affair. When three American diplomats approached the French foreign minister, Talleyrand, to negotiate a settlement of the Quasi-War with France, Talleyrand asked for not only a loan from America to help France in the war with Britain but for a personal bribe of almost a quarter of a million dollars. The name of the incident stemmed from the agents making the proposal who were referred to secretly as X, Y, and Z. News of this offer enraged the American public and made it more difficult for Adams to stop the raiding of American shipping from becoming all-out war that he feared the country could not survive. The public outcry declared, "Millions for defense, but not a penny for tribute!"

## 19 Alien and Sedition Acts

During the 1798 dangerous episodes of the Adams presidency, Congress acted to change the naturalization laws to favor the Federalist party. The Alien Act changed the residency requirement for citizenship from five to fourteen years, thus delaying the time when immigrants would become voters who, as farmers, voted with the Anti-Federalists. The Sedition Act curbed the freedom of the press by making punishable by prison and a fine, "any false, scandalous, and malicious writing," directed at the federal government. Both these measures were passed to maintain a political advantage, but they were also enforced with partiality.

# 20 Kentucky and Virginia Resolutions

Anti-Federalist, or Jeffersonian Republican, reaction to the Alien and Sedition Acts was voiced by these two states through their state legislatures. Because Madison and Jefferson helped pen the bills the Resolutions represented a serious challenge to constitutional government by declaring null and void within the borders of their states the provisions they deemed unconstitutional. Southern states would resort to nullification to preserve slavery, and the northern states did so to protest a stringent fugitive slave law enacted just prior to the Civil War. One can only imagine the chaos that would ensue if every state could pick and choose which federal laws it would obey, but the Republicans found the Federalist laws so odious they were glad to test the constitutionality of their idea. The Alien and Sedition Acts were eventually agreed to be unjustified and erroneous, but in trying to solve a small crisis the Kentucky and Virginia Resolutions would set in motion a big one called the Nullification Crisis, one step before the Civil War.

## *The Big Picture*

1. Despite the degree of unity evidenced by the ratification of the U.S. Constitution, debates about the interpretation of the document and about the workings of government gave rise to the two-party system in American politics.

2. With the leadership of men like Washington, Adams, and Hamilton the Federalist Party established stability for the new nation but at the cost of its own popularity.

3. Economic stability was provided through Hamilton's Financial Program, the provisions of which followed loose construction of the U.S. Constitution to the consternation of Thomas Jefferson and the Anti-Federalists.

4. Domestic and national security were provided for by Washington's insistence on neutrality, assertion of territorial sovereignty in treaties, and use of the military to put down rebellion and to quell frontier attacks by American Indians.

5. John Adams maintained peace when war would have been popular but disastrous, but Federalist policies sparked such ire that the Anti-Federalists defied federal law, foreshadowing the North/South conflict over sovereignty that would lead toward the Civil War.

# The Jeffersonian Revolution and the Era of Good Feelings

*Still one thing more, fellow citizens—a wise and frugal Government, which shall restrain men from injuring one another, shall leave them otherwise free to regulate their own pursuits of industry and improvement, and shall not take from the mouth of labor the bread it has earned.*

—Thomas Jefferson's first inaugural address, 1801

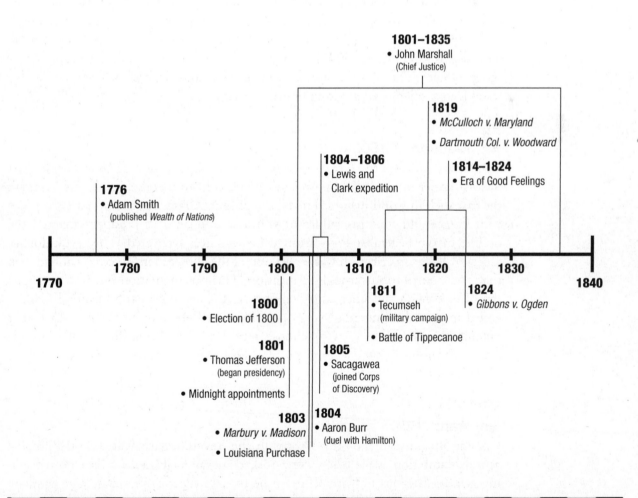

**1801–1835**
• John Marshall
(Chief Justice)

**1819**
• *McCulloch v. Maryland*
• *Dartmouth Col. v. Woodward*

**1804–1806**
• Lewis and
Clark expedition

**1814–1824**
• Era of Good Feelings

**1776**
• Adam Smith
(published *Wealth of Nations*)

1770    1780    1790    1800    1810    1820    1830    1840

**1800**
• Election of 1800

**1801**
• Thomas Jefferson
(began presidency)
• Midnight appointments

**1803**
• *Marbury v. Madison*
• Louisiana Purchase

**1804**
• Aaron Burr
(duel with Hamilton)

**1805**
• Sacagawea
(joined Corps
of Discovery)

**1811**
• Tecumseh
(military campaign)
• Battle of Tippecanoe

**1824**
• *Gibbons v. Ogden*

# Top 20 Things to Know

## 1 Thomas Jefferson

There are few aspects of the revolutionary and early national periods that were not fashioned in some measure by Thomas Jefferson's pen. A lawyer from Virginia, Jefferson rose through state and national offices forever putting his mark on the legacies of both his home state and the country. A short list of his accomplishments staggers the mind and includes the Declaration of Independence, the idea of public schools, the Virginia Statute on Religious Freedom (ending the establishment of the Episcopal Church), the Virginia and Kentucky Resolutions, the Louisiana Purchase, the Lewis and Clark expedition, the Embargo Act, and a revival of classical architecture. He also is directly responsible for the origins of the two-party system by leading the opposition to the Federalist Party, especially once he resigned his post as the secretary of state under Washington. Because of the original constitutional manner of electing the president, he wound up as the vice president to John Adams. His background made him influential enough to enforce his desire to weaken the central government while he was president while still being able to forge policy effectively. A true picture of the phenomenon of his achievements must include his lifelong attachment to and derision for slavery in which he personified America's entire dilemma regarding the peculiar institution. Jefferson died deep in debt on the same day as John Adams, exactly fifty years after the adoption of the Declaration of Independence. The two crucial advocates of independence had, before their deaths, reconciled as friends after a long political rivalry.

## 2 Election of 1800

Otherwise known as the Jeffersonian Revolution, the Election of 1800 was the first major transfer of ideological power in American history and, since it was peaceful, the first such in world history. The failure of John Adams to rally his party to peace with France and thus his failure to win a second term as president marked the decline of the Federalist Party from which it never recovered. The revolutionary aspect of Jefferson's election was a rejection of the elite leadership core that had seen the U.S. Constitution through ratification and implementation but had estranged the country with the Alien and Sedition Acts. The vote in the Electoral College ended in a tie that was resolved in the House of Representatives when Alexander Hamilton urged Federalists to choose Jefferson over Aaron Burr. This episode led to a revision in the electoral process through the Twelfth Amendment to the Constitution.

## 3 Aaron Burr

Coming up through the officer corps in the Revolutionary War, Aaron Burr had as much ambition as his fellow New Yorker, Alexander Hamilton, but no redeeming genius. After his tie with Jefferson he became the vice president, but was later defeated in a bid for governor of New York by the direct, public intervention of Hamilton. The two fought a duel over their differences in which Hamilton was killed. Eager to be president of something, Burr later attempted to carve out territory for a new country amid the vague borders of Spain and the Louisiana Territory in the West. The Burr Conspiracy fell through when a general in the U.S. Army who had conspired with Burr turned him in. He was acquitted of treason charges, however, and died in obscurity in New York City. His exploits revealed, in part, just how hard it was going to be for the U.S. government to manage westward expansion.

## 4 Mosquito Fleet

The area of Jefferson's Renaissance Man status lacking the most was in military acumen. Although he called for action that successfully humbled the Barbary pirates in Tripoli, he still tolerated the nuisance of paying tribute to the others dominant in the area. To cut expenses for the government, he reduced the size of the army and sold off the capital ships of the U.S. Navy that John Adams had painstakingly provided for national security. To attempt to patrol the national waters off the east coast, Jefferson developed a plan of using many small boats with minimal firepower. When contemplating the magnitude of either the French or especially the British navies, Jefferson's critics gave his idea the pejorative Mosquito Fleet title. The policy was in keeping with Jefferson's desire for a weaker central government and began the great debate in American history about the amount of resources to be dedicated to military readiness. From then on presidents and others either believed a strong military was the path to peace or the path to war.

## 5 Era of Good Feelings

The rest of the era of the Virginia dynasty saw Jefferson, Madison, and Monroe all enjoy two-term presidencies. With the demise of the Federalist Party, the Era of Good Feelings was the period when the notion of political parties gave way to the dream of national unity. Although factions did exist, the country experienced four presidencies, including that of John Quincy Adams, when the secretary of state from the previous administration became the next president. Such a predictable harmony was not destined to last long with the rise of Andrew Jackson or the events surrounding the War of 1812.

## 6 Congressional Committee System

As in the working out of kinks in the presidential election process, the relationship among the branches of government also experienced evolution. Although Federalist presidents worked with Federalist Congresses, policy had been driven by a centralized decision making focused on the president and his cabinet, another Washington precedent. When Jefferson actively set about reducing the power of the executive branch even in his personal leadership style, the resulting power vacuum was quickly filled by the legislative branch. Both houses of Congress established committees to review and to introduce legislation along a whole range of topics.

The committee system, once begun, was never undone, and even when presidents arose with forceful agendas the legislative process was thus all the more complex.

## 7 Louisiana Purchase

When the Haitian Revolution thwarted Napoleon's New World aspirations, he shrewdly backed out of having to build a more extensive navy, cut his losses, and sold out to the United States. He did so with the intention of raising America to one day humble the British whom he despised. Jefferson eagerly accepted the deal to double the size of the country for only $15 million even though to do so required him to use loose construction. He pushed the purchase through Congress as a treaty in 1803, and then hoped the massive addition of cheap land would allow his cherished yeoman farmers all the territory they would need for over a century of expansion. Nothing he did destabilized the relationship between North and South more, however. Federalists rallied against the purchase, but their irrelevance was evident in that no one listened.

## 8 Lewis and Clark expedition

The amazing journey of Meriwether Lewis and William Clark was only the most famous of the several expeditions dispatched to the new Louisiana Territory and beyond. For three years the Corps of Discovery set about following Jefferson's admonition to make friendly relations with the American Indians of the West while looking for economic opportunities. Although these goals eventually proved incompatible, Lewis and Clark succeeded in proving a river and land route existed that could get settlers all the way to the Pacific Ocean. Along the way they made several important scientific and geographical discoveries and returned alive. Their journal and other reports aroused great interest in western migration.

## 9 Sacagawea

This young Shoshone woman is a poignant symbol of the rivalry among American Indian tribes as well as the difficulties and opportunities of European/American encroachment into their territory. Having been sold to or captured by another tribe, Sacagawea wound up becoming one of the wives of a Frenchman. The two of them became a part of the Corps of Discovery, and Sacagawea provided crucial assistance as a guide, interpreter, and peaceful ambassador. He brother was a Shoshone chief who provided Lewis and Clark and their men horses with which to cross the Rocky Mountains. The bond was such among the erstwhile band of explorers that when Sacagawea died prematurely in 1812, William Clark raised her two children.

## 10 Tecumseh

The other most famous American Indian of the Era of Good Feelings did not seek cooperation with whites as Sacagawea did. In 1791 he attacked an American military force and dealt it a blow only to be surpassed by the complete annihilation of the force under George Armstrong Custer. A Shawnee chief, Tecumseh exhibited an unusual tendency to cooperate with American Indians of other tribes in opposition to white settlement in Tennessee. He conceived a plan with his brother, known as the Prophet, to combine American Indians of the West into a confederacy that could stop American expansion. When the plan was launched prematurely by his brother, the Battle of Tippecanoe undermined Tecumseh's authority while launching the career of the victor, William Henry Harrison. Tecumseh, who had been supplied by the British all along, joined the British military in the War of 1812 during which he was killed in battle.

## 11 Battle of Tippecanoe

This battle was the climax of Tecumseh's career as a coalition builder among American Indian tribes. William Henry Harrison mounted a military campaign as the governor of the Indiana Territory to put a stop to Tecumseh's offensive raids. When Tecumseh's forces attacked the Americans by surprise at dawn in 1811, all seemed to be going in his favor, but Harrison's men won despite heavy losses. Whether Tecumseh had manipulated the British in Canada to help him or the British had used Tecumseh as a pawn is hard to determine, but British support for American Indian resistance eroded. Harrison's victory would eventually earn him the presidency and immediately heightened tensions between the United States and Great Britain. Some western leaders called for the forceful annexation of Canada as a result.

## 12 Virginia Dynasty

Of the first five presidents, four of them were from Virginia. This curious circumstance belied the fact that the population of the North and West was growing to challenge Virginia's preeminence. Washington, Jefferson, Madison, and Monroe gave at least tacit support to slavery as well as set in motion events that would bring about the very sectionalism of which Washington had warned the nation in his Farewell Address. Of course, this collection of statesmen established the precedents of the most prominent professions to dominate the presidency, attorneys, and military officers. Since the last three members of the Virginia dynasty were Jeffersonian Republicans, the people of especially New England began to resent an apparent executive bias toward states' rights and the planter aristocrats of the South. The Virginia dynasty ended when John Quincy Adams became president in 1825.

## 13 Midnight Appointments

This derisive nickname was given to the federal judges put in office by John Adams on his last day as president of the United States. The divisive nature of Adams's political style contributed to the tendency of others to scorn him, but this shrewd measure provided for at least some balance in the federal government going into the Era of Good Feelings. John Marshall's appointment as chief justice of the Supreme Court proved to be a turning point in the status of the court as an equal member of the three branches of government established by the Constitution.

## 14 John Marshall

Another prominent Virginian, John Marshall served in the military under George Washington during the Revolutionary War and then held posts in government up to and including service as secretary of state under John Adams. Marshall was appointed to the Supreme Court as its chief justice during the fallout from the Election of 1800 and remained on the bench for over thirty years. As the last prominent Federalist who outlived his own party, Marshall placed his stamp on the workings of the Supreme Court and on the American economy. His cases were landmark decisions in the assertion of federal authority over individuals and states and in the establishment of judicial review, the concept that the Supreme Court was the final determiner of what was and was not constitutional.

## 15 Adam Smith

This British economist's book, *The Wealth of Nations*, was published the same year as the Declaration of Independence and proved equally revolutionary. Smith attacked mercantilism by arguing the law of supply and demand should determine the priorities of a country's economy rather than its government. He reasoned that people knew instinctively what would work to produce wealth and were best suited to make the adjustments in their practices according to market forces. His phrase, "the invisible hand," achieved lasting fame as the underpinnings for laissez-faire, the American political philosophy of the nineteenth century that advocated government support for economic growth with a minimum of interference. Smith's theories were based on observations of the economic dynamic that would become known as capitalism and served to popularize this economic philosophy that supplanted mercantilism.

## 16 *Marbury v. Madison*

William Marbury had been one of John Adams's midnight appointments (although all of the appointments had been signed by 9:00 P.M.). Secretary of State James Madison from the Jefferson administration, however, declined in 1801 to forward Marbury's commission as justice of the peace for Washington, D.C. When Federalist Marbury sued Madison, the case came before Federalist John Marshall in 1803. Marshall denied his fellow Federalist had a right to bring the suit because the Judiciary Act of 1789 whereby he based his claim granted powers to the Supreme Court that the Constitution did not contain. Incredibly, here was a Federalist justice writing a strict construction opinion denying a Federalist a position when the Anti-Federalists had denied Marbury the job. The Anti-Federalists were speechless, which is exactly what Marshall intended. Heretofore, ambiguity existed as to who would be the final arbiter of what the Constitution actually said. Whereas Thomas Jefferson believed the states were the best to judge the constitutionality of laws, his cousin John Marshall established the precedent of judicial review and dramatically increased the power and significance of Supreme Court rulings.

## 17 *McCulloch v. Maryland*

Many years later in 1819 the Marshall Court struck a blow maintaining a powerful central government when Maryland attempted to tax a branch of the Bank of the United States in order to check its influence. After the wrangling over Hamilton's Financial Plan in the Congress, this case was the first opportunity for the Supreme Court to weigh the concept of implied powers. Saying that "The power to tax involves the power to destroy," Marshall voiced the majority opinion on the Court that the federal government's institutions were impervious to state control just as federal law was superior to state law. He forever established the use of the elastic clause with the assertion, "Let the end be legitimate, let it be within the scope of the Constitution, and all means which are appropriate, which are plainly adapted to that end, which are not prohibited, but consist with the letter and spirit of the Constitution, are constitutional." Of course, this phrase also forever established the power of the Supreme Court to decide what was "appropriate," "plainly adapted," and so forth.

## 18 *Dartmouth College v. Woodward*

Also in 1819, this case clearly established the superiority of federal law over state law. Dartmouth College had existed since before the American Revolution and was chartered by King George III. When New Hampshire became a state the state legislature eventually sought to change the original charter, something the college resisted. The most distinguished graduate of Dartmouth, Daniel Webster, came to the defense of his alma mater and argued the case before the Supreme Court. Marshall merely pronounced that the original charter had been a contract and that New Hampshire had no power to break a contract. The college survived, but more importantly the states were humbled. The long-term result was to aid businesses of all types by protecting the sanctity of all contracts before the law.

## 19 *Gibbons v. Ogden*

Known as the "steamboat case," this 1824 suit symbolized both the continuing strength of the federal government but also the rising importance of interstate transportation and commerce. Alexander Hamilton's state of New York attempted to grant a monopoly on water transportation between New York and New Jersey to one company operated by Aaron Ogden but with the backing of Robert Fulton, the inventor of the first practical steamboat. Although the Constitution protected contracts and inventors' patents, Marshall said it did not grant to states the power to control interstate commerce. That arena was the sole prerogative of the federal government, and another giant precedent was set just as the nation was moving toward national markets for products.

# 20 Judicial Review

This concept in American law was the chief legacy of the Marshall Court, although judicial review also contributed to the continuing centralization of power in Washington in an era when those in power in Washington allowed it to lapse. No document would have been able to anticipate all the workings of government and all the pitfalls, certainly not the "bundle of compromises" that was the U.S. Constitution. Men like Hamilton and Marshall were instrumental in sifting through the ambiguities to hammer out hard and fast principles for practical application. The questions of which law was the supreme law of the land and which institution in the United States had the final say over what was constitutional and what was not were major causes of the Civil War and nearly destroyed the country within the lifetime of people who were young when the country was born. One can only wonder what would have happened had not the precedents of judicial review, contractual obligations, and the balance between federal power and states' rights been set at the opening of the nineteenth century.

## The Big Picture

1. The viability of the American republic was proven in the smooth transition between the Federalists and the Jeffersonian Repbulicans after the Election of 1800.

2. While the Era of Good Feelings experienced a period of one-party rule, events during the presidencies of the Jeffersonian Republicans revealed that factionalism and political parties were natural and would become a permanent part of American society.

3. Westward expansion, exploration, and settlement were established as the great national themes of the nineteenth century by the excitement generated by the Louisiana Purchase and the Lewis and Clark expedition.

4. As migration west commenced in earnest, violent clashes with Indians broke out and ambiguities in the relationship between federal authority and states' rights were revealed.

5. John Marshall was a stabilizing influence for American law and the American economy as he presided over a nationalist Supreme Court and asserted the power of the judicial branch through the concept of judicial review.

# The War of 1812 and the Age of Jackson

*The progress of the United States under our free and happy institutions has surpassed the most sanguine hopes of the founders of the Republic.*

—Andrew Jackson, farewell address, 1837

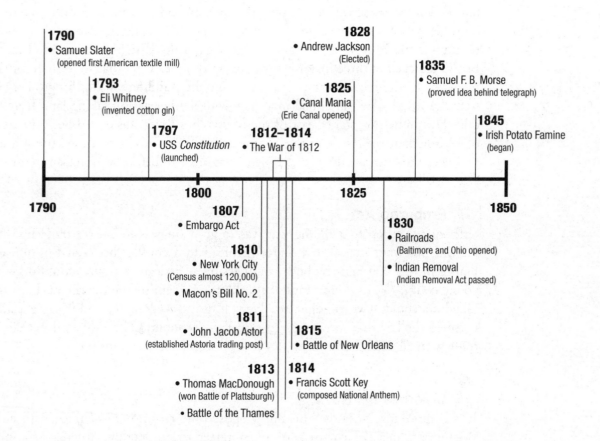

**1790**
• Samuel Slater
(opened first American textile mill)

**1793**
• Eli Whitney
(invented cotton gin)

**1797**
• USS *Constitution*
(launched)

**1812–1814**
• The War of 1812

**1828**
• Andrew Jackson
(Elected)

**1825**
• Canal Mania
(Erie Canal opened)

**1835**
• Samuel F. B. Morse
(proved idea behind telegraph)

**1845**
• Irish Potato Famine
(began)

1790    **1800**    **1825**    1850

**1807**
• Embargo Act

**1810**
• New York City
(Census almost 120,000)
• Macon's Bill No. 2

**1811**
• John Jacob Astor
(established Astoria trading post)

**1813**
• Thomas MacDonough
(won Battle of Plattsburgh)
• Battle of the Thames

**1814**
• Francis Scott Key
(composed National Anthem)

**1815**
• Battle of New Orleans

**1830**
• Railroads
(Baltimore and Ohio opened)
• Indian Removal
(Indian Removal Act passed)

# Top 20 Things to Know

## 1 Andrew Jackson

The epitome of a self-made man, Andrew Jackson was orphaned by the Revolutionary War but then pulled himself up from poverty, taught himself enough law to practice on the frontier, and wound up a planter aristocrat of the South. He got into politics but proved too hot-headed and combative. These qualities served him well on a military campaign against the Creek Indians, however, which brought him in close proximity to New Orleans, the defense of which he took on himself. The Battle of New Orleans catapulted him to national fame and eventually the presidency. His forceful style of leadership manifested itself in prolific use of the veto, Indian removal, the Bank War, and other episodes of a career that led historians to name the period from 1820 to 1840 the Age of Jackson.

## 2 War of 1812

This second war against the mother country occurred because neither Great Britain nor the United States respected each other or could do without each other economically. Napoleon provoked animosity between the British and the Americans in order to humble the British. When James Madison got the Congress to declare war, the British attacked in three major campaigns on American soil that were all eventually repulsed. In the second campaign, major public buildings in Washington, D.C., were destroyed. The war ended in a draw with neither nation taking land from the other. All Indian resistance east of the Mississippi River was ended with the death of Tecumseh at the Battle of the Thames. The Treaty of Ghent ended the war and propelled Americans into a brief time of nationalism before sectionalism returned.

## 3 Embargo Act

Jefferson's solution to avoiding war was to get Congress to cut off trade in 1807. He did not want the United States involved in a conflict between England and France in fear that raids by both countries on American shipping would draw the young country to its doom. Only a southern president before the rise of the cotton kingdom could have thought so. New England Federalists and Yankee traders despised the law that threatened to ruin their economy. The Embargo Act cut off trade with all foreign countries, not just the combatant nations.

## 4 Macon's Bill No. 2

In a compromise position, this bill proposed the resumption of trade with either Britain or France, whichever nation first agreed to stop raiding American shipping. Although the Federalists still did not like any restrictions on their trade, the bill became law. Napoleon saw a chance to move the United States toward war with Great Britain and vowed to stop French predation of American merchant vessels.

President Madison trusted Napoleon and reopened commerce with France, an act the British regarded as tantamount to war.

## 5 War Hawks

Young Congressmen from the western states made it clear that they favored war with Great Britain. While not seafaring people themselves, they claimed the British practice of impressment, or forcible drafting of even American seamen into the British navy, was a violation of the dignity of the nation. The War Hawks, led by Henry Clay of Kentucky, said they would rather fight for American rights on the high seas than cower behind shady agreements with nations that viewed America as a pawn. When James Madison blamed the British for all of the affronts to American shipping (rather than the French who were also guilty), the War Hawks led Congress to declare war.

## 6 Impressment

Service in the British navy occurred under such harsh conditions that men had to be drafted in order to fill crews. Press gangs came ashore in England and in other countries and essentially kidnapped men, especially those lying drunk on wharves in harbors. Because it was hard to determine whether any given seaman was of English or American origin, confusion abounded. Mistaken identities regarding those who might have escaped from British ships did not erase the fact that some men were simply shanghaied, or stolen outright. The harsh discipline aboard ship was capable of keeping involuntary recruits at work, usually. Impressment was considered an odious violation of national sovereignty by the War Hawks and by most Americans.

## 7 Battle of the Thames

In a largely bungled series of clashes along the Great Lakes in the War of 1812, the Battle of the Thames stands out as a singular success. Fresh from the Battle of Tippecanoe, William Henry Harrison took advantage of the naval victories of Oliver Hazard Perry on the Great Lakes to move troops north of Lake Erie into Canada. Although the American forces had higher casualties at the ensuing battle, 477 British soldiers were captured and Tecumseh was killed. Tecumseh's death ended the confederacy of American Indian tribes and opened the way for white settlement of land all the way to the Mississippi River at the end of the war. Especially because all other attempts to invade Canada failed, Harrison's two victories in the area launched him toward the presidency.

## 8 Thomas MacDonough

The British in Canada eventually had enough of pesky invasions from the south and sent eleven thousand troops in four ships accompanied by twelve gunboats to invade the United States via Lake Champlain. A successful insertion through this route threatened New York City and the cutting off of New England. Thomas

MacDonough, a young naval captain, built and/or assembled a fleet almost as large as that of the British. MacDonough's clever positioning of his fleet and his clear-headed thinking during the battle allowed his shorter-ranged guns to prevail over the longer-ranged British cannon. When the British surrendered, the Americans took all the supplies for the invasion, and stopping the invasion saved the war in the North from being a total disaster.

# 9 USS *Constitution*

This American war vessel was made of thick Virginia oak and proved to be the major symbolic protector of the U.S. Constitution during the War of 1812. She bested four British frigates, once taking on two at a time and capturing both. The nickname "Old Ironsides" was given her by her crew after they observed British cannon balls ricocheting off the hull. Now, the USS *Constitution* is the oldest commissioned ship in the world and is preserved as a symbol of the war that first brought the United States to prominence in world affairs.

# 10 Francis Scott Key

Kept overnight during the Battle of Fort McHenry by the British on a prisoner ship, Francis Scott Key was thus given an excellent vantage point as an eyewitness of the attempt to invade the United States via the Chesapeake Bay and Baltimore. He deserves mention because of the poignant way in which he captured his observations on some notes on the back of a letter. The notes eventually became the *Star-Spangled Banner*, honored as the national anthem of the United States ever since. The actual flag that Key observed "was still there" is still here, restored and on display in Washington, D.C. These items were the stuff and symbols of which nations are made.

# 11 Battle of New Orleans

The Battle of New Orleans was a terrible slaughter that need not have happened. The Treaty of Ghent had already been signed ending hostilities, but the news of the peace had not arrived by the time of the battle. Through arrogance and lack of coordination, the British plan to assault Andrew Jackson's forces ensconced behind breastworks failed utterly, and the British soldiers were caught in murderous fire from American muskets and cannon. The casualties were lopsided with the British receiving over two thousand and the Americans only seventy-one. The War of 1812 had been ended by a treaty, but the Battle of New Orleans contributed greatly to intellectual independence for the American people from their British heritage and launched Jackson to national fame.

# 12 Irish Potato Famine

A sudden blight caused by a fungus in September 1845 destroyed the potato crop in Ireland. The disease lingered, and tariff laws protecting the wealthy classes prevented the importation of grain to stave off the hunger stalking the land, as the lower classes of Ireland subsisted almost entirely on potatoes. Estimates range from four hundred thousand to one million Irish succumbed to starvation while much of what food was produced continued to be shipped to England according to existing contracts. Under conditions like these, almost two million Irish migrated to the United States in the middle of the nineteenth century. The Irish arrived impoverished and had little hope at first of anything beyond meager factory wages to keep them alive in eastern cities. In time, however, the Irish made a lasting cultural contribution to America and became important in the power structures of New York, Boston, and Chicago among other cities.

## 13 Canal Mania

A crucial step in the transportation revolution that opened the West for settlement was the era of canal building known as Canal Mania. Beginning with the Erie Canal, which was constructed from 1817 to 1825, states and private companies sought to dig canals wherever they appeared to be feasible. Although canal boats traveled no faster than the horses or people pulling them along, they could more easily transfer large cargoes than wagons over land. Canals facilitated the migration of people west and the shipping of grain back east. Canals also bred an endearing folk hero in flatboat men like Mike Fink, who were said to embody the great enterprising spirit and wildness of the frontier that so captivated the imaginations of Americans and stimulated westward migration.

## 14 New York City

Because of the Erie Canal's connecting of Buffalo on the Great Lakes with the Hudson River, New York City became the transit point for oceangoing goods and people coming into the country, while goods, especially grain, were funneled in from the West. Even cotton was brought up from the South to New York in order to be shipped from there to Europe. The natural advantages of the harbor discerned by the first Dutch settlers of New Amsterdam worked to the advantage of this city, the first in America to have one million inhabitants. Because of its early diversity, wealth, and population, New York City became and remains a driving force in American and world culture.

## 15 Samuel Slater

Slater left England secretly and migrated to the United States in 1789 as the first Englishman who could construct a textile factory. He built a mill in Rhode Island by 1793. Just as in England, water-powered mills spread across the land, and the manufacture of textiles was the main industry prior to the Civil War. The ease with which cotton fabric was made by machine, along with the invention of the cotton gin, dramatically increased the demand for cotton from the South and thus the demand for slaves. As the industrial revolution began in America, laborers clustered in towns provided by mill owners. Native-born men, women, and children, as well as increasing numbers of immigrants, found work in mills. Industrialists craved efficiency and set about organizing the lives of the workers in ways that were eventually considered restrictive of workers' freedoms.

# 16 Eli Whitney

Whitney was the other great founder of American industry. A mechanical genius with a degree from Yale, he seized on the problem of processing raw cotton while traveling in the South. In 1793 he invented the cotton engine, or gin, to separate the cotton fibers from the seeds ten times faster than could be done by hand. With improvements to the machine and a patent in hand, he set about revolutionizing the production of cotton for market. Along the way he sought to expand his manufacturing business by earning a contract with the federal government to make muskets rapidly. To speed the process and to make the finished muskets uniform and easily repaired, Whitney used machines to manufacture interchangeable parts. His manufacturing process for both the cotton gin and muskets was the basis for modern mass production once Henry Ford put the process in motion on a continuously moving assembly line.

# 17 Railroads

Although the original steam engines and steam locomotives were made practical in Great Britain, only the sweeping geography of North America (or later Russia) would unlock the potential of railroads to shrink space. As roads, bridges, canals, and steamboats advanced transportation, railroads revolutionized it by allowing travel faster than ever before. Railroads could go up and down hill much faster than the lock systems of canals and could carry heavier loads. If mountains were too high to cross, tunnels allowed railroads to pass through. Because railroads were foundational to the expansion of commerce, travel, and thus industry, they became the first big business. Therefore, managers and lawyers invented business practices working for railroads that all other industries and corporations copied. Walt Whitman selected the steam locomotive for one of his poems as the symbol of American energy, innovation, and potential for greatness.

# 18 Samuel F. B. Morse

Another in a growing series of inventors who transformed life on earth, Morse contributed to a communications revolution with his development of the telegraph and the code that bears his name. The communication revolution literally paralleled the transportation revolution as telegraph wires were strung on poles alongside railroad tracks. These two inventions together made time zones necessary because rapid travel and almost instantaneous communication required a relative concept of time. Morse was an artist who became fascinated with the concepts of electromagnetism and proved that messages could be sent over vast distances along a continuous wire.

# 19 John Jacob Astor

Astor deserves mention as the first of many rags-to-riches stories that are associated with the American Dream. He is also an example of how German immigrants had a smoother transition to success in American society than other groups like the Irish. Born at the end of the French and Indian War in 1763, by the end of the Revolutionary War in 1783 Astor had worked and saved enough money for passage to New York City. He and his wife embodied the typical path to wealth followed by so many who came after. They lived frugally, worked diligently in their business, and watched for good investments. His original business was the organization of the fur trade taking some of the most independent-minded men in America, fur trappers, and creating a system of regular trafficking that benefited all. Astor traveled extensively and was the first to set up a trading post at the mouth of the Columbia River on the Pacific coast at what would become Astoria. When the fur trade declined he sold out and shrewdly managed his profits. At his death he was the richest man in America.

# 20 Indian Removal

As the population climbed Americans hungered for more land. Treaties established locations for American Indian tribes in their ancestral hunting grounds and villages, but those treaties were shunted aside. The Indian Removal Act was controversial even in its day, but it passed in 1830. As a result, the Cherokee, Creek, Chickasaw, Choctaw, and Seminole tribes were given land in what would become the state of Oklahoma. When they protested, Andrew Jackson commanded the military to forcibly remove the American Indians, and thousands of them were evacuated in winter on what was known as the Trail of Tears. The removal policy was based on the assumption that the two peoples could never coexist peacefully despite the fact that many of the American Indians had converted to Christianity and settled on farms. These and other policies would lead by 1890 to the placement of all American Indians on tribal reservations.

## *The Big Picture*

1. Controversies over trade and encroachments on the citizens and property of the United States led to a second war of American independence known as the War of 1812.

2. The War of 1812 revealed the lack of preparedness of the American military and the lack of unity of the American people, but by the end in 1815 both were remedied.

3. Immigration picked up in the middle of the nineteenth century with Irish and Germans helping to swell eastern cities just in time for the beginnings of the Industrial Revolution.

4. Transportation and communication were both revolutionized and contributed dramatically to the transformation of the American economy.

5. Economic growth and westward settlement provided a higher standard of living for most, created vast fortunes for some, and powerfully impacted the less fortunate like immigrant factory workers and southeastern American Indian tribes.

# Mini Quiz

1. The reason the Stamp Act caused such alarm among Americans in 1765 was that the new tax

   (A) showed that George III and Parliament intended to control the colonial economy.
   (B) highlighted colonial dependence on England for manufactured goods like paper.
   (C) was intended to control colonial court proceedings by the stamp requirement.
   (D) was the first direct tax merely for revenue rather than mercantilist control.
   (E) made it impossible for Americans to advance in professional careers.

2. The colonial representative assembly to issue the Declaration of Independence was the

   (A) Albany Congress.
   (B) First Continental Congress.
   (C) Second Continental Congress.
   (D) Stamp Act Congress.
   (E) Philadelphia Convention.

3. Among which of the following factors was the chief reason the United States won its independence?

   (A) The Continental Army and the French Navy together amounted to a superior military force.
   (B) George Washington was a brilliant military strategist.
   (C) Large portions of the British military deserted to join the American forces.
   (D) The growing free market economy of America outpaced that of mercantilist England.
   (E) British resolve was insufficient to surmount the tremendous physical challenges of the war.

4. The foundation of the American republic depended on all of the following principles EXCEPT

   (A) the national government would be divided into three branches.
   (B) the power in the country was exercised by the voting citizens.
   (C) the government operated through representatives rather than through direct democracy.
   (D) legislators expressed the will of the people by making laws.
   (E) all citizens, even the rulers, were subject to the country's laws.

5. The leader of the American Revolution NOT present at the Constitutional Convention was

   (A) Benjamin Franklin.
   (B) George Washington.
   (C) Thomas Jefferson.
   (D) Roger Sherman.
   (E) Alexander Hamilton.

6. What attitude toward state governments existed after the ratification of the U.S. Constitution and the Bill of Rights?

   (A) State governments would lose all importance once the central government got on its feet.
   (B) State governments would share some powers with the central government and lose others.
   (C) State governments would continue just as they were from the founding of the country.
   (D) State governments would gain new powers to hold the new central government in check.
   (E) State governments would forfeit all access to military power.

7. George Washington's chief political and administrative adviser in his new government was

   (A) Secretary of State Thomas Jefferson.
   (B) Secretary of War Henry Knox.
   (C) Chief Justice of the Supreme Court John Jay.
   (D) Secretary of Treasury Alexander Hamilton.
   (E) Attorney General Edmund Randolph.

8. The first compromise hammered out in the U.S. Congress that could be said to be a North/South compromise was over what issue(s)?

   (A) The slave trade in the national capital
   (B) The excise tax on whiskey
   (C) The national debt and payment of war bonds at par
   (D) The Bank of the United States and the location of the national capital
   (E) The representation of slaveholding states in the House of Representatives

9. George Washington's foreign policy position is best expressed how?

   (A) Foreign powers should not interfere in America nor fear American interference.
   (B) The United States needed to test its military prowess against some European power.
   (C) The United States should acquire territories at sea to facilitate foreign trade.
   (D) France could count on the United States for a long-term military alliance against England.
   (E) The United States should join in an association of nations dedicated to world peace.

10. Thomas Jefferson's political views could be summed up with what phrase?

    (A) A strong central government was the best assurance of national unity.
    (B) The U.S. Constitution should be viewed as a general guide for shaping policy.
    (C) The American economy needed to diversify in the quest for world power status.
    (D) An educated elite made up the natural rulers of any society.
    (E) Whatever was good for simple rural citizens was good for America.

11. Which two men were most responsible for the Louisiana Purchase?

    (A) Thomas Jefferson and French Foreign Minister Talleyrand
    (B) Aaron Burr and Robert Livingston
    (C) Napoleon Bonaparte and Toussaint L'Ouverture
    (D) Meriwether Lewis and William Clark
    (E) John Quincy Adams and James Madison

12. Which position in the government usually produced the next president during the Virginia dynasty?

    (A) Vice president
    (B) Secretary of state
    (C) Secretary of war
    (D) Secretary of treasury
    (E) General in the U.S. Army

13. Which previous treaty was most responsible for the breakdown in relations that led to the War of 1812?

    (A) The 1763 Treaty of Paris
    (B) Pinckney's Treaty
    (C) The Treaty of Greenville
    (D) Jay's Treaty
    (E) The Treaty of Washington

14. In which region did the United States experience its greatest success against the British military in the fighting associated with the War of 1812?

    (A) The Chesapeake region
    (B) The region nearest the border with Canada
    (C) The Great Lakes region
    (D) The region around New York
    (E) The region around New Orleans

15. Which technological advance did NOT occur prior to 1850?

    (A) Interchangeable parts as the basis for mass production
    (B) The cotton gin
    (C) Textile manufacturing mills
    (D) The steam locomotive
    (E) The assembly line

# Answer Explanations

1. **D**  The Stamp Act's primary offense in the eyes of Americans was its departure from indirect taxation designed to control the economy to direct taxation designed merely to raise money to pay the war debt.

2. **C**  The famous gathering of the Founding Fathers that declared American independence was the Second Continental Congress.

3. **E**  Choice E is the only answer that was true of the Revolutionary War.

4. **A**  This principle was not a part of the Articles of Confederation but came later with the U.S. Constitution.

5. **C**  Thomas Jefferson, although often assumed to have written the U.S. Constitution, was away from the country as an ambassador to France during the Constitutional Convention.

6. **B**  A major part of the revision of the government in the Critical Period was the removal of certain powers from the states, like issuing currency and charging tariffs, but the definition of a federal government is also that states would share power with the central government.

7. **D**  Although George Washington selected and respected all of these men for their roles in the new government, Alexander Hamilton organized the finances of the new government, the beginnings of the Federalist Party, and the practical workings of government through several precedents supported by President Washington.

8. **D**  The Bank of the United States and the moving of the national capital was the direct swap between Federalists in the North and Anti-Federalists from the South.  No compromise was reached on answer A until 1850, whereas answers B and C were a part of the general financial program proposed by Hamilton that antagonized others than just southerners. Answer E occurred during the Constitutional Convention in Philadelphia.

9. **A**  Washington's policy was isolationist and was either directly or indirectly opposed to all the other choices.

10. **E**  Thomas Jefferson was opposed to all the rest of the ideas even though he was an elite aristocrat. He was a strict constructionist and believed America should retain an agrarian economy. He valued yeoman farmers above all other citizens and acted as their chief advocate.

11. **C**  All these men played a role directly or indirectly in the Louisiana Purchase or in the Louisiana Territory, but Napoleon's plans set all the rest in motion until thwarted by L'Ouverture's Haitian Revolution, which caused Napoleon to choose to sell the land to Jefferson through Livingston's negotiations with Talleyrand.

12. **B**  All of the Virginia dynasty presidents were first secretaries of state except for Washington.

13. **D**  Of these only Jay's Treaty had any relevant bearing on the British during the era of the War of 1812, and the failure of the treaty strained Anglo-American relations to the breaking point.

14. **E**  Most of these regions saw mostly American failures, some that were atrocious. One small victory on the Great Lakes and a significant turning point at Lake Champlain could not compare with the glory of the lopsided victory at New Orleans.

15. **E**  All of these advances occurred before 1850 except for Henry Ford's assembly line that was not perfected until the 1920s.

# Political Evolution in the Age of Jackson

*Get up on all occasions, and sometimes on no occasion at all, and make long-winded speeches, though composed of nothing else than wind.*
—Davy Crockett's advice to politicians, 1836

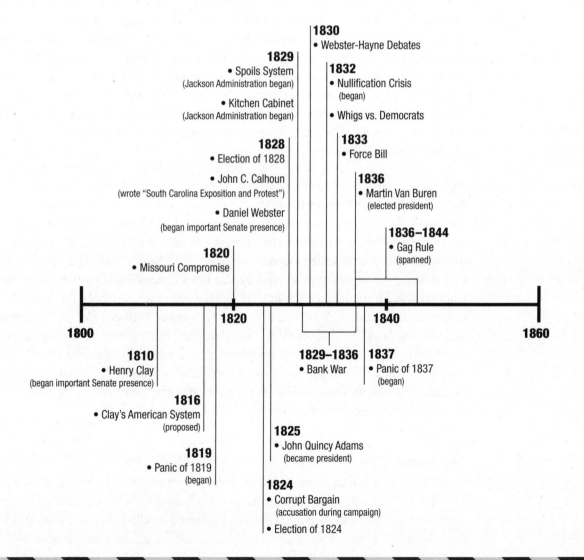

**1830**
• Webster-Hayne Debates

**1829**
• Spoils System
(Jackson Administration began)

• Kitchen Cabinet
(Jackson Administration began)

**1832**
• Nullification Crisis
(began)

• Whigs vs. Democrats

**1828**
• Election of 1828

• John C. Calhoun
(wrote "South Carolina Exposition and Protest")

• Daniel Webster
(began important Senate presence)

**1833**
• Force Bill

**1836**
• Martin Van Buren
(elected president)

**1820**
• Missouri Compromise

**1836–1844**
• Gag Rule
(spanned)

**1800**

**1820**

**1840**

**1860**

**1810**
• Henry Clay
(began important Senate presence)

**1829–1836**
• Bank War

**1837**
• Panic of 1837
(began)

**1816**
• Clay's American System
(proposed)

**1819**
• Panic of 1819
(began)

**1825**
• John Quincy Adams
(became president)

**1824**
• Corrupt Bargain
(accusation during campaign)

• Election of 1824

# Top 20 Things to Know

## 1 Panics of 1819 and 1837

These opening panics, or depressions, were the first in a series of economic crashes that grew successively worse until the Great Depression of the 1930s. The Panic of 1819 resulted from economic adjustments after the War of 1812. The Panic of 1837 stemmed largely from the manipulation of the financial industry by the Jackson and Van Buren administrations. The Bank War caused federal money to flood into state banks, and the resulting risk-laden investments led to a boom that busted. These two panics clearly illustrated the natural cycle of economic ups and downs in a capitalist society and the detrimental nature of some government policies.

## 2 Missouri Compromise

This legislative compromise was the first engineered by Henry Clay of Kentucky. When Missouri wanted to enter the Union as a slave state, Clay's idea was to keep the balance of slave and free states in the Senate by bringing in Maine, a part of Massachusetts, as a free state. To stave off further disunion, no state other than Missouri carved out of the Louisiana Purchase north of the 36°30' line of latitude would ever be a slave state. New states below the line would be slave states. Thus Clay began his career as the Great Compromiser by avoiding further North/South conflict for a time. The debates over the compromise frightened the South into adamant defense of slavery.

## 3 Gentlemen's Agreement

Just as in the Second Continental Congress and the Constitutional Convention, an understood truce had to be maintained between the North and the South over the issue of slavery in order to preserve peace. The North had to accept the notion that slaves were property protected by the Fifth Amendment to the Constitution, whereas the South had to agree that slavery was such a troubling issue that all means necessary should be taken to end the institution as soon as economically and socially possible. The problem was that the North found references to people as property distasteful, and few people in the South really planned for the end of slavery. A fear of disunion and war as well as a pretended civility in both houses of Congress did prevent conflict for a time, but the Gentlemen's Agreement also prevented any serious unified attempt to resolve the issue.

## 4 Henry Clay

As influential a senator and failed presidential candidate as there has ever been, Henry Clay was a slave-owning attorney from Kentucky who represented his young state from his old War Hawk days until his death in 1852. He was responsible for the Missouri Compromise, the compromise tariff, and the Compromise of 1850, partly due to his ability to cooperate with John C. Calhoun as a planter aristocrat and with Daniel Webster as a Whig, the opposition party Clay helped to found. He was the first major statesman of the Age of Jackson to follow through with Alexander Hamilton's vision of a national economy. Clay's American System attempted to use the influence of the federal government to stimulate the economy and to stabilize it at the same time. He supported the Second Bank of the United States, a high protective tariff, and internal transportation improvements using federal dollars.

## 5 Elections of 1824 and 1828

These presidential elections were the first modern elections with strategies and procedures recognizable today. John Quincy Adams won in 1824 over Andrew Jackson in the House of Representatives because no clear majority existed in the Electoral College. The result infuriated Jackson because he had won the popular vote in the election and believed that Henry Clay and Adams had conspired to steal the election. Jackson won outright in 1828, however, and brought his common man democratic values to bear on the nation's problems. These two elections ended the Era of Good Feelings, and Americans have embraced the two-party system ever since.

## 6 Corrupt Bargain

Jackson's (and his supporters') belief that the Election of 1824 was stolen stemmed from his accusation that Henry Clay dropped out of the election in order to be president later. Clay did throw his support behind John Quincy Adams thereby securing the vote in the House of Representatives for Adams, but Jackson accused the two of conspiring to bring Clay into the cabinet as secretary of state. Most presidents to that point had been the secretary of state of the previous president, so when Clay was chosen for the slot Jackson cried foul. No evidence exists to prove that Adams and Clay actually made a deal, but Jackson was Clay's sworn enemy for the rest of their lives.

## 7 John Quincy Adams

This eldest son of one of the Founding Fathers was also the most traveled American of his day having been raised on international relations. He served in several diplomatic posts and in the Senate until becoming Monroe's secretary of state and the mastermind behind the Monroe Doctrine. While president he tried to remain above political wrangling and to accomplish great goals for domestic development, but he failed to acquire the latter without the former. He was elected to the House of Representatives after leaving the presidency and remained all his life an indefatigable opponent of slavery and its expansion. He later stood against Texas annexation and the Gag Rule and personally argued the case in the Supreme Court of the slaves aboard the *Amistad* who had taken over their slave ship in transit from Africa. The slaves were freed. As proof that he dedicated his life to his country he died at his desk as the only ex-president to go into the House of Representatives.

## 8 Spoils System

This name for patronage is associated with Andrew Jackson's presidency because he quoted the phrase from the classical world, "To the victor belong the spoils." All presidents before his time and since selected many of their supporters as advisers and to hold positions in government. Jackson was simply the first to do so after the Era of Good Feelings when one-party rule had left a class of civil servants in power for almost three decades. Jackson said rotation in office was necessary to prevent these individuals from becoming parasites or from acquiring too much influence even though they were not elected to office. In the context of his campaign and subsequent political struggles Jackson's supporters viewed the measures as "cleaning house," whereas his enemies accused him of giving away the government to his friends. Of course, most presidents of the nineteenth century gave the government away to their friends.

## 9 Kitchen Cabinet

Speaking of the friends and associates of Andrew Jackson, he liked to meet with them in the kitchen after state dinners to discuss policy where they could feel free to spit tobacco on the floor. Jackson's informal advisers were usually more important in his decision-making process than his actual cabinet. His enemies therefore used this pejorative phrase to portray these closed-door sessions with cronies as giving them undue influence. All presidents, however, have trusted private advisers to help them accomplish the monumental task of running the executive branch.

## 10 National Nominating Convention

Another lasting legacy to arise from the Age of Jackson was the national nominating convention. In an age of growing democracy, the shady caucus system of the party leadership's selecting the candidates for president and vice president in secret was replaced with a more open system. By 1832, the modern Democratic Party was born and selected Jackson as their candidate. The conventions also served to let delegates debate and hammer out a party platform that their chosen candidate was supposed to go out and stump for on the campaign trail and implement if and when he took office.

## 11 Nullification Crisis

The 1828 tariff was a protective tariff so high as to earn the title the Tariff of Abominations in the South. Tariffs helped northern manufacturers compete with cheaper imported goods therefore making manufactured products more expensive while alienating foreign customers of exports like cotton. Although the 1832 tariff was slightly lower, it was still protective, and South Carolina nullified it. This step threatened national unity with secession. Andrew Jackson firmly supported the Union and threatened to invade South Carolina if she seceded. Again, Henry Clay calmed the crisis with a compromise tariff reduced annually over nine years.

## 12 John C. Calhoun

Another constellation of the antebellum political sky was John C. Calhoun of South Carolina. He also held cabinet positions and desired the presidency but rose to prominence only in the Senate. Despite his stint as vice president under Jackson, Calhoun took South Carolina's side in the Nullification Crisis and anonymously published editorials against Jackson's policies. Calhoun was an ardent believer in states' rights, slavery, and thus nullification and eventually secession. He abandoned the Calvinist doctrines of his Scots-Irish heritage but kept all of the stubbornness. He was the southern star in the powerful triumvirate of senators who opposed Andrew Jackson but compromised in order to keep the peace.

## 13 Martin Van Buren

Affectionately known as "Old Kinderhook" because of his birthplace in New York, his campaigns may be the origin of the Americanism, "OK." He transformed a keen legal mind into a keen political one that rose from obscurity to become the intellect behind the bluster and force of Andrew Jackson as one of Old Hickory's top advisers. In doing so, Van Buren was the organizing force behind the first political party to survive into the modern day, the Democratic Party. Unlike his fierce friend from Tennessee, however, Van Buren opposed the extension of slavery and thus blocked the annexation of Texas. As president, he stuck to Jackson's policy of allowing public land to be bought only with gold or silver and was thus partly responsible for the Panic of 1837, the worst depression the country had ever seen to that point. When the blow fell, Van Buren attempted to stop speculation by taking federal money out of state banks and keeping it in independent treasuries where it was unable to do anybody any good. The panic deepened, and Van Buren was rejected even by his own party in favor of James K. Polk in 1844.

## 14 Force Bill

The Force Bill was a sign of the severity of the conflict between South Carolina and President Andrew Jackson during the Nullification Crisis. If the customs agents in South Carolina refused to collect the protective tariff, Jackson vowed to prosecute them as traitors. The Force Bill said that the president could use the military to enforce the law. Jackson said, "If you secede, we will invade." South Carolina nullified the Force Bill, which implied that if the president led the U.S. Army into South Carolina that the Force Bill would not be in effect the moment they entered the state. Jackson refrained when he realized it was an election year and he needed the southern planter aristocratic class to win. Instead of pressing the Force Bill, Jackson made a peaceful gesture of stopping the mail service of the abolitionist press. South Carolina accepted the offered gesture and cooperated with Henry Clay's compromise tariff plan.

## 15 Gag Rule

This resolution in the House of Representatives is as responsible for the onset of the Civil War as any of the other more famous causes. The Gag Rule was adopted in 1836 and remained in effect until 1844 during the very time the constitutional process of debate and majority rule could have helped both sides toward gradual emancipation of slaves and compensation for their owners. Instead, where the debates were most intense because of the South's handicap in representation due to its lower population, the capacity for peaceful debate was silenced. The rules stated that any abolitionist resolution or bill brought before the House would be immediately tabled, or postponed indefinitely. While this kept arguments from arising in the Congress, they arose later anyway when tempers were hotter, the compromising Senate leaders were dead, and the conflict between North and South inevitably ended in a terrible war.

## 16 Bank War

Jackson's other big confrontation with his rivals in the Senate was the conflict over the Bank of the United States (BUS). Jackson had publicly called the bank and its national currency a conspiracy against the rights of the people. In trying to diminish Jackson's popularity, Henry Clay and Daniel Webster sought to recharter the BUS early during a presidential election year. While the Whig Party and business interests of the country had come to think of the bank as a necessary part of the economy, Jackson saw it as an enemy of the common man. The showdown came when Jackson vetoed the recharter bill and began the transfer of federal funds into his supporter's private banks in various states. Drained of funds, the BUS was bankrupted and Jackson was more popular than ever. The machinations of Nicholas Biddle, the bank's director, contributed to the coming Panic of 1837, however, as did Jackson's "pet banks" by encouraging rampant speculation in a burgeoning economy.

## 17 Daniel Webster

Considered the greatest political orator of his day, this Massachusetts senator embodied New England principles of education and commerce. Famous for his defense of his alma mater, Dartmouth, before the Supreme Court, he applied his oratory to larger issues as the Age of Jackson unfolded. As a Whig leader he cooperated with Henry Clay in defending the BUS and promoting the American System, but his singular contribution was enunciating the North's view that secession was unconstitutional. In a debate with Senator Hayne from South Carolina, Webster agreed with Jackson in one regard: that secession would never occur peacefully. His ringing line was, "Liberty and Union, now and forever, one and inseparable." Before the days of the Pledge of Allegiance, Webster voiced the principles that would carry the country toward actual nationhood through the trials of the Civil War.

## 18 Whigs Versus Democrats

These were the two significant parties that restored the two-party system to American politics. The Democrats coalesced around the heroic stature of Andrew Jackson as a champion of the common man, an instigator of westward expansion, and a member of the aristocratic planter class. The Whigs derived their party name from the traditional name for an opposition party in English politics. Henry Clay, Daniel Webster, and even Abraham Lincoln were Whigs. The first split of the Jeffersonian Republican Party that ended the Era of Good Feelings was that of the National Republicans and the Democratic Republicans. The National Republicans became the Whigs and the Democratic Republicans became the Democrats. While the Democrats remain a party today, northern Whigs were later absorbed with other smaller parties into the modern Republican Party in 1854. As to policy, the Democratic Party originally adopted the notion that common people deserved a voice in government just as did the Jeffersonian Republicans, but after Andrew Jackson was president they adopted the desire to have a strong central government from the Federalists. The main plank of the Whig Party was to block whatever Andrew Jackson wanted to do.

## 19 Webster-Hayne Debates

These 1830 debates in the Senate began over a Connecticut senator's desire to slow down the sale of western lands. What they became was a showdown between those who interpreted the Constitution as creating a nation and those who still viewed it as continuing a league of friendship among states. Northerners feared that open access to land in the West would drain the new factories of their laborers. The nationalism born of the War of 1812 was clearly dissipated when Robert Hayne of South Carolina created an alliance of the South and the West against the North by insisting that the lands remain open for sale as a source of new slave territories. Daniel Webster exploded in oratory about all the issues then dividing the nation including the sale of lands, the tariff, the spread of slavery, and especially states' rights. Webster made it clear that he was a unionist and that all talk of one state or section going its own way was detrimental to the core understanding of the American republic, a nation created by the will of the people, not the will of states. The rancor over these and other issues revealed that, while the Founding Fathers were astute in forming the U.S. Constitution, certain intentional and inadvertent ambiguities dangerously threatened the Union when men from every section differed over the very nature of the republic.

## 20 Clay's American System

Henry Clay was the first statesman to articulate a plan that tied the strengths and weaknesses of the three sections of the nation together in a viable national economy. His principles of a high protective tariff, a high demand for land in the West, the stabilizing influence of the BUS, and the use of public money to build roads and canals were all designed to improve the economy on a national scale. A weakness of his plan was that few others could understand the concept of national markets when he first used the term *American System* in 1824. Clay wanted the West to feed grain to the East and the South to feed cotton to northern mills. He wanted transportation improvements to facilitate this commerce in order to boost the role of America in the world economy. His vision came true but not in his lifetime.

## *The Big Picture*

**1.** The Age of Jackson was a time of tremendous energy and volatile sentiments much like the man for whom it was named.

**2.** Slavery and the spread of slavery were contentious issues throughout the period and were not far below the surface of every other political and economic issue discussed.

**3.** The North, South, and West each had differing needs and goals, and each section had a proponent in the Senate (Webster, Calhoun, and Clay, respectively) who personified the ideals of his section.

**4.** Andrew Jackson restored the executive branch to its prominent position in the federal government through several presidential legacies including the spoils system, actual use of the veto, and the national nominating convention.

**5.** Through the ups and downs of antebellum economic and political changes, the two-party system was restored to American political life and has endured ever since.

# The Reform Impulse

# CHAPTER 13

*Gentlemen, I commit to you this sacred cause. Your action upon this subject will affect the present and future condition of hundreds and of thousands.*
—Dorothea Dix, report to the Massachusetts legislature, 1843

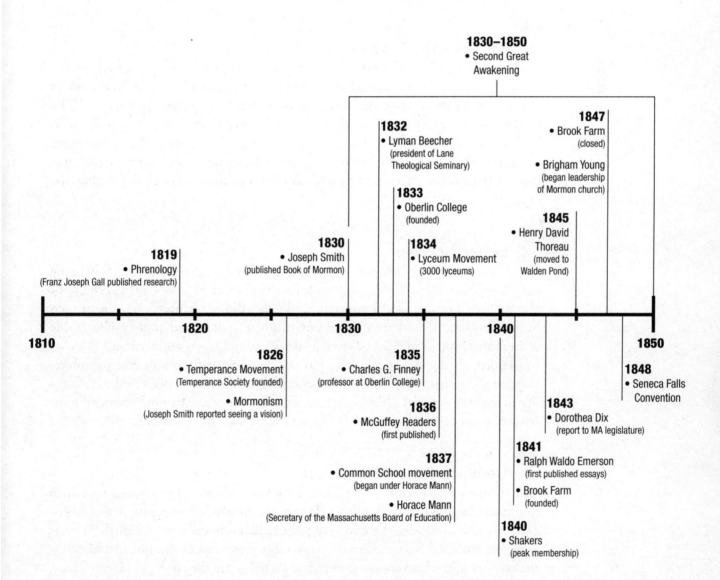

**1830–1850**
• Second Great Awakening

**1847**
• Brook Farm (closed)
• Brigham Young (began leadership of Mormon church)

**1832**
• Lyman Beecher (president of Lane Theological Seminary)

**1833**
• Oberlin College (founded)

**1845**
• Henry David Thoreau (moved to Walden Pond)

**1819**
• Phrenology (Franz Joseph Gall published research)

**1830**
• Joseph Smith (published Book of Mormon)

**1834**
• Lyceum Movement (3000 lyceums)

**1810**    **1820**    **1830**    **1840**    **1850**

**1826**
• Temperance Movement (Temperance Society founded)
• Mormonism (Joseph Smith reported seeing a vision)

**1835**
• Charles G. Finney (professor at Oberlin College)

**1836**
• McGuffey Readers (first published)

**1837**
• Common School movement (began under Horace Mann)
• Horace Mann (Secretary of the Massachusetts Board of Education)

**1848**
• Seneca Falls Convention

**1843**
• Dorothea Dix (report to MA legislature)

**1841**
• Ralph Waldo Emerson (first published essays)
• Brook Farm (founded)

**1840**
• Shakers (peak membership)

# Top 20 Things to Know

## 1 Dorothea Dix

The headmistress at a Boston school for girls, Dorothea Dix dedicated her life to reforming prisons, almshouses, and asylums. She gathered data on the conditions in these institutions in Massachusetts and other states and presented her findings in 1843 to the Massachusetts legislature. Her efforts led to the improvement of conditions for the mentally ill in at least fifteen states, and she was placed in charge of all female nurses during the Civil War. One can hardly imagine a more ardent pioneer in any field, and she established the techniques of investigation and reform that applied to many later humanitarian efforts.

## 2 Seneca Falls Convention

Lucretia Mott and Elizabeth Cady Stanton launched the women's suffrage movement at this meeting of around three hundred women and men in New York in 1848. Beyond demanding the vote, the document listing their grievances, "The Declaration of Sentiments," called for the ending of discriminatory practices and lay the groundwork for the modern feminist movement. From there, Mott and Stanton worked with Susan B. Anthony and other activists to secure women's suffrage, although the movement paused its efforts at the climax of the abolitionist crusade.

## 3 Lyman Beecher

This Connecticut minister was not only the father of Harriet Beecher Stowe, the author of *Uncle Tom's Cabin*, and abolitionist preacher Henry Ward Beecher, but also the father of the reform association. Beecher did not believe government even in a democratic republic was sufficient to guide morals and protect liberty. He insisted that American citizens needed education and Christian teachings to properly reform themselves and society. His widely circulated sermons and pamphlets inspired the formation of numerous associations, or societies, dedicated to reforming all manner of social ills. He was a perfect example of the twofold nature of most reformers as educators and as religious leaders because he was both.

## 4 Common School Movement

Like so many other reforms, the common school movement originated up out of the Massachusetts Puritan tradition that sought to both convert people to Christianity but also to educate them so as to prepare them for callings. Although Thomas Jefferson espoused public education, tax-supported schools did not spread across the country as the basis for modern public schools until the efforts of Horace Mann and others picked up after Jefferson's death. With the influx of large immigrant populations, common schools provided a shared educational experience to assimilate Americans from differing backgrounds into a common culture. In the nineteenth century, this culture was Protestant, hence the formation of Catholic school systems. Educational reform was seen by nearly all reformers as a key investment in the long-term preservation of American civilization. Education was made available for free but was not compulsory at first.

## 5 Horace Mann

An attorney and humanitarian reformer, Horace Mann became a legislator and educational advocate on the Massachusetts State Board of Education. He was responsible for implementing almost all of the aspects of public schooling as a pioneer of modern school systems. Common schools were open for a minimum of six months of the year. Mann secured increased funding for the schools and for teacher salaries and revised curriculums and methods of instruction. He also founded the first state-operated teacher-training school in the country. The Massachusetts common school movement was picked up as a model in western states first, then back East in Virginia, and then became universal as the twentieth century opened.

## 6 McGuffey Readers

William McGuffey was another minister/educator who was asked by a publishing company to produce a series of readers for children to use as textbooks. He began publishing the series in the 1830s so its use coincided nicely with the rise of common schools. The books were designed to progressively improve the students' reading ability, literary taste, and morals, and espoused a set of values descended from the Puritans. Widely criticized for emphasizing white, Anglo-Saxon Protestant values as superior to others, the books still were instrumental in educating generations of Americans even on the frontier.

## 7 Oberlin College

Oberlin College was founded by missionaries in 1833 when northeastern Ohio was still a frontier. The express mission of the school was to educate teachers and other leaders to help develop the frontier both morally and intellectually. In keeping with the atmosphere of reform, Oberlin allowed women and minorities to enroll and graduated the first women with college degrees from an American university. The school early on became associated with Presbyterian minister Charles G. Finney and the style of revivalism prevalent on the frontier during the Second Great Awakening.

## 8 Second Great Awakening

Beginning as early as the first decade of the nineteenth century, Christian revivals appeared in Virginia, Pennsylvania, Kentucky, and Tennessee. By the 1830s and 1840s the revivals had spread across the country including eastern cities by the 1850s. The widespread impulse to reform society was at first an extension of these revivals as newly converted Christians sought to improve their own lives and the lives of those around them. Reform itself became a sort of religious revival that spread beyond the bounds of traditional Christianity as it was taken up by secular leaders as well. The doctrines prevalent in the churches founded during the Second Great Awakening departed from the Calvinist and Reformed doctrines of early colonial America. A more self-help approach became popular and led to an increase in the variety of churches and the forms of worship in American religion.

# 9 Charles G. Finney

This Presbyterian minister was singularly responsible for departing from the Calvinist doctrines of traditional Presbyterianism and for ushering in new methods of seeking converts. Finney organized camp meetings during the Second Great Awakening where fervent, less polished preaching was combined with techniques designed to soften the hearts of those in attendance. Camp meetings were gatherings in the open air where one or more revival preachers exhorted frontier families to change their own lives in response to the message of the Christian Gospel. Modern evangelicalism received its emotionalism and persuasive tendencies from Finney's New Light methods. Conservative, or Old Light Christian leaders criticized Finney for abandoning orthodoxy and for using empty spiritual enthusiasm to make superficial converts. Finney became the president of Oberlin College after leaving the frontier for a time to test his methods in the urban East.

# 10 Circuit-riding Preachers

These men were about as popular a frontier folk hero stereotype as that of riverboat men or long hunters. Since there were too few ministers to fill the need for preaching in churches founded during the Second Great Awakening, missionary preachers would ride on a circuit like circuit judges and preach in a different church each Sunday. Their temporal news was as readily devoured as their eternal news, and their appearances became popular community events because marriages, baptisms, and funerals were conducted while they were present. The difficulty for frontier Christianity, however, was that in their absence lay leaders would conduct services and minister to the church members that over time served to decrease adherence to orthodoxy, or sound doctrine. Some frontier lay preachers preached without actually being able to read the scriptures, but such was the nature of American culture during the new era of the common man that men like Charles G. Finney appealed to the democratic and enterprising spirit of the age just as Andrew Jackson did.

# 11 Temperance Movement

At the bottom of many of societies' evils, according to many of the preachers of the Second Great Awakening, was the excessive consumption of alcohol. Domestic abuse and other crimes were blamed on "demon rum." Of course societies were formed to attack this vice behind the vices, including the Women's Christian Temperance Union and the Anti-Saloon League. The original purpose of these reformers was to encourage moderate use of alcohol, but the temperance movement eventually turned into the Prohibition movement that ultimately amended the Constitution to outlaw even the production and sale of alcoholic beverages. Those opposed to the legislation inspired by the temperance movements said that the reform violated their freedom to both sell alcohol and consume it. Slaveholders later used the same argument against abolition with much less success.

## 12 Lyceum Movement

The secular answer to the Second Great Awakening was the Lyceum movement. The aura of self-improvement inspired even non-Christians and nontraditional Christians to desire societal reform. The original Lyceum was Aristotle's school, and the movement in America in the Age of Jackson was also an educational institution. Lyceums were public lecture halls dedicated to adult education and public debate. These halls were favorite venues for Transcendentalists to discuss their philosophy and for scientists to astound audiences with experiments and with new machines. Some of the presenters and lecturers in Lyceums were charlatans, but the fact that people actually came to hear information just to better themselves speaks to the ongoing prevalence of optimism in American society.

## 13 Phrenology

Originated by Franz Joseph Gall, this pseudoscience became popular during the reform era as a means of explaining human behavior and personality. Phrenologists posited maps of the human brain that placed various aspects of temperament, talent, and proclivities in various regions that could be assessed by measuring the skull. Lyceums gave phrenologists the opportunity to perform public demonstrations and schedule private screenings. The new confidence in science as a method of investigating and explaining all natural phenomena contributed to the popularity of such a system, and for a time phrenology was given by some serious consideration in screening individuals for employment and other purposes as another method of self-improvement.

## 14 Brook Farm

This utopian community was the most interesting of its type largely due to the luminaries who attempted to join in creating a perfect alternate society there. A Unitarian minister named George Ripley purchased a farm outside Boston, and from 1841 until 1847 the likes of Ralph Waldo Emerson, Henry David Thoreau, Margaret Fuller, and Nathaniel Hawthorne made varying degrees of physical and financial commitments to creating a model society. Thus the community was based on Unitarian and Transcendentalist principles, although the intense individualism of the latter undermined the communal impulse. Brook Farm practiced radical forms of equality and universal education that made the society certainly different than typical American society, but most of the better-educated members chafed under the rigors of farm life. Those who found the atmosphere too stifling left, and Ripley's mismanagement led the community toward bankruptcy.

## 15 Shakers

Celibate neighbors to the free-love Oneida community, the Shakers were founded even before the United States in 1774 by a woman named Mother Ann Lee. They were a monastic sect of Christianity that devoted themselves to work and worship. Shaker villages were organized into families, although males and females led segregated lives. The Shakers founded villages in New York but then spread out to New England and beyond until they reached a peak membership in 1830. Shaker villages declined over the next century because celibacy left no other way to propagate their faith except through conversions. Shaker missionaries were less and less successful as the reform era passed and their doctrine of pacifism estranged them from other Americans who fought the first modern wars. The Shaker lifestyle was simple as was their elegant furniture. Shakers represented not only the reform impulse but also a millennial view of Christianity that taught humanitarian reforms as utopian communities were trying to perfect society so that Christ would return.

## 16 Ralph Waldo Emerson

This star of the Lyceum circuit was a scholar and minister who found Unitarianism too constraining and thus founded Transcendentalism, a romantic philosophy that combined idealism and Eastern mysticism. With Margaret Fuller and others he published *The Dial* in the 1840s to spread transcendental ideas. Emerson became an abolitionist and published many of his lectures, like "Self-Reliance." He captured the individualism and optimism of American society as a chief proponent of these ideas for a wide audience.

## 17 Henry David Thoreau

Thoreau was accused of being a Harvard graduate with no ambition, but he taught school and made pencils, as well as wrote poems, essays, and philosophical works like *Walden*. A close associate of Emerson, Thoreau experimented with a simple life by living alone on Walden Pond outside Concord, Massachusetts, for over two years. While observing minute details in nature he wrote of higher laws available for guidance beyond the established institutions of human society. His opposition to the Mexican War and to slavery led him to write the essay "Civil Disobedience" that codified a pattern of passive resistance popular in the civil rights movement and in Gandhi's movement for Indian independence from the British Empire.

## 18 Joseph Smith

Joseph Smith published the *Book of Mormon* in the 1830s that became the foundation of a new religion calling itself the Church of Jesus Christ of Latter-Day Saints. Smith claimed to have translated the book with the help of an angel from golden tablets he had discovered. In the Burned-Over District of New York, called such because of the fervent revivals of the Second Great Awakening in the area, Smith garnered some followers. The Mormons, as they were called, founded settlements and thus were a new type of utopian communalists that sought to reform society. Smith instituted militaristic tendencies as the Mormons experienced persecution as well as the practice of polygamy. While jailed for destruction of property and for treason, a mob murdered Smith and his brother who then became martyrs inspiring their roughly eighteen thousand followers to move west to escape persecution.

## 19 Brigham Young

A laborer and farmer in his youth, Brigham Young was an early convert to Mormonism. After the death of Joseph Smith he became the head of the religion and moved Mormons west. His leadership held the Mormons together and guided their settlement of Deseret, their colony or new country in the Valley of the Great Salt Lake. The government recognized their settlement as the Utah Territory in 1850, but after claiming to have seceded from the United States Brigham Young was removed as the territorial governor. Young still led the Mormon community, however, and put in place an administrative structure that far outlived his own impact. Brigham Young had twenty-three wives and fathered fifty-six children.

## 20 Mormonism

The *Book of Mormon* gave rise to Mormonism, the first religion born in the United States. Converts came from as far away as Europe, for while the Mormons were moving west they were also sending out missionaries. Their settlements in the West forged trails to Utah and to California that eventually opened up the path of the first transcontinental railroad. Mormons worked diligently to irrigate the soil in arid climates and otherwise proved to be hard workers living in close-knit communities. With their legal, and nearly military, clash with the federal government they were the prime example of the extent to which reformers and utopian communalists could exist in the United States without so alienating their fellow citizens as to spark expulsion or destruction. Intense persecution displaced the Mormons, but it did not intimidate or silence them. Therefore, they were also a prime example of the ability of a tradition of religious freedom to keep the peace in a pluralist society.

## The Big Picture

1. The Age of Jackson was an era of humanitarian reforms as well the era of political advancement for the common man.

2. Religious revivals stimulated associations of reformers to assault numerous societal evils including drunkenness, abuse of the mentally ill, discrimination against women, and slavery.

3. Religion and education worked together as ministers of the Second Great Awakening either directly or indirectly supported the common school movement and the development of universities on the frontier.

4. Secular and nontraditional religious reforms included Transcendentalism, Unitarianism, and the Lyceum movement that mutually elevated their ideas before a listening and reading public.

5. Numerous communal societies sprang up as groups formed radical alternative programs for the pursuit of utopia, but none were so successful and lasting as Mormonism.

# The Ramifications of Slavery

# CHAPTER 14

*Our fancies with regard to the condition of the slaves proceed from our northern repugnance to slavery, stimulated by many things that we read.*
—Nehemiah Adams, *A South-Side View of Slavery*, 1854

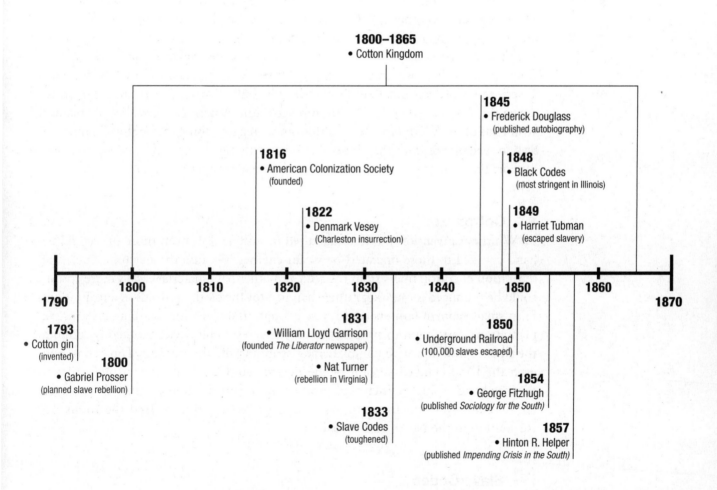

# Top 20 Things to Know

## 1 Peculiar Institution

A euphemism for slavery used by John C. Calhoun and other southerners who either were proud of the unique nature of American slavery or ashamed of it and wanting to avoid directly naming it for what it was. Calhoun and other defenders of slavery, especially after the 1830s when the abolitionist crusade began, tried to explain that the institution of slavery was beneficial to the country and to the African-Americans themselves. Other young men in planter families rued the day they would inherit a plantation and become directly responsible for the peculiar institution as slave owners. This sentiment among southern gentlemen, like that of Thomas Jefferson, either amounted to little or was drowned out.

## 2 Cotton Kingdom

This title glorified the importance of cotton to the American and world economies. The Deep South and parts of Texas were ideally suited in climate, soil, and length of the growing season for the production of cotton. Once inventions like the cotton gin and the screw press made the production of cotton lucrative, more and more southerners planted this cash crop. Cotton was the raw material needed by British and American textile factories. Cotton made up the bulk of what Americans exported to the world as well as what the British imported from America. The zeal of the planter aristocrats of the South to make wealth from such a sure thing inexorably led them to seek independence from the United States even though their society could not long support their participation in a drawn-out war with modern weapons.

## 3 Cotton Gin

Eli Whitney's invention was manufactured in various sizes from those that could be hand cranked to those operated by steam engines. Because the machine made the separation of cotton fibers from the seed and other base material easier, more cotton could be produced for market rather than just for the clothing needs of a plantation. Even small yeoman farmers could raise enough to make a little cash after renting a plantation's cotton gin to process the year's harvest. The device worked by pulling the fibers through a wire comb thereby stripping off the unwanted material, and even the hand-cranked version of the device could "gin" fifty times more cotton than by hand. With the increased production of cotton came a higher demand for cotton cloth and thus for more slaves to pick more cotton to feed the Industrial Revolution in the North and abroad.

## 4 Slave Codes

These laws controlled slaves but also slave owners. A general understanding of slavery was that if masters were allowed to be too harsh with their own slaves, fugitive slaves would incite uprisings. Therefore, egregious abuse was forbidden, but harsh punishments and even murder of slaves was tolerated in many cases. In regard to the slaves themselves, Slave Codes enforced the white supremacy of the South by considering slaves to be clever subhumans capable of crimes but not capable of testifying against criminals as witnesses. Slaves could not own property or travel freely without written permission from their masters. Slaves could work for money, but the use of the pay was at the discretion of the master.

## 5 Manumission

Manumission was the legal term for formal freeing of slaves by their masters. Some of the Founding Fathers, like George Washington, freed their slaves especially in their wills. Other slaves could be freed or were permitted to buy their way out of bondage if they had the means to make and keep money. The earliest slaves in colonial Virginia were manumitted just as indentured servants were, but as the Age of Jackson became identifiably the antebellum period, laws on manumission were tightened to prevent increase in the free African-American population of the South. By and large, few planter aristocrats condoned or practiced manumission because so few could imagine either how the plantations could be run any other way or how free African-Americans could support themselves.

## 6 Christian Paternalism

Although the Second Great Awakening stimulated northerners to begin the abolitionist crusade, the revivals in the South were often shared by slave owners and slaves alike. Christian masters in the wake of revivals treated their slaves better and saw themselves as having the responsibility to see to the salvation of their own slaves. Some churches in the South admitted African-Americans to full membership and even to church office, but even paternalistic masters were often against manumission. When slaves were treated better with more favorable living conditions and medical care, production on the plantations improved, a fact not lost on Christian and non-Christian masters alike.

## 7 Gabriel Prosser

The first leader of a significant slave insurrection since the formation of the United States was Gabriel Prosser of Virginia. In 1800, Prosser and other leaders plotted and amassed weapons and ammunition and were said to have hundreds if not thousands of slaves ready to rise up. The original attack was thwarted by a heavy rain, but word of the conspiracy was leaked to the governor of Virginia who mobilized militia forces immediately. Prosser and over thirty other conspirators were hanged. The quick response was indicative of the unity of the people of Virginia, and soon of other states, to prepare for the possibility of a slave revolt.

# 8 Denmark Vesey

Vesey was a Charleston, South Carolina, slave who acquired an education as well as his freedom by purchasing it from his master with six hundred dollars of lottery winnings. He established himself as a carpenter in Charleston but grew increasingly dissatisfied with the condition of slaves by reading abolitionist literature. By 1822, Denmark Vesey had amassed nine thousand Charleston slaves ready to rise up, storm arsenals in order to commandeer weapons, and slaughter all whites in the city. A servant divulged the plot and Vesey and over thirty other leaders were hanged. Vesey wanted to model his insurrection after the revolution in Haiti, and it is said that John Brown's later plot was so similar as to likely have been inspired by Vesey's plan.

# 9 Nat Turner

The most successful slave uprising in the history of the United States was another plot in Virginia, this one led by a black slave preacher named Nat Turner. In 1831, Turner and his followers killed almost sixty white men, women, and children. In the move to put down the revolt, over one hundred blacks were killed, and Turner and nineteen other leaders were captured and hanged. This crescendo of slave rebellions caused the South to become more militantly supportive of slavery in political battles, and the Nat Turner rebellion served to silence all abolitionist sentiment in the slaveholding states.

# 10 Frederick Douglass

Douglass began as the son of a slave and a white man and rose to become the nation's noted black abolitionist, author, and orator. He was educated in secret as a house servant in Baltimore, and he acquired a trade as a ship's caulker. He escaped from Baltimore and moved to New York and Massachusetts where he supported a wife by working at his trade. He began giving abolitionist speeches in 1841 and wrote his famous *Narrative of the Life of Frederick Douglass* in 1845. He traveled abroad and returned to the United States with enough in donations to purchase his freedom. His stirring oratory moved audiences across the North, and he edited an abolitionist newspaper called the *North Star*. He was an adviser to John Brown before the Civil War and to Abraham Lincoln during the war in which he was responsible for raising black regiments for the Union Army. His efforts inspired white abolitionists as well as Sojourner Truth, a woman who had also escaped slavery and toured as an abolitionist orator.

# 11 Negro Spirituals

Like the other forms of unique culture created by American slaves, "negro spirituals" were a combination of African and American influences, in this case rhythms and lyrics. Slaves often converted to Christianity in the South prior to the Civil War, and after the normal worship services they sometimes held singings where illiterate worshippers could learn and enjoy the hymns of slavery. Negro spirituals were also used to pass the time in the fields or to coordinate hauling and other especially difficult labor. A slave song leader often sang out calls to the rest of the slave teams, who answered in unison. In conjunction with the Underground Railroad, several "negro spirituals" were later shown to be coded messages regarding places and times of departure for escaping slaves.

## 12 Slave Society

Slave societies existed throughout the world and far back into ancient times. The American South under the cotton kingdom was such a society where the laws and customs elevated to power those who held property and acquired wealth through the labor of slaves. The planter aristocrats of the South held political and economic power with roughly three thousand families in the top class with large plantations holding two to four hundred slaves. These families maintained the apparatus of slavery like cotton gins and screw presses to make bales easily, as well as the horses, dogs, and weapons necessary to form slave posses. Slave posses were dispatched to round up escaped slaves, and in the case of slave revolts they formed the nucleus of state militias. Although most white people of the South owned few or no slaves, the entire society was based on not only an acceptance of the peculiar institution but also an aspiration on the part of yeoman farmers to one day acquire enough slaves to join the leisure class.

## 13 Black Codes

Since a population of free African-Americans existed in the South from the colonial period and through manumission, laws were passed by the states in the slave society to keep them "in their place." That place was considered to be as laborers and craftsmen who did not aspire to education or equality. To prevent the fomenting of slave insurrections on the part of free African-Americans, the Black Codes forbade meetings after dark, freedom of travel, the ownership of guns, and participation in the political process. This institutionalized racism would continue even after the Civil War and was the basis for segregation and other forms of discrimination that lingered through the twentieth-century civil rights movement and beyond.

## 14 Hinton R. Helper

Helper was a southerner and a failed gold prospector returned from California who took up printing and writing while living in the North. He published the book *The Impending Crisis of the South* that used statistics from the 1850 census to examine the economic weaknesses of the slaveholding states. The book was popular in the North not only because of its abolitionist message but because of how Helper praised the society and economy of the free states. His book also lambasted the leaders of the slave society for unfairly keeping not only blacks but also lower-class whites from rising up. His analysis was used before the war to mobilize the abolitionist cause but after the war, coupled with his later writings, dismissed as violent racism against blacks whom he wanted deported to Africa.

## 15 Positive Good Theory

Although men like Thomas Jefferson referred to slavery as a "necessary evil," the next generations of southern leaders developed the notion that slavery was a "positive good," to borrow a phrase from John C. Calhoun. When slavery came under renewed scrutiny in the Missouri Compromise and the Nullification Crisis, the South developed defenses of slavery against the rising abolitionist crusade. Among other defenses, supporters of slavery said that slaves had lives that were better than Africans in Africa and even better lives than northern factory workers who were essentially wage slaves. Christian paternalism sanctioned slavery as perhaps the only opportunity Africans would have to hear the Christian message. Because of racist views of negro inferiority, supporters of slavery maintained that African-Americans needed the guidance and provision of their white masters to organize their lives.

## 16 George Fitzhugh

One of the most outspoken proponents of the positive good theory was the Virginian lawyer and author George Fitzhugh. He originated the argument that African slaves in the South were better off than wage slaves in the North who never saw the sun because they worked from before dawn to after dark in factories. His views were not only racist but bordered on evoking the ideas of class warfare. Because he viewed the slave society of the South as the ideal society, he advocated the expansion of slavery virtually globally as he recognized the free labor and slave labor systems were incompatible. Fitzhugh predicted that if African-Americans were ever freed and sent North, they would be unable to function in the free labor system.

## 17 William Lloyd Garrison

A background in the newspaper business and a talent for virulent writing propelled William Lloyd Garrison to prominence as the editor of *The Liberator*, the leading abolitionist newspaper. While his inflammatory editorials bordered on libel and led him to actually burn a copy of the U.S. Constitution, he organized abolitionist societies and published his newspaper for thirty-five years. Garrison espoused northern secession in order to cut off ties with the compromises that had kept peace with the South. He also preached the breaking of the Fugitive Slave Law. Once Abraham Lincoln issued the Emancipation Proclamation his rhetoric toned down to full support for the war effort. After the war, Garrison continued agitating for reform in the fight to ban alcohol and in the women's suffrage movement. As an advocate for women's rights, Garrison was at least partly responsible for delaying votes for women until after slavery was abolished.

## 18 Harriet Tubman

As an escaped slave, Harriet Tubman became a leading "conductor" on the Underground Railroad. In other words, she was a guide who helped other slaves escape and make their way north to Canada by way of a series of safe houses supported by northerners. Tubman is thought to have personally guided as many as three hundred slaves from Maryland to Canada despite chronic headaches resulting from an injury to the head received from her master. For her efforts before the Civil War she was known as "Moses," and she even served as a guide for black soldiers during the war.

# 19 Underground Railroad

By 1840 a secret series of houses and people supportive of the emancipation of individual slaves had formed in defiance of federal laws regarding the return of fugitive slaves to the South. The Underground Railroad assisted and transported escaped slaves to safety in sympathetic communities in the North or to complete freedom from recapture in Canada. From 1830 to 1860 as many as 3,200 black and white workers helped as many as fifty thousand slaves escape. Sung about in "negro spirituals," the Underground Railroad was a network of Quakers and other abolitionists, including Senator William H. Seward of New York, who actively pursued their principles rather than just reading and writing about them. Certain northern states passed personal liberty laws to protect escaped slaves as a result of widespread support for the activities of the Underground Railroad "conductors."

# 20 American Colonization Society

Founded in 1817 and headed by presidents Monroe and Madison and by other such luminaries as John Marshall and Henry Clay, the American Colonization Society (ACS) advocated the transportation of free American blacks back to Africa. At first Sierra Leone was a transfer point, but eventually the Republic of Liberia was founded when land was purchased by the ACS in Africa to establish a permanent location. Over fifteen thousand blacks left the United States to join the colony by 1860, but most black emigration from the South was shut down after the Nat Turner rebellion in 1831. While the mission of the ACS was popular for a time, the motives of the society were more to rid the United States of what was considered to be an unsolvable problem rather than to elevate blacks or to encourage African development.

## The Big Picture

1. Slavery and cotton shaped the economic, societal, and political dynamics of the South into a culture in dramatic contrast with that of the North.

2. Although the reform impulse based on humanitarian and religious principles in the North created the abolitionist crusade, southerners were bent on reforming the institution of black slavery as a positive good.

3. Black slaves developed a unique culture of their own that saw varying degrees of cooperation with and resistance toward their white masters, up to and including violent rebellion.

4. Northern abolitionists used powerful oral and written rhetoric to gradually develop animosity toward the institution of black slavery, but the quest for an end to slavery did not immediately equate to a quest for black equality.

5. As their peculiar institution came under attack, southerners developed pro-slavery arguments and political tactics that nearly thwarted the abolitionist crusade largely because of the demand in the North for southern cotton.

# Expansion and Two Wars with Mexico

CHAPTER **15**

*I consider the annexation of Texas . . . as a measure compromising the national character,*
*involving us certainly in war with Mexico . . . [and] dangerous to the integrity of the Union.*
—Henry Clay, "Raleigh Letter," 1844

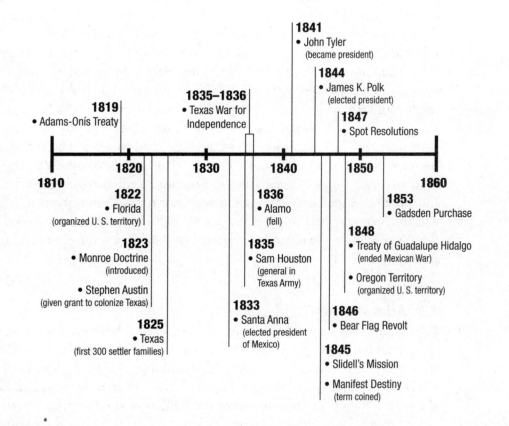

**1841**
• John Tyler
  (became president)

**1844**
• James K. Polk
  (elected president)

**1835–1836**
• Texas War for
  Independence

**1847**
• Spot Resolutions

**1819**
• Adams-Onís Treaty

**1810**

**1820**

**1830**

**1840**

**1850**

**1860**

**1822**
• Florida
(organized U. S. territory)

**1836**
• Alamo
  (fell)

**1853**
• Gadsden Purchase

**1823**
• Monroe Doctrine
  (introduced)

• Stephen Austin
(given grant to colonize Texas)

**1835**
• Sam Houston
  (general in
  Texas Army)

**1848**
• Treaty of Guadalupe Hidalgo
  (ended Mexican War)

• Oregon Territory
  (organized U. S. territory)

**1825**
• Texas
(first 300 settler families)

**1833**
• Santa Anna
  (elected president
  of Mexico)

**1846**
• Bear Flag Revolt

**1845**
• Slidell's Mission

• Manifest Destiny
  (term coined)

# Top 20 Things to Know

## 1 Anglophobia

Whether it was personal, as with Andrew Jackson, or philosophical, as with Thomas Jefferson, American presidents from Washington to James K. Polk operated under the assumption that America's mother country was out to get them. The War of 1812 was clear evidence that the fear was grounded in fact, but at some point in the early nineteenth century the excuse that America should annex territory or else the British would take it began to wear thin. Dependence on the British for trade contributed to anxiety when markets became strained or tariff wars erupted, and Great Britain was moving into its heyday as an expansionist world empire. The refusal of Canada to join the American republic also caused suspicion. The "natural enemy" status between the two powers would last until after the American Civil War.

## 2 Florida

This peninsula had changed hands through the colonial wars but wound up with Spain after the American Revolution. Like France, Spain had backed American independence as a way to humble Great Britain. But the Spanish Empire was in decline by the opening of the nineteenth century. The Spanish colonial administration was growing weaker and claimed it was unable to stop African-American slaves from escaping into Florida and American Indians from raiding American settlements. Andrew Jackson had pursued Creek and Seminole Indians into Florida as a result. While there, Jackson confirmed fears that Great Britain had designs for a new colony in Florida by capturing two British agents supplying the American Indians with weapons. Jackson promptly hanged the men as spies. The events surrounding Jackson's invasion of Spanish Florida led to conflicts known as the Seminole Wars that saw around three thousand American soldiers fighting against Seminole Indians and escaped slaves. The issues were not resolved until the British backed off and the Spanish caved in. The war against the Seminole Indians proved to be the fiercest conflict in the history of warfare between the United States and indigenous peoples.

## 3 Adams-Onís Treaty

John Quincy Adams skillfully capitalized on Andrew Jackson's aggression in Florida even though he privately complained to the hero of the Battle of New Orleans that he had no authorization to invade a foreign country. Of all the Spanish holdings in the New World, however, foreign minister Luis de Onís recognized that Florida was the most tenuous. In order to clarify the borders of the Louisiana Purchase, Spain agreed to sell Florida to the United States in this treaty ratified by both countries in 1821. The United States gave up claim to Texas, and Spain gave up claim to the Oregon Territory in the Northwest. Florida entered the United States as a slave state in 1845.

## 4 Monroe Doctrine

This landmark in American foreign policy was another brainchild of John Q. Adams who served as James Monroe's secretary of state. With a crumbling Spanish Empire and encroachments in the Western Hemisphere by the British, French, and Russians, President Monroe agreed to make a stand. The Monroe Doctrine stated that the United States desired no participation in the affairs of Europe and that Europeans should no longer consider the Western Hemisphere open to colonization or any European involvement. The United States considered any violation of this policy a threat to America's national security. The Monroe Doctrine extended Washington's isolationism, and in the years to come Monroe's claim would be tested by various nations that all felt varying degrees of American ire as a result.

## 5 Mountain Men

Various intrepid individualistic men, and at least one woman, departed from civilized society and forged paths into the wilderness in pursuit of furs and, presumably, freedom from constraints. Men from Daniel Boone to Jim Bridger conducted extensive forays into the unchartered wilderness of unsettled American territory. Mountain men negotiated with various American Indian tribes for permission to trap, hunt, and trade on tribal lands and were thus often the first white men known intimately on the frontier. The great service these lone explorers performed was to open up trails for western settlement and to send back rumors of, say, the fertile soil of the Oregon Territory. Like the cowboy, mountain men were an iconic American stereotype whose image lasted far longer than the actual era when such a lifestyle was possible.

## 6 Stephen Austin

Austin was the founder of Texas in the northern province of Mexico by virtue of a grant from the Mexican government as it became free from Spain. Despite the abolition of slavery by the Mexican government, Austin negotiated permission for American slaves to enter Texas as indentured servants, but the southern Americans who came believed they were merely expanding the cotton kingdom and the plantation lifestyle. As war broke out between Texans and Mexico, Austin became the chief liaison between Texas and the United States.

## 7 Texas

The Mexican government encouraged settlement of their northern provinces by Americans because of the ferocity of the Apache and Comanche Indians. Neither the Spanish nor the Mexicans made successful incursions into the region, but men like Stephen Austin and Jim Bowie did. Santa Anna, the president of Mexico, attempted to ban the further importation of slaves as well as any further settlement by American immigrants. He also chose to operate as an authoritarian dictator rather than a constitutional executive. As Texans experienced success in the production of cotton and in cattle ranching, they chafed under the confines of a system worse than that of British colonies prior to the American Revolution. Texans likewise decided to declare independence, and the Texas War for Independence was the result.

## 8 Santa Anna

His full name was Antonio López de Santa Anna, and he rose up through the ranks of the officer corps of the Spanish military to eventually lead in the Mexican Revolution. He liberated his birthplace, Vera Cruz, and declared Mexico to be a free republic. When independence from Spain was secure, he put down insurrections for the new Mexican government and rose to the top of the rival factions struggling for power by 1834. To quell further internal strife, Santa Anna was granted dictatorial powers backed up by an army of men famous for their ability to endure the hot climate and infamous for the atrocities they committed on Santa Anna's opponents.

## 9 Texas War for Independence

Texans declared their independence from Mexico in 1836 and appointed Sam Houston as the commander of the military. Volunteers from Tennessee, including Davy Crockett, joined the militia. Houston ordered William Travis and other volunteers to hold the mission church called the Alamo in San Antonio while he set about organizing and training the rest of the army. After massacres at the Alamo and at Goliad, Houston drew Santa Anna's remaining army into a chase across Texas that ended at the Battle of San Jacinto. Texans cried, "Remember the Alamo!" as they assaulted the Mexican positions, defeated the remnants of the Mexican army, and captured Santa Anna. The war ended when Santa Anna was forced at gunpoint to sign a treaty declaring Texas independent with a border along the Rio Grande River.

## 10 Alamo

One of the many Spanish mission sites in San Antonio, the Alamo became the hallowed ground of the Texas Republic. Santa Anna's three thousand troops attacked the Alamo's garrison of 187 men for thirteen days. When the walls were finally breached all of the defenders of the Alamo were killed and their bodies burned. Their sacrifice, however, took many times their number of Mexican lives and allowed Sam Houston to mount an effective strategic retreat all the way to San Jacinto and victory. A larger massacre of over three hundred men at Goliad was perpetrated by Santa Anna even after the defenders surrendered, which William Travis had refused to do at the Alamo. Perhaps the refusal to surrender earned for Travis, Crockett, Bowie, and the other defenders of the Alamo the immortal love of Texans.

## 11 Sam Houston

Houston fought in Andrew Jackson's militia army from Tennessee in the war against the Creeks and other American Indians marauding in the Southeast during the War of 1812. He lived for three years among the Cherokee Indians who had been his allies in the Creek War, and he was eventually adopted into the Creek nation.

Between the War of 1812 and the Texas War for Independence, he studied law, served as a congressman, and became the governor of Tennessee. After a failed marriage, Houston was sent to Texas by President Jackson to negotiate with American Indians. He moved to Texas and became the commander of its army fighting Santa Anna. He was elected president of the Republic of Texas and negotiated with the United States for recognition and then annexation of Texas at which point he became a senator. He was elected governor of Texas just prior to the Civil War, but opposed secession and was deposed, dying in 1861 just as war commenced.

## 12 John Tyler

Tyler was a lawyer from Virginia and rose from being governor there to being vice president under William Henry Harrison, the hero of the Battle of Tippecanoe. Thus was born the slogan, "Tippecanoe and Tyler, too" in the "Log Cabin and Hard Cider" campaign for the Election of 1840 (although Harrison was a wealthy planter, he had been born in a log cabin). As a result of Harrison's premature death, Tyler became the first "accidental" president, or the first vice president to succeed a fallen president. Harrison had been a Whig and had placed Whigs in his cabinet, but when Tyler took office his policies clashed with the Whigs who resigned en masse. To the horror of northern Whigs and the consternation of Henry Clay and John Quincy Adams, Tyler backed the annexation of Texas by a joint resolution of Congress, and the Republic of Texas became a giant slave state.

## 13 James K. Polk

Another Tennessee lawyer-turned-statesman was James K. Polk who made a conscious point to follow in Andrew Jackson's footsteps. Polk was thus a Democrat who favored expansion of the country and expansion of slavery. As the winner of the presidential election of 1844, he accomplished everything he promised in his campaign including the acquisition of the Oregon Territory, overseeing Texas statehood, reestablishing Van Buren's independent treasury system, and settling the border dispute and debt issues with Mexico by starting and winning the Mexican War. Polk thus brought in every territory of the American West beyond the Louisiana Purchase except that of the Gadsden Purchase and therefore is responsible for enlarging the country more than any other president. For all his acquiring of land at the expense of Mexico, he did stop forces within his own party from annexing "all of Mexico." He accomplished his final pledge made during his campaign of holding only one term as president by refusing to seek reelection.

## 14 Oregon Territory

The far Northwest was desired for settlement by the United States, Great Britain, and even Russia. John Jacob Astor had founded an American trading post at the mouth of the Columbia River as early as 1811, and mountain men regularly harvested furs from the region throughout the early nineteenth century. Missionaries Marcus and Narcissa Whitman established contacts with American Indians and a permanent settlement before being killed by those they were trying to convert.

Stories from mountain men and the missionaries, however, ignited a land fever causing settlers to take the Oregon Trail to claim land. Because more Americans moved to Oregon than did Canadians or Russians, President Polk seized the initiative to annex the territory to the United States. Despite some Americans' desire to take all of the territory with the slogan, "54°40' or fight," Polk negotiated a settlement with Great Britain establishing the border with Canada along the 49th parallel of latitude, the longest unfortified border in the world. The North was relieved that while slavery was expanding west, the nation also acquired territory where slavery would never be feasible.

# 15 Manifest Destiny

Polk's acquisitions and the Mexican War were motivated not only by a desire to expand the country to spread slavery but to expand the American way of life generally. The phrase, "Manifest Destiny," was coined by John L. Sullivan, an editor of an expansionist magazine. Although the words simply mean "apparent future," in the wake of the Second Great Awakening they took on a quasi-religious significance. Americans generally believed in the nineteenth century that God had placed Protestant Christian Anglo-Saxons in the New World as a part of a plan to free people from religious and political oppression. Although this idea was popular with northerners and southerners alike, when it became clear that southerners were going west first and spreading slavery there, northern humanitarian reformers resisted expansion.

# 16 Bear Flag Revolt

When hostilities broke out between Mexico and the United States, Polk had not only provoked the clash but positioned American military forces in California in anticipation of war. John C. Fremont led the expedition across the Rocky Mountains, and the Bear Flag Revolt was the result. With Fremont's assistance, Californians of Spanish descent as well as American settlers rose up against the Mexican government to secure California's independence. Fremont's campaign was joined by that of Stephen Kearney who traveled from Kansas to California as the Mexican War commenced, and thus the Bear Flag Revolt became a theater of that war. The name comes from the flag created for the original indigenous rebellion, which remains the flag of the state of California. California was eventually brought into the United States as a part of the Mexican Cession.

# 17 Slidell's Mission

Revealing of Polk's willingness to start the Mexican War, John Slidell was sent to Santa Anna to first offer to purchase the northern provinces of Mexico for up to $40 million. The Mexican government originally agreed to negotiate, but when the nature of Slidell's offer became known, the people of Mexico raised such complaints that negotiations were called off. Part of the negotiations were to include the erasing of the debts Mexico owed to the United States, but when the Slidell Mission ended in failure, Polk was willing to start the war just to force the Mexicans to pay the debt he had offered to pay for them. Before protests from Whigs could gain ground, provocations from military maneuvers on the Rio Grande River had ignited an exchange of fire. Polk used the clash to get Congress to declare war against Mexico in 1846.

# 18 Spot Resolutions

Abraham Lincoln and other Whigs in Congress attempted to stop the expansionist policies motivated by Manifest Destiny that were dragging the nation to war against Mexico by offering the Spot Resolutions in Congress. In his war message, President Polk had said, "American blood has been spilled on American soil." The Spot Resolutions drew into question who had shot whom first by asking the president to show the Congress where the blood was spilled on American soil on a map of the region. Although the Spot Resolutions failed to stop the war, they did give voice to the coming sectional debate between expansionist southern Democrats interested in spreading and protecting slavery and those northerners from many political parties who would eventually form the modern Republican Party and run John C. Fremont as their first presidential candidate in 1856.

# 19 Treaty of Guadalupe Hidalgo

Nicolas Trist negotiated this treaty as Polk's envoy to the Mexican government. After systematically invading Mexico and Mexico City and beating armies larger than their own, U.S. Army generals like Winfield Scott and Zachary Taylor humbled Santa Anna who consented to surrender in 1848. The Treaty of Guadalupe Hidalgo provided that the United States would pay $15 million for the territory known as the Mexican Cession and for the confirmation that the Rio Grande River was the border between Texas and Mexico. Trist even agreed for the United States to write off the over $3 million in debt the Mexican government had earlier refused to pay. This generous settlement with a beaten foe revealed that the level of resistance toward the expansion of slave territories required a magnanimous gesture to Mexico or else the Senate would never ratify the treaty. A deep division was revealed within the United States by the Mexican War just as many of the men who would lead the opposing armies in the Civil War were gaining military experience as comrades against the Mexicans.

# 20 Gadsden Purchase

A final adjustment to the border between the United States and Mexico was gained at the expense of another $10 million in 1853. James Gadsden was sent to negotiate by Franklin Pierce. The small piece of land was desirable as the best route for a southern transcontinental railroad across the mountains and to the Pacific Ocean. Although construction of the railroad was delayed by the Civil War, the addition of the Gadsden Purchase marked the end of the addition of contiguous territory to the United States.

## *The Big Picture*

1.  The era from 1803 to 1853 saw the major expansion of the contiguous territory of the United States, and the driving force behind it was the notion of Manifest Destiny.

2.  The region of Texas was settled by Americans and became the cause of two wars with Santa Anna, the dictator of Mexico.

3.  The Whigs and the Democrats were national parties compelled by the events surrounding the Mexican War to operate along sectional lines.

4.  Although many Americans sought new opportunities by migrating west, southerners went west first in greater numbers, and their desire to expand slavery antagonized northerners motivated by humanitarian reforms to abolish slavery.

5.  The annexation of Florida, Texas, and Oregon Territory along with the Mexican Cession unlocked great potential for Americans to pursue national greatness and world power status but not without unleashing a deadly Civil War.

# The Last Attempts at Compromise

*The constitutional compact has been deliberately broken
and disregarded by the nonslaveholding states; and . . .
South Carolina is released from her obligation.*
—South Carolina Declaration, 1860

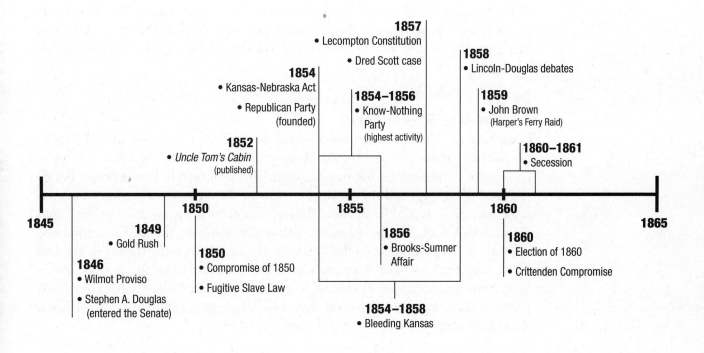

**1857**
• Lecompton Constitution
• Dred Scott case

**1854**
• Kansas-Nebraska Act
• Republican Party
  (founded)

**1854–1856**
• Know-Nothing
  Party
  (highest activity)

**1858**
• Lincoln-Douglas debates

**1859**
• John Brown
  (Harper's Ferry Raid)

**1852**
• *Uncle Tom's Cabin*
  (published)

**1860–1861**
• Secession

1845          1850          1855          1860          1865

**1849**
• Gold Rush

**1846**
• Wilmot Proviso
• Stephen A. Douglas
  (entered the Senate)

**1850**
• Compromise of 1850
• Fugitive Slave Law

**1856**
• Brooks-Sumner
  Affair

**1854–1858**
• Bleeding Kansas

**1860**
• Election of 1860
• Crittenden Compromise

# Top 20 Things to Know

## 1 Know-Nothing Party

Stemming from violent clashes in Philadelphia between Protestants and Catholics that killed twenty and injured one hundred people in 1844, a nativist party arose in the 1850s. Calling itself the American Party, the members tried to maintain secrecy by responding, "I know nothing," if questioned. Opponents then called the American Party the Know-Nothing Party. The real nucleus of the political movement was the clandestine fraternal order called the Order of the Star Spangled Banner. The Know-Nothings were anti-Catholic and anti-immigration and proposed barring both groups from holding public office and for immigrants to have to wait twenty-one years for citizenship. The American Party sidestepped the slavery issue and thus made itself irrelevant by the Election of 1856.

## 2 Wilmot Proviso

During the Mexican War, Pennsylvania representative David Wilmot proposed that any land acquired from Mexico would be closed to slavery. Wilmot entered the bill in the House, and northern congressmen passed the bill over the objections of their southern colleagues. The bill was defeated in the Senate. The debate over the Wilmot Proviso revealed the tenuous party unity of both the Democratic and Whig parties because members of both parties voted for sectional loyalties rather than party lines.

## 3 Popular Sovereignty

Lewis Cass, a northern senator, developed the notion of a democratic solution to the nation's debate over the spread of slavery into the territories. Senator Stephen Douglas of Illinois coined the ringing phrase that promised to let the people decide the issue. Cass suggested that a vote be taken by the settlers of a territory to determine whether it would be open to slavery or not. In the major bills of the 1850s the idea took root. Abraham Lincoln eventually dismissed the idea as amoral and opposed to the precedents of the central government's banning slavery in the Old Northwest Territory. The Supreme Court also disapproved of the practice in the Dred Scott case because the pro-slavery justices feared slaveholders would have their property taken away from them if they took slaves west and then their neighbors voted for freedom.

## 4 Gold Rush

Gold was discovered in the American River near Sacramento, California, in 1848 by a crew working to build a sawmill for John Sutter. News of the discovery spread, and the influx of gold hunters in 1849 from across the United States and overseas was called the gold rush. Prospectors came from as far away as Australia and China, and by the next year one hundred thousand "Forty-niners" had swelled California's population putting it on the fast track to statehood. Miners kept coming for over two years, but few small speculators struck it rich. Fifty-five million dollars in gold was gleaned mostly by large operators by the year 1851.

## 5 Compromise of 1850

The gold rush set in motion the disruptive news that California wanted to join the Union as a free state. This proposition would not only cut off the Pacific coast from slaveholding states but also upset the balance of power in the Senate that had been maintained since the Missouri Compromise in 1820. The furor was temporarily settled by the last great compromise from Henry Clay who entered resolutions that were eventually passed as five separate laws collectively known as the Compromise of 1850. The North was pleased that California did come in as a free state, but the South demanded that popular sovereignty decide the question in the rest of the territories acquired from Mexico. Texas was reduced in size to make more potential slave states but was compensated with $10 million. Northerners seized the opportunity to ban the slave trade in Washington, D.C., while southerners demanded a more stringent Fugitive Slave Law. The Compromise of 1850 did keep the peace, but its measures were poorly enforced. As the great senators began to die off, the country lacked confidence that the Congress could withstand another such shock without coming apart.

## 6 Stephen Douglas

Douglas himself revealed the wisdom in going west as a young man. He was born in Vermont but moved to Illinois where he taught school and became a lawyer. He rose steadily through the ranks of state politics and by the years of crisis was a U.S. senator. He came to power as the chairman of the Committee on Territories and, as the champion of popular sovereignty seemed to want to make peace in the slavery controversy. His actions were also directed toward his ambition to become president, however, and his Kansas-Nebraska Bill created nothing but strife. He sparred with Abraham Lincoln for the Senate seat in 1858 and then again in the Election of 1860 for the presidency. Known as the "Little Giant" for his powerful oratory despite his small stature, he eventually supported Lincoln's measures once the Civil War began.

## 7 Fugitive Slave Law

This component of the Compromise of 1850 was especially odious to northerners. As the Underground Railroad continued its work and as abolition gained more and more supporters, the South accused the North of violating the provisions in the Constitution for the return of escaped slaves. When the southerners in Congress discovered how objectionable the slave trade in Washington, D.C., was to northern congressmen, they saw their chance to stiffen the laws for the return of escaped slaves. Furthermore, as the law was implemented in the North, judges were paid

$10 per case if they determined an African-American was an escaped slave and only $5 if they freed him or her. Under these circumstances, even African-Americans born free in the North were sent south into slavery. Among the other causes of the demise of the capacity to compromise was the passive and active resistance to the Fugitive Slave Law by the increasingly determined humanitarian reformers of the North. Even Walt Whitman wrote in a poem about helping an escaped slave on to Canada and freedom.

## 8 *Uncle Tom's Cabin*

Harriet Beecher Stowe had grown up in reformer Lyman Beecher's home. Her husband was a professor at Lane Theological Seminary, her father's seminary that turned out many ardent abolitionists. She saw in the controversy over the Fugitive Slave Law a chance to produce a work that would not only stir hearts to end slavery but also sell well. *Uncle Tom's Cabin* was the melodramatic story of the ruination of a slave's family and life after he was sold to pay off his master's gambling debts. Uncle Tom faced fiercer oppression the farther south he went as the whites involved in slavery became more and more degenerate. The book, and the play derived from it, received heated criticism in the South and just as emotional a reception in the North and around the world.

## 9 Nativism

This belief derived largely from animosity between Protestants and Catholics but extended to all immigrants, especially to those from Southern and Eastern Europe. As the United States received waves of immigrants starting in the 1840s, more and more Americans already living in the country began to attribute the ills in society to this influx. Many eastern cities were made up of predominantly immigrant populations, and although these workers filled factories, the problems of overpopulation and urban sprawl were blamed on them. In the early nineteenth century nativism inspired the Know-Nothing Party, but as urbanization and migration increased even further, nativism contributed to the rise of the Ku Klux Klan and the anti-immigrant episodes of the 1920s.

## 10 Kansas-Nebraska Act

This law was the brainchild of Senator Stephen Douglas who wanted to facilitate the construction of the first transcontinental railroad and his own path to the presidency. In order to make the railroad worth the investment, the Indian Territory from which Kansas, Nebraska, and other states were carved needed to be organized and civilized. Deeply committed to his ideal of popular sovereignty, Douglas and other backers in the North garnered support by promising southerners the chance to vote on extending slavery far north of the Missouri Compromise line. The Missouri Compromise had to be repealed. The sudden possibility of slavery's spread into the northern reaches of the Louisiana Purchase galvanized several parties to join forces and form the modern Republican Party in 1854, the year the Kansas-Nebraska Act passed.

## 11 Republican Party

Numerous parties in the North and West realigned in response to the Kansas-Nebraska Act. The shock that slavery could jump the 36°30' line awakened fears that it would gain ground in the West and enough political momentum to restart the slave trade from Africa. The Republican Party thus began as a coalition among the Free Soil and Liberty Parties, as well as northern Whigs and even northern anti-slavery Democrats. The new party originally called for the repeal of the Kansas-Nebraska Act and the Fugitive Slave Law, and the abolition of slavery in Washington, D.C. Because many of those who joined were abolitionists, the Republican Party began with a curious mix of radical social ideas and conservative economic ideas. John C. Fremont of Bear Flag Revolt fame was the party's first presidential candidate in the Election of 1856.

## 12 John Brown

A divisive figure, John Brown was beloved by some, demonized by others, and lamented by the rest. From a family that participated in the Underground Railroad, Brown was a failed businessman who became obsessed with the idea of a slave insurrection. He led a local militia in Kansas in the midst of the events known as Bleeding Kansas and began terrorist attacks with the Pottawatomie Massacre. After murdering five pro-slavery Kansans there, Brown came to the attention of ardent abolitionists in New England who funded his mission into the South known as the Harpers Ferry Raid. When captured after the mission failed, Brown was executed in Virginia and became a martyr for the abolitionist cause. Historians agree that Brown's actions were the major cause of the formation of militias in the South by an aggrieved people who said those who condemned Brown in the North did so only because his raid failed.

## 13 Bleeding Kansas

During the period from 1854 to 1858 much blood was shed in the violence ignited by popular sovereignty at the organization of a territorial government of Kansas. Two governments were formed, a pro-slavery one at Lecompton and an anti-slavery one in Topeka. By 1856 clashes between the rival factions led to the destruction of the free-soil settlement of Lawrence and to Brown's Pottawatomie slayings. Brown's militia defended another free-soil town from an attack, and a murderous Civil War ensued. The violence stemmed from the fraudulent nature of the vote to organize a government due to the presence in Kansas of Missourians and others who voted illegally just to spread slavery. Between two and three hundred people died in the fighting prior to the Civil War during which Kansas entered the Union as a free state in 1861.

## 14 Brooks-Sumner Affair

After lambasting the slavery interests in the Senate in a speech about the rape of Kansas, Charles Sumner sat down at his desk in the Senate chamber. Preston Brooks, a senator from South Carolina, then beat Sumner with a cane so badly that Sumner could not return to his seat in the Senate for three years. Brooks resigned amid horrified northern criticism but widespread praise in the South. He was reelected to his seat unanimously. Meanwhile, Sumner's seat was left vacant for symbolic effect. Tempers flared around the country when it became known that the violence in Kansas had reached the floor of the nation's highest deliberative body.

## 15 Lecompton Constitution

In the midst of the strife in Kansas, four separate constitutions were submitted to organize the government. The Lecompton Constitution was a pro-slavery foundation for statehood that was supported by President James Buchanan who agreed with popular sovereignty so much that he would later do nothing to stop secession of the southern states. He also proposed an amendment to the U.S. Constitution that would directly legalize slavery once and for all. While the Congress accepted the Lecompton Constitution, its opponents demanded another vote in Kansas to ratify it before it could take effect. The second vote on the Lecompton Constitution was ten to one against it. The rejection of the pro-slavery government of Kansas ensured entry as a free state, but also served to enrage the forces in Kansas and in Congress who wanted the peculiar institution not only to survive but to grow.

## 16 Dred Scott case

Dred Scott was a household slave of an army surgeon whose master had taken him to both a free state and a free territory. Therefore, Scott had lived as a slave for around four years where slavery was illegal. With the help of abolitionists, Scott sued his master for his liberty at first in 1846. A Missouri court agreed with Scott, but that decision was overturned in 1852 by the state supreme court. When the case came to the U.S. Supreme Court in 1856, a majority of the justices determined that neither Dred Scott nor any slave or descendant of slaves was a citizen of the country and were not able to sue in the federal court system. In the process, the Supreme Court declared the Missouri Compromise to have been unconstitutional since it deprived citizens of their Fifth Amendment rights to property, their slaves. This case, then, was only the second time the Supreme Court had declared an act of Congress unconstitutional, the last being in the *Marbury v. Madison* case that had established judicial review back in 1803. In short, the South was jubilant and the North was aghast. The grip of the Democratic Party on the presidency for the bulk of the Age of Jackson, with only two Whigs holding the presidency and both of them dying in office, had established a solidly pro-slavery, pro-expansionist court by the eve of the Civil War.

## 17 Lincoln-Douglas Debates

Lincoln challenged his opponent for the Senate seat of Illinois to a series of debates in 1858. Seven debates between Abraham Lincoln and Stephen A. Douglas, then, were held in a statewide campaign. At Freeport, Lincoln pointed out the inconsistency of Douglas's position of popular sovereignty with the heavily Democratic Supreme Court's decision in the *Dred Scott* case. Douglas's response became known as the Freeport Doctrine. Douglas said the vote for or against slavery would occur before a state was in the Union and that slavery would only exist if the people were willing to use force to maintain it. Douglas therefore was caught in a position as a northern Democrat of sidestepping the Supreme Court ruling that the South cherished, so a fatal split in the Democratic Party was opened. Lincoln came out and said he regarded slavery as "a moral, a social, and a political wrong" although he backed away from supporting the equality of all races. The debates in Illinois did not win Lincoln the Senate seat but did win him national fame. His reputation for homegrown wit and sagacity was captured in his famous line, "You can fool all of the people some of the time, and some of the people all of the time, but you cannot fool all of the people all of the time."

## 18 Election of 1860

Two years after the famous Lincoln-Douglas debates for the Senate seat in Illinois, Lincoln and Douglas squared off again, but this time for the presidency. In addition, the southern Democrats had split off in a bid to support states' rights and slavery with John C. Breckinridge as their candidate. John Bell of Tennessee also headed a ticket for what was known as the Constitutional Union Party. The Republican Party seized the opportunity of a divided opposition to put forward a platform of national advancement that garnered support not only in the North but also in the West. Lincoln campaigned for a transcontinental railroad, the Homestead Act, and a protective tariff and against reopening the African slave trade and the spread of slavery into any territories. Lincoln won even though he was not on the ballot in ten southern states. Lincoln's election was the last straw for South Carolina and six other southern states that then seceded from the Union.

## 19 Crittenden Compromise

With secession looming, Senator John Crittenden of Kentucky attempted a last effort at peace in the spirit of his predecessor, Henry Clay. With the lame duck president James Buchanan doing nothing to stop secession, Crittenden proposed the reestablishment of the 36°30' line and its extension to the Pacific Ocean. Crittenden hoped that if such a definitive boundary could be drawn between slavery and freedom that the seceding states would return and war could be averted. Abraham Lincoln made it clear, however, that the Republican Party meant what it said in the campaign, that slavery should not expand into any territories, not even those from the Mexican Cession that were below the proposed compromise line.

The fact that this compromise was rejected and that nothing came from a peace convention held in Washington, D.C., revealed that the era of compromise over the issues of slavery and federal authority were over.

# 20 Secession

Aside from the firing on Fort Sumter, secession was the last cause in the unfortunate series of events that led the nation to the Civil War. Southern secessionists reasoned that they had the constitutional right to back out of the Union that they had only joined as a league of friendship in opposition to the British in the American Revolution. The U.S. Constitution had replaced the Articles of Confederation but had not codified that status of states in subordination to the federal government clearly enough to avoid differing interpretations. South Carolina led the way out of the United States in February of 1861. Abraham Lincoln said the states had no right to leave the Union or to take the mouth of the Mississippi River with them. The six states that followed South Carolina met in Montgomery, Alabama, to write a new constitution for a new country, the Confederate States of America. Lincoln called for seventy-five thousand volunteers to form an army to put down the rebellion in the South.

## *The Big Picture*

1. The capacity of the Congress to compromise over the spread of slavery into the territories was slowly eroded by the accelerating events of the 1850s.

2. The crusade to abolish slavery escalated as a result of popular works of literature, continued agitation for humanitarian reforms, and dramatic events.

3. The South was more and more determined to defend slavery once the Congress opened territories to its spread through popular sovereignty and the Supreme Court determined that slaves were property protected by the Bill of Rights.

4. Violence between anti-slavery and pro-slavery forces erupted in the territories, at a federal arsenal, and even in the U.S. Senate.

5. A crescendo of divisive events culminated with the election of Abraham Lincoln in 1860 and the rapid secession of seven southern states that formed the Confederate States of America.

# Mini Quiz

1. In the Election of 1824, John Quincy Adams

   (A) became the last of the Virginia dynasty presidents.
   (B) won with more electoral votes even though Andrew Jackson won the popular vote.
   (C) won when the election was decided in the House of Representatives.
   (D) lost to Andrew Jackson in the first election with only two political parties represented.
   (E) won because he exchanged the vice presidency for Henry Clay's support.

2. The Nullification Crisis was resolved in 1833 when

   (A) Andrew Jackson invaded South Carolina to stop secession.
   (B) the Congress voted to end the use of high protective tariffs.
   (C) John C. Calhoun proved nullification was constitutional.
   (D) the Gag Rule was passed to end the discussion.
   (E) Henry Clay negotiated the reduction of the tariff over nine years.

3. Andrew Jackson's presidency possessed all of the following legacies EXCEPT

   (A) the president's reliance upon a team of trusted advisers other than his cabinet.
   (B) a shift in power west as the population moved in that direction.
   (C) frequent use of the veto to increase the executive branch's power and influence.
   (D) a growing focus on the interests of merchants and bankers in government policy.
   (E) the placing of political supporters in government jobs, or rotation in office.

4. Which reformer in the antebellum period established common, or public, schools?

   (A) Dorothea Dix
   (B) Horace Mann
   (C) William Lloyd Garrison
   (D) Bronson Alcott
   (E) Ralph Waldo Emerson

5. Which of the experiences below would likely NOT occur at a Lyceum meeting?

   (A) A scientist demonstrates a laboratory experiment
   (B) A transcendentalist delivers a lecture on self-reliance
   (C) A Methodist revival preacher delivers a sermon
   (D) A phrenologist demonstrates analysis of the brain and then offers private screenings
   (E) A local orchestra performs a new composition from Europe

6. The clash between the Mormon settlers of Utah and the federal government ended when

   (A) the Mormons burned Salt Lake City before federal troops arrived.
   (B) Joseph Smith was captured and killed by a mob.
   (C) federal troops soundly defeated the Mormon militia.
   (D) federal troops arrived to find Salt Lake City deserted and then left.
   (E) neighboring settlers drove the Mormons from their homes and burned Salt Lake City.

7. What was the impact of Eli Whitney's cotton gin on the South?

   (A) The cotton gin convinced the South to begin the cultivation of cotton.
   (B) The cotton gin dramatically eased the labor involved in the harvesting of cotton.
   (C) The cotton gin had little to no impact on the demand for slaves.
   (D) The cotton gin reduced the demand for slaves by saving on manual labor.
   (E) The cotton gin made cotton lucrative and thus increased the demand for slaves.

8. Which activity below was forbidden in connection with slavery by federal law prior to the Civil War?

   (A) Buying Africans directly from Africa
   (B) Manumission, or freeing of slaves by choice
   (C) Separating slave families and marriages by selling them as individuals
   (D) Allowing slaves to work for money for self-purchase
   (E) Teaching slaves to read

9. The experience of African-Americans in slavery

   (A) was uniformly harsh because slavery was an institution based on violence.
   (B) varied widely depending on their particular role and their masters' temperaments.
   (C) was so harsh as to lead to constant slave rebellions.
   (D) grew harsher the closer they lived to the North.
   (E) erased the opportunity for expressions of human culture because slaves were property.

10. Which answer below best summarizes America's relationship with Great Britain before the Civil War?

    (A) The United States and England were allies against the Spanish as Spain's Empire crumbled.
    (B) Britain feared the rise of the United States as a world power and thus actively thwarted it.
    (C) The United States feared British encroachment on any territory in the New World.
    (D) The two nations saw each other as economic equals and thus experienced competition.
    (E) The United States leaned toward annexation of Canada regardless of British protests.

11. Which two men made unlikely allies in stopping Texas annexation immediately following the Lone Star Republic's independence from Mexico?

    (A) Andrew Jackson and John Quincy Adams
    (B) Andrew Jackson and John C. Calhoun
    (C) Andrew Jackson and Henry Clay
    (D) Henry Clay and James K. Polk
    (E) Sam Houston and Daniel Webster

12. What made the Gadsden Purchase so valuable as the last addition of contiguous territory to the continental United States?

    (A) More gold deposits had been discovered there.
    (B) The territory supplied a seaport on the Gulf of California.
    (C) The territory contained the best pass through the Rockies for a railroad.
    (D) The Apache and Comanche Indians refused to go there for religious reasons.
    (E) The border with Mexico became more defensible because of natural boundaries.

13. The Wilmot Proviso suggested that

    (A) the Gadsden Purchase be extended to the sea.
    (B) the United States annex all of Mexico.
    (C) popular sovereignty be used to determine the status of slavery in the Mexican Cession.
    (D) no territory acquired from Mexico would become open to slavery.
    (E) a canal in Central America be exclusively the property of the United States.

14. The South interpreted the U.S. Constitution in the slavery debates to mean that

 (A) the federal government had the right to block the spread of slavery in the territories.
 (B) states that disagreed with the trends of federal power could constitutionally leave the union.
 (C) state law must always defer to federal law in times of disagreement.
 (D) slavery's extent was governed by natural geographic and climatic boundaries.
 (E) the reference in the Bill of Rights to due process did not extend to slaves as property.

15. Abraham Lincoln's stated position on slavery was that slavery

 (A) should be abolished because it was immoral despite federal laws protecting it.
 (B) should be decided in the territories by the will of the people, or popular sovereignty.
 (C) violated the natural equality of all men that was established by God.
 (D) should end by allowing each new African-American born into slavery to be freed.
 (E) would end naturally as long as the federal government banned its spread.

# Answer Explanations

1. **C**   Adams was from Massachusetts and received fewer popular and electoral votes than Jackson, who still did not gain enough electoral votes to win among four challengers. Adams thus won in the House of Representatives, and the "corrupt bargain" hinted at in answer E involved Clay's becoming the secretary of state.

2. **E**   Henry Clay negotiated the compromise tariff as stated, whereas the rest of the items were related to the Nullification Crisis; none of them are true as stated.

3. **D**   All of the items listed were major legacies of Andrew Jackson's presidency except answer D because Jackson was the president who advanced the interests of the common man, not commercial interests.

4. **B**   Horace Mann was the secretary of the Massachusetts Board of Education who advanced the common school movement, the origin of modern public schools.

5. **C**   A sermon would not likely happen at a Lyceum because the types of reform embodied in the Lyceum movement were secular, not religious.

6. **D**   When Albert Sydney Johnston's troops arrived in Salt Lake City the Mormons had evacuated to avoid a violent clash, although all but answer A either happened or were possibilities in the history of the Church of Jesus Christ of Latter Day Saints.

7. **E**   Because the cotton gin dramatically cut the labor required not to harvest but to process cotton by removing the seeds and other material from the cotton fiber, many more slaves were needed to perform all the other tasks of cotton cultivation that was turned into a lucrative cash crop.

8. **A**   The U.S. Congress banned the African slave trade in 1808. All of the other activities were either legal or banned only by state laws.

9. **B**   Slaves who were field hands, especially those of the Deep South, had much harsher lives than household slaves or those living in the border states. Such slave rebellions that occurred were by no means constant, and although oppressed, slaves developed their own unique cultures and maintained family ties as proofs of their participation in human culture.

10. **C**   Only this choice is true and is the background for the Monroe Doctrine as well as the expansion associated with Manifest Destiny. All hopes of annexing Canada were given up after the War of 1812.

11. **A**   Although all of these pairings would have made unlikely alliances in the 1830s and 1840s, Jackson and Adams were by no means fond of each other but agreed that Texas annexation would be too hazardous for the nation right after it broke free from Mexico. Both men thwarted annexation if for different reasons.

12. **C**   Only this choice was in the minds of those who purchased this afterthought on the Mexican Cession.

13. **D**   Although all of these ideas were expressed in this era at one time or another, David Wilmot was most concerned to prevent slavery being restored by the United States where the dictator Santa Anna had abolished it. Yet the Wilmot Proviso failed to pass both houses of Congress.

14. **B**   This choice was the whole basis for secession and the formation of the Confederacy, whereas few Southerners, if any, would have believed or openly acknowledged the others.

15. **E** This choice was not only Lincoln's position but part of the official platform of the Republican Party. Lincoln actively opposed or disagreed with the other ideas that were indeed held by others of his day.

# The Civil War

CHAPTER **17**

*. . . and the war came.*

—Abraham Lincoln's second inaugural address, 1865

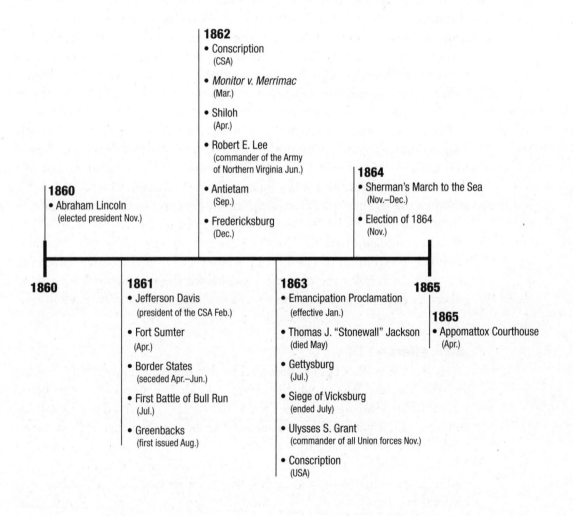

**1862**
- Conscription
  (CSA)

- *Monitor v. Merrimac*
  (Mar.)

- Shiloh
  (Apr.)

- Robert E. Lee
  (commander of the Army
  of Northern Virginia Jun.)

- Antietam
  (Sep.)

- Fredericksburg
  (Dec.)

**1864**
- Sherman's March to the Sea
  (Nov.–Dec.)

- Election of 1864
  (Nov.)

**1860**
- Abraham Lincoln
  (elected president Nov.)

**1860**

**1861**
- Jefferson Davis
  (president of the CSA Feb.)

- Fort Sumter
  (Apr.)

- Border States
  (seceded Apr.–Jun.)

- First Battle of Bull Run
  (Jul.)

- Greenbacks
  (first issued Aug.)

**1863**
- Emancipation Proclamation
  (effective Jan.)

- Thomas J. "Stonewall" Jackson
  (died May)

- Gettysburg
  (Jul.)

- Siege of Vicksburg
  (ended July)

- Ulysses S. Grant
  (commander of all Union forces Nov.)

- Conscription
  (USA)

**1865**

**1865**
- Appomattox Courthouse
  (Apr.)

# Top 20 Things to Know

## 1 Abraham Lincoln

Son of an illiterate father, Lincoln rose from a storekeeper and militia captain in Illinois to a postmaster and a successful lawyer in Springfield. He belonged to the Whig party and then in 1856 joined the new Republican Party founded in 1854 in response to the Kansas-Nebraska Act. Having served a term in the House of Representatives, Lincoln ran in 1858 against the incumbent senator Stephen A. Douglas. Lincoln read predominantly from the Bible, from which he used the line, "A house divided against itself cannot stand," and from Shakespeare, and these sources helped him craft the original rhetorical style that became famous in the Lincoln-Douglas debates, in his first and second inaugural addresses, and in the Gettysburg Address delivered at the dedication of the Union cemetery after the Battle of Gettysburg. Winning the Election of 1860 with no southern electoral votes, his presidency marked the last straw for the seceding South. Lincoln proposed that the federal government should purchase the emancipation of southern slaves but otherwise opposed abolition saying, "My paramount objective is to save the Union, and not either to save or destroy slavery." Lincoln used a trial and error system in search of a fighting, winning general until he settled on U. S. Grant. After the Battle of Antietam, he issued the Emancipation Proclamation in an effort to support the flagging morale of the Union in the face of Confederate victories. He chose Andrew Johnson as his vice president for the Election of 1864 as a gesture of conciliation to the South in that Johnson was a unionist from Tennessee. Having won the election and then the war and advocated a prompt restoration of the seceded states, Lincoln was assassinated by John Wilkes Booth. When he died on April 14, 1865, Secretary of War Edwin Stanton said, "Now he belongs to the ages." No other president, with the possible exception of Franklin D. Roosevelt, has had to carry such a burden or face such dangers for the country. Lincoln was the first major leader in American history to refer to the United States as a singular noun, and he made it one.

## 2 Jefferson Davis

Davis was a West Point graduate who served in the Black Hawk War (as did Lincoln) and the Mexican War in which he was wounded. Between the wars he opened a plantation in Mississippi that he called "Brierfield." He served as a Democratic U.S. congressman, senator, and secretary of War for Franklin Pierce. These experiences made him a clear choice to lead the Confederate States of America (CSA) once Mississippi seceded, but once he was elected president his authoritarian demeanor and military opinions did not endear him to other Confederate leaders, military or civilian. His heavy hand partly undid the Confederacy, but in his defense he was constantly hampered in leading the central government by the very principle upon which the CSA was founded—states' rights. Warned by Robert E. Lee to flee Richmond, President Davis was captured, charged with treason, and imprisoned from 1865 through 1867 when the charges were dropped.

## 3 Fort Sumter

Fort Sumter was a federal installation located at the opening of Charleston harbor off the coast of South Carolina. Although it was not the first fort fired upon (that was in Pensacola, Florida), South Carolinians were the first to secede and considered by the North to be the culprits who started the war. Intolerable to southern pride and impossible to ignore because Charleston was one of the largest cities in the South, Confederate batteries opened fire on the fort at 4:30 A.M. on April 12, 1861. The fort returned fire, but after thirty-four hours of sustained bombardment the commander inside Ft. Sumter, Major Robert Anderson, surrendered. Neither the Confederate nor the Union forces sustained any casualties, but four additional states seceded to make eleven, and Lincoln decided to respond militarily instead of diplomatically. Lincoln is said to have engineered the whole episode by sending a supply ship that he calculated would provoke the South to attack but also not be considered by objective observers to have been an act of aggression. Lincoln and others claimed, therefore, that the Confederacy started the Civil War.

## 4 Border States

Missouri, Kentucky, Maryland, and Delaware were slave states that remained loyal to the Union (later to include West Virginia). The Republican Party platform mandated that slavery be left alone where it existed, and Lincoln strove to convince these four states not to secede. He reasoned that if these states left, the Union would be dissolved. In convincing the citizens of especially Missouri, Kentucky, and Maryland he did not hesitate to use military force and the police powers of the federal government in ways that were later deemed to be unconstitutional.

## 5 Robert E. Lee

A descendant of one of the first families of Virginia, he declined President Lincoln's offer to command the Union Army in 1861. Although opposed to both slavery and secession, he joined the Confederate cause and was given command of the Army of Northern Virginia. Lee's iron will and unimpeachable character provided much of the Confederacy's resolve. After his army was whittled down to thirty thousand troops, he surrendered to General U. S. Grant at Appomattox in 1865. Lee is credited with using his influence over his countrymen to urge a peaceful resolution to the war by resisting all efforts to continue armed conflict that might have prolonged the war.

## 6 Ulysses S. Grant

A West Point graduate from Ohio, Grant was decorated for gallantry in the Mexican War and was said to be an excellent horseman. While pulling off some astounding tactical victories during the Civil War in the West, including the reduction of Vicksburg and the freeing of the Mississippi River, as Grant rose in responsibility he relied on attrition. Therefore, this other memorable top general of the Civil War is also not considered a tactical genius, and he is often remembered as a butcher of his own men. The numbers were all in Grant's favor, however, and the brutal wearing down of the Confederate army prevailed. As a war hero, Grant was elected president in 1868 and served two terms. His was the first scandal-ridden presidency of the Gilded Age.

## 7 First Battle of Bull Run

The Battle of Bull Run, or Manassas, was the first major conflict (1861) of what many politicians said would be a short war. Thomas J. Jackson's example rallied fleeing Confederate forces and earned him the nickname "Stonewall." Confederate reinforcements were brought by train for the first time in warfare and allowed the South to turn the tide. The Confederate rout of the Union Army and the five thousand casualties caused many U.S. leaders to realize the Civil War could be long and bloody.

## 8 Shiloh

This battle was fought in western Tennessee in 1862 with the Union Army prevailing, barely. But more Americans—North and South—fell at Shiloh than in all previous American wars combined. In particular, the Confederacy lost its then commanding general, Albert Sydney Johnston. On the Union side the actions of Grant's undisciplined troops almost ended his career before it got off the ground.

## 9 *Monitor v. Merrimac*

This clash of ironclad ships marked a turning point in world naval conflicts and is part of the reason the Civil War was the first modern war. The Confederate ship *Virginia* (the refitted *Merrimac*) was wreaking havoc with wooden Union ships until the newly designed *Monitor* arrived. The two ironclad ships pounded each other for five hours before calling it a draw. The Confederates later scuttled the *Virginia* rather than allowing it to be captured. The Confederacy foreshadowed modern naval warfare even more with the first successful combatant submarine, the *Hunley*.

## 10 Thomas J. "Stonewall" Jackson

One of the Confederacy's brilliant commanders, General Jackson's army defeated larger Union forces in the Shenandoah Valley of Virginia. After achieving yet another victory at Chancellorsville, "Stonewall" was accidentally shot and killed by some of his own men upon his return from a night reconnaissance. His death proved a severe blow to Confederate military capacity.

## 11 Antietam

Antietam was the bloodiest one-day battle of the war with twenty-three thousand casualties from both sides and the one time George McClellan thwarted Robert E. Lee's plans. The retreat of Lee into Virginia was the first significant good news for the Union forces and spurred Lincoln to issue the Emancipation Proclamation. Foreign recognition of the Confederacy was also stymied, a fact that severely crippled Confederate hopes for European aid or intervention.

## 12 Emancipation Proclamation

Lincoln's issuance of this document was his single most important act in saving the Union by providing a moral justification for continuing the war. It provided that after January 1, 1863, all slaves in states still in rebellion would be "then, thenceforward, and forever free." Black soldiers were also permitted to fight for the freedom of their race after this document met with popular approval. While no states still in rebellion would honor Lincoln's executive order, every subsequently conquered state had to. Thus Lincoln made the war about "a new birth of freedom" and boosted the nation's morale.

## 13 Fredericksburg

This Virginia battle was among the most disturbing early setbacks of the war for the North, in 1862. It caused another shakeup in the high command of the Union Army, the leadership of which wasn't effective until General Grant assumed control in 1863. Because of the nature of the battle in which the Confederate soldiers sheltered behind a stone wall in a sunken road, Union casualties were severe after several frontal assaults failed. Union soldiers at the Battle of Gettysburg then chanted the name "Fredericksburg," as Confederate soldiers made Pickett's Charge (an infantry assault) against their line.

## 14 Gettysburg

This battle was the largest ever fought in the Western Hemisphere and the most crucial of the Civil War. It marked the Confederate Army's last invasion of the North and started when the forces unexpectedly ran into one another in a small Pennsylvania town in July of 1863. Lee unsuccessfully attacked the Union forces several times including the disastrous Pickett's Charge. The Confederates retreated into Virginia, but the new Union commander, George Meade, refused Lincoln's orders to give chase. Over fifty thousand men were killed or wounded. Lee's offer to resign after the battle was ignored by the Confederate government that struggled on, but most people even in the South realized that Gettysburg spelled the doom of the Confederacy.

## 15 Siege of Vicksburg

This last Confederate stronghold on the Mississippi River fell on July 4, 1863, after a six-week siege by General Grant's army. The Union victory came the same day General Lee's army retreated from Gettysburg. This double blow demoralized southerners for the first time. The fall of the city of Vicksburg meant the Union controlled the Mississippi River, a key aim in its original war strategy to split the Confederacy geographically.

## 16 Sherman's March to the Sea

This military campaign proceeded not only from Atlanta to Savannah, but turned northward and destroyed Columbia, South Carolina, the birthplace of secession. Along the way Sherman's men cut their ties to any supply lines and then destroyed or stole everything of value in a path sixty miles wide. Sherman's making war on civilians' property is the first prominent example of the modern concept of "total war." As he promised, Sherman made ". . . the South howl."

## 17 Election of 1864

Lincoln won reelection to a second term. His replacement of first-term vice president Hannibal Hamlin with Andrew Johnson had a significant impact on Reconstruction. Johnson succeeded Lincoln as president after his assassination. Lincoln insisted on holding the election during the war even though his loss to the Democrat, former General George McClellan, probably would have meant the dissolution of the Union. But Lincoln defeated the Copperheads, a derogatory term for northerners opposed to the war. In his second inaugural address, Lincoln said he sought a "lasting peace" and one "With malice toward none; with charity for all…."

## 18 Appomattox Courthouse

With Union armies encircling the Army of Northern Virginia, General Lee surrendered to General Grant in April 1865. Lee received rations for his men and permission for officers to keep their swords and all soldiers to keep their own horses and mules. Lee's urging of his men to surrender and return to civilian life was his greatest contribution to peace.

## 19 Conscription

This new governmental power arose from the need for troops in both armies by 1863. All men ages twenty to forty-five were eligible for the draft. When news of the names being drafted appeared in New York City newspapers alongside a long list of the casualties from Gettysburg, the New York Draft Riots erupted. Four days of rampaging, in which Irish immigrants lynched African-Americans and destroyed their property, were finally put down by exhausted troops marched north from Gettysburg.

## 20 Greenbacks

This war-time emergency remedy that persisted after the Civil War was not the first but the most extensive issuing of paper currency. Both the North and the South eventually circulated paper currencies backed with no precious metals and touched off intense inflation. The Union currency was printed with green ink, hence its "colorful" name.

## *The Big Picture*

1. The Civil War was a tragic clash of forces holding opposing interpretations of the powers of the federal government, and the Union victory established the United States as a more unified nation with new perspectives on both the U.S. Constitution and the Declaration of Independence.

2. Both sides in the Civil War originally employed military tactics unsuited to their modern weaponry and infrastructure, but the North adopted techniques of total warfare that foreshadowed the terrible nature of twentieth-century conflicts in which civilian populations and resources were attacked and destroyed.

3. Abraham Lincoln's skillful management of the war earned him the top rank among presidents, status as a model for all subsequent presidents, and the legacy of being a martyr for American freedom.

4. By surviving this harrowing national ordeal, the federal government emerged from the Civil War with greater powers and authority not only over states but also over individuals.

5. Major consequences of the war included defining the ever-changing relationships between the races and economic transformations that launched the settlement of the West and the rise of industrialized big business.

# Reconstruction

# CHAPTER 18

*This is the most important subject which now engages the attention
of the American people, for on it depends the future welfare of the nation,
and the destinies of a race but partially redeemed from bondage.*
—Philip A. Bell, editorial in the *Elevator*, 1865

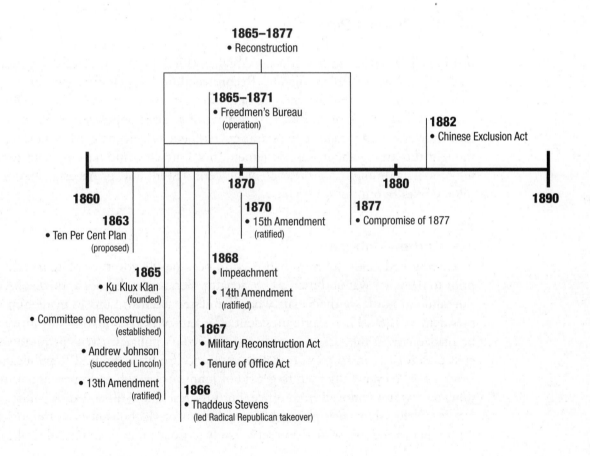

**1865–1877**
• Reconstruction

**1865–1871**
• Freedmen's Bureau
(operation)

**1882**
• Chinese Exclusion Act

**1870**

**1880**

**1860**

**1863**
• Ten Per Cent Plan
(proposed)

**1870**
• 15th Amendment
(ratified)

**1877**
• Compromise of 1877

**1890**

**1865**
• Ku Klux Klan
(founded)

• Committee on Reconstruction
(established)

• Andrew Johnson
(succeeded Lincoln)

• 13th Amendment
(ratified)

**1868**
• Impeachment

• 14th Amendment
(ratified)

**1867**
• Military Reconstruction Act

• Tenure of Office Act

**1866**
• Thaddeus Stevens
(led Radical Republican takeover)

# Top 20 Things to Know

## 1 Reconstruction

This word is a name for an era and a process. The era ran roughly from 1863 to 1877, whereas the process continued much later. After the horror of the Civil War the country had to rebuild destroyed infrastructure like buildings and railroads, but the more difficult Reconstruction was the attempt to reunite the states as a nation. Throughout the period political forces struggled to determine whether the defeated states should be punished or not and what should or should not be done to help the freed slaves. All the while the resentment of the southern people smoldered at their humbled status in the hands of a federal government several times more powerful than it had ever been.

## 2 Ten Percent Plan

Based on his belief that the seceded states had never left the country because they had lost their war for independence, Abraham Lincoln sought to ease the country back to peace with a lenient plan for Reconstruction. His plan first gave amnesty to almost all Confederates, and then he called for states to emancipate their slaves and swear loyalty to the Union. Once 10 percent of a state's population took the oath, Lincoln planned to recognize the state's government as legitimate. Most northerners thought this arrangement was too lenient, but Lincoln could have perhaps guided his proposals through to a benevolent peace if it were not for his assassination by John Wilkes Booth.

## 3 Andrew Johnson

A self-educated tailor, Johnson had risen to become the governor of Tennessee just prior to the Civil War and then a U.S. senator. Because he did not approve of secession and did not leave the Senate when Tennessee seceded, Lincoln made him vice president in 1864. He became president after Lincoln's assassination but proved to be inadequate to the task of carrying out Lincoln's policies. Even his more stringent plan for Reconstruction met with resistance from the Radical Republicans in Congress who eventually tried to get rid of Johnson through an impeachment trial. Johnson was not removed from office, but his presidency still ended in failure. He, like President Grant, was plagued by accusations of alcoholism. His attempts as a southerner to end Reconstruction served only to isolate him from his political party.

## 4 Thirteenth Amendment

This amendment to the Constitution was foreshadowed by the Emancipation Proclamation and was a penalty for the secession of the slaveholding states and the Civil War. Once Lincoln issued his proclamation, the Union fought on to secure emancipation as its new unifying impulse. This step, completed with ratification late in 1865, was the one measure that Lincoln, Johnson, and the Radical Republicans all agreed should occur before Reconstruction could be considered a success. The Thirteenth Amendment was considered by some to be the end of the abolitionist movement and its crowning achievement. The events of Reconstruction, however, left the freedmen in a general condition not much different from their status before the war.

## 5 Radical Republicans

This wing of the Republican Party in Congress sought to punish the South for having caused the Civil War and to elevate the freedmen. Some viewed the latter issue as another attempt to humiliate the South, whereas others were sincerely interested in advancing African-Americans to a position of equality. All the Radicals were said to "wave the bloody shirt," or to continually gain political advantage by blaming the Democratic Party for the war. The Radicals used their numerical advantage in the Congress to vie for control of Reconstruction with President Johnson, and they represented the only opportunity to secure the Thirteenth, Fourteenth, and Fifteenth Amendments to the Constitution for nearly a century because they held complete control while most southern whites could not vote.

## 6 Freedmen's Bureau

In response to the southern states' laws known as the Black Codes, the federal government expanded this agency originally formed to transfer abandoned land to former slaves. Under the leadership of Oliver O. Howard, the Bureau sought to provide freedmen with basic necessities until they could either own land or secure jobs. Bureau agents were supposed to monitor the working conditions to which African-Americans were subjected, but the land for distribution and the staff were never enough. The Freedmen's Bureau's greatest success was the establishment of the first serious efforts to educate African-Americans in the South. President Johnson vetoed the legislation saying that the U.S. Constitution did not call for the federal government to set up welfare agencies looking out for individual citizens' needs. The attempt to elevate African-Americans for their sakes and to humiliate the South saw this first welfare agency established when the Radical Republicans overrode the president's veto.

## 7 Sharecropping

This form of tenant farming permitted workers, black and white, to live on a former plantation's land while working the cotton or tobacco crops for the landowner. When the crop was harvested, a portion of the proceeds would be given to the workers as income, share by share. Most former slaves and many poor whites displaced by the Civil War accepted this arrangement as their only viable option to make a living. Sharecropping generally provided a meager existence, however, due to manipulation by the landowner or by merchants who supplied the sharecroppers with tools and seed on credit. Furthermore, natural agricultural problems like drought or hailstorms could ruin crops and leave sharecropping families in debt for generations. Families falling prey to the system lived little better than the serfs of the medieval period in Europe, and the existence for former slaves was almost exactly reminiscent of slavery. As the only plausible labor arrangement for the ruined cotton kingdom, however, sharecropping existed in the South through the Great Depression and World War II.

## 8  Thaddeus Stevens

This Pennsylvania lawyer and politician practiced, ironically, in Gettysburg before the Civil War. With the rise of the Republican Party, Stevens rose to national prominence as the leader of the Radical Republicans in the House of Representatives. He and his counterpart in the Senate, the caned Senator Charles Sumner, formulated Reconstruction policies meant to force a punitive peace upon the South. He chaired the Committee on Reconstruction and organized the impeachment of President Johnson. Whether he believed in complete equality of the races is impossible to tell, but at death he did have himself buried in an African-American cemetery.

## 9  Committee on Reconstruction

This joint committee of six members of the Senate and nine members of the House of Representatives was appointed to guide matters like the ratification of the Thirteenth Amendment and other Reconstruction policies. Thaddeus Stevens wielded the solid Radical Republican majority power in Congress to impose his will on the "conquered provinces," as Stevens referred to the former Confederate states. The Committee declared Congress to be the sole power in the land regarding Reconstruction. They were largely responsible for the Fourteenth Amendment and the idea of military Reconstruction, a fate only escaped by the state of Tennessee because of its early compliance. The ten other seceded states faced the wrath of Stevens, the Committee, and the Radical Republicans.

## 10  Fourteenth Amendment

When the Congress tried to confer citizenship rights on freedmen with the Civil Rights Act of 1866, the law was considered such a usurpation of the rights of states to determine citizenship that the Committee on Reconstruction resolved to amend the Constitution. Once it was ratified in the North, the Committee demanded that each southern state do so as a condition of Reconstruction. The amendment clarified the citizenship status of African-Americans and of all people born on American soil. Furthermore, the federal government was put in charge of monitoring whether or not states abused the civil rights of their citizens. Provisions of the amendment were also designed to punish high-ranking Confederate leaders by barring them from holding public office. The Committee on Reconstruction designed the policies to further punish the South, and the Fourteenth Amendment was the basis for federal action during the civil rights movement.

## 11  Military Reconstruction Act

After issuing his own Reconstruction program, Andrew Johnson had to bow to the will of Congress who rejected the governments and representatives thus assembled. With the Military Reconstruction Act of 1867, Congress added the indignity of combining the seceded states, except for Tennessee, into five military districts each headed by a general with regular army and African-American militia troops to impose order and to protect African-American voters once the Fifteenth Amendment was passed. During military Reconstruction those southerners who cooperated with the process were known as scalawags, whereas the northerners who came to the South to participate were known as carpetbaggers.

## 12 Tenure of Office Act

In a quest to rid themselves of Andrew Johnson in order to freely reshape the South in Reconstruction, the Radical Republicans passed the Tenure of Office Act. This innocuous-sounding name hid the fact that the law was a trap. Reasoning from the constitutional power of the Congress to review appointments of the executive branch, they sought to require Congressional consent for any firings as well. In his ongoing animosity for the legislative assertion of one-party power, Johnson tested the law by firing Secretary of War Edwin Stanton. He had first asked permission from the Congress, but they said no. Johnson's going ahead with the firing was the grounds whereby the Radical Republicans impeached him for "high crimes and misdemeanors."

## 13 Impeachment

Although a constitutional process, impeachment was used during Reconstruction as a political weapon. The House of Representatives reviewed the case against Andrew Johnson for his violation of the Tenure of Office Act and determined that there was enough evidence to send him to the Senate for trial. At that point the president was impeached. In his trial in the Senate, however, the senators came one vote short of the two-thirds majority necessary for removal from office.

## 14 Chinese Exclusion Act

Chinese immigrants had flocked to California during the gold rush and were still around when construction of the transcontinental railroad began in 1862. The Chinese workers were instrumental in the success of the Central Pacific Railroad in crossing the Sierra Nevada Mountains from Sacramento all the way to Promontory Point, Utah. Tensions arose in San Francisco and other California cities when it became apparent that not only were the Chinese not going back to China, they were taking over segments of the economy and establishing themselves permanently. The first expression of nativist immigration law was passed in 1882 and barred any further Chinese immigration for ten years.

## 15 Louis Agassiz

A Swiss-born scientist with an emphasis in zoology, Louis Agassiz came to the United States in 1846 to give a series of lectures. The advantages of American life and the opportunities for research, especially on fishes of the Western Hemisphere, impelled him to stay. He is noted as the first scientist to propose the idea, derived from studying the boulder-strewn reaches of upper North America, that an ice age had once gripped the earth and carved the landscape with glaciers. With his fame as a preeminent scientist, Agassiz's statements on race were used as justification for the racist policies of the South during and after Reconstruction. Although he defied the theory of evolution in his studies of animals until his death in 1873, he considered African-Americans inferior and believed in natural selection in so far as it applied to them. Agassiz predicted that African-Americans would die off because of an inability to organize, a condition that if true anecdotally, could easily be explained by their recent escape from bondage. The acceptance of Agassiz's views and the theories about race derived from Darwinism were continuing evidence of the latent racism and white supremacy of both the North and the South.

## 16 Fifteenth Amendment

The Radical Republicans' final constitutional blow against the former Confederate states was the Fifteenth Amendment. African-American males were given the right to vote in local and national elections before many white southern men and before all white women. Ratified in 1870, the Fifteenth Amendment was used to legalize African-American male suffrage even in the North where only a small minority of states permitted blacks to vote. The Radical Republicans further humiliated the South by finally providing full citizenship rights to former slaves. Women suffragists rallied against both the Fourteenth and the Fifteenth Amendments because they were the first uses of the word *male* in the U.S. Constitution and were another hurdle women would have to leap before they could claim full citizenship.

## 17 Ku Klux Klan

At the close of the Civil War the Ku Klux Klan was founded in Pulaski, Tennessee, as a social and commemorative club lamenting the Lost Cause. Nathan Bedford Forrest, the Confederate cavalry genius, became its first Grand Wizard. As Reconstruction progressed the Klan became more a force for intimidation and terrorism. The use of violence included the burning of African-American's churches and schools, forcible displacement from homes, lynching, and outright murder. Lynching was the process of violently executing a supposed criminal without a trial. Both African-Americans and whites fell prey to the Klan's intimidation and murder because the Klansmen targeted anyone who supported congressional and military Reconstruction. The early goal of the Klan was Home Rule, that is, the return of state governments under the control of the Democratic Party with the ability to enact Black Codes to "keep the negro in his place." As this goal was achieved, the Klan's violent intimidation tapered off, but not entirely, and the main focus became political organization to maintain southern autonomy. Whole states were led by members of the Ku Klux Klan, and as rising nativism spread up through the 1920s, some of the states controlled by the Klan were in the North.

## 18 Compromise of 1877

Because the returns from the three states still unreconstructed by the Election of 1876 sent in disputed election returns, the country experienced a constitutional crisis. Florida, South Carolina, and Louisiana had failed to jump through all the hoops set out for them by the Radical Republicans, and these states were still under military occupation. A congressional committee was formed to review the election returns, but the committee was skewed with eight Republicans and only seven Democrats. The Republicans said they believed Rutherford B. Hayes had won the three states, whereas the Democrats looked at the same evidence and determined that Samuel B. Tilden, the Democratic challenger, had won. The South was outraged that the election might be stolen by stacking the deck, and trouble was brewing until a compromise was reached. In an unspecified process, what became known as the Compromise of 1877 saw the South trade the presidency for receiving the three states back under Home Rule. The military was withdrawn from the states in question and Reconstruction was considered to be over. Because of the fatigue resulting from decades of wrangling over slavery and its consequences, northern and southern racism, and constitutional limitations on federal power, African-Americans were left at the mercy of their former masters who were quickly restored across the South as a political ruling class.

## 19 Disenfranchisement

Despite the ratification of the Fifteenth Amendment, when states received self-government again they instituted policies that systematically limited or removed African-Americans' voting rights. The discrimination was originally hidden in that the regulations applied to all voters, but the regulations were not equally enforced. Literacy tests hampered the right to vote of freedmen for obvious reasons, but even literate, articulate African-Americans could not interpret sections of state constitutions to "the satisfaction of the registrar." In other words, the voting officials could in almost all cases tell if a person was of African descent and simply disallow any attempt on the part of that person to pass the test. Poll taxes, even if low, barred sharecropping African-Americans from voting because they existed in a nearly cashless economy near to the life of serfs. Remarkably, tacit restrictions on voting for African-Americans were not entirely eliminated in the South until nearly one hundred years after the ratification of the Fifteenth Amendment.

## 20 Jim Crow

Jim Crow was the name of a comic Vaudeville character of a white comedian whose act mocked African-American stereotypes. During Reconstruction the character's name came to symbolize the institutionalized racism of the Solid South. As each southern state was restored to self-government, the Democratic Party enacted restrictions on the personal freedom and on the new constitutional rights of the freedmen. These laws included poll taxes and literacy tests that disenfranchised African-American voters. In addition to losing their right to vote, segregation laws deeply divided southern society by banning African-Americans from public facilities like schools, restaurants, transportation, and even restrooms and water fountains. As the grip of these laws returned freedmen almost to the impotence of their life as slaves, Jim Crow was a descriptor for all of southern society after Home Rule was reestablished and the North ended efforts at Reconstruction.

## The Big Picture

1. The period known as Reconstruction proved to be a difficult era of social, political, and economic strife as the country tried to heal the wounds of the Civil War.

2. The main political battles occurred between the restored national political parties but also between the executive and legislative branches of the federal government.

3. Radical Republicans were intent on punishing the South for starting the Civil War and enacted reform laws, policies, and even constitutional amendments while they held a powerful majority in the U.S. Congress.

4. The capacity for change in southern society regarding the status of African-Americans was severely hampered by racism and the difficulty in rebuilding the southern economy without the institution of slavery.

5. Crippling laws and poor economic conditions reduced the freedmen of the South to a status not far removed from that of slaves, and African-Americans found themselves working on plantations without voting or other civil rights and with little to no opportunities to advance.

# The Settlement of the West

*Hear me, my Chiefs! I am tired; my heart is sick and sad.*
*From where the sun now stands I will fight no more forever.*
—Chief Joseph of the Nez Perce Tribe, surrender speech, 1877

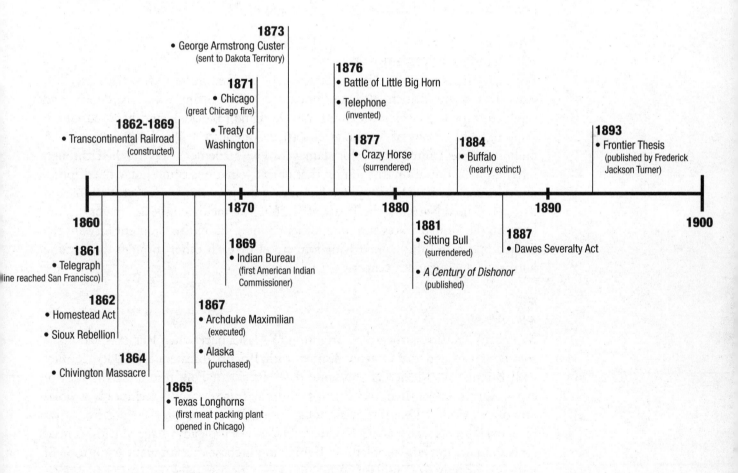

**1873**
• George Armstrong Custer
(sent to Dakota Territory)

**1871**
• Chicago
(great Chicago fire)

• Treaty of
Washington

**1862-1869**
• Transcontinental Railroad
(constructed)

**1876**
• Battle of Little Big Horn

• Telephone
(invented)

**1877**
• Crazy Horse
(surrendered)

**1884**
• Buffalo
(nearly extinct)

**1893**
• Frontier Thesis
(published by Frederick
Jackson Turner)

**1860**

**1870**

**1880**

**1890**

**1900**

**1861**
• Telegraph
(line reached San Francisco)

**1869**
• Indian Bureau
(first American Indian
Commissioner)

**1881**
• Sitting Bull
(surrendered)

• *A Century of Dishonor*
(published)

**1887**
• Dawes Severalty Act

**1862**
• Homestead Act

• Sioux Rebellion

**1867**
• Archduke Maximilian
(executed)

• Alaska
(purchased)

**1864**
• Chivington Massacre

**1865**
• Texas Longhorns
(first meat packing plant
opened in Chicago)

# Top 20 Things to Know

## 1 Archduke Maximilian

Maximilian was a clear example of the difficulty of placing an extra Hapsburg brother of an emperor of Austria in meaningful work fit for royalty. His career in the navy led him to travel widely, rub shoulders with the emperor of France, and get caught up in leading the joint kingdom of Lombardy-Venice after a revolution there. When his brother disapproved, Maximilian went back to running the Austrian Navy. In the unrest following Napoleon's placing his family in positions of power and the revolutions of 1848, the Hapsburg family forged alliances with the Bonapartes. It fell to Maximilian to be sent to Mexico in 1863 to bring stability to the region the Spanish had pushed toward ruin. The government of Mexico owed money to France (and to the United States), but Maximilian's presence antagonized the Mexican people. In an uprising he was executed in 1867. William H. Seward had voiced support for deposing Maximilian because the presence of a new European ruler in Central America was a violation of the Monroe Doctrine.

## 2 Treaty of Washington

British relations with the United States were strained at best after the Civil War years because the British, although not directly supporting the Confederacy, had supplied ships with which the South ran the Union blockade and harassed Union shipping. The Treaty of Washington settled American claims by granting $15.5 million to the United States for damages. The settlement was reached through international arbitration, the notion that objective nations could judge the disputes of other nations to achieve peace. The idea grew into the League of Nations and then the United Nations. The Treaty of Washington mediated the last major dispute between the United States and her mother country. From this moment forward the United States and the United Kingdom stood by each other through the coming horrors of the twentieth century.

## 3 Alaska

Americans had first turned their attention to Alaska back when Russians had made colonies there and the Oregon dispute with Britain threatened military conflict with Britain and Mexico at the same time. President Polk restrained the idea of expansion to Alaska then, but Russia's continued presence was technically a violation of the Monroe Doctrine even though relations with Russia were positive. After the Civil War, Secretary of State William H. Seward took advantage of Russia's need for cash in her imperial problems in Europe to purchase this last giant acquisition of territory for only $7.2 million. While most Americans could not conceive of what could come from a frozen wilderness one fifth the size of the rest of the country, Seward's Folly, as the purchase was known, not only prevented instability in Russia from opening up a new foothold for other European powers in North America, but opened up vast mineral wealth. Alaska's natural resources are still largely untapped even after the Klondike gold rush and an oil boom.

## 4 Indian Bureau

Created by John C. Calhoun in the War Department back in 1824, the Indian Bureau was the agency managing the interaction of the United States with over five hundred American Indian tribes. In 1849, the Bureau was transferred to the Department of the Interior, and after the Civil War its agenda was to assimilate American Indians into American life by working to end tribal governments and communal ownership of land. Bureau agents were supposed to Christianize and civilize those in their charge, but during the Gilded Age most agents skimmed off the top of the supplies they were given for their wards. The Indian Bureau did not have a commissioner who understood and appreciated tribal cultures until 1869, and even then it was not until 1934 that the Indian Reorganization Act sought to restore tribal governments. Through the long history of territorial and cultural conflict between American Indians and the United States, tribes were considered foreign powers operating under the sanctions of the original treaties negotiated as civilization advanced. The 1924 Indian Citizenship Act, however, transferred to all American Indians the same citizenship rights protected in the Fourteenth Amendment.

## 5 Sioux Rebellion

The Dakota Sioux recognized that their Indian Bureau agents on their Minnesota reservation were unscrupulous. All game on the reservation was hunted to extinction, and the Sioux were near starvation, yet the agents would not release warehouses filled with food. The agents had designed to sell the food to white pioneers. In 1862, young Sioux warriors left the reservation and killed a family on a neighboring farm. Minor victories over responding American forces encouraged wider resistance and sporadic fighting on the part of the Sioux. When the Sioux were once again defeated, thirty-eight of those responsible were hanged in what remains the largest mass execution in American history. The rest of the Sioux were split up and distributed to various new reservations. The whole episode illustrated the unfortunate circumstances of Gilded Age corruption exacerbating already tense relations between American Indians, who were considered savages, and the increasing numbers of white settlers.

## 6 Chivington Massacre

This event, otherwise known as the Sand Creek Massacre, was an unfortunate clash based on conflict, misunderstanding, and superior force. In the Colorado Territory in 1864 young Cheyenne and Arapaho warriors raided traffic traveling to and from Denver. The isolated citizens of Denver asked for rescue. The Cheyenne chief Black Kettle declared that he could not control his young warriors, and other chiefs negotiated a settlement requiring the Cheyenne to come to forts in the territory to register as a peaceful tribe. Black Kettle merely put an American flag and a white flag up over his tepee at a settlement of around five hundred warriors and their families at Sand Creek. Colonel John Chivington and seven hundred or more troopers descended on the technically unauthorized camp and killed around two hundred Indians, two-thirds of whom were women and children. In the review of his actions Chivington was found to have gone beyond his orders although he acted on a sentiment that was prevalent in the territory after the raids by the infamous Cheyenne Dog Soldiers. Although Chivington retired from the army before receiving any formal punishment, he faced divided opinions about his actions for the rest of his life. As for the Cheyenne, their power structure was undone by the massacre because of the loss of so many chiefs.

## 7 Crazy Horse

This Lakota Sioux chief was a fierce warrior even as a young man, and he led the resistance against the United States after 1876 when all Cheyenne and Sioux were ordered to go to reservations provided by the government from public lands. He was adamant about maintaining traditional Sioux ways even to the point of never allowing himself to be photographed. During the events leading up to the slaughter of Custer's force at Little Big Horn, Crazy Horse not only solidified the alliance between the Sioux and the Cheyenne, he personally led the war party that stopped the unification of Custer's forces. He then took his force to help Sitting Bull annihilate Custer and his Seventh Cavalry. After the campaign to subdue the Plains Indians was successful, however, Crazy Horse left the reservation without permission, was captured, and bayoneted to death in a struggle. The image of Crazy Horse is being captured in stone in a Mount Rushmore-size memorial to all American Indians, so his legacy will be the poignant reminder of the war on the Great Plains long into the future.

## 8 Sitting Bull

Sitting Bull was a Dakota Sioux medicine man and chief whose reservation in the Black Hills in South Dakota became the location of intense strife after the discovery of gold there. His vision partly inspired the resistance that led to the Battle of Little Big Horn in which he foresaw that all of the white soldiers would be killed. Escaping into Canada for a time, Sitting Bull held out until his tribe's resources were entirely expended by the demise of the buffalo. He was the last Sioux chief to surrender to federal authority. As late as 1885 Sitting Bull was famous as a novelty in Buffalo Bill's Wild West show. A revival of the traditional religion of the Sioux was manifested in a ceremony called the Ghost Dance during which Sioux warriors believed their shirts were made impervious to bullets. In the clashes that resulted from this inspiring but incorrect assumption, Sioux factions struggled for leadership of the movement. Sitting Bull was shot and killed in 1890, perhaps by rivals, while being arrested by American Indian police officers for being an ongoing symbol of resistance.

# 9 George Armstrong Custer

Little could match the tale of Custer's bravado and gallantry during the Civil War. He was the youngest general officer of the Union Army, a rank he achieved through repeated acts of daring that some called reckless. In total he had eleven horses shot from beneath him in his fourteen years of nearly constant warfare, plus one he accidentally shot from under himself. After the Civil War Custer headed the Seventh Cavalry in the war against the Sioux in which he planned an attack in the region of the Little Big Horn River and the Black Hills in South Dakota. Without knowing the strength of the united Sioux tribes, Custer divided his forces for a three-pronged attack on Sioux and Cheyenne settlements off their reservations. The villages together contained nine thousand Indians, approximately four thousand of whom were warriors. Custer, with 1,100 troopers, had calculated his odds were far better based on fraudulent Indian Bureau statistics submitted by crooked agents lining their own pockets. He and a third of his divided cavalry force numbering some 270 men were isolated and killed by the combined forces of Crazy Horse and Sitting Bull. The Battle of Little Big Horn was the most significant defeat inflicted by Indians in American history.

# 10 Battle of Little Big Horn

This battle, otherwise known as Custer's Last Stand, has been blamed on George Armstrong Custer's hot-headedness, but with false statistics from the Indian Bureau Custer assumed he would be facing a smaller enemy force than he found in 1876 in what would become Montana. He did divide his forces in the face of an enemy of unknown number and attacked without properly scouting in fear that the elusive Dog Warriors of Crazy Horse's renegade Sioux would escape. The pyrrhic nature of this victory in which Custer and his force of 267 men were killed was evident in that it confirmed in the American public's mind that the Plains Indians were savages who refused to cooperate with federal policy designed to keep the peace. Forgetting that the sudden influx of fifteen thousand miners into the sacred territory of the Black Hills had provoked the Sioux in the first place, the U.S. Army continued to hound them until both Sitting Bull and Crazy Horse were defeated. The Great Plains War continued with little public dissent until the Battle of Wounded Knee when another Sioux uprising ended in a massacre in 1890.

# 11 Buffalo

Properly called bison, these animals ranged across the Great Prairie of North America and were the source of sustenance for American Indians, especially when Europeans reintroduced the horse. Upwards of two hundred million buffalo are thought to have existed before this time. American Indians became proficient buffalo killers, but their cultural values mandated the killing of just what was needed and the use of nearly every part of each buffalo carcass. White hunters began actively killing buffalo for their hides in the nineteenth century. In the winter of 1872 alone 1.5

million buffalo were killed and their carcasses shipped east. Buffalo Bill earned his name by killing four thousand in just two years by order of the federal government that determined the solution to the American Indian problem was the elimination of the buffalo. The herds that used to range as far as the eye could see were reduced by 1880 to just a few thousand animals. The Great Plains Indians lost their way of life with the near extinction of this iconic American creature.

## 12 *A Century of Dishonor*

Helen Hunt Jackson was a Massachusetts novelist and friend of poet Emily Dickinson. However, with her 1881 nonfiction exposé, *A Century of Dishonor*, she became nearly the lone voice of protest against the treatment of American Indians during the nineteenth century. Her work catalogs the violations of treaties and other repressions that she was among the first to call a violation of American Indians' human rights. She traveled personally to collect data, presented her book to the Indian Bureau, and then sent a copy to every member of Congress. In the style of the antebellum humanitarian reformers, she lectured continually and advocated for better treatment for American Indians for the last four years of her life.

## 13 Dawes Severalty Act

In keeping with its policy to assimilate American Indians into American culture and to reduce the authority of tribal governments, the federal government abandoned the policy of giving land to tribes to be owned communally. The Dawes Act of 1887 granted 160 acres of land to heads of American Indian families as the Homestead Act had done for white settlers. American Indians were encouraged to farm their private land and to abandon their tribal affiliations and traditional religion. Just as with the Freedman's Bureau and the Indian Bureau, however, government ineptitude and corruption hampered the implementation of the Dawes Act that was abandoned. The attempt to turn Plains Indians into American citizens and farmers failed and for a time merely increased American Indian resistance.

## 14 Homestead Act

The federal government enacted this plank of the Republican Party's 1860 campaign platform by 1862. In an effort to encourage settlement of the West, the government surveyed 160-acre tracts of land for any twenty-one-year-old head of household, citizen or immigrant, who would work the land and reside there for five years. The only cost to the settler was a small registration fee. After six months, the land could be purchased outright for $1.25 per acre. The invention of barbed wire by Joseph Glidden in 1874 and the pacification of the Plains Indians helped settlers protect their lands from trespass. The era of long cattle drives over public lands ended as a result. Two-thirds of the homesteaders, however, failed to establish viable agriculture in the dry west, and much of the land given to private individuals was eventually sold to large companies and real estate speculators.

## 15 Frontier Thesis

Frederick Jackson Turner delivered a paper called "The Significance of the Frontier in American History" at a conference for historians in Chicago in 1893. His thesis for the paper stated that the frontier experiences had transformed American society and democracy into more robust institutions and Americans into rugged individualists. The essay was an expression of nationalism maintaining that Americans were to be distinguished from their European ancestors as more enterprising, dynamic, and innovative. The failure of many homesteaders, however, belied Turner's assertion that the frontier was a "pressure valve" that eased societal tension by giving any American with pluck the opportunity for a new life in the West.

## 16 Telegraph

Samuel F. B. Morse invented the telegraph in 1844, and he first successfully transmitted a message from Baltimore to Washington, D.C., about the nomination of James K. Polk for the presidency. By 1860, 50,000 miles of telegraph wire were strewn across America connecting most parts of the country to the communication revolution. A direct line almost 3,600 miles long connected New York to San Francisco in time to relay news about the Civil War to the West. The Western Union Telegraph Company monopolized the telegraph from that point on. Never had people been able to communicate virtually instantly over such vast distances before, and because the dots and dashes of Morse code could be perceived over greater distances on radio waves than the human voice, the influence of Samuel Morse outlasted the telegraph itself. A transatlantic cable laid between the United States and Great Britain in 1866 opened instantaneous communication with Europe. Subsequent cables were a chief source of information until they were replaced by satellite communication beginning in the 1960s.

## 17 Telephone

The invention of a teacher of the deaf, Alexander Graham Bell, the first practical telephone service connecting American cities was in place by 1877. There were nearly as many miles of telephone wires as telegraph wires by 1890, and by 1895 New York and Chicago were connected. Many smaller companies were consolidated into the American Telephone and Telegraph Company. The awareness of the need for time zones occurred because of the communication revolution and began as early as 1883. The boost to the American economy of the inventions of the telegraph and the telephone is impossible to calculate, but the ease with which business could be conducted granted America an advantage in achieving national and international markets.

## 18 Transcontinental Railroad

The first railroad line to span the continent was begun in 1862 by two companies and completed in 1869 with a ceremony at Promontory Point, Utah, near Salt Lake

City. The Central Pacific began in Sacramento, California, and had the daunting task of crossing the Sierra Nevada Mountains. The Union Pacific railroad was built from Omaha, Nebraska. The Union Pacific was built largely by Irish immigrants and the Central Pacific was built with the help of Chinese immigrants who came to California during the gold rush. Both crews built the many miles of track and all the trestles and bridges virtually by hand and often under the threat of American Indian attack. The transcontinental railroad when finished was considered the greatest civil engineering feat in American history to that time, and it reduced the time of travel across the continent from two months to ten days. National markets for all American products were achieved by 1874 as a result. Five transcontinental railroads existed by 1900. These railroads took homesteaders west and their products back east and contributed to the decimation of buffalo herds with shooting excursion trains. The Plains Indians resisted the construction of the railroad across their lands but held grudging admiration for a society that could bring such a machine into the wilds.

## 19 Texas Longhorns

These cattle were free-ranging by the time the West was being settled because the Spanish had left them, and the cattle's horns provided ample protection from predators. The wild cattle fed on the grasses of the Trans-Mississippi West until cowboys rounded them up on long drives to railheads for shipment to meat-packing plants in Chicago. Few such bonanzas of wealth in livestock have ever occurred, and the process continued until barbed wire closed off most of the land. The era of the cowboy was thus short but remains the most lasting iconographic image of the Wild West and of the capacity of America to tame the land but not all of its young men.

## 20 Chicago

The end of the line for the Texas longhorns and for swine and other livestock was at the meat-packing plants of Chicago. Because of its location near the origin of the first transcontinental railroad and on Lake Michigan, Chicago became the next great transportation hub in American history after New York City and New Orleans. Because of the network of railroads that centered on Chicago and because of the invention of the refrigerated railroad car, the United States became the first country to have an economy that provided meat in the daily diet of its average citizens. The meat-packing industry in Chicago was the setting for *The Jungle*, by Upton Sinclair, a book that rivals *Uncle Tom's Cabin* as a work that inspired radical change to American life and politics. Begun as a village in 1833 and achieving a population of over a million inhabitants by 1890, Chicago overcame the Great Fire that destroyed a third of its buildings to build the world's first skyscraper in 1885. Few other urban centers in history experienced such rapid growth.

## *The Big Picture*

1. After enduring the threat of the Civil War, the United States finally got down to the business of settling the vast lands acquired in the antebellum period, a process that lasted from 1862 to 1890.

2. White encroachment on tribal lands and territorial reserves of the Great Plains Indians touched off violent conflict that escalated from sporadic fighting to an intensive effort to eliminate the Plains Indian culture.

3. The availability of and increasing access to free land in the West set in motion one of history's vast human migrations as immigrants and citizens moved to take advantage of vast natural resources.

4. A communication and a transportation revolution accompanied westward migration and transformed the way in which Americans, and indeed all the people of the world, viewed space and time and lived their lives.

5. Because of the largely untapped resources of the West, the spanning of the continent with a railroad set in motion an incredible economic boom that built huge cities and distributed all American products to national markets by 1874.

# The New American Economy

# CHAPTER 20

*This, then, is held to be the duty of the man of wealth: . . . to consider all surplus revenues which come to him simply as trust funds . . . to administer in the manner which, in his judgment, is best calculated to produce the most beneficial results for the community. . . ."*
—Andrew Carnegie, "The Gospel of Wealth," 1889

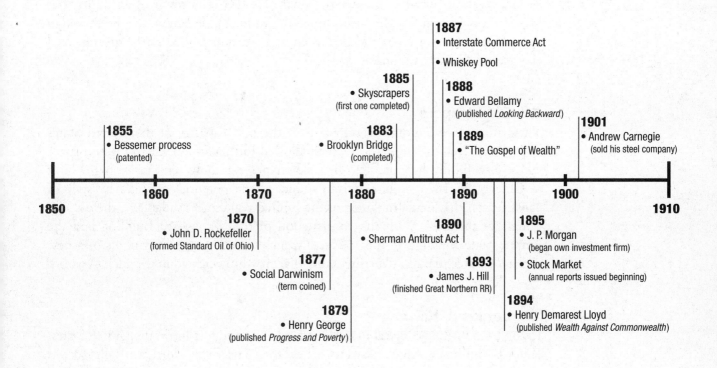

**1887**
• Interstate Commerce Act
• Whiskey Pool

**1885**
• Skyscrapers
(first one completed)

**1888**
• Edward Bellamy
(published *Looking Backward*)

**1855**
• Bessemer process
(patented)

**1883**
• Brooklyn Bridge
(completed)

**1889**
• "The Gospel of Wealth"

**1901**
• Andrew Carnegie
(sold his steel company)

1850    1860    1870    1880    1890    1900    1910

**1870**
• John D. Rockefeller
(formed Standard Oil of Ohio)

**1890**
• Sherman Antitrust Act

**1895**
• J. P. Morgan
(began own investment firm)
• Stock Market
(annual reports issued beginning)

**1877**
• Social Darwinism
(term coined)

**1893**
• James J. Hill
(finished Great Northern RR)

**1894**
• Henry Demarest Lloyd
(published *Wealth Against Commonwealth*)

**1879**
• Henry George
(published *Progress and Poverty*)

# Top 20 Things to Know

## 1  Patents

Originally a British idea, patents were instrumental in the expansion of the new American economy of the nineteenth century. The Founding Fathers sewed this incentive into the Constitution in 1790 along with copyright laws. Writers and inventors were thus assured the ability to benefit from their intellectual property and to defend their products from imitators. A total reorganization of patent law, along with the construction of a Patent Office, occurred in 1836 just in time for the spate of inventions and innovations that began to transform American industry and society. Both inventions and significant alterations of existing technology earned patents, and by the end of the nineteenth century thousands of patents were being issued annually.

## 2  Brooklyn Bridge

John Roebling was a manufacturer of steel cable who proposed the idea of spanning the East River in New York City with a suspension bridge, and he convinced city leaders that bridges were the key to growth. He died as a result of an injury, but his son, Washington Roebling, continued the work as chief engineer. The Brooklyn Bridge was begun in 1870 and dedicated in 1883 and ranked as the greatest civil engineering feat of its kind for decades.

## 3  Skyscrapers

These innovative buildings capitalized on the new capacity of the United States to produce steel, the strength of which allowed for maximum use of interior space and ever-climbing heights. The first skyscraper was only ten stories high, built in Chicago in 1874. Louis Sullivan unlocked the potential of this new style of construction that made the most of the limited real estate available in the old city centers of the East. With the construction of the Woolworth Building and the Empire State Building in the 1920s, skyscrapers became status symbols of a new civilization able to build structures taller than anything created in the ancient world.

## 4  James J. Hill

Rising from birth in a log cabin in Canada to fame and fortune in the United States, James J. Hill had a singular rags-to-riches story. His Great Northern Railroad was the only transcontinental line built without government assistance. He built the railroad in increments across the unchartered wilderness of the Rocky and Cascade Mountains in the United States and Canada. From 1878 until he reached Seattle in 1893, Hill built segments of the railway and then attracted settlers until each segment was prospering. Hill also innovated by building trunk lines off from his mainline to access specific mines, logging operations, and ranches. His mansion completed in 1891 was a far cry from the log cabin of his origins and at the time of completion the largest and most expensive home in all of Minnesota.

## 5 John D. Rockefeller

Rockefeller was a pioneer of the oil industry and of business combination. His company, Standard Oil of Ohio, became the model for all subsequent large corporations. Rockefeller capitalized on the new petroleum industry by building his first oil refinery with his own funds in 1863 in Cleveland. Standard Oil was a prime example of efficiency and technical innovation. By 1882 Rockefeller monopolized the oil industry through horizontal combination, and his success attracted attacks by individuals and regulation by the U.S. government. This notoriety culminated in the 1911 breakup of Standard Oil under the Sherman Antitrust Act. By 1897, however, Rockefeller had dedicated his life to philanthropy and before his death given more than $500 million to various foundations and charities.

## 6 Bessemer Process

American William Kelly invented a process whereby air was forced up through molten iron, raising the temperature and burning off more carbon to make steel. At the same time, Henry Bessemer had been making similar strides in Great Britain. After a bankruptcy, Kelly sold his patent to Bessemer who developed the process that was the height of steel-making technology in the nineteenth century. The Bessemer process allowed the cheaper manufacture of better steel, and readily available sources of steel were instrumental in the construction of railroads, bridges, and skyscrapers that formed the crucial infrastructure of the new American economy.

## 7 Stock Market

Bond trading in American history goes back at least to the American Revolution, and a market in such commodities has existed ever since. Private banks also raised capital by issuing stocks following the colonial model of a joint-stock company. Several merchants in New York City began trading these commodities in 1792 in the open air on Wall Street, and thus the New York Stock Exchange was born. The rapid growth of the American economy after the Civil War found companies hungry for sources of capital to expand their business. The chief source of this capital by 1900 was the sale of stocks on Wall Street, still conducted in the open air until 1921. By then investors realized that the stocks themselves could be bought and sold depending on the public perception of a company's soundness or potential for expansion. With some obvious setbacks, the stock market expanded throughout the twentieth century as a wealth builder for the rich and an overall reliable investment for the masses.

## 8 Andrew Carnegie

As a young Scottish immigrant to the United States, Carnegie mastered the telegraph with such skill that he became the personal secretary sending the messages of the manager of the Pennsylvania Railroad. Thus Carnegie learned business sense directly, and he saved money and made wise investments. He foresaw an opportunity in the iron bridges being built across the United States and entered the steel industry by use of the Bessemer process. His company by 1900 produced more steel than all of Great Britain, and through vertical combination employed 170,000 workers. After selling his steel company, Carnegie turned to philanthropy. He believed his funding of 2,500 public libraries across the country far more beneficial than merely giving money to poor individuals. He had gained much of his own education and personal growth by visiting a small library for working class youths. By the end of his life he had donated $350 million to various foundations and causes and is famous for his "Gospel of Wealth," an essay explaining his economic and societal views.

## 9 The Gospel of Wealth

Andrew Carnegie's manifesto expressed his firm belief that "The man who dies rich dies disgraced." Published in 1889, the essay explained his view that the amassing of large fortunes by capable entrepreneurs was a natural process with which the government should not interfere. The wealthy held their accumulated resources in trust and were by their accomplishments proven to be wise judges of how the wealth should be used for the benefit of the entire community that produced it. Considered inspirational at the time, the essay is now usually interpreted to be an egregious example of Social Darwinism.

## 10 Social Darwinism

A contemporary biologist with Charles Darwin, British philosopher Herbert Spencer coined the phrase "survival of the fittest." When he applied this notion to ethics and sociology, the theory of Social Darwinism was born. Spencer claimed that the rich deserved to be rich because of their superior capacity for adaptation, but most interpreters of his ideas could not help but see him as an elitist who associated being rich with being good. Critics of his philosophy said he was too quick to believe that whatever he observed in the natural world justified the abuse of the weak by the strong in human society. At best, the theories of Social Darwinism could be said to have both inspired the philanthropy of the great industrialists but also channeled the donations toward long-term productive ends rather than merely passing charity toward individuals. At worst, Social Darwinism was a justification for social engineering (including eugenics) and policies that unfairly favored the wealthy.

## 11 Robber Barons Versus Lions of Capitalism

A difficult yet crucial distinction to make is whether men like Rockefeller and Carnegie were heroes or villains. The great industrialists argued that the consolidation of their businesses was necessary to survive competition. They also parried envious attacks against their success by pointing to the fact that they were the only Americans who could accomplish the growth of the industrial strength of America that proved to be so crucial to the country's victories in the coming global conflicts. Their wealth, however, staggered the imagination in an era when there were no income taxes and no inheritance taxes; hence the phrase "Robber Baron" stemmed from the fact that inherited wealth was not earned and could establish an impregnable aristocracy threatening American democracy. The growing gap between the rich and the poor in nineteenth-century America made the majority of Americans suspicious of the industrialists despite their philanthropic endeavors. The political views of the major parties in the twentieth century were largely shaped by the nineteenth-century debate over the wealth created by the rise of big business, the use of that wealth for gaining political influence, and the attempts to check the economic and political power of the trusts.

# 12 Whiskey Pool

Distilleries in the late 1800s sought to reduce competition in an effort to maintain a strong demand for whiskey and thus a higher price. A pool was an informal alliance of producers in any industry, even railroads, who agreed to share markets at specified rates, and among whiskey distillers the pool agreed to reduce output in order to create an artificial shortage. Because the agreement was entirely based on the integrity of industry leaders willing to cheat the public, during economic downturns the members of the pool were also willing to cheat each other. In the Whiskey Pool this fact meant that some distillers secretly increased their production beyond what they agreed in order to garner more profits for themselves. The failure of some pool members to keep their word led many business leaders to seek a more binding form of business combination.

# 13 Horizontal Combination

This form of trust was maintained by industries that cooperated in business combinations consisting of many companies involved in the production of a given commodity. A single company, like Standard Oil of Ohio, would organize the trust based on its complete control over one step in the production process. In using horizontal combination, John D. Rockefeller invited the owners of other companies to sit on the Board of Directors of Standard Oil and thus to share in decisions and inside information regarding the entire oil industry. These interlocking directorates agreed on rates their companies would charge each other and the prices at which the commodity would be sold to the public. If any company stepped out of line, the trust could punish it by cutting it out of the system and replace it with a competitor that would stick to the plan.

# 14 Vertical Combination

A much simpler form of business monopoly occurred when a company owned facilities in every stage of the production process as did Andrew Carnegie in the steel industry and Gustavus Swift in the meat-packing industry. From ore mines to marketing of finished steel products, Carnegie employed experts and maintained state-of-the-art technology in each type of facility required to gather natural resources, transport them, and turn them into marketable shapes. The total control of a corporation by one man and his hand-picked managers permitted a maximum level of efficiency in an industry and thus both cheaper prices for consumers and higher profits for the company.

## 15 J. P. Morgan

One of the giant tycoons who was not a rags-to-riches self-made man, John Pierpont Morgan was a New England banker's son who was educated both in the United States and abroad. Morgan returned home and opened up a branch bank for his father in New York City just before the Civil War. By 1871 he had expanded his banking business with branches in London and Paris to become one of the leading banks in the world. He acquired companies and railroads as other men acquired farms or fine horses. Morgan's influence and wealth stabilized the entire American economy, especially during the Panics of 1893 and 1907 when he personally bailed out the U.S. Treasury. He purchased Carnegie's steel company and turned it into U.S. Steel. Always a target of envy and scrutiny, Morgan was the dark face of the Robber Baron class to those who believed such wealth and influence should not be under the control of one man.

## 16 Henry George

After a varied background as a seaman, typesetter, and prospector, Henry George settled down as a journalist and economic reformer. He originated the idea of a single tax in 1871, and by 1879 had published his theories in the book *Progress and Poverty.* The single-tax idea stemmed from George's belief that all people share the earth in common and thus the wealth derived from owning land should be the only source of tax revenue. He was thus opposed to taxation on the incomes of wage-earning laborers or any other form of tax other than property taxes on land. He believed that such a tax would raise sufficient revenue to operate the government while not burdening the classes of people who could least afford to pay. His ideas were never seriously applied in the United States but formed some of the incentive for Americans to move toward a graduated income tax.

## 17 Edward Bellamy

In an age where questions of wealth and class were experiencing dramatic debate, Bellamy promoted a utopian philosophy that he expressed in his 1888 novel, *Looking Backward.* In the bestselling book he posited that within one century the United States would have nationalized its economy, removed all class consciousness and strife, and equalized the distribution of wealth. Although his predictions proved false, in his day they inspired a new spate of utopian communities filled with intellectuals who once again proved that perfect societies could not exist on earth. Not revolutionary enough for actual Socialists like Eugene V. Debs, and not practical enough for the masses of Americans alienated by the elitist tendencies in Bellamy's vision, his ideas faded from popularity even before the nineteenth century ended.

## 18 Henry Demarest Lloyd

This minister's son was a graduate of law school who saw it as his calling to wield his pen against the societal injustices he observed around him in New York City and

Chicago. Lloyd was thus a forerunner of the muckraking journalists associated with Progressivism. He scooped Ida Tarbell by writing about the practices of Standard Oil of Ohio through the 1870s and 1880s while he was on the staff of the *Chicago Tribune.* He used these exposé articles as the background for his most famous book, *Wealth Against Commonwealth*, published in 1894. In this regard Lloyd could have been merely an investigative journalist, but his work championing the cause of laborers inspired the likes of Samuel Gompers, the leader of the American Federation of Labor. His defense of the accused in the Haymarket Square Riots cost him his job at the *Tribune* even though his father-in-law was the one doing the firing. His journalism turned into activism, which led to his being a Populist candidate for president, but never quite a Socialist. Upon his death, however, his son helped found the Communist Labor Party of America. Just as H. L. Mencken would later inspire the Lost Generation of the 1920s, Lloyd's work inspired Progressive journalists and politicians alike.

## 19 Interstate Commerce Act

As the centrality of railroad companies to the success of the American economy became evident in the 1870s, the practices of railroads came under close scrutiny. States attempted to regulate railroad rates and other policies within their borders, but railroads defied these regulations saying that their business was interstate, not intrastate, and they should not be subject to state laws. The Supreme Court decided in *Munn v. Illinois* in 1877 that state laws and regulations did apply, but the Congress went further with the Interstate Commerce Act. If a railroad went beyond a single state's border, the law said the rates charged had to be just and that pools were illegal. To monitor such behavior the law called into being the first federal regulatory agency in American history, the Interstate Commerce Commission. By the end of the nineteenth century, however, corporate lawyers working for railroads had devised ways to circumvent the actions of the Commission, which was reduced to a bureau collecting statistics as a result.

## 20 Sherman Antitrust Act

As a sign of the response to large business combinations, Senator John Sherman of Ohio was able to garner widespread support for this law in 1890. It stated that "Every contract, or conspiracy, in restraint of trade or commerce among the several states, or with foreign nations, is hereby declared illegal." The law authorized the federal court system to prosecute trusts thought to be guilty of monopolistic conspiracies. With a legacy of federal judges placed by Gilded Age Republican presidents, however, the ambiguity of terms like *trust* and *restraint* led to few trusts being prosecuted before 1901. Only eighteen suits were pursued, and four of those were against labor unions. Once trustbuster Theodore Roosevelt arrived on the scene, however, this law became (and remains) the chief legal grounds for enforcing federal regulatory policy.

## The Big Picture

1. Profound developments in technology and infrastructure engineering led to a dramatic expansion of the American economy after the Civil War.

2. Individuals who organized large business enterprises formed giant corporations that allowed them to amass immense personal fortunes.

3. In the face of competition in major industries, industrialists combined markets and resources to stabilize the business cycle, maintain efficiency, and support long-term economic growth.

4. The growing gap between the rich and the poor as a result of the rise of big business led to the search for the means to regulate business practices and to limit the economic and political power of individual business tycoons and their trusts.

5. The U.S. Congress passed legislation that clarified the power of the federal government to control corporations by monitoring business practices and by prosecuting monopolistic conspiracies in the federal courts.

# Gilded Age Politics

# CHAPTER 21

*Everybody is talkin' these days about Tammany men growin' rich on graft, but nobody thinks of drawin' the distinction between honest graft and dishonest graft.*
—George Washington Plunkitt, in the *New York Evening Post*, 1905

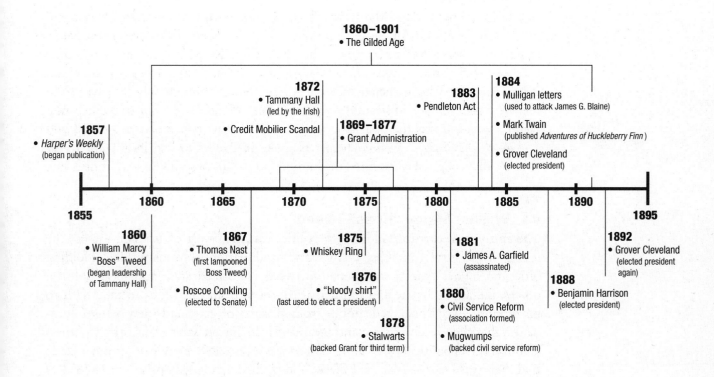

**1860–1901**
• The Gilded Age

**1872**
• Tammany Hall
(led by the Irish)

• Credit Mobilier Scandal

**1869–1877**
• Grant Administration

**1883**
• Pendleton Act

**1884**
• Mulligan letters
(used to attack James G. Blaine)

• Mark Twain
(published *Adventures of Huckleberry Finn*)

• Grover Cleveland
(elected president)

**1857**
• *Harper's Weekly*
(began publication)

1855    1860    1865    1870    1875    1880    1885    1890    1895

**1860**
• William Marcy
"Boss" Tweed
(began leadership
of Tammany Hall)

**1867**
• Thomas Nast
(first lampooned
Boss Tweed)

• Roscoe Conkling
(elected to Senate)

**1875**
• Whiskey Ring

**1876**
• "bloody shirt"
(last used to elect a president)

**1878**
• Stalwarts
(backed Grant for third term)

**1881**
• James A. Garfield
(assassinated)

**1880**
• Civil Service Reform
(association formed)

• Mugwumps
(backed civil service reform)

**1888**
• Benjamin Harrison
(elected president)

**1892**
• Grover Cleveland
(elected president
again)

# Top 20 Things to Know

## 1 The Gilded Age

This phrase, taken from the title of a book by Mark Twain, reflected the nature of the era from 1865 to 1900 so well that historians seized on it as the basis for their own interpretations. The postwar time period was one of rapid, unprecedented economic growth, hence the golden exterior. The undue influence of business tycoons in politics as well as the corrupt actions of politicians from both major parties formed the dark inner core of American power. Although the standard of living rose considerably for most Americans, the cost of living rose also. A wide gap developed between the upper and lower classes, and local, state, and federal government agencies and leaders were often steeped in scandals involving expanding the privileges and profits of the wealthy at the expense of the working class.

## 2 Mark Twain

The Gilded Age was also Mark Twain's era, a time when this southern writer could say, "I am not just an American; I am *the* American." Mark Twain was a pen name, taken from steamboat parlance on the Mississippi River, for Samuel Langhorne Clemens. Twain was a humorist and novelist who began as a newspaperman and steamboat pilot who gathered material for his books through traveling widely in the West and abroad. His famous works include *Huckleberry Finn* (a book Ernest Hemingway said was the first American novel), *Roughing It, Innocents Abroad,* and *Life on the Mississippi.* Twain's characters spoke in dialect to add local color to his writings that collectively captured the humor and pathos of southern and frontier life.

## 3 William Marcy "Boss" Tweed

The epitome of corrupt Gilded Age politics was the career of William Tweed, the leader of the New York City Democratic headquarters, Tammany Hall. Holding office no higher than a state senator, Tweed controlled state and local political offices and allotted state and municipal contracts from the 1850s to the 1870s to his cronies. Tweed pocketed money from all sorts of graft and then bought companies that then received state and local contracts for business. A favorite victim of Thomas Nast's political cartooning, Tweed was arrested after some of his inner circle told their story to *The New York Times,* and he died in a federal prison in 1878 after being convicted for 204 of the 220 charges against him.

## 4 Tammany Hall

The name for the headquarters of the Democratic Party in New York City was likely taken from that of an American Indian chief. Tammany Hall was the epicenter of the Tweed Ring's exploits. The Tweed Ring consisted of William Tweed, George Washington Plunkitt, and other corrupt managers who not only selected who would run for which office, but used unscrupulous practices to fix who would win. The Tweed Ring stole between $75 million and $200 million from taxpayers for overcharged bills, false vouchers, fake contracts, and kickbacks from real contracts.

# 5 Credit Mobilier Scandal

In 1864 executives of the Union Pacific Railroad organized a construction company called the Credit Mobilier for building their part of the transcontinental railroad. Even though the leaders of the railroad and the construction company were the same individuals, the construction firm kept charging higher prices that the railroad passed onto the taxpayer through a deal with Congress. By 1873 an investigation was underway, but Vice President Schuyler Colfax diverted it, a service for which he was given stock in the railroad.

# 6 Grant Administration

Having led the Union Army to victory in the Civil War, Ulysses S. Grant won the presidency in 1868 and again in 1872, the second time with the help of the newly enfranchised black voters of the South. His judgment of men's character, however, was less well developed than his military prowess. Grant's advisers, cabinet members, and staff saw their monopoly on power as an opportunity to become wealthy. Although remaining above suspicion, Grant had the first scandal-ridden presidency in American history with the Credit Mobilier scandal and the Whiskey Ring scandal originating under his nose. His brother-in-law also attempted to engineer a run on gold reserves after Jay Gould and Jim Fisk conspired to buy up as much gold as possible in order to profit from a bull market. Grant was an honest man who ended as a failure in the presidency because his associates destroyed the moral high ground the Republican Party had enjoyed since the Emancipation Proclamation. Although Grant did crack down on the Ku Klux Klan in the South, he was unable to bring about any serious change in the condition of freedmen under the rule of Jim Crow.

# 7 Whiskey Ring

One of Grant's own appointees ran a conspiracy among revenue agents and whiskey distillers to tip off the Whiskey Ring when tax inspections were scheduled. The plot originated in St. Louis but was modeled in other major cities around the country. As more and more inspections turned up empty warehouses, the secretary of the treasury ordered an investigation. When evidence of corruption began to surface, President Grant said, "Let no guilty man escape." In total 238 people were indicted for their participation including Orville E. Babcock, the president's private secretary who had been bribed. Babcock avoided prosecution because President Grant testified on his behalf.

## 8 Civil Service Reform

A Civil Service Commission was formed as early as 1871, but the federal agency designed to ferret out political corruption instead fell prey to it. The first commission was disbanded after its chairman resigned when his investigations were ignored by the Grant administration. Only after the assassination of President James Garfield did the continued clamoring for reform take the shape of actual legislation. The Pendleton Act was the first concrete step in a long road of making it more difficult for corrupt politicians and civil servants to get away with graft. Not until Theodore Roosevelt was placed on a new Civil Service Commission by Benjamin Harrison did the agency begin to perform it duties thoroughly.

## 9 *Harper's Weekly*

A prime example of an early news magazine, *Harper's Weekly* was published by four brothers (the Harpers) and had a circulation of over two hundred thousand by the outbreak of the Civil War. Along with political commentary, the magazine launched the career of the cartoonist Thomas Nast. The magazine was so influential in spreading Republican Party ideas that it was said to be responsible for the elections of Ulysses S. Grant and Rutherford B. Hayes. Perhaps it was more the influence of Thomas Nast's cartoons, for when Nast switched his support to Grover Cleveland, Cleveland became the only Democrat elected to the presidency in the entire Gilded Age.

## 10 Thomas Nast

Illustrator and cartoonist Thomas Nast was a German immigrant intent on making his adopted country free from the evils of political corruption and other societal ills. He worked for *Harper's Weekly* for twenty years and established such lasting icons as the Democratic donkey, the Republican elephant, the image of Santa Claus, and that of Uncle Sam himself. Nast distorted the features of those he wanted to attack and thus created the genre of caricature. He was instrumental in the downfall of Boss Tweed even after Tweed offered him a $200,000 bribe to stop making the unflattering pictures.

## 11 Roscoe Conkling

A New York lawyer and Radical Republican congressman, Conkling rose through the House of Representatives and the Senate to become a chief adviser to President Grant. His abrasive personality and flamboyant style limited his success in the Victorian Era, but he was to the Republican Party what Boss Tweed was to the Democrats, the quintessential grafter. He disbursed patronage for the Stalwart segment of the Republican Party, a group sometimes known as the Conklingites. Republicans like Rutherford B. Hayes, James G. Blaine, and James Garfield began to pull their party out of his clutches, and as civil service reform became more popular with the public, Conkling was not returned to the Senate by the legislature of New York.

## 12 Stalwarts

The Stalwarts were the wing of the Republican Party fully in agreement with Democrat Andrew Jackson's notion that "To the victor belong the spoils." Appointments, contracts, grants, and other privileges were the bread and butter of patronage within a political party that maintained its power for so long. Roscoe Conkling led the Stalwarts, and Grant's men used the system of graft to exchange influence and preferences for votes.

## 13 Mugwumps

Otherwise known as the Half-Breeds, this wing of the Republican Party favored civil service reform. James Garfield led the fight by standing against Conkling in regard to appointments within his administration and even in what amounted to the Tammany Hall of the New York Republican Party, the New York Customs House. Garfield installed Half-Breed Republicans against Conkling's recommendations, and Conkling resigned from the Senate in protest.

## 14 James A. Garfield

A decent man and a Civil War veteran with a distinguished military record, Garfield became a lawyer in Ohio and then a congressman. He used his oratorical skills to begin to chip away at his own party's corruption, and he even escaped scandal when accusations about his involvement in the Credit Mobilier Scandal proved groundless. He was elected to the Senate in 1880 and immediately to the presidency. His campaign included as vice president Chester A. Arthur, a notorious Stalwart from the New York Customs House, as a concession to unify the party. When Garfield was assassinated by Charles Guiteau, the killer said, "I am a Stalwart, and now Arthur is president!" Since Garfield was ending gratuitous patronage, Guiteau had been rejected for a job, so Garfield became a martyr for the civil service reform movement.

## 15 Pendleton Act

Garfield's assassination made even many Stalwarts favor reform in the face of Democratic advances and public outcry. Senator George Pendleton sponsored this bill that called for a new Civil Service Commission. The commission was to have three administrators to guard against patronage by, among other things, issuing competency tests for prospective civil servants. By the time the bill made it through the Congress, the Pendleton Act issued exams for only one-tenth of federal jobs. With this start, however, future presidents were able to expand this amount and create a civil service hiring process based more on merit than on patronage. Chester Arthur signed the Pendleton Act into law but set about dispensing patronage in the form of jobs just as if he were back at the New York Customs House.

## 16 "Bloody Shirt"

In an age when political oratory was more eloquent but also more melodramatic, "waving the bloody shirt" was a rhetorical device that reminded listeners that the southerners who started the Civil War were Democrats. This device preserved the grip of the Republican Party on power in the federal government throughout the Gilded Age. The phrase is thought to have been developed when a Massachusetts member of the House of Representatives was given a blood-stained shirt from a carpetbagger in the South who had been attacked by the Ku Klux Klan.

## 17 Grover Cleveland

The only president to win nonconsecutive terms, Grover Cleveland had been the reform governor of New York. As president he had the odd distinction of being a conservative Democrat holding Republicans in check in the Congress. He fought off attempts to expand the federal government as an instrument of welfare for individuals, even Civil War veterans, saying that such expenditures would only encourage dependency on the government. His desire to reduce the tariff cost him the support of reform-minded Republicans, and Benjamin Harrison won a term in between Cleveland's two. When he regained the presidency, Cleveland walked straight into the Panic of 1893, the worst depression the country had ever seen. He is one of two presidents to seek the support of J. P. Morgan to jump-start the Treasury and stabilize the currency (Theodore Roosevelt did, too). Grover Cleveland not only did not support striking workers during the panic, he sent in troops to disperse them. He was also so conservative as to reject the annexation of Hawaii and to return the nation closer to the gold standard by leading the effort to repeal the Sherman Silver Purchase Act. No other type of Democrat would have been able to wrest control away from the Republicans during the Gilded Age. For all his principles regarding civil service reform, Cleveland was depressed to find a long line of Democratic job seekers outside his office from the first day of his presidency.

## 18 Mulligan Letters

During the election of 1876 and again in 1884, these letters to and from a bookkeeper, James Mulligan, haunted James G. Blaine. Mulligan testified about the letters and gave oral testimony about Blaine's grafting days as the Speaker of the House of Representatives. Curiously, Blaine had written at the bottom of the letters, "Burn this letter," which was an invitation for the detail-oriented Mulligan to keep the letters for blackmail. When exposed to the public these letters were used by the Democrats to vilify Blaine and were partly responsible for Cleveland's victory.

## 19 Benjamin Harrison

This grandson of William Henry Harrison was also a warrior who led an Indiana regiment in the Civil War. This background is perhaps why he backed Cleveland's civil service reforms but not the Democrat's (and draft dodger) desire to roll back pensions for Union Army veterans. Although pro-imperialism, pro-tariff, and pro-silver policies marked him as opposed to Cleveland's core principles, Harrison's greatest act for reform was placing Theodore Roosevelt on the Civil Service Commission.

# 20 Custodial Presidency

This term was used to define the role of the presidents of the Gilded Age, collectively known as the "forgotten presidents" or merely custodial in their impact. After Lincoln and before Theodore Roosevelt was a difficult time to make a lasting impression on the country, but the nature of the Gilded Age was one of maintaining the status quo. In an era when the only winning Democrat was also a conservative, most presidential tickets presented much the same policies for governing as did their opponents. The executive branch of the federal government waned in power while Congress waxed, and behind Congress stood the industrialists and their wealth.

## The Big Picture

1. The Gilded Age was an era of unprecedented economic growth, but nearly one-party rule on the federal level and the duplicity of individual politicians led to an atmosphere of rampant corruption.

2. The political corruption of the Gilded Age extended from either giving undue influence and privileges to one's political supporters or merely stealing taxpayer money through falsified accounting practices.

3. The rise of the importance of investigative journalism was evident in the success of writers, humorists, and even cartoonists who used satire and statistics to expose political hypocrisy and conspiracy.

4. The attempt to reform government and purge it from corruption did not gain ground until after the assassination of a president by a frustrated job seeker, and even then those involved in graft were slow to relinquish their abuses of power.

5. If the control of the federal government by Democrats in the early nineteenth century led to the Civil War, the control by the Republicans in the Gilded Age proved that prolonged periods of unchecked power in the hands of either party were detrimental to the nation.

# Mini Quiz

1. Abraham Lincoln did not consider the abolition of slavery as an option at the beginning of the Civil War because he

   (A) wanted abolition but had no plan for what to do with the freed slaves.
   (B) knew there was no serious support for abolition in the North.
   (C) feared that the slave states still in the Union would also secede.
   (D) knew slavery was necessary to supply cotton to the textile mills of the North.
   (E) did not think the country could afford to pay compensation to slave owners.

2. The Union strategy to conquer the South in the Civil War was called the
   (A) Ten Percent Plan.
   (B) Border State Plan.
   (C) McClellan Plan.
   (D) Anaconda Plan.
   (E) Elephant Plan.

3. The most devastating turning point for the Confederacy came

   (A) at Shiloh in Tennessee where more Americans fell than in all previous wars.
   (B) with Sherman's devastating March to the Sea from Atlanta to Savannah.
   (C) at Gettysburg and Vicksburg ending Southern offenses and control of the Mississippi.
   (D) at Antietam, the bloodiest single day of the war.
   (E) at First Bull Run, when Stonewall Jackson was accidentally killed.

4. The Freedman's Bureau's main success came with which one of its initiatives?

   (A) Creating the first systematic effort to educate African-Americans in southern history
   (B) Confiscating plantation land and redistributing it to former slaves
   (C) Overseeing work relations between former slaves and their new employers
   (D) Providing basic necessities for former slaves and war refugees
   (E) Initiating African-Americans' entry into the political process

5. All of the following realities were limitations on the rise of freedmen out of slavery toward a new social standing EXCEPT

   (A) southern society in general maintained a belief in white supremacy.
   (B) southern racism had a repressive militant wing in the Ku Klux Klan.
   (C) the theories of American followers of Charles Darwin encouraged even northern racism.
   (D) the readily viable economic arrangement of sharecropping strongly resembled slavery.
   (E) the Radical Republicans in Congress did nothing to elevate the status of former slaves.

6. President Andrew Johnson was impeached because he

   (A) held strong views against Reconstruction's goals.
   (B) believed the South had never successfully seceded and blocked the return of the states.
   (C) was guilty of a high crime and misdemeanor and the U.S. Constitution had to be followed.
   (D) wrestled with the Congress for control of the Reconstruction process.
   (E) exceeded the powers of the executive branch according to the Supreme Court.

7. The most severe blow to the American Indians in the Great Plains War was the

   (A) completion of the transcontinental railroad.
   (B) Dawes Severalty Act's enticing of American Indians away from tribal loyalties.
   (C) Sand Creek, or Chivington, Massacre.
   (D) near extinction of the American bison through deliberate slaughter.
   (E) execution of thirty-eight chiefs after the Sioux Rebellion was crushed.

8. Where were most of the cattle rounded up by cowboys in Texas taken for slaughter in the years following the Civil War?

   (A) Abilene
   (B) Baltimore
   (C) Chicago
   (D) Denver
   (E) New York City

9. Which treaty brought lasting peace between Great Britain and the United States?

   (A) The Treaty of Paris, 1783
   (B) Jay's Treaty
   (C) The Treaty of Ghent
   (D) The Webster-Ashburton Treaty
   (E) The Treaty of Washington

10. The "Gospel of Wealth" by Andrew Carnegie was an argument for what principle?

   (A) Government regulation of business through redistribution of wealth
   (B) Leaving the decision of the use of wealth to philanthropic capitalists
   (C) Consolidation of all corporations through vertical integration
   (D) The amassing of vast fortunes by families over generations
   (E) The role of providence in determining which individuals would become wealthy

11. Which individual was the strongest and most influential financier through the Gilded Age?

   (A) Andrew Carnegie
   (B) John D. Rockefeller
   (C) J. P. Morgan
   (D) Samuel C. T. Dodd
   (E) Cornelius Vanderbilt

12. Which law eventually became the most successful in checking the power of big business?

   (A) The Sherman Antitrust Act
   (B) The Sherman Silver Purchase Act
   (C) The Interstate Commerce Act
   (D) The Clayton Antitrust Act
   (E) The Morrill Land Grant Act

13. The cover up of the Credit Mobilier Scandal occurred when the

   (A) Central Pacific Railroad lied about who was constructing their railroad.
   (B) former Union military officer building the Union Pacific was cleared by President Grant.
   (C) owners of the railroad company gave stock in their company to Vice President Colfax.
   (D) Credit Mobilier board of directors turned on the owners of the Union Pacific Railroad.
   (E) attorney general received kickbacks from both transcontinental railroad companies.

14. Which Gilded Age president was assassinated by a frustrated office seeker as a result of the graft of the spoils system?

(A) Ulysses S. Grant
(B) Rutherford B. Hayes
(C) Chester A. Arthur
(D) James A. Garfield
(E) William McKinley

15. How did the Pendleton Act seek to reform the civil service?

(A) By preventing labor unions from contributing to the campaigns of political candidates
(B) By preventing corporations from contributing to the campaigns of political candidates
(C) By forcing presidential administrations to honor the appointments of previous administrations
(D) By preventing office holders from appointing friends and relatives to civil service jobs
(E) By requiring those working in the civil service to pass tests proving their competence

# Answer Explanations

1. **C** Lincoln guessed that the slave-owning border states would secede if he pressed for abolition and feared it because the South would likely win its independence if they did.

2. **D** The name of the Anaconda Plan referred to the process of blockading the South with the Union navy while dividing the Confederacy into thirds by taking the Mississippi River and the Shenandoah Valley to squeeze each third into submission.

3. **C** All of the choices occurred except Stonewall Jackson did not die at First Bull Run. Gettysburg and Vicksburg, however, were the dual blows suffered by the Confederacy from which even southerners realized they could not recover.

4. **A** Although answers B, C, and D were goals of the Freedman's Bureau, the success of these initiatives was limited. The Bureau did produce the first successful effort to educate large numbers of African-Americans in the South. Selection E was only indirectly a result of the Bureau's work.

5. **E** All of the other conditions were true, and although the Radical Republicans had other goals for the Thirteenth, Fourteenth, and Fifteenth Amendments and military occupation than just helping former slaves, their basic goal was to advance the social, economic, and political standing of African-Americans.

6. **D** Some of the selections have shades of truth in them, but the bottom line was that the Congress wanted Johnson out of the way so they could conduct a punitive Reconstruction plan without interference from the executive branch.

7. **D** Although all of the choices were part of the destruction of the Plains Indian cultures, the systematic destruction of the vast herds of bison accomplished its intended goal of breaking the capacity of the Plains Indians to resist federal authority.

8. **C** Although some of these other cities were a part of the long drives or destinations for the processed beef, Chicago became the meat-packing capital of America because the railroads running west converged there on the way to the large markets of the East.

9. **E** Serious conflicts between Great Britain and the United States erupted after each of these treaties except the Treaty of Washington that forged a peace that lasted until the present day.

10. **B** Andrew Carnegie would have disagreed all or in part with all the rest of the principles, and his essay made the case that successful businessmen were the citizens with the most wisdom about how the nation's surplus wealth should be used for the good of all.

11. **C**   J. P. Morgan was the only individual in the list that could be strictly classified as a financier, and he was even the strongest and most influential of all those in America who could be classified as financiers.

12. **A**   Although the Interstate Commerce Act and the Clayton Antitrust Act both tried to regulate businesses to prevent monopolistic behavior, only the Sherman Antitrust Act proved to be a workable piece of legislation despite its rocky start.

13. **C**   All of the other scenarios are merely plausible fabrications, whereas Schuyler Colfax did accept gifts of stocks in order to thwart the investigations into the allegations of corruption.

14. **D**   William McKinley was the only other assassinated president in the list, and he was killed by an anarchist, whereas Garfield was killed by a job seeker whom he had denied a position.

15. **E**   Although nearly all of these ideas have occurred to various reformers, only the civil service exam system became a reality and grew into a successful tool for warding off rampant corruption.

# The Revolt of the Common Man

CHAPTER

*. . .the union of the labor forces of the United States this day consummated shall be permanent and perpetual; may its spirit enter all hearts for the salvation of the republic and the uplifting of mankind!*
—*Populist Party Platform*, July 4, 1892

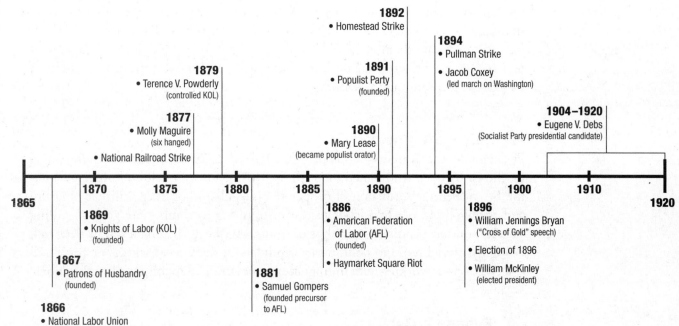

# Top 20 Things to Know

## 1 National Labor Union

Organized by the Boston machinist Ira Stewart, the National Labor Union was the first attempt to build a labor movement on a national scale. The National Labor Union met first in Baltimore in 1866 and declared their goal to be an eight-hour work day. Later labor movements would pursue this goal with the slogan, "Eight hours for work, eight hours for sleep, and eight hours for what we will." While the National Labor Union unraveled during the Panic of 1873, the federal government did begin a federal eight-hour work day for laborers and mechanics working on behalf of the United States.

## 2 Knights of Labor

Uriah Stephens began the Knights of Labor (KOL) in Philadelphia in 1871. Under Terence Powderly in 1879 the KOL included all industrial laborers, including skilled and unskilled workers, regardless of sex or race. Powderly preferred boycotts over strikes, and this tactic succeeded in forcing negotiations between the KOL and the Union Pacific Railroad in 1884. While more and more of the seven hundred thousand or so members of the KOL wanted to use strikes, Powderly urged them instead to educate themselves and stand together in brotherhood. The Haymarket Square Riot precipitated the decline of the KOL, and the American Federation of Labor rose to prominence as a result.

## 3 Terence V. Powderly

President of the Knights of Labor (KOL) from 1879 to 1893, Powderly was a machinist by trade who joined the KOL in 1872. More of a reformer than an agitator, he stressed the formation of cooperatives, regulation of trusts, currency reform, and the abolition of child labor instead of pushing for immediate goals regarding wages, working conditions, or shorter hours. As the KOL organization declined, Powderly turned more to politics as a candidate of the Greenback Labor Party and as a civil servant working with immigration issues under Republican administrations.

## 4 Eugene V. Debs

A railroad worker and socialist labor organizer, Debs organized the American Railway Union in 1893. He organized the Pullman Strike and was sentenced to jail for contempt of court for defying Cleveland's injunction to start the trains moving again. After his release he worked to establish the Social Democratic Party by 1897. Debs ran five times for the presidency as a Socialist and was sentenced to ten years in jail for violating the World War I Sedition and Espionage Acts. While there Debs received almost one million votes in the Election of 1920. Warren G. Harding had Debs released from jail after serving only three years but did not restore his citizenship. Debs edited Socialist periodicals until his death in 1926.

## 5 Molly Maguires

The Molly Maguires were a secret organization of miners imported from Ireland who began promoting labor violence in Pennsylvania as early as 1862. The Ancient Order of the Hibernians had been organized in Ireland to combat the encroachments of landlords, and when members of the Order migrated to the United States they employed intimidation tactics and murdered managers. The Philadelphia and Reading Railroad employed the Pinkerton Detective Agency to infiltrate the Molly Maguires. As a result, twenty-four of the organization's leaders were prosecuted. Fourteen spent from two to seven years in jail, and ten were hanged for murder. The reputation of all other labor movements suffered in the public eye because of the actions of subversive and violent individuals and groups like the Molly Maguires.

## 6 Pinkerton Detectives

Allan Pinkerton was a Scottish immigrant who stumbled on the hideout of a counterfeiting gang outside Chicago and thus began a career as a private detective. His successes led him to become the head of spying on the Confederacy during the Civil War after which he returned to his detective agency. The Pinkertons continued after the death of their founder and were often hired by large corporations to protect property and scabs, or workers hired to replace workers on strike. The use of armed Pinkerton detectives alienated corporate leaders like Andrew Carnegie even further from those sympathetic to labor interests.

## 7 National Railroad Strike

Just as railroads had many "firsts" as they formed the first giant corporations in American history, the first major strike also occurred in this industry. As a result of the Panic of 1873, railroads sought to cut costs by reducing workers' wages. The National Railroad Strike began in 1877 when the workers of the Baltimore and Ohio Railroad went on strike after receiving their second pay cut. The strike spread across the nation, and violence erupted. President Hayes even sent the U.S. military into West Virginia at the request of the governor, the first time a president intervened in a strike in this way. Hayes said he was protecting the U.S. Mail, but workers blamed him for merely protecting the railroad's private property. The strikers backed down, but an era of labor violence had begun.

## 8 Haymarket Square Riot

In Chicago in 1886, workers at the McCormick Harvesting Machine Company organized a strike trying to reduce their twelve-hour work days to the eight-hour Knights of Labor (KOL) goal. The first day of the strike demonstrators struggled with the police and a worker was killed. A second day of demonstrations was planned in protest of the killing, and around two thousand people assembled in Haymarket Square. When police advanced to clear the square, anarchists in the crowd threw a bomb that killed seven police officers and injured sixty. The two hundred policemen then fired into the crowd killing four and injuring dozens. Eight anarchists were put on trial and seven were sentenced to be executed. The KOL reputation was tarnished by the riot, and Americans assumed that anarchists and socialists filled the unions.

# 9 Samuel Gompers

Gompers's was the tale of millions of immigrants in that he arrived in New York City, a Dutch Jew from London, and lived in a tenement apartment. He picked up the trade of making cigars as a boy and by 1875 rose to be the local president of the international union for such workers. Gompers recognized the limitations of the Knights of Labor after the Haymarket Square Riot and in 1886 organized the American Federation of Labor (AFL), which became the most successful national labor organization in American history. Except for one year, Gompers was the president of the AFL from its founding until his death in 1924. Gompers stressed practical measures to achieve practical ends and distanced himself from the radical elements in the American labor movement.

# 10 American Federation of Labor

Under Gompers's leadership the American Federation of Labor (AFL) gained 150,000 members its first year. Much of the membership of the Knights of Labor (KOL) joined the AFL, and by his death Gompers led three million skilled workers in America's largest union. The AFL was a craft or trade union made up of unions of skilled workers who had organized together locally. Gompers said that skilled and unskilled workers had nothing in common. Furthermore, although Powderly and the KOL were not supposed to advocate strikes, the AFL readily used strikes and other forms of demonstrations to achieve shorter hours, higher wages, and safer working conditions. Before these victories, however, the AFL had to achieve recognition of their right to collective bargaining in the first place. The practical nature of the AFL approach and the leadership of Gompers went a long way in overcoming the negative reputation of labor unions.

# 11 Closed Versus Open Shop

A goal of many unions was to acquire complete compliance with all workers in a factory, mine, railroad, or other industrial facility working together as members of the same union. If every worker in the "shop" belonged, and if the union had negotiated with management the exclusion of all nonunion workers, the union was said to have achieved a "closed shop." Closed shops could conceivably demand higher wages, shorter hours, and better working conditions than the open shops where nonunion workers could still find work. Employers sought to prevent closed shops by issuing what unions called "yellow-dog contracts," or documents signed by prospective employees saying they would never join a union.

## 12 Homestead Strike

Although Andrew Carnegie had negotiated with unions among his workers, when he left his Homestead steel plant in the care of Henry Clay Frick, Frick took measures to break them. A workers' demonstration turned violent, and Frick closed down the plant in a "lockout." To protect the plant's property, Frick hired three hundred Pinkerton detectives who landed a barge at the plant's dock on the Monongahela River. The workers attacked, and three Pinkertons and seven workers were killed. The governor of Pennsylvania then called out the National Guard and after five months the workers gave in. Some Homestead workers were hired again, whereas many were "blacklisted" or placed on a list shared with other plants to prevent their ever securing jobs in the steel industry again. The Homestead plant was without a viable union for the next forty years as a result.

## 13 Pullman Strike

Eugene V. Debs called a strike against the Pullman Palace Car Company by the American Railway Union in 1894. In less than two weeks, every railroad in the Midwest was incapacitated. The attorney general sent in 3,400 men to move the trains and restart mail service, but violence broke out between these federal "scabs" and the striking workers. Grover Cleveland sent in federal troops to restore order, move the U.S. Mail, and to reestablish general commerce. A federal court backed the president's actions with an injunction, or court order, forbidding the interference with transit. When Debs resisted he was found guilty of contempt of court and jailed, and the strikers gave up. Nearly three hundred injunctions followed this method of ending strikes by 1928.

## 14 Jacob Coxey

Coxey was a Pennsylvania mill worker who opened a quarry in Ohio and became a successful businessman, reformer, and Populist political candidate. He ran for the House of Representatives, the Senate, the governorship, and the presidency, and lost every time. In the depths of the Panic of 1893, Coxey supported the idea of public works providing jobs for the poor by leading a march on Washington, D.C. He wanted the federal government to fund a road-building campaign to employ men who had lost jobs in the Depression. While his technique of a demonstration march would be picked up by dozens of causes, his own collection of around five hundred marchers were referred to as "Coxey's Army" and dispersed by the police immediately upon arriving in the national capital. Coxey and other leaders were arrested for trespassing in 1894. His actions generated national publicity but his proposals were ignored, that is, until the Great Depression when they were applied on a massive scale in the New Deal. Coxey did win one public office, the mayor of a small town.

## 15 Patrons of Husbandry

Otherwise known as the Grange, the Patrons of Husbandry was a secret fraternal organization designed to advance the interests of agriculture beginning in 1867. Farmers who joined the Grange sought to reduce the influence of corporate monopolies, especially railroads whose rates the Grangers wanted fixed with no rebates to large corporate shippers. Positive aims were the establishment of agricultural and mechanical universities and the cooperation of farmers in purchasing supplies and in marketing their products. Small merchants and other businessmen were also their allies in that they supported laws that made it illegal for a railroad to charge more for shipment of loads short distances than for long-distance loads. Such regulations were collectively known as Granger laws. Although the Patrons of Husbandry was not a political organization, the Populist Party sprang up from the collective action of farmers through their Grange chapters across the South and the West.

## 16 Populist Party

As the Patrons of Husbandry, or the Grange, developed political will they formed Farmers' Alliances and other national organizations to lobby for laws attacking eastern moneyed interests. By 1891 these efforts coalesced into the People's Party, otherwise known as the Populist Party. The Populist Party sought to unite industrial laborers and agricultural laborers in a movement to stand against the capitalists for the advancement of the common man. The first national convention of the new third party met in Omaha, Nebraska, in 1892 and selected James B. Weaver as its presidential candidate. The Populists wanted a long list of reforms that included a new national currency, the free coinage of silver, government ownership of all transportation and communication components, a graduated income tax, direct election of senators, shorter working hours for industrial laborers, and restrictions on immigration. While the new party lost the presidential election, they gained ground in the farming states, and even though their party did not live to see their ideas implemented, nearly every one of the Populist Party's issues from the 1892 platform became a part of American political and economic life.

## 17 Mary Lease

An early example of the new generation of politically active women, Mary Lease was a lawyer, orator, and founding member of the Populist Party leadership. Her potent quotes included "Raise less corn and more hell!" and "The country belongs to Wall Street." She gave over 160 speeches in the campaign to elect James B. Weaver whose nomination she had seconded at the national convention in Omaha. She resisted the Populist Party's self-destructive support for William Jennings Bryan in the Election of 1896, but she continued to fight for progressive causes including women's suffrage and prohibition.

## 18 William Jennings Bryan

An Illinois lawyer who backed the Democratic Party and the free coinage of silver, Bryan was elected to the Congress just as the Populist Party was getting started in his adopted state of Nebraska. His powers of oratory kept him in demand as a public speaker even after losing a bid for the Senate in 1894. At the Democratic National Convention in Chicago in 1896 he delivered his most famous "Cross of Gold" speech against the gold standard and for inflation as a means of easing the plight of farmers. He was awarded the nomination for the Democratic presidential candidate and launched a national speaking tour. His message gained the support of the Populists who were dismayed that their crusading hero went on to lose the election. He strove to obtain the presidency but rose only to be the secretary of state under Woodrow Wilson whom he served until Wilson went against the original position of U.S. neutrality in World War I. Bryan opposed the teaching of the theory of evolution in schools and appeared on the public stage one last time in the Scopes Trial in 1925, dying two weeks after winning the case for the prosecution but losing the war of ideas.

## 19 William McKinley

Civil War officer William McKinley became a lawyer in Ohio and ultimately served in the Congress and as the state's governor. He was a typical Republican Party political machine candidate for the presidency in 1896 after gaining attention supporting the protective tariff that bore his name in 1890. Marcus A. Hanna, the Ohio Republican boss, backed McKinley's candidacy on a platform of a high tariff and the gold standard for a sound currency. As president he signed the Dingley Tariff, the highest tariff rate in American history. He led the country through the Spanish-American War and won a second term to the presidency but was assassinated in 1901 by an anarchist.

## 20 Election of 1896

The next presidential election marking a turning point in American history, the Election of 1896 surpasses even the elections of 1800 and 1860 in the impact on the nation's direction. After William Jennings Bryan said at the Democratic convention, "You shall not press down upon the brow of labor this crown of thorns, you shall not crucify mankind upon a cross of gold!" the campaign became a battle between the silver interests, including farmers, and the urban capitalists in favor of the gold standard. Bryan traveled 13,000 miles through twenty-nine states and trumpeted about the debtor and the farmer while William McKinley sat in Ohio and campaigned for the creditor and sound money. The election results put yet another Gilded Age Republican in the presidency, but its real significance lay in who would be McKinley's vice president in his bid for a second term. Mark Hanna had fought the choice of Theodore Roosevelt by asking, "Don't you realize there's only one heartbeat between that madman and the presidency?" The Republicans wanted to capitalize on Roosevelt's tremendous popularity earned in the Spanish-American War, however, and when McKinley was assassinated Roosevelt was catapulted into power.

## *The Big Picture*

1. An awareness arose among American laborers after the Civil War that collective action on their part could alleviate their grievances regarding their wages, hours, and working conditions.

2. Labor demonstrations and strikes resulted in violence so often that labor unions were stigmatized as subversive elements in American society.

3. After many trials a national labor organization finally shunned radicalism in favor of practical goals reached through practical means, and the path toward acceptance of collective bargaining was opened.

4. American farmers also sought collective action to address their economic grievances in the first grassroots movement resulting in the most successful third party in American political history.

5. The end of the Gilded Age was in sight after the Election of 1896 since the Republican winner chose Theodore Roosevelt for his vice presidential running mate in a bid for a second term.

# CHAPTER 23

# The Progressive Reform Movement

*We have in America a fast-growing number of cultivated young people who have no recognized outlet for the active faculties . . . [who] feel nervously the need for putting theory into action, and respond quickly to the Settlement form of activity.*
—Jane Addams, *The Subjective Necessity for Social Settlements,* 1892

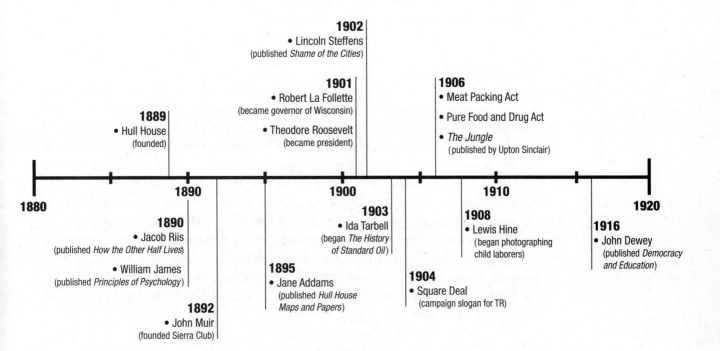

**1902**
• Lincoln Steffens
(published *Shame of the Cities*)

**1901**
• Robert La Follette
(became governor of Wisconsin)

• Theodore Roosevelt
(became president)

**1906**
• Meat Packing Act

• Pure Food and Drug Act

• *The Jungle*
(published by Upton Sinclair)

**1889**
• Hull House
(founded)

**1880**

**1890**

**1900**

**1910**

**1920**

**1890**
• Jacob Riis
(published *How the Other Half Lives*)

• William James
(published *Principles of Psychology*)

**1892**
• John Muir
(founded Sierra Club)

**1895**
• Jane Addams
(published *Hull House
Maps and Papers*)

**1903**
• Ida Tarbell
(began *The History
of Standard Oil*)

**1904**
• Square Deal
(campaign slogan for TR)

**1908**
• Lewis Hine
(began photographing
child laborers)

**1916**
• John Dewey
(published *Democracy
and Education*)

# Top 20 Things to Know

## 1 Progressive Reform

After the collapse of the Populist Revolt, Progressivism became America's last great reform movement reshaping all aspects of the relationship between the American government and the American people. A set of reform principles received bipartisan support in the last decade of the nineteenth century that grew in influence until they became the predominant view of American political life. Progressives were more successful than Populists because they came more from the middle class and included more educated and articulate spokespersons. Whereas in early American history the political consensus was in the limiting of government power, Progressives sought to expand government power by including more citizens in the political process and by putting government in charge of more and more aspects of life in the name of ridding the government of corruption and improving life for more people. The Progressive movement effectively ended the Gilded Age and its rampant political corruption, but in the name of progress Progressives did not stop there. Progressivism built on the precedents of the Indian Bureau and the Freedmen's Bureau to create the modern welfare state.

## 2 Social Gospel

The Social Gospel was a reform movement within American Christianity that sought to deemphasize doctrinal purity and traditional worship in favor of social activism. In working out the implications of the antebellum Second Great Awakening, Social Gospelites attempted to continue the ardor created by the humanitarian reform movements in order to boost church attendance. In the classical balance between faith and works, then, the Social Gospel became more interested in works. Largely an urban phenomenon, Social Gospel advocates reached out to the poor, especially immigrants, in an effort to help the needy but also to make religion more practical and inspiring. Critics of the Social Gospel claimed that the movement sacrificed spiritual solutions for merely pragmatic solutions that addressed only physical needs. Young, college-educated women were often the chief activists of the Social Gospel who were thus transformed into soldiers on the front lines of the Progressive movement.

## 3 Jane Addams

The chief female social reformer and Progressive activist was Jane Addams from Illinois. She founded Hull House in Chicago in 1889 as the first of many centers of the settlement house movement. Her actions virtually created the field of social work as she attempted to improve the lives of the immigrant poor. Addams was a leading advocate for other Progressive causes like women's suffrage and prohibition as well as a world-renowned pacifist who eventually received the Nobel Peace Prize for her efforts in 1931. Her books based on her experiences during forty years of settlement house work became models for scientific inquiry into social problems because they were the first systematic compilation of statistics and observation techniques that became the mainstay of several social sciences.

## 4 Hull House

The settlement house founded by Jane Addams was the first dedicated to community intervention and improvement of civic life in a slum, the Nineteenth Ward of Chicago. Beginning in 1889, Addams sought to provide cultural instruction for immigrant children. Hull House programs shifted to practical assimilation instruction in personal hygiene and the English language. The settlement house movement spread to other cities where immigrant families were separated as both parents worked long hours in factories. Settlement houses provided day care, educational materials and periodicals in reading rooms, and medical care. The movement was a training ground for Social Gospel workers and anti-child labor activists who awakened American women to political activity.

## 5 Hazen Pingree

Pingree ran a shoe factory in Detroit and became a Progressive from inside the Republican Party. He became Detroit's mayor in 1890 and enacted several Progressive reforms. His goal was to break up the system of graft associated with city contracts and to create municipal utility companies to compete with the privately owned utilities in order to lower rates through competition. In the Panic of 1893 Pingree created relief programs to public works projects that built schools, parks, and bathhouses. He gained notoriety by turning vacant lots into gardens for the growing of potatoes to feed the city's poor. Pingree was eventually elected as governor of Michigan and exemplified the type of Republican Progressivism that became the driving force of the political career of Theodore Roosevelt.

## 6 Tom Johnson

In contrast to Pingree, Tom Johnson was a Progressive Democrat who became the mayor of Cleveland, Ohio. He was also a Confederate veteran, whereas Pingree had fought in the Union Army. After a business apprenticeship working for others, Johnson opened his own streetcar company in Indianapolis, Indiana, that soon expanded to other major cities. Johnson sparred with the Ohio Republican boss Marcus Hanna in both business and political struggles. He became a congressman and then ran for the mayor of Cleveland in order to pursue all of the Progressive goals for which Pingree was famous. He was elected in 1901 and succeeded in a nearly identical career to Pingree's proving that Progressivism emanated from both major parties. He ran for governor of Ohio but lost even though the famous muckraking journalist, Lincoln Steffens, had described him as the best mayor in the United States.

## 7 William James

A Harvard-educated medical doctor, William James pioneered in the fields of psychology and physiology but gravitated toward a professorship in philosophy. As an empiricist, James originated the indigenous American philosophy of pragmatism, or the testing of truth based on the practical consequences of ideas. He praised American cultural values like individuality, initiative, drive, spontaneity, and a love of novelty. He opposed the excesses of Transcendentalism, and saying truth must come down to reform reality both described and inspired the Progressive Reform movement.

## 8 John Dewey

A philosopher and professor, John Dewey's career led him to Columbia University, which became a fount of Progressive ideas. Dewey applied the pragmatism of William James to his own field of education and developed the notion of functional reality. He advocated a new approach to education where children would be freer to explore knowledge and come to their own conclusions about truth. He wrote widely and in his books and classes advocated the relativism that increasingly pervaded American culture as the country developed a pluralist society.

## 9 Lewis Hine

Hine was an educator who developed an interest in photography more as a tool than a hobby. He went on to study sociology at Columbia University and became the official photographer of an organization trying to end child labor. In this pursuit he photographed child workers in mines, factories, canneries, textile mills, and farms. His photographs implied that child labor led to widespread deprivation and cultural desolation and were instrumental in the advance of anti-child labor laws. Hine worked for the Red Cross in Europe during World War I and returned to the United States to take a famous series of photographs documenting the construction of the Empire State Building. During the Great Depression he was the head photographer for the New Deal Works Progress Administration.

## 10 Jacob Riis

The most famous muckraking photographer was Jacob Riis. His life exemplified the struggle of immigrants as he came to America from Denmark in 1870 and did not find employment until 1877. As a reporter for a New York newspaper he developed an interest in photography. His book, *How the Other Half Lives* (1890), was a classic work of muckraking journalism that brought him to the attention of Theodore Roosevelt. Riis cataloged the various types of poor who lived in the Lower East Side of New York City and documented their plight with photographs and rather prejudiced ethnic stereotypes. He portrayed women and children in need of assistance but men as less deserving if they were poor. His book contributed to Progressive Reform, but he did not proscribe an active welfare state because he portrayed many of the immigrant poor's problems as being self-inflicted.

## 11  Lincoln Steffens

Steffens settled in New York City by 1892. He eventually rose to be the editor of *McClure's* magazine, a major muckraking periodical that advanced the careers of Jack London, Ida Tarbell, Upton Sinclair, Willa Cather, and Ray Stannard Baker. That list alone is enough to seal Steffens a place in American letters, but his own articles were collected by 1904 in a book titled *The Shame of the Cities*. His style of journalism became the model for future investigative journalists. His articles attacked machine politics for election tampering, police corruption, and graft, as well as questionable business practices. Steffens became enamored of Lenin and communism on a trip to Bolshevik Russia and advocated Progressive, or liberal, political reforms the rest of his life. Having lived in Mussolini's Italy, however, he recognized that both fascism and communism denied the freedoms of speech, press, and assembly but also freedom of thought. He ultimately denounced communism in his 1931 autobiography.

## 12  Ida Tarbell

Reared in the oil fields of Pennsylvania, Ida Tarbell went on to be the only woman in her college graduating class and a muckraking journalist for *McClure's*. She became the magazine's most popular writer with serialized biographies of Lincoln and Napoleon, but her most influential work was called *The History of the Standard Oil Company*. This investigative report appeared in nineteen separate articles from 1902 to 1904 and was written as an exposé of the type of business practices that Rockefeller had used to absorb independent oilmen like her father. The articles did not condemn capitalism and actually acknowledged Rockefeller's genius and efficiency, but they ended in a personal attack that revealed her deep animosity and obsession with her target. Rockefeller never responded to her attacks and referred to Ida Tarbell only as a "misguided woman." Interestingly, Tarbell disagreed with woman's suffrage despite her being recognized as one of the most important women in America. She said the suffrage movement had gone too far in belittling the contributions of women who chose traditional roles.

## 13  Robert La Follette

A Wisconsin lawyer and three-term congressman, La Follette was a typical Republican until his constituents fired him for supporting the McKinley Tariff. By the 1890s he was a pariah among Republicans until he bolted the party, barnstormed around the state, and became a three-term independent Progressive governor. What Roosevelt would go on to do for the nation, La Follette did in Wisconsin by pushing a broad spectrum of reforms. La Follette moved into the Senate and became a presidential contender. Shoved aside by Roosevelt in 1912, La Follette did run as the Progressive Party candidate in 1924. He received almost five million votes but took them mostly from Democrats giving Republican Calvin Coolidge a solid victory. His use of independent regulatory commissions filled with experts as sources of policy ideas became known as the Wisconsin Idea and was the basis of much of Progressive Reform.

## 14 Wisconsin Idea

As the governor of Wisconsin, Robert La Follette hit upon the strategy of gaining advice from university professors and other "leading experts" to help him shape Reform policies. Just as in the independent regulatory commissions established in Progressive cities, La Follette invited his experts to sit on regulatory agencies but now at the state level. Professors and their universities received prestige, and La Follette received ideas that "Back to the people Bob" could take back to the people and popularize through his passionate oratory. When expanded to the national level, the Wisconsin Idea became the mechanism whereby a more and more populous middle class consented to be ruled by the educated elite of the country. In the process the American people grew accustomed to turning to government for solutions to problems, and hence the Wisconsin Idea was part of the end of "rugged individualism."

## 15 Theodore Roosevelt

Theodore Roosevelt, or TR, both wrote about and lived what he called "the strenuous life." Born in the family of a New York banker, TR rejected any notion that he continue in the family business or even take up the legal profession for which he began studies after graduating from Harvard. Instead, he dove into New York City and state politics and other jungles. He spent his entire adult life following his motto of "Get action; do things!" TR served as a sort of police chief for New York City, a state legislator, a civil service reform commissioner, an assistant secretary of the Navy, a soldier in the Spanish-American War, governor of New York, vice president, and eventually president upon William McKinley's assassination. Throughout his many experiences he wrote articles and books that earned him as much as $750,000 per year in modern dollars. As president, Roosevelt launched Progressive Reform on the national level. After his presidency he went on safari in Africa and toured Europe, becoming the most famous American of his day. His fame and ambition drew him back into politics in the Election of 1912 when he and his supporters split the Republican Party by forming the "Bull Moose" Progressive Party. The split ensured the victory of Woodrow Wilson in 1912. In regard to foreign policy, TR was aggressively nationalistic and even imperialistic. He claimed to be single-handedly responsible for the construction of the Panama Canal by the United States. TR's presidency and personal style ended the Gilded Age string of forgotten presidents in an unforgettable way, and every subsequent American president inherited from him the capacity to act as the most powerful individual on the planet. For good and for ill, TR's political talents entirely altered the American political landscape. For this reason he is the only twentieth-century president to alter the landscape of Mt. Rushmore with his visage.

## 16 Square Deal

Theodore Roosevelt's (TR's) coined phrase for his Progressive agenda was the Square Deal. Among his reform principles the three most important were controlling corporations, consumer protection, and conservation of natural resources. TR wielded the Sherman Antitrust Act effectively for the first time and earned the title, the "Great Trustbuster," by bringing antitrust suits against corporations he deemed to be "bad trusts." He backed the Pure Food and Drug and the Meat Packing Acts as a result of reading *The Jungle* (1906) by Upton Sinclair. As a result of his love of the outdoors and his friendship with John Muir, TR was also known as the "Great Conservationist" for the reserving of land for national parks and national forests as well as coal reserves. Together these initiatives created a government with an entirely new orientation as a "watchdog," protecting it citizens and its resources in unprecedented ways. In some sense TR's Square Deal was continued by future presidents as the New Freedom, the New Deal, the Fair Deal, the New Frontier, the Great Society, the Bridge to the Twenty-first Century, and even Hope and Change.

## 17 *The Jungle*

The most sensational muckraking novel of the Progressive Era was *The Jungle* (1906) by Upton Sinclair. The book contained actual scenes of muckraking on the floors of Chicago's hog and cattle meat-packing slaughterhouses, and the tales of what went into the nation's sausage turned many stomachs including that of President Roosevelt. Sinclair had gone undercover into the meat-packing industry in a classic example of investigative journalism to reveal the plight of the workers, not the animals or the customers. The novel traces the struggle of Jurgis, a Lithuanian immigrant, and his family to survive in the slipshod housing and brutal conditions associated with the workers of the meat-packing plants. As many in the family perish, Jurgis grows increasingly embittered. As his character moved toward socialism, so Sinclair wanted to move the nation, but as he said, "I aimed at the public's heart, and by accident I hit it in the stomach." The novel was a main impetus toward the Progressive initiative of consumer protection through increased regulation of the food and drug industries. Because it contributed to Roosevelt's support for Progressivism, *The Jungle* proved to be one of the most influential books in all American literature in bringing about societal change.

## 18 Pure Food and Drug Act

This 1906 law was a direct assault on the quackery associated with nineteenth-century remedies that were peddled about the country as well as the use of fillers and otherwise tainted food products. The Pure Food and Drug Act forbade the manufacture, sale, or shipping of impure or fraudulently labeled foodstuffs or drugs involved in interstate commerce. The law served as a forerunner of the later Food and Drug Administration (FDA), and its language was ultimately applied to alcoholic beverages by the Volstead Act during prohibition.

## 19 Meat Packing Act

Otherwise known as the Meat Inspection Act, this law was also passed in 1906 on the heels of the publication of *The Jungle* in that year. Although it did have provisions to address the dangers to meat packers, the law also addressed the disreputable practices in the industry as cited in Sinclair's exposé novel. Sanitary regulations were enforced by making all meat-packing plants selling their products in interstate commerce susceptible to surprise inspections by federal regulators. The price of meat went up as a result of the new federal regulations, and many smaller packers were forced into bankruptcy.

# 20 John Muir

Muir was a Scottish immigrant who came to the United States as a child in 1849. The boy grew up on a Wisconsin farm where he gained a deep appreciation for nature. After some college training, Muir worked odd jobs that allowed him to pursue his passion of tramping about as a sauntering naturalist in the spirit of Henry David Thoreau. He traveled to California and Alaska, and after some time as a fruit grower expanded his travels to South America, Europe, and Asia. He best loved the Sierra Mountains range of California, though, and founded the Sierra Club in 1892 to act on his passion for conservation. He wrote extensively about his struggles to preserve various natural wonders and was befriended by Theodore Roosevelt who camped with Muir in Yosemite National Park. He acted as the nation's conscience in the conservation of natural resources with a quasi-religious adoration of wilderness places and was the major influence in preserving the natural heritage of the nation until his death in 1914.

## *The Big Picture*

1. The backlash to the corruption and scandals of the Gilded Age came in the form of a widening series of ideas called the Progressive Reform movement.

2. Progressives originally came from the ranks of social workers trying to aid in the assimilation of immigrants into American urban life.

3. Professionals from all walks of life quickly picked up the ideas of Progressive Reform and expanded their application until states like Wisconsin implemented a wide series of political reforms.

4. Investigative studies done by historians, writers, social workers, and photographers exposed the problems of American society and compelled widespread support for Progressive reforms.

5. The Gilded Age came to a close with the rise to the presidency of Theodore Roosevelt whose Square Deal policies revolutionized American government and made many Progressive policies permanent fixtures in American life.

# Domestic Policy Debate

*In a very few years, with our free and compulsory schools, our free libraries, and the economic opportunities which this country has to offer, these people were transformed into ambitious, self-respecting, public-spirited citizens.*
—Harvard professor A. Piatt Andrew, *North American Review*, 1914

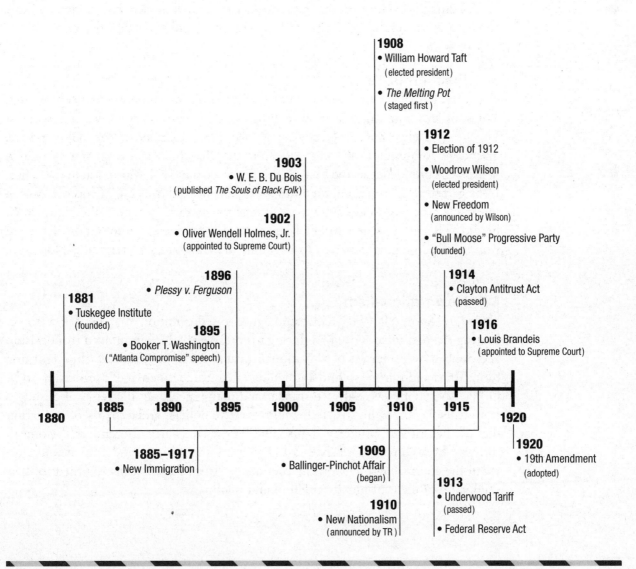

**1908**
- William Howard Taft (elected president)
- *The Melting Pot* (staged first)

**1903**
- W. E. B. Du Bois (published *The Souls of Black Folk*)

**1902**
- Oliver Wendell Holmes, Jr. (appointed to Supreme Court)

**1912**
- Election of 1912
- Woodrow Wilson (elected president)
- New Freedom (announced by Wilson)
- "Bull Moose" Progressive Party (founded)

**1896**
- *Plessy v. Ferguson*

**1881**
- Tuskegee Institute (founded)

**1895**
- Booker T. Washington ("Atlanta Compromise" speech)

**1914**
- Clayton Antitrust Act (passed)

**1916**
- Louis Brandeis (appointed to Supreme Court)

1880   1885   1890   1895   1900   1905   1910   1915   1920

**1885–1917**
- New Immigration

**1909**
- Ballinger-Pinchot Affair (began)

**1910**
- New Nationalism (announced by TR)

**1913**
- Underwood Tariff (passed)
- Federal Reserve Act

**1920**
- 19th Amendment (adopted)

# Top 20 Things to Know

## 1 William Howard Taft

This Ohio attorney and judge was appointed by William McKinley as the first governor of the Philippines after the islands became U.S. territory. He performed so well in this task that Theodore Roosevelt (TR) made him secretary of war and then suggested the American people elect him president, which they did upon TR's departure in 1908. Taft busted trusts like Standard Oil and American Tobacco, but he favored the highly protective Payne-Aldrich Tariff and lost the confidence of TR and other Progressives. TR tried to win the Republican nomination for the presidency in 1912 to reclaim ground from the Republican Old Guard, but was rejected by his old party. Taft went on to lose the election when TR helped launch the Progressive Party and ran against his protégé. The split between TR and Taft was a bitter personal feud, but Taft eventually received the slot he most desired. Warren G. Harding placed him on the Supreme Court as chief justice. He formed a solidly conservative bench in the 1920s with pro-business and anti-labor decisions.

## 2 Election of 1912

This presidential election was a major turning point in modern American politics. Three of the four candidates were Progressive or ultra-Progressive (the socialist Eugene V. Debs) and Progressivism gained three-quarters of the popular vote. Theodore Roosevelt (TR) and Taft split the Republican vote giving Woodrow Wilson the presidency as the first southerner since the Civil War to attain the office. Debs gained nearly one million votes, or 6 percent of those cast. Woodrow Wilson interpreted the election as a mandate to take the country in a new direction, which he did. TR's assertiveness might have been well received by the nation if he had won, but in losing he departed from public life except as a writer and explorer.

## 3 New Nationalism

Theodore Roosevelt (TR) had campaigned on the notion that he could go on busting the bad trusts as he had during his presidency. He announced this decision and dubbed his principles New Nationalism at Osawatomie, Kansas, after returning from Africa and Europe to find Taft failing to continue his energetic leadership style. Other aspects of New Nationalism alarmed many including the removal of judges from federal courts who struck down Progressive policies and a theory of regulation that assailed private property rights. The Progressive Party also endorsed women's suffrage. Even some Progressives feared where TR's ambition and fame would have taken the country had he won the presidency again. Republicans returned to their original assessment of him as a radical and madman.

## 4 Woodrow Wilson

Wilson was born in Virginia and rose in fame as a lawyer, professor, and expert on political economics and constitutional law. He became the president of his alma mater, Princeton University, and eventually the governor of New Jersey just before being elected to the presidency in the Election of 1912. The reform governor proved to be a Reform president, and the Wilson administration oversaw a lowered tariff, the creation of the Federal Reserve and the Federal Trade Commission, and passage of the Clayton Antitrust Act. As war erupted in Europe in 1914, Wilson maintained neutrality and was elected in 1916 on a platform of staying out of the war. Events after his election pushed him toward war, however, and he wound up bringing the United States into World War I as the war to "make the world safe for democracy." He shaped much of the future of international relations with his proposal of a League of Nations but could not bring the Senate to support his ideas. In attempting to persuade the people to force the Senate to accept membership in the League, Wilson had a stroke and never fully recovered his faculties but lived out his second term while communicating with his cabinet through his wife.

## 5 New Freedom

Taking a cue from his rival, Theodore Roosevelt (TR), Wilson coined a phrase to sell his domestic agenda to the American people. New Freedom was a response to TR's desire within New Nationalism to discern between "good trusts" and "bad trusts." Wilson said all trusts were bad and that a powerful president needed to end all monopolistic business combinations intended to reduce competition so the American people could be free from corporate control. As president, however, Wilson could only practically pursue a limited number of the most egregious violators of the Clayton Antitrust Act. Thus, Wilson's idealism gravitated toward TR's policy of regulation and limited use of antitrust suits.

## 6 Old Guard

The conservative wing of the Republican Party that attempted to put the brakes on Progressive reforms was called the Old Guard. In an era of radical change, the normal policies of the Republicans appeared reactionary, and in certain circumstances they actively became so. Henry Cabot Lodge in the Senate led the conservatives who worked with Taft, rejected Theodore Roosevelt's bid for the Republican nomination, and were so adamantly against Wilson's policies as to be called the Irreconcilables in the wake of World War I. Because civil service reform had become a plank in the Republican Party as well as the other two major parties, the Old Guard is not to be confused with the Stalwarts of the Gilded Age.

## 7 Ballinger-Pinchot Affair

Reminiscent of the Gilded Age was this scandal erupting during the Taft administration. In 1910, Secretary of the Interior Richard Ballinger reversed a decision made by the Theodore Roosevelt (TR) administration concerning some land in Wyoming, Montana, and Alaska. Gifford Pinchot of the U.S. Forest Service accused Ballinger publically of allowing corporations to abuse the land. Taft backed Ballinger, and as the controversy heated up he sacked Pinchot. A congressional committee investigated and agreed that Ballinger had acted properly in questioning the legality of some of TR's conservation policies, a fact that irrevocably deepened the split between TR and Taft. Ballinger, although exonerated, resigned in an effort to spare Taft's presidency from any further public outcry.

## 8 Oliver Wendell Holmes, Jr.

Famous son of a famous father, Oliver Wendell Holmes, Jr. graduated from Harvard and fought with distinction in the Civil War. After advancing American law as a lawyer, professor, and judge, Theodore Roosevelt nominated him in 1902 to the Supreme Court where he stayed until his death at the age of ninety. Although most of the Court was held over from the Gilded Age, Holmes dissented regularly from the majority opinions and ultimately led the way in increasing the federal government's power to regulate commerce. He stood against child labor, intellectual oppression, and wiretapping and gave American law the phrase, "clear and present danger."

## 9 Louis Brandeis

A legal and economic scholar from Harvard, Brandeis was routinely tapped for "Wisconsin Idea" advice by Woodrow Wilson in trust legislation, currency, and labor problems. For his efforts Brandeis was placed on the Supreme Court by Wilson in 1916 and formed the more liberal base for the Court with Oliver Wendell Holmes, Jr. He was the first Jewish justice on the Supreme Court and thus marked a turning point in American pluralism. He urged his fellow justices not to stand against the social and economic reforms of the Progressive Reform movement.

## 10 "Bull Moose" Progressive Party

When the Republican nominating convention in Chicago refused to nominate Theodore Roosevelt (TR) in 1912, TR and other Progressives bolted the party and formed the Progressive Party on the spot. The Progressive platform was called "A Contract with the People," and TR launched a bitter campaign through which he accused the Republicans of using unscrupulous practices to steal the nomination from him in the first place. The Progressive Party trumpeted its characteristic reforms including the direct election of senators and a push for nationwide primaries for choosing presidential candidates. The initiative, referendum, and recall were planks in the platform as well as women's suffrage and even minimum wage laws for women workers. Together Taft and TR received over 7.5 million popular votes in the Election of 1912 compared to Wilson's 6.2 million. TR had named the party by another inspired quip when asked about his fitness to run again for the presidency, but after his defeat he retreated from public life. The Progressive Party went through many iterations but disappeared from American political life by 1952.

## 11 New Immigration

As prosperity returned to Germany fewer and fewer Germans migrated to the United States. As all northern and western European migration waned, that from southern and eastern Europe waxed until a definite trend existed. From 1885 to 1917 almost 70 percent of immigrants were from these new regions. Major migrations from Russia, Poland, Austria-Hungary, Italy, and the Balkans brought many Slavic peoples into America. Most of these immigrants were Roman Catholic, Greek or Russian Orthodox, or Jewish. This new group of immigrants either found it difficult to assimilate into American culture or chose not to do so. Most of the New Immigration settled in eastern cities or in Chicago and found work in factories, mills, construction, or the meat-packing industry. Most Progressives and Populists opposed this influx of people from such different cultures, and the nativism that had been directed toward the Irish was now directed with greater severity toward the New Immigration peoples. As a result, immigration legislation was enacted during the 1920s that attempted to systematically reduce immigration from these regions.

## 12 *The Melting Pot*

Israel Zangwill's 1908 play of this title was a smash hit on Broadway with a plot somewhere between *Romeo and Juliet* and *Fiddler on the Roof.* In the story a Russian Jewish immigrant to America falls in love with a Russian Orthodox immigrant, and Zangwill attempted to show that such distinctions were pointless in the new country and should not keep the lovers apart. He attributed the foundation of the United States to a plan in God's providence to purify all of the European cultures into a new alloy called the American people. Zangwill's metaphor was appealing to a newly industrialized steel-producing nation, and the idea has remained popular ever since, although in his day, it was largely a myth. The numerous ethnically segregated neighborhoods in American cities belied the assimilation into a superior new culture that Zangwill described in the play.

## 13 Booker T. Washington

Like Frederick Douglass, Booker T. Washington was the son of an African-American slave and white man. He worked his way through school after being freed from slavery. As a distinguished educator in Virginia, he was chosen by the Alabama legislature to start a vocational school for African-Americans in Tuskegee, Alabama. Tuskegee Institute became a normal and industrial school for African-American students, that is, it trained teachers and workers in the trades. As the foremost educator of his race in his day he was a sought-after speaker on race relations, and he clashed with W. E. B. Du Bois over strategy. Washington stressed the importance of giving African-Americans in the South skills that would get them off the plantations and give them an opportunity to pursue the American Dream, which for him meant a gradual march toward self-respect and the respect of white Americans. He rejected the idea that political and civil rights were the first priority for African-Americans and that they should be demanded.

## 14 W. E. B. Du Bois

Born in Massachusetts, Du Bois (pronounced "duh boyz") was the first African-American graduate of Harvard University and became a professor at Atlanta University in history and economics from 1896 to 1910. He studied and wrote about the sociology of the African-American experience and became a more militant advocate for civil rights than Booker T. Washington. His famous 1903 book, *The Souls of Black Folk*, traced case studies of the lives of African-Americans after he conducted research similar to that done by Jane Addams with immigrants in Chicago. Du Bois helped lead the National Association for the Advancement of Colored People (NAACP) and many other organizations and conferences dealing with race relations. As opposed to Washington, Du Bois demanded that American society grant immediate equality to African-Americans, including the removal of all restrictions on the right to vote that had thwarted the Fifteenth Amendment in the Jim Crow South. Frustrated with the slow pace of change, Du Bois expatriated to Ghana where he developed Marxist leanings and died in 1963.

## 15 Tuskegee Institute

Claiming that the opportunity to earn a dollar was more important than the opportunity to spend a dollar in an opera house, Booker T. Washington established Tuskegee Institute in 1881. Starting with only thirty students and no buildings, Washington developed a program that turned out African-American teachers, prepared others for work in trades and modern agriculture, and wove into all instruction the cultivation of dignity through cleanliness, orderliness, and thrift. As a result of Washington's extensive speaking tours, donations came in from North and South, and Tuskegee Institute became a major recipient of philanthropy from great industrialists. By 1915 the campus came to consist of almost 300 acres and over five thousand faculty and students. Among its most famous benefactors was George Washington Carver, who headed the Department of Agriculture at Tuskegee Institute for almost fifty years, all the while making great strides in the development of uses for southern agricultural products.

## 16 *Plessy v. Ferguson*

In 1896, the Supreme Court upheld a Louisiana law that segregated passenger trains and railroad facilities. The Court determined that as long as the facilities were "separate but equal" then such separation did not violate the civil rights of African-Americans as constituted in the Fourteenth Amendment. *Plessy v. Ferguson*, therefore, justified and extended the Jim Crow policies of the South and not only denied African-Americans equal protection under the law but also access to equal facilities. In practice, segregation usually led to the facilities reserved for African-Americans receiving poor maintenance and funding and their generally falling into disrepair. The findings in the case were applied not only to railroads but to schools across the South, and not until the Supreme Court picked up the issue again in the 1950s did it acknowledge that the whole premise behind "separate but equal" was flawed.

## 17 Nineteenth Amendment

After the Reconstruction amendments were in place for African-Americans and other reforms were enacted like the income tax, direct election of senators, and prohibition, the U.S. Constitution was finally amended to permit women the right to vote. The Nineteenth Amendment was proposed in 1919 and ratified by 1920, just in time to inspire the flappers of the Roaring Twenties to flaunt their equality. The goal of the women's suffrage movement was at last attained (embarrassingly after the Soviet Union had led the way), but women tended to vote just as their husbands did. The success of the women's suffrage movement, however, led women to push for equality in other respects and the modern feminist movement was the result.

## 18 Underwood Tariff

The origins of the income tax lay in the effort of Woodrow Wilson, as the first southern president since the Civil War, to reduce the tariff further than any Republican administration since Lincoln was elected. Wilson went personally to Congress to ask for a reduced tariff, the first time a president directly addressed a Congress since Thomas Jefferson stopped the practice. The Underwood Tariff of 1913 lowered customs duties to 30 percent, and duties were removed entirely from iron, steel, raw wool, and sugar. The income tax was enacted, after the Sixteenth Amendment legalized it, to make up for the lost revenue from tariffs. Together the lowering of the tariff and the first income tax were blows against the wealthy industrialists long desired by Progressives and therefore major successes of Wilson's domestic agenda.

## 19 Clayton Antitrust Act

The Wilson administration pushed the Clayton Antitrust Act of 1914. This new trustbuster law was designed to close some of the loopholes in the Sherman Antitrust Act that corporate America had exploited since 1890. The legislation established labor unions as legitimate institutions in American society, and Samuel Gompers called the law the "Magna Carta of labor" because it legalized collective bargaining and protected labor unions from attacks using antitrust legislation. The Clayton Antitrust Act was to be enforced by the Federal Trade Commission. Wilson's antitrust legislation specifically targeted the interlocking directorates and the exclusion from prosecution of individual business leaders that had so strengthened Standard Oil and other trusts. Due to the need for American industry to produce for World War I and to the interpretations by the Taft Court, the Clayton Antitrust Act proved unworkable.

# 20 Federal Reserve Act

The establishment of the Federal Reserve by this law in 1913 was the first major reform of the national banking system since the Civil War. Twelve regions contained a Federal Reserve Bank to which private banks could belong. The system was overseen by up to eight members of the Federal Reserve Board who set the rate at which banks could borrow money from the national system, and thus determined the basic rate at which private banks could loan money to individuals and businesses. Both the interest rates and the amount of the new national currency, the Federal Reserve Notes, could fluctuate according to the rising and falling of the business cycle in an effort to stabilize the American economy.

## *The Big Picture*

1. The Election of 1912 was a major turning point in American politics in that most voters after the Gilded Age voted for some type of Progressive Reform candidate.

2. Progressive Reform was established in all three branches of the federal government, which enacted legislation and interpreted the Constitution to permit greater involvement of government in actively regulating business and shepherding the lives of American citizens.

3. The diversity of American society was enhanced by an influx of southern and eastern European immigrants who were not as well received as previous waves of immigrants nor as readily assimilated into American culture.

4. Although women finally received the right to vote in national elections in this era, African-Americans still struggled under repressive policies, and their efforts to attain civil rights were hampered by disagreement within the African-American community as to proper goals and strategies.

5. The Wilson administration revised the federal government's involvement in the American economy in ways that have had lasting impact by establishing the taxation, regulation, and banking systems still in place today.

# The Spanish-American War and the Imperialism Debate

 CHAPTER **25**

*The obligations of humanity demanded that we take possession of the Philippine Islands
in order to prevent the anarchy which would certainly have followed had we taken
any other course than that which we did.*

—Joseph Henry Crooker decrying a popular argument for imperialism, 1900

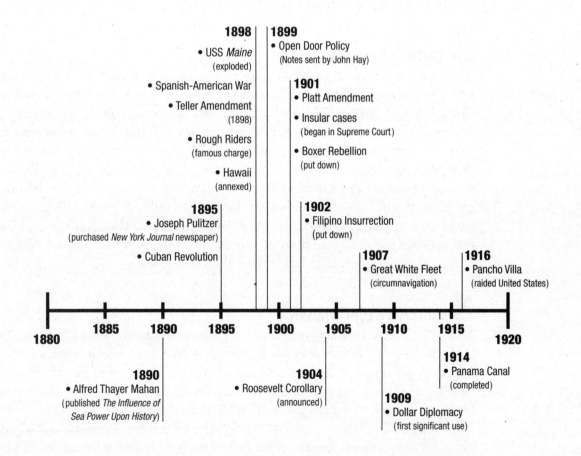

# Top 20 Things to Know

## 1 Imperialism Debate

What was a maritime nation to do with the potential of world power and world trade? After the growth of the American economy through the Gilded Age, manufacturers sought new markets. Other nations were expanding their empires rapidly as the world was shrinking because of new transportation and communication technologies. Some in the United States believed that America should try to keep pace, to acquire spheres of influence for economic competition and for national defense in times of trouble. Others believed such a step would violate the core principles that had caused the American colonies to seek independence in the first place. Isolationists, as they were called, believed the United States should not acquire influence or territory just as the nations of Europe had always done. Pacifists and humanitarian reformers believed to do so would be the ultimate in hypocrisy. Imperialists believed that America would spread the best way of life along with trade and that to sit by idly while more aggressive nations carved up the world was folly, maybe even suicide. The Spanish-American War forced the debate onto the front pages of American newspapers and into the U.S. Congress.

## 2 Spheres of Influence

When nations in the nineteenth century expanded economic or military control into specific regions, the territories in question were called spheres of influence. The essence of imperialism involved a nation's acquiring control or ownership of territory beyond its national boundaries. Spheres of influence were different from colonies in that an imperialistic nation's control came by privileges that had been granted by sovereign nations or tribal regions. These privileges might be the exclusive right to secure raw materials and/or sell products in a region or the right to use the territory as a base of operations in the event of military conflict. Regions of the world that were undeveloped, like Africa, or falling into decline, like China, became ripe pickings for the acquisition of spheres of influence by the United Kingdom, France, Germany, Japan, and eventually the United States.

## 3 Alfred Thayer Mahan

Mahan lectured on naval history and tactics at the Newport War College. In 1890, he published *The Influence of Sea Power upon History* in which he examined the impact of naval power, strategy, and technology during the time period from 1660 to 1783. He later illustrated how British sea power held Napoleon in check despite his land victories. Mahan's ideas led to a buildup of the U.S. Navy and made imperialists desire naval bases around the world. The United Kingdom acknowledged his praise for the accomplishments of the British Navy by building the largest empire in world history, and the United States and Germany both tried to catch up.

## 4 Cuban Revolution

Spain held onto Cuba the longest of all of its New World Empire because of the lucrative nature of its sugar, tobacco, and coffee plantations. Early revolts in the 1860s led to two hundred thousand deaths, but Spain held on despite the animosity of world opinion against the continuation of African slavery. Exiled Cubans in the United States raised funding and public awareness of the plight of the Cuban people who were suffering far worse repression than Americans had prior to 1776. The United States responded with economic sanctions against Spain, but some Cuban slaves responded by launching another revolt in 1895. This revolt was also crushed by the Spanish military, but a firmer resistance was established with modern weapons supplied to Cuban revolutionaries by the Cuban Revolutionary Party and the exiles in America. As the revolutionary forces burned plantations and attacked Cuban cities, Spain sent General Valeriano "Butcher" Weyler who began a policy of placing peasants who supported the rebels into concentration camps. Tortures and murders committed by the Spanish were reported in American newspapers, and many Americans came to believe intervention was a duty.

## 5 Spanish-American War

Because of numerous atrocities reported from Cuba in the American press, the public clamored for President McKinley to declare war against Spain. The Cuban Revolution had reached a crisis point by 1898, and Americans were evacuated from Cuba. With the sinking of the USS *Maine* and other provocations, McKinley and the Congress authorized an invasion of Cuba and the Philippines. American fleets beat the Spanish fleets in the Atlantic and the Pacific Oceans, and the invasion of Cuba secured victory in just four months. The Spanish-American War was the background for the heroic rise of Theodore Roosevelt who had volunteered to lead the Rough Riders. The war also left the United States to decide what to do with Cuba, the Philippine Islands, Guam, and Puerto Rico, all of which were liberated from Spain. Spain's world power status, long on the wane, was shattered.

## 6 Joseph Pulitzer

Joseph Pulitzer's career after coming to the United States in 1864 foreshadowed that of Theodore Roosevelt's in that Pulitzer rose from being a soldier and a politician to a major shaper of public opinion. Pulitzer's "bully pulpit," however, was his newspaper empire culminating in publication of the *Evening World* beginning in 1887. Pulitzer employed the technique of "yellow journalism," or the sensationalizing of the news through large headlines and sleazy crime stories, in order to boost his circulation. This sensationalizing reached its peak in Pulitzer's competition with William Randolph Hearst's *Evening Journal* as the two publishers outdid each other in promoting war against Spain with their readers. Later Pulitzer's *World* developed higher standards and gained increasing credibility. In his will, Pulitzer left millions to start a School of Journalism at Columbia University and the prize that bears his name, which rewards singular achievements in many varied fields of publishing, public service, and the arts.

# 7 USS *Maine*

After riots in early 1898 in Havana, Cuba, the battleship *Maine* was ordered to protect American life and property there. On February 15 the battleship was destroyed and sunk in an explosion that killed 260 of its officers and crew. Yellow journalists pounced on the story as another Spanish atrocity and made "Remember the *Maine*!" the slogan of the campaign demanding American intervention in the Cuban Revolution. The U.S. Congress voted unanimously to spend $50 million on building up defenses. A naval court of inquiry confirmed what had been alleged in the newspapers, that the battleship had been destroyed by a submersible mine, but could not prove that Spain was the culprit. William McKinley tried to refrain from asking the Congress to declare war, but the sinking of the *Maine* was the last straw. Congress declared war on Spain by April. The mast of the USS *Maine* was recovered and placed as a memorial flagpole in Arlington National Cemetery.

# 8 Teller and Platt Amendments

The Teller Amendment to the war resolution against Spain declared the United States had no desire to make Cuba anything more than a sphere of influence. The government of Cuba would be left to Cubans after they were freed from Spain. At the end of the war Cuba was occupied militarily, and the American government decided not to withdraw immediately in fear that instability would threaten the Cuban people. A public health and sanitation campaign was launched and stamped out yellow fever. The U.S. military commander, General Leonard Wood, oversaw the establishment of a Cuban constitutional government. The Platt Amendment said that the United States would not withdraw until Cuba agreed not to sign a treaty with any foreign power threatening Cuban independence and not to acquire too much debt. Furthermore, Cuba had to agree that the United States could intervene if law and order or Cuban independence were ever threatened and to allow a U.S. naval base at Guantanamo Bay. The Platt Amendment rendered Cuba a protectorate of the United States.

# 9 Rough Riders

This volunteer cavalry unit was mustered by Leonard Wood and Theodore Roosevelt (TR) in San Antonio, Texas, in preparation for the invasion of Cuba during the Spanish-American War. Officially known as the First U.S. Volunteer Cavalry, the Rough Riders were a curious mix of around 1,250 cowboys, American Indians, desperadoes, athletes from Ivy League universities, and some aristocratic thrill seekers (like TR himself). Because of logistical problems only the officers could bring their horses to Cuba, so the Rough Riders walked instead of rode into history. They participated in two major actions, the second of which was an assault on the heights around Santiago where the Spanish were dug in to protect the city. TR led his Rough Riders and other troops, including African-American "buffalo soldiers," on the assault that proved victorious. TR exulted in the action despite being slightly wounded. During the entire Spanish-American War the Rough Riders experienced the highest casualty rate of any American unit. Thirty-seven percent were wounded, killed, or felled by disease. The fame of the Rough Riders was enhanced by TR's "strenuous life" rhetoric, and several survivors of the cavalry unit helped him campaign for his various political offices for the rest of his career.

## 10 Hawaii

The Spanish-American War drew attention to the convenience of Hawaii as a naval installation. Grover Cleveland had forestalled annexation of Hawaii after the 1893 overthrow of the autocratic government of Queen Liliuokalani by a committee of safety assembled by Americans who were sugar and fruit planters on the islands. While Sanford B. Dole was proclaimed president of Hawaii with the protection of U.S. marines, the Hawaii question languished until William McKinley was elected and the war with Spain was won. McKinley was pro-annexation, and when the Japanese complained about American interests in Hawaii, McKinley was all the more resolved to take them. A joint resolution of Congress annexed the Hawaiian Islands even before another Treaty of Paris officially ended the Spanish-American War. Hawaii was the only territory acquired in the era of American imperialism to eventually earn statehood, which it did right after Alaska in 1959.

## 11 Coaling Stations

As the era of the great clipper ships gave way to the power of the steam engine, coal became the indispensable material fueling national security and the merchant marine. The Pacific Ocean is the largest on earth, and American interests required that American ships conquer its vastness for military and economic reasons. The islands acquired from Spain in the Spanish-American War, as well as others picked up along the way, became the solution. Instead of filling a ship's hold with coal and a small amount of cargo, ships could be filled with cargo and pick up coal (and other supplies) along the way at the islands. When islands were stocked with coal for this purpose they were known as coaling stations, and the United States acquired enough of these by the turn of the twentieth century to help turn that era into what it became, the American Century.

## 12 Insular Cases

As the United States entered the debate over imperialism and actually acquired what amounted to colonies, thorny questions about the U.S. Constitution kept presenting themselves. Islands like the Philippines, Puerto Rico, and Guam were in a state of constitutional limbo in which they were not even considered territories, let alone states. Puerto Ricans, for example, were granted citizenship in the United States in 1917, but not self-government nor the ability to send voting representatives to the U.S. Congress. The question became whether U.S. law would apply equally to these islands, or as it was asked then, "Does the Constitution follow the flag?" The Supreme Court decided, in a series of cases called the Insular cases, that although the islanders in question were ruled by the United States, they would not receive full rights as American citizens.

## 13 Filipino Insurrection

During the Spanish-American War the United States helped the revolutionary leader, Emilio Aguinaldo, to throw off Spanish authority. Germany, however, had aspirations to take over the Philippine Islands, and the United States did not believe the Filipino people were ready for self-government or that they could mount a defense against German or British acquisition. McKinley decided it was the Manifest Destiny of the United States to help the Filipinos by governing them. After an incident in which three Filipinos were shot by American soldiers, fighting erupted that became the Filipino Insurrection. In two years of fighting, 4,200 Americans and 16,000 Filipinos were killed. During the transition to peaceful government over 200,000 civilians died from disease and deprivation. Emilio Aguinaldo directed the insurgency, which employed guerrilla warfare tactics in daunting jungle conditions. Aguinaldo was captured, however, in 1901 and called for an end to hostilities, but fighting continued another year.

## 14 Open Door Policy

With the urgings of Mahan and other imperialists, Secretary of State John Hay sent a diplomatic note to the nations carving up China at the turn of the century. Hay wanted these nations to keep China intact as a sovereign nation and to keep their encroachments from leading to a general conflict. In other words, Hay did not want other imperial powers to divide China and exclude the United States from trading there. Neither the United Kingdom, France, Germany, Russia, nor Japan assented to the proposal, but Hay announced to the world that the Open Door Policy was in effect. As feared, competition for spheres of influence did touch off the 1904 Russo-Japanese War, which was ultimately mediated by Theodore Roosevelt with the Portsmouth Treaty in 1905 (a feat for which he received the Nobel Peace Prize). The implications of the Open Door Policy would not be settled until after World War II.

## 15 Boxer Rebellion

As Hay distributed his Open Door Note, Chinese nationalists were forming a secret society called the Righteous and Harmonious Fists. Westerners referred to the group as the Boxers because of their public displays of martial arts. The Boxer Rebellion occurred because the nationalists wanted to overthrow the Qing Dynasty for their complicity with foreigners in allowing the type of incursions that prompted the Open Door Note. The Empress Dowager then backed the Boxers who set about trying to rid China of all foreigners by massacre. Missionaries and Chinese Christians were killed across China, but by 1900 the Boxers had moved into Peking and attacked foreigners there, even killing the German ambassador. Open Door nations including the United States sent troops to crush the Boxers, and the combined forces of the imperial armies recaptured Peking. By 1911, the Qing Dynasty was overthrown by a revolution that established a republic, but the subsequent instabilities prompted a civil war that paved the way for communism to control China after World War II.

# 16 Roosevelt Corollary

When the Dominican Republic collapsed in 1904, Theodore Roosevelt (TR) reiterated the principles of the Monroe Doctrine in a speech before Congress. His main concern was that a European power would do just what James K. Polk had done in regard to Mexico, that is, use military force for the stated purpose of collecting debts but with the real purpose of acquiring new territory. TR said that the United States wanted no new land, but he and the government of the United States did want stability, order, and prosperity across the Western Hemisphere. What TR did not want was a nation or nations guilty of "chronic wrongdoing" to ruin peace for the rest of the Americas. Therefore, he suggested that the United States act as an international police force since European nations had to stay away. Directly this meant that the United States intervened in short order in the Dominican Republic, Cuba, Nicaragua, Mexico, and Haiti. Indirectly, the Roosevelt Corollary led to the rise to world power status of the United States that exercised police powers across the world for the rest of the twentieth century and beyond. The difficulty faced by each president became where America should intervene when so much of the world routinely experienced conflict, instability, and even massacres.

# 17 Panama Canal

Picking up from failed French attempts at producing a canal in Central America that would join the Atlantic and Pacific Oceans, the United States pursued at first a route in Nicaragua but moved the project to Panama. Since Panama belonged to Colombia and Colombia appeared unwilling to negotiate with the United States, Theodore Roosevelt (TR) moved the U.S. Navy to Panama, landed a few U.S. marines, and otherwise encouraged Panama to revolt from Colombia. The 1903 Panamanian Revolution was nearly bloodless, and from its inception the new country allowed a 10-mile-wide canal zone to be leased by the United States as specified in the Hay-Bunau-Varilla Treaty of 1904. After herculean effort the Panama Canal was open for business by 1914. Therefore, TR set in motion what even the original Spanish explorers recognized would revolutionize world trade, a canal at the isthmus. The Panama Canal dramatically increased the speed with which American naval forces could switch oceans in times of crisis.

# 18 Great White Fleet

When Theodore Roosevelt (TR) said, "Speak softly and carry a big stick" as a principle of foreign policy, the stick was the U.S. Navy. If the world did not get the message about the ability to project power in the Panamanian Revolution, TR sent sixteen battleships painted white to circumnavigate the globe. The trip lasted from 1907 to 1909 and put into harbor at all major points along the way to display American might. Battleships were named after states, so their voyage inspired nationalism for the states thus represented and were an expression of collective militarism aided by the coaling stations acquired with imperialism. The future friends and enemies of the United States had to take into account that the Melting Pot was forging giant steel platforms for rifled cannons capable of firing many miles inland or at other ships in the open seas.

## 19 Dollar Diplomacy

William Howard Taft's twist on the Monroe Doctrine revealed Taft agreed with Theodore Roosevelt that America should intervene in the affairs of nations in the Western Hemisphere but not that the intervention should use the military. As a representative of the business community, Taft wanted stability in Latin America, too, in order for American investors to feel confident in helping develop commercial opportunities. In Nicaragua, for example, Taft allowed American dollars to support a revolution and guaranteed the new government loans. If nations in Latin America cooperated with the interests of the United States, Taft allowed more investment dollars to flow into those countries. If a country resisted American interests, it could find itself with a ban on such investment. This policy was extended on a global scale during and after the twentieth-century world wars and by no means precluded the use of military intervention, not even in Nicaragua where Taft began the policy. Ever since the Taft administration presidents have faced the accusation that the United States was bribing other nations and manipulating events for oil or other forms of wealth. A struggle within every presidential administration was whether or not this accusation was true.

## 20 Pancho Villa

Son of a sharecropper, Pancho Villa became a bandit leader who resisted the oppression by the upper classes of Mexico. As the Mexican revolution of 1911 unfolded, Villa became a guerrilla fighter joining Francisco Madero's forces. In the revolving loyalties and alliances of the crumbling revolution, Villa found himself in prison. He switched sides, then switched sides again and before 1914 had served under three separate aspirants to the presidency of Mexico. When the United States backed Venustiano Carranza, Villa led the first invasion on American soil since the War of 1812. His raid on Columbus, New Mexico, and other actions killed a total of thirty-seven Americans. Woodrow Wilson ordered American military forces to hunt down Villa in Mexico but after over a year of searching they failed to catch him. When Mexico stabilized in 1920, Villa retired but was murdered by 1923.

# The Big Picture

1. The Spanish-American War came as a result of Spanish actions and policies in Cuba and the sensationalizing of events by pro-war journalistic giants.

2. The United States found itself in the awkward position of mulling over what to do with colonial holdings acquired from Spain after winning the Spanish-American War.

3. Imperialists convinced the American government to hold on to useful territories in the Pacific Ocean as European nations and Japan jockeyed for position in seeking spheres of influence in China.

4. In the interests of increasing American sea power, Theodore Roosevelt began the process of constructing a canal in the newly formed nation of Panama and dispatched the Great White Fleet of battleships to sail around the world.

5. With America's new position as a rising world power, American presidents innovated new ways to protect interests and to exert influence on events on a global scale.

# American Involvement in the Great War

*We are disloyal to our ideals if we refuse to let our country enlist in this cause.*
—Senator James D. Phelan, in support of the League of Nations, 1919

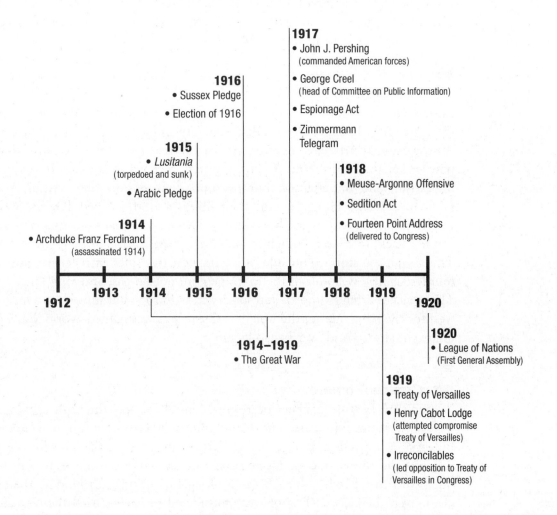

**1917**
- John J. Pershing
  (commanded American forces)
- George Creel
  (head of Committee on Public Information)
- Espionage Act
- Zimmermann Telegram

**1916**
- Sussex Pledge
- Election of 1916

**1915**
- *Lusitania*
  (torpedoed and sunk)
- Arabic Pledge

**1918**
- Meuse-Argonne Offensive
- Sedition Act
- Fourteen Point Address
  (delivered to Congress)

**1914**
- Archduke Franz Ferdinand
  (assassinated 1914)

1912   1913   1914   1915   1916   1917   1918   1919   1920

**1914–1919**
- The Great War

**1920**
- League of Nations
  (First General Assembly)

**1919**
- Treaty of Versailles
- Henry Cabot Lodge
  (attempted compromise
  Treaty of Versailles)
- Irreconcilables
  (led opposition to Treaty of
  Versailles in Congress)

# Top 20 Things to Know

## 1 Archduke Franz Ferdinand

As the heir apparent to the dual throne of the empire of Austria-Hungary, Franz Ferdinand was sent to inspect the army at Sarajevo in Bosnia in June 1914. Despite the fact that the Archduke had been searching for ways to reform imperial policy to satisfy Serbian and Slavic discontent, he was selected for assassination by a terrorist organization called the Black Hand. The Black Hand stood for Serbian nationalism and independence, and a push among Slavic peoples to create a Slavic country in the Balkans (Yugoslavia) perceived Germanic treatment of Serbia as a flashpoint for their ancestral ethnic conflict. The Archduke's motorcade had been attacked and the Archduke and his wife had escaped harm, but having taken a wrong turn the motorcade ironically brought the royal couple right by Gavrilo Princip, a conspirator in the Black Hand plot. Princip shot both Franz Ferdinand and his wife, Sophie, and the assassination was used as justification for the actions of Austria-Hungary and her ally Germany in starting World War I.

## 2 The Great War

Austria-Hungary gave Serbia a list of several demands after the assassination of their Archduke Franz Ferdinand that were impossible to meet. Backed by Germany, Austria-Hungary declared war on Serbia for revenge. These actions ignited the powder key that was the European continent. Steeped in competitive nationalism, militarism, and imperialism, Europe soon divided into the Central Powers of Germany, Austria-Hungary, and their allies, and the Allied Powers of France, England, Russia, and their allies. Germany recognized that both Russia and France would attack, so Kaiser Wilhelm's forces struck first through Belgium into France. This assault was stopped outside Paris where the two sides entrenched to survive the murderous new weapons of the machine gun, poison gas, and long-range artillery. The trenches extended north and south across Europe but moved very little east or west for the remainder of the war. The Great War was named World War I only in hindsight after World War II had begun.

## 3 Central Powers

Named such because of their location in central Europe, the Central Powers were Germany, Austria-Hungary, and their empires; the Ottoman Empire (Turkey); and Bulgaria. A previous alliance called the Triple Alliance was the basis for this grouping since the 1880s, but when war came Italy backed out of the Triple Alliance and sided with the Allied Powers. Because of legal questions surrounding the opening of the war, the Central Powers were considered to have started the war, although all combatant nations participated in imperialism and militarism as expression of ardent nationalism before the Great War commenced. Since the Central Powers were defeated, they bore the brunt of the blame, lost their empires, and were ordered to pay damages.

# 4 Allied Powers

In a counterpoint to the Triple Alliance, England, France, and Russia had formed the Triple Entente. Again, when imperial powers went to war so did their empires, so numerous other principalities supported the Allied war effort either directly or indirectly. Other significant combatant nations that joined the Allied Powers, however, included Italy, Japan, and the United States. Russia sought to fend off Germanic imperialism and to support its fellow Slavs against German aggression. France was allied with Russia against the German threat, and the United Kingdom joined the Allied Powers, as did Belgium, when Germany invaded France through neutral Belgium. The United States eventually joined the Allied Powers after, among other causes, the hostile provocations from German submarines.

# 5 U-boats

The German U-boats, or submarines, were the hope of the Central Powers in breaking the blockade of its shores by the British navy. The United States traded with both sides of the war prior to 1917, although the Allied blockade considerably reduced the supplies reaching the Central Powers. Germany possessed twenty-nine submarines at the start of World War I but by war's end had constructed 360. German U-boats attacked enemy naval vessels but also merchant ships, troop transport ships, and even passenger liners. Submarines could surface unexpectedly and capture enemy ships as prizes or simply sink the ships without warning by firing torpedoes from beneath the surface. After several warnings to stop what was then considered to be dishonorable attacks, Germany's unrestricted submarine warfare brought the United States into the war. U-boats sank passenger vessels with Americans on board and then American merchant vessels. These last were considered to be the final straw and the main justification for a reluctant president to seek a declaration of war.

# 6 *Lusitania*

The German embassy warned Americans not to board the *Lusitania*, a British passenger steamship that was sunk by a submarine in May of 1915. The attack killed 1,198 people including 128 Americans. Germany had accused the British of running small arms from America to Europe hidden aboard passenger ships. That this accusation was true did not keep Germany's enemies, and public opinion in the United States, from assuming the German people to be barbarous. The United States issued a demand that Germany stop unrestricted submarine warfare. Germany justified the sinking because of the weapons on board, but Wilson ordered his secretary of state, William Jennings Bryan, to issue another demand. Bryan, a pacifist and isolationist, refused on the grounds that the note would provoke a war with Germany, and Wilson accepted his resignation.

## 7 *Arabic* Pledge

Another British passenger steamer was sunk in August 1915. Two American lives were lost when the *Arabic* went down. The German Ambassador himself issued the *Arabic* Pledge saying, "Liners will not be sunk by our submarines without warning and without safety of the lives of non-combatants, provided that the liners do not try to escape or offer resistance." These words were not comforting, especially to people facing a plunge into the icy waters of the North Atlantic, but Germany did for a time focus attacks only on cargo ships. The United States claimed a diplomatic victory in this regard. Subsequent violations of the *Arabic* Pledge were all the more shocking as a result.

## 8 *Sussex* Pledge

The next year a German submarine sank the French passenger steamer, the *Sussex.* A secret order had gone out to German U-boat captains to sink all ships in the English Channel as possible troop transports. While no Americans were killed in the attack on the *Sussex,* some were injured. Wilson called the attack a violation of the *Arabic* Pledge. His advisers suggested an immediate break in diplomatic relations was necessary, but Wilson insisted on giving the Germans one more chance. In what amounted to the *Sussex* Pledge, Wilson said that unless Germany abandoned its method of submarine warfare that the United States would break off diplomatic ties, a classic step toward war. Wilson's unwillingness to respond after an incident he himself said violated the *Arabic* Pledge and his subsequent election to a second term on a neutrality platform only encouraged the Germans to think the United States was weak.

## 9 Zimmermann Telegram

The German attitude toward the United States was revealed in an intercepted telegram from Germany's foreign secretary, Arthur Zimmermann, to the German ambassador to Mexico. Believing that tensions between Mexico and the United States could serve the Central Powers, Zimmermann authorized the ambassador, in the event of war between Germany and the United States, to say, "That we shall make war together and together make peace. We shall give generous financial support, and it is understood that Mexico is to reconquer the lost territory in New Mexico, Texas, and Arizona." When this message was decoded, the state department released it to the press, and Woodrow Wilson, who had vacillated in his policy toward Mexico, was in exactly the same position as William McKinley after the release of the Depuy de Lome letter prior to the Spanish-American War. Wilson did not want a war, but if he failed to act he would appear weak. Before he could decide what to do, events exploded in the shape of four American merchant vessels sunk by submarines in less than two weeks, all within the same month the Zimmermann Telegram was released to the press. Just over a week later Wilson went to the Congress and secured a declaration of war against Germany because, as he said, Germany was making "warfare against mankind."

## 10 Election of 1916

The slogan "He kept us out of war" put Wilson back in the White House after campaigning against Supreme Court Justice Charles Evans Hughes who said the United States should enter the Great War and end it. Women were already getting the vote in some states, and Wilson's promise not to send their sons to war in Europe had dramatic appeal. Still, the election was so close that no decision could be rendered until California had voted. Wilson won California by fewer than four thousand votes, but his election was interpreted by Germany to mean the United States did not want to enter the war in Europe and would not do so even under continued provocation. Within just a few months of the election Wilson was preparing for war through funding measures and the Selective Service Act requiring all men between the ages of twenty-one and thirty to register for the draft. As the severity of a war that had been allowed to drift on became apparent, the draft age was increased to the ages of eighteen to forty-five in 1918.

## 11 Uncle Sam

The name came from a Samuel Wilson who in the War of 1812 supplied beef in barrels to American soldiers. Wilson stamped the barrels with the initials "U.S." for United States, but soldiers began to say the meat came from Uncle Sam. Before long "Uncle Sam" became a euphemism for the federal government. Thomas Nast picked up on the metaphor and personified the United States in the striped pants and top hat familiar today. James Flagg used the image in the most successful recruiting poster of World War I, or of any American war. The simple message, "I want you for the U.S. Army," was emblazoned across an image of Uncle Sam pointing at passersby. The eyes and the finger of the poster were designed to follow people and remain fixed upon them because of the use of foreshortening and an optical illusion in the eyes. Of the four million men and women who were in uniform during World War I, 2.5 million volunteered to serve their country.

## 12 John J. Pershing

Pershing was a cavalry officer who had fought American Indians and served in the Spanish-American War. He then served in the Philippines and was caught up in the Russo-Japanese War as an observer of the Japanese military. Pershing then returned to the United States in time to be dispatched by Wilson into Mexico to lead the hunt for Pancho Villa. As America's most seasoned cavalry commander, Pershing was promoted to major general at the outbreak of World War I and commander of the American Expeditionary Force, or AEF, when the United States entered the war. In leading the four million American personnel, Pershing insisted that Americans fight as separate units rather than be placed piecemeal into the trenches as reinforcements of the exhausted Allied Powers. For his efforts Pershing was promoted to full general and given the title "General of the Armies of the United States," a rank reminiscent of that of Napoleon. He served after the war in the more traditional role of army chief of staff and retired in 1924. Medium-range nuclear missiles later bore his name during the Cold War.

## 13 Meuse-Argonne Offensive

The Meuse-Argonne Offensive was the largest commitment of American fighting units of the war. As part of an overall offensive designed by the French commander, all available American forces were put into combat in September 1918 along a sector between the Meuse River and the Argonne Forest. The American force amounted to 1.2 million men whose objective was to cut the main German supply line to the Western Front. The Germans were worn down slowly through the autumn, but by the first of November they were in full retreat. On November 11, 1918, an armistice was called that ended the fighting and allowed the combatants to negotiate the Treaty of Versailles. In the Meuse-Argonne Offensive, America lost 120,000 wounded, dead, or missing casualties, or 10 percent of the force.

## 14 George Creel

Back home in the United States, Woodrow Wilson chose Madison Avenue advertising executive George Creel to head the Committee on Public Information. After his narrow victory in 1916, Wilson realized as war loomed that he needed some system to now sell the war to the American people. Creel had been steeped in the use of propaganda as a muckraking journalist, and he said his goal for the campaign was to create "a passionate belief in the justice of America's cause" and to turn that passion into recruits for the military and dollars for the war effort. The Committee on Public Information sponsored "Four Minute Men" who gave patriotic, pro-war speeches in movie theaters, produced films showcasing America's commitment, and published millions of posters that were distributed to increase the sale of war bonds and enlistment in the military. The activities of the Committee on Public Information were criticized even in their day as maudlin political propaganda, but a similar campaign was mounted again on a larger scale for World War II.

## 15 Espionage and Sedition Acts

Revealing even more insecurity about war aims, Wilson and a Democratic Congress passed the Espionage and Sedition Acts in a similar vein to the Alien and Sedition Acts passed by John Adams and the Federalists. The Espionage Act of 1917 imposed severe fines and up to twenty years' imprisonment for persons found guilty of aiding the enemy, obstructing recruiting, causing insubordination, stirring up disloyalty, or inspiring the refusal of duty in the military. Such a law served to touch off a wave of anti-German sentiments regarding German immigrants who had long been in the United States as citizens. In 1918, the Sedition Act was an amendment to the Espionage Act that applied the penalties to those proven to lie about the government or to use "disloyal, profane, scurrilous, or abusive language" about America, its government, its patriotic symbols, or its armed forces. The law was aimed mainly at socialists and pacifists because the Soviet Union had backed out of the Allied Powers just as the United States had joined the war effort. Breaking this law landed Eugene V. Debs in jail from where he ran for president in 1920.

# 16 Fourteen Point Address

After the Bolsheviks succeeded in the communist revolution that began the Soviet Union, Lenin pulled the new communist state out of the war and revealed documents that portrayed the alliance system agreed on by the czar as shamelessly imperialistic. In response, Woodrow Wilson addressed the U.S. Congress in January 1918 and delivered his Fourteen Point Address denying any desire on the part of the United States for acquisition of territory. Instead, the Fourteen Points were a series of principles that Wilson and his advisers thought were the only hope of a lasting peace. The first several points directly attacked the nationalism, imperialism, militarism, and alliances that had brought on the war and proposed measures to keep these forces in check in international relations. The rest of the points, except the last one, dealt with establishing self-government for various oppressed peoples in the empires of the Central Powers or struggling nationalities that lacked actual nations. The fourteenth point sought the formation of the League of Nations, a body where member nations would commit to collective security but also the arbitration of international disputes. Many of the provisions were adopted in the peace after World War I, but many were so idealistic as to require another world war before gaining wide support.

# 17 Treaty of Versailles

After heated discussion in Europe by the Big Four—the United States, the United Kingdom, France, and Italy—Wilson was unable to persuade the other leaders to grant the Central Powers a benevolent peace. The 1919 Treaty of Versailles, therefore, was a punitive peace. Germany, in particular, had to accept the blame for starting the war, give up all her colonies, give land back to France taken in a previous war, pay ultimately $56 billion in reparations, and relinquish any offensive military forces. The peace also ended the Austro-Hungarian Empire and the Ottoman Empire. The Treaty of Versailles also laid the groundwork for the League of Nations and excluded the Central Powers from membership. Wilson brought the treaty back to Washington for ratification by the Senate even though he was deeply dissatisfied. Adolph Hitler later pointed to the Treaty of Versailles as an injustice and used animosity toward the punitive peace as a key to unifying the German people behind the rule of the Nazi Party. Thus, the peace of World War I actually was a major cause of World War II. Even the Germans who signed the Treaty of Versailles said at the ceremony, "We will see you again in twenty years." Their prediction was nearly perfectly accurate because the official start of World War II came with Germany's invasion of Poland in 1939.

# 18 League of Nations

This provision of the Fourteen Points and the Treaty of Versailles was built on the nineteenth-century belief in arbitration as the miracle cure for international strife. The League had two great handicaps, however, as the member nations sought to keep the peace between World War I and World War II. First, Woodrow Wilson could not convince his own country to support the notion and to join the League, so his moral high ground as the "Savior of Europe" was lost. Whatever success American involvement might have accomplished will never be known, but the second handicap was simply that the League of Nations did not do what it said it would do. A few minor problems between small nations were solved without war, but when Japan and Italy began aggressively pursuing nationalistic, militaristic, and imperialistic goals in the 1920s and 1930s, the League did not respond. Hitler and the Germans learned that the League could be ignored, and Germany withdrew from membership in the League that had been granted as appeasement for the punitive nature of the Treaty of Versailles. The principles of the League of Nations were resurrected in the form of the United Nations after the League itself was destroyed by the horrible catastrophe that was World War II.

# 19 Henry Cabot Lodge

Woodrow Wilson's nemesis in the Senate was Massachusetts senator Henry Cabot Lodge. Lodge had received the first political science Ph.D. degree ever given by Harvard University in 1876. He went on to lecture there in American history. As a member of the House of Representatives he was a civil service reformer and personal friend of Theodore Roosevelt (TR) who helped draft much of the legislation behind the Square Deal, but the two men had a falling out over TR's bid for the presidency in 1912. By then Lodge was a prominent senator, imperialist, and leader of the Old Guard. He led the "Irreconcilables" in the battle against Woodrow Wilson's desire to draw the United States into the League of Nations.

# 20 Irreconcilables

Henry Cabot Lodge and other conservative Republicans in the Senate had supported the involvement of the United States in World War I but could not bring themselves to support the League of Nations. Much of the nation desired to "return to normalcy," a phrase that in part meant the restoring of isolationism as the mainstay of American foreign policy. The Irreconcilables opposed Wilson's collective security idea on the grounds that the United States had not had a military alliance in times of peace with any nation but France immediately after the War for Independence, and under the wise leadership of George Washington had dispensed with the alliance as soon as possible. Even during World War I the United States never formally joined the Allied Powers but merely declared war independently on the enemies of the Allied Powers. Lodge and the Irreconcilables said an alliance pledging the United States would go to war if other members of the League of Nations were attacked violated the constitutional power of the Congress to both make war and to declare peace. Many senators were, of course, skeptical of Wilson's notion that World War I had been the war to end all wars. The difficulty with this stance after World War I, however, was that the United States had become a creditor nation for the first time. On top of the food, oil, and men America had contributed to the war effort were loans granted to the Allied Powers that only one, Finland, ever actually paid off. Dollar diplomacy and the possession of spheres of influence around the globe created a situation where the isolationist policies of the Irreconcilables proved impossible to maintain.

## The Big Picture

1. The United States was drawn into the worst war the world had ever seen by a series of events that made it impossible to remain neutral in World War I.

2. Once the decision to enter World War I was made, the United States mobilized the tremendous manpower and natural resources of the nation to make a significant contribution toward the victory of the Allied Powers.

3. Although the most significant contribution made by the United States was the economic support provided by American food, oil, and money, the American Expeditionary Force distinguished itself on the battlefield and contributed to forcing the Central Powers to surrender.

4. Woodrow Wilson conceived of a plan for world peace that proved impossible to implement successfully in his lifetime, but the visionary ideals of the Fourteen Point Address became the model for a more lasting peace after World War II.

5. The American system of constitutional checks and balances served to avoid the extremes of one-man rule or those of ceaseless parliamentary debate in order to allow the United States to become a more balanced world power.

# Mini Quiz

1. The first organization that could be termed a national labor union was the

   (A) Molly Maguires.
   (B) American Federation of Labor.
   (C) American Railway Union.
   (D) National Labor Union.
   (E) The Knights of Labor.

2. The Granger Laws included a regulation that

   (A) limited the number of attorneys a corporation could employ in its defense in a federal lawsuit.
   (B) granted a ten-year period of use before an inventor could earn profits on agricultural patents.
   (C) kept railroads from charging higher prices for carrying loads shorter distances than for long.
   (D) set aside some western land in each state for agricultural and mechanical universities.
   (E) increased the number of silos in the West where farmers could store their grain.

3. William Jennings Bryan delivered his famous "Cross of Gold" speech while he was

   (A) campaigning as the Democratic candidate for the Election of 1896.
   (B) preaching to his congregation and contemplating a bid for the presidency.
   (C) speaking about currency issues at the World's Fair in Chicago.
   (D) addressing a crowd of Populists trying to persuade them to join the Democrats.
   (E) attempting to secure the nomination for the presidency for the Democratic Party.

4. Jane Addams was considered a pioneer in

   (A) social work among urban dwellers.
   (B) international relations with countries sending immigrants to the United States.
   (C) municipal government reforms.
   (D) modern library management.
   (E) activism on behalf of farmers in the Populist movement.

5. Which of the following is an example of how Theodore Roosevelt used the Wisconsin Idea?

   (A) Development of more modern dairy facilities to produce cleaner products for consumers
   (B) The collection of large game animals as specimens for museums around the world
   (C) Singling out some bad trusts to be prosecuted by federal law while advancing other trusts
   (D) Personally intervening in the coal miners' strike as a matter of national security
   (E) Consulting with John Muir about natural resource management in national forests and parks

6. Muckraking journalist Ida Tarbell wrote exposés about the

   (A) insurance industry.
   (B) oil industry.
   (C) meat-packing industry.
   (D) steel industry.
   (E) transportation industry.

7. William Howard Taft most disagreed with Theodore Roosevelt over

   (A) intervention in Central America with American money and military power.
   (B) American control of the Panama Canal.
   (C) conservation of natural resources like timber and coal.
   (D) intervention in World War I in Europe.
   (E) domestic regulatory and tariff policies.

8. The first federal income tax legalized by the Sixteenth Amendment to the U.S. Constitution was intended to raise funds as a result of

   (A) American involvement in World War I.
   (B) a recession that lasted from 1910 to 1911.
   (C) a push to expand telephone wires to connect all American towns and cities.
   (D) a lowered tariff's reducing of federal revenues.
   (E) the formation of the federal reserve system.

9. Besides being from a different part of Europe, most immigrants to America from 1885 to 1917 were also different in that they

   (A) were war refugees.
   (B) came fleeing famines.
   (C) were not Protestant Christians.
   (D) established businesses in urban centers upon their arrival.
   (E) were already accustomed to factory work.

10. All of the following arguments were used to attack support for imperialism EXCEPT

   (A) the U.S. Constitution made no provision for creating spheres of influence abroad.
   (B) subjecting others to American rule violated the principles of the Declaration of Independence.
   (C) the United States did not need to add more nonwhite people to its concerns.
   (D) America's military was already stretched beyond its capacity to protect American interests.
   (E) the rhetoric about spreading a better way of life was just a cover for greed for more profits.

11. The annexation of Hawaii was reminiscent of that of Texas because

   (A) the president of the United States made a treaty to acquire the territory.
   (B) a joint resolution of Congress approved the annexation.
   (C) the land was purchased from a foreign power.
   (D) the annexation occurred without the approval of the people living in the annexed territory.
   (E) a monarch was toppled in order for the land to be available for annexation.

12. Which of the following statements is most accurate in regard to the role of the United States in the building of the Panama Canal?

   (A) After taking over the isthmus from Colombia, the United States built the canal from scratch.
   (B) The United States took over a construction project in Panama that had been abandoned by the French.
   (C) After helping the Panamanians acquire freedom, the United States then bought the Canal Zone.
   (D) The United States built a naval base on the tip of the Yucatan Peninsula to protect the Panama Canal.
   (E) An American's plan to control malaria made construction of the canal feasible.

13. The most significant factor in bringing the United States into World War I was the

    (A)  use of propaganda by the British in imploring the United States to uphold a shared heritage.
    (B)  domestic propaganda created by the Committee on Public Information.
    (C)  diplomatic crisis created by the leaking of secret German-Mexican negotiations.
    (D)  desperation of Germany to break the Allied blockade by using submarine warfare.
    (E)  increase in anti-German sentiment after the discovery of spies operating in the United States.

14. The most important contribution of the United States in winning World War I was the

    (A)  demand by John J. Pershing that American forces fight together.
    (B)  heroism and skill of individual Americans in battle.
    (C)  diplomatic skill of Woodrow Wilson, the first president to go to Europe while in office.
    (D)  economic boost through supplying food, fuel oil, and financial backing to allies.
    (E)  American invention of the tank to combat machine guns in trench warfare.

15. A main theme of Woodrow Wilson's Fourteen Points Address besides the quest for world peace was the

    (A)  diplomatic isolation of Germany, Austria, and Hungary.
    (B)  right of small nations released from empires to determine their own destinies.
    (C)  elimination of military power as an instrument of national policies.
    (D)  recognition of the rise of Russia as a force to be contended with in the twentieth century.
    (E)  reparations to be paid to the victors by the aggressor nations that started the war.

# Answer Explanations

1. **D**  Neither the Molly Maguires nor the American Railway Union could be called national labor unions, and both the Knights of Labor and the American Federation of Labor followed the National Labor Union as the first successful organization to achieve a national voice.

2. **C**  Although farmers associated with the Grange or the Populist Party might have approved of all of these measures, only answer D was a real action on the part of the government. Answer C describes the law meant to address the circumstances farmers in the West found so frustrating, that a man like John D. Rockefeller could get rebates for shipping a large volume of product that would allow him to pay less to ship oil farther than he paid to ship his grain.

3. **E**  All of the answers evoke images of the Great Commoner in action, and answer D conveys the results of the "Cross of Gold" speech, but the speech was delivered at the Democratic National Convention and not only secured Bryan the nomination but swept the Populists into his ill-fated campaign against William McKinley in 1896.

4. **A**  Although answer A is close to the truth in that Jane Addams criticized the municipal government of Chicago and pressured them into making changes, the reason they listened to her at all was because she had already made a name for herself as the Mother of Social Work in reaching out to the immigrant poor through the urban settlement house movement she began at Hull House.

5. **E**  Answers B, C, and D are certainly pursuits in which Theodore Roosevelt (TR) participated and/or led, and answer A is a nod to Wisconsin's dairy industry. The Wisconsin Idea, however, had nothing to do with dairies directly. The Wisconsin Idea was that government leaders should consult with "experts" like John Muir in order to determine what policies to apply to problems like the conservation of natural resources. TR took Muir's advice in many cases, and although the two did not see eye to eye in all matters, they maintained a powerful working relationship when it came to preserving the American wilderness.

6. **B**  Ida Tarbell wrote her serialized "History of Standard Oil" for *McClure's* magazine in an attempt to expose what she considered to be the nefarious business practices of John D. Rockefeller. Other muckrakers focused on each of the other industries as targets of what was coming into vogue, "investigative" journalism.

7. **E**  Although Republican presidents Theodore Roosevelt (TR) and Taft agreed in their earlier days about the Progressive Reform movement, as President Taft began to go his own way he operated more in tune with the Old Guard Republicans. This stance led him to approve of the Payne-Aldrich Tariff that began as a bill to lower the tariff but wound up a law to raise the tariff. In this regard in which trusts should be targeted for busting and in other domestic policies TR was horrified that his protégé was not following in his footsteps. TR and Taft largely agreed in the areas of policy referred to in the other answers.

8. **D** When Woodrow Wilson won the Election of 1912, one of his first acts was to push the Underwood Tariff through Congress in order to lower taxes on imported goods. He then backed the Sixteenth Amendment to make income taxes constitutional in order to replace the revenue lost by the lowered tariff rates. Answer A certainly was grounds for raising income tax rates, but answer B was not true because the United States had not yet resorted to deficit spending and higher taxation to address recessions or depressions (panics). Neither the Federal Reserve mentioned in answer E nor internal improvements like the expansion of telephone lines in answer C were used as a justification to legalize an income tax.

9. **C** Answers A and B would not have made the immigrants of the New Immigration unique because both were causes of immigration to America before and after the time period mentioned in the question. Few of these new types of immigrant families could afford to establish businesses in their first generations, although many did in the next generation. Most stepped into factory jobs upon their arrival, although most did not have experience with this type of work back in their regions of Europe. Answer C is correct in that most of these immigrants were Roman Catholics, Jews, and Eastern Orthodox Christians. Even though most Irish coming to America were Catholics, most immigrants prior to 1885 were Protestant.

10. **D** All of the other answers were actively used by anti-imperialists to make their case. Answer D was not true in that anti-imperialists said the military would be stretched, not that it was already beyond its capacity. To acknowledge that the U.S. military was stretched beyond its capacity just after the Spanish-American War and after the voyage of the Great White Fleet might have been interpreted as a severe lack of patriotism in such a nationalistic era, and anti-imperialists were careful to maintain the stance that they were the true patriots guarding the cherished principles of the founding principles recorded in the venerated founding documents.

11. **B** Answers A and C are references to the Louisiana Purchase and the Alaska Purchase, respectively. Answer D was not the case in either Texas or Hawaii because both populations earnestly sought entrance into the United States. Answer E refers to the deposing of Queen Liliuokalani, but Texans did not topple a monarch; they declared independence from an autocratic leader who called himself a president.

12. **E** All of the other answers are twists on the story of the Panama Canal in that the United States did not take over Panama but instead helped the Panamanians break free from Colombia. American engineers did start from scratch after a treaty granted the United States the right to build the canal, but they took over the project from the French who had failed in Nicaragua, partly due to the debilitating effects of malaria. The United States leased the Canal Zone instead of purchasing it. Answer D is a reference to the naval base at Guantanamo Bay on the tip of Cuba, not the Yucatan region of Mexico. Walter Reed confirmed the

discoveries of other scientists about the transmission of malaria by mosquitoes and developed a plan to control the disease's spread. Of these choices, answer E best expresses how Americans achieved this monumental task.

13. **D** All of the answers either contributed to the decision of the U.S. Congress to enter the Great War on the side of the Allied Powers or increased support for the war once Americans were fighting. Only answer D, however, can be said to be the most significant factor. The sinking of passenger ships with Americans on board and the sinking of unarmed American merchant vessels compelled a reluctant Woodrow Wilson to ask the Congress for a declaration of war. Wilson considered unrestricted submarine warfare a sign of German barbarism, especially after the Germans had pledged not to do it. Resorting to such a measure, new to warfare, was a sign of how desperate the Germans were to break the Allied blockade that threatened their supplies, many of which they received from the United States prior to American involvement.

14. **D** Answers A, B, and C were all important contributions even though Wilson's diplomatic intervention failed to avoid a punitive peace. Answer E is incorrect in that the British invented the first practical tanks to combat machine gun emplacements. The invention of the airplane by the United States had little impact on the outcome of World War I, but in the deadly attrition created by trench warfare, the Allied Powers would likely not have prevailed without American food, oil, and money. World War I made the U.S. transition away from being a debtor nation to being a creditor nation.

15. **B** Answer B conveys Wilson's cherished notion of self-determination, and many nations were created out of the four collapsed empires at the end of the war partly because of Wilson's firm stand. Wilson actually opposed the punitive nature of the provisions expressed in answers A and E. Answer C is incorrect in that, although Wilson urged disarmament, even he was not as idealistic as the authors of the Kellogg-Briand Peace Pact to which answer C refers. Wilson had used military power in Central America enough to know it was sometimes necessary, let alone having sent Americans into Europe. Neither Wilson nor many other observers could have looked at the chaos of the Bolshevik Revolution in Russia during World War I and predicted the role the Soviet Union would eventually play as suggested in answer D.

# The Roaring Twenties: Sex, Alcohol, and Jazz

# CHAPTER 27

*With but little equipment one can call the life of the rest of the world from the air, and this equipment can be purchased piecemeal at the ten-cent store.*
—Robert S. Lynd and Helen Merrell Lynd, *Middletown*, 1929

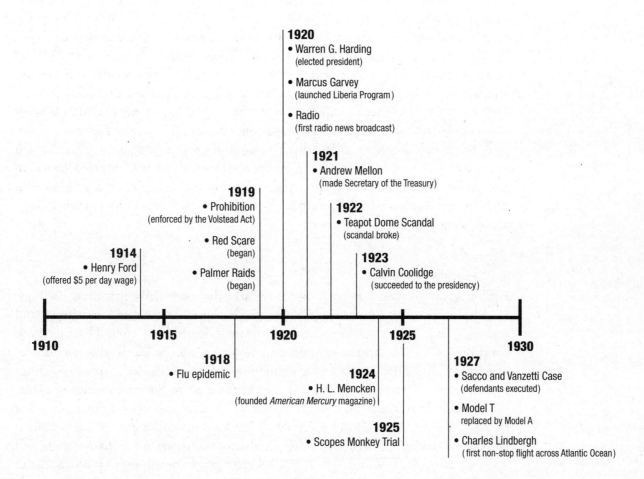

**1920**
• Warren G. Harding
(elected president)

• Marcus Garvey
(launched Liberia Program)

• Radio
(first radio news broadcast)

**1921**
• Andrew Mellon
(made Secretary of the Treasury)

**1919**
• Prohibition
(enforced by the Volstead Act)

• Red Scare
(began)

• Palmer Raids
(began)

**1922**
• Teapot Dome Scandal
(scandal broke)

**1914**
• Henry Ford
(offered $5 per day wage)

**1923**
• Calvin Coolidge
(succeeded to the presidency)

1910      1915      1920      1925      1930

**1918**
• Flu epidemic

**1924**
• H. L. Mencken
(founded *American Mercury* magazine)

**1927**
• Sacco and Vanzetti Case
(defendants executed)

• Model T
replaced by Model A

**1925**
• Scopes Monkey Trial

• Charles Lindbergh
(first non-stop flight across Atlantic Ocean)

# Top 20 Things to Know

## 1 Flu Epidemic

From 1918 to 1919 an influenza epidemic spread from the trenches of World War I around the world and killed from twenty-five to fifty million people. The disease spread in the United States across military installations and then broke out in the general public. The proximity of military personnel and workers in cities made the death toll particularly severe among those between the ages of twenty and forty. In the United States the flu killed more Americans than had the Civil War, roughly 675,000. These deaths were also far more than those of Americans killed in Europe, and the combined effects of war and one of the worst outbreaks of disease dramatically impacted the social fabric of the United States.

## 2 Jazz Age

This nickname for the Roaring Twenties paid homage to one of America's great cultural innovations, jazz music. Called "negro music" because its origins lay in the syncopated rhythms of the legacy of African music among American slaves, jazz led the way for country, rockabilly, and rock 'n' roll as indigenous musical forms. Jazz became a major avenue for cultural exchange between African-American musicians and white youths frequenting famous dance clubs like the Cotton Club in New York City. Jazz expressed a spirit of revolt from traditional musical standards as musicians performed through improvisation, and its spontaneity became a metaphor for the youth revolt. The cultural impact of jazz was evident in that the first motion picture with sound was *The Jazz Singer* in which a white actor portrayed an African-American performer. The style of dancing that accompanied jazz music at nightclubs also expressed deliberate revolt in that couples moved in a manner rarely if ever seen in public.

## 3 Henry Ford

Ford was one of the last great industrialists who personally manifested a rags-to-riches story of the American Dream. He began in Detroit as a machinist and mechanic but began building custom automobiles for the rich. His ingenious contribution to the American economy, however, was in pioneering techniques of mass production that allowed a standardized car, the Model T, to come within the means of the average citizen. He also introduced in his manufacturing plants the eight-hour workday and the $5-a-day minimum wage (twice that for other factory workers). Ford Motor Company therefore avoided many of the problems with labor unions that plagued other industries. Ford was a key manufacturer of war material during World War I, but his attempts to break into a political career ended in failure. He and his son, Edsel, began the Ford Foundation that eventually became a major philanthropic contributor to American society. Ford believed that if Americans could just obtain more individual mobility, then a great equalizing force would alter society. He was right, even though he did not understand what General

Motors learned early on, that Americans wanted cars in colors other than just black. Cars became status symbols rather than merely means of transportation, but they also contributed to the youth revolt in that couples could escape supervision and the traditional courtship process.

# 4 Model T

Henry Ford created the next giant leap in the transportation revolution by making a nearly indestructible product cheaply by use of the continuously moving assembly line. Workers mastered a few tasks in the construction of the Model T and repeated them endlessly as the product moved instead of the workers. During Ford's lifetime this level of efficiency rose until a new car was being driven off the end of the assembly line every ten minutes. This level of productivity not only lowered the price of the car to under $300 (within the capacity of the average person to buy with cash after saving for a year) but also prepared the industrial might with which the United States won both world wars. While Ford stubbornly kept producing his one successful product, his competitors at General Motors experimented with colors other than black and a new model change each year. General Motors could not match Ford's efficiency but they sold their cars on credit, another major innovation creating the modern consumer-based American economy.

# 5 Radio

The entertainment and advertising industries were revolutionized by the invention of the radio. The wireless communication first proven possible before the turn of the century came into nearly every household by the end of the Roaring Twenties. AM radio allowed for far-flung broadcasting, and the KDKA station in Pittsburgh, Pennsylvania, became the first to air election results when Warren G. Harding was elected president in 1920. Music, sports, and drama programs were interspersed with numerous advertisements for household products and ever more numerous consumer goods. The radio was not grasped as a political tool until the fireside chats by Franklin D. Roosevelt in the 1930s, but before then it had become a major producer of a standardized American culture.

# 6 Red Scare

With the creation of the world's first communist state in Russia, the Soviets set about propagandizing against Western nations, and this rhetoric created a panic in American society. The Communist Party in America existed as early as 1919 even before the death of Lenin. The already tenuous history of the labor movement in America made nativist and anticommunist fears erupt in the anti-immigration laws of the 1920s, which were another decade of the repression of labor interests. Americans feared that Bolsheviks, or communists, were infiltrating labor unions, universities, and other institutions with the purpose of plotting the overthrow of the government. Enough evidence of such infiltration was discovered to raise public hysteria. During the Roaring Twenties the civil liberties of certain elements of society were sacrificed in the process of ferreting out radicals.

# 7 Palmer Raids

Attorney General A. Mitchell Palmer began a series of mass arrests of subversives and agitators in the country's labor unions. Those immigrants arrested who had not yet received citizenship were simply deported. Anarchists, socialists, and communists, as well as innocent bystanders were all caught in the net of the many Palmer Raids in what became the First Red Scare. In January 1920, Palmer ordered raids in thirty-three cities that took 2,700 people into custody. Palmer cited the phrase from Oliver Wendell Holmes Jr. regarding a "clear and present danger" to national security in justifying the arrests and the confiscation of labor publications with suspicious content. A. Mitchell Palmer was nearly killed by a mail bomb after which point the Palmer Raids diminished, but a fear of communist infiltration remained as a basis for the Cold War.

# 8 Sacco and Vanzetti Case

Nicola Sacco and Bartolomeo Vanzetti were two Italian immigrants who were arrested in 1927 for murder. They were convicted after one of America's first show trials on what many considered insufficient evidence, and a widespread belief developed that they were only found guilty because they were anarchists. The two men were sentenced to death, but when defense attorneys succeeded in throwing enough doubt on their convictions as to secure a stay of their executions, liberal and radical Americans resorted to mass demonstrations to secure their release. As a result of the protests, the governor of Massachusetts (the original murders were committed in Braintree, Massachusetts) ordered a review of the case by a special commission. The commission ruled that the men actually were guilty and that the trial had been conducted appropriately, so Sacco and Vanzetti were each executed in the electric chair. Their case was considered by some to be the result of the mass hysteria created by the civil liberties abuses of the Red Scare.

# 9 Warren G. Harding

Harding was a flashback to the Gilded Age in that he was a Republican with strong ties to the political machine created in Ohio by Marcus Hanna. He rose from editing a newspaper up through Ohio politics and into the U.S. Senate. He was nominated as a dependable and predictable Republican to run for the presidency in 1920, and his plea for America to "return to normalcy" struck a chord with American voters tired of Progressive Reform and the horrors of World War I. He achieved the largest margin of victory yet in a presidential election but proved to be an incompetent administrator who, like Ulysses S. Grant, surrounded himself with unscrupulous men. His one foreign policy coup, the Washington Naval Conference, seemed to end the dangerous arms race among the United Kingdom, the United States, France, Italy, and Japan but it did not spare him from a growing public frustration with a return to corruption instead of normalcy. After traveling to Alaska on a tour to regain the respect of the American people he died on the return trip leaving Calvin Coolidge in the White House.

## 10 Teapot Dome Scandal

This scandal reminiscent of the Ballinger-Pinchot Affair in the Taft administration was the most widely known case of corruption in the Harding administration. Reports of wrongdoing in the Navy, Justice, and Interior Departments were only the tip of the iceberg. Members of the executive branch were indicted for fraud, conspiracy, and bribery. Albert B. Fall was the best example of the "Ohio Gang," the group of grafters using their connections to Harding to line their own pockets. Fall was appointed by Harding in 1924 to oversee the oil reserves at Teapot Dome, Wyoming, that were supposed to be set aside for the national security needs of the U.S. Navy. Fall leased the Wyoming oil fields, and others in California, to private developers. The developers paid Fall at least $125,000 for the access. Fall, who had tried to retire, was sentenced to prison and fined $100,000. Before Warren G. Harding died nearly every member of his cabinet had fallen under suspicion. The character and reputation of Calvin Coolidge were all the more remarkable after the Harding administration in that Vice President Coolidge was never connected to any of the Harding scandals.

## 11 Calvin Coolidge

The integrity of Calvin Coolidge had propelled him up through Massachusetts politics even as a Vermonter, and as governor of Massachusetts during the Boston police strike he gained national fame for saying "There is no right to strike against the public safety by anybody, anywhere, any time." This reputation led to his election as vice president that led to his ascension to the presidency after Harding's death. Coolidge had the good fortune to preside over a booming economy and a calm world. His hands-off policy was nearly a flashback to laissez-faire and Jeffersonian principles of limited government. In other words, whatever Theodore Roosevelt had done as a Republican president, Calvin Coolidge did not. After winning a term to the presidency in his own right, he did not seek a second term and went off as had John Adams to work his New England farm. He left Herbert Hoover to deal with the inevitable crash after a decade of wild economic growth.

## 12 Andrew Mellon

As a Pennsylvania banker Andrew Mellon made himself rich by backing successful businessmen and investing in their companies. In 1921, President Harding chose Mellon as secretary of the Treasury, a post he manned all the way through the incredible prosperity of the Roaring Twenties. He sought efficiency in government and developed the idea of cutting taxes and reducing spending in order to lower deficits and boost the economy. He proved that when Americans kept more of their own money they did not all waste it in conspicuous consumption of consumer goods and luxuries. Instead, they invested the money in business enterprises through the stock market and created unprecedented financial prosperity. The Stock Market Crash, however, ruined Mellon's reputation even though the practices of banks in speculation were more to blame than federal policies. Mellon resigned from public office to devote his energies to philanthropy and art collecting, and before his death his contributions and his private collection became the nucleus of the National Gallery of Art in Washington, D.C.

## 13 Marcus Garvey

Garvey was born in Jamaica and rose from being a printer to being a journalist and editor of radical newspapers. After traveling widely and reading Booker T. Washington's *Up from Slavery*, Garvey became a passionate supporter of African nationalism. He formed the Universal Negro Improvement Association, or UNIA, "to work for the general uplift of the Negro peoples of the world." Garvey brought his message to America in 1916 and resurrected the idea that the descendants of American slaves should go back to Africa to develop an independent civilization of their own. Until that goal could be reached, Garvey dressed flamboyantly in flashy military-style uniforms and spread the word that "black is beautiful." He supported segregated African-American churches and maintained that Jesus and Mary were of African descent, and Garvey went so far as to say African-American children should play with black dolls. Garvey suggested African-Americans should become businessmen and achieve economic independence. Through scandals in the financing of a shipping company, Garvey was convicted of squandering investors' money and served two years in prison. He was then deported back to Jamaica as his land grants and early attempts at colonizing in Liberia also fell through. His movement at its peak consisted of eight million readers and followers, and he laid the groundwork for much of the modern emphasis on African-American history and African heritage.

## 14 Lost Generation

This phrase was a reference to the generation of European youth whose lives were literally or figuratively blasted into smithereens by World War I, but it was applied in the 1920s in America to certain literary figures who expatriated. Gertrude Stein famously used the phrase in reference to Ernest Hemingway, and the writings of many of the American authors who lived abroad reflected the fact that American youth had lost a moral compass. The Lost Generation is evidence that Western Civilization was alienated from its traditional values by the collapse into the chaos of World War I. Many of these poets and novelists lived in Paris or London and from that distance portrayed American society as materialistic and devoid of substantive values. Among them were Hemingway, F. Scott Fitzgerald, and T. S. Eliot. Their portrayal of society both reflected and encouraged the esoteric, the eccentric, and the amoral values of the urban youth revolt as it searched for meaning in gin and jazz music.

## 15 Scopes Monkey Trial

Sixty-six years after the debate opened with the publication of *On the Origin of Species* by Charles Darwin, the state of Tennessee banned the teaching of the theory of evolution in public schools. John T. Scopes, a biology teacher in Dayton, Tennessee, agreed to test the law when approached by the American Civil Liberties Union (ACLU). Scopes was arrested, and his trial turned into a part-circus, part-epicenter show trial that became the focus of the debate between Fundamentalist Christianity and Modernism, a movement that tried to reconcile Darwinism and the Bible. Clarence Darrow, a famous agnostic defense attorney, took up Scopes's case while William Jennings Bryan acted as the prosecutor. Darrow trapped the aging Bryan into testifying on the stand, and Darrow went on to befuddle Bryan with a series of questions about the veracity of the Bible. Scopes was eventually found guilty and fined, but the case brought derision on Tennessee in particular and the South in general. William Jennings Bryan died shortly after the trial, which became a milestone of revolutionary changes in values.

## 16 Flappers

Flappers were not in the majority among young women even in the Roaring Twenties, but they represented what was chic and daring in American cities. Some were obvious in that they cut their hair short as well as their hemlines. Others simply embraced the spirit of looseness bordering on hedonism exhibited by their more daring sisters' flapping dresses. The lifestyle of flappers involved more open use of tobacco and alcohol even though the latter was made illegal by Prohibition. Young women also pursued greater romantic and sexual freedom apart from the supervision of their families. One cannot say which led this cultural revolution, the young people or the advertisers who marketed products in the new consumer economy. Although the older generations were shocked at the behavior of young women and decried their degeneracy, it should be pointed out that for every flapper there was a male companion, or many, actively rejecting traditional values that had been drawn into question in the aftermath of World War I.

## 17 Prohibition

This term applies to a period of about fourteen years in length between the passage of the Eighteenth Amendment and the Twenty-first Amendment that repealed it. The Prohibition movement, however, extended back to the Second Great Awakening preachers decrying "demon rum" and the activities of the Women's Christian Temperance Union. The 1919 amendment to the Constitution was enforced by the Volstead Act that defined alcoholic beverages as any that were more than 0.5 percent alcohol by volume. Specifically, the Eighteenth Amendment did not outlaw the consumption of alcoholic beverages but their "manufacture, sale, or transportation." Al Capone of Chicago and other gangsters took advantage of the laws to develop a network of bootleggers to distribute liquor illegally. The Mafia and other nefarious organizations also opened speakeasies, or secret bars, that were frequented by flappers and their dates. The illegal manufacture of alcoholic beverages also skyrocketed in home or backwoods stills. During the Great Depression the government realized that more tax dollars could be had if the legal alcohol industry were restored. America's experiment with Prohibition led to the only repeal of a constitutional amendment and a general loosening of morals resulting from a conspiracy of deliberate revolt against a federal law.

## 18 Speakeasies

The enforcement of Prohibition proved beyond the capacity of the federal government. Halfway into the Prohibition era it was estimated that one hundred thousand of these small, secret bars existed in New York City alone. The corrupting influence of bootlegging went beyond the running of liquor to the bribing of law enforcement officials to avoid prosecution. The term *speakeasies* derives from the bars that attempted to avoid prosecution not by bribing but by making the customers remember secret passwords to gain admittance. The existence of sophisticated smuggling rings and subversive hideouts made the youth revolt all the more exciting and the lack of respect for the law all the more pervasive, but just as the majority of young women were not flappers, the majority of Americans curtailed the consumption of alcohol markedly during Prohibition.

## 19 H. L. Mencken

Nietzsche spoke, and there was H. L. Mencken. Mencken was a journalist from Baltimore whose talents lay in the clever use of language to criticize virtually everything and everyone around him. His cynicism proved addictive to many other writers and thinkers who followed Mencken's biting wit through the pages of his *The American Mercury* magazine. He referred to his fellow Americans as of the species, "Boobus Americanus," and he wrote disparagingly of American democracy. He personally covered the Scopes Monkey Trial for his magazine and wrote that Dayton, Tennessee, was a medieval town that would soon burn John T. Scopes at the stake. His style of muckraking journalism channeled the disillusion with Western Civilization and traditional values that was the spirit of the age. Later, when Americans were depressed enough by the Great Depression, his readers grew weary of Mencken's continued scorn and sought authors who were more constructive than destructive in their criticism.

## 20 Charles Lindbergh

As evidence of the frivolous nature of American culture, the public idolized sports heroes like Babe Ruth, people who sat atop flagpoles for days on end, and pioneer aviator Charles Lindbergh. Lindbergh was an airmail pilot and plane mechanic who pursued a $25,000 prize for the first person to fly a nonstop flight from New York to Paris. With backing from investors in St. Louis, Missouri, Lindbergh designed a plane he dubbed "The Spirit of St. Louis" and flew the distance to Paris in 33.5 hours. Bemedaled and promoted, Lindbergh returned a national hero. He married, but his first child was kidnapped and murdered, the news of which was a sensationalized national crime story. Having toured Germany between the world wars, Lindbergh returned to America saying Hitler was a "great man" and headed the America First Committee, an isolationist organization that opposed American involvement in World War II. When war came, however, Lindbergh again moved up the ranks of the American military as a test pilot and eventually as a combat pilot. His fame was evidence of the new American fascination with aeronautical technology, travel, and celebrities that became hallmarks of the postwar world.

## *The Big Picture*

1. The Roaring Twenties was an era of societal change as many young war veterans and their female companions rejected traditional values and participated in a moral and sexual revolution.

2. Technological breakthroughs on the consumer level revolutionized daily life and the American economy.

3. Fears of radical infiltration of labor organizations led to a constriction of civil liberties during a period of mass hysteria based on nativism and the deaths resulting from the war and a flu epidemic.

4. A lack of forceful leadership contributed to cultural drift that resulted in the rejection of American society by many intellectuals and artists as well as a general decline of belief in traditional Christianity.

5. The era of Prohibition was a climax of the temperance movement but proved to undermine respect for lawmaking and for authority in general.

# The Stock Market Crash and the Great Depression

*The selling pressure was wholly without precedent. It was coming from everywhere. When the closing bell rang, the great bull market was dead and buried. Not only the little speculators, but the lordly, experienced big traders had been wiped out by the violence of the crash, and the whole financial structure of the nation had been shaken to its foundations.*

—Jonathan Norton Leonard, journalist, 1929

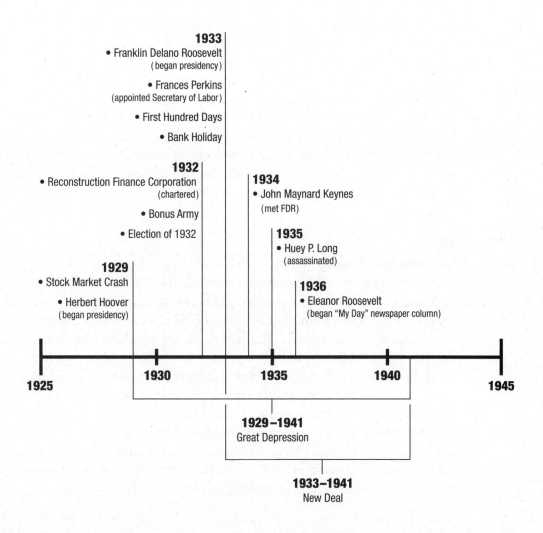

# Top 20 Things to Know

## 1 Stock Market Crash

The period from 1922 to 1929 was one of an unprecedented rise in speculation in stocks and other securities. The subsequent Stock Market Crash was the major sign that the world was facing a global Great Depression. The Crash came after thirteen million shares sold on October 24, 1929. On October 29, sixteen million shares were sold with very few buyers buying. The result was a precipitous drop in the value of stocks and the evaporation of the theoretical wealth created after nearly a decade of margin buying, pumping and dumping, and other inflationary practices.

## 2 Great Depression

Although not entirely caused by the Stock Market Crash, the worst depression the country had ever seen occurred in the wake of the 1929 disaster. Despite the actions of the Hoover administration, the economy of the United States was in critical condition by the time Franklin D. Roosevelt (FDR) took the reins. Citizens lost confidence in the American banking system and rushed to withdraw their savings before bank runs made their banks bankrupt. People hoarded what cash and other valuables they possessed, and the ensuing drop in consumption in a consumer-based economy closed factories and created massive unemployment. Before FDR could act, 5,504 banks closed, and their account holders lost whatever assets they had deposited, an amount estimated at over $3.4 billion. Unemployment rose to a high of nearly 25 percent nationally, and in some cities as many as a third of adults lost their jobs. The Great Depression spanned the globe as international trade diminished causing some countries to experience crippling hyperinflation and bankruptcy.

## 3 Margin Buying

During the years of wild speculation on the stock market, stock values climbed so high and so fast that it was possible to borrow as much as 90 percent of the purchase price of a stock from one's broker, pay the payments for a few months, sell the stock, and still make a profit after paying off the purchase loan. Most speculators then used that profit as another 10 percent down on another even larger purchase of stocks on margin. The repetition of this process contributed to the value of stocks on the stock market being widely separated from the actual value of the American economy. When the Stock Market Crash hit, brokers called in their margin loans. This step meant that the creditors demanded all the money from the purchase loans of their clients who had little to no cash to cover the expense. As stock prices fell, investors sold their stocks at a fraction of their original value and wound up defaulting on their margin loans and walking out into the street penniless.

## 4 Pumping and Dumping

Rings of large speculators used pump-and-dump schemes to dupe the public into raising the artificial value of certain stocks even faster than the speculative boom would have done on its own. A few rich investors would sell a certain stock among themselves while bribing journalists to write glowing reports of the business's potential for growth. The volume of shares being exchanged made small investors believe it was a hot stock, and masses of unsuspecting Americans would jump on board. That open-market sale of the stock would also boost the price higher until the original conspirators sold all their shares at considerable profits. The conspirators would own so much of the stock, however, that their sell-off would catch the market by surprise and create a crash in value. Thankfully, just as most young people in the 1920s were not flappers and most Americans drank less liquor during Prohibition, most Americans thought the stock market was too risky to participate. Until laws were passed to regulate the market and make severe margin-buying and pump-and-dump schemes illegal, it was too risky.

## 5 Herbert Hoover

The man who had the unfortunate timing to become president before the Stock Market Crash was really something of an economic genius and a self-made millionaire. Herbert Hoover was a mining engineer who traveled the globe overseeing numerous projects. During World War I his organizational skills were instrumental in running the U.S. Food Administration, which was responsible for supporting the Allies with food they could not grow for themselves. Hoover served as secretary of Commerce in the biggest decade of commerce in American history, the Roaring Twenties. Once the Great Depression began during his presidential administration, Hoover hoped natural economic forces would fix the problem. He was eventually convinced, however, to extend federal loans to banks and large corporations through his Reconstruction Finance Corporation. Defeated in the landslide victory of Franklin Roosevelt in 1932, Hoover applied his organizational skills to a review of how the executive branch of the United States government was run, otherwise known as the Hoover Commission. Herbert Hoover was another capable man who, like Martin Van Buren, assumed the presidency at a time when nothing he did would be viewed positively. He was, and likely will remain, America's last isolationist president.

## 6 Charles Mitchell

Mitchell was a fast learner like Andrew Carnegie who rose by serving capable men and learning from them before starting out on his own as a New York City financier. By 1921 he was elected president of the National City Bank. He, more than other financial wizards, believed stocks would be popular investments for even the middle class, and he organized the sale of millions of dollars of stock in his own bank. Mitchell in turn used that money for investment schemes, a practice later blamed for the crash and which became either highly regulated or outright illegal after the Stock Market Crash depending on the nature and risk of the investments. When stock prices dropped on October 24, 1929, Charles Mitchell and his associates were so wealthy as to be able to turn the market around by simply putting in their personal wealth (and their banks' wealth) as buyers. When the Stock Market Crash happened, however, Mitchell and his partners were ruined. Unlike some great financiers who either committed suicide or died impoverished, Mitchell made a comeback, regained respect, and left a fortune to his children.

## 7 Joseph P. Kennedy

The father of John, Robert, and Ted Kennedy was so well connected as an Irish banker's son in Boston that because of a shrewd maneuver to save Boston's only Irish-owned bank he was appointed president of the bank at the age of twenty-five. He dabbled in other businesses, including liquor importing (allegedly during Prohibition) and through shrewd investments became the richest man in America. He played the stock market all through the 1920s but pulled out all of his cash just before the Crash. During the Great Depression Franklin Roosevelt made him the head of the new Securities and Exchange Commission that was the New Deal agency designed to regulate the stock market. Some considered this appointment similar to letting a wolf loose among sheep, but Kennedy actually established the agency's integrity as John Marshall had done for the Supreme Court. Joseph Kennedy was later appointed as ambassador to the United Kingdom, a prestigious position from which Kennedy attempted to use his wealth to back his sons as presidential candidates.

## 8 Reconstruction Finance Corporation

When Hoover relented and began to use the federal government as a tool to attempt recovery from the Great Depression, the Reconstruction Finance Corporation (RFC) used federal monies to make loans to banks and large corporations like railroads. Hoover hoped that these loans would stop deflation and maintain the financial structure that would allow consumption and employment to rebound. The Congress authorized Hoover to disperse $500 million through the RFC at first, an amount later extended to $2 billion of borrowed money to in turn be loaned to banks in emergencies. The RFC could even buy corporations and run them directly if such a measure seemed necessary. Hoover signed the RFC into law in 1932 and within six months had loaned out $1.2 billion. The first step of Franklin Roosevelt's New Deal was to continue the RFC and to expand its operations.

## 9 Bonus Army

World War I veterans called for their promised retirement bonuses to be issued early because of the severity of the Great Depression. In July 1932, about one thousand veterans marched on Washington, D.C., to make the request of Congress in person. When Congress failed to act, a total of seventeen thousand veterans and their families descended on the national capital and resolved to camp there until their demands were met. The House of Representatives passed a bill to issue $2.4

billion, but the Senate defeated it. The Congress then offered money to pay for the veterans' expenses to get home, and most took advantage of that offer and left town. About two thousand veterans refused to leave, however, and when Washington police tried to force their evacuation an altercation killed two protestors and two policemen. Hoover then called out the U.S. Army and drove the veterans away using infantry and cavalry, including tanks. In some sense Hoover's reputation never recovered from this act, but he maintained that the situation was dangerous and merited the response.

# 10 Election of 1932

When nominated by the Democratic Party for the 1932 presidential campaign, Franklin D. Roosevelt (FDR) appeared in Chicago in person and delivered an acceptance speech, something only done once before at Theodore Roosevelt's (TR's) acceptance of the nomination of the Progressive Party in 1912. In the speech, the second Roosevelt said, "I pledge you, I pledge myself, to a new deal for the American people." In many other ways did FDR's rise to political power mirror that of TR, his cousin. FDR proposed sweeping government involvement in the direct operation of the American economy in order to help the "forgotten man at the bottom of the economic pyramid," but he said such measures should be "only as a last resort." When he won a landslide victory of Hoover (472 electoral votes to 59) and the Democratic Party won both branches of Congress, FDR immediately set about resorting to his last resort. The result was a reassertion of the principles of Progressive Reform on a massive scale, and to one degree or another Progressivism has been the style of government management considered normal and proper ever since.

# 11 Franklin Delano Roosevelt

Just like his cousin Theodore Roosevelt (TR), Franklin D. Roosevelt (FDR) graduated from Harvard, studied law, served in the state legislature of New York, was the assistant secretary of the Navy, and eventually governor of New York. In the course of his political career he contracted polio and suffered paralysis of his legs. He differed from TR in that his Progressivism originated up out of the Democratic Party. He defeated Herbert Hoover in a landslide victory in the Election of 1932 and told the nation, "the only thing we have to fear is fear itself." His New Deal promised relief, recovery, and reform. FDR's preferred approach to providing relief was through public works projects financed with deficit spending as advised by John Maynard Keynes, a British economist. He faced the Great Depression with a willingness to try any solution, and he inspired the American people through fireside chats on the radio to hang on through the struggle. He also exceeded the traditional restraints on executive power, not the least of which was George Washington's two-term precedent that FDR smashed by being elected four times to the presidency. Facing World War II on top of the Great Depression, however, Americans largely accepted the campaign notion of not switching horses in midstream. FDR and the leaders of Allied nations were largely responsible for fighting the Axis Powers until they submitted to unconditional surrender and for designing the international relationships of the postwar world. FDR died of a brain hemorrhage just three months after his fourth election and within a few weeks of being able to see the victory over the Axis he had worked so hard to achieve.

# 12 New Deal

Upon being inaugurated to the presidency in 1933, Franklin D. Roosevelt (FDR) immediately set about sending proposed pieces of legislation to his "Rubber Stamp" Congress. The New Deal was a flurry of the laws that established agencies within a sweeping bureaucracy that aimed money at the problems of the Great Depression. Each agency was targeted to address relief, recovery, or reform—or all three. Through a system of trial and error, the Roosevelt administration enacted regulations, incentives, and grants to put people back to work. New Deal agencies became known by the three or four initials of their names such as CCC, TVA, FDIC, and the WPA. Although FDR was getting action and doing things in pure Rooseveltian Progressive style, the New Deal failed to organize the sometimes contradictory programs into a comprehensive plan. Some economic historians believe that the New Deal actually prolonged the Great Depression, which was declared only after World War II required a full-scale mobilization of the economy.

# 13 Eleanor Roosevelt

The daughter of Theodore Roosevelt's alcoholic younger brother, Elliott, Eleanor Roosevelt rose from a childhood of neglect to the most influential First Lady to date after marrying Franklin D. Roosevelet (FDR), a distant cousin. Her activism was a powerful counterpoint to FDR's stricken physical condition. Not only did she perform the normal hospitality duties of a president's wife, Eleanor Roosevelt traveled across the country, gave lectures and radio broadcasts, and wrote a newspaper column in which she recounted her daily activities. In this capacity she informed her husband about conditions of average Americans and presented a caring face for the impersonal forces of the New Deal bureaucracy. During World War II she even visited soldiers abroad. Upon her husband's death she made what she considered her greatest contribution by leading in the formation of the United Nations Universal Declaration of Human Rights.

# 14 Frances Perkins

A sociologist and economist, Frances Perkins possessed the best Progressive pedigree possible in that she had worked at Hull House in Chicago. She moved to New York City where she studied industrial conditions and became an advocate for hygiene and safety for workers, especially after the Triangle Shirtwaist Factory fire in 1911 that killed 146 young women. She also helped guide legislation that reduced the work week for women from fifty-four to forty-eight hours. Through her work on many other industrial boards and commissions she came to the attention of Franklin Roosevelt who made her secretary of Labor and the first woman to hold a cabinet post. Throughout the New Deal she guided policies and laws pertaining to labor relations and working conditions that embroiled her in controversy as she advocated the fixing of wages and prices. She supported laws that limited the employment of children under the age of sixteen, pushed for unemployment compensation, and championed the Civilian Conservation Corps (CCC), which employed young men in forestry and other public works.

# 15 Brains Trust

Frances Perkins was only one of the formal and informal advisers to Franklin D. Roosevelt (FDR) known as his "Brains Trust." The New Deal required the "Wisconsin Idea" to be in operation constantly developing innovative ways to either attack the Great Depression or create activity that would assure people that the Roosevelt administration was doing everything in its power to end the crisis. In the early New Deal era, several handpicked professors provided FDR with ideas for bank regulation and other aspects of the First Hundred Days. In the later New Deal the group widened to include lawyers, military officers, and even more academicians (usually economists). The leftward leanings of some of FDR's advisors and New Deal administrators attracted criticism, especially after some toured the Soviet Union and returned with glowing reports. By and large, however, the Brains Trust did assure the American people that the best minds in the country were contributing to the government's grip on the situation.

# 16 Relief, Recovery, and Reform

As Theodore Roosevelt's Square Deal had three Cs, Franklin D. Roosevelt (FDR) imposed at least that level of organization on the New Deal. With the history of the Freedmen's Bureau and the Indian Bureau as precedents, the federal government actively began providing for the welfare of citizens in the relief measures. While there were some direct welfare payments, FDR preferred providing public works projects that employed those who had lost their jobs in various trades including the arts. Therefore, the first goal of the New Deal was to provide for the basic needs of the unemployed. Recovery New Deal measures were designed to take care of the basic needs of the whole economy, that is, to boost consumption, restore the confidence of employers, and raise farm prices. Reform measures were aimed at preventing an economic crisis of the magnitude of the Great Depression from ever happening again. These policies involved regulation of the banking industry and the stock market as well as the general notions of deficit spending and Progressive Reform that have become the norm in American politics.

# 17 First Hundred Days

Franklin D. Roosevelt (FDR) had promised immediate action and delivered by setting to work right after his inauguration. Within the first one hundred days the executive branch had sent an unprecedented number of prospective bills to Congress in consultation with the new Democratic majorities in both houses of the legislative branch. These first measures of the New Deal were aimed at fixing banking, bolstering industry and agriculture, managing labor issues, and giving relief to the unemployed. Eight major components of the New Deal and several more minor ones were established starting with the Emergency Banking Relief Act in March of 1933 running through the National Industrial Recovery Act in June. The special session of Congress FDR had called to deal with the economic emergency then adjourned. Critics dubbed the Seventy-third Congress the "Rubber Stamp" Congress because it did nothing to challenge the will of the executive branch. Two major pieces of New Deal legislation passed during the First Hundred Days, the Agricultural Adjustment Act and the National Industrial Recovery Act, were later judged to be unconstitutional by the Supreme Court. Still, presidents ever since FDR have felt compelled to accomplish significant strides within the first hundred days of their administrations.

## 18 Bank Holiday

To stop bank runs the first act Franklin D. Roosevelt (FDR) did to address the emergency was to declare a four-day national bank holiday that officially ended all transactions of banks and other financial organizations. Having said "The only thing we have to fear is fear itself," FDR thus stopped panic from sending even more banks into bankruptcy. After the bank holiday, over five thousand banks reopened within the first three days. Therefore, three-quarters of all the banks that belonged to the Federal Reserve System were supported through the initial panic. Two weeks later stock prices began to rise and banks reported that people were putting currency and gold back into their bank accounts. One week after starting the Bank Holiday FDR delivered his first fireside chat, a national radio address in which he explained his actions in simple language in an effort to reassure the American people that the crisis had passed. Then because fear subsided, a worse crisis was avoided.

## 19 Huey P. Long

Jumping on the Progressive Reform resurgence bandwagon, certain national figures and politicians claimed that Franklin D. Roosevelt (FDR) had not gone far enough in the first New Deal measures. Governor Huey P. Long of Louisiana wanted more radical change. Long had been a populist lawyer who entered politics as a commissioner for a state transportation and communication agency through which he pushed Progressive reforms. He ran for governor against the oil-industry-backed New Orleans Democratic Party machine and won in 1928. He immediately taxed the oil interests to fund state projects like highways and schools. He then co-opted the political machine and engineered his election to the U.S. Senate while retaining the governorship. Back home he built highways and hospitals and expanded Louisiana State University while pushing radical reforms in Washington, D.C. By then the state referred to Huey Long as the "Kingfish," and Long capitalized on the name saying he wanted to make every man a king. He proposed that the federal government guarantee every American family a minimum annual income of $2,500. While running Louisiana as a virtual dictator, Long announced he would run for the presidency to further his agenda. In 1935, before his campaign could gain ground, Long was assassinated at the Capitol Building in Baton Rouge. Huey Long, Dr. Francis E. Townsend, and Father Charles E. Coughlin all presented the radical fringe that allowed the later New Deal to forward the legislation that led to Social Security.

# 20 John Maynard Keynes

Keynes was a British economist whose revolutionary theories were so controversial as to become a whole school of thought called Keynesian economics, and his work marked a turning point in the twentieth century. Having risen to a position of prominence in the Treasury, Keynes was sent to Versailles as England's main economic adviser. He viewed the Treaty of Versailles to be economically unfeasible for the Germans to endure and resigned in protest. He published a book in 1919 that won him fame, especially after his predictions regarding Germany came true. His *Economic Consequences of the Peace* was only one of his many major works analyzing the economic problems of England, her allies, and her enemies. Keynes advocated the type of interest rate adjustments on the part of governments that were embodied in Woodrow Wilson's Federal Reserve System, but during the Great Depression he suggested that the central governments of countries should abandon balanced budgets and use deficit spending to "prime the pump" by hiring unemployed people to work on public works. Franklin Roosevelt adopted Keynesian economics and agreed that in the absence of progress from corporate America that the federal government should act in the stead of big business to mobilize the economic resources of the country.

## The Big Picture

1. After a decade of wild speculation and unscrupulous investment schemes, the stock market collapsed as one more domino in the series of events leading to the Great Depression.

2. Rampant unemployment resulted from the collective awareness that a consumer-based economy could not survive without consumption.

3. Herbert Hoover was principally opposed to using the federal government as an instrument of social welfare, and when he did decide to buttress the banking system with federal dollars it was too little too late.

4. Franklin D. Roosevelt won a landslide victory in 1932 and began to push for radical new ways to salvage the American economy in a loosely organized plan he called the New Deal.

5. Employing trial and error, the New Deal pursued economic relief, recovery, and reform in an effort to reverse the effects of the Great Depression through public works and new federal regulations.

# The Rise and Fall
# of the New Deal

*The issue of Government has always been whether individual men and women
will have to serve some system of Government or economics, or whether a system
of Government and economics exists to serve individual men and women. . . .*

—Franklin D. Roosevelt, speech before the Commonwealth Club, 1932

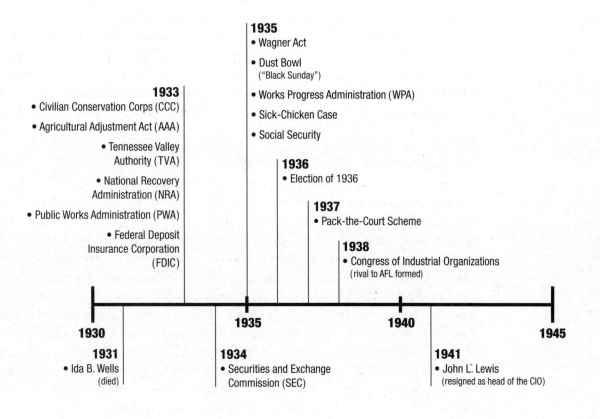

**1935**
- Wagner Act
- Dust Bowl
  ("Black Sunday")
- Works Progress Administration (WPA)
- Sick-Chicken Case
- Social Security

**1933**
- Civilian Conservation Corps (CCC)
- Agricultural Adjustment Act (AAA)
- Tennessee Valley Authority (TVA)
- National Recovery Administration (NRA)
- Public Works Administration (PWA)
- Federal Deposit Insurance Corporation (FDIC)

**1936**
- Election of 1936

**1937**
- Pack-the-Court Scheme

**1938**
- Congress of Industrial Organizations
  (rival to AFL formed)

**1930**

**1931**
- Ida B. Wells
  (died)

**1935**

**1934**
- Securities and Exchange Commission (SEC)

**1940**

**1941**
- John L. Lewis
  (resigned as head of the CIO)

**1945**

# Top 20 Things to Know

## 1 "Alphabet Soup" Agencies

As the New Deal agencies began to pile up critics and supporters alike marveled at the sheer number of laws passed by the Rubber Stamp Congress. The practice of bureaucrats to abbreviate the names of the agencies and the seemingly endless supply of the measures drew the witticism "Alphabet Soup," which highlighted the confusing nature of the barrage. The phrase, when used by critics, also decried the apparent disorganization of the New Deal as ideas were implemented through trial and error.

## 2 Civilian Conservation Corps

The Civilian Conservation Corps (CCC) provided work for unemployed young men ages eighteen to twenty-five in projects ranging from planting trees to building hiking trails, roads, structures, and flood-control facilities for national parks. The young men lived in camps, wore uniforms, and were led by army officers. A portion of their $30/month salary was automatically sent to their families to provide relief. As many as five hundred thousand young men worked for the CCC at a time, and by the opening of World War II two million had been employed. CCC corpsmen were preconditioned to military life prior to the entry of the United States in the war. Reforestation had never received such a focus by any government in history.

## 3 Agricultural Adjustment Act

The Agricultural Adjustment Act (AAA) addressed the prices for agricultural products that collapsed since the end of World War I. The government tried to eliminate farm surpluses by paying farmers not to produce with the goal of reducing supply in order to boost prices. The Populist Party's idea of farm subsidies had arrived as farmers were paid to cut the supply of corn, cotton, wheat, rice, hogs, and dairy products. The AAA established the Agricultural Adjustment Administration to monitor compliance as well as to tax companies that processed food in order to fund distributions to farmers. Refinancing of farm mortgages was also included to slow foreclosures. The AAA also authorized the president to create inflation with silver coinage and paper currency. The Supreme Court determined that the AAA was unconstitutional in 1936, but when Franklin D. Roosevelt was reelected he stepped around the ruling by couching the subsidies in terms of soil conservation, another Progressive goal with clear precedents in the Square Deal.

## 4 Tennessee Valley Authority

The Tennessee Valley Authority (TVA) arose from a World War I installation at Muscle Shoals on the Tennessee River in Alabama. A hydroelectric dam had been constructed that powered two munitions plants. Senator George Norris of Nebraska attempted to have the federal government operate the plants to produce fertilizer, but both Calvin Coolidge and Herbert Hoover opposed the idea saying the government should not compete with private industry. Franklin D. Roosevelt (FDR) was not averse to the possibility having pursued similar policies as governor of New York. After FDR visited Muscle Shoals in 1933, the TVA was begun both to provide electricity through water power but also to control flooding. Dams and power plants were constructed beginning in a model town in Tennessee that was named for Senator Norris. The goals of the TVA went beyond rural electrification to include conservation measures as well as the wider development of social programs in the region. TVA built nine dams before the end of World War II that helped provide electricity for the Manhattan Project and aluminum smelting facilities as well as the production of fertilizers and explosives. Because the TVA competed directly with private utilities it was considered by critics of the New Deal to be the most socialistic agency, but it has remained in operation as a public utility company ever since.

## 5 National Recovery Administration

The National Recovery Administration (NRA) was begun by the National Industrial Recovery Act during the First Hundred Days and was designed to boost employment but also industrial and business activity. Modeled after the voluntary compliance system developed during World War I, the NRA relied on self-regulation by business owners according to a set of standards, or codes, created by the federal government. The president was also permitted to enforce the codes, and any agreements made with the president by an industry were exempt from prosecution under the Sherman or Clayton Antitrust Acts. The NRA reiterated the Clayton Antitrust Act's affirmation of collective bargaining. At its peak the NRA controlled five hundred separate industries, and its policies impacted around twenty-two million employees. The NRA was another New Deal agency determined to be unconstitutional by the Supreme Court in 1935.

## 6 Public Works Administration

The Public Works Administration (PWA) extended from a provision of the National Industrial Recovery Act (NIRA) and was a widespread program funding the construction of roads, post offices, and other public buildings. Over $4.2 billion was spent on over thirty-four thousand projects to provide relief for workers and recovery once the money given to construction workers was spent on consumer goods. The PWA was the last New Deal agency passed during the First Hundred Days and revealed the extent of Franklin D. Roosevelt's belief in Keynesian theories of the government's responsibility to "prime the pump" of the economy through deficit spending. The idea of public works for the pump priming came from Frances Perkins as the Roosevelt administration sought to spend "big bucks on big projects." Although the PWA did not reverse the Depression, such activity encouraged American citizens that something was happening until World War II and the need for production for the war effort made it obsolete. The PWA was discontinued in 1941 as a result.

# 7 Works Progress Administration

The Works Progress Administration (WPA) was the significant relief agency of the second New Deal that channeled $11 billion into public works projects between 1935 and 1943. The administrators of the WPA held down the numbers of hours each worker could work in a week in order to provide an income to as many unemployed people as possible, and they spent 85 percent of all the funds on wages. When it was terminated in 1943, the WPA had provided jobs for 8.5 million people involved in over 1.4 billion projects. Most public works were focused on manual labor, but the WPA also hired writers, actors, artists, and musicians. Historians, for example, were hired to write histories of every state, and John Steinbeck was paid to write *The Grapes of Wrath*. Artists painted murals that featured New Deal accomplishments in nearly every post office in America. The WPA also built over 650,000 miles of roads, almost 125,000 bridges, over 125,000 public buildings, over 8,000 parks, and 853 landing fields for airplanes. WPA workers also managed the recreational facilities they had built. Extensive waste associated with the projects angered critics, but defenders of the New Deal said that those who were employed were now consumers again.

# 8 Federal Deposit Insurance Corporation

The Federal Deposit Insurance Corporation (FDIC) was created in 1933 by the Glass-Steagall Banking Act and guaranteed individual banking deposits up to $5,000 per account. The call for deposit insurance arose from the collapse of banks in the early part of the Great Depression. The language of the Glass-Steagall Act clearly blamed the Stock Market Crash and the subsequent Depression on the banking industry, and the law gave the Federal Reserve more power to prevent unsound banking practices in the future. The FDIC, then, was a reform measure designed to prevent a panic of the severity of the Great Depression from ever happening again, and the agency did restore confidence in the nation's banks over time. More banks were permitted to join the Federal Reserve and more branches of the Federal Reserve banks were opened. The main reforms of banking included the power to curtail speculative investments using credit as well as the prevention of the banks' use of depositor's money in investment schemes.

# 9 Securities and Exchange Commission

The Securities and Exchange Commission (SEC) was a New Deal measure aimed at the third R, reform. The SEC became a licensing agency with the power to regulate the sale of stocks and other securities by denying licenses to those exchanges using unscrupulous practices. Begun by the Securities and Exchange Act of 1934, the SEC prohibited price-manipulation schemes like the pump-and-dump conspiracies, insider trading, and excessive margin buying. All of these measures were designed to hold in check the wild speculation that had led to the Stock Market Crash, but the SEC went on to develop a system of breaks to slow the market in times of large sell-offs, and today it requires corporations trading on licensed stock exchanges to publish reports of their companies' financial information.

# 10 Social Security

As a result of some of the radical critics of the New Deal, Franklin D. Roosevelt pursued policies of unemployment insurance, old-age insurance, and a system of social services all wrapped up in the economic safety net called Social Security. Although some states had unemployment insurance, the New Deal federalized the program and began to collect taxes from employers that would be redistributed to the unemployed. Employees as well as employers were taxed to support the Social Security measures designed to help the old, orphans, and widows. Individuals who retired at the age of sixty-five beginning in 1942 would receive what amounted to federal pensions ranging from $10 to $85 per month depending on how many years the retirees had paid taxes into the system. Other payments were authorized to states to help them provide relief for the blind, the homeless, the crippled, and for dependent and delinquent children. The Social Security Administration also provided public health care for indigents, especially mothers with dependent children, as well as vocational training and job-seeking assistance to the unemployed. Of all the New Deal measures, the Social Security Administration has had the longest-lasting impact on American society even as it became increasingly hard to fund.

# 11 Wagner Act

This law created the National Labor Relations Board (NLRB) in 1935. The NLRB was to review the elections of labor leaders and certify them as legitimate in an effort to eliminate corruption in the collective bargaining process. The NLRB also heard testimony about workers' grievances and was the official agency through which the Roosevelt administration sought to intervene in labor issues. Along with the injunctions the president or federal courts could issue, the NLRB could issue cease–and-desist orders to address abuses. The Wagner Act reiterated that even in times of depression workers could join unions and bargain collectively with their employers through their chosen representatives. Similar to William Howard Taft's labor board during World War I, the NLRB allowed direct management of labor relations and therefore prevented many strikes in a time when the American economy could least afford them.

# 12 Rubber Stamp Congress

Because Franklin D. Roosevelt (FDR) had Democratic majorities in the House of Representatives and in the Senate upon his election in 1932, the legislation of the New Deal passed during the First Hundred Days worked its way through the Congress with unprecedented speed. The emergency banking measures were passed on the day they were presented and thus went into effect immediately to address the banking crisis. Critics of the New Deal, however, said the Congress was simply a rubber stamp for whatever ideas FDR and his advisers presented and were thereby abdicating their responsibility to use checks and balances to prevent the executive branch from wielding dictatorial powers. Since FDR attempted to alter the Supreme Court and, for example, personally set the price of gold each day, it was disturbing to people to find their president wielding such power even in a crisis. Defenders of the Roosevelt administration said that FDR was using extreme measures to attempt to preserve the existing institutions of the American economy and government in a situation that otherwise might have led to widespread civic unrest and even revolution. Other presidents with substantial majorities in both houses of Congress have faced the "Rubber Stamp" charge when the phenomenon is really a natural part of the electoral process in a republic. The pendulum of power has swung back and forth through the twentieth century and maintained an overall moderate course. This fact still does not prevent both major parties from hurling identical slurs at each other.

## 13 Boondoggling

Another criticism of the New Deal was that it wasted money on useless projects. *The New York Times* reported in 1935 that over $3 million was spent on a project to teach unemployed workers how to make crafts out of leather and rope of the type that Boy Scouts had made to decorate their uniforms. The word was quickly applied to any New Deal example of make-work jobs in which useless projects were completed by shiftless workers on relief or to the skill of simply appearing to be busy while accomplishing nothing of value.

## 14 Dust Bowl

The Dust Bowl referred to the drought that struck during the 1930s during the Great Depression. Giant dust storms were created when the topsoil from tilled fields that bore no crops was simply blown away in vast clouds that traveled hundreds of miles. Dust storms occurred with increasing severity and frequency from 1932 until they reached their peak in 1935 when it was estimated that one hundred million acres of land had been stripped. Dust clouds blocked out the sun and forced dirt into every crevice in homes throughout the Great Plains and the Midwest reaching as far east as Washington, D.C., where lawmakers passed the Soil Conservation Act to require the Department of Agriculture to prevent soil erosion. The drought helped farmers who could produce grain receive higher prices for their crops, and the Dust Bowl became the symbolic background for the entire Depression in Steinbeck's classic *The Grapes of Wrath* in which ruined farmers sold out to large corporate farms and moved west to California.

## 15 Election of 1936

The Republican Party attacked the New Deal in the Election of 1936 saying that Franklin D. Roosevelt (FDR) had begun to make laws himself, many of which were unconstitutional. They decried the violation of free enterprise represented by the federal government's participation in the economy. By 1936 even some conservative Democrats supported a curtailment of New Deal policies. Even FDR had slowed the use of deficit spending prior to the election. Still, the Republicans and their Democratic allies submitted no specific plan to the people of America that they could perceive as helpful during the ongoing Depression. FDR merely stood on his record of action, and the Dust Bowl and downturn in the economy after the easing of federal spending did the rest. He said, "The true conservative seeks to protect the system of private property and free enterprise by correcting such injustices and inequalities as arise from it." In the election, FDR carried every state but Maine and Vermont, piling up a smashing 523 to 8 margin in the Electoral College. Majorities were maintained for the Democratic Party in both houses of Congress. FDR interpreted the Election of 1936 as a mandate from the American people to restart deficit spending, which he did in earnest. The false conclusion about the spending was revealed, however, in that the American economy did not rebound in the latter half of the 1930s despite larger expenditures than ever before. FDR went on to say, famously, in his inauguration that, "I see one-third of a nation ill-housed, ill-clad, ill-nourished."

## 16 Ida B. Wells

Like most early Progressives, Franklin D. Roosevelt (FDR) paid little attention to the ongoing plight of African-Americans. He promoted a few African-Americans into positions of importance in administration of the New Deal but ignored accusations of segregation and discrimination in New Deal projects. He also failed to take any steps on the federal level to address the issue of lynching. Ida B. Wells was a Mississippi teacher and journalist who had been born into slavery and in the 1890s had launched a nationwide anti-lynching campaign. Wells had helped found the National Association for the Advancement of Colored People (NAACP) but resigned from the organization because she said it was not going far enough to address the lack of civil rights for African-American citizens. She and Jane Addams fought to prevent Chicago from segregating its schools as well as led in the women's suffrage movement together. Her editorials and journals fought to expose the cruelty of lynching and to dispel the myth that African-American men raped white women. Ida B. Wells died in 1931 just prior to FDR's first election having failed to secure any support from either major party for her cause.

## 17 Pack-the-Court Scheme

After his landslide victory in the Election of 1936, Franklin D. Roosevelt (FDR) chafed under the continued resistance toward the New Deal by the Supreme Court. Early in 1937 he submitted a plan to Congress to reorganize the Court by increasing the number of judges from nine to as many as fifteen if those over the age of seventy failed to retire. He also proposed many changes to the lower federal courts that would make it more difficult for the judicial branch to impede the progress of his second New Deal. The proposal met with sharp criticism and the accusation that FDR was merely trying to "pack" the Supreme Court with his pliant appointees to overbalance the conservatives who lingered there. Opponents of the measure claimed that it would destroy the independence of the Court and effectively end the checks and balances inherent in the U.S. Constitution on an already overpowerful executive. Even Democrats in Congress broke with FDR over the proposed changes. Chief Justice Charles Evans Hughes pointed out that the Supreme Court was not behind in its caseload. FDR defended the measures in speeches and fireside chats. Meanwhile, the Supreme Court actually supported the constitutionality of the Social Security Act and the Wagner Labor Relations Act and other New Deal measures. The original proposal thus never made it out of the Senate. FDR's image was tainted by his impatience, and legislation became harder to achieve. By constitutional means FDR was later able to replace seven justices on the Supreme Court before his death in 1945.

# 18 Sick-Chicken Case

This 1935 Supreme Court case was just the type of obstructionism that caused Franklin D. Roosevelt (FDR) such consternation. His National Recovery Administration (NRA) set up by the National Industrial Recovery Act was deemed unconstitutional as it applied to the operation of the Schechter Poultry Corporation. The NRA set codes for poultry workers including maximum hours of work and minimum wages. The suit against the Schechter company claimed that the poultry supplier had resisted the codes and the inspections that were meant to enforce them. The Supreme Court in its ruling first declared that the executive branch was exerting too much power over the economy. The Court said that FDR's codes against "unfair competition" were too ambiguous to actually enforce and that federal law did not apply to the Schechter Corporation because its alleged offenses occurred entirely within one state, New York.

# 19 John L. Lewis

Lewis was an Illinois coal miner who became a representative for the American Federation of Labor (AFL) and eventually the president of the United Mine Workers (UMW) in 1920. He called crippling strikes in bituminous coal mines that led to victories for the mine workers. Lewis rose to be the vice president of the AFL but split off in 1938 to form the Congress of Industrial Organizations or CIO. He supported Franklin D. Roosevelt (FDR) in the Election of 1936 but later withdrew his support. After World War II, Lewis called another massive strike that caused President Harry Truman to seize the mines just as Theodore Roosevelt had threatened to do. Lewis defied an injunction and was convicted of contempt of court, but after the strike received all the UMW demands from the mine owners. Lewis was venerated by coal miners as a result and remained president of the UMW until his death in 1960.

# 20 Congress of Industrial Organizations

Begun by John L. Lewis as the Committee for Industrial Organizations (CIO) within the American Federation of Labor (AFL), the CIO eventually split off to become its own organization. Lewis believed that industries like coal mining, steel and rubber production, and automobile manufacturing were thwarting the goals of labor because they involved so much unskilled labor. He parted from the AFL to include skilled and unskilled workers in a successful national organization that became the AFL's chief rival. Four million laborers bolted the AFL to join the CIO when it formed in 1938, and by 1945 CIO membership rose to six million. The CIO moved next to purge its ranks of communists and expelled eleven unions with communist ties. By 1955 the old division about skilled and unskilled workers had become so ambiguous that the two major unions joined to become the AFL-CIO.

## *The Big Picture*

1. The climax of Progressive Reform came in the New Deal policies of Franklin D. Roosevelt during the Great Depression.

2. The Roosevelt administration, backed by a Democratic Congress, experimented boldly with the power of the federal government to regulate the economy and to provide for the welfare of its citizens.

3. The extent to which the New Deal controlled the economy with social welfare programs and business regulation became controversial, especially because the funding of the programs came from deficit spending.

4. Critics of the New Deal ranged from those who thought Franklin D. Roosevelt had not gone far enough to those who believed he abused the powers of the executive branch and undermined the foundation of free-market capitalism that was the basis of the American Dream.

5. An objective assessment of the New Deal era must balance the prolonging of the Great Depression through often contradictory federal policies with the fact the Franklin D. Roosevelt was personally responsible for maintaining the unity and tenacity of the American people in the face of both the Great Depression and World War II.

# World War II

# CHAPTER 30

*No realistic American can expect from a dictator's peace, international generosity,
or return to true independence, or world disarmament, or freedom
of expression, or freedom of religion—or even good business."*
—Franklin D. Roosevelt, State of the Union address, 1941

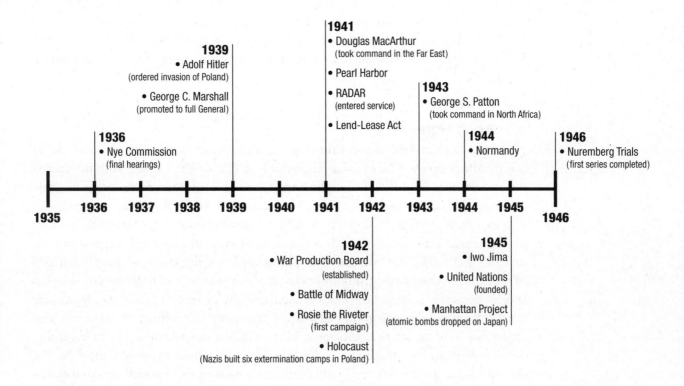

**1941**
- Douglas MacArthur
  (took command in the Far East)
- Pearl Harbor
- RADAR
  (entered service)
- Lend-Lease Act

**1939**
- Adolf Hitler
  (ordered invasion of Poland)
- George C. Marshall
  (promoted to full General)

**1943**
- George S. Patton
  (took command in North Africa)

**1936**
- Nye Commission
  (final hearings)

**1944**
- Normandy

**1946**
- Nuremberg Trials
  (first series completed)

1935   1936   1937   1938   1939   1940   1941   1942   1943   1944   1945   1946

**1942**
- War Production Board
  (established)
- Battle of Midway
- Rosie the Riveter
  (first campaign)
- Holocaust
  (Nazis built six extermination camps in Poland)

**1945**
- Iwo Jima
- United Nations
  (founded)
- Manhattan Project
  (atomic bombs dropped on Japan)

# Top 20 Things to Know

## 1 Fascism

Fascism was an economic, political, and societal system whereby intense nationalism subsumed individual citizens into a coordinated militancy. Fascist nations were run by dictators who mobilized the aggrieved sentiments of their nations through powerful rhetoric and patriotic spectacles in order to achieve totalitarian control. Fascist governments had control of the means of production and were thus a form of socialism but left industry in private hands and openly attacked Marxists, socialists, and communists. Dissenters were harassed, imprisoned, or murdered just as in other totalitarian states. Benito Mussolini fabricated fascism as a replacement for the Marxism he abandoned during World War I, and in his own words as the fascist leader of Italy he described fascism thus: "The citizen in the Fascist State is no longer a selfish individual who has the anti-social right of rebelling against any law of the Collectivity. The Fascist State with its cooperative conception puts men and their possibilities into productive work and interprets for them the duties they have to fulfill." For the fascist leaders of World War II, the work their citizens had to fulfill was the domination of their neighbors in aggressive imperialism and militant nationalism.

## 2 Adolf Hitler

Hitler was born in Austria and aspired to the life of an artist, but the best he could do was peddle his postcards. He was relieved when World War I broke out and offered the opportunity for a life of discipline and heroism. Hitler served on the front lines and was highly decorated for valor even as a corporal. After the war he rose to leadership in a political organization that would eventually become the National Socialist, or Nazi Party. His oratorical skills inspired an attempted attack on the government in 1923 that failed, but while in prison he crafted his life vision in a work entitled *Mein Kampf.* After serving nine months of a five-year prison term he was released and immediately returned to political agitation. Hitler rose to power in a legitimate appointment as chancellor but ultimately combined the offices of president and chancellor to become a fascist dictator. Hitler's railing against the Treaty of Versailles, communism, and a supposed conspiracy of Jews increased his power until he was able to silence his enemies and launch the expansion of the Third Reich that began World War II. The Nazi Party used propaganda, intimidation, and terrorism to launch both a seemingly unstoppable blitzkrieg attack on neighboring countries in Europe, and also the Holocaust. When the Nazi forces were forced back to Berlin, Hitler committed suicide in an underground bunker in 1945.

## 3 The Axis Powers

After annexing Austria and stealing parts of France and Czechoslovakia, the Nazi war machine of Germany combined forces with the fascist dictator of Italy, Benito Mussolini, and the fascist war ministers of Japan to form the Rome/Berlin/Tokyo

Axis. Hungary, Romania, and Bulgaria also joined the Axis Powers. Hitler's forces invaded Poland and divided it with the Soviet Union and then expanded into Scandinavia and France. Then the Axis turned to Eastern Europe and North Africa for resources to fuel Germany's professed need for "living space" by which ruse Hitler masked his obsessive compulsion to destroy Europe's Jews as well as Russians and other Slavs.

## 4 Nye Commission

In 1934, the U.S. Senate had set up a commission under Senator Gerald Nye of North Dakota to investigate any connection between American munitions manufacturers and the country's involvement in World War I. The Nye Commission focused on the large profits such companies had made even before America entered the war and asserted, without conclusive evidence, that lobbying on the part of the munitions manufacturers had persuaded President Wilson and the Congress to declare war against the Central Powers. As Hitler rose to power in Germany, the Nye Committee worked until 1936 to preserve an isolationist stance in American foreign policy. The Neutrality Acts of 1935, 1936, and 1937 were a direct result and forbade American manufacturers to sell war materials to combatant nations if war erupted. Neutrality of this extent was designed to prevent American ships from being sunk by German submarines and repeating the process that dragged the United States into the Great War. A 1939 Neutrality Act eventually permitted combatant nations to buy American arms as long as they shipped the goods on their own ships in a policy called "cash and carry."

## 5 The Lend-Lease Act

In early 1941, Franklin D. Roosevelt (FDR) signed into law the Lend-Lease Act, a measure to help primarily Great Britain receive war supplies despite having run out of credit. The law allowed the president to designate which countries were acting in the interests of the United States and, in a massive outpouring of Dollar Diplomacy, to open the faucet wide for the transfer of resources. Originally designed to keep America from having to enter World War II, the Lend-Lease Act continued until 1945 long after the United States had joined the Allied Powers. In total, $50.6 billion worth of supplies was given in this manner.

## 6 Pearl Harbor

On Sunday, December 7, 1941, the naval and air forces of Japan conducted a sneak attack on the U.S. naval base at Pearl Harbor, Hawaii. The attack damaged all eight of the American battleships moored in the harbor and destroyed three. Nineteen total ships were lost along with around 150 planes. Of casualties there were over 2,400 killed and nearly 1,200 wounded. The next day the U.S. Congress declared war on Japan with only one dissenting vote. Three days later Germany and Italy declared war against the United States. Because of the nature of naval warfare in World War II, the United States was extremely fortunate that her aircraft carriers were at sea at the time of the Pearl Harbor attack.

## 7 Allied Powers

After Hitler's successful expansion of Nazi control over much of Continental Europe, the United Kingdom stood virtually alone against the German menace. The Soviet Union had at first cooperated with Germany in partitioning Poland, but when Hitler ordered an invasion of Russia Josef Stalin allied with the British. After Pearl Harbor, both the United States and China joined the Allies, and as nations were liberated from Nazi control the ranks of the Allied Powers swelled. Eventually twenty-six nations allied together by 1942 and formed the core of what would become the United Nations.

## 8 Douglas MacArthur

Having graduated from the U.S. Military Academy in 1903, Douglas MacArthur saw service in the Philippines and Japan in peacekeeping forces and saw combat in World War I. MacArthur was wounded twice during World War I despite the fact that he was the commanding general of an infantry brigade. He spent the rest of his career in the Far East, which made him the perfect candidate to command all the American forces in the Pacific Theater of World War II. After escaping the Japanese as they took over the Philippines, MacArthur employed a strategy of "leapfrogging" around unnecessary targets in Japan's empire and led the Allied campaigns that eventually threatened the Japanese mainland. After the war was over he commanded the occupation of Japan and the United Nations forces that repelled a communist attack on South Korea in the Korean War. As a result of a disagreement about strategy, MacArthur was fired by President Harry Truman in 1951 and said in a famous address to Congress: "Old soldiers never die, they just fade away."

## 9 War Production Board

Franklin D. Roosevelt launched the War Production Board (WPB) in 1942 to mobilize all aspects of the American economy to fight and win the war. The WPB halted on nonessential domestic New Deal projects and redirected all major industries from making consumer products to making war material including jeeps, trucks, tanks, ships, and planes. The WPB achieved almost complete employment, especially because so many men from the ages of eighteen to forty-four were drafted for military service. Having helped America win the war and end the Great Depression, the WPB disbanded and allowed the American economy to return to civilian uses in the control of private industry.

## 10 Rosie the Riveter

Even though women had worked in war industries during World War I, the New Deal era frowned on their participation in industry when so many men were out of work. When large numbers of men were drafted into the military for World War II, however, women helped fulfill the requirements of the War Production Board. Rosie the Riveter became an iconographic example of the importance of women to the war effort as the accomplishments of an actual riveter in an airplane factory were celebrated in order to draw more women into the workforce. At the beginning of World War II, women made up only one-quarter of the workforce, but by the end they made up one-third. Proving the slogan, "We Can Do It," six million women entered the workforce during the war years, half working in war factories in traditionally male jobs.

## 11 Radar

After the crash of the *Titanic* into an iceberg, an effort was made to develop a device to discern the presence of objects just as a bat does by sending out a signal and listening for it to rebound. Progress in radio technology by Marconi and some American physicists contributed to the first effective radar device in Great Britain just in time for World War II. During the Battle of Britain from 1939 to 1941 a significantly smaller Royal Air Force was able to intercept the waves of German planes because radar installations pinpointed their locations. Radar operators' claims that a large wave of planes was coming into Pearl Harbor were ignored, making such warnings all the more important in later years. Even during World War II, however, countermeasures were developed to trick radar operators, and planes could simply fly low toward a target to avoid detection. Still, ships and planes were able to engage in combat far more effectively and even at night because of radar technology.

## 12 George C. Marshall

This Pennsylvanian became what America has a genius for producing—military scholars and statesmen. Marshall rose in rank from captain to colonel in World War I, served as a military instructor, and was immediately promoted to general upon Germany's invasion of Poland in 1939. He became the chief of staff of the army and is largely forgotten for his World War II service because the more famous generals were the ones he assigned. Still, Marshall's was the grand, master strategy that the Allies pursued to beat back the Axis Powers. After the war he became the secretary of state and the architect of the plan to aid European nations that bears his name. The Marshall Plan sought to stave off Soviet influence in Europe by sending billions of dollars to help with rebuilding Western Europe.

## 13 George S. Patton

A Scots-Irish Californian, Patton graduated from West Point and was a veteran of Pershing's hunt for Pancho Villa as well as World War I where he first studied tank warfare. In World War II Patton commanded armored cavalry units in nearly every major campaign in North Africa and Europe. His insistence on rigorous discipline and aggressive offensive tactics belied the fact that his troops sustained fewer casualties than the units serving under other generals. General Patton vied for prominence in key actions with British general Bernard Montgomery such that one of General Dwight Eisenhower's main accomplishments was keeping these rivals for glory fighting the Germans instead of each other. In the campaign on the European mainland Patton's forces routinely outdistanced both supply lines and other Allied forces. General Patton was a man of many faults, but his contemporaries said of him that he was, ". . . unrivalled in his ability to inspire and lead large forces of men in a desperate and ultimately victorious struggle against a determined enemy." Patton died in an automobile accident in Europe shortly after World War II ended.

## 14  Battle of Midway

This battle was the turning point in the Allied victory over Japan. For three days American carrier-based aircraft exchanged fire with the invasion force of Admiral Yamamoto. Admiral Chester W. Nimitz had guessed the Japanese plan based on intelligence reports, and through valorous service and good fortune the navy bombers destroyed four of Japan's aircraft carriers. The U.S. Navy lost only one carrier and not only saved Midway Island as a crucial military base but equalized Japanese and American naval strength from that point on.

## 15  Normandy

Though Allied forces had clawed their way onto the European continent in Italy, the invasion of Normandy beginning on June 6, 1944, was the largest and most important amphibious assault in world history. While the Russians pushed Germany from the east, the D-Day invasion was the crucial "Second Front" to divide Germany's forces and bring about the end of the Nazi regime. U.S. General Dwight D. Eisenhower planned and ordered Operation Overlord that saw three divisions of American and British paratroopers dropped behind enemy lines and the main American, British, and Canadian forces land on Utah, Omaha, Gold, Juno, and Sword beaches. A beachhead was established from which more and more men and machines were unloaded that eventually allowed the Allied Powers to reclaim France and push the Nazis back to Germany and destruction.

## 16  Iwo Jima

This island became the most famous of the amphibious assaults that were part of Douglas MacArthur's island-hopping strategy largely because of Joe Rosenthal's famous photograph of the raising of an American flag on Mount Suribachi, the island's dormant volcano. Before surmounting that obstacle, however, American Marines suffered horrendously violent assaults from the Japanese forces that had burrowed into the volcanic rock of the island to make defenses. Sworn to fight to the end, only 212 of the twenty-two thousand Japanese defenders were taken prisoner. Almost seven thousand Marines were killed and over eighteen thousand wounded. The importance of Iwo Jima and Okinawa was that these islands were "unsinkable aircraft carriers" from which long-range bombers could attack the mainland of Japan.

## 17  Manhattan Project

Named such because it was conceived of in an office in New York City, the Manhattan Project was America's secret race with the Germans and the Japanese to create atomic bombs. Albert Einstein had warned Franklin D. Roosevelt that the Germans were conducting research in atomic energy for this purpose, and the United States responded by pouring incredible amounts of natural resources, manpower, and technical expertise into the effort. Installations at Hanford, Washington, and Oak Ridge, Tennessee, were designed to produce the enriched uranium fuel for three bombs, one of which was detonated as a test in Los Alamos, New Mexico. J. Robert Oppenheimer was responsible for overseeing the production of the bombs, and in six years he spent $2 billion to succeed. When Japan was warned that the United States would destroy cities and refused to surrender, the atomic bombs were dropped on Hiroshima and then on Nagasaki. Over 105,000 people were killed immediately in the two cities with severe lasting health consequences for thousands more. Each bomb destroyed everything within a mile of its detonation site and caused serious damage as far as three miles away. Although the firebombing of Tokyo had killed more civilians, the shock of the two atomic bombs caused the Japanese to surrender within days of this only use of nuclear weapons in the history of warfare. The implications of what the Manhattan Project created led to the Cold War after World War II was over.

## 18 United Nations

The phrase *United Nations* came from a term Franklin D. Roosevelt (FDR) used to refer to the Allied Powers. The idea of the United Nations arose from the International Peace Conference that established the International Court at The Hague, but was more fully elaborated by Woodrow Wilson in his Fourteen Point Address. The League of Nations was founded as a result of the Treaty of Versailles that ended World War I. FDR and Winston Churchill reiterated the need for such an organization during their Atlantic Conference even though the League of Nations had been unable or unwilling to stop the rise of fascist empires. In 1945, fifty nations met at the San Francisco Conference to establish a charter for the United Nations even before the end of World War II. When the document was ratified by the five permanent members of the Security Council (China, France, the Soviet Union, the United Kingdom, and the United States), in October of 1945 the United Nations was born. The first resolution adopted by the General Assembly of the United Nations was for the peaceful use of atomic energy and the elimination of atomic weapons.

## 19 Nuremberg Trials

A body called the International Military Tribunal tried twenty-two Nazi leaders who survived the war for crimes against peace, crimes against humanity, and other war crimes. The trials lasted from late 1945 into 1946 and established a precedent of holding the instigators of aggressive war accountable as well as perpetrators of atrocities and genocides like the Holocaust. Twelve of the defendants were sentenced to death. The rest were given varying prison sentences from life down to ten years while three were acquitted. A similar trial of twenty-eight Japanese war criminals was held in Tokyo. Seven of the Japanese defendants, including Hideki Tojo, were sentenced to death. As for the fascist leader of Italy, Benito Mussolini, he was mobbed when caught trying to escape Italy in 1945 and shot by his own people.

# 20 Holocaust

Having claimed that the Jews of Europe were conspiring for the destruction of Germany, Hitler set about isolating and persecuting them immediately upon taking office in 1933. The nine million Jews of Europe lived largely in countries that would eventually fall under German control, and as the Nazis consolidated power over Central Europe they initiated what they called the Final Solution. The word *Holocaust* meant "sacrifice by fire," and the Final Solution would eventually kill six million Jews and hundreds of thousands of other victims the Nazis found undesirable like Gypsies, the physically and mentally handicapped, socialists, communists, Jehovah's Witnesses, and homosexuals. Jews under German occupation were first quarantined in ghettos. Killing squads followed the front-line German troops and committed mass murder, but then Jews and other victims were rounded up into concentration camps to perform slave labor for the Nazi war machine. Ultimately, many of the concentration camps became death camps as Jews were exterminated and their bodies burned with mass-production efficiency. Hitler diverted large amounts of resources to the Final Solution that did not stop until Allied forces liberated the camps by force.

---

## *The Big Picture*

1. The menace of aggressive war was unleashed upon Europe and Asia by fascist regimes in Italy, Germany, and Japan beginning in 1937 with the Japanese invasion of China and in 1939 with the German invasion of Poland.

2. The United States tried to remain neutral as World War II erupted, but the surprise attack by the Japanese on Pearl Harbor, Hawaii, forced the nation to join the Allied Powers in the war against the Axis Powers.

3. A full-scale mobilization of the American economy was initiated to meet the demands of war production, and women swelled the ranks of the workforce as millions of American men served in the military.

4. World War II was the worst war in history because of its global scale but also because of new technical innovations that made aerial bombing, ground warfare, and sea warfare more deadly.

5. The United States helped the Allies secure victory in Europe but fought largely alone against the Japanese who were turned back at the Battle of Midway and finally surrendered after two atomic bombs were dropped on cities on the Japanese mainland.

# Truman and Eisenhower in Post-War America

*The main element of any United States policy toward the Soviet Union must be that of a long-term, patient but firm and vigilant containment of Russian expansive tendencies.*
—George F. Kennan, "The Sources of Soviet Conflict," 1947

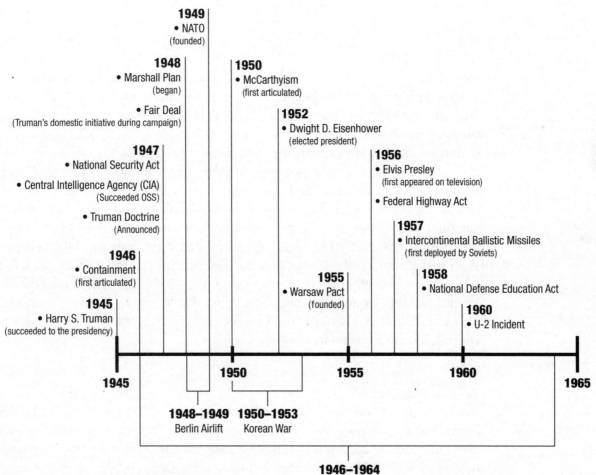

**1949**
• NATO
(founded)

**1948**
• Marshall Plan
(began)

• Fair Deal
(Truman's domestic initiative during campaign)

**1947**
• National Security Act

• Central Intelligence Agency (CIA)
(Succeeded OSS)

• Truman Doctrine
(Announced)

**1946**
• Containment
(first articulated)

**1945**
• Harry S. Truman
(succeeded to the presidency)

**1950**
• McCarthyism
(first articulated)

**1952**
• Dwight D. Eisenhower
(elected president)

**1956**
• Elvis Presley
(first appeared on television)

• Federal Highway Act

**1957**
• Intercontinental Ballistic Missiles
(first deployed by Soviets)

**1955**
• Warsaw Pact
(founded)

**1958**
• National Defense Education Act

**1960**
• U-2 Incident

1945     1950     1955     1960     1965

**1948–1949**
Berlin Airlift

**1950–1953**
Korean War

**1946–1964**
Baby Boom

# Top 20 Things to Know

## 1 Harry S. Truman

Truman served in the First World War as a captain of artillery and returned to enter Missouri politics as a part of the Pendergrass machine, an association he later repudiated. He rose to be a senator and vice president for Franklin D. Roosevelt's (FDR's) last election in 1944. He became president upon FDR's death in office, and then won the Election of 1948 in his own right. Overnight Truman had to learn of the secret atomic bomb project and then decided to authorize use of the bombs to end the war with Japan. He won reelection even though he lost the Congress in the midterm elections by coming out against the antilabor Taft-Hartley Act and coming out for an extension of New Deal programs Truman called the Fair Deal. No other peacetime president had ever faced such daunting foreign policy challenges as Truman who in his second term had to deal with the Cold War Soviet aggression in Europe *and* Chinese and North Korean aggression in Asia while negotiating the peace treaties with Germany and Japan.

## 2 Cold War

After World War II the United States and the Soviet Union, former allies, began to view each other with suspicion. The two superpowers wound up controlling the East and the West, but each viewed the actions of the other as aggressively expansionist. The conflict known as the Cold War became a bizarre chess game where espionage, the space race, and the arms race caused the opponents to feed off of each other's insecurities in a global competition where the stakes were total annihilation of the human race. The bizarre aspect of the conflict was that the threat of thermonuclear war kept the conflict from escalating to that point and prevented any direct clash between the superpowers or their surrogate nations from widening into a third world war. The Cold War lasted over forty years until the collapse of the Soviet Union left the United States as the incredulous victor. Along the way the superpowers used all possible means to align the rest of the nations into the "Free World" and the "Communist Bloc." The Cold War following so closely on the heels of World War II is what kept the United States from ever being able to seriously contemplate isolationism as a viable policy again.

## 3 Containment

After Winston Churchill's 1946 observation that an "Iron Curtain," had fallen across Europe, the Western nations contemplated Russian imperial tendencies, now animated by communist zeal. The idea of containment of Soviet expansion originated with diplomat George Kennan, a Russian specialist in the American Foreign Service who later served as ambassador to the Soviet Union. He explained his policy in a famous 1947 article that he signed only as "X." He said containment was a political solution to a political problem rather than a military solution to a military problem. Still, he recommended the consistent application of counterforce to any shifting Soviet geographical designs to spread communism throughout the world. Containment drove the foreign policy decisions of the United States for the next forty years even though Kennan himself thought it became obsolete upon the death of Joseph Stalin and the discovery of animosity between Soviet and Chinese communists.

## 4 National Security Act

Congress passed the National Security Act in 1947 after summing up the new position of the United States as the leader of the Free World. The law coordinated the Army, Navy, and the new Air Force in a single organized administration centered in the person of the secretary of defense in the presidential cabinet. The law created the National Security Council of direct advisers to the president and the Central Intelligence Agency (CIA) to conduct espionage and to process information regarding national security. The CIA was forbidden to conduct domestic espionage that, if necessary, would fall under the authority of the Federal Bureau of Investigation (FBI).

## 5 Central Intelligence Agency

While spying was nothing new in American history, the high stakes of the Cold War compelled the federal government to organize intelligence gathering on a global scale. The forerunner of the Central Intelligence Agency (CIA) was the World War II agency known as the Office of Strategic Services (OSS). Harry Truman discovered after the OSS was disbanded after the war that the position of the United States demanded the greater coordination and sophistication provided by the National Security Act. The CIA was charged with not only the responsibility of gathering intelligence but of coordinating with other branches of the government like the Secret Service (also begun under Truman after a nearly successful assassination attempt) and the FBI. The CIA was therefore the warehouse for all military, diplomatic, and other forms of monitoring of information for national security purposes, and the director of the CIA operated as the chairman of the National Security Council. After a second National Security Act in 1949 the budget of the CIA was permitted to be clandestine as well as its activities.

## 6 Truman Doctrine

Harry Truman acted on behalf of Turkey and Greece when the British announced in 1947 that they no longer possessed the means to look after these countries' welfare. In an address to Congress, Truman asked for $400 million to aid the countries saying that the United States should help any European nation in order to "support free peoples who are resisting attempted subjugation by armed minorities or outside pressures." Some critics noted that this policy was the exact opposite of the Monroe Doctrine and that the United Nations should take the lead role in organizing resistance to communist aggression, but Truman noted that the Soviet Union and the Chinese were able to thwart the designs of the United Nations by using their permanent seats on the Security Council. Therefore Truman committed the United States to leadership in keeping Europe free from communism, a burden that subsequent Cold War presidents expanded.

# 7 Marshall Plan

In keeping with the Truman Doctrine, George C. Marshall as secretary of state proposed that European nations should cooperate in a coordinated effort to rebuild their countries and keep them free from communist influence. By 1948 he proposed that the United States should pay for it. The Marshall Plan was said to be directed "not against any country or doctrine but against hunger, poverty, desperation, and chaos." The intentions of the aid, however, were to build up strong economies in Western Europe in order to maintain political stability and to thwart communist infiltration. The Soviets interpreted the generous measure as an imperialist plot, but the original pledge of $12 billion was provided without American territorial designs. The amount of aid rose to over $22 billion in four years as Truman expanded the Marshall Plan into his European Recovery Program. Analysts concluded that the plan was imminently successful and cheaper than the maintenance of conventional military forces that would have rendered the free nations of Europe merely American proxies. The expenditures of the Marshall Plan, the Truman Doctrine, the formation of the United Nations, the formation of the nation of Israel, and many others revealed the United States to have become the most generous nation of any in history during the Truman presidency alone.

# 8 Berlin Airlift

After General Eisenhower allowed the Soviets the glory (and the casualties) of capturing the German capital city of Berlin, the Soviets occupied half of the city. American, British, and French forces established zones in the western half. In the period of determining what should be done with Germany, the Soviets gradually cut off access to the city by ground because it lay entirely inside the eastern portion of Germany that they controlled. By 1948 this blockade of Berlin was total. The three western powers decided to supply the more than two million residents of West Berlin food, coal, and medical supplies via round-the-clock flights known as the Berlin Airlift. When the matter was referred to the United Nations, the Soviet Union used its veto power on the Security Council to block a compromise and then boycotted any further discussions. The Soviets watched the resolve of the West to maintain the flights for 321 days. Over 270,000 flights delivered 2.3 million tons of supplies as American policy toward the Soviets hardened. When the blockade was finally lifted in 1949, Berlin became a symbol of American resolve to win the Cold War. In response to massive migration from communist Berlin to free Berlin, the Soviets built the Berlin Wall.

# 9 Fair Deal

Despite being preoccupied with the difficulties of the Cold War, Truman did propose in his campaign for the Election of 1948 a domestic agenda he called the Fair Deal.

His vision of expanding the New Deal included national health insurance, federal aid to education, an increased minimum wage, expanded Social Security benefits, greater farm subsidies, expansion of federal housing programs for the poor, and even civil rights legislation. Although these promises and his prolabor stand against the Taft-Hartley Act won him a surprise victory over Thomas Dewey, the Congress after the election showed that it had moved Right during the war years. Conservatives in both parties prevented much of the Fair Deal from being implemented, although the minimum wage was almost doubled from forty cents an hour to seventy-five cents and social security benefits were expanded. Soon the Korean War distracted even President Truman from pursuing more domestic reforms.

## 10 McCarthyism

Joseph McCarthy represented a backlash against the liberal policies that had brewed in Wisconsin since the opening of the Progressive Reform movement under Robert La Follette. McCarthy served in World War II in the Marine Corps after practicing law and holding a minor political office. After the war he was elected to the U.S. Senate. In 1950, Senator McCarthy delivered a speech in Wheeling, West Virginia, in which he declared he possessed a list of "card-carrying" members of the Communist Party who worked in the State Department. Without ever having named a single State Department official who was a communist, McCarthy started the Second Red Scare by holding a series of televised hearings from 1951 to 1954. During the hearings, McCarthy charged civil servants, writers, actors, professors, labor leaders, and eventually even army officers as having membership in the Communist Party or communist leanings. Such accusations spurred the House of Representatives to open their own hearings of a body called the House Un-American Activities Committee (HUAC). As a new wave of hysteria swept the nation in the Cold War, such accusations ruined the careers of many innocent and some guilty individuals who were together blacklisted, or barred from working in their professions. Civil rights advocates attacked McCarthy as a bully and someone who did not truly believe in the freedoms enshrined in the Bill of Rights. Among the accused were even such leaders as George C. Marshall and Adlai E. Stevenson, and when McCarthy pursued more attacks against U.S. Army personnel the Senate moved to censure him for his abuses. His influence diminished rapidly and he soon died of the effects of alcoholism.

## 11 NATO

The North Atlantic Treaty Organization (NATO) was formed when President Truman sought an arrangement with Canada for mutual security and wound up attracting twelve nations to the idea. A treaty was signed in Washington, D.C., in 1949 that committed all the NATO nations to the idea that an attack on one of their number was an attack on all of them. Each NATO nation was to take "individually and in concert with the other Parties, such action as it deems necessary, including the use of armed force, to restore and maintain the security of the North Atlantic area." NATO nations were to permit new nations to join the alliance upon the unanimous vote of the existing members, and Greece and Turkey joined by 1952. General Dwight D. Eisenhower was picked to coordinate the military component of the agreement, and his skill in diplomacy evidenced through the war years made NATO all the more successful in unifying the security effort. The treaty forming NATO marked the first time since abandoning the treaty with France after the War for Independence that the United States made a peacetime alliance. By 2009, twenty-eight nations belonged to NATO, many of them having previously been Soviet Bloc satellite nations.

# 12 Warsaw Pact

In a classic Cold War response the Soviet Union answered the formation of NATO with an organization of their own erroneously named the Warsaw Pact. Eight nations did meet in Poland in 1955 to form the alliance based on mutual security, but it quickly appeared evident that the Soviet Union considered the Eastern European Warsaw Pact nations to be its own empire. During the Cold War the Warsaw Pact nations combined their militaries under Soviet control twice to attack their own members, Hungary and Czechoslovakia, when the nations sought to operate independently. After the collapse of the Soviet Union the Warsaw Pact was dissolved in 1991.

# 13 Korean War

Korea had also been divided between Soviet and American influence after World War II and as a result two competing worldviews took up residence on the Korean Peninsula. The United Nations tried merely to divide the country at the thirty-eighth parallel of latitude, but in 1950, North Korea crossed the border and invaded South Korea with the intention of uniting all of Korea under communist rule by force. Because North Korea was backed by the Soviet Union and later by Communist China, the Korean War became another dangerous Cold War showdown. Douglas MacArthur landed United Nations forces at both the southern extremity of the peninsula and behind North Korean lines at Inchon. This maneuver forced the communist aggressors back across the thirty-eighth parallel, and MacArthur's assault drove them up against the Chinese border. When massive wave attacks indicated that Chinese forces were invading the peninsula, the United Nations forces were driven back to a cease-fire line at the thirty-eighth parallel by 1953. The Korean Peninsula remains divided at this heavily fortified border to this day without any peace treaty to enforce the cease-fire. Over one million Koreans and Chinese were killed in the war, and over fifty-four thousand Americans died in battle or of other causes. During the conflict disagreements between General MacArthur and President Truman led to MacArthur's being fired and replaced, proving America's tradition of the subordination of military leaders to civilian rulers. The Korean War heightened tensions in America during the Second Red Scare and led to the election of Dwight Eisenhower to the presidency as the first Republican since Franklin D. Roosevelt had beaten Hoover twenty years earlier in the Election of 1932.

# 14 Dwight D. Eisenhower

Eisenhower graduated from the U.S. Military Academy in 1915 and rose to the rank of captain by the end of World War I, but only as a training officer. Eisenhower did not lead troops into combat until Operation Torch when American troops landed in North Africa to begin to push the German armies back toward Italy and Germany. Eisenhower, or Ike, exhibited crucial diplomatic skill in coordinating the efforts of the various Allied forces and rose to the rank of the supreme commander in Europe. He organized the D-Day invasion of Normandy and the broad-front strategy encircling Berlin that ended the war in Europe. After the war he served as the chief of staff of the military and eventually the commander of North Atlantic Treaty Organization (NATO) forces. He was elected to the presidency in 1952 with the largest popular vote to that time in history saying he would personally go to Korea to end the war there, which he did by 1953. He won a second term to the presidency and was the chief architect of the Cold War policies of the United States through the decade of tension and high stakes. Meanwhile he managed several domestic crises as the cultural changes of the 1950s developed. Like Coolidge, he was president during a period of widespread prosperity, but unlike any other president Eisenhower was the first to have to contemplate the implications of the existence of intercontinental ballistic missiles with nuclear warheads.

# 15 Elvis Presley

Few kings have risen from such obscurity to change the world as did the king of rock 'n' roll. Elvis Aaron Presley picked up a guitar at the age of ten and cut his first single record in 1954. As he began touring, the young people of America were drawn to his style of singing and dancing that for his producer was like having an African-American man in a white man's body. Elvis's mix of Negro spiritual roots with jazz, the blues, and country music produced rockabilly and ultimately rock 'n' roll. Presley's musical career was interrupted by a stint in the military, but upon completing his service he entered into a movie career. He personified the new youth culture that was coming out of the stresses of World War II and the ongoing Cold War seeking a freer lifestyle, and he set the pattern for dissipation and untimely death through drug addiction that so many rock 'n' roll performers would follow. His work, which included eighteen number-one hit songs, and his image became so iconographic that he remains one of the richest dead men in history, that is, his estate still makes millions of dollars for his heirs.

# 16 Baby Boom

Contributing to the cultural changes of the 1950s was the release of the pent-up urge to procreate that had plagued the dark years of World War II and the Great Depression. Suburbia was born and rampant consumerism was reborn as the baby boom, a huge increase in the number of births, expanded through the decade. At its peak, 4.3 million babies were born in two separate years during the era. From 1946 to 1964 a total of seventy-nine million babies swelled the population of the country. As baby boomers retire, however, the federal government will face a significant burden in meeting its commitments from the New Deal program of social security.

# 17 Federal Highway Act

Dwight Eisenhower advanced a New Deal public works project of his own by backing the 1956 Federal Highway Act. Having seen the German autobahn system in Europe, Ike envisioned creating the Interstate Highway System to facilitate military travel during times of national emergencies. Larger than any other single public works project in American history, the law authorized the expenditure of $30 billion to construct 41,000 miles of state-of-the-art highways over thirteen years. The federal highway system employed tens of thousands of citizens and contributed to the automobile, recreational, and entertainment industries so significantly that through the 1960s one in seven Americans had their livelihood from some economic endeavor connected to this new transportation revolution. Just like the railroad before it, however, the highway system chose some areas for greatness and doomed others to obscurity. The Eisenhower Interstate System has never been used for its original purpose of fending off invading armies, although its design as emergency landing fields for airplanes has from time to time saved lives.

# 18 National Defense Education Act

Along with the G.I. Bill that funded the college educations of war veterans, the National Defense Education Act represented millions of dollars of federal spending for education. After the Soviet Union placed the first artificial satellite, *Sputnik*, into orbit, the federal government in 1958 sought to boost instruction in math, the sciences, and foreign languages to help the country catch up to the Soviets. Grants were given to college students who were studying to become teachers and directly to school systems to fund facilities and curriculum development. This response to having been beaten by the Soviets into outer space was the origin of the Space Race, another area of Cold War competition between the superpowers.

# 19 U-2 Incident

As the Arms Race continued between the United States and the Soviet Union, high-flying espionage aircraft helped the American military keep tabs on the development and deployment of Soviet missile technology. In 1960, an American pilot named Francis Gary Powers had his U-2 reconnaissance aircraft shot down by a Soviet missile 1,200 miles inside the Soviet Union. Eisenhower and National Aeronautics and Space Administration (NASA) had tried to cover up the secret surveillance flights by claiming the plane was a weather research plane that had flown off course, but Powers survived and confessed to being a Central Intelligence Agency (CIA) agent. Caught red-handed by the gloating Reds, Eisenhower made an unprecedented disclosure of international espionage by a world leader. A planned Summit Conference was boycotted by the Soviets because of this admission, and

Eisenhower's reputation as a Cold War master strategist was tarnished. Powers was convicted of espionage by the righteously indignant Soviet government, but his release was secured by an exchange of a convicted Russian spy in an effort to show the world the Soviets were not innocent victims.

# 20 Intercontinental Ballistic Missiles

Intercontinental ballistic missiles (ICBMs) were developed during the Cold War to launch under power from their respective superpowers and then to follow a trajectory out of Earth's atmosphere calculated to cause their nuclear warheads to fall onto enemy cities. German scientists had developed technologies before the end of World War II that had enabled them to fire V-1 and V-2 rockets into Great Britain, but the Cold War warheads contained atomic weapons. As atomic bombs became smaller and lighter, rockets became larger and more powerful until the entire earth could be considered in range in the event of a thermonuclear war. American missiles went through the stages of the *Atlas*, the *Titan*, the *Minuteman*, and then the *Peacekeeper* missiles while the Soviet Union followed suit with their own array of ICBMs. Nuclear weapons, especially after the development of the one thousand times more powerful hydrogen bomb, struck fear into the hearts of whole generations of world citizens.

## *The Big Picture*

1. Harry Truman and Dwight Eisenhower were the first presidents of the United States to wrestle with the problems of world leadership thrust upon them by the end of World War II and the opening of the Cold War.

2. The federal government of the United States organized new agencies to manage national security issues and designed programs using deficit spending to support and stabilize nations in an effort to contain the spread of communism.

3. Massive military expenditures fueled massive domestic economic growth that, coupled with an extensive new highway system, returned America to prosperity and launched unprecedented consumerism.

4. The Cold War competition between the superpowers of the United States and the Soviet Union involved the application of resources around the globe to everything from symbolic showdowns to actual shooting wars, all with the backdrop of a potentially deadly exchange of nuclear weapons.

5. Americans in the 1950s swallowed their Cold War fears and lived the "good life" with a burgeoning population, suburbanization, and the development of whole new forms of entertainment including amusement parks, power cars, and rock 'n' roll music.

# Mini Quiz

1. The Ford Motor Company transformed the automobile industry by

   (A) making the first functional automobiles with internal combustion gasoline engines.
   (B) producing new model innovations and color choices each year to increase consumer interest.
   (C) being the first major automobile manufacturer to sell cars using installment credit.
   (D) producing cars efficiently and making the price within the means of the average person.
   (E) borrowing the technologies used in racing vehicles to improve cars for the general public.

2. Attorney General A. Mitchell Palmer responded to the hysteria associated with the first Red Scare in the 1920s by

   (A) declaring the influx of radicals among immigrants to be an act of war by Soviet Russia.
   (B) requiring all rail and ship passengers to be searched for weapons before boarding.
   (C) raiding the headquarters of labor organizations looking for subversive literature.
   (D) arresting immigrants who could not produce the proper paperwork in roadblocks.
   (E) censoring the publications of radical organizations and stopping their mail service.

3. Warren G. Harding's major failure as president was his

   (A) inability to judge the character of those working for him in the executive branch.
   (B) overemphasis on foreign policy in an era of extreme domestic societal change.
   (C) misinterpreting his landslide victory as a mandate to expand the power of the government.
   (D) lack of sincere, moral leadership because of his personal character flaws.
   (E) unfamiliarity with the world of journalism during a new era of mass communication.

4. Margin buying allowed investors to

   (A) purchase stock in many companies at once.
   (B) borrow money to buy stocks with only a small cash payment.
   (C) pool capital to allow more leverage in company takeovers.
   (D) buy and sell stocks through second-party transactions by brokers.
   (E) sell stock in companies that owned no assets and produced no products.

5. Herbert Hoover's approach toward the growing depression in the wake of the Stock Market Crash was to

   (A) order the Federal Reserve to restrict access to capital to prevent wild speculation.
   (B) appeal to major banking firms for support in issuing gold bonds to stabilize the dollar.
   (C) give Americans scapegoats by arresting bankers and stock brokers guilty of insider trading.
   (D) slowly mobilize the resources of the federal government to support the financial industry.
   (E) enact a series of laws to provide for the basic needs of the people who had lost their jobs.

6. All of the following attributes linked Franklin D. Roosevelt's New Deal to the earlier goals of Progressive Reform EXCEPT

   (A) a focus on new regulations on the economy enforced by the federal government.
   (B) collective action of a broad spectrum of American citizens seeking reform.
   (C) isolating a segment of the population as those who selfishly ruined the economy for others.
   (D) popularizing reform measures through the skillful use of rhetorical devices.
   (E) taking an expert's advice to use deficit spending to "prime" the economic "pump."

7. The agency of the New Deal most criticized as an expression of socialism was the

   (A) National Recovery Administration.
   (B) Agricultural Adjustment Administration.
   (C) Tennessee Valley Authority.
   (D) Securities and Exchange Commission.
   (E) Works Progress Administration.

8. Franklin D. Roosevelt justified the radical nature of some New Deal programs by stating his position that

   (A) the government should take from each according to his or her ability and give to each according to his or her need.
   (B) the businesses of the United States were cooperating with the New Deal measures out of voluntary compliance because of patriotism just like back in World War I.
   (C) the people demanded the specific programs he was championing and he was merely acting as a public servant carrying out their wishes.
   (D) the New Deal was protecting private property and free enterprise by preventing a revolution based on injustices and inequalities that had arisen in the American economic system.
   (E) whatever excesses were committed by his desire to provide relief, recovery, and reform to the American people would be corrected because these emergency measures were temporary.

9. John L. Lewis broke away from the American Federation of Labor (AFL) and formed the Congress of Industrial Organizations because he believed that

   (A) the AFL had been infiltrated by too many socialists and communists from abroad.
   (B) in the crisis of the Great Depression skilled and unskilled workers needed to stick together.
   (C) the AFL was ignoring the needs of Appalachian coal miners because they were southerners.
   (D) although the AFL looked out for Jewish workers, it did not respect African-Americans.
   (E) a more radical approach was necessary requiring an alliance with the Socialist Party.

10. The findings of the Nye Commission led the United States between the world wars to

   (A) institute the first peacetime draft in American history.
   (B) provide all aid short of war to the Allies standing against Nazi aggression in Europe.
   (C) mobilize the American economy for the production of weapons and armored vehicles.
   (D) ban all Americans from participating in war in Europe even as volunteers.
   (E) pass laws restricting trade with combatant nations.

11. American women could help the war effort during World War II in all of the following ways EXCEPT

   (A) helping comfort female prisoners when concentration camps were liberated.
   (B) enduring the hardships associated with the rationing of many staple products.
   (C) working in war industries to replace the labor of men called off to war.
   (D) serving in uniform as nurses, signal corps personnel, and clerical staff.
   (E) touring American military bases as entertainers for the United Service Organization (USO).

12. The primary goal of Douglas MacArthur's "island-hopping" strategy in the Pacific during World War II was to

   (A) conserve his dwindling number of transport ships that were falling to kamikaze attacks.
   (B) confuse the Japanese as to which of their fortified islands he would attack next.
   (C) take only necessary islands, especially those from which airplanes could attack Japan.
   (D) prevent loss of Japanese lives because their soldiers were sworn to fight to the death.
   (E) fight the least fortified Japanese-held islands first before coming back to tougher targets.

13. The general opinion of Harry Truman held by most Americans when he succeeded to the presidency after the death of Franklin D. Roosevelt (FDR) was that

   (A) they trusted FDR's judgment and Truman must be the best successor.
   (B) as a World War I veteran he was better able to lead the country in war than FDR.
   (C) as a former businessman he would be well equipped to restart the peacetime economy.
   (D) he was a tough leader who had fought political corruption and would fight to win the war.
   (E) he was not up to the challenges America faced in World War II and the Great Depression.

14. The first American politician to effectively use the potential of television to spread a political message was

    (A)  Harry Truman.
    (B)  Dwight Eisenhower.
    (C)  Adlai E. Stevenson.
    (D)  Joseph McCarthy.
    (E)  George C. Marshall.

15. The Soviet Union's launch of the first artificial satellite into orbit around the earth impacted the United States most by

    (A)  proving that the nation was vulnerable to nuclear attack from space.
    (B)  causing Americans to doubt the free enterprise system because communists won the space race.
    (C)  mandating a higher percentage of America's gross domestic product be spent on defense than the Soviets spent.
    (D)  increasing federal support for educational goals that would increase national security.
    (E)  causing the Congress to authorize the development of a missile defense system.

# Answer Explanations

1. **D**  Answer A is incorrect in that European and American companies had been making gasoline-powered automobiles even before the turn of the twentieth century. Ford's genius was in making a simple, durable model on an assembly line, thus reducing overhead costs and bringing the cost of a car within the reach of the middle class. Answers B and C were innovations General Motors used to try to compete with Ford, and answer E was a later step in the automobile industry.

2. **C**  The Palmer Raids of the first Red Scare were focused on subversive elements like socialists and communists in existing labor organizations. Palmer authorized the raids to seize both literature and immigrants, but he did not use roadblocks as suggested in answer D.

3. **A**  In the same way President Grant's administration became scandal ridden, the Harding administration suffered from the corruption of the president's subordinates. Harding tried to contract the power of government and had been a newspaper editor himself, so answers C and E are the opposite of the truth. Answers B and D could be said to be true of Harding, but the scandals erupted when men he thought were befriending him for the good of the country had other intentions.

4. **B**  The inflation of stock prices that led to the Stock Market Crash in 1929 was largely due to the rampant speculation produced by the ability of buyers to borrow most of the money they invested. In the rapid rise of stock prices in the 1920s they could make profits for a while, but when prices fell they could not cover their debts.

5. **D**  All of the other answers reflect the actions of other presidents under similar and different economic conditions, but answer D was Hoover's approach during his crisis management. He originally balked at profound intervention in the economy, but as the Depression deepened he resorted to attempts to stem the tide that actually formed a model for some of the measures of the New Deal like the Reconstruction Finance Corporation.

6. **E**  Because Progressive Reform was begun during the upswing from a depression, Progressives did not resort to deficit spending as a purposeful policy nor see it as their duty to do so. Franklin D. Roosevelt's (FDR's) taking the advice of John Maynard Keynes to "prime the pump" was an example of the Wisconsin Idea in action, but unlike all the other answers, was not practiced extensively in peacetime until the Great Depression. All of the other answers express ideas and actions that could be said to be shared values between Theodore Roosevelt's Square Deal and FDR's New Deal.

7. **C**  Since the Tennessee Valley Authority (TVA) "took over the means of production" by producing electrical power in such a way that private companies could not compete, critics identified it with socialism. The other agencies in the

other answers were viewed this way by some, but the TVA was a government-owned utility company that transformed an area of the Southeast that had little to no industrial potential into one with great potential but no competition in providing electrical power.

8. **D**   Answers B, C, and E are plausible explanations except that many of the New Deal measures were intended as permanent reforms and are still operating today. Answers B and C would serve as justifications for typical government involvement in setting economic policy, but Franklin D. Roosevelt (FDR) specifically stated the position in answer D to explain his belief that the government had to be radicalized for a time. He believed his actions were conservative in that they were using liberal policies to guard against an overthrow of the status quo. Answer A is an example of Marxist rhetoric that FDR did not employ.

9. **B**   The Congress of Industrial Organizations (CIO) allowed skilled and unskilled workers to unite in industrial unions unlike the American Federation of Labor (AFL) that had broken away from the Knights of Labor to focus on the needs only of skilled workers. Later the AFL and the CIO united to form the AFL-CIO.

10. **E**   Answers A, B, and C described actual actions of the Roosevelt administration in preparation for American involvement in World War II prior to his overcoming of the Neutrality Acts inspired by the Nye Committee as stated in answer E. After Pearl Harbor, Franklin D. Roosevelt did not have to convince the American people to set aside their traditional isolationism; it had been set aside for them. Answer D is a reference to the voluntary service of Americans in the British military and that of other nations prior to Pearl Harbor.

11. **A**   All of the other answers were paths open to women in supporting the war effort. By its nature the liberation of Nazi concentration camps was a combat operation, and women in World War II were barred from serving in combat roles.

12. **C**   All of the answers hint at realities of the terrible warfare faced by Americans and their allies in the Pacific Theater of World War II, and some were partially used to justify MacArthur's innovative strategy. The overall goal of the whole procedure, however, was to focus on acquiring islands like Iwo Jima and Okinawa to use as "unsinkable aircraft carriers" from which constant bombing of the Japanese mainland could help end the war as it had in Europe.

13. **E**   Although Truman later proved to be a tough fighter who made sure "the buck stops here" at his desk, he was originally thought to be inadequate as stated in answer E. He had fought in World War I and had run a gentleman's clothing store, but these were not foremost in the minds of the American public when Franklin D. Roosevelt (FDR) died after being elected to an unprecedented fourth term as president. No one could have taken the office at that moment with the full confidence of the American people, especially because a good portion of the people fighting the war had never known another president besides FDR.

14. **D**  Whereas Franklin D. Roosevelt had shown all politicians the path toward mass communication with his fireside chats, Joseph McCarthy first seized on television as a political tool. His hearings, when broadcast on television, won for him and for his cause the heartfelt support of the majority of Americans until McCarthy's campaign to root out communists from the government backfired on himself. Richard Nixon, for one, never forgot how powerful a tool television could be; he saved his political career by delivering his "Checkers" speech but lost the presidency to John Kennedy who proved an even better master of the new medium.

15. **D**  Answers A, B, and C are the opposite of the truth in that despite hysteria President Eisenhower and the government knew the Russian's launch of *Sputnik* did not immediately threaten the United States. Americans turned all the more toward private enterprise to devise new technologies, and the spending on national defense by the United States during the Cold War as a percentage of the gross domestic product (GDP) never approached the nearly 50-percent mark the Soviets had to expend to keep up. The two philosophical and economic systems were sharply contrasted by the fact that the United States never spent more than about 4 percent of its GDP on national defense during the height of the Cold War. A missile defense shield was a goal much later in the Cold War than in 1957 when *Sputnik* orbited the earth. The original strategy of the Cold War was to have a strong defense by maintaining a strong offense, one so strong it could destroy the planet several times over. The direct and most significant impact of the launch of *Sputnik* was passage of the National Defense Education Act the next year to boost instruction in math, sciences, and foreign languages. These courses were offered at the college level in high school by funding the College Board and other initiatives in an attempt to catch and to surpass the Soviets.

# The Changing Values of the 1960s

# CHAPTER 32

*We are people of this generation, bred in at least modest comfort, housed now in universities, looking uncomfortably to the world we inherit.*
—Tom Hayden, "The Port Huron Statement," 1962

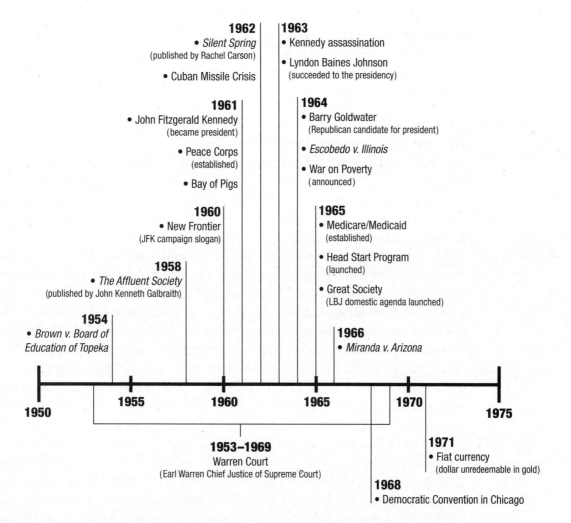

**1962**
• *Silent Spring*
(published by Rachel Carson)

• Cuban Missile Crisis

**1963**
• Kennedy assassination

• Lyndon Baines Johnson
(succeeded to the presidency)

**1961**
• John Fitzgerald Kennedy
(became president)

• Peace Corps
(established)

• Bay of Pigs

**1964**
• Barry Goldwater
(Republican candidate for president)

• *Escobedo v. Illinois*

• War on Poverty
(announced)

**1960**
• New Frontier
(JFK campaign slogan)

**1965**
• Medicare/Medicaid
(established)

• Head Start Program
(launched)

• Great Society
(LBJ domestic agenda launched)

**1958**
• *The Affluent Society*
(published by John Kenneth Galbraith)

**1954**
• *Brown v. Board of
Education of Topeka*

**1966**
• *Miranda v. Arizona*

1950    1955    1960    1965    1970    1975

**1953–1969**
Warren Court
(Earl Warren Chief Justice of Supreme Court)

**1971**
• Fiat currency
(dollar unredeemable in gold)

**1968**
• Democratic Convention in Chicago

# Top 20 Things to Know

## 1 *The Affluent Society*

This book by John Kenneth Galbraith sparked discussion as the United States moved into the 1960s after a large expansion of the American economy in the 1950s. Published in 1958, *The Affluent Society* criticized the consumerism and waste of a society obsessed with increasing productivity managed by private industries bent on making profits. Galbraith identified postwar America as the richest society in history, but he also criticized the advertising industry for making Americans want to consume more resources than any previous society. Because Americans, he said, had not developed an adequate system of managing unprecedented affluence, the government should moderate the excesses of consumerism by devoting more resources to the public sector, especially to public education. Galbraith's ideas rejected traditional economic views and professed that poverty could be eradicated from society, but many Americans recognized that the productivity of the United States had won World War II and were suspicious of intellectuals who told them their spending on themselves was ultimately destructive. Galbraith's ideas, however, were the natural extension of Keynesian economics and Progressive Reform and won him fame and influence among political liberals, including John F. Kennedy who made Galbraith one of his chief advisers.

## 2 John Fitzgerald Kennedy

Kennedy was the son of the wealthy banker and realtor, Joseph P. Kennedy, who brought his Harvard-educated son to London while ambassador to England. John F. Kennedy (JFK) was critical of England's lack of preparedness and foresight in the face of the rise of Nazism, and when the United States entered World War II he became a decorated war hero. He entered politics upon returning to the United States and served three terms in the House of Representatives. His defeat of veteran Republican Senator Henry Cabot Lodge in the 1952 Senate race won Kennedy fame with Democrats around the nation, and his dashing good looks and attractive wife appealed to a nation becoming fixated on youthfulness. After a failed bid for the vice presidency, JFK returned to the Senate. In the Election of 1960, however, he won the presidency and became the first Roman Catholic and the youngest man elected to the executive branch (Theodore Roosevelt had been younger when he replaced McKinley but was not elected to do so). Kennedy inherited many dangerous Cold War threats from the Eisenhower administration and made strong showings against communists in Cuba and in Berlin. He was assassinated by Lee Harvey Oswald in Dallas, Texas, in November 1963, just as he was beginning to mature in the presidential office. His policies on civil rights had waivered and then become so firm as to alienate southern Democrats, hence the trip to Dallas. The president's being cut down in the apparent prime of life after beginning to make strides in both foreign and domestic issues caused shock and grief across the nation and instability in the world.

## 3 New Frontier

John F. Kennedy (JFK) called his Progressive agenda the New Frontier, and because he entered the presidency with a Democratic Congress as had Franklin D. Roosevelt, expectations were high that sweeping reforms would be passed in another First Hundred Days. The results were disappointing to liberals, however, despite Kennedy's capable advisers and popularity. Kennedy's cabinet overhauled the executive branch's operations, but Kennedy failed to install a new Department of Urban Affairs. Congress also defeated his proposed measures on housing, medical care for the elderly, and federal grants for public education. He did succeed in securing an increase in the minimum wage to $1.25 per hour, but despite stirring rhetoric could not make the plight of African-Americans a viable goal of white Progressives. The phrase *New Frontier* seemed more applicable to his outreach to the world in the Peace Corps and his announcement that the United States was planning on "landing a man on the moon and returning him safely to earth" by the end of the decade.

## 4 Peace Corps

John F. Kennedy (JFK) launched this program by executive order as a new component of the involvement of the United States in global issues. By the time Congress approved the measure and established it as a permanent volunteer organization, over thirteen thousand Americans had answered JFK's call in his inaugural address to "Ask not what your country can do for you, but what you can do for your country." Young Americans served two-year stints in developing nations as teachers, medical workers, and technical advisers in implementing economic and human resource development strategies. A similar program was launched to subsidize volunteer work at home called VISTA. Since its launch in 1961, the Peace Corps has now sent over two hundred thousand volunteers into 139 countries.

## 5 Bay of Pigs

President Eisenhower had authorized the training of Cuban exiles for a mission to return to Cuba to overthrow Fidel Castro, the communist dictator who led a coup against Fulgencio Batista. Under the advice of the Central Intelligence Agency (CIA) and other national security advisers, John F. Kennedy (JFK) allowed the mission to go forward despite his own misgivings. Kennedy denied the revolutionaries any direct support from the American military, however, and when the fifteen hundred-man invasion force landed at the Bay of Pigs, they were all killed or captured in just three days. The incident drew international criticism of Kennedy and the United States and made a permanent breech in negotiations with Castro. A meeting of the Organization of American States (OAS) condemned Castro's loyalty to Marxism-Leninism and initiated an embargo against Cuba that remains in place today.

## 6 Cuban Missile Crisis

The Soviet Union had been supplying Castro with the resources he used to consolidate his control of Cuba, but by 1962 this support took the form of missile installations in Cuba just 90 miles away from Florida. The Kennedy administration pronounced that the United States would deter any further expansion of communism on the part of Castro or the Soviets and would respond with force if the Soviets used Cuba as a base from which to threaten the nation's security. When photographic evidence proved that missile bases were being constructed in Cuba, Kennedy demanded their removal and blockaded the island nation. Kennedy called on the Organization of American States (OAS) and the United Nations to intervene and called on Nikita Khrushchev to personally take responsibility for the threat to peace. After the U.S. Navy began stopping Soviet ships, Khrushchev offered to remove the missiles under United Nation's supervision if Kennedy would pledge not to attack Cuba and if the United States would dismantle similar missile installations in Turkey. Kennedy ended the standoff by pledging not to attack and standing down the American missiles aimed at the Soviet Union from Turkey. Kennedy was able to save face, but Nikita Khrushchev could not and was removed from office as the leader of the Soviet Union. Just how dangerous the tense situation was became apparent later when it was revealed that the Soviets had to restrain Castro from firing missiles into the United States, a step that would have likely resulted in thermonuclear war.

# 7 Kennedy Assassination

Having gone to Dallas to shore up support from the Democrats of Texas, Kennedy was shot twice while traveling in an open car in a motorcade. Lee Harvey Oswald, a former Marine who had visited the Soviet Union and exhibited leftist leanings, was apprehended after killing a Dallas policeman and accused of assassinating the president. Kennedy was pronounced dead thirty minutes after the shooting. Lyndon B. Johnson was sworn in as president. While Oswald was being moved from a prison cell he was shot by nightclub owner Jack Ruby as America watched on television. Chief Justice Earl Warren headed a commission investigating the assassination that announced that Oswald had acted alone. A later report by a committee of the House of Representatives concluded that an unknown assailant had fired a shot that perhaps had delivered the mortal wound to the head. Kennedy's assassination shocked the world and devastated the grief-stricken nation, but Lyndon Johnson was able to present Kennedy as a martyr, thereby making way for many of Kennedy's (and his own) policies' passage by Congress.

# 8 Lyndon Baines Johnson

Another World War II naval-hero-turned-politician was the big Texan, Lyndon B. Johnson (LBJ), although Johnson was already in the House of Representatives when he joined the navy. He was elected to the Senate in 1949 and became the Democratic Majority Leader by 1955. He was elected vice president under John F. Kennedy in 1960. After becoming president because of Kennedy's assassination, LBJ won in his own right in 1964 against Barry Goldwater. Lyndon Johnson's presidency was one of tremendous advance for the welfare programs and civil rights legislation of the liberal version of Progressive Reform, but his escalation of the Vietnam War without developing a winning strategy was his undoing. Although constitutionally able to run in the Election of 1968 he declined to do so.

## 9 Great Society

Lyndon B. Johnson's (LBJ's) reform agenda outstripped any previous presidential liberal initiative save the New Deal. Whereas John F. Kennedy had been stymied in his attempts at reform, LBJ was able to turn the nation's injury in losing its youthful president into solid legislative advances. His advances included civil rights legislation, the War on Poverty, VISTA, Head Start, and even a resurrection of the Civilian Conservation Corps (CCC) called the Job Corps. After soundly beating Barry Goldwater, LBJ was able to receive passage of pollution control laws and other environmental legislation, the National Endowment for the Arts, funding to public schools, Medicare and Medicaid, the end of discriminatory immigration quotas, consumer safety regulations for products, and funding for public housing for low-income families. The Great Society began to unravel, though, as more federal dollars were diverted to the Vietnam War. Conservatives decried his spending for liberal domestic programs, and liberals decried his spending for a flawed foreign policy commitment.

## 10 War on Poverty

Lyndon B. Johnson (LBJ) declared in a state of the union address that the United States would fight an "unconditional war on poverty." He said in the affluent society created after World War II there should not be thirty million people living in poverty, thirteen million of whom were children. The Head Start program was aimed at reaching the disadvantaged children, the first one opening in rural Mississippi, which was the most impoverished state. Urban programs, however, were also begun to address a lack of housing and jobs. LBJ addressed the symptoms of poverty by stressing education and jobs training without acknowledging that because of the development of the welfare state a crisis lay in the fact that certain citizens chose to receive a meager existence from the government rather than to better themselves through government programs. Poverty rates in the United States dropped at the onset of the War on Poverty but have remained largely the same since the 1970s.

## 11 Barry Goldwater

Barry Goldwater inherited a department store chain from his father in Arizona and ran the business until World War II when he entered the Army Air Corps. He rose to the rank of brigadier general and after the war became a senator. As a strong anticommunist he supported Joseph McCarthy and was critical of Harry Truman. Within the Republican Party Goldwater was more conservative than Dwight Eisenhower and most other national leaders. Goldwater ran against Lyndon B. Johnson for the presidency in 1964, but his voting record in the Senate, which stood against the Fair Deal, the New Frontier, and the Great Society, led people to believe LBJ's campaign ads that claimed Goldwater would start a nuclear war. Goldwater returned to the Senate where he advocated a more aggressive offensive war in Vietnam. He backed Richard Nixon for the presidency but was among the Republicans who talked Nixon into resigning for the good of the country after the Watergate Scandal. Staying true to conservative principles for the remainder of his career in public life, Goldwater opposed Jimmy Carter and backed Ronald Reagan. He has been called one of the most successful politicians of the twentieth century because he is attributed with the beginning of the conservative movement and lived to hear Bill Clinton pronounce "The era of big government is over," after losing the Congress to the Republicans for the first time in forty years.

## 12 Medicare/Medicaid

Lyndon B. Johnson (LBJ) backed a 1965 change in the Social Security Administration to incorporate an idea Harry Truman initiated in the Fair Deal, saying that the elderly in America were the most likely to live in poverty and that half of them did not have health insurance. Medicare was designed to provide medical care for the elderly attached to their social security payments and funded by social security taxes, which had to be raised. Those citizens sixty-five or older receiving social security also received hospitalization insurance, coverage of physicians' and surgeons' expenses, and home health care. Medicaid was designed to provide similar benefits for the poor and disabled. Costs for Medicaid were divided between the states and the federal government. Nineteen million elderly Americans were receiving Medicare payments by 1966, and the programs have been routinely expanded every three to five years since.

## 13 Head Start Program

One of the War on Poverty programs was known as Head Start, originally a summer program for disadvantaged children overseen by the Office of Economic Opportunity. The program was designed to build the emotional and physical health of preschool children in order to help them overcome the social and economic conditions into which they were born. Children as young as three participated in the program when it started in 1965. In 1969, the Head Start program came under the oversight of the new Department of Health, Education, and Welfare. The summer program model was transformed into year-round day care and preschool instruction as early as 1967. The age at which children could enter an Early Head Start program was dropped to zero, or infancy, and was the source of critics' phrase "from the cradle to the grave" in complaining of the desire of the federal government to control citizens' lives through the extension of the welfare state.

## 14 Fiat Currency

The Coinage Act of 1965 eliminated all silver from American coins except for the Kennedy half-dollar that retained only 40 percent silver. By 1968, Lyndon B. Johnson proclaimed that the paper currency of the United States could no longer be redeemed for silver creating a nearly fiat currency, a process Richard Nixon completed in 1971 by ending the international gold standard touching off soaring inflation. Fiat currencies contain value only because a society accepts them as a means of exchange by faith in the government that issues the currency. The inflation that results from fiat currencies has ruined many nations as the shrinking value of the fiat currencies undermines confidence in the governments that possess the ability to print money at will.

## 15 *Silent Spring*

Published by scientist and naturalist Rachel Carson in 1962, *Silent Spring* launched the modern environmentalist movement. The book attacked the use of DDT, an insecticide used by the government to fight mosquitoes during World War II, which had come into common use in the United States. After three years of research she reported in the book that DDT built up in the food chain over time and thus poisoned top predators like the bald eagle. An attempt by chemical companies to stop the publication of the book only increased its sales, and by 1963 President Kennedy had set up a committee to investigate environmental issues. DDT was banned in 1972 after the National Cancer Institute published findings that it could cause cancer. Rachel Carson combined her scientific background with literary talent to popularize ecology.

## 16 Democratic Convention in Chicago

The national nominating convention for the Democratic Party in 1968 occurred during one of the most tumultuous years in American history. Both Martin Luther King Jr. and Robert Kennedy had been assassinated, and the Vietnam War had become so unpopular that Lyndon B. Johnson's (LBJ) support for it had wrecked his presidency. Johnson stepped aside and did not seek reelection. Mayor Richard Daley had turned the convention center into a fortification manned with around twelve thousand policemen and the National Guard. Antiwar protestors turned out in great numbers and clashed with the established leaders of the Democratic Party who nominated Hubert Humphrey, LBJ's vice president and a supporter of Johnson's escalation of the war. When police moved on the crowd and began using nightsticks and tear gas to disperse them, a riot ensued that was caught on television. Around one hundred protestors and one hundred policemen were injured, and many young people decided the political system of the United States was irrevocably damaged. After a long summer of riots in Los Angeles and other cities around the country, Richard Nixon's law-and-order campaign won him the Election of 1968.

## 17 Warren Court

Earl Warren was such a popular governor of California that both the Republican and the Democratic parties nominated him for the office in 1946. He became the chief justice of the Supreme Court under Eisenhower and served from 1953 to 1969. Apart from serving as the chairman of the Warren Commission that investigated the Kennedy assassination, Earl Warren and his colleagues guided the Court through its most activist era during another time period of great societal flux. The Warren Court fostered such sweeping changes in the application of the U.S. Constitution that some said the Supreme Court was making laws rather than interpreting them, whereas others rejoiced that aspects of the Bill of Rights were being applied to certain minorities in particular cases for the first time in history. The Warren Court promoted a radically equal society as well as one in which civil liberties were secured and preserved for all Americans regardless of race, religion, or other attributes that might have placed them outside the mainstream. The most important decision of the Warren Court was the landmark case *Brown v. Board of Education of Topeka, Kansas*, but other cases contributed to redefining First Amendment rights, the right to privacy, law enforcement procedures, and voting and representation issues.

# 18 *Brown v. Board of Education of Topeka, Kansas*

The U.S. Supreme Court under Earl Warren voted unanimously in 1954 that segregation of African-American and white students in schools denied children the equal protection of the laws. The Warren Court directed public schools to admit African-American students to schools with white children "with all deliberate speed." That clause was interpreted to admit a wide range of speeds by states, some of which complied immediately and others of which staged protests in the form of administrative hurdles all the way to a resolution for nullification in Alabama. The activities of the National Association for the Advancement of Colored People (NAACP) to advance desegregation were met with the activities of White Citizens' Councils to hamper it. In 1956, a document called the "Southern Manifesto" was signed by over one hundred members of the U.S. Congress saying that the South would use "all lawful means" to resist the Supreme Court's decision.

# 19 *Escobedo v. Illinois*

Danny Escobedo was arrested, freed, and rearrested for the murder of his brother-in-law in 1960. During police questioning, Escobedo asked repeatedly to talk to his lawyer. When police said they had an eyewitness accusing Escobedo of the murder, Escobedo denied killing the man but gave information that led police to believe he had been at the scene of the killing. Escobedo was thus charged with the murder of his brother-in-law after being tripped up in the investigation, and his case was appealed ultimately to the Warren Court. The majority opinion of the Court was that Escobedo's prosecution had been based on evidence obtained while the police were denying the accused the right to have legal counsel. This case laid the groundwork for the *Miranda* case by setting the precedent of an accused criminal's right to remain silent until a lawyer could be provided. Law enforcement advocates decried the decision as one that would make convictions far more difficult to obtain, which is exactly what the civil rights advocates on the Court intended.

# 20 *Miranda v. Arizona*

In 1966, the Warren Court followed the *Escobedo* case with a more specific ruling after Ernesto Miranda was arrested and coerced into confessing to a kidnapping and rape of an eighteen-year-old woman. The Supreme Court ruled that the original evidence had been circumstantial and that the conviction could not stand because Miranda had at no time been informed of his rights to legal counsel. Miranda was retried and convicted again on more substantial evidence and went on to serve five years of a much longer sentence before he was paroled and later stabbed to death in a bar fight. His name has been turned into a verb, though, as police officers "mirandize" anyone being arrested by telling the person that he or she has the right to remain silent, that anything said could be used against him or her, that he or she has the right to consult with an attorney, and that if the person could not afford an attorney, a public defender would be appointed for him or her. The Supreme Court thereby effectively made a new law in that statements obtained before the Miranda rights were read to a suspect would be inadmissible in courts as evidence.

## The Big Picture

1. The Kennedy administration grappled with foreign affairs and achieved some successes in the Cold War without being able to match that success with the advance of a Progressive domestic agenda.

2. After the Kennedy assassination, the Johnson administration successfully passed a wide range of measures addressing domestic reforms in Johnson's Great Society program.

3. A conservative backlash began to take shape in America as a result of the succession of presidential programs from the Square Deal to the New Deal, the Fair Deal, the New Frontier, and the Great Society.

4. The Cold War competition between the superpowers of the United States and the Soviet Union involved the application of resources around the globe to everything from symbolic showdowns to actual shooting wars, all with the backdrop of a potentially deadly exchange of nuclear weapons.

5. The Supreme Court under Chief Justice Earl Warren advanced numerous civil rights issues with such force as to give the nine members of the Court the ability to virtually make laws outside the legislative powers of states and of the U.S. Congress.

# The Civil Rights Movement

*We have waited for more than three hundred and forty years
for our constitutional and God-given rights.*

—Martin Luther King Jr., "Letter from Birmingham Jail," 1963

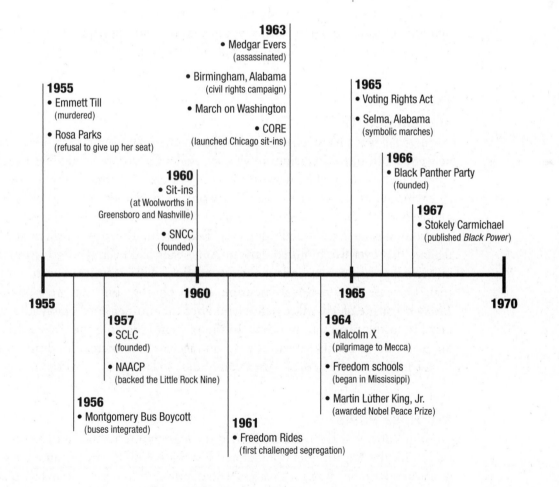

**1963**
- Medgar Evers
  (assassinated)
- Birmingham, Alabama
  (civil rights campaign)
- March on Washington
- CORE
  (launched Chicago sit-ins)

**1955**
- Emmett Till
  (murdered)
- Rosa Parks
  (refusal to give up her seat)

**1965**
- Voting Rights Act
- Selma, Alabama
  (symbolic marches)

**1966**
- Black Panther Party
  (founded)

**1967**
- Stokely Carmichael
  (published *Black Power*)

**1960**
- Sit-ins
  (at Woolworths in
  Greensboro and Nashville)
- SNCC
  (founded)

**1957**
- SCLC
  (founded)
- NAACP
  (backed the Little Rock Nine)

**1956**
- Montgomery Bus Boycott
  (buses integrated)

**1961**
- Freedom Rides
  (first challenged segregation)

**1964**
- Malcolm X
  (pilgrimage to Mecca)
- Freedom schools
  (began in Mississippi)
- Martin Luther King, Jr.
  (awarded Nobel Peace Prize)

1955     1960     1965     1970

# Top 20 Things to Know

## 1 Segregation

Segregation was a key component of the Jim Crow laws that survived the Reconstruction era. Such laws mandated that African-Americans and white Americans should not share schools, restaurant facilities, public bathrooms and water fountains, public transportation, playgrounds, or even jails. Although churches were segregated by the Freedman's Bureau in some states, the long-standing segregation that occurred in churches was by choice rather than by state or federal law. Racial segregation was sanctioned by the Supreme Court in *Plessy v. Ferguson* in 1896, although dissenting justices claimed such laws would only fan racial hatred and mistrust. A chief strategy of the civil rights movement was to purposefully break segregation laws in acts of civil disobedience. The 1954 *Brown v. Board of Education of Topeka, Kansas* case called for the end of segregation in public schools after Harry Truman had desegregated the U.S. Armed Forces in the Korean War. The Warren Court also struck down laws barring interracial marriage in 1967, and by 1971 the Supreme Court banned all forms of segregation and approved of a wide range of tools governments could use to end practices like busing and the reapportioning of school districts.

## 2 Emmett Till

Emmett Till was a fourteen-year-old African-American from Chicago in 1955 when he went south into Mississippi to visit an uncle. On a dare from a local youth, Till approached a young white woman working at a grocery store and said, "Bye, baby," and whistled as he left the store. The woman's husband and brother-in-law later removed Till from his uncle's home by force and beat and shot the boy to death. His body was later recovered out of the Tallahatchie River by a fisherman. Despite the fact that over five hundred African-Americans had been lynched with impunity in Mississippi since the end of Reconstruction, Till's murderers were brought to trial. The case drew national attention as did photographs that were published in *Ebony* magazine of Till's face before and after the murder. Predictably, the all-white jury found the two men innocent. In the tension following the *Brown* decision by the Supreme Court the previous year, outrage over Emmett Till's death prompted Rosa Parks and other African-American leaders to launch the civil rights movement.

## 3 Rosa Parks

During World War II Rosa Parks joined the Montgomery, Alabama, National Association for the Advancement of Colored People (NAACP) and became the secretary to its president. She was a seamstress who commuted to her work on city buses, and in 1955, three months after the Emmett Till murder case, she was asked to move from the front of the "black section" of the bus to allow a white man to sit because the "white section" was full. This practice sometimes made African-American passengers have to exit the bus entirely if enough whites boarded to fill a bus. Rosa Parks said, "Why do you push us around?" and refused to move. The protest of her arrest prompted the Montgomery Bus Boycott and launched the activities of Martin Luther King Jr. Parks moved north upon release and served as a secretary to a member of the House of Representatives. She remained a leader and iconic symbol of the civil rights movement for the rest of her life.

## 4 Montgomery Bus Boycott

Martin Luther King Jr. began his leadership in the civil rights movement by organizing the Montgomery Bus Boycott, a protest on the part of African-Americans for the arrest and fine imposed on Rosa Parks. In Montgomery, Alabama, African-Americans walked and carpooled to work, whereas before the boycott they had made up the majority of the passengers riding the buses. The boycott lasted 381 days and cost the bus company 65 percent of its normal income. The Warren Court decreed that the segregation of the buses should end.

## 5 Martin Luther King Jr.

For his efforts in the Montgomery Bus Boycott, the Rev. Martin Luther King's church was machine-gunned. Like his namesake, however, attacks simply hardened his resolve to fight on. As a leader of the Southern Christian Leadership Conference (SCLC), King advocated nonviolent resistance modeled after that of Henry David Thoreau and Gandhi. The SCLC prompted African-Americans to rally in churches and to launch voter registration drives, boycotts, sit-ins, and freedom rides. King was arrested in 1963 after leading demonstrations in Birmingham, Alabama, and eloquently defended his actions in a document called "Letter from Birmingham Jail" written to local white ministers. The episode moved John F. Kennedy to push for stronger civil rights measures that alienated southern Democrats, leading Kennedy to Dallas and his death. As one of the leaders of a March on Washington, King addressed more than two hundred thousand people with his "I have a dream" speech. For his moral courage, eloquence, and activism King was awarded the Nobel Peace Prize in 1964. He led a march from Selma, Alabama, to Montgomery in 1965 and had begun to protest de facto segregation, the plight of the poor, and the Vietnam War when he was killed in Memphis, Tennessee, in 1968.

## 6 The Southern Christian Leadership Conference

The Southern Christian Leadership Conference (SCLC) was formed to coordinate protests around the South in the wake of the Montgomery Bus Boycott. Sixty people, mostly African-American ministers, from ten states created the organization and resolved that the civil rights of all citizens are necessary for true democracy to work. The SCLC sought to end segregation by urging African-Americans to resist the practice in all its forms and to do so nonviolently. The first convention of the SCLC was held in Montgomery, Alabama, in 1957 where Dr. Martin Luther King Jr. was elected president. Other leaders in the organization included Dr. Ralph

David Abernathy, whose house and church were bombed, and the Reverend C. K. Steele. The SCLC also resolved to open its membership to all regardless of race, religion, or background. The organization revealed the centrality of African-American churches to the early civil rights movement.

# 7 National Association for the Advancement of Colored People

The National Association for the Advancement of Colored People (NAACP) had been in existence since its founding by W. E. B. Du Bois, Ida B. Wells, and others in 1909 as a result of a lynching and racial riot in Springfield, Illinois, the hometown of Abraham Lincoln. Both whites and blacks joined the organization dedicated to securing the rights within the Thirteenth, Fourteenth, and Fifteenth Amendments for African-Americans across the nation. Further goals were to secure the political, educational, social, and economic equality of minorities and people of color and to end racial prejudice. As the oldest civil rights organization, the NAACP hired Thurgood Marshall to argue the 1954 *Brown* case before the Supreme Court, and Marshall went on to become the first African-American justice on the Court. In the civil rights era of the 1950s and 1960s, NAACP leaders became targets of Ku Klux Klan reprisals and were sometimes murdered. The organization focused more on lobbying government to achieve legislative and judicial advances, but during the height of the activist period of civil rights protests the NAACP provided legal counsel and representation to participants across the civil rights spectrum.

# 8 Congress of Racial Equality

Formed in 1942 by James Farmer, the Congress of Racial Equality (CORE) stood against racial segregation of public transportation and other public facilities in the North prior to the civil rights era. Mainly white members joined starting from the University of Chicago, but the organization spread nationally and inspired African-Americans to employ direct protest tactics like sit-ins and freedom rides. When these tactics led to arrests, CORE members said they were also employing jail-ins. These same tactics were picked up by the Southern Christian Leadership Conference (SCLC) and other organizations on a wider scale through the 1960s, and CORE continued its operations as well.

# 9 Sit-ins

In a reenactment of the Congress of Racial Equality's (CORE's) first sit-in that took place in North Carolina in 1947, four African-American males sat down at a Woolworth's department store lunch counter in Greensboro early in 1960. The four politely asked for service but were refused according to the South's segregation policies. When asked to leave, the four young men refused. The students asserted that they were able to purchase goods from other parts of the store so they should be able to buy lunch. At the store's closing, protestors were forced to leave. They returned the next day, however, and their sit-in touched off a six-month protest that culminated in the desegregation of Greensboro's lunch counters. Other students across the South picked up the tactic and also staged sit-ins at Woolworth's stores because the department store was a national chain. Even northern students picketed outside the stores, and sit-ins became a chief strategy of the subsequent antiwar protests of the youth revolt.

## 10 Student Nonviolent Coordinating Committee

The Student Nonviolent Coordinating Committee (SNCC or Snick) formed as a youth spin-off from the Southern Christian Leadership Conference (SCLC) in the wake of the Montgomery Bus Boycott, and after the Greensboro sit-in they launched a sit-in at a Woolworth's in Nashville, Tennessee. Forty students of local African-American colleges initiated the sit-in, but as they were arrested, hundreds more replaced them at the lunch counter. Despite beatings, verbal abuse, and other forms of intimidation by white youths, the SNCC protestors did not strike back. After three months the city of Nashville ordered the integration of public dining facilities. SNCC widened its sit-in tactics to target public parks, swimming pools, theaters, churches, libraries, museums, and beaches. John Lewis, a seminary student and later U.S. congressman, became the chairman of SNCC in 1963 and helped organize the March on Washington, the Selma march, freedom rides, and freedom schools in cooperation with the Congress of Racial Equality (CORE) and the National Association for the Advancement of Colored People (NAACP). Stokely Carmichael became the chairman in 1966 and moved SNCC toward a more militant position of Black Power. As more extremists took up leadership in the organization, SNCC lost membership and ceased to exist in 1970.

## 11 Freedom Rides

Northern lawyers, teachers, and students of both races organized bus rides of activists and protestors to enter the South during what became known as the long, hot summers of the civil rights era. The protestors helped challenge the segregation laws and the practices that had disenfranchised African-Americans and helped establish and staff Freedom schools. As tension mounted, the voter registration drives inaugurated by Freedom Riders led to reprisals like beatings and the burning of buses. This tactic was especially designed to raise awareness in the North as the family members, neighbors, and colleagues of the protestors followed the events that resulted from the confrontations. White supremacists in the South said they were motivated by a desire to defend their way of life, but the violence aimed at the Freedom Riders served only to expose the injustices of southern society in the media, especially television, and to harden the resolve of all ranks of civil rights protestors. The murder of three Freedom Riders by Klansmen during the Johnson administration led to passage of the Civil Rights Act and the Voting Rights Act for which Lyndon B. Johnson was famous.

## 12 Medgar Evers

Evers was an African-American World War II veteran who returned to Mississippi and resolved to end racial discrimination in his home state after defending freedom in Europe. He rose in the ranks of the National Association for the Advancement of Colored People (NAACP) to become the field secretary, an office through which he organized new chapters of the organization and voter registration drives across the state as well as African-American boycotts of white businesses. As the face of the NAACP, Evers and his family received numerous threats, and their house in the state capital of Jackson was firebombed. Medgar Evers was shot in the back by a sniper in the summer of 1963 and died. Not until after thirty-one years was the killer brought to justice.

## 13 Birmingham, Alabama

Birmingham had been the site of eighteen unsolved bombings of African-American neighborhoods in six years and was thus nicknamed "Bombingham." A mob in the city had attacked a Freedom Rider bus in 1961. Martin Luther King Jr. was invited to the city by a local African-American minister in 1963 during protests that saw commissioner of public safety, Bull Connor, use police dogs to disperse crowds. King was arrested after leading a march and wrote "Letter from Birmingham Jail" while in custody. After King's release from jail, he and other leaders organized a walkout by school children who gathered and marched downtown singing the civil rights anthem, "We Shall Overcome." Almost one thousand students were arrested, filling Birmingham's jails. When another thousand students protested the next day, Bull Connor had the fire department turn high-pressure hoses on the children as well as using dogs again. By then pictures of the confrontation had received world-wide attention and drew the ire of President Kennedy who went on television to decry the events in Birmingham with his famous "Race has no place in American life or law" speech. Birmingham business leaders agreed to open lunch counters and to hire more African-American workers as a result.

## 14 March on Washington

After John F. Kennedy announced his support for the end of segregation before his assassination, two hundred thousand demonstrators marched on the national capital in August 1963 demanding "jobs and freedom." John Lewis and Dr. King delivered famous speeches (King's "I have a dream" speech) during an event that marked the high point of civil rights activists' unity and nonviolent "soul force." The march was also designed to lobby leaders in Washington to support a Civil Rights Bill that passed the House early in 1964 and later the Senate. President Johnson signed the Civil Rights Act almost a year after the March on Washington, and the law banned segregation in public facilities; discrimination in employment based on race, color, religion, sex, or national origin; and the denial of registration to vote based on immaterial errors on registration forms. The law also authorized the attorney general to sue agencies, businesses, and school systems that barred desegregation.

## 15 Voting Rights Act

In 1965, the Johnson administration followed the Civil Rights Act with the Voting Rights Act. The law removed all bars toward voting for African-Americans in the

South including literacy and other tests. The federal government was also given the task to supervise voting registration in state and local voting districts where fewer than half of potential voters were registered or had voted. At the time of the passage of the Voting Rights Act, seven states in the South still used Reconstruction era literacy tests.

## 16 Freedom Schools

One goal of the Freedom Rides of the 1960s was to instill greater pride in southern African-American communities. Freedom schools were held during the summers and taught African-American history and the nonviolent philosophies of the civil rights movement in order to prepare the next generation to continue the struggle. Proposed as early as 1963, freedom schools spread across Mississippi in 1964 and 1965 until over three thousand children were meeting in over forty organized efforts. The meeting places of the schools and the homes of the organizers were often targets of firebombing and some schools were attacked by white mobs. The founder of the freedom school movement, Charles Cobb, said the purpose of the schools was "to create an educational experience for students which will make it possible for them to challenge the myths of our society, to perceive more clearly its realities, and to find alternatives—ultimately new directions for action."

## 17 Selma, Alabama

Selma was the scene of a climactic series of marches in which the first march of Student Nonviolent Coordinating Committee (SNCC) leaders organized as a protest turned into a televised riot. As a peaceful line of marchers approached the Edmund Pettus Bridge in the spring of 1965, the local sheriff and highway patrolmen dispersed the march using tear gas. Television cameras caught the scene of the troopers wailing away at the marchers with clubs while wearing gas masks to protect themselves from the tear gas. This coverage prompted Martin Luther King Jr. to bring support from the Southern Christian Leadership Conference (SCLC) and lead another march, this time having sought protection under the law from a federal district court. Over three thousand people, five times the number of marchers in the original attempt, began a five-day 54-mile march to Montgomery, Alabama. By the time the march arrived in Montgomery, twenty-five thousand people had joined in order to help the protestors petition their government with grievances regarding racial discrimination. Within five months the U.S. Congress passed the Voting Rights Act.

## 18 Malcolm X

Malcolm X was born Malcolm Little in the home of a Baptist minister who was a follower of Marcus Garvey. After his family fled reprisals for his father's activities and moved to Michigan, the family home was burned and his father killed. Little dropped out of school and moved to New York City and to Boston where he was arrested for burglary. While in prison, Little came under the influence of the Nation of Islam, a Muslim religious organization led by Elijah Muhammad. After converting to Islam, Malcolm Little changed his last name to "X" to symbolize the loss of his African ancestors' tribal name. With Malcolm X's articulate and charismatic leadership the Nation of Islam increased its membership from five hundred to thirty thousand in just nine years. Malcom X adhered strictly to celibacy before marriage as a Muslim teaching, but discovered that Elijah Muhammad was having sexual relations with six different women. Over time, Malcolm X severed his ties to the Nation of Islam, and after making a pilgrimage to Mecca renounced his racist views that sought separation from white society. After giving a speech in New York City in 1965, Malcolm X was assassinated by three gunmen from the Nation of Islam.

## 19 Stokely Carmichael

Another spin on African-American civil rights came from Stokely Carmichael who became the leader of a movement called "black nationalism." Carmichael coined the phrase "Black Power," and rejected the nonviolent strategies espoused by earlier leaders. Having come through the Student Nonviolent Coordinating Committee (SNCC) organization and participated in Freedom Rides, Carmichael's break with the majority opinion caused a rift in the civil rights movement. As chairman of SNCC, in 1966 he espoused self-defense training, self-determination, the pursuit of political and economic power, and racial pride. A political organization he helped found in Alabama was the first to adopt a black panther as its symbol. Carmichael left the United States and moved to West Africa taking the name Kwame Toure.

## 20 Black Panther Party

This organization was founded in Oakland, California, in 1966 by Huey Newton and Bobby Seale. The Black Panthers formed a militant wing of the "black nationalism" movement and patrolled in African-American neighborhoods protecting residents from police brutality. The Black Panthers adopted Marxist ideology and called for all African-Americans to arm themselves. The group demanded from the federal government the release of all African-Americans from jails, their exemption from the draft, and reparation payments for the history of white oppression in America. After several shoot-outs with police in California, Huey Newton was arrested for murdering a policeman. The Black Panther Party's goals and tactics were shunned by most other civil rights leaders. The Black Panthers grew less militant over time and were disbanded in the 1980s.

## The Big Picture

1. After a century of repression after the Civil War, the actions of a few individuals ignited the activism on behalf of African-Americans known as the civil rights movement.

2. Prominent ministers and other leaders organized national reform associations to coordinate protests and to mobilize African-American communities in the face of segregation and other forms of racial discrimination.

3. African-American protestors and those of other races gathered in the South from all over America to help advance the causes of voter registration and desegregation through sit-ins, marches, and other forms of nonviolent protest that resulted in important federal legislation promoting equality.

4. A campaign on the part of white supremacist organizations and individuals in the South harassed civil rights leaders and murdered several prominent as well as many average citizens involved in civil rights activism.

5. Several African-American activists grew impatient with the pace of change through nonviolent means and advocated a more militant approach through "black pride," "black power," and "black nationalism" to achieve a separation of the races as racist as that espoused by white supremacists.

# Foreign and Domestic Crises of the Vietnam Era

*Over this war—and all Asia—is another reality: the deepening shadow of Communist China. . . . The contest in Vietnam is part of a wider pattern of aggressive purposes.*
—Lyndon B. Johnson, speech at Johns Hopkins University, 1965

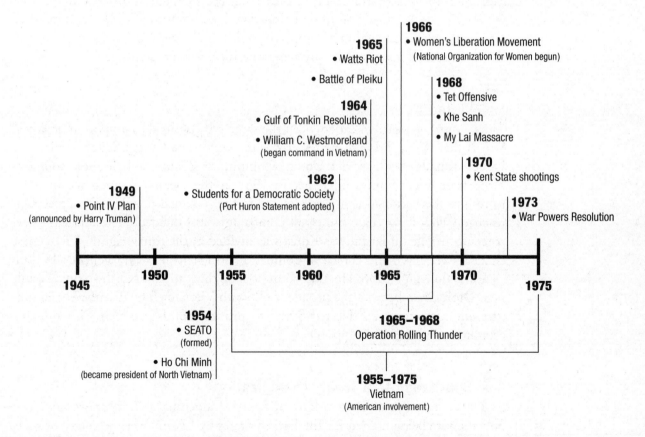

**1966**
• Women's Liberation Movement
(National Organization for Women begun)

**1965**
• Watts Riot
• Battle of Pleiku

**1968**
• Tet Offensive
• Khe Sanh
• My Lai Massacre

**1964**
• Gulf of Tonkin Resolution
• William C. Westmoreland
(began command in Vietnam)

**1970**
• Kent State shootings

**1962**
• Students for a Democratic Society
(Port Huron Statement adopted)

**1973**
• War Powers Resolution

**1949**
• Point IV Plan
(announced by Harry Truman)

1945    1950    1955    1960    1965    1970    1975

**1954**
• SEATO
(formed)
• Ho Chi Minh
(became president of North Vietnam)

**1965–1968**
Operation Rolling Thunder

**1955–1975**
Vietnam
(American involvement)

# Top 20 Things to Know

## 1 Point IV Plan

The name of this plan was taken from the section of Harry Truman's inaugural address in which he called for a "bold new program" of assistance to developing countries. Truman sought permission from the Congress to allow dollar diplomacy and American technical assistance in these areas, and by 1950 $35 million had been allocated. The Point IV Plan extended the Truman Doctrine to include areas of the world like Indochina that would play key roles in the Cold War.

## 2 Youth Revolt

The civil rights movement became connected to a wider display of unrest among young people of all races in America in the 1960s and 1970s. The Youth Revolt used strategies of nonviolent disobedience and staged demonstrations just as the civil rights activists had done, but the goals of the movement varied from self-expression to pointless rebellion to protesting the Vietnam War. Centered in universities across America, youthful demonstrations often turned violent and involved arson and other destruction of property as well as takeovers of public buildings by sit-ins and teach-ins sponsored by sympathetic university faculty.

## 3 Vietnam

The country of Vietnam experienced the same type of divided support after World War II that Korea did and the result was the same. The United States, France, the United Kingdom, the Soviet Union, Communist China, and the new countries made from French Indochina met in 1954 at the Geneva Conference in order to resolve the nationalist impulses of the former colonial peoples. The agreement reached called for a cease-fire of all combatants and divided Vietnam at the seventeenth parallel of latitude as Korea was divided at the thirty-eighth. Vietnamese citizens were given the choice of country in which to live, and general elections were scheduled for 1956. Ho Chi Minh became the leader of North Vietnam while Ngo Dinh Diem became the president of South Vietnam. The Eisenhower administration committed the United States to provide South Vietnam with military, economic, and political support.

## 4 Southeast Asia Treaty Organization

As France lost control of its colony of French Indochina in 1954, new Cold War policies were being crafted for the United States by Eisenhower's secretary of state, John Foster Dulles. The "New Look" in national security policy departed from the containment policies of the Truman administration and began to discuss "rolling back" communism and responding to any aggression on the part of the Soviet Union with "massive retaliation." As French Indochina was broken up by the

United Nations and nationalist forces created North and South Vietnam, Laos, and Cambodia, Eisenhower presented the idea that if one of these nations fell to communism, then the rest would fall like dominoes. The Domino Theory prompted the formation of the Southeast Asia Treaty Organization (SEATO), a mutual defense treaty modeled after the North Atlantic Treaty Organization (NATO). Unlike NATO, however, the treaty did not create a unified military command and left the United States to defend South Vietnam alone.

## 5 Vietcong

The Vietcong were the guerrilla fighters within South Vietnam who represented the National Liberation Front, a nationalist yet communist organization fighting to unite all of Vietnam under one communist government. Vietcong fighters coordinated their attacks on a national basis but could also operate as tiny insurgents assassinating South Vietnamese leaders and sabotaging American installations. Although supplied with modern weaponry by the Soviet and Chinese governments, the Vietcong also employed booby traps made from simple materials from the jungle and unexploded bombs dropped by the United States. Extensive tunnel systems helped hide the Vietcong soldiers who also used sewer drains to infiltrate cities. A major difficulty in the war in Vietnam was in distinguishing which Vietnamese were peaceful and which were the enemy.

## 6 Gulf of Tonkin Resolution

Under the Kennedy administration the United States looked the other way while a military coup deposed and assassinated Ngo Dinh Diem, the president of South Vietnam. The Vietcong increased their activities in South Vietnam, and under Lyndon B. Johnson (LBJ) the surveillance of North Vietnam using clandestine military operations began. In the summer of 1964 North Vietnamese forces attacked the destroyer *Maddux*, an American naval vessel involved in gathering intelligence. President Johnson asked the Congress to authorize reprisal air strikes for the attacks. The Congress was not informed of the provocative nature of the American military in spying on the North Vietnamese in the Gulf of Tonkin, but they responded with the Gulf of Tonkin Resolution. The resolution granted the president their support to "take all necessary measures to repel any armed attack against forces of the United States and to prevent further aggression." This wording gave Johnson a "blank check" to wage war and was the sole premise for fighting the Vietnam War, a war in which the United States never actually declared war against any nation or nations. LBJ dramatically escalated the presence and activity of the American military in the region for the rest of his presidency.

## 7 William C. Westmoreland

Westmoreland was a decorated veteran of both World War II and the Korean War who became the superintendent of West Point before being sent to Vietnam. Within a few months he became the commander of American forces in South

Vietnam and he oversaw the increase of American troops from under twenty thousand in 1964 to almost five hundred thousand by 1968. General Westmoreland developed the "search and destroy" strategy that relied on a war of attrition dependent on a body count of the number of enemy soldiers killed as progress toward victory. After the Tet Offensive in 1968, Westmoreland's strategies fell from favor and he was replaced.

## 8 Body Count

The key to the "search-and-destroy" strategy of fighting guerrilla forces in the Vietnam War was the belief that the United States would win if combat resulted in a death ratio of four enemy soldiers killed for every one American soldier killed. The nature of such warfare conducted in a rural country with thick jungles and the enemy's operating in tunnels made an accurate count nearly impossible, and inflation of body count estimates led to a false belief in progress. The strategy also neglected the total commitment of the Vietnamese insurgents and the North Vietnamese not only to support the existing forces but to produce more soldiers indefinitely for their nationalistic and communistic goals. The population of the enemy forces in the Vietnam War outlasted the resolve of the United States to kill them, and thus the strategy failed.

## 9 Women's Liberation Movement

The "Second Wave" of the feminist movement occurred in the 1960s and 1970s amid the societal upheaval of the Vietnam era. Building on the success of the suffrage movement, women's liberation activities sprang from the 1963 book, *The Feminine Mystique*, by Betty Friedan. Friedan chronicled the dissatisfaction of women coming out of the materialism of the 1950s who sought to move outside the traditional women's role of housewives and mothers into a more overtly political stance that opposed all forms of sexist discrimination in American society and culture. By 1966 Friedan was elected president of a new civil rights organization called the National Organization for Women (NOW). The members of NOW and other feminists advocated greater equality of the sexes in educational and employment opportunities as well as in political office. The women's liberation movement also lobbied the government to reform family, marriage, and divorce laws and generally sought to redefine gender roles in American culture. As in the African-American civil rights movement, tactics of the women's liberation movement varied widely from nonviolent marches and bra burnings to protests against beauty pageants.

## 10 Hippies

In a similar fashion to the moral revolution of the 1920s, the hippie culture developed out of the Beat Generation of writers and artists who lived a Bohemian lifestyle and experimented with drugs and free love in San Francisco. Spreading from California in the 1960s, the culture of youth revolt advocated the abandonment of traditional lifestyles and advanced the idea that no one over the age of thirty could be trusted. What began as a pursuit of freedom and indifference to social norms expressed through long hair, sexual license, and drug use became a cultural revolution that used folk music and psychedelic art forms to protest racial and sexual discrimination and the Vietnam War. Hippies burned their draft cards and performed other acts of nonviolent resistance but also resorted to violence and arson at extreme moments of societal tension in the Vietnam era. The hippie culture created lasting manifestations through greater sexual promiscuity, tolerance for greater cultural diversity, environmentalism, ongoing pacifist crusades, and even a natural foods movement.

## 11 Watts Riot

The Watts Riot was just one of the outbreaks of severe racial tension during the 1960s. The atmosphere of social activism coupled with frustration at setbacks touched off the Watts Riot in 1965 when African-Americans began burning and looting in their own neighborhood in Los Angeles. The rioting claimed twenty-eight lives and caused $200 million in damages. Riots erupted in Chicago in 1966 and in Newark, New Jersey, and Detroit in 1967. In Detroit, forty people died, two thousand were injured, and five thousand homes were burned. The assassination of Martin Luther King Jr. in 1968 caused a wave of riots in 125 cities across twenty-nine states. This background of street violence prompted Richard Nixon to run a "law–and-order" campaign that won him the presidency in the Election of 1968.

## 12 Students for a Democratic Society

Beginning in 1960, the campuses of American universities experienced political and social activism on the part of the Students for a Democratic Society (SDS). SDS was associated with the New Left movement and consisted of college students who protested social injustices and the Vietnam War. In the Port Huron Statement of 1962, SDS leaders decried the materialism and discrimination of American society and advocated the takeover of university campuses as instruments of political change. The SDS claimed alliance with the National Liberation Front in Vietnam and called for the immediate withdrawal of troops from the war zone. By the late 1960s, SDS had moved even farther left toward radical Marxist revolutionary rhetoric. After prompting campus takeovers at Columbia University and New York University as well as the protests that led to the Kent State shootings in Ohio, SDS splintered into various other groups including the terrorist organization that called itself the Weathermen. As tensions deescalated in the 1970s, the fragmentation of the SDS led to its end as an organizing force.

## 13 Kent State Shootings

Early in 1970 the U.S. military and the South Vietnamese forces attacked across the border into Cambodia to search out and destroy communist sanctuaries from which attacks had been made into South Vietnam. Cambodia had claimed to be neutral in the Vietnam War but regularly supplied Vietcong forces within South Vietnam. The expansion of the war into a neighboring country set off large antiwar demonstrations on college campuses across the nation. Reserve Officers' Training Corps (ROTC) buildings were burned and protestors confronted police and other forces sent to contain the damage and end the riots. At Kent State in Ohio, National Guard forces fired into a crowd of protestors after being cornered against a fence, and four students were killed. Two more students were killed at Jackson State College in Mississippi ten days later. As many as one hundred thousand protestors marched on Washington, D.C., to stage a massive antiwar rally in the nation's capital.

## 14 Ho Chi Minh

Ho was a Vietnamese nationalist under French colonial rule who went to France for an education and was converted to communism. During World War II he led guerrilla attacks against Japan from just across the border with China, and when the war was over Ho sought to establish a new Vietnamese nation. When the French refused to give up their colony of French Indochina, Ho also helped lead an insurgency against them. After the departure of the French and the division of the country, Ho helped found the National Liberation Front and supplied Vietcong guerrillas from within North Vietnam along the trail through Laos that bore his name. Having firmly established the goal of spreading communism through a united Vietnam, Ho Chi Minh died in 1969 within a few years of seeing it happen.

## 15 Operation Rolling Thunder

Once the Gulf of Tonkin Resolution authorized retaliation, Lyndon Johnson ordered large-scale bombing of North Vietnam. The bombing campaign was named Operation Rolling Thunder and dropped over one million tons of bombs in three years. When the campaign proved ineffectual after dropping more bombs than had been dropped in all of World War II, Johnson decided to escalate the number of troops on the ground in Vietnam. After the war it was revealed that Operation Rolling Thunder had failed to force North Vietnam to negotiate a peace because the essential military assets of North Vietnam were located in underground tunnels.

## 16 Pleiku

American military advisers had been located in Vietnam since before the Kennedy administration escalated their number to seventeen thousand, but at the Battle of Pleiku in 1965 an attack by the Vietcong killed eight Americans and injured 128. The Johnson administration responded with Operation Rolling Thunder but also with the placement of the first actual American ground troops into Vietnam. The large number of casualties suffered by the Vietnamese during the Pleiku clash encouraged the development of the search and destroy missions that moved American soldiers into combat with helicopters.

## 17 Tet Offensive

During a supposed cease-fire to allow the observance of the New Year holiday in 1968, Vietcong and North Vietnamese forces attacked all of the major cities of South Vietnam, including the capital of Saigon, as well as many small towns. Other attacks occurred at Khe Sanh and in the countryside and were all designed to demonstrate the ease with which the communist forces could coordinate widespread attacks. Although the casualties received by American forces over the weeks of fighting were the highest to that date in the Vietnam War, the casualties incurred by the attackers were considerably higher. Still, the Tet Offensive made Americans back home watching on television doubt whether the United States could win the war. General Westmoreland was denied his request to raise the number of American forces in Vietnam to over 730,000 and was eventually replaced. As a result of the Tet Offensive, stronger calls for peace back home in America revealed that although the campaign had ended in military failure, the attacks had achieved a psychological victory. The Tet Offensive and the Election of 1968 were thus major turning points in the American effort to win in Vietnam.

## 18 Khe Sanh

When North Vietnamese soldiers began to cut off supplies and make raids around Khe Sanh village in northwest South Vietnam, General Westmoreland decided to fortify the position and supply the Marines inside the fortifications by air. Late in 1967 the North Vietnamese lay siege to the base and began attacking. By early 1968 the situation grew increasingly serious causing Westmoreland to launch Operation Niagara, the largest bombing mission in the history of aerial bombing to that point. The equivalent of five atomic bombs was dropped in an effort to eliminate the besieging enemy forces. After seventy-seven days the siege was broken, but after General Westmoreland was removed from Vietnam, the next commander abandoned the position after destroying it. The entire engagement cost over seven hundred American lives and ten thousand to fifteen thousand enemy lives, but the North Vietnamese likely staged the whole battle as a diversion to help the Tet Offensive succeed. The Battle of Khe Sanh evidenced the courage and sacrifice of American and South Vietnamese forces in the midst of strategic decisions that confused the American people.

## 19 My Lai Massacre

In 1969, American infantrymen apparently "snapped" and murdered at least 450 unarmed South Vietnamese villagers, mostly women, children, and old men, at the village of My Lai. The shooting only stopped when an American helicopter pilot observed what was happening and landed his aircraft between the infantry patrol and the survivors telling his gunner to open fire on the Americans if they did not stop the massacre. My Lai revealed the dark side of the pressure, confusion, drug abuse, and protracted nature of the war that undermined the morale of American military personnel. The events were reported to the press and led to the court martial on charges of premeditated murder of the lieutenant in charge of the patrol.

# 20   War Powers Resolution

Congress asserted its role in the foreign policy of the United States in 1973 by issuing the War Powers Resolution. This law, in the context of the end of the Vietnam era and during the Watergate Crisis, reduced the power of the president to wage war without congressional consent. War had been declared only five times in American history, but the Korean and Vietnam Wars were presidential wars fought in often clandestine ways. A credibility gap opened between the American people and the presidents after revelations of the deception in how America entered into the war in Vietnam. The War Powers Resolution said that a president was to consult with Congress before employing military force and to notify the Congress within forty-eight hours of deployment. The law also required an end to any conflict of this nature within sixty days unless withdrawing American forces at that time would endanger them, in which case a total of ninety days were permitted before the action had to stop, unless Congress had declared war. Several subsequent presidents expressed doubts as to the constitutionality of the resolution, and some have tested the law by ignoring it.

## *The Big Picture*

1. Various presidents after World War II committed the United States to policies that ultimately led to American involvement in Southeast Asia as a theater in the Cold War.

2. After some American forces were attacked by North Vietnam, the U.S. Congress granted Lyndon B. Johnson a "blank check" with which he escalated the war.

3. Confusion and disagreement about the goals and merits of the war prompted an antiwar movement that accompanied other protest movements like those for African-American's civil rights and women's rights in a general youth revolt through the 1960s and 1970s.

4. Protests during the Vietnam era grew particularly violent as an antiauthoritarian drug culture incited riots and demonstrations in which protestors clashed with government security forces.

5. The excesses of the protracted conflict in Vietnam as well as a flawed military strategy led to the failure of the U.S. government to achieve its objectives and a revision of the abilities of American presidents to wage war by executive action alone.

# Nixon and the Arms and Space Races

*I believe that this Nation should commit itself to achieving the goal, before this decade is out, of landing a man on the moon and returning him safely to earth.*
—John F. Kennedy, speech before a joint session of Congress, 1961

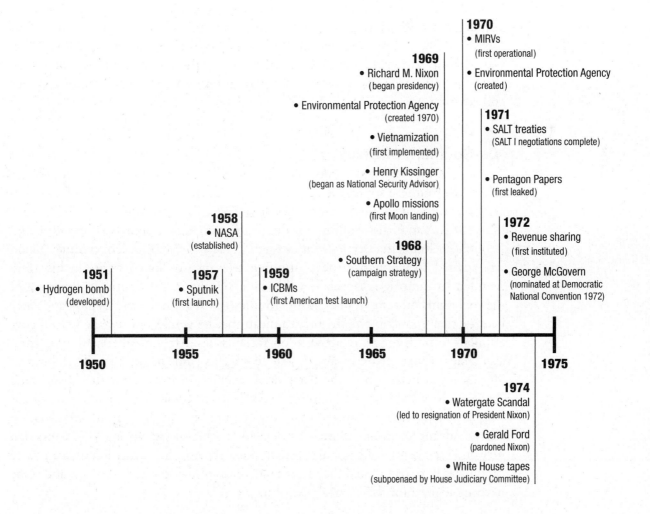

**1970**
- MIRVs
  (first operational)
- Environmental Protection Agency
  (created)

**1969**
- Richard M. Nixon
  (began presidency)
- Environmental Protection Agency
  (created 1970)
- Vietnamization
  (first implemented)
- Henry Kissinger
  (began as National Security Advisor)
- Apollo missions
  (first Moon landing)

**1971**
- SALT treaties
  (SALT I negotiations complete)
- Pentagon Papers
  (first leaked)

**1972**
- Revenue sharing
  (first instituted)
- George McGovern
  (nominated at Democratic National Convention 1972)

**1968**
- Southern Strategy
  (campaign strategy)

**1958**
- NASA
  (established)

**1951**
- Hydrogen bomb
  (developed)

**1957**
- Sputnik
  (first launch)

**1959**
- ICBMs
  (first American test launch)

1950    1955    1960    1965    1970    1975

**1974**
- Watergate Scandal
  (led to resignation of President Nixon)
- Gerald Ford
  (pardoned Nixon)
- White House tapes
  (subpoenaed by House Judiciary Committee)

# Top 20 Things to Know

## 1 Richard M. Nixon

Richard Nixon was a lawyer and World War II Navy veteran who became a congressman after the war. He was a red hunter on the House Un-American Activities Committee (HUAC) in tandem with Joseph McCarthy's investigations looking for communists in the government, and Nixon led the investigation of Alger Hiss. He went on to serve as a senator and as vice president under Dwight Eisenhower. While traveling in Latin America Nixon was attacked by mobs, and while traveling in the Soviet Union he sparred with Nikita Khrushchev in the famous Kitchen Debate about capitalism versus communism. Nixon was narrowly defeated for the presidency by John F. Kennedy in the Election of 1960 and two years later for the governorship of California, his home state. Many thought his career in politics over until he won the Election of 1968. As president, Nixon opened communist China to relations with the United States in an effort to alienate the Chinese from the Soviets. Nixon won again in 1972 but quickly became embroiled in the Watergate Scandal. After obstructing justice through passive and active resistance to investigators, Nixon faced impeachment but resigned from the presidency instead in 1974. Gerald Ford pardoned Nixon for any crimes he might have committed, and Nixon spent the rest of his life recovering his reputation by writing about foreign policy and advising subsequent presidents.

## 2 Southern Strategy

Among the most curious components of the back and forth of American political values, the southern strategy led to a wholesale realignment of the former Confederate states from the Solid South of the Democratic Party to support for the Republican Party. A strategist working for the Nixon campaign popularized the idea, and Republican strategists employed it through the rest of the twentieth century. Nixon was advised to emphasize the continuing relevance of states' rights in his 1968 presidential campaign, especially while campaigning in the South. In the wake of the civil rights movement many white southerners abandoned the Democratic Party because they took Nixon's rhetoric to mean that he would not use the federal government to push for more activism on racial issues. African-Americans apparently also believed that Nixon meant to stall civil rights gains or roll them back because 90 percent switched from the party of emancipation to vote for the Democratic Party. As to what Richard Nixon actually believed about civil rights, part of his enigmatic political identity was that he was a member of the National Association for the Advancement of Colored People (NAACP). Still, by Nixon's 1972 campaign he won 70 percent of the popular vote in the Deep South. Recent Republican Party candidates have repudiated the underhandedness of the southern strategy, and some have apologized for their party's use of it.

# 3 Revenue Sharing

Another apparent nod from the Nixon administration toward states' rights was revenue sharing. Having said, "We're all Keynesians, now," Richard Nixon attempted a decentralization of expenditures that placed federal tax revenues in the hands of state and local governments. Therefore, after an era of massive deficit spending that seemed perpetual, Nixon advocated spreading the spending of federal money at levels that were also hungry for cash and readily took the money. More conservative leaders recognized that federal money always came with strings attached, however, and future Republican presidents Gerald Ford and Ronald Reagan proposed cutting taxes and lowering federal revenue rather than sharing the money and the philosophy of government involvement at deeper and deeper levels that prolonged the years of overtaxed budgets. Reagan preferred to disburse federal money in smaller amounts in block grants.

# 4 Environmental Protection Agency

When Congress passed the National Environmental Policy Act (NEPA), which took effect in 1970, the work of Rachel Carson and others had achieved its goal, making protection of the environment a matter of national policy. The NEPA required all federal agencies to publish an environmental impact statement regarding all their major activities, especially in matters of new pieces of legislation. The law established an advisory council to the president on environmental quality and required the president to submit to Congress an annual environmental quality report. Richard Nixon later consolidated all major programs to combat pollution and other environmental damage into the Environmental Protection Agency, or EPA, which was independent of all other existing government departments. The EPA became responsible for managing stringent controls on all federally owned public land and for enforcing laws relating to endangered species and other conservation measures. A reasonable balance was difficult to achieve between economic progress and environmental protection, and some have interpreted the activities of the EPA to be too restrictive.

# 5 Vietnamization

Richard Nixon entered office with the troop level in the Vietnam War at its peak of 541,500 American military personnel. As a response to the Vietcong's use of Cambodia as a route into South Vietnam, he secretly authorized bombing of that nation in 1969. Then Nixon ordered the first troop withdrawal. As the first twenty-five thousand soldiers came home, Nixon explained on television that his goal was to gradually withdraw all American forces with a flexible schedule related to Vietnamization, the effort to support, train, and equip South Vietnamese soldiers to defend their own country. With negotiations backed by food embargoes to the Soviet Union going on in Paris, Nixon set in motion the end of America's involvement in the Vietnam War, which came about by 1973 before he left office in disgrace. Because of Nixon's failed presidency, his successful policy of Vietnamization did not receive the necessary funding to aid South Vietnam, which fell to communism by 1975.

# 6 Henry Kissinger

A German immigrant, Kissinger served in the U.S. Army during World War II and returned to take a Ph.D. in government at Harvard. He was a noted scholar in the study of diplomacy, nuclear strategy, and American foreign policy and defense. He was a consultant to the National Security Council during the Berlin Crisis before becoming an actual assistant to the president for national security under Richard Nixon. Nixon then made Kissinger the secretary of state in 1973, an office Kissinger held through the Ford administration. While at the top of diplomatic circles Kissinger became famous for tremendous energy, personal and secret negotiations, and surprises like President Nixon's visit to China. Kissinger believed that the momentum of the Cold War would eventually build toward an American victory. He was the chief strategist for opening China, ending the Vietnam War, achieving détente with the Soviet Union, and supporting Israel through the Yom Kippur War. He and his Vietnamese counterpart received the Nobel Peace Prize for ending the war, and then Kissinger returned to academia.

# 7 *Sputnik*

During the Eisenhower administration the Soviet Union started the space race and the arms race of the Cold War by launching the first artificial satellite into orbit around the Earth. *Sputnik I* was launched in 1957 almost four months before the United States responded with *Explorer I*. The space race reflected the Cold War fears of both superpowers that each other's technology would outpace the opposing side and achieve an advantage in rocket technology. *Sputnik I* precipitated large federal expenditures of money to boost math, science, and foreign language instruction in public schools through the National Defense Education Act. Over $500 million was dedicated to provide scholarships for prospective teachers and direct grants to schools. Although the *Sputnik* satellites were merely roving radio transmitters, the impression that the Soviets could be dropping atomic bombs on the United States from space spurred the creation of the National Aeronautics and Space Administration (NASA) and the development of the capacity for both nations to actually drop atomic weapons on each other from space using intercontinental ballistic missiles (ICBMs).

# 8 Intercontinental Ballistic Missiles

Intercontinental ballistic missiles (ICBMs) are missiles, like the ones launching astronauts into space, which were large enough to exit the Earth's atmosphere and then descend over targets on other continents to deliver atomic bombs. During the Cold War, both the United States and the Soviet Union developed the capacity to strike any part of each other's countries. Based on the research begun by American and German scientists during World War II, the United States developed the Atlas missile program followed by the creation of the Titan missiles that were even larger than the Atlas rockets that were used in the *Apollo* space missions. In the 1960s, the solid-fuel Minuteman rocket was developed that was more stable and easier to maintain, and at the peak of the Cold War one thousand Minuteman rockets were deployed, ready to launch on short notice by an authorization from the president. Other missiles could also be launched from submarines, and eventually multiple individually targeted reentry vehicles (MIRVs) were developed. MIRVs had the capacity to deliver multiple nuclear warheads on each ballistic missile. The aptly named Peacekeeper missiles, otherwise known as the MX missiles, were the last stage of the nuclear arms race in that these missiles could be launched from mobile launchers rather than fixed missile silos. MX missiles were operational by 1972, but retired with the ending of the Cold War.

## 9  Strategic Arms Limitation Treaties

Under Richard Nixon and Henry Kissinger's skillful guidance of American foreign policy, negotiations opened to pursue a freeze on nuclear weapons and the systems that deployed them. Meetings in Helsinki and Vienna led to two separate agreements that were signed in Moscow. The Strategic Arms Limitation Treaty (SALT) agreements recognized that the aggressive offensive strategy of the superpowers ensured that both sides could deliver destructive blows to each other in the event of one superpower's launching of intercontinental ballistic missiles (ICBMs) and other delivery systems. Therefore, the mutual assurance of destruction deterred the outbreak of war. The SALT I agreement of 1972 permitted a limited deployment of defensive antiballistic missiles and limited the production of missiles by both superpowers. The later SALT II treaty negotiated by President Carter called for limitations on missile launchers and other delivery systems but was never ratified by the U.S. Senate. The SALT approach was later abandoned by the Reagan administration in the process of ending the Cold War and dismantling the Soviet Union.

## 10  Hydrogen Bomb

The United States wanted to regain the "lead" in the arms race after the Rosenbergs and other Americans spying for the Soviets transferred critical bomb-making secrets to allow the Russians to catch up. American scientists first tested a hydrogen bomb in 1952. Whereas the atomic bomb had the explosive power of thousands of tons of TNT, the hydrogen bombs were approximately one thousand times more destructive. The H-Bomb used a fission bomb to accomplish fusion, the power of the sun. The scientist who led the construction of the A-Bomb, Robert Oppenheimer, opposed the H-Bomb on moral grounds, but President Truman pushed for the test on November 1, 1952, on Bikini Atoll in the Marshall Islands in the Pacific Ocean. When the bomb was detonated, a radioactive cloud was shot 25 miles into the sky. The blast made a canyon in the floor of the ocean 1 mile wide and 175 feet deep. The world was frightened to learn that the Soviets had an H-Bomb by 1953, and even the British did by 1957. Dwight Eisenhower viewed the development of nuclear weapons as a way to reduce military budgets because they provided "more bang for the buck." The goal was not only to make the deployment of American military forces cheaper but also to bring down the cost of maintaining peace. As revealed at Dien Bien Phu in 1954, however, Ike was reluctant to nuke. What followed was the Vietnam War.

## 11 Multiple Individually Targeted Reentry Vehicles

Multiple individually targeted reentry vehicles (MIRVs) were new types of inter-continental ballistic missiles (ICBMs) created by the United States to answer the Soviet's development of larger and larger ICBMs. MIRVs could be launched from missile silos in North America or from submarines, and upon reentry into Earth's atmosphere as many as ten warheads could be delivered by one missile. Delivering multiple warheads with each American missile drove the cost of attacking down and the cost of Soviet defense up, the equation that ultimately ended the Cold War by bankrupting the Soviet Union faster. The first missile of this type was the Minuteman III deployed as an ICBM in 1970. New technology of this type drove the Soviet Union to the negotiating table with Strategic Arms Limitation Treaty (SALT) talks and Strategic Arms Reduction Treaty (START) talks, but the actual treaty banning MIRVs was never approved by the Soviet Duma.

## 12 National Aeronautics and Space Administration

One year after Sputnik, in 1958, President Eisenhower started the National Aeronautics and Space Administration, or NASA, to conduct scientific space exploration. NASA combined all previous research agencies under one organization with eight thousand employees and an annual budget of $100 million. America's own first satellite in orbit, *Explorer I*, symbolized the scientific emphasis of NASA by confirming the existence of radiation belts around the earth but also the military competitiveness of the superpowers. *Mercury* and *Gemini* missions tested manned space flight, and the *Apollo* missions succeeded in landing a man on the moon in 1969 six months ahead of President Kennedy's schedule. Various probes were launched into the solar system and beyond to explore the outer planets while NASA scientists developed more and more sophisticated technologies, and scientific and then communications satellites (as well as secret military satellites) were launched into orbit. NASA then placed a laboratory for astronauts called Skylab in space and developed the Shuttle program to create a vehicle that could launch and service satellites and return to earth only to be used again like a space truck. Through various tragedies and glorious achievements that fascinated the nation and worried the Soviets (although the Soviets launched the first satellite, the first man, and the first woman into space), NASA embodied the American spirit and spun off hundreds of technologies for civilian use to improve the American standard of living. As the Cold War waned, however, the costs involved in, for example, exploring Mars with robots in preparation for a manned mission, have come under greater and greater scrutiny.

## 13 *Apollo* Missions

The most gripping of all the National Aeronautics and Space Administration (NASA) programs placed Neil Armstrong and Buzz Aldrin on the moon in 1969 but also twelve other astronauts in five other missions in subsequent years. Tragedies occurred on either side of this achievement believed by some to be mankind's greatest technological accomplishment. A fire in a capsule in 1967 killed three astronauts on the ground in a preflight test, but then *Apollo Eleven* successfully placed the Lunar Excursion Module, or LEM, on the surface of the moon where Neil Armstrong announced to the world "The Eagle has landed." The first man on the moon then backed down a ladder and jumped to the surface while the world watched spellbound on television. That jump was his famous "One small step. . . ." This moment, which even some Americans believed was faked, was followed by a near disaster when *Apollo Thirteen* had an explosion of an oxygen tank that crippled the mission. The astronauts were miraculously able to return home alive, however, and the *Apollo* missions wound down without further mishap in 1972. Before leaving the moon, however, American astronauts had run, jumped, explored, collected moon rocks, and even driven a Moon Rover there. Apollo astronauts left a plaque on the moon that says "We came in peace for all mankind." When asked why all the expense was necessary, however, and what NASA expected to find on the moon, a U.S. Air Force general responded, "Russians."

# 14 George McGovern

If Barry Goldwater was "Mr. Conservative," George McGovern was the self-styled "Mr. Liberal." He was the first senator (Democrat from South Dakota) to come out against the Vietnam War even though he had stuck by Lyndon Johnson and voted for the Gulf of Tonkin Resolution. While McGovern considered a presidential run in 1968, the varied field and his emotional trauma resulting from the assassination of Robert Kennedy made him step aside for Hubert Humphrey. McGovern ran against Nixon in 1972, however, on a platform of immediate withdrawal from Vietnam and a domestic agenda that included a guaranteed income for every American family of anywhere from $6,500 to $10,000. In a period of high inflation some analysts viewed this last suggestion as a sign of insanity, and McGovern himself exhibited some rather un-presidential behavior in response to a heckler. These proposals and actions made McGovern popular with his base, however, and his more moderate voting record in the Senate was abandoned for increasingly radical rhetoric. McGovern is thus considered to have been the most politically radical candidate of any major party to run for the presidency. The Election of 1972 turned out to be the second biggest landslide victory to date in modern American history with an Electoral College vote of 520 for Nixon to McGovern's seventeen votes.

# 15 Watergate Scandal

Watergate was the name of an apartment and hotel complex in Washington, D.C., that housed the Democratic National Committee offices during the campaign for the Election of 1972. Five men were caught breaking into the campaign headquarters in June 1972 and were linked to G. Gordon Liddy, an adviser to the Committee to Reelect the President (dubbed CREEP in the press). When President Nixon denied any involvement on the part of his staff and began a cover-up, reporters Bob Woodward and Carl Bernstein of the *Washington Post* began an investigation that led to Nixon's downfall. In the weeks and months that ensued, Nixon dismissed some of his staff and others resigned. Other break-ins were revealed, and when a Senate investigation opened to look into the allegations, disturbing revelations about the Nixon administration became regular fare in the press. Members of the president's staff confessed to perjury, and the existence of an "Enemies List" of politicians, journalists, scholars, and others was revealed. Those on the list were targeted for harassment by various agencies of the federal government. The existence of a group called the "Plumbers" was also revealed, their task being to stop the leaks to the press from within the administration by wiretapping, bugging, and discrediting whistleblowers. The deeper the investigations went, the less the American people felt confident in the word of their president as deception, unscrupulous campaign financing, and other nefarious practices came to light all the way back to the Johnson administration. Finally, President Nixon was accused in early impeachment proceedings of "violating the constitutional rights of citizens [and] impairing the due and proper administration of justice." Before the impeachment got underway, however, Richard Nixon announced his resignation from the presidency on television on August 8, 1974.

# 16 Pentagon Papers

The Pentagon Papers is the popular name for a Department of Defense study outlining the events surrounding American involvement in Vietnam from 1945 to 1967. The papers included four thousand pages of government documents and three thousand pages of analysis that was considered "Top Secret-Sensitive" because they revealed, among other embarrassing facts, that President Johnson had misrepresented events and, according to the *New York Times*, lied to the American people. Daniel Ellsberg, a military analyst working as an employee at the Pentagon for the secretary of defense, released the Pentagon Papers in 1971 during the Nixon presidency, a fact that Nixon called a threat to national security. A credibility gap was thus opened in the Nixon administration that had its own problems telling the truth about its actions in prosecuting the war, and an attempt to discredit Ellsberg through divulging his mental health records involved a break-in similar to those that led to the Watergate Scandal. The Pentagon Papers eventually sullied the images of the Kennedy, Johnson, and Nixon administrations and opened up a possibly permanent level of distrust between the American people, specifically journalists, and the executive branch of the federal government.

# 17 G. Gordon Liddy

A participant in the break-in searching for Daniel Ellsberg's mental health records was former Federal Bureau of Investigation (FBI) agent G. Gordon Liddy. He went on to lead the team of "Plumbers" seeking to stop leaks to the press as an employee of the Nixon administration. In this position Liddy masterminded the break-ins of the Democratic National Headquarters in the Watergate Hotel and Office Complex during the 1972 presidential campaign. Since Liddy supervised the break-ins he was convicted of burglary, conspiracy, and other crimes. His twenty-year sentence was reduced by President Jimmy Carter to eight, and Liddy was paroled after serving over four years in federal prisons. Seven other members of the Nixon administration were indicted for crimes and four of these also served prison time, but because

Liddy refused to testify before a Senate committee he served almost as much as the other four of the president's men, combined.

# 18 John Dean

The Nixon administration counsel to the president who did testify before the Senate committee was John Dean. His testimony not only implicated the other administration officials but the president himself. Dean was the first of the president's men to accuse Nixon of direct involvement in the Watergate Scandal. For his involvement, Dean was sentenced to one to four years in prison, but he wound up being held in a witness protection program instead of prison and for only four months. He was disbarred and unable to practice law, however. Dean's actions in implicating his fellow conspirators in the Watergate Scandal appeared to be motivated by his fear that he was targeted as the fall guy in the cover-up, and Liddy and Dean have published warring books and given contrasting interviews ever since.

# 19 White House Tapes

Central to the impeachment process that was building steam against Richard Nixon was the Senate committee's desire to know what the president knew and when he knew it. A Nixon staffer inadvertently revealed the existence of a taping system that recorded all Oval Office conversations (even those on the phone) during his testimony. The Senate committee seized on the "Nixon tapes" as a key to the investigation of the Watergate Scandal and demanded they be released. The existence of a taping system only fed the popular notion that Nixon was paranoid and devious even though the taping system had been installed by Lyndon Johnson. President Nixon instigated a series of obstructions of justice delaying the release of the tapes by claiming executive privilege. When the Supreme Court ruled that he had to release the tapes he released them slowly and with many long silences. The silences were explained by saying Nixon's secretary had accidentally erased those portions while recording the tapes. Finally, however, the tape known as the "smoking-gun tape" was released in which Nixon was recorded in 1972 instructing a staffer to contact the Central Intelligence Agency (CIA) to get the Federal Bureau of Investigation (FBI) to back down on the investigation in the interests of national security. Such a revelation caused support for Nixon to disappear and led to impeachment proceedings on the grounds that the president was guilty of obstruction of justice.

# 20 Gerald Ford

Gerald Ford was born Leslie King Jr., but was adopted by a stepfather and changed his name. The most athletic man to ever attain the presidency, Ford turned down a professional football career to enter a twenty-five year career as a congressman. After Spiro Agnew resigned as Nixon's first vice-president, he appointed Ford to fill his place according to the Twenty-fifth Amendment's provisions. As a universally respected and honest man, Gerald Ford set about healing the nation's wounds from Watergate and the Vietnam War, but his pardon of Nixon was so unpopular that he lost the Election of 1980 to Jimmy Carter.

## *The Big Picture*

1. The Nixon administration employed a successful foreign policy but was undone by domestic issues arising from Nixon's own temperament and the atmosphere of suspicion prevalent in the Vietnam era.

2. Richard Nixon was a political moderate who began the return to law and order by expanding the power and size of the federal government.

3. Along with the brewing domestic crisis of the Nixon administration, the ongoing Cold War tensions manifested themselves in massive expenditures by both superpowers in the Arms Race and the Space Race.

4. After being beaten twice by the Soviet Union in making advances in space technology, the United States ultimately exceeded the capacity of the Soviets by attaining the ability to come and go from the moon.

5. As the Vietnam War wound down the Watergate Scandal erupted, and the combined impact of these events created a lasting credibility gap between the American people and their presidents.

# Presidents Looking for America

*The erosion of our confidence in the future is threatening to destroy
the social and the political fabric of America.*

—Jimmy Carter, televised speech, 1979

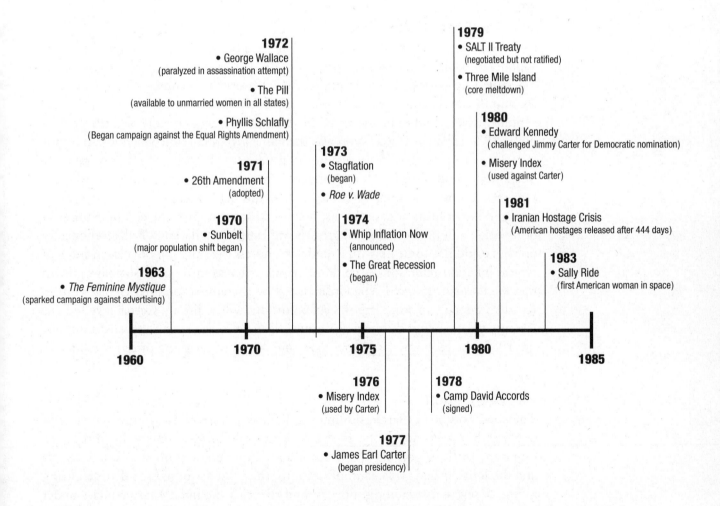

# Top 20 Things to Know

## 1 George Wallace

George Wallace was a World War II veteran from Alabama who entered law school upon his return from the war. Early in the 1960s he was elected governor of Alabama as a segregationist and as an advocate of states' rights. He served four terms as governor and went on to run for the presidency four times. In 1963, he blocked a doorway at the University of Alabama in an attempt to dissuade two black students from enrolling there, but federal marshals forced him aside. His notoriety led him to win five southern states in the presidential Election of 1968, almost enough to throw the outcome into the House of Representatives. While campaigning again in 1972 Wallace was shot in an assassination attempt and lost the use of his legs. His popularity for his racist views was a disturbing reminder of the racial tensions in American society, and his repudiation of those views after converting to Christianity in the 1970s was a symbol of increasing toleration among the races.

## 2 The Great Recession

As a result of the oil crisis caused by the Arab embargo in retaliation for American support for Israel, the 1970s experienced a deep recession. A recession is defined as a decline in the gross domestic product (GDP) over two consecutive quarters, or six months. Syria and Egypt attacked Israel in 1973, and when the United States supplied Israel to aid in her defense, the Arab Oil Embargo quadrupled the price of oil by 1974. The Great Recession was the name given to a time when inflation was over 14 percent because of the connection between the price of oil and the price of all other goods raised with tractors, manufactured with oil, or shipped in trucks (which is almost everything). The scarcity of affordable fuel not only created inflation and lines of cars at gas stations, it slowed the economy. The combined impact of inflation at a time of stagnant growth was called "stagflation." Federal monetary policies could not come up with a model to address the situation because in times of typical inflation interest rates could be raised, whereas in times of stagnant growth they were usually lowered. The Great Recession therefore prompted Gerald Ford to resort to tax cuts to stimulate the economy, and when Jimmy Carter reversed the tax cuts the economy slumped again until Ronald Reagan again lowered taxes. By the 1980s the economy also benefited from a steadily declining price for crude oil.

## 3 Stagflation

The condition of stagflation flummoxed Keynesian economists in the government because they were not prone to examine the role of government in hurting an economy. In the highly regulated economy that emerged from the New Deal era and the Johnson and Nixon administrations, the existence of severe inflation during a time of severe recession did not respond to either the inflationary policies under a Democrat or Republican president nor to the stimulation of their economy by deficit spending. Stagflation thus called the Keynesian economic consensus into question for the first time since the time of Franklin D. Roosevelt. Supply-side economics arose in the thinking of economists in the late 1970s as a possible solution to stagflation, and an increase in productivity coupled with tax cuts during the 1980s caused the economy to grow and conservative politicians to embrace this policy counterpoint.

# 4 Whip Inflation Now

Gerald Ford embraced the notion that the American people could reverse stagflation themselves by reducing consumption, saving money, and feeling the solidarity of a World War II-era type of civic pride in a public drive of sacrifice for the common good. Ford was concerned about inflation and the "energy crisis" as a dual blow to the American economy. He held an economic "summit" meeting where he and his advisers debated solutions. Their idea was a voluntary anti-inflation crusade that would be led by the president who would even wear a Whip Inflation Now (WIN) button during the speech in which he launched his proposals. Ford outlined twelve steps families could take without the need for expensive government programs. Among the ways families could ". . . grow more and waste less," Ford advocated balancing family budgets, using credit wisely, economizing, recycling, and reusing. He told Americans to look for bargains while shopping and to brag about being bargain hunters. He said Americans had an "international reputation as the world's worst wasters," and said they should inventory their trash to reduce waste. Finally, Americans should all guard their health, as days lost through illness constituted terrible waste. Although this all sounded rather bizarre for presidential attention, these were new ideas in the 1970s that have since become commonplace. Despite the number of supporters who wrote the White House describing their home gardens or telling what they gave up for the good of the country, the whole WIN campaign came off rather flat.

# 5 *Saturday Night Live*

Accompanying the credibility gap left over from the Vietnam era was this landmark television show in the history of comic social commentary. The show premiered in 1975 and developed a water-cooler effect that caused especially young, upcoming professionals to discuss the parodies of social and political issues on Mondays that had appeared the previous Saturday night. Chevy Chase made his career as a comic by whacking people with golf balls, stumbling, breaking podiums, and other antics designed to subject President Ford to ridicule. Ever since, comics from Will Ferrell to Tina Fey have lampooned presidents and presidential candidates so successfully that polls reveal the show has had a demonstrable effect on elections. The influence *Saturday Night Live* has had on political contests led many candidates to appear on the show in person to combat accusations of stodginess. The popularity of skits and parodies of news casts revealed that the propensity of journalism to shape ideas and even to ruin presidents like Johnson and Nixon could itself become a form of entertainment. The result has been a plethora of media outlets, news channels, and talk show hosts whose purpose is not only to inform but to entertain. Critics decry how these media diminish objective discourse because most citizens select the venues that entertain them with their own ideas.

## 6 The Pill

Research on an oral contraceptive began as early as the 1950s. By 1960 the first pill believed to be 100 percent effective at preventing pregnancy was marketed and became immediately popular. The Pill contained a synthetic hormone (progesterone) that convinced a woman's body she was already pregnant and therefore suppressed ovulation. What the Pill did not suppress was sexual activity, which increased among unmarried women as a result of the sexual and moral revolution of the 1960s and 1970s. A convenient oral contraceptive increased promiscuity and often resulted in unwanted pregnancies if women accidentally skipped some of the daily doses of the pills. By 1968 six million American women, or nearly 20 percent of all women of child-bearing age, used the Pill.

## 7 Roe v. Wade

This Supreme Court case in 1973 struck down state antiabortion laws saying that such laws violated a woman's right to privacy. The Court said that the Fourteenth Amendment guaranteed the personal liberty of women in deciding to terminate a pregnancy. The court specified that these laws could not interfere through the first trimester, or the first three months, of a pregnancy. Second-trimester abortions could be regulated by state laws as they pertained to the mother's health, and last-trimester abortions could be banned. The decision of the Supreme Court launched an ongoing debate about the legality and morality of abortion that endures to this day. Pro-choice groups sought to expand abortion rights while antiabortion groups sought to define life as beginning at the moment of conception and to restore states' abilities to ban the practice entirely or in varying degrees of permissible abortions due to rape or a threat to the mother's life. During the 1970s and 1980s Congress limited the use of federal funds for abortions through Medicaid, and the Supreme Court upheld a state's right not to fund an abortion. Opponents of bans on abortions argued that making the practice illegal would only return women to seeking the termination of pregnancies through more dangerous means, and the number of legalized abortions increased steadily. Since the *Roe v. Wade* decision in 1973 there have been an estimated forty-six million abortions performed in the United States.

## 8 The Feminine Mystique

The 1960s and 1970s were the era of the modern women's liberation movement, or the feminist movement. In this era women made up more than half of the population of America but struggled under sexual discrimination. The momentum that began with the Nineteenth Amendment to the Constitution had dwindled, but the publication of *The Feminine Mystique* by Betty Friedan in 1963 sparked a revival of female activism. Through interviews with suburban women, Friedan exposed a general lack of enthusiasm for the postwar American Dream being lived out in row after row of houses that exactly resembled those of their neighbors. Friedan said that this new version of the cult of domesticity, for which her book's title was a synonym, said that deeply frustrated and unhappy women were being buried alive, and she called the American suburb a "comfortable concentration camp." Friedan and other feminists identified discrimination spanning from sexual harassment to the "glass ceiling," the practice of passing over competent women for promotion to the highest levels of corporate power. In response, the largest women's liberation organization was founded by Betty Friedan in 1966, the National Organization for Women, or NOW.

## 9 National Organization for Women

This organization demanded better educational opportunities for women and more outlets for suburban housewives and denounced traditional marriage and family values. The National Organization for Women (NOW) called for "a fully equal partnership of the sexes, as part of the worldwide revolution of human rights," and the organization took action to "bring women into full participation in the mainstream of American society now, exercising all privileges and responsibilities thereof. . . ." Over half a million women belong to this, the largest feminist organization in America. National conferences and campaigns organized by the various chapters across the country have mobilized women in dozens of legislative and legal battles since NOW was founded. The organization particularly focuses on issues concerning access to abortions, domestic abuse, Constitutional rights for women, diversity, rights for homosexuals, and economic factors that pertain specifically to women.

## 10 Sally Ride

A milestone for women and for the American space program came in 1983 when Sally Ride became the first woman (and the youngest American) to go to space as an astronaut. She flew aboard the Space Shuttle *Challenger* as an operator of the shuttle's robot arm, a machine she helped develop. After her career as an astronaut ended, Ride became a physics professor and developed educational materials designed to encourage children, especially girls, to enjoy learning about science. Her careers and many awards were evidence of progress that the "glass ceiling" for women in the United States was being shattered.

## 11 Phyllis Schlafly

As a counterpoint to the feminist movement, Phyllis Schlafly wrote the book *A Choice Not an Echo,* in 1964 and led the movement to stop the ratification of the equal rights amendment (ERA) to the U.S. Constitution. An attorney, Mrs. Schlafly's other writings and conservative activism came as part of her leadership of the Eagle Forum, an organization she founded in 1972. The ERA sought to eliminate all discrimination based on sex, but when the 1979 deadline for ratification came only thirty-five of the required thirty-eight states had adopted the amendment. In a ten-year campaign Schlafly and other leaders warned that women would no longer be able to be supported by husbands and that divorces would increase. She also feared that women's privacy would be violated and that they would be sent into combat. An effort to ratify the ERA was begun again in 1982.

# 12 James Earl Carter

Another Navy veteran-turned-president, James (Jimmy) Carter studied nuclear physics and engineering before returning home to Georgia to take over the family business upon his father's death. Carter thus ran a business raising peanuts, ginning cotton, and warehousing. His moderate policies as a Georgia Democrat won him the governorship by 1970. He then enacted state-level reforms including an end to racial discrimination. Carter was perceived as a relaxed Washington outsider in a bid for the presidency and won over Gerald Ford in the Election of 1976, the nation's bicentennial year. Carter's open and unpretentious style won him the election but did not serve him well as president. Through the Iranian Hostage Crisis, the Soviet invasion of Afghanistan, ongoing Cold War negotiations, and the Energy Crisis he was criticized for vacillation in decision making, but his strong stance on human rights was praised by the left and influenced the United Nations. After seeming unable to solve the problem of the United States that he called "malaise," Carter lost the Election of 1980 to Ronald Reagan. After the presidency Carter and his wife, Rosalyn, devoted themselves to domestic and international humanitarian causes.

# 13 Edward Kennedy

The sole surviving son of Joseph Kennedy was a long-standing senator from Massachusetts who for a time was considered a presidential hopeful with the potential to advance the Kennedy legacy beyond two assassinations and the oldest son's tragic death in World War II. "Ted" Kennedy, was known eventually as "The Lion of the Senate," but when he made a bid for the presidency in 1976, another Kennedy-with-another-woman story surfaced. In 1969, Ted Kennedy had driven his car off a bridge at Chappaquiddick Island. In the car with him was his young female staffer named Mary Jo Kopechne. Kennedy said that he tried to save Miss Kopechne, that he had no immoral relations with her, and that he was not under the influence of alcohol at the time of the accident; but he left the scene. He did not report the incident to the police before someone had found the overturned car in the water. Unanswered questions about the incident stymied any chance for the Democratic nomination in 1976, and Senator Kennedy's one serious bid lost to President Jimmy Carter who was trying for a second term. Kennedy supported over three hundred bills in his long career in the Senate, mostly dealing with health care and education. Although he was considered a champion of liberal policies, Senator Kennedy cooperated at times with Republicans to pass legislation. He died of a brain tumor in 2009.

## 14 Misery Index

Jimmy Carter used this calculation to criticize the Ford administration and to win the presidency in 1976, but the same numbers came back to haunt him in 1980 when he ran for a second term and lost to Ronald Reagan. The misery index is determined by adding the unemployment rate to the inflation rate, and the result in 1976 was over 13.5 percent. On television Carter asked a simple question: "Are you better off today than you were four years ago?" His question earned Carter 51 percent of the popular vote over Ford's 48 percent but four years later in debates with Ronald Reagan the Republican challenger asked the question and the answer was still the same for most Americans: "No." By then the misery index stood at almost 22 percent. The greatest drop in the misery index occurred during the Reagan administration, whereas the lowest average of the misery index over the course of a presidency belongs to the Clinton administration.

## 15 SALT II Treaty

President Carter negotiated the SALT II Treaty with Leonid Brezhnev by 1979 in which the two superpower leaders agreed to halt the manufacture of new nuclear weapons or launching systems and to reduce the operational force of nuclear weapons. The treaty stalled Soviet progress toward the deployment of multiple individually targeted reentry vehicle (MIRV) technology. Just a few months after the treaty was signed, however, the Soviet Union invaded Afghanistan, and the U.S. Senate retaliated by refusing to ratify the SALT II Treaty. Both sides abided by the negotiated limitations, however, until President Reagan ended American cooperation in 1982 because of Soviet violations. This step gave the Reagan administration the premise whereby the Strategic Defense Initiative (SDI) could be funded for research and development until President Reagan could negotiate treaties with Mikhail Gorbachev that led to the end of the Cold War.

## 16 Twenty-sixth Amendment

As early as World War II, when the draft age was dropped to eighteen, Americans under the age of twenty-one lobbied the government for the right to vote. The idea of "Old enough to fight, old enough to vote," became particularly acute during the Vietnam War as a result of the antiwar movement. The constitutionality of laws lowering the voting age to eighteen was debated by the Supreme Court in 1970, which determined that full voting rights to Americans as young as eighteen would have to be established by a Constitutional amendment, and by 1971 the Twenty-sixth Amendment was passed by both houses of Congress. In the shortest time of any other amendment's becoming law, the states ratified it within just over two months. Eleven million new voters existed in the country, but over the years the percentage of these young voters who actually voted steadily declined. After over half of them voted in the Election of 1972 and Richard Nixon still won a second term that level of participation was not again approached until the Election of 2008 with 49 percent.

## 17 Sun Belt

During the 1960s and 1970s over seven million Americans left the Northeast and the Midwest to move into the warmer fifteen southern states that became known as the Sun Belt. The advent of air conditioning made the warmer climate endurable in the summers, and retired Americans preferred the warmer winters. The migration was also a result of a decline in the manufacturing industries that had been located from Pittsburgh to Cleveland, an area dubbed the Rust Belt. Heavy industries and manufacturing jobs were shifted overseas after American unions fought for higher and higher wages. Workers in Mexico would work for a week for less money than American workers were paid in an hour, and what had been a thriving iron and steel industry had by the 1980s largely disappeared. The move to the Sun Belt altered the American political equation and led to the first big boost to the economy of the South since the Civil War.

## 18 Three Mile Island

The 1979 failure of the cooling system of the Three Mile Island nuclear plant outside Harrisburg, Pennsylvania, raised fears of a "meltdown" of the reactor core that would lead to a catastrophic release of radiation into the atmosphere. Under the Carter administration the incident led to a shakeup of the Nuclear Regulatory Commission and a deeper focus on plant safety for the seventy-two nuclear plants in America. Although these plants produced 12 percent of the nation's electricity without any other serious incident, the 125 reactors under construction were put on hold. As of now most of those new reactors were never completed.

## 19 Camp David Accords

President Carter's biggest foreign policy success was his participation in negotiating the Camp David Accords, an agreement between Egypt and Israel named such because the principal parties met at the American presidential retreat in Maryland. Carter met with Anwar el-Sadat of Egypt and Menachem Begin of Israel in 1978 after relations between the two had broken down. Sadat had realized after losing two wars to Israel that diplomacy was necessary, and he had become the first Arab leader to go to Israel on a visit. The two men accepted Carter's invitation and met in secret with the president for twelve days to restart negotiations. The Camp David Accords brought about an end to hostilities between the two nations by calling for a withdrawal of Israeli forces from the Sinai Peninsula they had conquered in return for free passage of Israeli ships through the Suez Canal, an end to boycotts between the nations, access for Israel to purchase Arab oil, and a proposed settlement of the problems of the Palestinian people. Sadat was assassinated by some of his own military personnel in 1981, however, and full implementation of the Camp David Accords was thwarted.

# 20 Iranian Hostage Crisis

The Shah of Iran, an American-backed ally named Mohammed Reza Pahlavi, fled the country after a fundamentalist Islamic revolt established an Islamic republic under the Ayatollah Ruhollah Khomeini in 1979. When the United States allowed Pahlavi to enter America to receive medical treatment for cancer, hundreds of militant students stormed the American Embassy in Teheran and took fifty-three American personnel hostage. President Carter boycotted Iranian oil, froze Iranian assets in America, and broke off diplomatic relations with the revolutionary government of Iran. While waiting for the United Nations to intervene, Carter allowed the crisis to drag on for over a year after threatening to go to war in the Persian Gulf. United Nations efforts proved ineffectual, and Carter's one attempt at a rescue ended in disaster when two American military aircraft collided and killed eight rescuers. The constant media coverage of the crisis made it the focus of American foreign policy during the campaign for the Election of 1980, and the frustration of the American people with the insult of the hostage crisis led to victory for Ronald Reagan. After consenting to several of the Iranian demands, the Carter administration successfully negotiated the release of the hostages, but the Iranian government refused to allow the plane carrying them to leave until after Ronald Reagan finished his inaugural address.

## The Big Picture

1. Gerald Ford managed to calm the nation after the crises of the Vietnam War and the Watergate Scandal, but his pardon of Richard Nixon was unpopular and paved the way for Jimmy Carter to win the Election of 1976.

2. The 1970s experienced high inflation but also a stagnant economy due to oil shortages and federal monetary policies that together produced the Great Recession, the worst recession to that time in American history.

3. Women experienced significant societal changes as feminists organized a civil rights movement to address sexual discrimination, the Supreme Court legalized abortion, and an oral contraceptive contributed to another sexual revolution.

4. President Carter's administration faced daunting foreign issues and continuing domestic woes that together created what Carter called a crisis of confidence, a challenge he proved unequal to meet.

5. As a result of the Energy Crisis and other economic issues, large numbers of Americans moved into the South to find jobs but also to enjoy warmer temperatures in what became known as the Sun Belt.

# Mini Quiz

1. By the time of his assassination, an assessment of the Kennedy presidency might be that he

    (A) revitalized Progressive Reform through his New Frontier agenda.
    (B) finally placed African-American civil rights at the forefront of domestic politics.
    (C) was overshadowed by his ambitious vice president, Lyndon Johnson.
    (D) grew in his mastery of foreign policy but was still stalled on the domestic front.
    (E) was popular in the South and in New England, but would not likely have won reelection.

2. Lyndon Johnson's War on Poverty stressed which type of solution?

    (A) Deficit spending to provide jobs as under the New Deal
    (B) Federally funded educational and jobs-training programs
    (C) Welfare reform by reducing the time a citizen could receive government support
    (D) Tax relief for businesses hiring people who had been unemployed for at least two years
    (E) Emphasis on expanding markets through trade negotiations with other nations

3. After President Eisenhower placed Earl Warren on the Supreme Court, the highest court in the land

    (A) retreated from participating in civil rights cases.
    (B) returned to a more traditional role for the judiciary branch.
    (C) cracked down on criminals fulfilling Eisenhower's promise to restore law and order.
    (D) lost a great deal of its prestige because of impeachment proceedings against two justices.
    (E) undertook a liberal agenda unanticipated by the Eisenhower administration.

4. The Montgomery Bus Boycott in the wake of the arrest and fine of Rosa Parks

    (A) seriously lowered the bus company's revenues for over a year.

    (B) relied almost entirely on the national reputation of Martin Luther King Jr. to succeed.

    (C) had no appreciable impact as a boycott because most African-Americans never rode the buses.

    (D) inspired a march on Washington, D.C., at which point the Supreme Court intervened.

    (E) ended when African-Americans could no longer afford to carpool to work.

5. Which of the following was the oldest civil rights organization addressing the concerns of African-Americans?

    (A) The American Civil Liberties Union

    (B) The Southern Christian Leadership Conference

    (C) The Congress of Racial Equality

    (D) The National Association for the Advancement of Colored People

    (E) The Student Non-violent Coordinating Committee

6. The Voting Rights Act of 1965 primarily addressed the continued use of

    (A) poll taxes to place economic hurdles for African-American voters in the South.

    (B) complex ballots in the North that made the voting process confusing to immigrants.

    (C) literacy tests that were interpreted by southern voting registrars to favor white voters.

    (D) labor racketeering to deliver the votes of union members to the Democratic Party.

    (E) unreasonable residency requirements before citizens could register to vote in the South.

7. The "New Look" in regard to national security policy under the Eisenhower administration sought to

    (A) achieve supremacy in satellite surveillance of the Soviet Union and its allies.

    (B) close the missile gap revealed by the launch of *Sputnik* by using the National Aeronautics and Space Administration for military purposes.

    (C) take a more aggressive stance toward communist expansion rather than merely contain it.

    (D) seek some other means of keeping the peace besides mutually assured destruction.

    (E) separate American foreign policy more and more from control of the United Nations.

8. Lyndon Johnson's approach to the Vietnam War was to

(A) allow his generals to exercise nearly complete control over strategy and military operations.

(B) increase the number of American military personnel even though fighting a limited war.

(C) respond to attacks in a purely defensive war until the Congress agreed to declare war.

(D) pressure the Chinese and Soviet governments using economic threats to end their support role.

(E) maintain a front of restraint while sending special forces to assassinate communist leaders.

9. All of the following protest movements challenged American societal norms during the Vietnam era EXCEPT the

(A) women's liberation movement.

(B) African-American civil rights movement.

(C) antiwar protest movement.

(D) antinuclear energy movement.

(E) hippie youth revolt.

10. Richard Nixon's "southern strategy" directly resulted in

(A) many southerners' switching from the Democratic to the Republican Party.

(B) more federal dollars supporting projects in the South through "revenue sharing."

(C) most African-Americans voting for the Republican Party again.

(D) racial riots in towns and cities through which Nixon campaigned for the presidency.

(E) the assassination attempt on his independent opponent, the segregationist George Wallace.

11. The first Strategic Arms Limitation Treaty (SALT I) differed from the SALT II in that SALT I

(A) limited nuclear missile manufacture, and SALT II called for destroying weapons.

(B) limited missile delivery systems, and SALT II limited the actual missiles.

(C) was initiated by the United States, and SALT II was initiated by the Soviet Union.

(D) was approved by the U.S. Senate, and SALT II was not approved by the Senate.

(E) was begun by President Nixon, and SALT II was begun by President Ford.

12. The Watergate scandal in the Nixon administration was investigated primarily by

 (A) the Federal Bureau of Investigation.
 (B) the Supreme Court.
 (C) an independent counsel assigned by the House of Representatives.
 (D) a grand jury from the District of Columbia.
 (E) a Senate committee.

13. Migration to the Sun Belt during the 1960s and 1970s occurred as a result of all of the following EXCEPT the

 (A) invention of reliable air-conditioning systems for homes and offices.
 (B) collapse of the heavy industries of the Rust Belt.
 (C) lowering of fares through regulation of the commercial airline industry.
 (D) increasing number of retirees seeking warmer winters.
 (E) greater influence of labor unions in the North.

14. The Camp David Accords resulted in

 (A) an increase in the territory under the control of Israel.
 (B) a settlement of the displacement problem of the Palestinian people.
 (C) a foreign policy success for President Carter with small expense to the American people.
 (D) a lessening of hostilities between Egypt and Israel.
 (E) the formation of an Islamic republic in Iran.

15. Jimmy Carter's response to the 1970s recession was most like

 (A) Franklin Roosevelt's response to the Great Depression.
 (B) Theodore Roosevelt's use of the presidency as a "bully pulpit."
 (C) Calvin Coolidge's hands-off approach to leadership.
 (D) Lyndon Johnson's launch of massive new welfare programs in his Great Society.
 (E) Gerald Ford's experimentation with voluntary compliance and tax cuts.

# Answer Explanations

1. **D** Some would suggest answer C as a function of an overall conspiracy theory that Lyndon B. Johnson participated in planning the assassination of John F. Kennedy (JFK), but new evidence suggests an even stronger case that Lee Harvey Oswald acted entirely alone in that he had eleven seconds to fire three shots at the president. Answers A and B are incorrect in that Kennedy's domestic agenda was mostly stalled in Congress even though his own party controlled it. Kennedy did state on national television that "race has no place in American life or law," a stance that made him decidedly unpopular in the South contrary to answer E. His fateful trip to Dallas, Texas, was intended to shore up support in the former Confederacy. Answer D points to the fact that the Bay of Pigs was a foreign policy debacle, but Kennedy had reversed this initial failure by careful management of the Cuban Missile Crisis and his bold stand at the Berlin Wall.

2. **B** Johnson's War on Poverty included Head Start and other educational and job-training programs designed to lift people out of poverty. Answer C did not occur until President Bill Clinton and a Republican Congress worked out welfare reform legislation. Answers A, D, and E are more the approach of the Obama administration.

3. **E** Although Earl Warren had been a member of the Republican Party, when he became chief justice of the Supreme Court he led in or cooperated with liberal policies advanced not in the Congress but by judicial activism. Therefore, answer B is incorrect, and answers A and C are the opposite of the truth. Opponents of the Warren Court's procedures claimed they did cause the Court to lose prestige, but not for the reasons stated in answer D, which is a fabrication.

4. **A** Although the segregation of buses in Montgomery was ended as a result of a ruling of the Supreme Court, the boycott did hurt the bus company economically because, contrary to answer C, most of those riding the buses before the boycott were African-Americans. Answer D hints at the intervention of the Supreme Court, but the march on Washington came much later in the civil rights movement. Answer E is incorrect in that African-Americans were walking and carpooling to the end of the boycott, and answer B is incorrect because the boycott did not rely on a national reputation of Martin Luther King Jr., but rather gave this young, local minister his national reputation as he went on to launch the Southern Christian Leadership Conference (SCLC).

5. **D** The roots of the American Civil Liberties Union mentioned in answer A go back only to 1917, whereas the National Association for the Advancement of Colored People was founded in 1909. The other civil rights organizations were founded in the civil rights era between 1941 and 1960.

6. **C** As Lyndon Johnson said when he signed this legislation into law, it addresses all limitations on the right to vote, but at the time the literacy tests mentioned in answer C were the most egregious violation of the rights of African-Americans

granted by the Fifteenth Amendment to the U.S. Constitution. In 1965, seven southern states still used this practice to limit access to voting for African-Americans. The other answers address problems with ballots and voting that existed before and after 1965 but were not the primary target of the Voting Rights Act.

7. **C** Answers A, B, and D were the initiatives of other presidential administrations throughout the Cold War, and even Eisenhower had to respond to criticisms about a "missile gap." The "New Look" referred to in the question mainly implied a departure with containment in favor of "rolling back" communism, if need be through "massive retaliation" up to and including the use of nuclear weapons. Answer E belies the fact that American foreign policy has never been under the control of the United Nations.

8. **B** Answer B refers to Lyndon B. Johnson's tendency to escalate the commitment of the United States without escalating the mission of the United States until almost five hundred thousand American service personnel were "in country." Answers A and C are the opposite of the truth in that Johnson micromanaged the war, and Congress never declared war. Answer E would be the more devious approach of Eisenhower or Nixon but was never documented, and answer D was Nixon's almost successful approach that accompanied his policy of Vietnamization.

9. **D** All of these protests occurred during the 1960s and early 1970s (and beyond) but the antinuclear movement only began in the United States at the very tail end of American involvement in Vietnam. Large-scale protests did not occur until late in the 1970s, especially after the 1979 Three Mile Island accident in Pennsylvania. American involvement in Vietnam slowed with an armistice in 1973 and ended in 1975 with the fall of Saigon to North Vietnamese and Vietcong forces.

10. **A** Nixon's campaign rhetoric emphasized states' rights, which southerners interpreted to mean that if he were elected president he would not continue the executive activism of the Johnson administration. For the first time since the Civil War, large numbers of southern voters voted for Nixon, the Republican candidate in 1968. This shift continued a trend begun under the administration of Franklin D. Roosevelt that for a time caused most African-American voters to support the Democratic Party. Answer B refers to Nixon's policy of revenue sharing, but federal funds were not distributed largely to southern states in any sort of quid pro quo arrangement. Racial riots were occurring throughout this time period and cannot be directly tied to Nixon's or any other candidate's campaign. George Wallace was a segregationist who ran on an independent ticket for the presidency against Nixon, but not until 1972 after the "southern strategy" was not needed to give Nixon a massive landslide victory that he soon squandered in the Watergate scandal.

11. **D** Answer B is the opposite of the truth of these treaties negotiated by Nixon and Carter, respectively. The one difference correctly stated is that the Senate never got around to ratifying the treaty until after American Cold War

policy took a different turn under President Reagan who repudiated both SALT agreements.

12. **E** Although both the Federal Bureau of Investigation and the Supreme Court played a role in the investigation, and there were even independent counsels assigned (and fired) by Nixon himself, the drama unfolded in the main investigation carried out by a Senate committee.

13. **C** Answers A and D are obvious reasons for the migration to the Sun Belt. Answer E hints at the increasing demands labor unions placed on the steel industry and other heavy industries that partly led to their demise suggested in answer B. Although the expansion of the commercial airline industry could have conceivably shrunk the time for families seeking to visit relatives over large distances, the regulation of the industry by the federal government did not lower airfares. Deregulation put more airlines in competition and lowered fares after the Sun Belt migration was largely over.

14. **D** The best that can be claimed for the Camp David Accords is hinted at in answer D, a fact reversed by the assassination of Anwar Sadat by his own people for his agreement to negotiate with the Israelis. Answer E hints at the revolution in Iran that deposed the Shah and installed the Ayatollah Khomeini as the Supreme Leader unrelated to the meetings between Egypt and Israel at Camp David. Answer A is incorrect in that Israel gave up land it had conquered on the Sinai Peninsula in return for access to the Suez Canal. Answer B is unfortunately still not achieved, and although the Camp David Accords were a success for President Carter as stated in answer C, they were not cheap. The Egyptians and the Israelis agreed to Carter's terms partly because they were offered the largest single dispersal of U.S. foreign aid to two individual countries to that time in history.

15. **B** Franklin D. Roosevelt would have initiated massive deficit spending to start federal programs, a tactic that looked impossible and even irresponsible in the 1970s situation. Coolidge would have pushed for tax cuts, done little, and said less. Carter did not launch any massive Johnsonesque welfare spending in an era when American resources seemed tapped out, and he did not agree with Ford's experiment with small tax cuts. He raised taxes. Carter consulted with Americans of all kinds as Theodore Roosevelt (TR) did on occasion, but he limited his action to speaking to the American people as TR did in a sort of moral lecture series, the exact thing TR described as a "bully pulpit." Without any other actions to back up his words, however, Carter followed in the footsteps of neither Roosevelt and lost the Election of 1980 to Ronald Reagan.

# Conservative Resurgence

*The American spirit is still there, ready to blaze into life.*
—Ronald Reagan, acceptance speech at the Republican National Convention, 1980

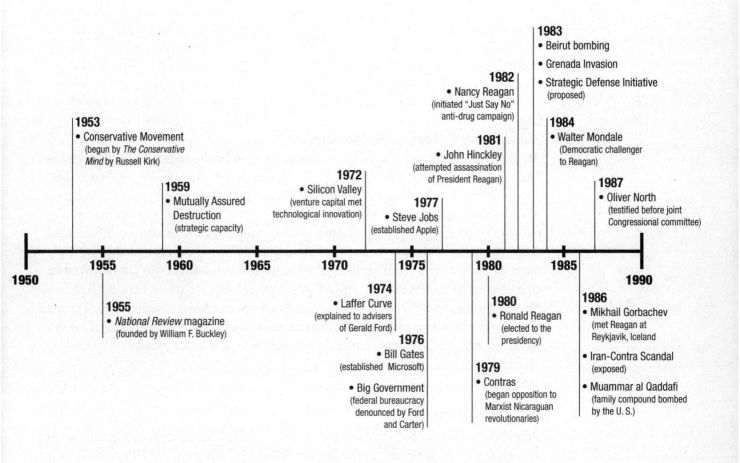

**1953**
• Conservative Movement
(begun by *The Conservative Mind* by Russell Kirk)

**1959**
• Mutually Assured Destruction
(strategic capacity)

**1972**
• Silicon Valley
(venture capital met technological innovation)

**1977**
• Steve Jobs
(established Apple)

**1982**
• Nancy Reagan
(initiated "Just Say No" anti-drug campaign)

**1981**
• John Hinckley
(attempted assassination of President Reagan)

**1983**
• Beirut bombing
• Grenada Invasion
• Strategic Defense Initiative
(proposed)

**1984**
• Walter Mondale
(Democratic challenger to Reagan)

**1987**
• Oliver North
(testified before joint Congressional committee)

1950  1955  1960  1965  1970  1975  1980  1985  1990

**1955**
• *National Review* magazine
(founded by William F. Buckley)

**1974**
• Laffer Curve
(explained to advisers of Gerald Ford)

**1976**
• Bill Gates
(established Microsoft)

• Big Government
(federal bureaucracy denounced by Ford and Carter)

**1980**
• Ronald Reagan
(elected to the presidency)

**1979**
• Contras
(began opposition to Marxist Nicaraguan revolutionaries)

**1986**
• Mikhail Gorbachev
(met Reagan at Reykjavik, Iceland

• Iran-Contra Scandal
(exposed)

• Muammar al Qaddafi
(family compound bombed by the U. S.)

# Top 20 Things to Know

## 1 Conservative Movement

Barry Goldwater's title of "Mr. Conservative" did not fall out of the sky. There had been since the 1950s a group of thinkers who espoused ideas trying to take the country back to principles that were held before Progressivism gained such successes through the Square Deal and the New Deal. The conservative movement attempted to revive traditional ideas of individualism with patriotism, religion, and capitalism all tinged with optimism. Fears about the growth of government and "creeping socialism," as Eisenhower called it, united various traditional, capitalist, and anticommunism strands of conservatism into a political agenda. Statesmen like Edmund Burke and John Adams and economists like Adam Smith were cited as intellectual lights, and Russell Kirk, Milton Friedman, Friedrich Hayek, and William F. Buckley were contemporary leaders. Buckley published the *National Review* magazine that popularized conservative ideas, but Ronald Reagan became the most successful conservative spokesman after his speech in support of Goldwater's 1964 campaign for the presidency. Conservatives stood for individual freedoms, free-market economics, the rule of law, respect for traditions within Western Civilization, lower taxes, less regulation of business, equality of opportunity, a transcendent moral order, property rights, and in some cases isolationism.

## 2 *National Review* Magazine

After Russell Kirk wove the threads of conservatism into a coherent legacy with his book *The Conservative Mind*, William F. Buckley Jr. set about trying to disseminate conservative ideas by founding *National Review* magazine in 1955. Since the conservative movement lacked any driving force other than the anticommunist editorializing of several popular magazines and authors, Buckley turned his Yale-honed debating skills, acerbic wit, and infamously large vocabulary to pushing a wide range of conservative ideas. Among the magazine's subscribers was Ronald Reagan who is said to have read the biweekly periodical from cover to cover. *National Review* attacked the liberal consensus but also more extremist conservative elements like Ayn Rand, the author of *The Fountainhead* and *Atlas Shrugged*, and the John Birch Society. Buckley also shunned anti-Semitism and segregationists like George Wallace.

## 3 Ronald Reagan

Reagan was an actor through the 1940s, even making training films as a soldier in World War II. As president of the Screen Actors Guild during the 1950s, he fought communism and changed from being a New Deal Democrat and fan of Franklin D. Roosevelt into being a political conservative. As his film career waned, Reagan became a spokesman for the General Electric Company and appeared regularly on television as a host of the corporation's sponsored programs. After becoming a

Republican his speech in support of Barry Goldwater for president brought Reagan to national attention. As governor of California in the 1960s he cut the welfare caseload while increasing benefits, reduced the size of the state bureaucracy, and squelched student protests on university campuses. After failing twice, Reagan was elected to the presidency in 1980 and again in a landslide victory in 1984. As president, Reagan survived being shot in the chest in an assassination attempt. He also cut taxes but at the same time called for a massive buildup of military power that created huge deficits. Reagan used this military might and optimistic and moralistic rhetoric in cooperation with leaders like Margaret Thatcher of Great Britain, Pope John Paul II, and Mikhail Gorbachev of the Soviet Union to set in motion events that led to the end of the Soviet Empire. His reputation was marred by the Iran-Contra Scandal and the bankruptcy of nearly 750 savings and loans due to deregulation policies.

## 4 Nancy Reagan

As a former actress, Nancy Reagan brought to the White House and the role as First Lady a touch of glamour and an interest in fashion reminiscent of the popularity of Jackie Kennedy. After having a conversation with a child about illegal drugs while on a school visit in 1982, Reagan launched a campaign to encourage all American youth to "Just Say No" to drug abuse. A result of a widespread national and international media initiative was a drug enforcement bill signed by President Reagan in 1986. After the president's near death in an assassination attempt, Nancy Reagan took a more assertive role in monitoring her husband's schedule, even to the point of consulting an astrologer for advice. Having been instrumental in converting her husband to conservative principles away from his support for the New Deal, the First Lady is said to have had unusual influence in the decision-making process of the Reagan administration. The active role Mrs. Reagan took in her husband's administration was reminiscent of Eleanor Roosevelt's and foreshadowed that of Hillary Clinton.

## 5 John Hinckley

In a bizarre fact follow fiction cycle, John Hinckley became obsessed with actress Jodie Foster after watching a movie based on the life of the man who attempted to assassinate George Wallace. Hinckley stalked Foster at Yale University and then hatched the plot to kill President Reagan to impress her, an idea derived from the plot of the movie *Taxi Driver*. Hinckley acted on these fantasies in 1981 by emptying a .22 caliber revolver toward President Reagan as the president entered his car in Washington, D.C. Hinckley hit three members of Reagan's staff and security detail and a ricocheted bullet hit the president in the chest. The assassination attempt was almost successful except for the surgical skills of doctors at a nearby hospital. Having survived a bullet in the chest served to enhance President Reagan's reputation as a Cold War warrior and a man's man, and Hinckley was found not guilty by reason of insanity and confined to a psychiatric hosptial.

## 6 Laffer Curve

Economist Arthur Laffer used an upside-down parabola to illustrate the notion that lowering taxes would boost the economy when he explained the idea to members of the Ford and Reagan administrations. Laffer theorized that there exists an optimal tax rate to maximize government revenue while at the same time stimulating economic growth. Building on the notions of Andrew Mellon who advised tax cuts would accomplish both goals as secretary of treasury under Calvin Coolidge, Laffer attempted to pinpoint the best level of taxation. If taxes were too low, the government would not make enough money to fulfill its obligations. If taxes were too high, as conservative economists thought they were in the 1970s, then individuals and businesses would refrain from investing in the economy because too much of their money was siphoned off by the government. If investment ceased, then the economy would sink and there would be too little tax revenue regardless of how high the tax rate was set. The Reagan administration used this theory to propound supply-side economics, the belief that job creation and economic expansion could be produced by lower taxes on the wealthiest Americans. Prosperity would then "trickle down" to the middle and lower classes. While tax cuts were enacted and the economy of the 1980s did soar, compensating cuts in spending were not enacted by Congress to balance Reagan's military spending, and deep deficits resulted.

## 7 Silicon Valley

Silicon Valley is the name of an actual region in California that turned from the growing of fruit to the production of Apple computers in the 1970s. As a concept, Silicon Valley represents the history of the personal computer. Computers that used to fill entire rooms were shrunk by the invention in 1971 of the microprocessor, or the silicon microchip. Intel Corporation invented and produced the chips outside San Francisco in the Santa Clara Valley. Desktop-size personal computers were available as kits as early as 1974, and mass production was achieved for marketing by Radio Shack in 1977. Steve Jobs and Steve Wozniak founded Apple Computer, Inc., in a garage in that same year. The Apple II was the first personal computer designed for use by people other than electronics enthusiasts in the mass marketplace. IBM followed suit by 1981, and computers have continually increased in memory capacity and decreased in size ever since. Bill Gates of Microsoft Corporation introduced an operating system that put computing within the capacity of the average citizen, and devices like the computer mouse increased usability. Since the 1980s the personal computer has developed into an essential business tool and an iconic aspect of the entertainment industry. American productivity experienced a phenomenal burst as American ingenuity ushered in the Information Age.

## 8 Bill Gates

A modern-day wealthy industrialist and philanthropist on a level with those of the Gilded Age revolutionized the personal computer industry by founding the software company Microsoft. Just as Andrew Carnegie did of old, Gates used cutting-edge technology, sharp dealing tactics in business competition, and sophisticated marketing strategies to make himself off and on again the richest man in the world, and then he became a philanthropist. In the process he brought personal computing to the business and entertainment world and revolutionized nearly all aspects of societal interaction. Through the 1990s Gates was involved in antitrust cases in which he was accused of forcing computer manufacturers to install Windows as the operating system on their machines along with Internet Explorer, the Microsoft web browser. Gates defended his business practices in these suits saying that he was not stopping competition in the computer industry but merely trying to survive it. As a result Microsoft was not broken up by the government in the way that Bell Telephone had been.

# 9 Steve Jobs

World War II had spun off the computer in the form of the giant ENIAC system. This computer was "giant" not in its computing capacity but in its sheer size. Not until 1952 did Texas Instruments develop silicon-sealed transistors that could withstand high temperatures and allow computers to decrease in size. By 1971 Intel managed to shrink computers further with their microprocessor. By 1977 Steve Jobs and Steve Wozniak founded Apple Computers, Inc. in a garage. Their company then joined the Fortune 500 in less time than any other company in American history. Apple developed a more user-friendly operating system for its Macintosh line of computers than IBM created to be used with Microsoft software. In contrasting the personas of Jobs and Gates, Bill Gates appeared to the public to be a more calculating, business-oriented intellect, whereas Steve Jobs cultivated a reputation as a mystic or guru out to change the world. Jobs died in 2011 after a long battle with pancreatic cancer.

# 10 Big Government

In his inaugural address President Reagan said, "Government is not the solution to our problem; government is the problem." With these words he expressed the frustration of the majority of voting Americans with the increasing size of the federal bureaucracy. Although conservatives held that government had legitimate duties, like providing justice to all and protecting American interests at home and abroad, the so-called "Reagan Revolution" sought to roll back both the Soviet Union and the federal government's size. The Reagan administration made efforts to turn back some of the spending on domestic welfare programs that went all the way back to Lyndon Johnson's Great Society. Reagan's New Federalism sought to transfer federally funded social programs to the management of the states where more efficient and knowledgeable monitoring could reduce waste. Through the 1988 Family Welfare Reform Act the Congress performed the most important restructuring of the welfare system since the New Deal era in order to shift the emphasis to job training. Reagan attempted to place conservatives on the Supreme Court to prolong the influence of these ideas. After leaving office, however, Reagan said the one disappointment of his presidency was his failure to seriously diminish the size of government or its pervasive influence on American life.

## 11 Muammar al Qaddafi

Qaddafi began his career as a dictator as a lieutenant in the Libyan military, not much higher than Corporal Hitler. Still, when he seized power in 1969 he was able to erase the constitution and impose his own will. He and his family took over the country with the backing of the military, yet curiously this dictator for a time provided his people with the highest standard of living in Africa. Qaddafi dabbled in chemical weapons and acts of terrorism, though, a fact that made him the target of a bombing raid by the U.S. military in 1986 after a bombing of a disco in Germany frequented by American service personnel. Escaping several assassination attempts by various groups, Qaddafi renounced his weapons of mass destruction after Saddam Hussein was captured, tried, and hanged. The Libyan people, however, rose against him in 2011 to end his career as a leader guilty of crimes against humanity both at home and abroad. He was deposed in a revolt by the Libyan people that was aided by NATO forces, including American military personnel, and killed while being captured.

## 12 Contras

After sending one authoritarian dictator a message, President Reagan wanted to take a stand against communist revolutionaries in Central and South America. Reagan believed Cuba was exporting socialism to its neighbors and that Daniel Ortega, who rose to power at the head of a revolutionary group in Nicaragua called the Sandinistas, was on his way to becoming another Castro. The U.S. Congress originally backed the Reagan administration and the Central Intelligence Agency's (CIA's) desire to aid the Contras, a rebel group that opposed Ortega and the Sandinistas, however, whispers of "Vietnam quagmire" soon arose when the Contras failed to achieve victory. Aid to the Contras was cut off by the Congress by 1985 at which time covert operations were begun to keep aiding them as an expression of containment of communism right in the Western Hemisphere. The Iran-Contra scandal was the result.

## 13 Beirut Bombing

President Reagan sent U.S. Marines on a peacekeeping mission in Lebanon in 1982 as a result of the activities of the Palestinian Liberation Organization in that country. The Marines were to come between two or more sides of an internecine Islamic conflict. After Christian militia forces and even Israeli troops became involved, violence escalated, and in 1983 terrorist truck bombs destroyed both the U.S. Embassy in Beirut and the Marines' barracks killing 241 American servicemen and seventeen other Americans and wounding one hundred. Congress had authorized the participation of the Marines and naval personnel in a multinational force, but after the bombing Reagan withdrew all American military forces from Lebanon. After this first of America's lethal experiences with terrorism, President Reagan issued a new set of four parameters for American military involvement abroad. First, the cause must be "vital to our national interest." Second, the commitment must have a "clear intent and support needed to win the conflict." Third, there must be "reasonable assurance" that the cause "will have the support of the American people and Congress." Finally, military intervention must always be the last resort when no other choices remain. After his presidency, in two out of the three times American troops were deployed between 1988 and 2002 all four of these conditions were met, revealing that Reagan might have hit upon a sound policy that could avoid a quagmire.

# 14 Grenada Invasion

The Soviets began to see that the Reagan administration would use the military to protect Americans and American interests around the world, a fact that hastened the end of the Cold War in the most dangerous form of brinkmanship. After a leftist government of the island nation of Grenada (just off the coast of Venezuela) slid into instability when the revolutionary leader was killed, the U.S. military invaded in 1983 to protect American citizens who were attending medical school on the island. The invasion cost nineteen American servicemen their lives, but it was largely supported by the American public. Other countries, however, claimed that the United States had violated several diplomatic agreements. Norman Schwarzkopf was second in command of the invasion and observed several weaknesses in the military preparedness of the American forces, a fact he corrected prior to the Persian Gulf War.

# 15 Mutually Assured Destruction

After the Soviet Union acquired a comparable ability to destroy life on the planet with that of the United States, the Cold War rested on the notion of mutually assured destruction, or MAD. Since the Kennedy sdministration the vulnerability of the populations of both superpowers to destruction by the other made a twisted sort of stasis possible. This equilibrium was captured in the pithy phrase, "Whoever shoots first dies second." Military leaders said that if the technology existed to form a shield over the country that would stop any nuclear attack, then the United States would immediately need to put it in place no matter how much it cost because the Soviet Union would immediately fire their intercontinental ballistic missiles (ICBMs) in self-defense. Although there is some evidence that MAD prevented even some conventional warfare and any actual thermonuclear exchange, the Reagan administration took the position that MAD was an immoral defense philosophy. Once technology existed that seemed promising regarding a strong missile defense, Reagan advocated its implementation as a way to end the Cold War.

# 16 Strategic Defense Initiative

In his pursuit of a strategy other than mutually assured destruction, Ronald Reagan announced in 1983 his support for the development of a defensive system designed to eliminate or minimize the threat of incoming missiles. Technologies under development included rail guns, laser beams, and particle beams as well as antimissile missiles, all guided by supercomputers. The Congress authorized as much as $30 billion toward research and development of these technologies under the broad umbrella of the Strategic Defense Initiative, or SDI. Because President Reagan had referred to the Soviet Union as the evil empire, SDI was quickly dubbed "Star Wars" after the recent George Lucas and Steven Spielberg smash sci-fi hit movie. Although the technology never reached a level of implementation, Soviet and American science acknowledged it was feasible. Therefore, Reagan could use even the funding of the program as leverage in his negotiations with Soviet Premiere Mikhail Gorbachev. Gorbachev realized on top of all the funding committed toward existing Cold War rivalries that it could not keep pace with the United States. Russian analysts have asserted that the SDI program sped up the collapse of the crumbling Soviet Union by at least five years. The United States recently improved antimissile technology sufficiently to acquire the capacity likened to "shooting a bullet with another bullet."

## 17 Mikhail Gorbachev

Gorbachev was the youngest general secretary in the history of the Communist Party when he took office in 1982. He took power in the climax of the Cold War and faced huge domestic problems, and he took the unique step of criticizing the Soviet system. In an attempt to improve the standard of living in the Soviet "utopia," Gorbachev instituted a series of domestic reforms designed to increase productivity and to provide a measure of freedom. He advocated *glasnost* and *perestroika*, or openness and restructuring, respectively. Gorbachev and Reagan began a series of summit meetings through which the two men developed respect and even friendship, and after overcoming some disagreements signed the first treaty to reduce the numbers of nuclear weapons in their stockpiles. Working with the American president and advocating reforms accelerated the end of the Cold War and won Gorbachev the Nobel Peace Prize in 1990, but because his reforms did not achieve immediate success in boosting the Soviet economy he was ultimately forced to resign in 1991. By then, however, Gorbachev had dissolved the Soviet Union.

## 18 Walter Mondale

Mondale was a Minnesota lawyer who began political life working for Hubert Humphrey and then became a senator and eventually vice president under Jimmy Carter in 1976. He took an active part in the Carter administration, something unusual in the modern vice presidency to that point. After Carter was defeated by Ronald Reagan in 1980, Mondale became the Democratic candidate to run against President Reagan in 1984. The Election of 1984 proved to be the last landslide victory to date with Reagan receiving 525 electoral votes, the highest of any candidate for the presidency in history. Mondale won only the District of Columbia and his home state of Minnesota (by a margin of just over three thousand votes) for a total of thirteen electoral votes. The economic turnaround during Reagan's first term led many to interpret the Election of 1984 as an endorsement of supply-side economics and a death knell to liberalism, but recent events revealed the Reagan Revolution to be merely another pendulum swing. After losing the election, Mondale later served under Bill Clinton as the ambassador to Japan.

# 19 Iran-Contra Scandal

After Reagan said that the United States would not negotiate with terrorists, a secret plan was revealed in 1986 that he had done just that. The Iran part of the scandal was the sale of antiaircraft missiles and other weapons to Iran in order to leverage release of American hostages being held in Lebanon. The Contra part of the scandal came in the form of funding of the Contra rebels, a group in Nicaragua fighting to overthrow the communist leader of the Sandinistas, Daniel Ortega. Because Congress would not authorize the expenditure, the secret proceeds of the arms sales to Iran were diverted for this purpose. Three hostages were released, but three more were taken. When Reagan's national security adviser, the director of the Central Intelligence Agency, and U.S. Marine Corps Lieutenant Colonel Oliver North all either resigned or were fired for their part in the scheme, Reagan appeared to have been asleep at the wheel or willfully negligent of his duty to uphold the law. Another "all-the-president's-men" Watergate-type coverup was discovered, and Reagan's ability to lead during his last two years as president was crippled.

# 20 Oliver North

North was a U.S. Marine Corps officer who worked in the Reagan administration for the National Security Council and ran the secret operation leading to the Iran-Contra Scandal. North took the money from weapons sales to Iran and orchestrated the supply of the Contras in Nicaragua. Before going to trial for numerous felonies, North testified to a Congressional committee about his involvement. Despite the hope of opponents of the Reagan administration that North would try to save his military career by implicating the president in the scandal, North took the blame and said Reagan knew nothing of the operation. In the subsequent trial, North was found guilty of three felonies, but the agreement for immunity from prosecution that prompted North to testify to Congress led to the dismissal of the case. Even though Oliver North's stance resembled that of G. Gordon Liddy in the Nixon administration, President Reagan could not avoid the implication that he had been asleep at the wheel and unaware of what his subordinates were doing.

## The Big Picture

1. The pendulum of American politics swung back to the right during the 1980s after five decades of government expansion, and Ronald Reagan became the central figure in a conservative resurgence.

2. Tax cuts and increased productivity due to the development of the personal computer dramatically increased the power of the American economy, which left the Great Recession to begin a period of phenomenal growth.

3. The optimism at home was matched by progress in the Cold War through a combination of firm rhetoric and technological breakthroughs that made the leaders of the Soviet Union realize they could not keep up the economic and ideological competition with the United States.

4. The attention of U.S. foreign policy became increasingly drawn to the Middle East as the first serious terrorist attacks on Americans further destabilized the troubled region.

5. After winning reelection in 1984 in the greatest landslide since that of Franklin D. Roosevelt in 1936, Ronald Reagan's presidency proved that despite great accomplishments all presidents are capable of serious errors in judgment that undermine their ability to govern.

# Moderate America

# CHAPTER 38

*. . . I am reaching out to President Gorbachev, asking him to work with me to bring down the last barriers to a new world of freedom. Let us move beyond containment and once and for all end the cold war.*

—George H. W. Bush, Thanksgiving message, 1989

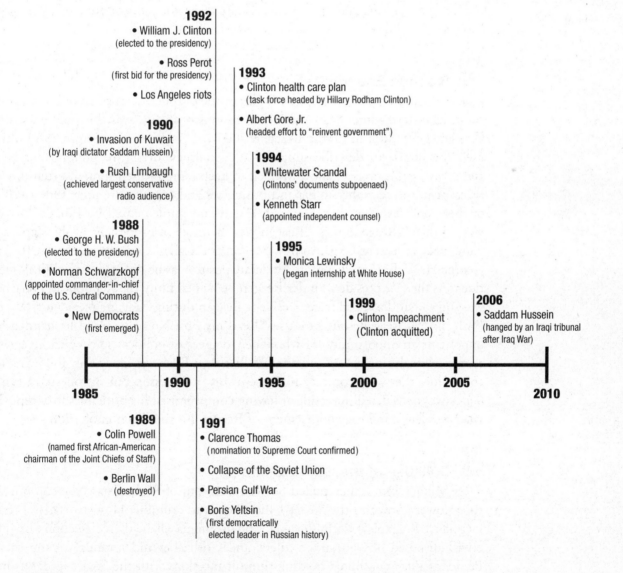

**1992**
- William J. Clinton
(elected to the presidency)

- Ross Perot
(first bid for the presidency)

- Los Angeles riots

**1990**
- Invasion of Kuwait
(by Iraqi dictator Saddam Hussein)

- Rush Limbaugh
(achieved largest conservative
radio audience)

**1988**
- George H. W. Bush
(elected to the presidency)

- Norman Schwarzkopf
(appointed commander-in-chief
of the U.S. Central Command)

- New Democrats
(first emerged)

**1993**
- Clinton health care plan
(task force headed by Hillary Rodham Clinton)

- Albert Gore Jr.
(headed effort to "reinvent government")

**1994**
- Whitewater Scandal
(Clintons' documents subpoenaed)

- Kenneth Starr
(appointed independent counsel)

**1995**
- Monica Lewinsky
(began internship at White House)

**1999**
- Clinton Impeachment
(Clinton acquitted)

**2006**
- Saddam Hussein
(hanged by an Iraqi tribunal
after Iraq War)

1985  1990  1995  2000  2005  2010

**1989**
- Colin Powell
(named first African-American
chairman of the Joint Chiefs of Staff)

- Berlin Wall
(destroyed)

**1991**
- Clarence Thomas
( nomination to Supreme Court confirmed)

- Collapse of the Soviet Union

- Persian Gulf War

- Boris Yeltsin
(first democratically
elected leader in Russian history)

# Top 20 Things to Know

## 1 George H. W. Bush

Son of Senator Prescott Bush, George H. W. Bush was a decorated World War II naval pilot who finished a bombing run even though his plane was hit by antiaircraft fire. After the war, Bush became wealthy as a Texas oilman. After serving as a congressman he was the ambassador to the United Nations and director of the Central Intelligence Agency among other posts. Bush was a moderate Republican who first opposed Ronald Reagan and then served as his vice president. Never truly believing in the conservative principles of his predecessor but basking in his popularity led Bush toward a collision with public opinion after winning the presidency in 1988. He was immensely popular after his handling of the first Persian Gulf War but slipped in domestic policy after agreeing to a compromise with Congress over raising taxes. Having promised to never raise taxes, the public doubted his integrity and even his ability.

## 2 "Voodoo Economics"

One of the more telling examples of spin, or the purposeful representation of political ideas in terms intended to alter perceptions of reality, was this phrase used by George H. W. Bush in his bid to secure the Republican nomination in 1980. Bush used the phrase to describe supply-side economics, or the reduction of income and capital gains taxes to allow the rich to keep more of their money, ostensibly to invest it in the economy to expand businesses and create more jobs. Other critics of these policies when they were advocated and implemented by Ronald Reagan termed them "Reaganomics." Reagan was the modern proponent of this approach going back at least as far as Andrew Mellon and Calvin Coolidge in the 1920s, but George H. W. Bush took a more moderate position as he did in most political questions. As the vice president under Reagan he helped unify the Republican Party but was somewhat distanced from President Reagan during Reagan's presidency. When Bush made a Reaganesque promise, "Read my lips: No new taxes," he handed his opponents an opportunity for whole new degrees of political spin when he agreed to raise taxes during his administration. President Bush was likely only following his core values that were contrary to those of his predecessor, but his one-term presidency was considered the result of having compromised his principles to accept the vice presidency and the endorsement of Reagan for the Election of 1988.

## 3 Collapse of the Soviet Union

After Mikhail Gorbachev pulled Soviet troops out of Afghanistan, the communist superpower known as the Soviet Union began to crumble. Hungary, Poland, East Germany, Bulgaria, Czechoslovakia, and Romania all held free elections or otherwise disposed of communist rulers, and Gorbachev did nothing to stop them. President Bush continued holding summit meetings with the Soviet leader as had Reagan, and Gorbachev boldly held the first free elections in the Soviet Union since the vote in 1917 that Lenin had ignored. Gorbachev assumed he would win because of his reforms, and he won the presidency of the Soviet Union in 1990, but Boris Yeltsin won as president of the Russian Republic. Bush and Gorbachev signed the START treaty that further reduced the number of nuclear weapons and agreed to the eradication of chemical weapons. Instead of winning him support, these steps and the winning of the Nobel Prize only caused communist hardliners to attempt a coup. Gorbachev held on but his power was diminished as was that of the Communist Party. With the destruction of the Berlin Wall in 1989, the dissolution of the Warsaw Pact, and the fact that Estonia, Latvia, and Lithuania again became independent countries by 1991, Gorbachev resigned by the end of that year. The Union of Soviet Socialist Republics, or USSR, ceased to exist. A Commonwealth of Independent States retained a loose organization, and Boris Yeltsin took up the mantle of establishing a free Russia and continued détente with the West. The Cold War was over. The United States won.

## 4  Boris Yeltsin

In a time of rapid change in the Russian government that survived the collapse of the Soviet Union, all eyes turned to the silver-haired and slightly inebriated reformer Boris Yeltsin. Once having stood atop a tank to rally support for Mikhail Gorbachev against a coup, Yeltsin became both the first democratically elected leader in Russian history in 1996 and the first Russian leader to voluntarily resign and give his power to someone else in 1999. Whereas Gorbachev had reformed the Soviet government with the aim of maintaining Communist Party control, Yeltsin instituted reforms that sought to decentralize control and create a more democratic Russia. He stopped government censorship of the news media, tolerated criticism of himself and the government, and even experimented with free markets. He did not see these reforms through, however, and presented an unstable face for Russia to the world with aberrant behavior associated with alcoholism that only served to feed anti-Russian stereotypes. He did convince the world that a new Russia was possible, a fact he later undermined by placing former KGB agent Vladimir Putin in the interim president job upon his surprising resignation.

## 5  Saddam Hussein

Hussein joined the Ba'ath Party of Iraqi nationalists and helped in an assassination attempt on the British-backed prime minister of colonial Iraq. When his party eventually took power in a free Iraq, he returned from exile only to be sent to prison when the Ba'ath Party fell from power briefly. Hussein escaped from prison, rose in rank, and became Iraq's president by 1979. He led Iraq in a war against Iran in the 1980s (in which the United States backed him) and through a civil war against the Kurdish people and throughout ruled as a harsh dictator. He ordered the use of chemical weapons against the Kurds of Iraq by which thousands of men, women, and children were killed. His invasion of Kuwait prompted the Persian Gulf War after which he withdrew from Kuwait but remained in power. After the Iraq War in 2003 Saddam Hussein was executed for his crimes against humanity in 2006 after being tried by an Iraqi tribunal.

## 6 Persian Gulf War

After Saddam Hussein, the dictator of Iraq, invaded Kuwait in 1990, King Fahd of Saudi Arabia allowed George H. W. Bush to send American troops to protect his country in Operation Desert Shield. This mobilization of American military power, the largest since World War II, eventually became Operation Desert Storm as the United States and twenty-seven other nations prepared to invade Kuwait in order to liberate it. As airstrikes pummeled Iraqi military targets in both Kuwait and Iraq for six weeks, Bush told Hussein to leave Kuwait or else. As the day of the ultimatum ended, the coalition force struck in Kuwait while an even larger attack swept into Iraq in a massive flanking maneuver designed by American General H. Norman Schwarzkopf. Americans watched on television as their military destroyed the most formidable army in the Middle East in 100 hours. Kuwait was liberated, but Saddam Hussein was allowed to stay in power and even to crush Shiite Muslim and Kurdish revolts. In accomplishing the original goals of the coalition, however, George H. W. Bush was lauded as a masterful diplomatic and military leader, for a time.

## 7 Colin Powell

Powell was a decorated Vietnam War veteran who rose in rank and influence as a military adviser to presidents of both parties from Richard Nixon and George W. Bush to Jimmy Carter and Bill Clinton. He was a national security adviser to President Reagan and became both the first African-American chairman of the Joint Chiefs of Staff under George H. W. Bush and the first African-American secretary of state under George W. Bush. He became widely known while leading in Washington during the Persian Gulf War and was instrumental in gaining support both in the United States and in the United Nations for the operations that became the Iraq War based on intelligence that Saddam Hussein was hiding a program to produce weapons of mass destruction. When no such weapons were found and the war was prolonged, Powell resigned from President Bush's cabinet after Bush won reelection in 2004. Powell was known for most of his career as a nonpartisan adviser who was unafraid to state any disagreements over policy he held with the presidents under whom he served, and was once considered a likely candidate for the presidency himself.

## 8 Norman Schwarzkopf

Another Vietnam-era officer who rose in rank prior to the Persian Gulf War was "Stormin' Norman" Schwarzkopf. He became a household name during the war and was responsible for everything from the design of the combat troops' desert camouflage uniforms to the winning strategy that beat most of Saddam Hussein's Republican Guard troops in four days. After prolonged bombardment and after fixing the Iraqi troops in Kuwait with a small frontal attack, Schwarzkopf sent the bulk of his armored divisions around Kuwait through a desert that had never been crossed by an army. This encircling maneuver caused a rapid retreat of Iraqi forces from Kuwait and the destruction of most of their vehicles by American air power.

# 9 Clarence Thomas

As the second African-American to attain a position on the Supreme Court, Clarence Thomas embodied the American Dream for his race. Abandoned by his father and raised in poverty in Georgia, Thomas was encouraged by his grandfather to pursue education. After facing intense racial discrimination in his quest to become a Catholic priest, he switched to the study of law at Yale University. As a leader among African-American conservatives, Thomas came to the attention of Ronald Reagan who placed Thomas in charge of the Equal Employment Opportunity Commission, or EEOC, where he enacted reforms that were not always well received by civil rights groups. After Thurgood Marshall retired from the Supreme Court, George H. W. Bush nominated Thomas. Clarence Thomas faced a typical confirmation process until a former staffer, Anita Hill, accused Thomas of sexual harassment while working at the EEOC. The hearings then became a media circus, but no convincing evidence ever surfaced to prove Hill's allegations. Thomas went on to be confirmed by the Senate and to vote with conservatives on the Supreme Court.

# 10 Los Angeles Riots

Revealing that deep undercurrents of racial tension still ran through American society, riots broke out in Los Angeles in 1992 as a result of frustration over the beating of an African-American named Rodney King by Los Angeles police. After leading law enforcement personnel on a chase at over 115 mph King was apprehended, tasered, and beaten when he resisted arrest. The beatings were caught on videotape that led to a trial of four officers involved for excessive use of force. Mostly white juries acquitted the officers, and Los Angeles erupted in six days of violent rioting. Acts of arson, looting, assault, and murder occurred, many on live television. Over $1 billion in damage was done, fifty-four people killed, and two thousand injured. During the riots, King appeared on television to say, "Can we all get along?" In interviews he said he originally fled the police because he was afraid a DUI would end his parole on a robbery charge. In an odd twist on American racism, Korean and other Asian stores in the Watts neighborhoods were targeted for looting, and the owners took up assault-style semiautomatic weapons to protect them. Later trials convicted two of the officers of violating King's civil rights, and Rodney King was awarded $3.8 million in damages.

# 11 William J. Clinton

William Jefferson Blythe never knew his father, who was killed in a car wreck before he was born as one of the first baby boomers. Bill Clinton thus took his name from a stepfather. Clinton went on to win a Rhodes Scholarship and study at Oxford University. He avoided the draft because he was opposed to the Vietnam War. He entered national politics as a campaign worker in 1972 and attended Yale Law School where he met his wife, Hillary Rodham. After law school Clinton taught and practiced law back in Arkansas where he was born. In 1978, he was elected there as the nation's youngest governor, an office he held for four terms. As governor he reformed education by employing the nation's first basic skills test for teachers. He formed a moderate wing of the national Democratic Party, and overcame criticism of his personal life to win the Election of 1992 as president. President Clinton harvested the fruits of the economic expansion of the 1980s in the lowest unemployment and inflation rates and the highest home ownership in modern history. He balanced the budget and even produced a budget surplus, that is, the stopping of the United States from going deeper into debt for a time. After failing to reform the health care system and losing the Congress to the Republicans in 1994, Clinton seized the political initiative and declared, ". . . the era of Big Government is over." At home he was thus able to begin the painful process of reforming the welfare system. Abroad, he tried to hold Saddam Hussein accountable to United Nations inspections because he feared the dictator was developing weapons of mass destruction, or WMDs. He worked to break down international trade barriers and to expand membership in the North Atlantic Treaty Organization (NATO). Despite being embroiled in several "-gate" scandals, Clinton remained a popular president and became a humanitarian spokesman after leaving office.

## 12 Ross Perot

Having been born in poverty in Texas, Perot won a nomination to the Naval Academy and served through the Korean War. After working for IBM for a time after leaving the Navy, Perot started his own business, Electronic Data Systems. Once this company became worth billions of dollars, Perot became something of a globe-trotting humanitarian crusader. He used much of his own money to run for president in 1992, splitting from the Republican Party with a third party as had Theodore Roosevelt in 1912. Perot received almost twenty million popular votes that, if they had gone to George H. W. Bush, would have given Bush a second term. He tallied over eight million votes in the much closer Election of 1996. During his 1992 campaign Perot criticized the North American Free Trade Agreement, or NAFTA, saying that the jobs departing the country for Mexico created "a giant sucking sound," and he gathered support by issuing dire warnings about the national debt on what became known as "infomericals," spots on television he paid for himself. Perot temporarily pulled out of the race only to reenter later, damaging his credibility. He remains a philanthropist, but has dropped from the public political debate.

## 13 Hillary Rodham Clinton

Undoubtedly the most politically active First Lady in American history, Hillary Rodham Clinton has served as a senator and secretary of state in addition to challenging Barack Obama for the Democratic nomination for the president in the Election of 2008. Like her husband, Bill Clinton, she was an attorney and law professor. She was a strong advocate for health issues and headed the task force to pursue a national health care program in the Clinton administration, and in a speech in China in 1995 linked human rights and women's rights. After the presidency of Bill Clinton ended, Hillary Clinton was elected to the senate for New York and worked to address national security and health concerns after the September 11, 2001, terrorist attacks. After being the first First Lady to become a senator, Senator Clinton became the woman to win the most primaries and delegates in a presidential campaign before conceding defeat and campaigning for Barack Obama.

# 14 Albert Gore Jr.

The son of a congressman, Albert Gore became a congressman himself and represented his home state of Tennessee until he was elected vice president with Bill Clinton in 1992. While serving in this capacity he led several economic initiatives in the Clinton administration including an effort to "reinvent government," by reviewing the operations of the federal government to eliminate waste. He also advocated the expansion of information technology and environmental issues. He ran against George W. Bush for the presidency in 2000 and conceded the race to Bush when the Supreme Court decided that voting irregularities in Florida could not be resolved constitutionally before an election deadline. After entering private life with several communications and other business interests, Gore received the Nobel Peace Prize for his global leadership in investigating the causes and consequences of climate change.

# 15 New Democrats

Bill Clinton and his vice president, Albert Gore Jr., represented what has been called a new brand of political leadership. In the wake of the smashing victories of Ronald Reagan and the Republican takeover of Congress in 1994, New Democrats moved to the center of the political debate and announced a third way beyond the traditional liberal versus conservative mainstream values. Focusing on the economy, New Democrats advocated a combination of moderate deregulation, tax cuts for low-income families and small businesses (made up for by tax increases on the wealthiest Americans), and the international quest for free trade that resulted in the passage of the North American Free Trade Agreement (NAFTA). The movement also espoused spending restraints that helped balance budgets. Combined with the investments made during the Reagan-era tax cuts, these policies resulted in the largest peacetime expansion of the American economy in history through the 1990s.

# 16 Rush Limbaugh

Limbaugh first experienced success in broadcasting in California and by 1988 had a nationally syndicated political commentary radio show where he expressed his conservative views. His satirical style and opposition to, among other things, the Clinton administration's national health care plan, won him by 1993 a daily audience of twenty million listeners. Limbaugh brought renewed vigor to the conservative movement that had lost much of its momentum after the Reagan years and became known as a leader of conservative Republican discourse. Like Father Coughlin of the 1930s, Limbaugh turned a caustic on-air persona into popularity among like-minded listeners. The *Rush Limbaugh* show became a lucrative franchise as he alienated opponents by launching diatribes against liberalism intended to break politically correct barriers for entertainment shock value among his devoted fans. Limbaugh was inducted into the Radio Hall of Fame for his popularizing of the talk show genre in a way that has spawned many imitators. His style is said by critics to have deepened the chasm between the Left and the Right in American politics.

# 17 Whitewater-gate

The name of this scandal of the Clinton administration was so reminiscent of the Watergate Scandal of the Nixon administration that the press began attaching the "-gate" suffix to a wide range of political intrigues. The Whitewater Development Corporation was a real estate firm in which the Clintons had invested. The company failed, but not before receiving several hundred thousand dollars in federally backed loans. The Securities and Exchange Commission investigated and found several of the Clintons' associates guilty of fraud, but the Clintons escaped prosecution because of a lack of evidence linking them to any criminal behavior. Before he left office President Clinton pardoned one of the Whitewater associates who was serving time in jail for contempt of court because she refused to testify in the matter.

# 18 Kenneth Starr

This lawyer and one-time federal judge was chosen to investigate the Whitewater situation as an independent counsel, but his investigation of the Clinton administration and of President Clinton widened to include a number of scandals or potential scandals. The Whitewater investigation was expanded to examine the death of a close Clinton adviser in an apparent suicide as well as allegations of the president's having had numerous extramarital affairs. The "Starr Report" was released to the public as a result of the investigation of accusations of several women of inappropriate sexual advances on the part of President Clinton going back as far as his tenure as governor of Arkansas. The often graphic details of the report fed the Monica Lewinsky scandal, but the impeachment of President Clinton originated in Kenneth Starr's assertion that the president had lied under oath when giving a deposition during his investigation.

# 19 Monica Lewinsky

Having taken an internship at the White House in 1995, Lewinsky became the center of the scandals of Bill Clinton's extramarital affairs. After a coworker secretly taped Lewinksy discussing sexual liaisons with the president, the story was leaked and led to the impeachment proceedings against Bill Clinton. Clinton denied any sexual relationship with the much younger woman, but during an investigation by a special prosecutor, Kenneth Starr, he lied under oath while giving a deposition. Allegations of several other affairs created yet another media circus, which President Clinton survived by apologizing to the nation on television. He also survived being impeached by the House of Representatives when the Senate voted to acquit him on the two charges, perjury and obstruction of justice. Although the nation was scandalized by the behavior of the president, Americans were comforted to know that not even the president was above the law. The Supreme Court ruled during the episode that a sitting president can be sued despite claims of executive privilege.

# 20 Clinton Impeachment

The nation wrestled with the unprecedented display of presidential infidelity during the Clinton years, although such infidelity was nothing new. The Clinton impeachment trial launched a debate in America about the different weight of public and private morality. The House of Representatives used a Republican majority to impeach the president, only the second time such a step had ever occurred. As in the Johnson impeachment trial, however, the prosecutors failed to achieve the two-thirds majority called for in the U.S. Constitution to remove the president from office. The Senate vote after the trial fell largely on party lines, and for one article was a 50-50 tie. The entire experience both fascinated and sickened much of the American people and filled late-night talk show hosts' monologues with material for years. Recent assessments of the conduct of the prosecution judge it to have been too motivated by partisan hatred than an impartial quest for justice or indignation over sexual harassment.

## *The Big Picture*

1. George H. W. Bush scored giant foreign policy successes by managing the end of the Cold War after the collapse of the Soviet Union and winning the Persian Gulf War against Iraqi dictator Saddam Hussein.

2. Dissatisfaction with the Bush administration on the domestic front was manifested in a prominent third-party candidate as well as the rise of the popularity of Bill Clinton caused the collapse of the Reagan-era Republican Party hold on the presidency.

3. After winning the Election of 1992, Bill Clinton faced Republican control of Congress by 1994 and followed through with his previous commitments to moderate political reforms.

4. The 1990s was a decade of phenomenal economic growth combining 1980s investments, the dot-com boom on the Internet, and the Clinton administration's commitments to free trade and balanced budgets.

5. Scandals in the president's personal life threatened to destroy the gains Clinton had made in his first term, but he weathered an impeachment storm and recovered much of his reputation as a successful president by the end.

# Presidential Pendulum
# in the Information Age

# CHAPTER 39

*If we work hard—and work together—if we rededicate ourselves to strengthening families, creating jobs, rewarding work, and reinventing government, we can lift America's fortunes once again.*
—Bill Clinton, speech before Congress, 1993

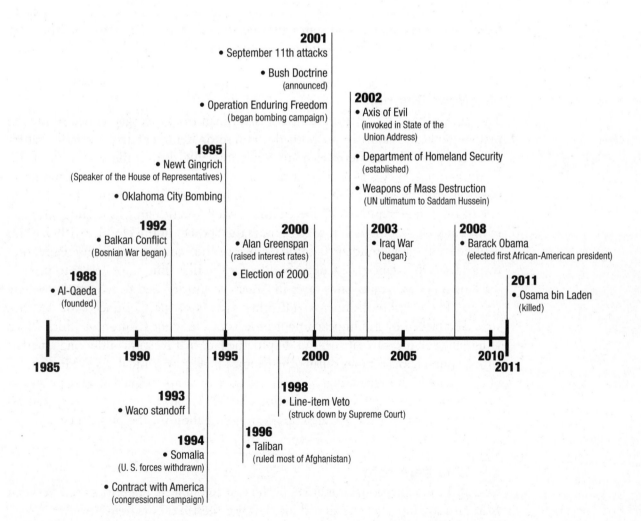

**2001**
• September 11th attacks

• Bush Doctrine
(announced)

• Operation Enduring Freedom
(began bombing campaign)

**2002**
• Axis of Evil
(invoked in State of the Union Address)

• Department of Homeland Security
(established)

• Weapons of Mass Destruction
(UN ultimatum to Saddam Hussein)

**1995**
• Newt Gingrich
(Speaker of the House of Representatives)

• Oklahoma City Bombing

**1992**
• Balkan Conflict
(Bosnian War began)

**2000**
• Alan Greenspan
(raised interest rates)

• Election of 2000

**2003**
• Iraq War
(began}

**2008**
• Barack Obama
(elected first African-American president)

**1988**
• Al-Qaeda
(founded)

**2011**
• Osama bin Laden
(killed)

1985    1990    1995    2000    2005    2010    2011

**1993**
• Waco standoff

**1998**
• Line-item Veto
(struck down by Supreme Court)

**1996**
• Taliban
(ruled most of Afghanistan)

**1994**
• Somalia
(U. S. forces withdrawn)

• Contract with America
(congressional campaign)

# Top 20 Things to Know

## 1 Contract with America

The 1994 the Republican Party won majorities in both houses of Congress for the first time in forty years. This victory was partly due to a series of ten proposals called the "Contract with America" that constituted the Republican agenda. After years of Big Government, the contract sought to decentralize power through deregulation, tax cuts, welfare reform, and a balanced federal budget. The House of Representatives passed nine of the measures, but the Senate passed only three. President Clinton had threatened to veto the more controversial measures if passed. Newt Gingrich, the chief architect of the contract and the congressman who became the new Speaker of the House, said the measures were intended "to restore the bonds of trust between the people and their elected representatives." One of the three points that became law required members of Congress to abide by the same workplace laws as regular Americans, especially those concerning sexual harassment. Another law reduced paperwork, and the final one banned the passage of unfunded mandates, or federal measures imposed on states with no source of funding. Laws to reform the legislative committee process and to install congressional term limits did not pass.

## 2 Newt Gingrich

This college history professor turned congressman from Georgia helped secure the first Republican majorities in both the House of Representatives and the Senate in forty years. The midterm election results in 1994 during the first term of Bill Clinton's presidency shocked political commentators and evoked more moderate positions from President Clinton who said "The era of Big Government is over." As one of the primary authors of the Contract with America and its leading advocate in the campaigns, Gingrich rose to become the Speaker of the House in 1995. With his leadership and President Clinton's move to the center, compromise legislation was enacted to balance the federal budget for the first time since 1969, to provide the largest cut in capital gains taxes in American history, and to reform the welfare system. These accomplishments and other aspects of the Contract with America were sidetracked by the impeachment process of President Clinton in which Newt Gingrich took obvious satisfaction despite the fact that he was conducting an affair with a young female staffer during the Monica Lewinsky scandal. As the figurehead of the Republican Party, Gingrich attracted criticism and resigned after Republicans lost ground in the next midterm elections. In 2011, Newt Gingrich announced his intentions to run for the 2012 Republican nomination for the presidency.

## 3 Line-item Veto

One of the Congressional initiatives of the new Republican majorities that President Clinton also supported and signed into law was the 1996 Line Item Veto Act. A line-item veto granted the president the power to selectively veto parts of a bill without having to veto a whole bill. The goal of such executive action was intended as a control on "pork barrel" spending, or the practice of attaching earmarks to legislation. Earmarks activate the expenditure of federal dollars for state and local projects and are attached as amendments to bills as one of the chief measures to funnel federal money into the home states of representatives and senators sponsoring the amendments. President Clinton used the line-item veto eighty-two times in signing just eleven bills before the Supreme Court struck down the measure as unconstitutional. Advocates for the establishment of a permanent line-item veto for the president say it is the most likely way to curb wasteful spending in Washington, D.C.

## 4 Waco Standoff

In 1993 agents with the federal Bureau of Alcohol, Tobacco, and Firearms surrounded a compound in Waco, Texas, occupied by a sect called the Branch Davidians that split from the Seventh-day Adventist Church. The leader of the movement, calling himself David Koresh, and others within the sect were suspected of child abuse and weapons violations. When the federal agents attempted to serve a warrant on the weapons charges, a shootout occurred in which both sides claimed the other fired first. The end result was the deaths of four agents and six Branch Davidians. A standoff then lasted fifty days until a second assault on the compound involving the Federal Bureau of Investigation employed an armored vehicle to open the wooden walls of the structure. A fire broke out that consumed the compound buildings and killed seventy-six people including twenty children. Both sides of the standoff claimed the other started the fire from which only nine Branch Davidians escaped alive.

## 5 Oklahoma City Bombing

Timothy McVeigh and Terry Nichols, with the complicity of several other individuals, constructed a bomb in a rental van and detonated the device next to the Alfred P. Murrah Building in Oklahoma City in 1995. The two men were Army veterans motivated by a desire to avenge the deaths of the people who died in the tragic encounter at Waco, Texas. The Oklahoma City domestic terrorist attack was the largest in American history until the September 11 attacks, and the blast killed 168 people including children in the facility's day care. McVeigh and Nichols represented what was called "right-wing militias," or groups of conspiracy theorists who armed themselves in fear of an oppressive federal government. McVeigh was captured and executed, and Nichols was given 160 consecutive life sentences in prison without the possibility of parole. President Clinton personally helped memorialize the victims and told the nation that a restriction of civil liberties would be necessary in the wake of such an attack.

## 6 Somalia

George H. W. Bush had ordered American troops into Somalia in 1992 to help distribute food during a severe famine amid factional warfare. The United Nations declared that a state of anarchy existed and took over control of food relief. When Bill Clinton became president, he changed the mission in Somalia to one of hunting down the most violent warlords who had caused the collapse of civilization in the first place. When militants shot down a Black Hawk helicopter during a raid in 1993 in search of one of the warlords, other American troops came to the rescue. In the ensuing firefight, eighteen U.S. soldiers were killed and some of their bodies were desecrated. In a Carter-style vacillation, Clinton ordered fifteen thousand troops into Somalia but then pulled them out within five months to seek a political solution.

## 7 Balkan Conflict

After the fall of the Soviet Union, the communist puppet-dictator of Yugoslavia was left dead in a street. The Balkans came apart. Various ethnic groups including the Croats, Serbs, Bosnians, Kosovars, and Albanians, many of whom were Muslims, all wanted autonomy in breakaway states. The North Atlantic Treaty Organization (NATO) stepped in, and President Clinton promised American support. Slobodan Milosevic, the Serbian leader, practiced ruthless displacement and genocide tactics that harkened back to those of Adolph Hitler. Three thousand Muslims were later discovered buried in a mass grave. Trying to avoid "another Vietnam," Clinton disallowed any American troops to go in on the ground. American pilots were given the mission to keep Kosovo safe for the Kosovars from no lower than 15,000 feet. Just as in Vietnam, a campaign of aerial bombardment proved ineffective against a determined enemy. Milosevic only agreed to negotiations after accomplishing what he called "ethnic cleansing" of Serbia. Another limited military engagement proved problematic because of fears that latent NATO versus Warsaw Pact tension would erupt in a larger war. The most internationally destabilizing event occurred when American aircraft accidentally bombed the Chinese embassy, straining relations with a rising superpower.

## 8 George W. Bush

The Republican Party's choice for a candidate for the Election of 2000 was not as clear. They looked desperately for a candidate who had strong conservative positions against gun control, abortion, and taxes. They found him in a surprising place, George H. W. Bush's family. George W. Bush graduated as a C student from Yale University and became a lieutenant in the Air National Guard where he flew F-102 fighter planes. He took his education more seriously in graduate school and became the first president to earn an MBA from Harvard. After a wild youth, where his wife told him to choose alcohol or her (he chose her), he failed in the oil business but succeeded as the part-owner/manager of the Texas Rangers professional baseball team. After serving as governor of Texas, he campaigned for the presidency becoming the first modern candidate to specifically name Jesus Christ as the chief influence on his life. The Reagan conservative revolution seemed to have new life, and George W. Bush became the greatest political fundraiser in American history, breaking the records set by Bill Clinton by a wide margin.

## 9  Weapons of Mass Destruction

In an era with attacks like the explosion inside the World Trade Center in New York City in 1993 and the Oklahoma City Bombing in 1995, Americans were afraid that terrorists would obtain even more serious weapons in the form of atomic, chemical, or biological weapons of mass destruction (WMDs). Saddam Hussein had used chemical weapons against his own people during the Kurdish uprising, and the United Nations attempted to enforce a series of inspections after the Persian Gulf War to ensure that he was not trying to rebuild his supply. When George W. Bush, the son of George H. W. Bush, won the Election of 2000, he and Tony Blair of the United Kingdom actively pursued the accountability of Hussein to live up to the commitments mandated by the United Nations. Although a direct attack on the United States from a rogue nation was unlikely, federal authorities feared unscrupulous leaders of what Bush called the "Axis of Evil" in a State of the Union Address in 2002—Iraq, Iran, and North Korea—would develop WMDs and allow terrorists to purchase them for smuggling into the United States.

## 10  Osama bin Laden

A member of a wealthy Saudi Arabian family, bin Laden financed the founding of al-Qaeda and became the organization's leader by 1988 after fighting against Soviet aggression in Afghanistan. He adhered to a militant form of Islam that interpreted the teachings of Mohammed about jihad to sanction making war against civilians even through the means of terrorist attacks. Before he could be brought to justice for his role in supporting the attacks on American embassies in Tanzania and Kenya in 1998, he authorized the September 11 attacks on American soil. An American invasion of Afghanistan after these terrorist attacks was intended to remove the Taliban from control of the country because of their harboring of bin Laden and al-Qaeda operatives. The mission of these attacks was also to hunt, capture, or kill bin Laden and other members of al-Qaeda's leadership. By the time U.S. intelligence operations could locate bin Laden, he was living in a secret compound in Pakistan. U.S. Navy SEALs and Central Intelligence Agency operatives stormed the compound in 2011 and killed Osama bin Laden when he resisted capture. Bin Laden's body was buried at sea.

## 11  Al-Qaeda

Or "the Base" in Arabic, is a terrorist organization founded by Osama bin Laden around 1988. After organizing to resist the invasion of Afghanistan by the Soviet Union, al-Qaeda expanded its goals to installing a Muslim Caliphate to control the world. As extremists from within Islam, the leaders of al-Qaeda first seek to purge the Muslim world from what they perceive as corruption from Western influences and secularizing elements. Al-Qaeda has trained over five thousand militants and cooperates with other terrorist organizations to conduct assassinations, bombings, hijackings, and kidnappings including suicide attacks in the quest for martyrdom. Operatives are organized in cells established across the world, and the organization is financed by the personal wealth of Osama bin Laden, the profits from various front businesses and Muslim charities, and direct donations.

## 12 Election of 2000

George W. Bush and Albert Gore Jr. ran close campaigns that ultimately hinged on the twenty-five Electoral College votes from Florida. Disputed elections returns showed Bush winning the state with a lead of only 1,700 votes out of over six million cast. In automatic recounts the margin was dropped to around three hundred votes in an election where Gore had won over five hundred thousand more votes nationally than did Bush. All eyes were on the Electoral College, however, and on the authenticity of the Florida vote. The Florida Supreme Court said manual recounting was permissible, but not all counties completed the recounts. When the period for recounting was over, the Bush lead had actually increased to 587 votes at which point the case went to the Supreme Court. In a 7 to 2 ruling the Court said that Florida should not have authorized recounts, and in a 5 to 4 decision declared that recounting only some of the votes amounted to a violation of equal protection under the law. The Supreme Court settled the election because Albert Gore decided not to pursue further appeals and conceded the election to Bush. Later recounts completed by investigative journalists concluded that George W. Bush would have maintained a narrow victory.

## 13 September 11 Attacks

The worst terrorist attacks in U.S. history occurred on September 11, 2001, when nineteen al-Qaeda operatives hijacked four jetliners and crashed them rather than merely making demands. Two planes struck the Twin Towers of the World Trade Center in New York City, and the fires ignited by the jet fuel eventually caused both towers to collapse. Another hijacked plane was flown into the Pentagon in Washington, D.C. The fourth plane was en route to the national capital and likely headed for an attack on the White House or the Capitol Building when passengers aboard the plane attacked the hijackers resulting in the plane's crashing in a field in Pennsylvania. Nearly three thousand victims, including rescue personnel, died in the crashes or as a result of the collapse of the Twin Towers. The attacks amounted to the first blow struck against the continental United States by a foreign enemy since the War of 1812. The United States retaliated by launching Operation Enduring Freedom in Afghanistan in what George W. Bush called the War on Terror. The attacks dealt a severe blow to the American economy and resulted in a streamlining of federal intelligence, national security, and law enforcement agencies into the Department of Homeland Security. Osama bin Laden and al-Qaeda claimed credit for the attacks and continued to plot other attacks on the United States, all of which have been thwarted so far.

## 14 Department of Homeland Security

Formed after the September 11 attacks, the Department of Homeland Security (DHS) quickly became the third largest department in the presidential cabinet.

Whereas the Department of Defense oversees the projection of American military force, the DHS is responsible for the protection of the borders and domestic territory of the United States and its protectorates. The chief mission of the DHS is in preventing and responding to terrorist attacks, but it also handles immigration and, among other issues, responses to natural disaster. Similarly to the reorganization and formation of federal agencies under the National Security Act in response to the new dangers during the Cold War, the formation of the DHS attempted to consolidate the efforts of the government to protect Americans and American interests in the "War on Terror." Twenty-two government agencies were placed under the department's umbrella, partly to avoid the failure to communicate across agencies that led to the success of the September 11 attacks.

## 15 Bush Doctrine

In the wake of the September 11 attacks, President Bush declared that the United States would find who had orchestrated the attacks and bring them to justice. After several events targeting the United States and its interests abroad since the Persian Gulf War, Bush declared that a War on Terror had reached a turning point. In a speech before Congress he said "We will pursue nations that provide aid or safe haven to terrorism. Every nation, in every region, now has a decision to make. Either you are with us, or you are with the terrorists. From this day forward, any nation that continues to harbor or support terrorism will be regarded by the United States as a hostile regime." The Bush Doctrine was used as a justification for labeling Iran, Iraq, and North Korea examples of an "Axis of Evil" and for the invasions of Afghanistan and Iraq. In the War on Terror the emphasis shifted from retaliating for attacks to preemptively striking to prevent attacks discovered by intelligence investigations.

## 16 Operation Enduring Freedom

Roughly one month after the September 11 terrorist attacks, the United States and the United Kingdom invaded Afghanistan because the Taliban regime in power there had sheltered and supported not only the 9/11 terrorists but Osama bin Laden himself. Freedom fighters from within Afghanistan allied with the invading Western powers to overthrow the repressive fundamentalist Islamic regime. While originally successful in displacing the Taliban and installing a democratic government in Afghanistan, the traditional instability of the region and a resurgence of the Taliban have required the continued presence of American military forces to maintain the freedom of the Afghan people and to prevent further terrorist attacks.

## 17 Taliban

These fundamentalist Islamist militants took over the majority of Afghanistan by 1996 and imposed Sharia law to such an extent that their major critics prior to their sheltering of Osama bin Laden were other Islamic leaders. Once the United States deposed them, most Taliban fighters fled to Pakistan where they received support and were allowed to regroup. As the war in Afghanistan continued, al-Qaeda and other organizations assisted the Taliban in counterattacking in their homeland through terrorist attacks on Afghanistan civilians. In 2010 alone they killed almost 2,500 people. Taliban leaders are the targets of special forces operations and predator drone attacks, but many fear the Taliban will return to power upon the withdrawal of American military forces.

# 18 Iraq War

After the Persian Gulf War the United Nations ordered Saddam Hussein to get rid of his weapons of mass destruction and not to build more, and inspectors were supposed to confirm his progress. A no-fly zone was established and enforced mostly with American and British war planes. After the September 11 attacks, the United States put increasing pressure on Hussein to comply with United Nations inspections. Because Hussein remained defiant the United Nations authorized a buildup of troops on the Iraqi border. When Hussein still refused to comply, President Bush issued an ultimatum for Saddam Hussein and his sons to leave Iraq in 2003. When they did not, Bush ordered the American invasion and bombing of Iraq that became known as the Iraq War. American and allied forces deposed Saddam Hussein, killed his sons, and captured the dictator by 2004. A new government in Iraq executed Hussein, but Iraqi insurgents and militant terrorists have kept up a steady series of attacks using improvised explosive devices (IEDs) and other means. Before leaving office, George W. Bush ordered a surge of American forces and sent an additional thirty thousand troops into Iraq in an attempt to stabilize the situation. The United States is now attempting under President Barack Obama to turn over the national security of Iraq to the Iraqis.

# 19 Axis of Evil

This phrase from a 2002 State of the Union address by George W. Bush identified Iran, Iraq, and North Korea as the chief rogue nations left in the world, or at least pointed to them as prime examples of latent problems facing the United States. All three nations had a record of sponsoring terrorism and attempting to produce or secure atomic, biological, or chemical weapons of mass destruction. North Korea remains one of the most repressive communist governments in the modern world, and attempts to negotiate with the government to curtail its missile and nuclear weapons programs have been largely rebuffed. Recent conflicts between North and South Korea have threatened to destabilize all of East Asia including Japan. Iraq remained a fragile government as the United States withdrew its military forces from the country in the wake of the Iraq War that led to the execution of Saddam Hussein. The encouraging outcomes of the "Arab Spring" uprisings in various countries in North Africa and the Middle East have not as yet manifested successful results in Iran, which remains a revolutionary Islamic republic under the supreme leadership of Ali Khamenei despite mass demonstrations in 2009. The president of Iran, Mahmoud Ahmadenijad, maintains that Iran should rise as the chief regional power and disregard the United States and Israel as checks on Iranian control of the Middle East. Despite his stated belief that the Holocaust never occurred during World War II and that Israel should be destroyed, Ahmadenijad assures the world that the Iranian nuclear program is for research, domestic power generation, and other civilian purposes.

# 20 Barack H. Obama

President Obama followed a similar path to the presidency to that of Bill Clinton by studying and teaching constitutional law and participating in community activism and state politics. Like Ronald Reagan he achieved national political prominence by delivering a speech at his party's convention in 2004. He won a Senate seat for Illinois in that same year. In 2008, he fought off a serious challenge from Hillary Rodham Clinton for the Democratic nomination for president and beat Senator John McCain in the general election to become the first African-American president of the United States. His accomplishments to date as president include the authorization of the expenditure of nearly $800 billion in economic stimulus in an attempt to reverse a recession and passage of national health care legislation. He has placed two justices on the Supreme Court and guided the process whereby homosexuals can serve openly in the U.S. military. He redirected the efforts of the National Aeronautics and Space Administration in the renewal of missions to the moon to more earthbound research. President Obama has stated his goals to end the wars in Afghanistan and Iraq (done in 2012) and authorized the missions to support the Libyan revolution that led to the capture and killing of Muammar Qaddafi and the mission that killed Osama bin Laden. Like his predecessors Reagan and Clinton, President Obama began his administration with high approval ratings that have steadily dropped, but like Reagan and Clinton he announced his intention to run for a second term as president.

## *The Big Picture*

1. After winning the presidency Bill Clinton lost the Congress to the Republican Party, and the balance struck between the executive and legislative branches caused the president to announce the end of Big Government.

2. Despite the dramatically expanding economy of the Clinton years, domestic terrorism and foreign conflicts in Somalia and the Balkans undermined a feeling of prosperity.

3. After a constitutional crisis surrounding the disputed Election of 2000, George W. Bush intended to spend his presidency building on the domestic reforms presaged in the Republican Contract with America.

4. Terrorist attacks on September 11, 2001, redirected the Bush administration toward launching the War on Terror and revamping homeland security.

5. The Bush Doctrine of retaliatory and preemptive attacks on terrorists and the nations that harbor them led to wars in both Afghanistan and Iraq, the consequences of which are still uncertain during the Obama administration.

# American Scientific and Technological Advances

*Be it known that we, ORVILLE WRIGHT and WILBUR WRIGHT, citizens of the United States . . . have invented certain new and useful Improvements in Flying-Machines. . . .*
—Wright Brothers' patent, 1906

**1744**
Benjamin Franklin (founded American Philosophical Society)

**1749**
Conestoga wagon (first built)

**1780**
Scientific societies (John Adams founded the American Academy of Arts and Sciences)

**1793**
Samuel Slater (opened first textile factory)

**1794**
Eli Whitney (patented cotton gin)

**1807**
Robert Fulton (built first commercial steamboat)

**1827**
John James Audubon (*Birds of America* first printed)

**1830**
Steam Locomotive (in operation)

**1834**
Cyrus McCormick (patented mechanical reaper)

**1836**
Smithsonian Institution (charitable trust founded)
Samuel Colt (patented a "revolving gun")

**1845**
Sewing machine (invented by Elias Howe)

**1847**
Samuel F. B. Morse (patented telegraph)

**1854**
Elisha G. Otis (invented elevator brake)

**1857**
Oliver F. Winchester (organized New Haven Arms Company)
William Kelly (patented steel-making process)

**1862**
Gatling gun (patented by Richard Gatling)

**1867**
Typewriter (invented)

**1874**
Barbed wire (patented by Joseph Glidden)

**1876**
Alexander Graham Bell (patented telephone)
Thomas Edison (built first industrial research laboratory)

**1888**
Camera (first Kodak sold)

**1893**
Automobile (first American manufacturing company founded)

**1897**
Radio (Nikola Tesla received first patents)

**1903**
Airplane (first successful flight)

**1916**
X-ray (improved tube patented)

**1926**
Rocket (first liquid-fueled launch)

**1939**
Television (demonstrated at World's Fair)

**1940**
Helicopter (first mass-produced model)

**1942**
Atomic energy (first sustained nuclear chain reaction)

**1943**
Penicillin (Margaret Rousseau designed first commercial production facility)

**1947**
Computer (first patented device ENIAC I)

**1954**
Transistor (first silicon version produced)

**1955**
Jonas Salk (introduced polio vaccine)

**1981**
Space shuttle (first orbital flight)

**1990**
Hubble space telescope (placed in orbit)

# Top 36 Things to Know

## 1 Benjamin Franklin

Franklin was more than a statesman. His electrical experiments discovered plus and minus charges and explained lightning as an electrical phenomenon and thus put American science on the map in the respected Royal Society of London. His inventions include a musical instrument called the armonica, the Franklin stove, the lightning rod, bifocal lenses, and the rocking chair. He conceived of daylight savings time and was the first scientist to measure and map the Gulf Stream. He invented an odometer to make post offices more efficient, and he tried to better society with libraries and to protect it with fire departments.

## 2 Scientific Societies

The American Academy of Arts and Sciences was founded as early as 1780 in Boston by John Adams. New Jersey founded a Society for the Promotion of Agriculture, Commerce, and Art in 1781. Other agricultural societies, chemical societies, and museums were founded by the end of the eighteenth century in an effort to elevate the useful discoveries of science and technology. Such organizations published journals that spread ideas and provided an incentive for research and development of inventions and innovations.

## 3 John James Audubon

Audubon was a storekeeper with drawing talent who turned his bankruptcy in the Panic of 1819 into a quest to draw and paint all of America's birds. His dramatic paintings appeared in Birds of America as early as 1827 but went through several reprints. His life story of roving about and adding to the advance of descriptive zoology appealed to readers during the Romantic period, and he made a living from selling his books that eventually turned to other fauna. His work bred in Americans a love of natural history, especially in the careers of zoologists like Louis Agassiz and naturalists like Henry David Thoreau, John Muir, and Theodore Roosevelt.

## 4 Smithsonian Institution

James Smithson, an English scientist, gave his fortune upon his death to found "an establishment for the increase and diffusion of knowledge" in Washington, D.C. The Congress accepted the gift and founded the Smithsonian Institution in 1846. The Smithsonian is now the largest museum and laboratory complex in the world housing nineteen museums, the National Zoo, and nine research facilities.

## 5  Samuel Slater

Slater has been called the father of the American Industrial Revolution. He came to the United States in 1789 as the first person who knew both how to make and to operate cloth-making machines. His first water-powered textile mill was operational by 1793 in Rhode Island. In a common system established in New England mills, Slater built three mill villages that housed his machines but also his workers, and whole families worked in the mills and shopped in the village stores. Textile manufacturing was the first large-scale process sparking industrial growth in both England and America.

## 6  Eli Whitney

Whitney solved the problem of making the production of cotton lucrative through the automation of the separation of the seeds from the fibers with his cotton gin. His original design could produce 50 pounds of cotton fibers per day, and this feat revolutionized the cultivation of cotton to become the central economic reality of many southern states. The rise of the Cotton Kingdom brought on a rise in the demand for African slaves to accomplish the other tedious tasks of growing cotton. Legal troubles hampered Whitney's production of his machines, but he grew wealthy from the manufacture of muskets for the government using interchangeable parts, a key facet of the principles of modern mass production.

## 7  Robert Fulton

Fulton was an artist born in Pennsylvania who also turned a love of mechanical things into the marriage of steam power to boats. He imported a steam engine from England and proved its feasibility aboard his first vessel, the *Clermont*, by 1807. Fulton had invented a submersible boat for naval warfare that he called a torpedo, but could not find a nation willing to purchase them. He therefore focused on a transportation business providing transit from New York City to Albany at 5 miles per hour. The use of steam-powered vessels spread across the United States and beyond as the most significant step in the transportation revolution next to the railroad.

## 8  Conestoga Wagon

This heavy-duty wagon was named for the Conestoga area of Pennsylvania where it was developed to carry goods back and forth across the Allegheny Mountains. In use as early as 1720, it remained the chief method of moving heavy goods until railroads, and a team of six horses could carry as much as 8 tons. A lighter version known as a prairie schooner became the classic means of transportation for pioneers as they traveled west. A canvas covering kept the elements out while allowing ventilation, and the boat-like shape of the wagon made it easier for horses or oxen to pull the wagon across rivers and streams. Wagon trains of travelers congregated together for safety. The invention of this device was how the West was won.

## 9 Cyrus McCormick

The first patent for this Virginian and mechanical genius was for a hillside plow in 1831. He then developed a mechanical reaping machine that used animal power to ease the job of harvesting grain. After his iron foundry failed in the Panic of 1837, McCormick began licensing manufacturers to build and sell his improved reaper. When quality control proved inadequate with this system, McCormick opened his own factory in Chicago in 1847. Later innovations in his machinery combined the process of harvesting and threshing grain in large machines drawn by as many as forty to sixty mules.

## 10 Samuel Colt

Colt was born in Connecticut and went to sea for adventure. His love of mechanical devices, however, led to his invention of the revolver, a firearm that could be loaded with multiple shots and fired rapidly. He obtained patents and operated a factory as early as 1837, but it was not until around 1855 that the U.S. Army increased the demand for his revolvers and made his business thrive. Colt developed new machinery and the largest firearm factory in the world just in time for the Civil War. Though he died in 1862, his weapons had become famous, and the Colt .45 caliber Peacemaker was the weapon of choice for gunslingers, lawmen, and cavalry soldiers alike in settling the West.

## 11 Steam Locomotive

The greatest transportation revolution until the invention of the automobile was the development of the steam locomotive. Although the steam engine and steam-powered vehicles were invented in England, American John Stevens demonstrated a practical railroad as early as 1826, three years before a railroad was developed in Great Britain. Peter Cooper made the Tom Thumb, the first American steam locomotive in 1830. Continual improvements in locomotives led to faster speeds and heavier loads as railroads crisscrossed the East during the 1850s, and the first transcontinental railroad helped open the West by 1869. George Pullman developed a comfortable sleeping car by 1857. Railroads remain such an integral part of the American economy that many foresee the use of high-speed bullet trains as the next significant step in revolutionized transportation.

## 12 Oliver F. Winchester

The only weapon that could rival the Colt revolver as the most important American firearm was the lever-action rifle developed by Oliver Winchester. Winchester gathered together various inventions like a self-contained brass cartridge, a tubular magazine, and the lever-action to create the repeating rifle used in the latter part of the Civil War. Improvements in manufacturing processes maintained quality while attaining the capacity for mass production. Settlement of the West was not entirely possible due to the ferocity of the Plains Indians until soldiers and even settlers could have a repeating revolver and a repeating rifle, especially when the two fired the same type of ammunition.

## 13 William Kelly

Kelly was the American ironworker who invented the process of making steel more easily by forcing air through molten iron. He made steel this way as early as 1850, but Sir Henry Bessemer patented a similar process in England and in America by 1855. By 1857 Kelly received a patent in America that supplanted Bessemer's, but the Panic of 1857 thwarted his efforts to make a successful steel plant. Kelly formed a later company bearing his name that competed with a rival plant that used the Bessemer process, but when the two combined their operations and Kelly's patent was extended in 1871, William Kelly finally achieved financial success. His career is the classic study in how trial-and-error innovation, patent law, and economic conditions can spell either success or ruin.

## 14 Elisha G. Otis

Louis Sullivan's skyscraper would hardly have been a practical invention had it not been for the elevator brake invented by Elisha Otis in 1852. Powered hoists existed previously, but Otis devised an automatic spring mechanism to catch the elevator car if the rope or cables suspending it failed. Otis demonstrated his invention at the famous Crystal Palace Exposition in 1854 after having the rope suspending his elevator cut dramatically before a rapt audience. Otis's device and the steel-framed structure developed by Sullivan transformed the look of cities across the world beginning with the ten-story Home Insurance Building built in Chicago in the 1880s.

## 15 Samuel F. B. Morse

The other famous painter-turned-inventor besides Robert Fulton, Samuel Morse patented a device that used electricity to send messages over wires in 1840 using his code consisting of long and short electric impulses. By 1844 a telegraph line was constructed between Baltimore and Washington, D.C., over which the first message, "What hath God wrought?" was sent. By 1861 a telegraph wire stretched from ocean to ocean across America, and by 1866 a transatlantic cable connected the United States and Europe. Morse is the reason that a communications revolution accompanied the transportation revolution, both of which dramatically boosted the eighteenth-century American economy.

## 16 Alexander Graham Bell

Bell was an educator of the deaf who opened a school in Boston in 1872. Bell's method used various devices to train his students to speak. His knowledge of acoustics led him to experiment with the telegraph invented by Morse. He demonstrated the first practical telephone in 1876 and founded the Bell Telephone Company the next year. His later work paved the way for the transmission of sound by light, metal detectors, and the phonograph. Communications thus took a giant leap forward in becoming accessible to everyone just by transmitting the human voice, and Bell company laboratories became a leading research facility.

## 17 Barbed Wire

The West could not have been tamed once it was won except for various patented stages in the invention of barbed wire. Joseph Glidden received the final patent in 1871. Ranchers therefore had a practical way of organizing the use of their private grasslands without the threat of free-ranging herds destroying fodder. The use of barbed wire ended the nostalgic lifestyles of cowboys herding cattle over long drives on public lands. Barbed wire also took on entirely new uses in fortifications in the trenches of World War I.

## 18 Gatling Gun

Richard Gatling studied the problem of battlefield injuries and deaths and came up with an interesting solution: the manufacture of the first successful machine gun. He believed his device would reduce the size of armies and therefore make war less deadly. The Gatling gun used six rotating barrels to fire ammunition at a rate of six hundred rounds per minute without overheating. His automatic weapon saw some use in the Civil War but was not adopted by the U.S. Army officially until 1866. The Gatling gun then played a role in the Great Plains warfare with American Indians and saw use around the world. Most battlefield machine guns eventually reverted to the use of a single barrel to achieve greater mobility, but Gatling's design formed the basis for several modern weapons mounted in aircraft.

## 19 Typewriter

Before the computer the most revolutionary tool for business was the typewriter invented in 1866 by Christopher Sholes. The device was manufactured by the Remington Arms Company. As typists' speed increased, Sholes changed the keyboard to spread out letters that were used frequently and created the QWERTY keyboard in use today. Touch typing, or the ability to type using all ten fingers while looking away from the keys, was developed by a court stenographer in 1878 and dramatically increased typing speed. The telephone and the typewriter together provided the first large boost to the employment of women outside the home in positions as telephone operators who manually connected calls and office clerks who typed business correspondence.

## 20 Sewing Machine

The invention of a practical sewing machine by Elias Howe in 1846 made possible the mass production of clothing for the first time. In 1851, Isaac Singer downsized Howe's industrial machine and added some technical innovations to produce a workable model for home use. Patent disputes between the two inventors were settled by royalty payments and then the formation of a company that combined several patents and created mass production. The first electric sewing machine was marketed in 1889 and by 1905 was in wide use across the country. The sewing machine was another labor-saving device that helped provide women with freedom from laborious hand stitching but also an employment opportunity outside the home.

## 21 Thomas Edison

Edison was homeschooled because he was considered a slow learner, but he became a telegraph operator in 1863 and pursued a passion for chemistry. By 1869 he received his first patent while working for the Western Union Telegraph Company for a device that could record votes. He invested in an electrical engineering firm that sold out and granted him a small fortune with which he started his own company. By 1876 he had founded the world's first research laboratory by hiring assistants with whom he collaborated in all his further inventions. Among these inventions were the incandescent electric lamp, an improved motion picture projector, storage battery, dictaphone, mimeograph, phonograph, and an electric locomotive. In all, Edison's laboratory received over one thousand patents, and his company was the foundation for General Electric Corporation.

## 22 Automobile

No one person invented the automobile. Over one hundred thousand separate patents led to the modern car. After steam-powered automobiles and a series of attempts at using internal combustion engines, two German engineers named Daimler and Benz developed successful four-wheeled gasoline-powered automobiles. French manufacturers like Peugeot were the first to make practical gasoline automobiles for sale but their products, along with those of the first American manufacturers (Duryea and Oldsmobile), were toys for the rich. Ransome Eli Olds had begun a rudimentary assembly line in Detroit, Michigan, but the first conveyor-belt-style assembly was installed by Henry Ford by 1914. Ford had built cars for his own company since 1903, but the assembly line sped up production until a Model T Ford was completed from start to finish in ninety-three minutes. That level of production dramatically lowered the cost of automobiles and brought them within the reach of the average American. Ford's plant had made fifteen million Model Ts by 1927. The transportation revolution turned into a social revolution as widespread mobility led to hundreds of other industries to accommodate the needs of travelers.

## 23 Camera

Two Frenchmen developed a device as early as the 1830s that used light coming through an orifice to draw images on chemicals on metal plates, but the process bore the name, daguerreotype, of the one who produced more lasting images in less time. American George Eastman invented a flexible celluloid film in 1889 that when coated with emulsions produced negative images that could then be used to make photographs. Eastman invented a small box camera that he marketed as the Kodak camera for use by amateur photographers. Eastman's company developed the negatives and produced photographs, but also sold chemicals so that individuals could produce their own photos. Innovations in the camera, lenses, flashbulbs, and film (including color by 1940) continued apace until the invention of the digital camera largely relegated Eastman's process to a hobby for purists. The widespread use of the camera was a paradigm shift in art, journalism, and history and, like the automobile, launched several spinoff industries.

# 24 Radio

French and German scientists discovered electromagnetic waves, but an American named Mahlon Loomis was the first person to demonstrate their use in sending a signal in 1866. In 1896, Italian Guglielmo Marconi was the first person to use radio waves to send a message in Morse code. Marconi's "radiotelegraph" received a message across the Atlantic Ocean by 1902. American Lee Deforest invented a sensitive radio receiver that amplified signals, thus the amplitude-modulated, or AM, radio was born and could receive many signals on different frequencies. American radio patents were used by the government exclusively through World War I, but their private inventors held them again in 1919 and continued development. Radio stations capable of broadcasting voice communications and music existed in America by 1915, and American Edwin Armstrong invented frequency-modulated equipment, or FM, that could dramatically quiet static. With the invention of the transistor by Bell Laboratories in 1947, the radio, along with all other electronic equipment, could be shrunk in size. In 1965, the first FM antenna system in the world designed to allow several FM stations to broadcast simultaneously was installed atop the Empire State Building in New York City. The collected impact of all of these stages of the development of radio technology led also to microwaves, cordless devices like phones, and remote control devices for televisions and other machines.

# 25 Airplane

Bicycle repairmen Orville and Wilbur Wright began tinkering with gliders prior to 1900 in a quest to create a flying machine. The brothers carefully modeled the curved wings of their Flyer that were able to change their shape by warping after the wings of birds. Their gliders grew in size until they launched a biplane version at Kitty Hawk, North Carolina, which they used as a testing site because of its remoteness, many sand dunes, and consistent winds. They successfully launched a manned glider in 1900. As design problems became more difficult, the Wrights invented a wind tunnel to test their designs. The first successful manned, powered flight lasted twelve seconds when they launched their Flyer off a downhill track at Kitty Hawk in 1903. The first death in a Wright Flyer occurred to one of Orville's passengers in 1908, but the American government began purchasing airplanes the next year. Airplanes were capable of being armed with machine guns by 1912 and began to make an impact on warfare in World War I. Another bicycle mechanic named Glenn Curtiss invented ailerons, a simpler method of steering airplanes than the Wright's wing-warping method. With continual innovations and the eventual manufacture using aluminum, planes developed from reconnaissance duties to serious aerial bombing. Commercial applications of air travel were not developed until after World War II.

# 26 X-ray

German physicist Wilhelm Roentgen discovered what he called X-rays being generated from a cathode ray generator in 1895. He became world famous by taking the first X-ray image, an "X-ray" of his wife's hand. The revolutionary medical implications of this technology became evident when American William Coolidge invented a better cathode tube using tungsten filaments. The Coolidge tube received a patent in 1916 and created the field of radiology because it could discern tissues more clearly and help in locating tumors.

# 27 Television

After studying the work of European scientists who developed vacuum tubes and the cathode ray tube, American Allen B. Du Mont made the first durable and commercially practical cathode ray tube for television. Cathode ray tubes produced images on their phosphorescent surfaces by channeling beams of electrons. Du Mont developed the high-speed equipment necessary to manufacture and test his tubes by 1932. He founded a production company in 1934 and an experimental broadcasting station in New York City as early as 1938. As he predicted, his work and that of the other inventors who developed television technology brought "about a new industry, a new means of entertainment, a new marketing medium, and a new age." Developments in antennae and tuning technology increased the feasibility of television through the 1940s, and color television was available as early as 1953. By 1960 the vast majority of Americans had at least one television in their homes.

# 28 Transistor

The transistor has been called the most important invention of the twentieth century. John Bardeen and Walter Brattain were researchers working for Bell Laboratories when they conceived of the idea of making a three-point contact using a semiconductor. An innovation made by William Shockley made the devices easier to manufacture, and the three men received the Nobel Prize in physics in 1956. Transistors accomplished the same task as vacuum tubes but without having to warm up. They also gave off less heat and took up a fraction of the space, so solid state electronic equipment could be smaller and easier to keep cool. Accomplishments of the transistor include tremendous commercial success in the handheld transistor radio as well as national scientific success with the only successful landings of men on the moon.

# 29 Computer

Two Harvard professors made the first modern computer for use by the U.S. Navy in 1944. The device, called the Mark I, filled a large room and weighed five tons. The Army sponsored the next generation, the ENIAC 1, which still filled a large room but was faster because it used vacuum tubes. The vacuum tubes were replaced by transistors by 1948, the transistors by the integrated circuit ("The Chip") in 1958, and the integrated circuit by the microprocessor in 1971 (the same year the "floppy" disk was introduced). Each advance in technology made computers smaller and faster. Small personal computers were first sold as kits, but Steve Wozniak and Steve Jobs began to manufacture Apple computers for the average consumer in 1976. Radio Shack and IBM marketed competitive models, and by 1981 Bill Gates offered DOS, the operating system that IBM used to allow the average person to use computers without knowing the BASIC computing language. Gates's Microsoft software company developed Windows in 1985 to compete with the user-friendly design of Macintosh computers. With computers being used to design computers, the pace of change became so fast that hardware and software suffered obsolescence every five years or less. No other technology in the history of the world has ever increased the productivity of mankind more or faster, with the possible exception of written language.

# 30 Penicillin

In 1928, Scottish scientist Alexander Fleming discovered by accident that cultures of bacteria were destroyed by a mold from which penicillin was derived. British scientists developed a technique for growing penicillin that was perfected by American scientist Andrew Moyer for production by 1943. Using a strain of the mold found in a cantaloupe in an American market, Moyer's process produced a stronger antibiotic result with much faster production, dropping the price for a dose of penicillin from $20.00 to fifty-five cents by 1946. Moyer was granted a patent for the production of penicillin in 1948, but as early as 1947 certain bacteria began mutating to acquire resistance to the drug. Hence began the war scientists wage to this day, saving millions of lives while trying to stay ahead in antibiotic research and development.

# 31 Atomic Energy

Once X-rays were recognized as a form of radiation, research by Pierre and Marie Curie and others uncovered the principles of radioactivity. Albert Einstein described the relationship between energy and matter theoretically by 1905. Understanding of the physics of the atom increased through the 1930s, and American scientist Enrico Fermi experimented with uranium testing the theory that nuclear fission could release tremendous energy in a sustained nuclear reaction. Einstein wrote a letter to Franklin Roosevelt stating that German scientists were working on the use of nuclear energy for military applications, and by 1942 the U.S. government devoted tremendous resources to the Manhattan Project, the attempt to construct atomic bombs before the Nazis. Enrico Fermi achieved the first controlled nuclear chain reaction in a graphite reactor at the University of Chicago before the end of 1942. While scientists worked in Oak Ridge, Tennessee, and Hanford, Washington, to produce the atomic material to fuel bombs, J. Robert Oppenheimer worked at the Los Alamos laboratory in New Mexico to design the bombs. In July of 1945 the first atomic bomb was tested at Los Alamos and was successful. The United States dropped two nuclear bombs on Japan before the Japanese government surrendered to end World War II. By 1960 nuclear reactors existed in the United States for the commercial production of electrical power that, since the tsunami-induced crisis in Japan in 2011, awaits further development as an energy solution.

# 32 Helicopter

After Russian Igor Sikorsky invented the first successful helicopter by 1940, American inventor Stanley Hiller Jr. made the first helicopter with all-metal rotor blades in 1944. Hiller's helicopter was thus much faster and more durable. Hiller proved the feasibility of helicopter flight by flying one across the United States in 1949. The Bell Aircraft company produced the first helicopter to have a bubble canopy. Bell helicopters and others revolutionized everything from law enforcement, traffic reporting, and tourism to ambulance service and the method of fighting wars. Later helicopters were tremendous antitank weapons and also crucial transport aircraft for the insertion and extraction of infantry troops in every war since the Vietnam War.

# 33 Rocket

Chinese gunpowder rockets had been used in both celebrations and warfare since the thirteenth century. As early as 1898 people envisioned using rockets to reach outer space, but the first practical experiments with solid-propellant rockets were done by American Robert H. Goddard. He desired to obtain meteorological data from greater heights than possible with hot-air balloons, and his research led to a publication in 1919 explaining the math. By 1929 he also developed liquid propellants to achieve higher altitudes. Goddard also developed the gyroscope to achieve better flight control and the concept of a payload space for his scientific experiments within the rockets as well as the idea of parachute recovery. German scientists developed military applications for liquid-propellant rockets by the end of World War II, and American and Soviet governments attracted German scientists to their own experimental programs after the war. Intercontinental ballistic missiles were developed by both superpowers, and in 1957 the Soviets succeeded in placing an object in orbit around the earth and the arms race turned into the space race. The United States formed the National Aeronautics and Space Administration (NASA) in 1958 as a civilian agency dedicated to the peaceful exploration of space.

# 34 Jonas Salk

Poliomyelitis, or polio, was a dreaded childhood disease that occasionally struck adults like President Franklin D. Roosevelt. Jonas Salk was an American medical student whose research with influenza paved the way for a flu vaccine as well as the research he began in 1947 on a vaccine for polio. After eight years of painstaking research, Salk not only proved his vaccine's effectiveness in human trials but refused to patent it. His selfless labor and miraculous success endeared him to people around the world, and polio has been eradicated in countries that use his vaccine.

## 35 Space Shuttle

President Richard Nixon directed National Aeronautics and Space Administration (NASA) after its successful moon landing in 1969 to devote its resources to develop a new system for space transportation. NASA engineers began working on the space shuttle program the next year. The ultimate solution was to create a reusable spaceship that would be launched with two reusable solid-propellant rockets and an expendable external liquid-repellant tank. The first test model of the shuttle was affectionately named *Enterprise* after the spaceship of *Star Trek* fame, and the integrity of the aerodynamics was proven by flying it atop a 747 jumbo jet. Five free flights proved that the shuttle could glide safely to a stop on the ground. After the *Columbia* was launched into space and successfully landed in 1981, the space shuttle program conducted over one hundred safe missions and two in which the entire crew was killed. The space shuttle program ended in 2011 in favor of more robotic explorations of space.

## 36 Hubble Space Telescope

While the space shuttle was considered the most complex technological achievement of the twentieth century, it was designed to carry payloads like the Hubble space telescope into space. Beyond the commercial implications of weightlessness, the space telescope was intended to achieve clearer pictures of deep space by escaping the interference of the earth's atmosphere. Edwin Hubble was an American astronomer credited with proving the existence of other galaxies beyond the Milky Way and for observing that the universe is expanding at a constant rate; the space telescope was named in his honor. The telescope was taken into space and released in orbit by a space shuttle in 1990. A flaw of one-fiftieth of the width of a human hair caused the pictures taken by the telescope to blur, but this defect in the telescope's primary mirror was corrected in 1993 by other shuttle astronauts. Notable discoveries of the Hubble telescope shine light on the future potential of space travel by confirming the existence of new planets and new stars in over 1,500 new galaxies. Just as NASA researchers began studying the feasibility of a space shuttle years before its success, research has now begun to provide for the transplant of portions of the earth's population to other planets.

# Essential Supreme Court Cases

*The judicial Power shall extend to all Cases, in Law and Equity,
arising under this Constitution, [and] the Laws of the United States. . . .*
—The United States Constitution, 1789

**1803**
Marbury v. Madison

**1810**
Fletcher v. Peck

**1819**
Dartmouth College v. Woodward
McCulloch v. Maryland

**1821**
Cohens v. Virgnia

**1824**
Gibbons v. Ogden

**1831–1832**
Cherokee Cases

**1857**
Dred Scott v. Sandford

**1877**
Munn v. Illinois

**1895**
In re Debs

**1896**
Plessy v. Ferguson

**1901–1905**
Insular Cases

**1904**
Northern Securities Co. v. United States

**1919**
Schenck v. United States

**1935**
Schechter Poultry Corp. v. United States

**1944**
Korematsu v. United States

**1954**
Brown v. Board of Education of Topeka, Kansas

**1962**
Engel v. Vitale

**1963**
Gideon v. Wainwright

**1966**
Miranda v. Arizona

**1973**
Roe v. Wade

**1974**
United States v. Nixon

**1978**
Board of Regents v. Bakke

**2000**
Bush v. Gore

# Top 24 Essential
# Supreme Court Cases to Know

## 1 *Marbury v. Madison*

As a result of the Jeffersonian Revolution in the Election of 1800, the Anti-Federalists came to power in Congress along with their chief in the executive branch. William Marbury was one of the late appointments to the federal court system by John Adams on his way out of office. Marbury was to be a justice of the peace for the District of Columbia, but the new secretary of state, James Madison, refused to give Marbury his commission, and thus Marbury sued Madison. Thomas Jefferson and other Anti-Federalists disliked President Adams's attempt to leave one branch of the central government in Federalist hands. In 1803, John Marshall, who also had been appointed to the Supreme Court by John Adams, wrote the unanimous decision that Marbury was due his commission, but Marbury's claim that the Supreme Court had jurisdiction in the case was based on the Judiciary Act of 1789, which in this case conflicted with the U.S. Constitution. Even though a decision in Marbury's favor would have helped a fellow Federalist, Marshall said the "essence of judicial duty" was to follow the Constitution when laws passed by the legislative branch and signed by the president conflicted with what the Constitution said. This case was the fundamental precedent establishing the right of the Supreme Court of judicial review as fulfilling its constitutional role to balance the power of the Congress. The case set in motion the process by which laws would be subject to constitutional examination and commanded justices to fulfill this duty. In limiting his own party's power as well as the jurisdiction of the Supreme Court, Marshall took a stance that no one could deny was impartial, yet at the same time increased the Supreme Court's and the federal government's power to protect the interests of minorities from the will of the majority. Marshall said a law that contradicted the Constitution was void.

## 2 *Fletcher v. Peck*

This case decided in 1810 was the classic natural rights defense of contracts. Corrupt Georgia state and federal politicians had been bribed to sell thirty-five million acres of land to speculators for 1.5 cents per acre. Outraged Georgians "threw the bums out," but much of the land had already been sold before that election cleaned up the corruption. Robert Fletcher sued John Peck because he tried to withhold the title to some of the property that Fletcher had bought saying the original land deal was corrupt and the sale of it was thus void. John Marshall and the majority of the Supreme Court justices said the second land purchase by Fletcher (and other new owners) was made in good faith according to the law, and the state legislature, even though filled with new representatives, could not void a legal contract. Here was an assertion of federal judgment over states' rights and an essential precedent for sound business contracts and property rights into the future. The Supreme Court was also trying to convince Americans to elect leaders with integrity.

# 3 *Dartmouth College v. Woodward*

This case decided in 1819 revealed that postsecondary education in America had not escaped the touch of politics. Jeffersonian-Republican leaders of New Hampshire took office and sought to dispense with the entrenched Federalists who ran the Dartmouth College by revising its charter. The Supreme Court that decided *Fletcher v. Peck* did not take kindly to having to teach another state about property rights and the sanctity of contracts before the law. Daniel Webster argued the case as an alumnus of Dartmouth College, and John Marshall specified in the majority ruling that the contract clause of the Constitution did apply to corporations like the one holding the original charter. The case revealed that a corporation could own property protected under the due process clause of the Bill of Rights. This determination stood even though the original charter had been granted by the king of England. The Marshall Court again limited the power of state legislatures to regulate private property and protected contracts setting a major precedent for future corporate legal interpretations.

# 4 *McCulloch v. Maryland*

In yet another pivotal case in 1819, Marshall pronounced Alexander Hamilton's interpretation of the Constitution to be the proper one regarding the Bank of the United States (BUS). In a direct assertion of federal power over state power, the Marshall Court said that James McCulloch, the cashier of the branch of the BUS in Maryland, was correct in refusing to pay tax to the state because the bank was a federal institution. While not denying the right of Maryland to tax those under her sovereignty, Marshall said emphatically that the BUS was not under the sovereignty of any state. His famous, "The power to tax is the power to destroy" did not sit well with Thomas Jefferson, James Madison, or Andrew Jackson who all disagreed with the Marshall Court's decision, and ultimately this Second Bank of the United States was the target of Jackson's wrath in the Bank War. As long as the Marshall Court was in power, however, loose construction of the Constitution provided for a stronger central government and a curtailment of states' rights.

# 5 *Cohens v. Virginia*

Since the ruling in *McCulloch v. Maryland* was so unpopular, Marshall took the opportunity to reiterate it in *Cohens v. Virginia* in 1821. The Cohens brothers had appealed their conviction for selling lottery tickets in Virginia when the state had passed a law banning the practice. The Cohens had based their sale on an act of the U.S. Congress that permitted them to hold the lottery for Washington, D.C. Lawyers representing Virginia claimed that the Supreme Court should not even be hearing the case because the Eleventh Amendment declared it outside the Court's jurisdiction. Although the Marshall Court asserted that Virginia was right to fine the Cohens brothers because the lottery law only applied locally to the District of Columbia, Marshall emphatically declared that the Supreme Court was the final arbiter of interpreting the Constitution. In other words, the Marshall Court did not permit a state to tell a branch of the federal government what it could and could not do because the Constitution was the supreme law of the land and the federal government it created was above the states.

# 6 *Gibbons v. Ogden*

This 1824 case was the first in the history of the Supreme Court involving the regulation of interstate trade, and the unanimous decision of the Marshall Court set a precedent for the nationalism associated with this federal power. After Robert Fulton proved the feasibility of commercial steamboat service, both Thomas Gibbons and Aaron Ogden developed steamboat lines. Gibbons took over Fulton's license from the state granting him a monopoly on the state's waterways, and Ogden had a license from the federal government allowing him a monopoly on coastal traffic between New York and New Jersey. While the New York courts upheld the monopoly granted to Gibbons, the Marshall Court said the federal permit trumped the state permit and allowed Ogden to proceed because he was involved in interstate shipping. Marshall said that states could regulate commerce within the confines of their borders, but in another assertion of centralized power over the business of the nation he set the precedent for the federal government's supremacy in regulating wider commerce. The enforcement of this decision was lax through the nineteenth century but picked up after the New Deal in the 1930s.

# 7 Cherokee Cases

The Marshall Court defined the legal status of Cherokee Indians and set precedents for future developments between the United States and other Indian tribes in two cases in 1831 and 1832. In *Cherokee Nation v. Georgia*, the Supreme Court denied it had jurisdiction to intervene in a dispute between the Cherokee Nation and Georgia over land rights because the Indian tribe was, according to John Marshall, a "domestic, dependent nation." This intriguing legal phrase denied the Cherokee Nation the status of a sovereign nation and declared that Indians were wards of the federal government. In *Worcester v. Georgia* the Marshall Court redefined its own ruling from the previous year and granted the Cherokee Nation sovereign rights to have Samuel Worcester, a Congregational minister, live on their lands as a missionary even though he did not seek a license required by state law. As Andrew Jackson's efforts to help Georgia remove the Cherokee Indians from their lands loomed, Marshall emphasized the "nation" part of "domestic, dependent nation" from the earlier case. He said the Cherokee tribe, as a nation, could make a treaty with the federal government and that a state could not interfere. Andrew Jackson illustrated the limitations on the power of the judicial branch by refusing to enforce the ruling, and the Trail of Tears commenced at the behest of Georgia and other southern states.

# 8 *Dred Scott v. Sandford*

Dred Scott was a slave whose original owner, Dr. John Emerson, had taken Scott into a free territory and a free state during his travels as an army surgeon. Scott sued for his liberty because he said that as he had spent most of the years from 1834 to

1838 on free soil that he should be freed. When the case came to the Supreme Court in 1857, Scott belonged to a man named John Sanford whose name was misspelled in the court records. In its ruling, the Supreme Court under Chief Justice Roger B. Taney said that neither Scott nor any African slave or descendant of slaves was a citizen of the United States and could thus not resort to the American court system. Furthermore, the Court said that the years on free soil were no help to Scott because he sued from within the state of Missouri, which was a slave state. The implications of these decisions led the Court to state that the Missouri Compromise had been unconstitutional because citizens in territories above the 36°30' line were subject to the loss of their private property. The Dred Scott case proved to be one of the most divisive issues of the 1850s as the decade surged toward the Civil War. Northerners feared the ruling would allow the federal government to legalize slavery in the North and to restart the slave trade with Africa. In this regard scholars have ranked this decision to be the worst ever handed down by the Supreme Court. Just when the federal court system was needed to help stabilize the country the most, the ruling destroyed northern confidence in the legal system. The Dred Scott case emboldened the South and infuriated the North and was itself a cause of the war. Dred Scott, however, died in 1858 and did not live to see the ruling overturned by the Thirteenth and Fourteenth Amendments to the Constitution after the Civil War.

# 9 *Munn v. Illinois*

In 1877, a series of cases coming before the Supreme Court were known as the Granger Cases because they involved suits against private businesses on behalf of associations of farmers known as the Grange, or the Patrons of Husbandry. Sympathetic legislators in Illinois had passed laws setting the price grain elevator operators in Chicago could charge farmers for storage of grain. The Supreme Court under Chief Justice Morrison Waite ruled that Illinois could regulate private businesses to the extent of fixing prices, especially those in which the public had an interest. Dissenting justices said that if this interpretation was true of grain elevators it would be true of any business. By virtue of *Munn v. Illinois* states attempted to exert the same regulatory power over the rates charged by railroads, but lawyers for private railroads later maintained that the ruling did not apply to them because they conducted interstate business. Still, the *Munn* case is regarded as a precedent for the support of government regulation, and the federal government took over where the states' jurisdiction ceased.

# 10 *In re Debs*

As a result of the Pullman Company's reduction in wages for its workers during the Panic of 1893, Eugene V. Debs organized a strike by the American Railway Union of which he was the president. Workers refused to handle trains with Pullman cars attached, and if any worker was fired because of the refusal, all the workers of the railroad would strike. The Pullman Strike thus immobilized the nation's railroads, and Attorney General Richard Olney sought a federal court injunction ordering the workers to get the trains moving. When violence erupted, President Grover Cleveland sent federal troops in to restore order. Eugene V. Debs was arrested for criminal conspiracy and later for contempt of court. Debs appealed his arrest and six-month jail sentence to the Supreme Court in 1895 because he had not been given a jury trial even though he was being treated as a criminal. The Supreme Court rejected Debs's plea saying the United States took the actions in question because the trains' not moving stopped mail service to the country. The Court called the Pullman Strike a public nuisance and an "unreasonable restraint of trade" as codified in the Sherman Antitrust Act. For several decades companies with labor troubles resorted to this ruling to secure court orders from compliant judges and then have the courts declare strikers in contempt of court rather than guilty of criminal offenses. Adjustments to labor laws eroded this interpretation during the New Deal of Franklin Roosevelt.

# 11 *Plessy v. Ferguson*

A mixed-race gentleman named Homer Plessy decided as a representative of a committee to test a Louisiana law that made African-Americans ride in separate cars on railroads within the state. He boarded a train on a trip within the confines of the state and refused to sit in the segregated car. When tried in the court of a Judge Ferguson, Plessy argued that the Thirteenth and Fourteenth Amendments ended Jim Crow laws like the one in Louisiana. When he lost the case and appealed to the Supreme Court in 1896, his arguments were rejected there, too. The majority opinion stated that those amendments to the Constitution abolished practices that were inclined to restore African-Americans to slavery and did not ban all distinctions based on race. The ruling stated that segregationist laws did not automatically imply that one race was inferior regardless of what people might perceive as their inherent assumption of white supremacy. The Supreme Court upheld Louisiana's law that stated, "separate but equal facilities" were constitutional, but in their arguments the justices on the majority likened transportation to education, and thus segregation in schools was tacitly sanctioned. The one dissenting justice, who interestingly was named John Marshall Harlan, said the "Constitution is colorblind, and neither knows nor tolerates classes among citizens." These words would form the basis for future arguments that overturned the ruling in the Plessy case.

# 12 Insular Cases

These fourteen cases occurred over a period from 1901 to 1905 and involved the application of the U.S. Constitution, including specifically the Bill of Rights, to territories acquired by the United States overseas (the word *insular* is a reference to islands). Echoing public opinion, the Supreme Court argued on the basis of race and background that the populations of the islands acquired during the Spanish-American War or those of Hawaii were not fit to become citizens and thus the territories were not fit to become states. Despite the jarring nature of possessing colonies in the minds of many Americans, the Court determined that the United States could possess them and could even incorporate them as territories just short of full statehood and far short of equal rights for their inhabitants. This ruling was set aside for Hawaii but not for the other islands to which the United States lays claim.

## 13 *Northern Securities Co. v. United States*

After Theodore Roosevelt began to apply the Sherman Antitrust Act in the way it was intended, as a law to regulate monopolistic corporations, the Supreme Court backed him up in this case in 1903. The Northern Securities Company belonged to J. P. Morgan and associates and held controlling stock in three railroads. Lawyers for the company argued that breaking up the conglomerate would have adverse effects on the business world. Again, John Marshall Harlan rose to the occasion and said the Supreme Court could not take into account the economic consequences of following the law. The majority ruling dealt with the nebulous "unreasonable restraint of trade" clause in the antitrust legislation by saying it certainly applied to this case. Another landmark aspect of this ruling was the application of the law not just to business practices but to the ownership of stock and the power that came with it.

## 14 *Schenck v. United States*

Interestingly it was not until the World War I era that the Supreme Court had to deal with the First Amendment rights regarding freedom of speech. This case in 1919 had to determine whether Charles Schenck and other socialists had violated the Espionage Act by distributing fifteen thousand leaflets that urged young men in Philadelphia to resist the draft. Schenck had mailed the papers, and several recipients complained to the Post Office that the federal mail was being used to invite citizens to join with the Socialist Party in signing a petition against "intimidation of war zealots." Schenck pled not guilty of breaking the Espionage Act but was convicted. He appealed to the Supreme Court saying his right to free speech was violated. His attorneys said his leaflet had only communicated an honest opinion and not incited anyone to do anything illegal. The case was set in the context of America's entry into the worst war the world had yet seen and the backlash in America of abuse toward German immigrants. Woodrow Wilson and leaders at all levels of government had taken the position that criticizing the war effort was unpatriotic. Justice Oliver Wendell Holmes spoke for the unanimous decision that Schenck had in fact broken the law by saying freedom of speech did not permit someone to conduct him- or herself in such a way that represented a "clear and present danger" to bring about illegal activity that, in this case, was thought to undermine national security. Charles Schenck thus had to serve out his six-month prison sentence, and the case opened the debate over what was protected and unprotected speech in American society.

## 15 *Schechter Poultry Corp. v. United States*

This unanimous ruling by the Supreme Court in 1935 undermined the National Industrial Recovery Act, a New Deal measure under Franklin D. Roosevelt (FDR) that attempted to increase employment and stimulate business activity during the Great Depression. The law declared a national emergency and called for industries to draw up codes of fair competition that effectively raised wages but also favored big business because industry leaders themselves set the codes. In just two years 750 codes were adopted that impacted around twenty-three million people. The case hinged on the accusation that the Schechter company sold sick chickens and also violated industry codes regarding wages and hours of workers. The Supreme Court, however, determined that the chicken slaughterhouse conducted an entirely local business and was therefore not susceptible to regulation by the federal government. The Court went on to declare that a declaration of an emergency did not create or enlarge power for the executive branch, which in effect was making laws as well as enforcing them. The National Recovery Administration was determined to be unconstitutional, which caused FDR to attack the Supreme Court in his rhetoric but also through the scheme to pack the Court with supporters of the New Deal.

# 16 *Korematsu v. United States*

This 1944 case focused on Fred Korematsu, whose very name revealed the circumstances that caused him to be in a predicament during World War II. Korematsu was a native-born American of Japanese descent who was rejected for military service for health reasons but still secured a job in a defense industry. As Japanese internment began, Korematsu moved away from his home (but not out of California), changed his name, and had cosmetic surgery that helped him claim to be a Mexican-American. Anti-Japanese sentiment in California had led to the internment program because the military claimed that Japanese-Americans threatened national security while living on the Pacific Coast. After refusing to comply with internment orders, Korematsu was apprehended, convicted, jailed, paroled, and then interned in a camp in Utah. The Supreme Court focused on the fact that Korematsu had remained in the restricted area rather than the constitutionality of internment. The majority opinion said the military urgency dictated the extreme measure and said it was not racist without explaining how that could be true. Dissenting justices said the case against Korematsu was motivated by a history of anti-Japanese discrimination that had not even been extended to Germans and Italians living in America during World War II. The Congress later declared in 1983 that the decision in this case had been "overruled in the court of history" and apologized. Japanese-Americans who had been interned were given monetary compensation, and Fred Korematsu was given the Medal of Freedom by President Bill Clinton.

# 17 *Brown v. Board of Education of Topeka, Kansas*

This first major case for Chief Justice Earl Warren was the culmination of growing animosity for Jim Crow laws, the civil rights stand of President Harry Truman, and a protracted assault on the ruling in *Plessy v. Ferguson* by the National Association for the Advancement of Colored People (NAACP). Together these threads were combined by the Warren Court in what was called "a legal and social revolution in race relations and constitutionalism." The NAACP had begun in the 1930s to challenge state-imposed racial segregation in public accommodations, especially in education, and some Supreme Court cases resulted that eroded support for Jim Crow. Oliver Brown was only one of many plaintiffs encouraged by the NAACP to sue school systems to obtain access for their children to integrated schools in the early 1950s. The Warren Court argued in a unanimous decision in 1954 that separate facilities for educating different races was an inherently unequal prospect that damaged the ability of African-American children to gain a good education in an era when education in general was becoming more significant and African-Americans were winning respect in various fields of life. This momentous decision that overruled the Plessy case and opened the door for desegregation of all public facilities had an unfortunate turn. The next unanimous decision in regard to the Brown case said that school systems should proceed with desegregation with "all deliberate speed." This phrase was notoriously used to justify the slowness of change that within ten years had only seen 2 percent of schools comply. Growing outrage over the continuing legacy of Jim Crow in the Brown case led to the Civil Rights Act and the Voting Rights Act of the 1960s in the context of the civil rights movement. The case also encouraged the Supreme Court to take on a greater role in societal reform and earned the Warren Court the reputation of being an activist court based more on personal convictions than on legal principle.

## 18 *Gideon v. Wainwright*

Another unanimous decision of the Warren Court resolved the case of Clarence Earl Gideon in 1963. Gideon had been charged with breaking in and entering a billiards hall and was convicted of a felony after representing himself. He took up his own defense because he could not afford an attorney, and when he was found guilty he appealed on the grounds that he had asked the Florida court of jurisdiction to provide him with legal counsel, which the court had failed to do. Wainwright was the named representative of the Florida Department of Corrections in the appeal. The Supreme Court did appoint a lawyer to take Gideon's case, which hinged on whether due process was given or his Fourteenth Amendment civil rights were violated by the state of Florida. With an attorney, Gideon's defense undermined the credibility of the one witness who had identified him and produced other witnesses eventually leading to Gideon's being acquitted. Previous cases had been handed down by the Supreme Court that built the very argument upon which Gideon had based his appeal, that to receive a fair trial people who could not afford an attorney should have one appointed for them. The Gideon case threatened to throw out any felony case in which the defendant did not have legal counsel, and later rulings extended the provision to misdemeanors. The office of the public defender originated in this ruling, and by 1984 a study showed that two-thirds of defendants resorted to this type of counsel. The study revealed that although private or public defense made little difference in the rate of convictions, defendants who represent themselves had a significantly lower chance of escaping conviction.

## 19 *Miranda v. Arizona*

The Warren Court's revolutionary changes to the criminal procedures in the United States climaxed with this case in 1966. The *Miranda* case proved to be one of the most controversial in the history of the Supreme Court in that some interpreted the ruling as a commitment to democratic values and fair treatment for all, whereas others attributed to the Warren Court the hamstringing of law enforcement. Ernesto

Miranda was arrested and charged with a rape upon being identified by the victim. After two hours of questioning by the police, Miranda changed his denial of guilt into a written confession. Throughout the interrogation Miranda had no access to legal counsel. The majority ruling of a divided Court stated that the freedom to not incriminate oneself did not just apply to courtrooms but also during interrogation. The fact a person was in police custody was also assumed to be a compulsion to speak. To solve the quandary of law enforcement after this ruling, the Supreme Court enunciated four provisions that all arrested people had to have read or recited to them immediately upon arrest including (1) you have the right to remain silent; (2) anything you say can and will be used against you; (3) you have the right to talk to a lawyer before being questioned and to have him present when you are being questioned; and (4) if you cannot afford a lawyer, one will be provided for you before any questioning if you so desire. Although law enforcement agencies originally decried the difficulty these steps added to their duties, most have become so accustomed to the *Miranda* warnings, as the legal notices are called, that the Warren Court's ruling has become a part of American culture. Studies have shown that arrested suspects still make confessions with some regularity.

# 20 *Engel v. Vitale*

While the words *wall of separation* regarding the relationship between church and state do not appear in the U.S. Constitution, they did exist in a letter by Thomas Jefferson that was quoted in Supreme Court cases considered by the Court when deciding this 1962 case. As late as 1952, the Court had refused to even hear a case that raised the constitutionality of Bible reading in public schools, but in the era of McCarthyism such a case might have led to accusations that communists had infiltrated the Supreme Court. The American Civil Liberties Union (ACLU), however, joined with ten public school students' parents in the *Engel v. Vitale* case to challenge a prayer authored by the state and read aloud over a school intercom system. The parents sued the State Board of Regents of New York saying the prayer violated their religious beliefs and went against the First Amendment's ban on the establishment of religion. The majority ruling in the case did not require that all religious values be purged from public life but that schools could not sponsor them. The dissenting opinion claimed that the First Amendment merely banned the power of the government to coerce citizens in regard to religion and that the "free exercise" clause of the amendment protected the rather bland prayer.

# 21 *Regents of the University of California v. Bakke*

Allan Bakke sought enrollment in the University of California Medical School and was twice turned down. Since the medical school was actively trying to create greater racial and ethnic diversity in its student body and Bakke was white, he sued the school for reverse discrimination. The *Bakke* case was thus an opportunity for the Supreme Court to rule regarding affirmative action, the practice of favoring minorities in selection and hiring in order to compensate for past social wrongs. Bakke said he was being treated unequally while the medical school was trying to increase equality. Sixteen of the one hundred slots in each entering class were reserved for minorities, and the entrance requirements were reduced for these applicants. A sharply divided Supreme Court ruled that although schools could consider applicants' race or ethnicity in the admissions process, a specific quota such as the sixteen slots denied Bakke equal protection under the law. While Bakke was permitted to enroll in the medical school as a result, the Court did not take up the whole notion of affirmative action in other applications as had been done in previous cases regarding race relations and equality.

## 22 *Roe v. Wade*

The increased availability of contraceptives did not end the increasing number of unwanted pregnancies associated with the sexual revolution of the 1960s, and the growing feminist movement sought to secure more of what was called "reproductive rights." Although state laws had been trying to reduce the number of abortions, publicized cases of birth defects caused by botched abortions and the unsanitary and dangerous conditions in which women often had the illegal procedure done prompted some states to permit abortions in cases when the mother's life was threatened. The Supreme Court in 1973 took up the case of Jane Roe, a name used to protect the privacy of the mother in question who was later revealed to be Norma McCorvey. McCorvey first said her pregnancy was the result of a gang rape and then admitted it was the result of voluntary sexual relations with a man with whom she no longer had a relationship. The majority opinion in the case divided pregnancy into three trimesters and established that an abortion was a private decision between a woman and her doctor all through the first trimester. Any restrictions a state had on abortions at this stage were unconstitutional, and the Court permitted abortions up through the second trimester if the health of a mother was in danger. This last standard was able to be considered up into the third trimester, but the Court allowed that states had an interest in protecting the lives of fetuses during the third trimester as well and permitted stronger restrictions on such late-term abortions. Dissenting opinions said the right to abortion on demand was not found in the Constitution and that the trimester system was arbitrary. If states had an interest in protecting the life of a fetus in the third trimester, they had an interest in protecting that life all through the pregnancy. The abortion debate between advocates of a woman's right to choose abortion and the right-to-life movement's assertion that life begins at conception and should be protected from destruction continues as an undercurrent in state and federal politics.

## 23 *United States v. Nixon*

This 1974 case was one of the most dramatic events in the saga that brought down the Nixon administration in the Watergate Scandal. When Nixon became more and more entangled in the web of deceit associated with the coverup of the Watergate break-in, his lawyers maintained that a president had nearly unlimited power, especially in matters of foreign policy and national security. The Nixon team tried to claim executive privilege and immunity from prosecution once the existence of tapes recording Oval Office conversations became known. A federal judge subpoenaed the tapes, and when the president refused to turn them over the case went to the Supreme Court. Despite the argument that the whole quandary was a dispute among the various departments within the executive branch, the Court agreed with a special prosecutor that the president had to turn over the tapes, especially because in the meantime President Nixon had released a few of the tapes. The Court did say that special deference was to be given to presidents in matters of defense and that they should not be thought of as normal citizens to be ordered about. Still, the U.S. government in two of its branches asserted that the third was not entirely immune from prosecution in criminal matters. When Nixon was forced to deliver all the tapes, the prosecution found what they called the "smoking gun," evidence that the president had conspired to obstruct justice in the prosecution of those in his administration responsible for the Watergate Scandal.

# 24 *Bush v. Gore*

In the other great modern saga of the Supreme Court's role in monitoring the executive branch, this case saw a divided Court settle the Election of 2000 that was disputed because of voting inconsistencies in Florida. When Florida's Supreme Court ordered one county to recount nine thousand votes by hand and every county to manually verify ballots that had been marked as not voting for any presidential candidate, the Bush/Cheney campaign asked the Supreme Court of the United States to intervene. The election had been so close that the electoral votes of Florida would determine the outcome, and the electoral votes would be determined by the popular vote, the results of which were within a few hundred votes between the candidates. The Supreme Court issued a stay on the recount and eventually determined by a 7–2 vote that the Florida court's actions had undermined the equal protection under the law of all Florida voters by making special rules for some Florida voters. Furthermore, in a 5–4 split decision the Court determined that a constitutional recount could not be accomplished by the deadline set by the Florida state constitution. Thus the meager lead George W. Bush held in Florida was unaltered and the election was decided in his favor. The legacy of the settlement of the Election of 2000 this way hampered the Bush administration's ability to lead for a time, and partisan interpretations of the decision are still too fresh to make a reasoned historical view of the significance of this precedent. In an almost irrelevant conclusion to the saga, the election results in Florida were later independently verified not only to maintain George Bush's lead but to expand it.

# Mini Quiz

1. An assessment of the Progressive Reform movement by a modern American politically conservative analyst might conclude that

    (A) government regulation was the key to efficient and fair economic progress.
    (B) democratic use of government power was the key to cleaning up corruption in government.
    (C) the government reforms were achieved at the expense of individual and property rights.
    (D) the federal government should become the largest employer through government contracts.
    (E) government bureaucracies were necessary to maintain order in a free society.

2. Ronald Reagan contributed to the end of the Cold War by

    (A) standing alone against communist countries' aggression in the United Nations.
    (B) negotiating new treaties calling for the reduction of intercontinental ballistic missiles (ICBMs).
    (C) restoring a fear of communism among Americans who had grown complacent to its threat.
    (D) increasing defense spending to fund technologies beyond what the Soviets could afford.
    (E) forcing Mikhail Gorbachev to pursue more openness in reforming Soviet communism.

3. The Iran-Contra scandal involved illegal, clandestine support for rebels in which country?

    (A) Iran
    (B) East Germany
    (C) Venezuela
    (D) Poland
    (E) Nicaragua

4. President H. W. Bush and Mikhail Gorbachev signed a treaty to

   (A) negotiate the transition of America's relationship to Russia as the
       Soviet Union collapsed.
   (B) discontinue the production of chemical weapons.
   (C) end Soviet involvement in Afghanistan.
   (D) eliminate medium-range nuclear weapons.
   (E) mutually agree to provide equal economic support to Israel.

5. The Persian Gulf War during George H. W. Bush's administration was
   fought to

   (A) force Saddam Hussein to submit to United Nations inspections regarding
       his weapons programs.
   (B) hunt down the terrorists responsible for the Beirut bombing that killed
       U.S. Marines.
   (C) remove Saddam Hussein from power in Iraq as a result of his use of
       chemical weapons.
   (D) intervene in the decade-long Iran-Iraq War to bring stability to the
       region.
   (E) liberate Kuwait from an invasion by Iraqi forces conducted despite
       United Nations sanctions.

6. The unusual hurdle Clarence Thomas faced in the confirmation process for
   his appointment to the Supreme Court was

   (A) accusations of racism against his white employees.
   (B) a secondary discussion about the constitutionality of affirmative action.
   (C) criticism that he would be taking the position away from an equally
       qualified woman.
   (D) sexual harassment charges brought by a former employee.
   (E) a delay in the procedure in order for the Supreme Court to decide about
       media access.

7. The strategy of the New Democrats of the 1990s was to

   (A) repudiate Progressivism in favor of more conservative approaches to
       government.
   (B) focus on issues relevant mostly to aging members of the baby boom
       generation.
   (C) move to the center of the political spectrum in an era of resurgent
       conservatism.
   (D) dismiss the use of tax cuts to boost the economy as irresponsible "voodoo
       economics."
   (E) advance the American economy at all costs regardless of political
       backlash.

8. The ruling of the Supreme Court in the matters surrounding the Starr report during the Clinton administration was that

   (A) President Clinton was guilty of perjury and obstruction of justice.
   (B) a mistrial had occurred in the impeachment process because of procedural errors.
   (C) the president was correct in invoking executive privilege over misdemeanor offenses.
   (D) the trial of President Clinton in the Senate was too marred by partisanship to be conclusive.
   (E) the president could be sued by a citizen during his term in office.

9. The main intention of giving a presidential line item veto was to

   (A) diminish the wasteful expenditure of federal monies for "pork barrel" projects.
   (B) accelerate the process whereby Congressional legislation could take effect in a crisis.
   (C) fine-tune the use of American military forces in cooperation with other countries.
   (D) advance the proposal for a new national health care system.
   (E) restore the integrity of the legislative process and close the "credibility gap."

10. The decision by the Supreme Court in *Bush v. Gore* in 2000 settled the disputed election on the premise that

   (A) the Electoral College is an outdated aspect of the presidential election process.
   (B) the Florida state Supreme Court's decision in the matter was unfair to some voters.
   (C) the type of ballot used by counties in Florida with disputed returns was unconstitutional.
   (D) a state deadline for the election returns violated the nation's need to have a recount.
   (E) once a candidate concedes the election to his or her opponent the election is decided.

11. The Smithsonian Institution was founded

   (A) as a private research facility that was donated to the federal government in the founder's will.
   (B) as a gift to honor the sacrifices Americans made to liberate France during World War II.
   (C) by order of James K. Polk with taxpayer dollars at first to house discoveries in the West.
   (D) by Congress after deliberation on how to use a private fortune donated to the United States.
   (E) by the Royal Society of London in honor of Benjamin Franklin, its first American member.

12. The invention of barbed wire in 1871 determined that

   (A) Americans could finally domesticate the buffalo.
   (B) American Indians could no longer use public land to graze their cattle.
   (C) the farmers of the Great Plains could now produce a surplus for export to Europe.
   (D) the trench warfare begun during the Civil War would become the main strategy of other wars.
   (E) American cowboys could no longer freely cross private lands during long drives to Chicago.

13. The two inventions below that most revolutionized the role of American women in the work force were

   (A) the sewing machine and the camera.
   (B) the radio and the practical elevator.
   (C) the automobile and the airplane.
   (D) Morse code and interchangeable parts.
   (E) the telephone and the typewriter.

14. The major principle decided by the Supreme Court in the *Northern Securities Co. v. United States* case that supported Theodore Roosevelt's trust busting with the Sherman Antitrust Act was that

   (A) there were some good trusts and some bad trusts.
   (B) all trusts were unreasonably restraining trade and needed to be systematically broken up.
   (C) the Court could not take into account the economic consequences of obeying the law.
   (D) the president had the duty to take the initiative in interpreting laws pertaining to the economy.
   (E) the president could order the prosecution of railroads because they crossed state lines.

15. The first case that came before the Supreme Court in which the Court had to decide a question about the First Amendment rights to free speech occurred in which context?

   (A) The restoration of the two-party system after the Era of Good Feelings
   (B) The Reconstruction era's debate about federal power in regulating states' rights
   (C) The imperialism debate prompted by territories won in the Spanish-American War
   (D) The wrangling over the Espionage and Sedition Acts passed during World War I
   (E) The African-American civil rights movement in the 1950s

# Answer Explanations

1. **C** Answers A and B were foundational principles of Progressivism, a movement that modern conservatives claim to be against, although most American politicians operate entirely within a Progressive political paradigm. Answer D is contrary to the stated goal of conservatives to shrink Big Government, and answer E is another notion that arose from Progressive reforms of which conservatives typically complain while doing little to amend. Only answer C would be agreed upon by most conservatives in that businessmen and corporations were identified as the culprits in the nineteenth century when Progressivism arose, and whether it was the Sherman Antitrust Act assailing the property of a giant trust or the later Environmental Protection Agency regulating a small farmer's use of his or her own property conservatives would say the government had shifted from protecting liberties to reducing them.

2. **D** President Reagan had allies like Margaret Thatcher, Pope John Paul II, and Polish labor organizer Lech Walesa (among countless others) so he could never be said to have stood alone in the Cold War, but he did engage with Mikhail Gorbachev man to man in order to reduce intermediate-range nuclear missiles in Europe, not intercontinental ballistic missiles (ICBMs). In the surprisingly warm relationship between Reagan and Gorbachev, however, Gorbachev was not forced to pursue *glasnost* and *perestroika*; they were his own ideas. Contrary to answer C, Reagan did not restore fear of communism through his rhetoric but openly mocked, criticized, and pronounced the coming doom of the Soviet Union on the "ash heap of history." What Reagan did almost single-handedly was change the discussion from combating the Soviet Union to ending the Soviet Union through large defense buildups, including the Strategic Defense Initiative, with which the Soviets could not keep pace. Later Russian analysts said that Reagan's stances sped up the collapse of the Soviet Union by at least five years.

3. **E** Oliver North's illegal and secret (he said even secret from President Reagan) operations involved using money acquired from selling weapons to Iran to support the Contra rebels fighting against Daniel Ortega's socialist regime in Nicaragua.

4. **B** Amid the rapidly transpiring events that led to the end of the Cold War and the nuclear arms race, almost forgotten is the agreement to both end the manufacture of chemical weapons on the part of the United States and the Soviet Union and the destruction of each nation's massive stockpiles of such weapons of mass destruction. Later START treaties hinted at in answer D led to the reduction of operational strengths of long-range intercontinental ballistic missiles (ICBMs) in the Cold War superpowers' arsenals. Gorbachev ended Soviet involvement in Afghanistan all on his own as he determined that the invasion of that country was the Soviet's "Vietnam." The other answers are fabrications based on peripheral issues in the Cold War.

5. **E** The Iran-Iraq War mentioned in answer D lasted ten years but was over before the Persian Gulf War began over the invasion of Kuwait by neighboring Iraq. Despite charges that the United States was mainly fighting to protect its own oil supply, the stated goal of the war was in answer E. Although the Beirut bombing that destroyed the Marine Corps barracks occurred before the Persian Gulf War, hunting down terrorists as well as the ideas expressed in answers A and C were more associated with the presidency of the second George Bush after the September 11 attacks in 2001.

6. **D** Although many issues were raised in the otherwise routine grilling during a confirmation hearing for a nominee to be a justice on the Supreme Court, Clarence Thomas's particularly provocative hurdle was a sexual harassment accusation by Anita Hill, his former staffer at the Equal Employment Opportunity Commission (EEOC). The EEOC was, ironically, a government agency partly responsible for investigating such accusations, and this fact along with the fact that Clarence Thomas was only the second African-American to be nominated as a justice turned the confirmation hearings into the "media circus" mentioned in answer E. All the other answers are fabrications based on the context of the hearings.

7. **C** Although Bill Clinton and Al Gore Jr., did position themselves as more moderate Democrats in the wake of the Republican takeover of the Congress, neither man nor any other New Democrats openly repudiated Progressivism as hinted in answer A. Most politicians of the era in question had to acknowledge the influence of the baby boom generation in that they made up the bloc of voters who voted most regularly as well as a large percentage of the population, so answer B is nothing unique to New Democrats. Contrary to answer D, New Democrats backed moderate tax cuts for the middle class while raising taxes for the wealthy, and these and other policies forged in compromises with Republicans helped create such a boom in the American economy that there was no political backlash as hinted in answer E. Instead, President Clinton attained high approval ratings.

8. **E** Answers B and C are fabrications nearly the opposite of the truth in that President Clinton was impeached for perjury and obstruction of justice. Answer A is incorrect, though, because that ruling was determined by the House of Representatives, not the Supreme Court. Answer D hints at the partisanship in the Senate, but the result was quite conclusive; President Clinton was not removed from office. The one comfort in the entire wrenching process for most Americans was the assurance that even the president, regardless of party, was not above the law. This conclusion is the ruling the Supreme Court delivered when asked about the president's reference to executive privilege just as President Nixon had in the Watergate scandal.

9. **A** Despite the facts that answer E would possibly be an indirect result of a line-item veto as would answer B, the main goal of political reformers in the Contract with America that led to President Clinton's being the first president to wield such a tool was to cut "pork barrel" spending attached to bills in Con-

gress to aggrandize members and their constituents back home. Answers C and D hint at initiatives and events of the Clinton administration that were not related to the line-item veto that was eventually found to be unconstitutional by the Supreme Court.

10. **B**   Many Americans came to the conclusion expressed in answer A, but the Supreme Court came to the conclusion in answer B in that the desire to recount only some of Florida's votes violated equal protection under the law provisions of voting laws for other Florida voters. Thus the recount desired by the Gore team was denied, and a deadline for counting Florida's votes that determined the outcome of the Election of 2000 was decided to stand. The infamous "butterfly" ballots used in this election gained much national attention but were not found to be unconstitutional in their design complexities. Although Al Gore did concede the election to George Bush and then reverse his decision in order to challenge the election, such a series of actions had no legal bearing on the election's outcome.

11. **D**   James Smithson did donate his fortune to the United States for the "diffusion of knowledge," but after much debate Congress founded the Smithsonian Institution. All of the other answers are fabrications although answer E correctly hints at the prestige enjoyed by Benjamin Franklin in Europe.

12. **E**   "Range wars" were touched off by the passing of the "Wild West" and the end of long drives of cattle up out of Texas toward rail heads in Kansas to ship cattle to Chicago. The other answers should be considered plausible fabrications except for answer A. Even "domesticated" buffalo think little of destroying barbed wire fences. American Indians did not need public land to graze their herds of cattle because they were given reservations for that purpose (albeit with inadequate pasturage to join the ranching industry). Because the herds of wild buffalo were largely eliminated by this time, farmers moving into the Trans-Mississippi West began producing surpluses right from the start. The reference to barbed wire in answer D as useful in war was true beginning in World War I, but it was the machine gun more than wire that made men fight in trenches.

13. **E**   Of this list the devices that became almost exclusively the jobs of women to operate in the increasingly urbanized American society, the telephone and the typewriter established entirely new opportunities for women to work outside the home and off the farm. The sewing machine was a similar boon to women's working, but the camera less so. The other answers were more gender neutral in their economic impact on the nation.

14. **C**   Answer A is the position Theodore Roosevelt (TR) took in his New Nationalism approach to the campaign for the presidency in 1912. Answer B is Woodrow Wilson's New Freedom stance. The Court's stance that gave TR greater leeway in enforcing the Sherman Antitrust Act was as stated in answer C in opposition to the defense of the Northern Securities Company that stated its dissolution would damage the American economy. Answer E was decided by the Supreme Court much earlier, and answer D is another Rooseveltian interpretation of a sort of domestic "Big Stick policy."

15. **D**  All of these historical moments of lively debate might have qualified as key opportunities to also debate free and open debate, but that moment actually came in 1919 in the case *Schenck v. United States*, especially because of the anti-German sentiment of World War I evoked by the defendant's name who was eventually found guilty of exercising his freedom of speech (and of the press) in such a way as to present a "clear and present danger" to national security.

# CHAPTER 42

## PRACTICE TESTS

# Answer Sheet

## PRACTICE TEST 1

| | | | |
|---|---|---|---|
| 1 Ⓐ Ⓑ Ⓒ Ⓓ Ⓔ | 24 Ⓐ Ⓑ Ⓒ Ⓓ Ⓔ | 47 Ⓐ Ⓑ Ⓒ Ⓓ Ⓔ | 70 Ⓐ Ⓑ Ⓒ Ⓓ Ⓔ |
| 2 Ⓐ Ⓑ Ⓒ Ⓓ Ⓔ | 25 Ⓐ Ⓑ Ⓒ Ⓓ Ⓔ | 48 Ⓐ Ⓑ Ⓒ Ⓓ Ⓔ | 71 Ⓐ Ⓑ Ⓒ Ⓓ Ⓔ |
| 3 Ⓐ Ⓑ Ⓒ Ⓓ Ⓔ | 26 Ⓐ Ⓑ Ⓒ Ⓓ Ⓔ | 49 Ⓐ Ⓑ Ⓒ Ⓓ Ⓔ | 72 Ⓐ Ⓑ Ⓒ Ⓓ Ⓔ |
| 4 Ⓐ Ⓑ Ⓒ Ⓓ Ⓔ | 27 Ⓐ Ⓑ Ⓒ Ⓓ Ⓔ | 50 Ⓐ Ⓑ Ⓒ Ⓓ Ⓔ | 73 Ⓐ Ⓑ Ⓒ Ⓓ Ⓔ |
| 5 Ⓐ Ⓑ Ⓒ Ⓓ Ⓔ | 28 Ⓐ Ⓑ Ⓒ Ⓓ Ⓔ | 51 Ⓐ Ⓑ Ⓒ Ⓓ Ⓔ | 74 Ⓐ Ⓑ Ⓒ Ⓓ Ⓔ |
| 6 Ⓐ Ⓑ Ⓒ Ⓓ Ⓔ | 29 Ⓐ Ⓑ Ⓒ Ⓓ Ⓔ | 52 Ⓐ Ⓑ Ⓒ Ⓓ Ⓔ | 75 Ⓐ Ⓑ Ⓒ Ⓓ Ⓔ |
| 7 Ⓐ Ⓑ Ⓒ Ⓓ Ⓔ | 30 Ⓐ Ⓑ Ⓒ Ⓓ Ⓔ | 53 Ⓐ Ⓑ Ⓒ Ⓓ Ⓔ | 76 Ⓐ Ⓑ Ⓒ Ⓓ Ⓔ |
| 8 Ⓐ Ⓑ Ⓒ Ⓓ Ⓔ | 31 Ⓐ Ⓑ Ⓒ Ⓓ Ⓔ | 54 Ⓐ Ⓑ Ⓒ Ⓓ Ⓔ | 77 Ⓐ Ⓑ Ⓒ Ⓓ Ⓔ |
| 9 Ⓐ Ⓑ Ⓒ Ⓓ Ⓔ | 32 Ⓐ Ⓑ Ⓒ Ⓓ Ⓔ | 55 Ⓐ Ⓑ Ⓒ Ⓓ Ⓔ | 78 Ⓐ Ⓑ Ⓒ Ⓓ Ⓔ |
| 10 Ⓐ Ⓑ Ⓒ Ⓓ Ⓔ | 33 Ⓐ Ⓑ Ⓒ Ⓓ Ⓔ | 56 Ⓐ Ⓑ Ⓒ Ⓓ Ⓔ | 79 Ⓐ Ⓑ Ⓒ Ⓓ Ⓔ |
| 11 Ⓐ Ⓑ Ⓒ Ⓓ Ⓔ | 34 Ⓐ Ⓑ Ⓒ Ⓓ Ⓔ | 57 Ⓐ Ⓑ Ⓒ Ⓓ Ⓔ | 80 Ⓐ Ⓑ Ⓒ Ⓓ Ⓔ |
| 12 Ⓐ Ⓑ Ⓒ Ⓓ Ⓔ | 35 Ⓐ Ⓑ Ⓒ Ⓓ Ⓔ | 58 Ⓐ Ⓑ Ⓒ Ⓓ Ⓔ | 81 Ⓐ Ⓑ Ⓒ Ⓓ Ⓔ |
| 13 Ⓐ Ⓑ Ⓒ Ⓓ Ⓔ | 36 Ⓐ Ⓑ Ⓒ Ⓓ Ⓔ | 59 Ⓐ Ⓑ Ⓒ Ⓓ Ⓔ | 82 Ⓐ Ⓑ Ⓒ Ⓓ Ⓔ |
| 14 Ⓐ Ⓑ Ⓒ Ⓓ Ⓔ | 37 Ⓐ Ⓑ Ⓒ Ⓓ Ⓔ | 60 Ⓐ Ⓑ Ⓒ Ⓓ Ⓔ | 83 Ⓐ Ⓑ Ⓒ Ⓓ Ⓔ |
| 15 Ⓐ Ⓑ Ⓒ Ⓓ Ⓔ | 38 Ⓐ Ⓑ Ⓒ Ⓓ Ⓔ | 61 Ⓐ Ⓑ Ⓒ Ⓓ Ⓔ | 84 Ⓐ Ⓑ Ⓒ Ⓓ Ⓔ |
| 16 Ⓐ Ⓑ Ⓒ Ⓓ Ⓔ | 39 Ⓐ Ⓑ Ⓒ Ⓓ Ⓔ | 62 Ⓐ Ⓑ Ⓒ Ⓓ Ⓔ | 85 Ⓐ Ⓑ Ⓒ Ⓓ Ⓔ |
| 17 Ⓐ Ⓑ Ⓒ Ⓓ Ⓔ | 40 Ⓐ Ⓑ Ⓒ Ⓓ Ⓔ | 63 Ⓐ Ⓑ Ⓒ Ⓓ Ⓔ | 86 Ⓐ Ⓑ Ⓒ Ⓓ Ⓔ |
| 18 Ⓐ Ⓑ Ⓒ Ⓓ Ⓔ | 41 Ⓐ Ⓑ Ⓒ Ⓓ Ⓔ | 64 Ⓐ Ⓑ Ⓒ Ⓓ Ⓔ | 87 Ⓐ Ⓑ Ⓒ Ⓓ Ⓔ |
| 19 Ⓐ Ⓑ Ⓒ Ⓓ Ⓔ | 42 Ⓐ Ⓑ Ⓒ Ⓓ Ⓔ | 65 Ⓐ Ⓑ Ⓒ Ⓓ Ⓔ | 88 Ⓐ Ⓑ Ⓒ Ⓓ Ⓔ |
| 20 Ⓐ Ⓑ Ⓒ Ⓓ Ⓔ | 43 Ⓐ Ⓑ Ⓒ Ⓓ Ⓔ | 66 Ⓐ Ⓑ Ⓒ Ⓓ Ⓔ | 89 Ⓐ Ⓑ Ⓒ Ⓓ Ⓔ |
| 21 Ⓐ Ⓑ Ⓒ Ⓓ Ⓔ | 44 Ⓐ Ⓑ Ⓒ Ⓓ Ⓔ | 67 Ⓐ Ⓑ Ⓒ Ⓓ Ⓔ | 90 Ⓐ Ⓑ Ⓒ Ⓓ Ⓔ |
| 22 Ⓐ Ⓑ Ⓒ Ⓓ Ⓔ | 45 Ⓐ Ⓑ Ⓒ Ⓓ Ⓔ | 68 Ⓐ Ⓑ Ⓒ Ⓓ Ⓔ | |
| 23 Ⓐ Ⓑ Ⓒ Ⓓ Ⓔ | 46 Ⓐ Ⓑ Ⓒ Ⓓ Ⓔ | 69 Ⓐ Ⓑ Ⓒ Ⓓ Ⓔ | |

# Practice Test 1

TIME—60 MINUTES

> **Directions:** Each of the questions or incomplete statements below is followed by five suggested answers or completions. Select the one that is best in each case and then fill in the corresponding circle on the answer sheet. You can cut the answer sheet along the dotted line to make recording your answers easier. Remember to give yourself only sixty minutes to complete this test in order to prepare for the pace of the real SAT Subject Test in U.S. History.

1. Which statement best relates the main contribution of Prince Henry of Portugal to European exploration during the sixteenth century?

   (A) He sought access to India via a water route around Africa.
   (B) He was fascinated by navigational instruments and collected them.
   (C) He was an accomplished sea captain who launched exploration personally.
   (D) He founded a school that advanced the science of navigation and trained skilled navigators.
   (E) He raced Spain to cross the Atlantic once Portuguese scientists proved the earth was round.

2. The Protestant Reformation altered colonial American society by

   (A) converting Spanish and French Roman Catholics to Protestantism in the New World and thus creating peace among the colonial neighbors of the English.
   (B) turning the minds of English colonists to spiritual ends thereby hampering the development of a thriving economy.
   (C) compelling a variety of dissenting religious groups to seek sanctuary in the English colonies leading to a higher level of cultural diversity compared to Spanish or French colonies.
   (D) narrowing public theological discourse in a strict doctrinal uniformity that led to higher levels of intolerance and persecution in the English colonies than existed in the mother country.
   (E) creating turmoil in societal values because of the questioning of the authority of the Roman Catholic Church that had guided European ethics for centuries.

467

3. Which statement best summarizes the results of England's original colonies being founded by joint-stock companies?

   (A) The British Crown took special interest in the progress of the colonies because English monarchs were chief investors in the companies.
   (B) Even though the companies failed as business projects the precedent of self-government was established by the relative inattention paid to the colonies by the English government.
   (C) Joint-stock companies that founded colonies in the South prospered because they were able to turn a profit for their investors by establishing a cash-crop economy.
   (D) Colonies founded by joint-stock companies in the North failed to produce cash crops but as a result turned to more diversified economies that produced higher profits for their investors.
   (E) Because many of the colonies were founded as business ventures the colonial population had a higher level of merchants, bankers, and lawyers per capita than the population of England.

4. The Federalist Papers were written to

   (A) combat the growing influence of the Anti-Federalist Party in American public discourse.
   (B) instruct political scientists in the nuances of interpretation of the U.S. Constitution.
   (C) persuade citizens of New York to support the ratification of the U.S. Constitution.
   (D) justify the need of a stronger central government in the minds of all Americans.
   (E) instruct the justices on the Supreme Court in the organization of American jurisprudence.

5. What was the main justification at the time of the purchase of Alaska for the expenditure of over $7 million for what some believed was just a vast territory of frozen wilderness?

   (A) To end encroachments on the part of Russia in keeping with the Monroe Doctrine
   (B) To tap into the vast territory of Alaska as a source of timber and other resources
   (C) To reserve the area for native species of wild animals that were already near extinction
   (D) To provide a region for expansion of the American population in the event of climate change
   (E) To acquire the vast reserves of oil and gold known to be present in the Yukon Territory

6. Which statement below best describes the status of closed and open shops as a part of the rise of the labor movement in the nineteenth and early twentieth centuries?

   (A) Closed shops were routinely found to lead to socialist subversion and were thus banned by law.
   (B) As the labor movement gained credibility and political power all major factories and trades were organized along the closed shop model.
   (C) Closed shops prevented labor unions from establishing in a given factory or trade, whereas open shops allowed labor unions to take part in collective bargaining.
   (D) When management rejected the demands of labor unions it always reserved the right to close factories because of private property rights.
   (E) Open shops were factories that still permitted nonunion laborers to work there, whereas closed shops were factories where unions had negotiated total unionization of the workforce.

7. Martin Luther King Jr. took his first major leadership role in the civil rights movement in which event?

   (A) The march on Washington, D.C.
   (B) The Selma march
   (C) The campaign in which he wrote a letter from the Birmingham jail
   (D) The Montgomery Bus Boycott
   (E) The sanitation workers' strike in Memphis

8. Which event in the Vietnam War directly sparked the protests at Kent State University in Ohio that led to the shooting of four students there?

   (A) The massive use of B-52 bombings at the Battle of Khe Sanh
   (B) The bombings of North Vietnam initiated by the Nixon administration
   (C) The passage of the Gulf of Tonkin Resolution in response to the Gulf of Tonkin incident
   (D) The My Lai Massacre in which American troops killed innocent civilians
   (E) The invasion of Cambodia by American troops attempting to shut down the Ho Chi Minh trail

9. What was the Congressional committee investigating the Watergate scandal looking for in the White House tapes that led the Supreme Court to grant access to these private recordings?

   (A) Proof of a conspiracy among President Nixon's staff to use any means necessary to win the Election of 1972
   (B) Infighting among the White House staffers to determine which Nixon adviser would give information leading to the prosecution of the others
   (C) Proof that President Nixon knew of the break-ins at the Watergate complex and was complicit in the attempt to cover them up
   (D) Proof that money was offered to White House staffers to encourage them to lie under oath
   (E) Signs that presidential advisers were trying to distance themselves from the president because they believed his actions were illegal

10. What role did Oliver North play in the Iran-Contra scandal of the Reagan administration?

    (A) He worked undercover for the Federal Bureau of Investigation to investigate the scandal from within the administration.
    (B) He led the Marine Corps Special Operations team that freed the hostages in Iran.
    (C) He organized the clandestine support for the Contra forces in Nicaragua using Iranian money.
    (D) He was the National Security Council adviser who exposed the illegal operation to the press.
    (E) He gave testimony in the Congressional investigation that incriminated President Reagan.

11. What was the result of soil depletion in the colonial era along the Coastal Plain in North America?

    (A) English colonists abandoned the cultivation of cotton and other crops that depleted the soil in favor of crops that replenished the soil.
    (B) More and more land was cleared and put under cultivation of tobacco and other crops thereby opening the frontier upriver from earlier settlements.
    (C) More intensive agriculture was practiced using natural fertilizers and crop rotation.
    (D) Peaceful relations with American Indian tribes were established as food shortages required the English colonists to make peace in order to survive.
    (E) Whole areas of colonial America were abandoned once their soil was incapable of producing a satisfactory yield.

12. What impact did passage of the Declaratory Act have on colonial Americans after the repeal of the hated Stamp Act in 1766?

    (A) The assertion of Parliamentary power after such a victory for the American cause emboldened colonists to view England with greater contempt.
    (B) The Declaratory Act forced colonists to accept the principle of direct taxation despite a lack of actual representation.
    (C) The repeal of the Stamp Act followed by such an arbitrary assertion of authority sparked immediate calls for American independence.
    (D) The Declaratory Act was met with such violent demonstrations that the standing army was put on high alert in New York and Boston.
    (E) The dispute over both acts of Parliament drained revolutionary sentiment and stalled the patriot cause for almost a decade.

13. Which statement best describes the significance of the Lewis and Clark expedition?

    (A) The expedition was a covert scouting mission for the military officers who accompanied the explorers in order to test the strength of American Indian tribes.
    (B) The expedition amounted to a race to determine whether Great Britain or the United States would control the unclaimed land between Spanish and British territory in the West.
    (C) The expedition was searching for the best route to build the first transcontinental railroad.
    (D) The expedition was searching for a water route to the Pacific Coast and, although unsuccessful in this quest, the safe return of the explorers sparked westward migration.
    (E) The collection of unique specimens by the explorers inspired the founding of the Smithsonian Institution.

14. ". . .those words of delusion and folly, 'Liberty first and Union afterward?'; but everywhere, spread all over in characters of living light . . . as they float over the sea and over the land . . . that other sentiment, dear to every true American heart—Liberty *and* Union, now and forever, one and inseparable!"

    These words most likely expressed the ideas of which leader and in which debate?

    (A) Henry Clay's call for his American System
    (B) John C. Calhoun's South Carolina Exposition and Protest in the Nullification Crisis
    (C) Henry Clay's compromise stance in the Nullification Crisis
    (D) Andrew Jackson's defense of his actions in the Bank War
    (E) Daniel Webster's stance in the Webster/Hayne Debates over the sale of western lands

15. Which action on the part of Joseph Smith led to his being arrested for treason in his leadership of the Church of Jesus Christ of Latter-Day Saints (The Mormons)?

    (A) His publishing of the Book of Mormon as an additional gospel account to the Bible
    (B) His establishing of a new city for his followers in Illinois
    (C) His drilling of militia forces while dressed in a military uniform
    (D) His instituting the practice of polygamy, or the marriage of one man to many wives
    (E) His leading his followers to establish a separate country in the unclaimed territory of the West

16. What was John C. Fremont's role in launching the Mexican War in 1846?

   (A) He was dispatched to the border of Mexico to instigate a clash that James K. Polk could use as a pretext for asking the Congress to declare war.
   (B) He led an expedition to California disguised as an exploratory journey that was designed to inspire Californians in the Bear Flag Revolt.
   (C) He was sent on a secret mission to try to negotiate a peace settlement of disputes between the two countries.
   (D) He led a larger army in the wake of Stephen Kearny's scouting mission to California.
   (E) He was the secretary of war who pushed James K. Polk to fight as an opportunity to expand slavery west.

17. What impact did the Supreme Court's decision in *Dred Scott v. Sandford* have on the sectional tensions prior to the Civil War?

   (A) Since the Supreme Court had no previous opportunity to give a ruling on slavery, the resolution of the case reduced sectionalism by exercising the balance of powers.
   (B) The presence of so many abolitionist justices on the Court exacerbated sectional tension and rendered the Court's decision of no value due to mistrust.
   (C) The decision angered the North by dismissing the rights of African-Americans and made the South jubilant.
   (D) The ruling failed to free Dred Scott but convinced the South that the Supreme Court would eventually declare slavery unconstitutional and thus abolish it.
   (E) The decision alienated the people of the West so much that to North/South tension was also added East/West tension.

18. Which new power for the federal government resulted from the Civil War?

   (A) The Congress was able to reverse a decision of the Supreme Court.
   (B) The president was able to declare a national observance of a day of prayer.
   (C) The military was able to enter a state for the purpose of protecting American citizens.
   (D) The Supreme Court was able to order the president to desist from an unconstitutional action.
   (E) The Congress was able to draft men into military service because volunteers were too few.

19. A. Mitchell Palmer was known in the 1920s for what activity as attorney general of the United States?

   (A) Cracking down on the activities of the resurgent Ku Klux Klan
   (B) Regulating corporations who used unscrupulous practices to ward off business competition
   (C) Bribing governors of states to obtain their cooperation with his family's road-paving company
   (D) Conducting surprise inspections of labor unions' headquarters looking for subversive material
   (E) Investigating the bootlegging operations of organized crime families during Prohibition

20. ". . . the general principle that the country can never again afford to let the prairies and the plantations drop lower and lower in poverty and discouragement just because its factories and brokerage houses are still flourishing may be taken as fairly established for 1934 and all future years."

   The above quotation was most likely made in reference to what aspect of the New Deal?

   (A) The Civilian Conservation Corps
   (B) The National Recovery Administration
   (C) The Works Progress Administration
   (D) The Agricultural Adjustment Act
   (E) The National Labor Relations Board

21. Which statement below best explains the reason the Navigation Acts became so problematic in the relationship between England and her American colonies?

   (A) The laws were based on mercantilism, an economic philosophy Americans dispensed with within one generation of the founding of the colonies.
   (B) The laws were only loosely enforced until England needed money to pay off the huge war debt from the French and Indian War.
   (C) The laws represented direct taxation of the lives and trade practices of the American colonists who agreed only to indirect taxation with the consent of their legislatures.
   (D) The laws were judged to be the punitive measures of a king seeking revenge for the temporary dissolution of the monarchy by the English Civil War.
   (E) The laws created hidden incentives for the American colonists to trade with the Spanish and the French in the New World, a practice most Americans found unpatriotic and disloyal.

22. Which event prior to the Constitutional Convention was the main factor that convinced leaders to create another form of government besides the Articles of Confederation?

    (A) British troops remained in forts on American soil around the Great Lakes Region.
    (B) The central government failed to force states to pay taxes to support the will of Congress.
    (C) Shays's Rebellion was barely put down by the Massachusetts militia.
    (D) The states disputed western land claims left over from colonial charters.
    (E) Tecumseh organized a coalition of American Indian tribes to resist westward expansion.

23. Which pairing below relates major causes of the War of 1812?

    (A) Impressment of American sailors and British aid to American Indians on the frontier
    (B) Disputes over British encroachments on American territory and on American trade routes
    (C) Mistrust of British designs in New World colonization and Napoleon's colonial ambitions
    (D) British cooperation with the French in foreign policy and Spanish intrigues in New Orleans
    (E) British destruction of American war vessels and support of the French in the XYZ Affair

24. All of the following people were abolitionists EXCEPT

    (A) Lewis Tappan.
    (B) George Fitzhugh.
    (C) William Lloyd Garrison.
    (D) Elijah P. Lovejoy.
    (E) Frederick Douglass.

25. What restriction was placed on the executive branch by the Tenure of Office Act during the Reconstruction era?

    (A) The president could no longer fire members of the executive branch without Congressional approval due to the struggle for power in the federal government.
    (B) The president could no longer run for reelection after serving for two terms.
    (C) The president could no longer commission general officers in the military branches due to the prolonging of the Civil War through political appointments.
    (D) The president could no longer take the lead in making appointments to his cabinet.
    (E) The president could no longer choose the leadership of federal agencies like the Indian Bureau and the Freedman's Bureau.

26. What was the significance of the Bessemer process to the American steel industry?

  (A) The dispute between Henry Bessemer and William Kelly was a landmark case for patent law.
  (B) The new manufacturing technique was Andrew Carnegie's first leap forward in his monopoly.
  (C) The technology was inexpensive to install and allowed Carnegie's competitors to catch up.
  (D) The process finally allowed the United States to exceed the British in production capacity.
  (E) The process made the production of steel cheaper because it required less energy.

Courtesy of the Bancroft Library, University of California, Berkeley

27. The circumstances portrayed in the 1881 political cartoon entitled, "The Proper Thing," revealed the need for Chester Arthur to

  (A) institute stricter security procedures in the wake of the Garfield assassination.
  (B) begin a new "open door" policy to finally allow citizens access to Gilded Age presidents.
  (C) support the Pendleton Act as a measure of civil service reform.
  (D) cooperate with labor unions in the growing gap between the rich and the poor.
  (E) come down from his views of the presidency as an imperial position.

28. The Social Gospel is expressed best by which statement of belief below?

    (A) Socialism is the political and economic system that best follows the teachings of Jesus Christ.
    (B) American Christians should place less emphasis on preaching and more on fellowship among believers.
    (C) The focus of church members should turn from an inward unity to outreach to unbelievers in the United States and abroad.
    (D) The American Church should focus less on converting individuals and more on addressing the problems of newly urbanized American society.
    (E) In the wake of the influx of immigrants from so many different backgrounds Christians should eliminate all doctrinal distinctions and form one church.

29. Which statement best summarizes Booker T. Washington's goals in founding the Tuskegee Institute in Alabama?

    (A) African-Americans should be trained for military service with the same rigor as white soldiers so they could become officers, not just enlisted men.
    (B) African-Americans should learn about their own history and cultural roots in Africa instead of trying to fit into Western culture as expressed in American society.
    (C) African-Americans should be steeped in classical literature and political theory so as to become activists who could debate the white power structure on its own terms.
    (D) African-Americans should not be prepared to enter professional careers as doctors, lawyers, and businessmen.
    (E) African-Americans should focus first on acquiring training to become skilled craftsmen and more qualified teachers so as to improve education and basic economic strength.

30. George Creel's task as the head of the Committee on Public Information during World War I was to

    (A) raise academic standards so as to help the United States better compete with the engineering prowess of Germany.
    (B) serve as the liaison between the federal government and American journalists to avoid the release of secret information that might jeopardize national security.
    (C) increase support for the war in enlistments and the purchase of war bonds through the skillful use of propaganda.
    (D) serve as a central location for the submitting of information on German-Americans and other citizens with connections to the Central Powers who might be spying for the enemy.
    (E) root out subversive elements in society who were sympathetic to the leftist ideas filtering in from the Bolshevik Revolution in Russia.

31. Which description below best states the role of Eleanor Roosevelt as a part of the Roosevelt administration?

    (A) She was a key influence in Franklin D. Roosevelt's Brains Trust.
    (B) She possessed great skill in entertaining and thus won her husband wider support.
    (C) She traveled across America to represent her husband and his policies.
    (D) She traveled abroad extensively and advised her husband on foreign policy.
    (E) She was the president's main contact with his cabinet after he suffered a stroke.

32. Which statement best expresses the Spanish conquistadors' important contribution to the establishment of colonies beyond their task of conquering new lands?

    (A) Every conquistador brought along friars or priests to convert American Indians to Roman Catholicism as the chief mechanism for societal control and cultural exchange.
    (B) Each conquistador had special talents in fields such as engineering, medicine, or law beyond mere military prowess and employed that expertise in organizing his colony.
    (C) Each conquistador founded a university in his area of conquest to transfer the highest forms of European culture as early as possible to the New World.
    (D) Every conquistador was required by the Spanish Crown to keep meticulous, personal accounts of his activities that would be published and studied in Spain as a guide for future efforts.
    (E) All conquistadors knew they had to send treasure fleets continually back to Spain to keep the attention of the Spanish monarchy focused on the significance of their efforts.

33. What was the main difference between the New Jersey Plan and the Virginia Plan expressed during the debates in the Constitutional Convention?

    (A) The New Jersey Plan expressed the goals and needs of the North, whereas the Virginia Plan expressed those of the South.
    (B) The New Jersey Plan represented the interests of states that were smaller in population, whereas the Virginia Plan represented those of states with large populations.
    (C) The New Jersey Plan sought to start from scratch and totally revise the government, whereas the Virginia Plan wanted merely to revise the Articles of Confederation.
    (D) The New Jersey Plan voiced the wishes of the Anti-Federalists to produce a weak central government, whereas the Virginia Plan voiced those of the Federalists for a strong one.
    (E) The New Jersey Plan demanded the national capital be placed near it in New York City, whereas the Virginia Plan sought the proximity of a capital on the Potomac River.

34. The "Corrupt Bargain" charge from the Election of 1824 was derived from the fact that

    (A) Andrew Jackson said, "To the victor belongs the spoils."
    (B) the election was thrown into the House of Representatives because there was no clear winner.
    (C) when John Quincy Adams won most Americans thought it was simply because of his father.
    (D) disputed election returns were received from Florida, South Carolina, and Louisiana.
    (E) John Quincy Adams made Henry Clay his secretary of state after Clay supported him.

35. Dorothea Dix was most closely associated as a leader in which antebellum reform movement?

    (A) The abolition of slavery
    (B) The women's suffrage movement
    (C) The temperance crusade against alcohol
    (D) The reform of the treatment of the mentally ill
    (E) The reform of prisons for juvenile delinquents

36. In what way did the Filipino Insurrection turn out to be worse than the Spanish-American War that brought the Philippine Islands under the control of the United States?

    (A) Involvement in the Philippines put the United States in conflict with Great Britain, a much more serious opponent than the declining Spanish nation.
    (B) Having the Philippines entangled the United States in the Chinese Revolution.
    (C) The insurrection lasted longer than the Spanish-American War and caused more casualties while sparking heated debates back home over imperialism.
    (D) The Spanish-American War made William McKinley popular, whereas the Filipino Insurrection led to his assassination that destabilized American politics.
    (E) The Philippine Islands required American soldiers to fight in desert-like conditions, whereas the fighting in Cuba took place in a temperate climate.

37. Which policy on the part of the Roosevelt administration prior to World War II was presented as an effort to keep the United States out of the fighting in Europe and Asia?

    (A) The formation of the War Production Board to make America the "arsenal of democracy"
    (B) The transformation of the Civilian Conservation Corps into a training branch of the military
    (C) The institution of the draft to increase the military preparedness of the United States
    (D) The transfer of money and military equipment to the Allies through the Lend/Lease program
    (E) The isolation of aggressor nations through the policies expressed in the Quarantine speech

38. What action on the part of President Eisenhower increased Cold War tensions with the Soviet Union when the two superpowers were on the verge of holding a peace summit in 1960?

    (A) Authorizing the production of the hydrogen bomb
    (B) Authorizing flyovers of the Soviet Union by spy planes
    (C) Authorizing the formation of the National Aeronautics and Space Administration to boost American rocket science
    (D) Alienating the Soviet allies, the Chinese, by staging military maneuvers near disputed islands
    (E) Alienating the Soviets by staging an insurrection in communist Cuba at the Bay of Pigs

39. Which landmark Supreme Court case below was decided by the Warren Court during the 1960s?

    (A) *Brown v. Board of Education of Topeka, Kansas*
    (B) *Engel v. Vitale*
    (C) *Korematsu v. the United States*
    (D) *Board of Regents v. Bakke*
    (E) *Roe v. Wade*

40. What role did Phyllis Schlafly play in the debate about the equal rights amendment?

    (A) She toured the country advocating ratification of this amendment to establish the equal rights of women in American constitutional law.
    (B) She joined with the National Organization for Women and wrote editorials supporting the amendment in *Ms.* magazine.
    (C) She mounted a national campaign to stop ratification of the amendment on the grounds that it demeaned the dignity of women to be subject to the military draft and other "male" roles.
    (D) She was instrumental in convincing her husband, a senator, to champion the ratification of the amendment in the Congress.
    (E) As the governor of Indiana she stopped the ratification vote in her state and rallied other Midwestern states to block it.

41. The Battle of Saratoga was significant in the American Revolution because the

    (A) Continental Army met an equally matched British force and defeated it for the first time.
    (B) American force assembled to meet the British was made up of patriot soldiers from every one of the thirteen states represented in the Continental Congress.
    (C) treachery of Benedict Arnold was finally exposed and this internal threat removed.
    (D) American victory in the battle prevented the British capture of New York City, the best seaport on the Atlantic Coast.
    (E) American victory convinced France the United States had a chance at winning the war so the French offered formal support.

42. How did President John Adams respond to the XYZ Affair?

    (A) He simultaneously built up the U.S. Navy while sending another delegation to sue for peace.
    (B) He pushed the Federalist-dominated Congress to declare war against the French.
    (C) He cut off all diplomatic channels with the French and made peace overtures to Great Britain.
    (D) He ignored the problem and focused on building up the economic strength of the new country.
    (E) He sent his son, John Quincy Adams, to visit the French foreign minister to clear the air.

43. How did President Jefferson respond to the outbreak of the Napoleonic Wars in Europe?

    (A) He doubled the number of frigates in the U.S. Navy.
    (B) He negotiated the Louisiana Purchase in an effort to fund French attacks on the British.
    (C) He sent an invasion force into Canada on an ill-fated winter attack.
    (D) He pushed the Embargo Act through Congress to avoid being drawn into the war.
    (E) He constructed a series of coastline forts, one of which saved Baltimore in the War of 1812.

44. What role did Stephen Austin play in Texas independence from Mexico?

    (A) He guided the original American settlers of the northern provinces of Mexico at the invitation of Santa Anna, the president of Mexico.
    (B) He organized the resistance at the Battle of the Alamo.
    (C) He rounded up volunteers from Tennessee to rescue the defenders of the Alamo.
    (D) He led the strategic retreat of Texan forces until he turned on his pursuers at the Battle of San Jacinto and captured Santa Anna himself.
    (E) He wrote the constitution of the Lone Star Republic and was elected its first president, then became governor when Texas was annexed by the United States.

45. "We have no power as citizens of the free states, or in our federal capacity as members of the federal Union through the general government, to disturb slavery in the states where it exists . . . . What I insist upon is that the new territories shall be kept free from it while in the territorial condition."

The quotation above was most likely the position of which individual in the debates about slavery prior to the Civil War?

(A) Henry Clay
(B) William H. Seward
(C) Stephen Douglas
(D) Abraham Lincoln
(E) James Buchanan

46. What practice made Union general William Tecumseh Sherman the first "modern" general during the Civil War but also foreshadowed the severity of warfare in the twentieth century?

(A) He ordered his troops to dig trenches that shielded them from enemy fire but turned battles into prolonged, murderous stalemates.
(B) He planted bombs in positions he knew his enemy would occupy before battles and detonated them once the battles commenced.
(C) He destroyed civilian property and confiscated scarce resources instead of just fighting the enemy's troops in order to break the opposing army's ability to wage war.
(D) He took prisoners of war and detained them in concentrated numbers in camps without adequate shelter or food and worked them as conscript laborers.
(E) He used sophisticated spy networks to improve his strategic advantage by studying the enemy's tactics so he could anticipate how a given general would respond when pressed.

47. What tactics characterized the presidential campaign between Grover Cleveland and James G. Blaine for the Election of 1884?

(A) Both campaigns took extensive "whistle-stop" railroad tours through the five states that were swing states during the Gilded Age.
(B) Both campaigns published book-length autobiographies that contrasted their candidates' personal and political differences based on their distinctive upbringings.
(C) Both campaigns sought common ground between their party platforms and emphasized the need for the United States to put to rest the latent animosity from the Civil War.
(D) Both campaigns pledged to cooperate with the winner of the election to rid both parties of the extensive corruption in government.
(E) Both campaigns resorted to mudslinging attacks on the opposing candidates because the platform of each party held relatively the same positions on most major issues.

48. In what way did Theodore Roosevelt reinterpret the Monroe Doctrine?

 (A) He worked to put aside the animosity previous presidents held for European nations and tried to reopen the Western Hemisphere for their active involvement.

 (B) He stated that because U. S. foreign policy prevented European nations from interfering in the affairs of Central and South America, the United States would have to act as the region's police force.

 (C) He stated that the Monroe Doctrine's prohibition on further European colonialism in the Western Hemisphere was an open door for American imperialism in the Americas.

 (D) He considered the building of the Panama Canal to be a mandate from world civilization and a feat that earned the United States exclusive rights to govern its use without European help.

 (E) He wielded his "Big Stick" foreign policy not only to ward off military intervention from Europe in the Western Hemisphere but also to permanently occupy neighboring countries.

49. In addressing the Great Depression, Franklin D. Roosevelt's (FDR) early administration

 (A) proposed a systematic plan for the relief, recovery, and reform of the American economy.

 (B) took a wait-and-see approach to determine whether the recent policies of President Hoover would bring about a change in the economy.

 (C) ushered an unprecedented amount of legislation through the Congress to establish any program that held promise for addressing the economic crisis.

 (D) held an economic summit with national and world leaders to get to the bottom of the problems that had brought about the worldwide Depression.

 (E) ignored the urgency of the economic crisis while captivating the nation with cheerful rhetoric broadcasts for the first time by radio in speeches FDR called "fireside chats."

50. What prompted President Harry Truman to go to extraordinary lengths to help the citizens of western Berlin in the Berlin Airlift?

 (A) The Soviet forces occupying East Germany ordered the immediate evacuation of the city.

 (B) The Soviet Union attacked the enclaves of Berlin that were under United Nations protection.

 (C) The Soviet Union built a barrier across the city of Berlin to prevent East Germans from trying to escape to the West through the zones of the city held by the United States, the United Kingdom, and France.

 (D) The Soviet Union cut off all access by road to supply the Berliners under American protection.

 (E) The Soviet Union was supplying Cuba by air and Truman wanted to show American resolve.

51. Which description below best summarizes the role of the viceroys in Spain's New World empire?

    (A) They served as commanders of the various conquistadors and their armies to provide a unified cooperation among usually competitive men.

    (B) They were the hand-picked legal representatives of the king of Spain and ruled their portion of the empire in his stead but also at his command.

    (C) They were priests vested with the highest civic and religious authority to represent both the monarchy but also the Roman Catholic Church.

    (D) They were tantamount to feudal lords who governed portions of the empire granted to them as their own private property that could be passed down to their sons.

    (E) They were salaried employees of the Crown who committed to live out their lives in the New World in order to transplant Spanish culture and to preserve societal stability.

52. Why did John Quincy Adams and later scholars refer to the time between 1783 and 1789 as the Critical Period in American history?

    (A) The ambiguity of government power in the new country under the Articles of Confederation jeopardized the gains of the successful American Revolution.

    (B) The continued presence of Great Britain's military forces on American soil posed a lethal threat to eastern cities.

    (C) The superiority of the British navy nearly stifled the fledgling American merchant fleet's ability to come and go to supply the country and to export American goods.

    (D) The sectionalism extending through the debates over whether to seek independence had already placed the North and the South on a war footing against each other.

    (E) The disunity of the new states and their lack of respect for Congress was apparent to the American Indian tribes who now knew the colonies were outside of British protection.

53. What was the direct, unintended consequence of Thomas Jefferson's desire to weaken the executive branch after Federalist presidents had created a strong central government?

    (A) The plan of the Founding Fathers to have a balanced, three-branch government was done away with.

    (B) Great Britain was encouraged by the power vacuum to actively plot for the restoration of the American colonies to the British Empire.

    (C) Most Americans began to think of their state governments as more important than the federal government in exerting authority in their lives.

    (D) Federalist policies like the charter for the Bank of the United States and the Alien and Sedition Acts were immediately repealed.

    (E) The Congress established its committee system in the vacuum left by Jefferson's lack of initiative and increased legislative control to provide leadership for the country.

54. Which of the political parties listed below set the precedent of holding a national nominating convention that all other parties adopted as more democratic than the caucus system?

    (A) The Federalist Party
    (B) The Anti-Federalist Party
    (C) The Whig Party
    (D) The Anti-Masonic Party
    (E) The Democratic Party

55. Why did the United States eventually possess the southern part of the Oregon Country rather than Great Britain?

    (A) James K. Polk sent the U.S. Navy into battle with the British Pacific fleet in a quasi-war off the coast, and the British retreated.
    (B) Mountain men had established forts throughout the territory that discouraged encroachments by British settlers.
    (C) More American citizens settled in the territory than did British or Canadian settlers, so when the dispute arose over ownership the British decided to withdraw.
    (D) The American Indians of the Pacific Northwest were peaceful and not as susceptible to British enticements with alcohol and European weapons, so they chose to become American.
    (E) American missionaries had converted American Indians to Protestant faiths other than the Anglicanism of the Church of England.

56. In what way did Abraham Lincoln attempt to slow down the rush toward war with Mexico?

    (A) He chastened President Polk publicly in newspaper editorials as a shameless pro-slavery expansionist.
    (B) He mounted a campaign in magazines like *Puck* and *Harper's Weekly* of excoriating essays that accompanied cartoons drawn by Thomas Nast.
    (C) He proposed resolutions in Congress that were skeptical of the president's claim that Mexico had provoked a war.
    (D) He toured the country by railroad saying that if Polk got his war, then the Union would be dissolved.
    (E) He highlighted the dangers of allowing slavery to spread west in a speech delivered at the Cooper Union in New York City before a spellbound crowd of over 1,500 listeners.

57. Which statement below best explains the impact of Darwinism on mainstream attitudes about race in the United States during the era of Reconstruction?

    (A) African-Americans were thought to be incapable of organizing their lives and that if the federal government did not step in, natural selection would eliminate their race.

    (B) Scientists like Louis Agassiz in New England were unmotivated to support help for African-Americans because evolution had destined them to a subordinate position in society.

    (C) Abolitionists like Frederick Douglass urged the government to leave African-Americans alone because now that they were free, they must be allowed to struggle to survive.

    (D) Because Darwinists said that human life originated in Africa, African-Americans were afforded special honor by the scientific community as fathers and mothers of all races.

    (E) Social Darwinism actively promoted the idea that with aid to African-Americans the federal government was working alongside evolution to better the whole human race.

58. "The interpretation of constitutional principles must not be too literal. We must remember that the machinery of government would not work if it were not allowed a little play in its joints."

    This 1928 quote by Justice Oliver Wendell Holmes Jr. revealed that he held which kind of views while on the Supreme Court?

    (A) Progressive
    (B) Loose constructionist
    (C) Strict constructionist
    (D) Democratic
    (E) Republican

59. What was Joseph Pulitzer's editorial position on the Spanish-American War?

    (A) Pulitzer demanded that his correspondents remain as objective as possible in their coverage of the war.

    (B) Pulitzer attempted to forestall the war by publishing daily reports of the Spanish perspective on the matters that alienated the two countries.

    (C) Pulitzer deeply criticized President McKinley for his lack of foreign policy experience in a time of national crisis.

    (D) Pulitzer actively promoted the oncoming war by giving his staff permission to print what amounted to propaganda.

    (E) Pulitzer considered the entire conflict an insignificant event not worthy of the attention of his newspaper, the largest one in the country, even though he was a Republican.

60. Which of the following best explains the rapid development of suburbs in America after World War II?

    (A) Americans had learned to fear living in urban centers because of what had happened to European cities bombed during the war.
    (B) After the war farm prices dropped suddenly and ruined American farmers who then sought a lifestyle halfway between country life and city life.
    (C) Presidents Roosevelt and Truman and General Eisenhower all returned from travels in Europe praising this manner of living that they had observed in Germany.
    (D) After the sacrifices of the war Americans could not afford to purchase homes in the cities so they sought less expensive real estate on the outskirts.
    (E) Companies that manufactured housing for the war developed uniform techniques that made home construction cheaper just in time for the baby boom.

61. Why were explorers working for the English Crown sent to look for a Northwest Passage in the era of European exploration of the Western Hemisphere?

    (A) Sir Francis Drake had proven that the passage through the Straits of Magellan below South America was too dangerous for routine travel.
    (B) The English government wanted easier access to the lucrative fishing and whaling grounds off the coast of North America in the Pacific Ocean.
    (C) Eskimo legend had indicated that such a route existed and led to a city filled with gold.
    (D) England was at war with Spain and sought a route to the Far East that would not run the risk of attack by the Spanish Armada patrolling the south Atlantic Ocean.
    (E) The wooden ships of the era could not sail efficiently through warm Atlantic routes because worms attacked their hulls and required refitting halfway through every voyage.

62. Which statement best explains why the Virginia House of Burgesses was founded as the first representative assembly in North America?

    (A) The British Crown ordered that because of its distance from England and Parliament Virginia needed a replacement legislature.
    (B) As prosperity came to the Virginia colonists they needed a body that could help mediate property disputes and pass laws to protect their rights as Englishmen.
    (C) As early as 1619 Virginians were contemplating independence from England and moved to organize themselves into a "civil body politic" to be ready when the opportunity arose to act.
    (D) The Virginia Company determined that having a legislature where colonists could air their grievances was the only hope of proving they were better than the French or Spanish.
    (E) The Virginia Company ordered the colonists to form the House of Burgesses in order to organize defense in the face of repeated attacks by the Spanish.

63. Why were the American colonists so angry over King George III's Proclamation of 1763?

   (A) They had just helped to win the French and Indian War because they wanted access to the land of the Ohio River Valley that the king now declared off limits.

   (B) They could not tolerate the fact that despite the English victory in the French and Indian War the Crown was expanding the boundary of French Canada southward.

   (C) They knew that the Proclamation of 1763 would incite attacks by American Indians on the frontier in retaliation for the English abandonment of allied tribes.

   (D) The Enlightenment had trained many leaders among the colonies to reject the actions of absolutist monarchs like George III.

   (E) The Proclamation of 1763 reflected that the people of America were no longer of interest to the British Crown on top of the indignities Americans suffered serving in the British Army.

64. Why were the Gag Rules of antebellum America so detrimental to the preservation of the Union?

   (A) No bills that provoked sectionalism were allowed to be debated during a national crisis.

   (B) In an era of latent animosity toward Great Britain, no congressman was allowed to appeal to the former mother country for help healing the North/South division.

   (C) The separation of church and state prevented the Congress from dealing effectively with the breakaway Mormon territory in Utah.

   (D) When the preservation of the Union depended on compromise, all abolitionist bills were tabled indefinitely so no reasonable approach to emancipation could be worked out.

   (E) Each new wave of immigrants further undermined the traditional values of American society but all nativist legislation was postponed without debate.

65. What was the impact of Helen Hunt Jackson's book *A Century of Dishonor* about the treatment of American Indians by the federal government?

   (A) The book was largely ignored and the settlement of the West continued apace.

   (B) The book sparked heated debate in the Congress and in American newspapers, but no action.

   (C) The book was dismissed for its overly melodramatic tone even though it was a fictional novel.

   (D) The book was criticized because Ms. Jackson had no first-person knowledge of the subject.

   (E) The book marked a turning point in the relations between Americans and American Indians.

66. Which statement below best depicts the workings of a corporation using vertical combination to organize its industry?

    (A) The leading corporation in an industry dictates the prices to be charged for its products by all lesser companies in the same industry.

    (B) One corporate leader amasses control of one step of an industrial process and then can force companies involved in the other steps to cooperate or drop out of the industry.

    (C) One corporation acquires companies that are involved in all stages of an industrial process and through efficiency and large economies of scale effectively runs that industry.

    (D) The largest corporation in an industry communicates to the federal government the standards that are best for the industry and the government then enforces those standards for all.

    (E) Experts in universities are hired by the federal government to advise corporate leaders in an industry on how best to run their businesses.

67. The problem with the original Civil Service Reform Commission begun under the Grant administration was that

    (A) the members of the Commission were gathered from among the very politicians and business leaders most guilty of peddling influence in the administration.

    (B) President Grant only hired the first commissioner to silence his criticism and then gave the Commission no enforcement power.

    (C) no systematic knowledge of the practices of graft and patronage existed because the outrage over political corruption in the Gilded Age had just begun.

    (D) the journalists asked to sit on the Commission merely argued about which of them would be able to publish their findings in his periodical first and thus accomplished little.

    (E) the Commission sat in New York City where the infamous Tweed Ring threatened them into silence.

68. What was the significance of the addition of multiple independently targeted reentry vehicles (MIRVs) to the American nuclear arsenal?

    (A) Because the United States had lost the Arms Race due to a missile gap, the existence of missiles with multiple warheads was the only way to keep pace with the Soviets.
    (B) The existence of such a terrifying weapon in the hands of the United States provided the last straw that caused the Soviet Union to acknowledge defeat in the Cold War.
    (C) The sophistication of the multiple-warhead technology was beyond the capacity of the Soviet Union and allayed Americans' fears that the Soviets would employ a first strike.
    (D) With such formidable weapons in existence, the Chinese finally decided to put pressure on their Soviet allies to end the madness of the Cold War.
    (E) The fear that terrorists would obtain nuclear warheads if a missile launched but failed to detonate all its payload led to the banning of these most lethal nuclear weapons.

69. "And this from a young Chicano: 'Some of us have suffered from recession all our lives.' The symptoms of this crisis of the American spirit are all around us. For the first time in the history of our country a majority of our people believe that the next 5 years will be worse than the past 5 years."

    The above quotation was most likely in a speech made by which president?

    (A) John F. Kennedy
    (B) Richard M. Nixon
    (C) Jimmy Carter
    (D) Ronald Reagan
    (E) Bill Clinton

70. Which candidate in the Election of 1992 mounted a third-party campaign that achieved sufficient success to alter the outcome of the election?

    (A) Former Ku Klux Klansman David Duke
    (B) Former columnist Pat Buchanan
    (C) Former businessman Ross Perot
    (D) Former consumer advocate Ralph Nader
    (E) Former governor of Minnesota Harold Stassen

71. The reason Viking discoveries of the New World were not recognized by Europeans as of great significance was that the

    (A) Vikings were considered barbarians with no cultural significance in world affairs.
    (B) Vikings did not even preserve knowledge of these accomplishments themselves.
    (C) Vikings reported the existence of humans already in North America who were there first.
    (D) settlements of the Vikings were not permanent and not widely known in Europe.
    (E) exploits of the Viking heroes like Leif Ericson were considered mythological.

72. What reform in criminal justice was a direct result of the successful American Revolution?

    (A) The end of the practice of burning dissenters from established religions as heretics
    (B) The creation of penitentiaries designed to reform criminals and cut down on the number of crimes for which capital punishment was the usual sentence
    (C) The closing of all American debtor prisons
    (D) The end of the practice of locking mentally ill people away as if they were criminals
    (E) The formation of prisons just for juvenile delinquents in order to keep them separate from hardened criminals who would only influence them to become worse

73. Why was the two-party system consisting of the Whigs and the Democrats able to avoid the outbreak of civil war while the Republicans and the Democrats could not?

    (A) Whigs and Democrats were both national parties who could more easily urge compromise to diminish the force of sectionalism.
    (B) Although the Whigs faced a national Democratic Party, the Republicans faced a Democratic Party that retained support only in the South.
    (C) The Whigs were able to ignore the influence of the nativist Know-Nothing Party, whereas the Republicans had to contend with them thereby diminishing their party's unity.
    (D) The Whigs were able to produce leaders skilled at oratory, whereas the Republicans had no such gifted speakers.
    (E) The Whigs were able to draw on a long heritage of British opposition parties, whereas the new Republican Party had no such honorable tradition.

74. What role stated below best describes how the notion of Manifest Destiny led to the settlement of the West?

    (A) A shared set of values like those expressed in Manifest Destiny allowed frontier towns to erase disparate Old World cultural differences and unify in one American culture.

    (B) The isolation of frontier life for pioneer families on the Great Plains could only be endured because the government routinely notified settlers of the mission of American society.

    (C) Immigrants aware of the concept of Manifest Destiny left Europe specifically to take part in this version of the American Dream and thus provided the manpower necessary to move West.

    (D) The national self-confidence created by the supposed superiority of the American way of life motivated expansionist politicians, pioneers, and missionaries alike to take on hardships.

    (E) The pristine nature of life on the frontier appeared to be the only solution to end the corruption that had taken root in the traditional power centers of the East.

75. Which statement below best describes the sentiment behind Abraham Lincoln's plan for Reconstruction of the South before his assassination ended its chance for implementation?

    (A) The southern states had never successfully left the Union so there was no need for them to do anything special to resume their status as states with full representation in the Congress.

    (B) Embittered by personal tragedies in his own family, Lincoln sought to punish the South for all the turmoil and bitterness it has caused in attempting to secede from the Union.

    (C) A benevolent approach to former Confederates was the only hope for healing the national wounds, yet some measure of repudiation of treason was necessary through loyalty oaths.

    (D) A serious determination needed to be made about which states would be allowed to reenter the Union and which would not depending on the relative culpability of each state.

    (E) If a state consented to submit to the rule of a governor picked by President Lincoln and adopted an amendment to the Constitution abolishing slavery, it should be let back in.

76. What was the decision in the "insular cases" before the Supreme Court regarding territories like the Philippine Islands acquired through the Spanish-American War?

    (A) Whereas the territories were U.S. property, people living there were not fully U.S. citizens.
    (B) The United States could not legally own territories outside its national boundaries.
    (C) The Filipinos and other islanders were not yet ready for civilization and democracy.
    (D) The United States should not hold colonies but could not let other countries have them, either.
    (E) Each of the island territories should be tutored until they could apply for statehood.

77. Which statement below best describes margin buying, a common practice in the stock market during the 1920s?

    (A) Stockholders took out insurance on their portfolios in case of setbacks in the market.
    (B) Stockbrokers carefully monitored the profit margin of clients' stocks to avoid risk.
    (C) Federal regulators monitored shareholders' accounts to prevent inflation of the market.
    (D) Consumers purchased small amounts of stocks in large mutual funds to spread out risk.
    (E) Stocks were purchased largely on credit with only a small cash down payment.

78. The reason stagflation was so difficult a problem for the American government and economy to endure during the 1970s was that

    (A) the costs of the Vietnam War had created such a deficit that even Keynesian economists feared a new series of measures using deficit spending would bankrupt the country.
    (B) a society accustomed to listening to the government for answers did not receive any because government experts had no viable solution or model for intervention.
    (C) inflationary currency policies of the federal government had removed the capacity of the Federal Reserve to boost the economy.
    (D) the crisis was the result of the Arab Oil Embargo, a situation beyond the control of either the private sector or the public sector to intervene.
    (E) the tax cuts with which President Ford had experimented had crippled the federal budget.

79. Which statement below best describes the dueling contributions of Bill Gates and Steve Jobs to the computer industry in the 1980s?

    (A) Gates assembled the best team of engineers, whereas Jobs assembled the best team of advertisers.
    (B) Gates was a pioneer in hardware, whereas Jobs was a pioneer in software.
    (C) Gates first made personal computers accessible, whereas Jobs made computing user-friendly.
    (D) Gates created an all-consuming monopoly, whereas Jobs set out to break it.
    (E) Gates's company was a one-man operation, whereas Jobs created a team approach to innovation.

80. President William Jefferson Clinton was impeached because he

    (A) had inappropriate sexual relations with a junior staffer.
    (B) used federal employees to solicit women for sexual favors.
    (C) had unscrupulous real estate investments back in Arkansas.
    (D) lied under oath and obstructed justice during a federal investigation.
    (E) defied the Supreme Court and refused to testify claiming executive privilege.

81. How did the French establish a presence in central North America before the English could?

    (A) Having founded New Orleans, French expeditions marched northward into the Ohio River Valley in advance of the English.
    (B) American Indians converted more readily to Roman Catholicism with its reverence for various saints, so French Catholics could obtain guides into the interior first.
    (C) With access to the Mississippi Basin from Canada, Rene-Robert de la Salle could explore the area and claim it for France before English colonists could cross the Appalachians.
    (D) The focus of the economy of New France on furs made them more prone to penetrate the wilderness.
    (E) The willingness of the French colonists to intermarry with American Indians led to more peaceful cultural exchanges of knowledge than with the English who only infrequently did so.

82. Which of the following events was most important in compelling Great Britain to end the policy of salutary neglect?

    (A) The Restoration of the British monarchy after the Puritan Revolution
    (B) The English Reformation
    (C) The Glorious Revolution
    (D) The French and Indian War
    (E) Pontiac's Rebellion

83. Which statement below best describes Alexander Hamilton's perspective on the national debt in the Early National Period?

    (A) Passing along the debts of one generation to the next was a national sin.
    (B) A national debt could be a useful unifying factor in national life.
    (C) Only debt incurred by the Continental Congress during the Revolutionary War should be paid by the federal government.
    (D) Every other mature nation had a national debt so the United States shouldn't feel bad about starting out with one.
    (E) The national debt was necessary but should be paid off as quickly as possible no matter what sacrifices were needed to accomplish this task.

84. What was the true significance of the buffalo, or the American bison, in the settlement of the West?

    (A) Destroying the buffalo population was the key to eliminating the threat posed by the Plains Indians who depended on the buffalo for their livelihood.
    (B) The vast herds of buffalo attracted tourists from all over the world and facilitated the construction of the first transcontinental railroad that ran hunting-excursion trains.
    (C) The manner in which Spanish vaqueros herded the buffalo was picked up by American cowboys for management of their herds of cattle.
    (D) Money secured from selling buffalo hides in Europe was the financial basis for the formation of most western towns.
    (E) Crossbreeding buffalo with European strains of cattle yielded the Texas Longhorn, the staple of the original American ranching industry.

85. Why did Henry Cabot Lodge and other senators block Woodrow Wilson's efforts to bring the United States into the League of Nations, the president's cherished solution to bring about world peace?

    (A) The Nye Commission had proven that American involvement in World War I was merely a conspiracy of munitions manufacturers who profited from the war.
    (B) The Republicans in the Senate believed that President Wilson was already too powerful and popular.
    (C) The senators did not believe the League of Nations could accomplish the lofty goal it had set out to do.
    (D) The senators believed that funding for the League of Nations would be the responsibility of the United States and the federal budget was already strained by the costs of the war.
    (E) The senators believed joining the League of Nations would remove the exclusive constitutional right of the U.S. Congress in deciding whether the country would go to war.

86. The outcry over the Sacco and Vanzetti case in the 1920s resulted from the

    (A) fact that the two men were proven innocent of murder after their executions.
    (B) growing influence of the indigenous American anarchy movement.
    (C) growing realization that anti-immigrant sentiment had gone too far in American life.
    (D) involvement of the Ku Klux Klan in the apprehension of the two criminals.
    (E) fact that evidence was discovered proving they were guilty after they were acquitted.

87. What impact did Franklin D. Roosevelt's Bank Holiday have on the nation?

    (A) The fact that the federal government had acted with such sweeping power caused leaders of many corporations to resolve to liquidate their businesses.
    (B) The lack of access to their accounts for two weeks caused many bank customers to withdraw all of their funds, which caused even more bank failures.
    (C) This action on the part of the president caused journalists and most Americans to focus on the banking industry as a scapegoat for the Great Depression.
    (D) After this period of quiet most Americans calmed down and the collapse of the banking industry was stopped.
    (E) The American people were frightened by the imperial powers assumed by Roosevelt and made the Election of 1936 the closest in history until the Election of 2000.

88. Which of the statements below best describes why the Vietnam War was so difficult for the American military to fight and to win?

    (A) The U.S. military had never fought in such a tropical climate or in such thick jungles.
    (B) The presence of Chinese and Soviet soldiers on the ground constantly threatened a wider war.
    (C) The supply of aircraft to the North Vietnamese by the Soviets prevented air superiority.
    (D) The enemy in South Vietnam, the Vietcong, were highly dedicated guerrilla fighters.
    (E) The micromanagement of President Johnson made his clear strategy impossible to implement.

89. How did the invention of the transistor radically alter the technology of Americans' daily lives and eventually that of the people of the world?

    (A) The manufacture of transistors was vastly less expensive than the technology they replaced, so personal electronic devices came within the means of the average consumer.

    (B) Having been created by Bell Laboratories, the transistor made the communications industry the focus of the twentieth-century economy in the same way railroads were for the nineteenth century.

    (C) New types of patents had to be developed because the transistor was invented by a team of researchers, and these patents provided an incentive for a flood of new technologies.

    (D) Transistors were dramatically smaller and more durable than the vacuum tubes they replaced so electronic devices became small enough to hold in the hand and thus more portable.

    (E) Transistors could better endure the conditions of outer space so communications satellites using them became more powerful and thus useful for global communications.

90. In what way did the actions of Muammar al Qaddafi of Libya represent the difficulties of combating global terrorism?

    (A) As a Sunni Muslim, any negotiations he initiated with the United States to temper his image as a dictator were perceived as an offense against Shiite Muslims.

    (B) While guilty of supporting terrorism against Americans in Europe he repudiated the use of weapons of mass destruction, so the American government viewed him as cooperative.

    (C) He violated United Nations resolutions regarding nuclear nonproliferation yet proved that his nuclear weapons program was strictly for self-defense.

    (D) As an ally of al-Qaeda, he sheltered Osama bin Laden while telling the United States that bin Laden was an evil man who did not represent Islam as a whole.

    (E) Even though he supported terrorism against American targets he was kind to his own people and led the only democratic Islamic country in the United Nations.

# Answer Key
## PRACTICE TEST 1

| | | | | | | | |
|---|---|---|---|---|---|---|---|
| 1. | D | 24. | B | 47. | E | 70. | C |
| 2. | C | 25. | A | 48. | B | 71. | D |
| 3. | B | 26. | E | 49. | C | 72. | B |
| 4. | C | 27. | C | 50. | D | 73. | A |
| 5. | B | 28. | D | 51. | B | 74. | D |
| 6. | E | 29. | E | 52. | A | 75. | C |
| 7. | D | 30. | C | 53. | E | 76. | A |
| 8. | E | 31. | C | 54. | D | 77. | E |
| 9. | C | 32. | A | 55. | C | 78. | B |
| 10. | C | 33. | B | 56. | C | 79. | C |
| 11. | B | 34. | E | 57. | A | 80. | D |
| 12. | A | 35. | D | 58. | B | 81. | C |
| 13. | D | 36. | C | 59. | D | 82. | D |
| 14. | E | 37. | D | 60. | E | 83. | B |
| 15. | C | 38. | B | 61. | D | 84. | A |
| 16. | B | 39. | B | 62. | B | 85. | E |
| 17. | C | 40. | C | 63. | A | 86. | C |
| 18. | E | 41. | E | 64. | D | 87. | D |
| 19. | D | 42. | A | 65. | A | 88. | D |
| 20. | D | 43. | D | 66. | C | 89. | D |
| 21. | B | 44. | A | 67. | B | 90. | B |
| 22. | C | 45. | D | 68. | C | | |
| 23. | A | 46. | C | 69. | C | | |

# Test Analysis

**Step 1: Count the number of correct answers.**

Enter the total here: _____

**Step 2: Count the number of incorrect answers.**

Enter the total here: _____

**Step 3: Multiply the number of incorrect answers by .250**

Enter the product here: _____

**Step 4: Subtract the results obtained in Step 3 from the total obtained in Step 1.**

Enter the total here: _____

**Step 5: Round the number obtained in Step 4 to the nearest whole number.**

Raw Score = _____

## Scaled Score Conversion Table

| Raw Score | Scaled Score | Raw Score | Scaled Score | Raw Score | Scaled Score |
|-----------|--------------|-----------|--------------|-----------|--------------|
| 90–79 | 800 | 46–45 | 600 | 8–7 | 400 |
| 78 | 790 | 44–43 | 590 | 6–5 | 390 |
| 77–76 | 780 | 42–41 | 580 | 4–3 | 380 |
| 75 | 770 | 40 | 570 | 2–1 | 370 |
| 74 | 760 | 39–38 | 560 | 0 – –1 | 360 |
| 73–72 | 750 | 37–36 | 550 | –2 – –3 | 350 |
| 71 | 740 | 35–34 | 540 | –4 | 340 |
| 70–69 | 730 | 33–32 | 530 | –5 – –6 | 330 |
| 68 | 720 | 31–30 | 520 | –7 | 320 |
| 67–66 | 710 | 29–28 | 510 | –8 – –9 | 310 |
| 65–64 | 700 | 27 | 500 | –10 | 300 |
| 63 | 690 | 26–25 | 490 | –11 – –12 | 290 |
| 62–61 | 680 | 24–23 | 480 | –13 | 280 |
| 60–59 | 670 | 22–21 | 470 | –14 – –15 | 270 |
| 58–57 | 660 | 20–19 | 460 | –16 – –17 | 260 |
| 56–55 | 650 | 18–17 | 450 | –18 – –19 | 250 |
| 54-53 | 640 | 16–15 | 440 | –20 | 240 |
| 52–51 | 630 | 14–13 | 430 | –21 – –22 | 230 |
| 50–49 | 620 | 12–11 | 420 | | |
| 48–47 | 610 | 10–9 | 410 | | |

# Answer Explanations

1. **D**  Although answers A and B are true, the main contribution of this fascinating man was the school mentioned in answer D. All European nations benefited from Prince Henry's school of navigation, which gave a leap forward for exploration and thus colonization. Henry was not a sea captain or really a navigator, even, nor did he race Spain. The main Portuguese endeavors across the Atlantic came over fifty years after those of Spain.

2. **C**  Answers A and D never occurred in significant enough numbers to alter colonial society. Answer B belies the fact that Protestantism made its followers harder workers in colonial America, not just otherworldly dreamers. Answer E had been going on so long in Europe that colonial America was a product of this fact, not a preexisting quantity altered by this fact. Answer C implies the reality that both French and Spanish colonies enforced a uniformity of religious belief, whereas England tried to rid itself of dissenters by granting them charters to found colonies.

3. **B**  No other answer is even approximately true. All eleven of the joint-stock companies that founded colonies in the New World went bankrupt.

4. **C**  Although the Federalist Papers have served many functions hinted at in the other answers, at the time of their writing New Yorker Alexander Hamilton (and Madison and Jay) were trying to convince the important state of New York to ratify the U.S. Constitution. The essays were thus published as editorials in New York newspapers.

5. **B**  Most of the answers hint at reasons "Seward's Folly" turned out to be an excellent idea, but only answer B was true at the time of the Alaska Purchase. Small amounts of gold were found, but the gold rush and oil bonanza days came later. Some propaganda and Russian bribes were used to convince Congress to ratify the purchase treaty, but Russia was not considered a threat. The greater fear was that Russia would sell the real estate to the United Kingdom instead of to the United States.

6. **E**  All of the answers twist the debate that led to closed shops versus open shops in the American labor movement, but answer E is the only one entirely true because it defines what closed and open shops actually were.

7. **D**  All of the answers are events in which Martin Luther King Jr. took a leading role, but his first major step was the Montgomery Bus Boycott.

8. **E**  Only answer C was ever popular with most of the American people, and only for a time. All the rest sparked immediate controversy among some or most elements of American society. The invasion of Cambodia, however, immediately sparked the protests at Kent State University when Nixon announced it on television because it seemed his actions violated a pledge to keep the war from expanding in Southeast Asia. The students were essentially protesting the credibility gap.

9. **C** The Congressional committee already had proof of a conspiracy, and the other answers address information that was known or would have been convenient to know. Only answer C describes what the committee was really hung for—the "smoking gun" that would prove Nixon had lied to them by denying any knowledge of the conspiracy in the Watergate scandal.

10. **C** Oliver North claimed the whole Contra angle was his idea and that he acted alone, which may or may not be the truth, but he did run the supply operation with money from the sale of weapons to Iran, something the Congress had forbidden. The other answers are fabrications, especially answer E, which is the opposite of North's goals in his testimony.

11. **B** Answer B was the reality that so frustrated the American Indians in the path of this launch of westward expansion. Although answers A and C are realities that later were somewhat true of American agriculture, in the colonial era the simple solution was to cultivate new land. This fact made answer D the exact opposite of the truth.

12. **A** Answer A could just as easily state the Declaratory Act sounded like a petulant whimper after the massive victory of the repeal of the hated Stamp Act. If answer B were true, the entire American Revolution would never have happened, nor would it have happened if answer E were true. Still, no Americans immediately called for independence. The first recorded suggestion of this desire occurred over a year later, and most Americans could not seriously contemplate independence for many years after that.

13. **D** All of the answers evoke images of real experiences of westward migration and settlement, but answer D was the stated purpose Thomas Jefferson set out for the expedition and speaks to the result.

14. **E** This quote is the famous end of Daniel Webster's plea in the Webster/Hayne Debates. The quote makes no reference to economics, the tariff of the Nullification Crisis, or to the Bank of the United States that Jackson hated so. The oratory nearly masks the land reference, but Webster was alarmed at the sectionalism North, South, and West evoked by the debate of the sale of western lands.

15. **C** Answer C, coupled with the fact that Smith announced he was running for president of the United States, made his neighbors so nervous that he was arrested for treason after an armed clash. While in jail on these charges he was killed by a mob and thus did not lead the Mormons to Utah and the subsequent brush with the U.S. Army there.

16. **B** Kearny followed Fremont on this expedition, not the other way around as suggested in answer D. Zachary Taylor performed the actions in answer A as John Slidell did for answer C. James K. Polk did not need any pushing to pick this fight with Mexico.

17. **C** All of the answers are fabrications except answer C, the unfortunate reasons the Dred Scott case was a major cause of the Civil War. The justices on the Court had been placed there by a long series of expansionist, pro-slavery Democratic presidents, so the balance of powers was leaning toward war.

18. **E** Answers B, C, and D were all true of the federal government already, although the U.S. Army could not enter a state without the permission of the governor (except when those states seceded from the Union). Answer A had not yet occurred in American history. Both the North and the South resorted to conscription before the Civil War ended, and the draft has been a part of American society ever since. Such conscription as existed in the Revolutionary War was done by the Continental Congress, not the federal government (which did not yet exist). No draft has been instituted since 1972.

19. **D** The infamous Palmer Raids were conducted against labor organizations in search of specifically Bolshevik literature. They are the classic example of a restriction on civil liberties from the First Red Scare.

20. **D** The reference to the prairies and the plantations indicates the agriculture bent to this quote that was stated in support of the Agricultural Adjustment Act that was later found to be unconstitutional.

21. **B** Answer B conveys a major cause of the American Revolution in that salutary neglect had turned American shippers into smugglers. When strict enforcement was enacted by William Pitt to pay the war debt, laws that were on the books for nearly a century were suddenly and harshly a part of colonists lives. Answer C is incorrect because the Navigation Acts were indirect taxes stemming from mercantilism, an economic philosophy Americans did not entirely reject until the American Revolution.

22. **C** This list of answers reveals how incredible it was that the country survived the critical period, but among these problems what motivated the formation of the Constitutional Convention the most was the internal rebellion within the very state where the American Revolution was born. Tecumseh's threat was greater but occurred several years after the Constitutional Convention was over.

23. **A** Only answer A contains two true causes, the latter of which is why the War of 1812 was the context of both Tecumseh's coalition of American Indian tribes and Andrew Jackson's wars against the Creek Indians and later the Seminole Indians.

24. **B** George Fitzhugh was the leading apologist for slavery who espoused the Positive Good theory in his writings and criticized the North for imposing wage slavery on immigrant factory workers. All the rest were abolitionists.

25. **A** All of the other answers are fabrications based on issues involved with the executive branch in the Civil War and Reconstruction except answer A. Andrew Johnson was caught in this trap by the Radical Republicans, but the Tenure of Office Act was later deemed unconstitutional.

26. **E** All of the answers evoke issues surrounding the steel industry but the only one entirely true or entirely the result of the Bessemer process was the fact that blowing air through molten iron produced steel more cheaply with less energy.

27. **C** Even though Garfield had been assassinated, the business dress of those wanting access to him reveals they were not assassins but job seekers and grafters wanting favors. Nothing indicates that they might be labor union leaders,

and Gilded Age presidents allowed all too much access to themselves through patronage. Chester Arthur, coming out of the New York Customs House, was a considerable grafter himself, yet he did sign the Pendleton Act. The next day, however, he kept handing out jobs to a long line of office seekers. The cartoon portrays the crying need for civil service reform.

28. **D**   All of the answers twist or actually state issues debated in American Christianity, and answer A was a criticism leveled at adherents of the Social Gospel. The chief theological shift, however, was in deemphasizing the traditional Gospel message in favor of political and social activism. The Populist Revolt and Progressive Reform were the result.

29. **E**   Tuskegee Institute was a vocational and normal school, or one that trained the craftsmen and teachers that Booker T. Washington saw as the essential first steps for African-Americans to come off the plantations and achieve status as more dignified economic necessities to the wider American culture. Washington thought that through achieving these goals African-Americans would be naturally set on the road to equality in contrast to the insistence by W. E. B. Du Bois for immediate equality. Washington thought that African-Americans then could and should move into professional careers to strengthen their communities even further.

30. **C**   George Creel was a successful Madison Avenue advertising executive hired by the Wilson administration to "sell" the war to the American people after Wilson had promised not to bring the country into the Great War. Creel's efforts were wildly successful in raising the amount of bonds sold to finance the war.

31. **C**   Answer E is a reference to Woodrow Wilson's wife, but the rest of the answers twist aspects of Franklin D. Rooosevelt's (FDR's) administration. Eleanor Roosevelt was the first First Lady to go into a coal mine and to dozens of other places across the United States where she actively represented her husband. Since FDR was stricken with polio as an adult and confined to a wheelchair, Eleanor Roosevelt was a big part of overcoming his physical impairments as she toured the country in his stead. She even wrote a newspaper column to discuss her experiences and was thus the most publicly politically minded, engaged wife of a president to that date in history.

32. **A**   Some of the answers hint at the realities of these incredible men, but Pizarro was illiterate and kept no records himself. Most conquistadors were uneducated and thus had no other trade or skill but military conquest. Their permitting Catholic missionaries to accompany them, however, became the chief way Spanish colonial governments pacified and organized American Indian laborers. The treasure fleet did bear New World wealth to the king of Spain, but that tribute had no direct impact on colonization; it just allowed the conquistadors to keep their jobs.

33. **B**   All of the answers refer to early issues surrounding the formation of the central, or federal government, but the competing plans are most associated with answer B. The issues in question were not resolved until the Great Compromise

provided proportional representation in the House of Representatives to please the large states while providing equal representation in the Senate to please the small states. The other issues espoused in the plans are the exact opposite of what is stated in answer C, and since James Madison's advocacy for the Virginia Plan prevailed, he was known as the Father of the U.S. Constitution.

34. **E**  Answers A and D refer to the Elections of 1828 and 1876, respectively. Answer B was associated with the Election of 1824 but led to the arrangement in answer E that infuriated Andrew Jackson who made the charge. Answer C may have been true for some but implied no direct corruption.

35. **D**  Dorothea Dix championed many of these causes but was personally responsible for the launch and the success of the cause in answer D.

36. **C**  All the answers twist the truth, especially answer E because fighting in the Philippines was America's first exposure to jungle warfare. Answer C states the true significance of this unfortunate conflict.

37. **D**  Answer D evokes Franklin D. Roosevelt's call to give the Allies, "All aid short of war." Answer E was tantamount to a declaration of war, especially to the Japanese, and the War Production Board was not formed until 1942 after Pearl Harbor. Roosevelt did institute a peacetime draft but it was because he seriously feared the United States would be drawn into the war, not a measure to bluff potential opponents.

38. **B**  Amazingly, President Eisenhower did all of these things, even setting up the invasion that was carried out under President Kennedy that led to the Bay of Pigs incident. The action that wrecked the peace summit with the Soviets, however, was the U-2 incident described in answer B.

39. **B**  Only *Engel v. Vitale* was decided by the Supreme Court in the 1960s while Earl Warren was the chief justice. The removal of prayer from public schools was part of the societal flux experienced during the 1960s and contributed to the decade's being a turning point in cultural values. All of the other cases were landmark cases, though, and should be understood as such; placing landmark cases in their decades correctly is useful in tracing changing social and political values.

40. **C**  Phyllis Schlafly did not single-handedly stop the equal rights amendment, but her prominent leadership in the movement to do so even though she was a woman focused much of the debate and the animosity on her.

41. **E**  Answer E reveals that what appears to be a military history question is actually a diplomatic history question. Saratoga was the turning point in the fledgling country's ability to attract support from France and Spain against the British. The money, troops, and naval support thus acquired was instrumental in the American victory.

42. **A**  None of the other answers is based in truth, and answer A is the essence of what Adams himself called "my greatest contribution to peace." The dual role of the presidency in diplomacy and in national defense is conveyed symbolically in the Great Seal of the United States. The eagle has arrows in one talon

and an olive branch in the other. Not all presidents got the balance right as did Adams who sacrificed his political career because his own party, the Federalists, clamored for war with France.

43. **D**   Answers A, C, and E were the actions of other presidents in national defense, and it was Napoleon who viewed the Louisiana Purchase as a source of cash. Jefferson saw the purchase as a source of land and left Napoleon to his own devices. Jefferson's attempt to keep the United States out of war infuriated the Federalist stronghold of New England because their economy was based on the very shipping of goods that was banned by the Embargo Act.

44. **A**   Answer B was the doing of William Travis. Answer C was Davy Crockett. Answer D was Sam Houston as was the president and governor parts of answer E. Answer A was Austin's contribution after his father negotiated with Santa Anna and then died.

45. **D**   Lincoln said these words during one of the Lincoln-Douglas debates, and it was his firm stand and the plank of the Republican Party until the Emancipation Proclamation and the Thirteenth Amendment to the Constitution. Douglas and President Buchanan would not have agreed with the need to stop slavery in the territories, and William H. Seward was the abolitionist senator who wound up as Lincoln's secretary of state. He would have supported the abolition of slavery where it existed. Henry Clay was a slaveholder himself who formed compromises that violated this premise.

46. **C**   Another seemingly military question that because of its correct answer foreshadowed why Winston Churchill would pronounce the twentieth century a great catastrophe. All diplomatic struggles in the twentieth century and the formation of the League of Nations and the United Nations were debated with the specter of total war grinning in the corner.

47. **E**   Answer E was the sad reality of this contest in the Gilded Age in which the only Democrat to win the presidency won one of his nonconsecutive terms. Answers A and B evoke ideas from future campaigns after 1884, and answers C and D would have been nice but are fabrications.

48. **B**   No president would be caught dead agreeing to answer A, and answer C goes beyond Theodore Roosevelt's actual stance that is expressed in answer B. Answers D and E twist the truth in that the Hay-Bunau-Varilla Treaty made sure the Panama Canal would be open to other nations besides the United States, and the United States did not permanently occupy a country in the Western Hemisphere. The United States leased the canal zone and retained a naval base in Cuba, but neither was an actual military occupation of a country.

49. **C**   Answer C conveys the reality of the First Hundred Days of the New Deal that Franklin D. Roosevelt (FDR) accomplished in the crisis of the Great Depression with the cooperation of a Rubber Stamp Congress. Some bills were written in the morning and passed in the afternoon! FDR certainly did not ignore the economic crisis, nor did he ever propose a systematic plan, although the New Deal was guided by the general goals of relief, recovery, and reform. He did not wait for Hoover's policies but started working on his own even during

his Inaugural Ball. Later presidents like Gerald Ford held economic summits on a global scale.

50. **D**   All the answers are either plausible fabrications or as in answer C, a reference to a later event (the Berlin Wall). Berlin was divided into four zones after World War II. The Soviets kept the east side of the city, whereas the United Kingdom, the United States, and France protected the west side. When the Soviet Union closed off all ground access to these three zones, Truman responded with the remarkable Berlin Airlift until the Soviets caved under such resolve.

51. **B**   Viceroys were essentially courtiers sent to the New World on temporary assignments to represent the Spanish monarchy. They were not allowed to cultivate any personal attachments as feudal lords would have done, and they never considered their stay in the Spanish Empire's farthest-flung provinces to be permanent. Although they may have dispatched conquistadors' armies in emergencies, they themselves were not generals who commanded military operations.

52. **A**   The term *critical period* was coined by John Q. Adams to convey the danger the central government faced until the U.S. Constitution stabilized the country by clarifying the organization of sovereignty in the American republic. The other answers exaggerate aspects of the period, none of which really amounted to a serious threat.

53. **E**   Although answer C was Jefferson's intention, the Congress made sure it did not happen by creating the committee system still in place today. Either answer A or B would have been disastrous if true, and curiously Jefferson did not push for repeal of the Federalist policies in answer D, which he hated but merely let them elapse according to their original charters.

54. **D**   Although the Democratic Party was the first major party to have a national nominating convention, a fact that Andrew Jackson and others touted as a major accomplishment for democracy, they got the idea from the mysterious Anti-Masonic Party. Andrew Jackson, himself a Mason, would have no interest in giving credit where credit was due.

55. **C**   All of the answers are at least half-truths regarding the situation on the ground (or at sea) in the Oregon Territory, but answer C was the simple truth that foreshadowed Nathan Bedford Forrest's famous dictum on how to win any battle, "Get there first with the most." Although Polk did dispatch the navy to ward off British intervention in the dispute, there was never any fleet engagement between the rivals.

56. **C**   All of the answers reflect circumstances of nineteenth-century political discourse, but the answer in C addresses the Spot Resolutions where Lincoln and other congressmen asked President Polk to show them the spot on a map where American blood was spilled on American soil. Most Whigs, like Lincoln, doubted the president's claims and believed he provoked the Mexican War on purpose. Critics like Henry David Thoreau claimed Polk did so just to expand slavery, and thus Lincoln was already involved in the issues that would bring on the Civil War.

57. **A** Answer A is actually a paraphrase of something Louis Agassiz, a leading scientist from New England, said. Agassiz, however, did not believe the government should abandon African-Americans in their plight, whereas Frederick Douglass did believe former slaves should be left alone by the government. Douglass's rationale for this position had nothing to do with Darwinism, though. Answers D and E are twists on stated positions of leading proponents of either the scientific or social implications of Darwin's writings.

58. **B** Although Justice Oliver Wendell Holmes Jr. was a Progressive who moved the Supreme Court to the left, the stated position is not necessarily exclusively Progressive in nature. All Progressives were loose constructionists, but not all loose constructionists were Progressives. Holmes was both. Furthermore, both Democrats and Republicans were persuaded by Progressive Reform to adopt Alexander Hamilton's view of the U.S. Constitution, that it contained implied powers.

59. **D** Although Pulitzer did possess the newspaper with the largest circulation in America, he considered the Spanish-American War a grandly significant event and plastered his correspondents' work all over the front pages through the march toward war (largely to increase circulation but also to increase support for the war and for the Republican Party). His correspondents included print journalists but also the artist Frederic Remington to whom Pulitzer said, "You provide the pictures, and I'll provide the war." Thus the propaganda he printed was a classic example of "yellow journalism."

60. **E** All of the answers are fabrications that belie the fact that prosperity quickly returned to most people in the United States after World War II and the Great Depression were both declared to be over. Then Mr. Levitt, who did build housing during the war, had difficulty building enough houses to keep up with the baby boom in what were derisively called Levittowns because of the uniformity of the construction of suburban homes.

61. **D** All of the answers are plausible fabrications, especially because Ferdinand Magellan had to entirely reconstruct the hulls of his ships that were eaten away by worms during his voyage! Later copper plating on hulls prevented this daunting turn of events, but the English were mostly afraid of having to run the gauntlet of Spanish fleets and fortifications to get to the Far East for trade. Spain and England were at war until the defeat of the Spanish Armada gave some respite in 1588. Even Jamestown settlers were sent out to search for the Northwest Passage, indicating the desperation the English had to find what did not exist (until climate change set in).

62. **B** Although answers D and E are twists on the truth that the legislature helped the colonists unify in the face of repeated attacks by American Indians, the colonists themselves discovered the need for a representative assembly for the purposes expressed in answer B, and the Virginia Company consented. No one contemplated independence in the seventeenth century, and the British Crown tolerated the Virginia House of Burgesses rather than ordering its formation. The Spanish did not repeatedly attack after 1588.

63. **A**   Answer B is a reference to the later Quebec Act. Answers C and E are distortions of realities in that the king was trying to stave off attacks rather than incite them, and he never lost interest in America even though Americans did suffer indignities. Answer D is wrong because, although George III was authoritarian, he was not an absolute monarch.

64. **D**   All of the answers are fabrications except for answer D, which states the tragedy of the Gag Rules, that the very power the Congress had to save the Union and settle the slavery question was silenced. The British Parliament was able to stumble its way to abolition through open debate. The American Civil War happened because the U.S. Congress ultimately could not.

65. **A**   Despite Ms. Jackson's best effort her work was largely ignored in her lifetime. Her work was nonfiction unlike *Uncle Tom's Cabin*, which was referred to in answers C and D (these were criticisms leveled at Harriet Beecher Stowe).

66. **C**   Answer B is actually horizontal combination or integration, whereas the other answers are fabrications or ideas well removed from the era of the rise of big business in which horizontal and vertical styles of business combination were formed. Answer C conveys the approach Andrew Carnegie took to the steel industry and Gustavus Swift took to the beef industry.

67. **B**   Answer B conveys the difficulty reformers were going to have in the Gilded Age in bringing about civil service reform. The other answers hint at the realities of Gilded Age corruption but are not true in regard to the Grant administration's actions.

68. **C**   All of the answers twist truths of the Cold War era except answer C. With much larger missiles than the Americans created, the Soviet Union contemplated the idea of a first strike with missiles that would destroy American missile silos. The chance that any multiple individually targeted reentry vehicles could be launched was a key deterrent to Soviet aggression, at least in the minds of Americans living at the time.

69. **C**   The quote is from Jimmy Carter and evokes the ideas associated with his notion of malaise and the misery index. The irony of the Election of 1980 was that Ronald Reagan was able to use the misery index to defeat President Carter because conditions had not improved during the Carter administration.

70. **C**   Although Ralph Nader is thought to have influenced the outcome of the Election of 2000, Texas businessman Ross Perot was a foil in the Election of 1992. The other candidates were minor players of fringe elements.

71. **D**   The Vikings' beating Columbus to the punch was not widely known until after their settlements in North America were discovered by archaeologists in the twentieth century. Even then the settlements were denigrated by supporters of Columbus as the discoverer of the New World because the Vikings abandoned them and did not capitalize on their incredible ocean voyages.

72. **B**   Answers C, D, and E were prison reforms in American history, but only answer B was a direct result of the optimism created by the successful American Revolution.

73. **A**  Answer A is the fortunate reality that men like Henry Clay could use to urge compromise. The Republican Party, however, began as an entirely sectional party with adherents only in the North. The Whigs were not able to ignore Know-Nothing advances. Answer B is close to the truth by 1860, but northern and southern Democrats still operated to balance their respective party platforms, and Republicans in previous elections (since 1854) faced a united Democratic Party. The Whigs were able to draw on the British heritage of an opposition party as in answer E, but so could the Republicans who attracted most northern Whigs, like Lincoln, to their party. As to oratory, although Webster was a giant in the Senate, Lincoln's rhetoric revealed an original political genius that has been unparalleled since his assassination.

74. **D**  All the answers hint at nineteenth-century realities associated with the West, but only answer D conveys the precise impact of the idea of Manifest Destiny on public opinion that motivated everything from the Mexican War to the missionary outpost of the Whitmans in the Oregon Territory.

75. **C**  Answer C is the only true perspective and the origin of Lincoln's Ten Per Cent Plan. The other answers twist the truth except for answer E that more closely matches the Reconstruction plan of Lincoln's successor, Andrew Johnson. Abraham Lincoln did believe that the Confederate states had never successfully seceded, but he also believed they had committed treason and needed a certain portion of their people to acknowledge this publicly before being restored to full status as states.

76. **A**  All of the answers are opinions held by sides of the imperialism debate, but only answer A was the determination of the Supreme Court in these troublesome cases.

77. **E**  The other answers are fabrications or, like answer D, foreshadowing of possibilities yet to come. Margin buying was one of the chief causes of the stock market crash because of the inflation in stock prices it created and the massive risk that buyers incurred the moment the market began to plummet. The rise was so incredible that debts could be paid off with buyers still making tidy profits, but in a crash margin calls by brokers required the full value of the stocks to be paid, which almost no one could cover.

78. **B**  Answer E is a fabrication, and all of the other answers hint at the difficulties of what was called the Great Recession of the 1970s. Answer B was the unfortunate backlash of the New Deal and other Progressive measures when even the government's experts could not come up with answers to meet the unprecedented stagflation. Not until Ford's and later Reagan's tax cuts did a solution come from government to boost the economy. Meanwhile, government regulations left over from the New Deal stifled any significant impact from private industry (or private companies purposefully refused to work for the larger good in an era of government intervention).

79. **C**  Most of the other answers are the opposite of the truth except for answer D that comes closest. In the beginning of the personal computing industry, however, Gates could not wield monopolistic control. This odd couple's transfor-

mation of world communications is best summed up in answer C. Microsoft's software made an electronic hobbyist's toy a major technological impact on people's daily lives, whereas Apple attempted to make the use of computers so simple anyone could use them.

80. **D**   The articles of impeachment had nothing to do with sex or real estate but rather with perjury and obstruction of justice. The other answers evoke the peripheral issues of this modern impeachment's proceedings.

81. **C**   After all the cultural differences between the French and the English are set aside, the head start accomplished by the French was merely geographical.

82. **D**   Although answer A set aside salutary neglect temporarily, the huge war debt created by the efforts of the British government to win the French and Indian War threatened to set it aside permanently, and before such control could be enforced the American Revolution ended English control over the thirteen colonies that made up the original United States.

83. **B**   Answer A was actually Thomas Jefferson's take on the debt. Answers C, D, and E are either the opposites of Hamilton's views or twists on the fact that Hamilton did model his Financial Program on British forms. Answer E is false because answer B is true.

84. **A**   Although answer B was true, answer A was the key to "winning the West." The other answers are fabrications, even dangerous ones. Do not try to lasso a buffalo.

85. **E**   Although all of the answers are close to the truth except for answer A, which had no bearing on the opinions of the Irreconcilables (and is not actually true), Lodge's great fear was a constitutional one, that the United States would be dragged into war against its will by the actions of tiny, squabbling nations in Europe.

86. **C**   Although Sacco and Vanzetti were almost certainly guilty of murder, the manner in which their case was handled was evidence of answer C in a growing number of Americans' minds. Answer E is false in that the men were executed, not acquitted.

87. **D**   Although all of the answers hint at truths associated with differing perspectives on the New Deal, fortunately Franklin D. Roosevelt's action in the Bank Holiday did slow the slide into disaster. His statement, "The only thing we have to fear is fear itself," was validated by the outcome, but the New Deal still had numerous detractors from those who said it went too far to those who said it did not go far enough.

88. **D**   Although answer E was true and troublesome, the real difficulty lay in the dedication of the Vietcong who had been fighting foreign invaders throughout the history of Vietnam. Furthermore, the clear strategy mentioned in answer E was not well suited for fighting insurgents.

89. **D**   The invention of the tiny transistor that accomplished the same task as hot, cumbersome vacuum tubes revolutionized electronics and thus life for people

around the world. Bell Laboratories did bring much attention to the communications industry, but small portable electronics have hundreds of applications beyond global communications that have literally transformed human life.

90. **B** Although all of the answers evoke problems associated with the "War on Terror," only answer B is entirely true. Answer C was what Qaddafi and others wanted the world to believe, and answer D is more true of Pakistan's government than that of Libya.

# Answer Sheet
## PRACTICE TEST 2

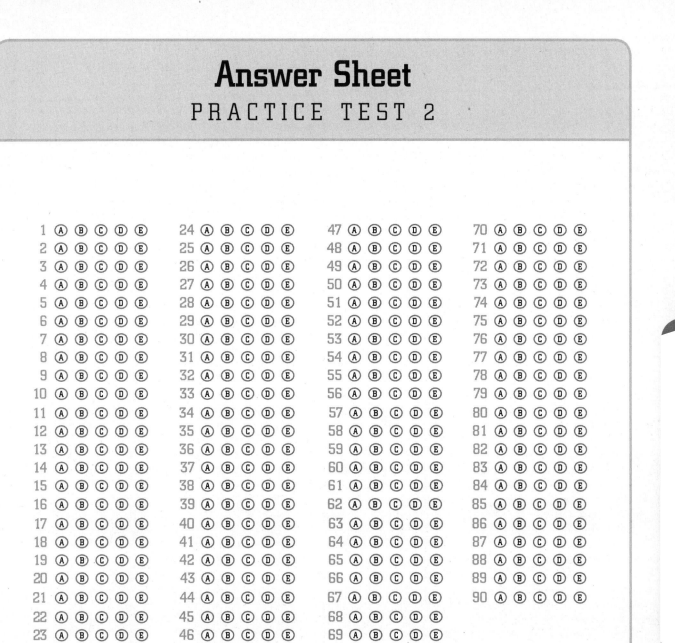

# Practice Test 2

TIME—60 MINUTES

**Directions:** Each of the questions or incomplete statements below is followed by five suggested answers or completions. Select the one that is best in each case and then fill in the corresponding circle on the answer sheet. You can cut the answer sheet along the dotted line to make recording your answers easier. Remember to give yourself only sixty minutes to complete this test in order to prepare for the pace of the real SAT Subject Test in U.S. History.

1. Which statement below best explains a difference between Hernando Cortés and Francisco Pizarro?

   (A) Cortés was more of an administrator, whereas Pizarro was a man of action.
   (B) Cortés was a staunch Roman Catholic, whereas Pizarro was a man with Protestant leanings.
   (C) Cortés conquered the Inca of Peru, whereas Pizarro conquered the Aztecs of Mexico.
   (D) Cortés was well educated, whereas Pizarro was entirely illiterate.
   (E) Cortés had a brutal disposition, whereas Pizarro was more compassionate to conquered peoples.

2. How did John Calvin contribute to the shaping of American society?

   (A) He wrote the Thirty-nine Articles of the Anglican Church that were crucial to colonial Virginia's unity in its early stages.
   (B) He convinced the French king to maintain peace between New France and England's North American colonies long enough for civilization to take root.
   (C) His teachings formed the doctrinal basis for both Puritanism and Scots-Irish Presbyterianism that in turn shaped the worldviews of most of England's first colonists.
   (D) He edited the first Bible written in the vernacular language in England that started the English Reformation.
   (E) His leadership in the churches of Zurich, Switzerland, established many political, social, and economic precedents that were instrumental in shaping the American republic.

3. The colony of Georgia was founded for all of the following reasons EXCEPT as

   (A) a humanitarian experimental society that banned African slavery.
   (B) a penal colony for Englishmen trapped in debtor prisons.
   (C) an attempt to produce an English silk industry.
   (D) a buffer between the English colonies and the Spanish colony in Florida.
   (E) a staging area for military maneuvers against the Spanish.

4. In the XYZ Affair in 1789, American diplomats responded to French demands for tribute money in exchange for access to the French foreign minister by

   (A) paying the bribe to meet with Talleyrand but refusing to heed his demands for more money.
   (B) remaining in France awaiting instructions after sending notice home to President Adams.
   (C) rebuffing the French agents from prison until being released in a prisoner exchange.
   (D) rejecting the French demands with such force that two of the diplomats were deported.
   (E) reporting to President Adams that he should immediately get Congress to declare war.

5. Why was the Gadsden Purchase of 1853 desirable after the huge Mexican Cession had already been added to the United States after the Mexican War?

   (A) Gold was discovered by American prospectors in this territory just across the border with Mexico.
   (B) The territory contained the best route across the Rocky Mountains for a southern transcontinental railroad.
   (C) Geronimo and his Apache warriors used the territory as a staging ground for repeated raids on American soil so the government needed unhindered access to hunt for him.
   (D) Cotton cultivation was proven to be feasible there so southerners saw it as the last chance to expand the cotton kingdom.
   (E) The Mormons had proven that the area contained the best route for wagon trains to reach California by the Mormon Trail and the Santa Fe Trail.

6. Which of the following facts about the Knights of Labor caused Samuel Gompers to form the separate organization known as the American Federation of Labor?

   (A) They called too many strikes and were thus damaging the reputation of the labor movement.
   (B) They tolerated too many socialists and communists among their leaders.
   (C) They staged demonstrations with the express purpose of destabilizing society by the use of violence.
   (D) They compromised with management too much and thus failed to represent worker's grievances forcefully enough to bring about change.
   (E) They allowed both skilled and unskilled workers to join their ranks and thus failed to achieve the specialized gains needed by either group.

7. Which statement below best explains the "Wisconsin Idea" popularized by that state's governor Robert La Follette?

   (A) A state needed in the early twentieth century to finally decide if it was going to be an agrarian state or an urban, industrialized state.
   (B) In times of societal reform better progress could be made by focusing the energies of activists on one reform rather than dissipating their efforts out over many reforms.
   (C) Charismatic leaders needed to rely on leading experts in a given field to provide rational policy steps that the leaders would in turn communicate convincingly to the people.
   (D) The federal government could most easily settle its national debt and deficit woes by merely printing enough paper money to pay off the debts and balance the federal budget.
   (E) Citizens of northern and southern states needed to experience exchanges where the latent animosity of the Civil War could be done away with through deeper cultural understanding.

8. How did Alfred Thayer Mahan's book, *The Influence of Sea Power on History*, shape American foreign or domestic policy?

   (A) The book's emphasis on the need for arms reduction led to an international crusade for world peace in which the United States took a leading role.
   (B) Nations around the world, including the United States, devoted more resources to building up powerful naval forces.
   (C) Several presidents in the early twentieth century sought to diminish the dependency of the American economy on foreign trade.
   (D) Government bureaus launched campaigns to encourage citizens living on the coasts to migrate inland away from dangerous hurricanes, tidal waves, and rising ocean levels.
   (E) The growing importance of China to world trade discussed in the book had the unintended consequence of the federal government's ban on Chinese immigration.

9. The Tet Offensive in 1968 weakened the morale of the American public during the Vietnam War by

(A) convincing them through this first invasion of South Vietnam by North Vietnamese forces that the war would be a long one.

(B) giving them the impression through these coordinated attacks by Vietcong insurgents across South Vietnam that the war was spinning out of control.

(C) outraging them because enemy soldiers committed atrocities against the very people they said they were trying to "liberate."

(D) making them believe that President Nixon was not up to the task of bringing peace in Southeast Asia as he had promised in his campaign.

(E) causing the highest number of American casualties of the whole war.

10. What policy proposal by Ronald Reagan did George H. W. Bush call "voodoo economics" during their campaigns to win the nomination to be the Republican presidential candidate in 1980?

(A) Supply-side economics, or Reagan's idea that tax cuts would provide incentives for businesses to cause prosperity to return to the United States

(B) Reagan's commitment to add even more deficit spending to the Keynesian model for the federal budget that was employed by the Carter administration

(C) Reagan's assertion that the federal government should become the chief employer of the majority of Americans who would then support tax increases to raise their own salaries

(D) Reagan's belief that all economic decisions should be made on rational grounds rather than on moral or ethical grounds

(E) Reagan's desire to double the salaries of the president, Supreme Court justices, and the members of Congress just on the heels of a deep recession

11. Which statement best describes the significance of the Mayflower Compact?

(A) The document was published in English newspapers as a means of attracting the first settlers of New England to hazard such a venture.

(B) The fact that it was written by John Locke, the greatest English political philosopher, gained for the Plymouth Colony an everlasting place in the history of English Common Law.

(C) The references to God and the spread of the gospel were evidence that English leaders were contemplating establishing the Anglican Church as the official Church of England.

(D) The document, although it was written in haste under desperate circumstances, was the first written attempt to establish a government for English-speaking peoples.

(E) The document was modeled after the document establishing the Virginia House of Burgesses from the previous year, thus revealing that the precedent of written constitutions would stick.

12. The concept of mercantilism alienated many of England's American colonies from their mother country by making many colonists believe that the English government

    (A) was giving the colonies too little economic direction.
    (B) had no right to pass laws like the Navigation or Molasses Acts.
    (C) was pitting the colonies against one another in unfair competition.
    (D) was stifling the successful agricultural base of the colonial economy in favor of industry.
    (E) had worked against the American economy in an unfavorable balance of trade.

13. What role did the early eighteenth-century exploits of mountain men, and at least one mountain woman, play in the settlement of the West?

    (A) Having been dispatched by eastern universities, mountain men collected specimens to fill museums with stuffed North American game animals that created interest in expansion.
    (B) Mountain men were among the first English-speaking peoples to intermarry with American Indian women and thus made favorable impressions for the larger culture on tribal leaders.
    (C) Mountain men created fortified stockades at critical points in the frontier that provided shelter and safety for the first pioneers.
    (D) Having been commissioned by the government as surveyors, mountain men supported themselves with fur trapping while they mapped the West for the U.S. Geological Survey.
    (E) Mountain men were among the first Americans to enter wilderness territories in the West and in their search for furs blazed trails that would later become major immigration routes.

14. In what way did many presidential administrations earn the designation of "custodial presidencies" during the Gilded Age?

    (A) The efforts of these presidents served to clean up political corruption at the highest levels of American government.
    (B) These presidents lacked any significant initiatives to bring about change, and their main goals were to maintain their political party's image while rewarding supporters with patronage.
    (C) The Gilded Age was a time of such high prosperity that the best approach for these presidential administrations was to do nothing except preside over America's success.
    (D) Since most of the Gilded Age presidents were Republicans, their main goal was to remake the South into a purer society that would come to terms with the harsh legacy of racism.
    (E) The main goal of all the presidents of the Gilded Age was to set aside party politics and to run the government not for their own fame or ambition but for the good of all Americans.

15. What assurances did Germany give, prior to American involvement in World War I, through agreements like the Arabic Pledge and the Sussex Pledge?

    (A) That Germany's objectives in Europe did not involve Napoleonic-type imperial designs but merely self-protection

    (B) That Germany would not use the technology it received from the United States for the manufacture of aircraft to harm American citizens

    (C) That Germany would limit the use of submarines against peaceful vessels in international waters

    (D) That the German blockade would allow merchant vessels and passenger ships of other nations to reach England safely but not military vessels

    (E) That if America entered the war in Europe that no German-Americans would be allowed to serve in the German military

16. What was unique about Franklin D. Roosevelt's (FDR's) collection of advisers and cabinet secretaries known collectively as his Brains Trust?

    (A) They were drawn from both the Democratic and Republican parties to provide unity in the crisis of the Great Depression.

    (B) All of the men and women in the Brains Trust had graduated from Harvard University as had FDR.

    (C) Of all the men and women in the Brains Trust working to solve the problems of the Great Depression, none of them had ever actually run a business.

    (D) The make-up of the Brains Trust remained largely unchanged over the entire course of the Roosevelt administration even though FDR was elected four times to the presidency.

    (E) Even though FDR led the nation through World War II, his administration was the first in American history not to contain any military veterans.

17. What strategy employed in fighting the Vietnam War prolonged the war and eventually caused it to become the first war where the United States "failed to achieve its objectives"?

    (A) American military missions were judged to be successful as long as there were four times the number of enemy deaths for every American death.

    (B) American missions were required to be accompanied by United Nations soldiers who were not authorized to use their weapons.

    (C) American bombing missions were not allowed to drop bombs on North Vietnam even though the North Vietnamese were the chief suppliers of the Vietcong guerrillas in South Vietnam.

    (D) American military forces were not authorized to attack the enemy unless attacked first.

    (E) American military search-and-destroy missions relied on the use of helicopters, which were inherently unreliable aircraft that were difficult to maintain.

18. What impact did the launch of the first artificial satellite, *Sputnik I*, by the Soviet Union have on American Cold War policy?

    (A) With the superiority in missile technology apparent in the Soviet launch, the United States resolved to fight only limited wars with the Soviet Union or its allies.

    (B) The United States used its position on the United Nations Security Council to veto all subsequent Soviet initiatives regarding the control of space technology.

    (C) The United States then kept all of its military forces involved with the delivery of atomic weapons on high alert so that they could strike the Soviet Union on a moment's notice.

    (D) As a result of this aggressive act on the part of the Soviet Union, the United States tried to save face by asserting influence in countries in Africa, Asia, and Latin America.

    (E) The U.S. government began to set aside revenues for the goal of strengthening the education of American students in math, science, and foreign language.

19. Which first significant act of terrorism against American interests occurred under the Reagan administration in 1983?

    (A) The attack on the USS *Cole*, an American destroyer docked in Yemen
    (B) The attack against the Marine Corps barracks in Beirut, Lebanon
    (C) The bombing of a disco in Germany that was frequented by U.S. military personnel
    (D) The first attack against the World Trade Center using a car bomb
    (E) The destruction of the U.S. embassies in Kenya and Tanzania

20. Five-time presidential candidate Ralph Nader first gained national attention as an activist for

    (A) the purity of America's water supply in an era of rampant industrial spills.
    (B) whistle-blowers, or individuals who expose corporate secrets that threaten the public.
    (C) stopping the use of nuclear power and nuclear weapons.
    (D) consumer protection by exposing safety problems in the automobile industry.
    (E) federal regulation to curtail the profit seeking of passenger airlines.

21. How did Samuel Slater change the American economy?

   (A) He developed the concept of interchangeable parts that formed the basis of mass production.
   (B) He was the first to successfully apply steam power to the propulsion of large ships.
   (C) He developed the first successful textile mill and thus began basic industrialization.
   (D) He invented barbed wire that began the decline of long cattle drives over open land.
   (E) He developed the first practical shutter camera and launched the photography industry.

22. In which of the following Supreme Court decisions handed down by the Marshall Court did John Marshall establish the precedent for the power of judicial review?

   (A) *McCulloch v. Maryland*
   (B) *Gibbons v. Ogden*
   (C) *Fletcher v. Peck*
   (D) *Marbury v. Madison*
   (E) *Dartmouth College v. Woodward*

23. Where did most Irish immigrants coming to the United States after the Potato Famine reside and why?

   (A) In the Midwest because, having been denied private property by the British Parliament, they craved nothing more than owning farms of their own
   (B) In Appalachia because of the basic cultural connection to the Scots-Irish citizens who were descended from the area's original colonial settlers
   (C) In western cities like Denver and San Francisco to put as much distance as they could between them and the British government whose policies had led to the famine
   (D) In the South because of the need for laborers to replace the slaves freed by the Civil War
   (E) In eastern cities because they arrived with so few resources they could not afford to buy their own land in the West and wound up working in northern factories

24. During the Nullification Crisis of the 1820s and 1830s, the Force Bill granted Andrew Jackson the power to

   (A) invade a state if the state seceded from the Union.
   (B) arrest the leaders of South Carolina who had organized a rebellious state convention.
   (C) use the military to enforce the collection of tariffs within a state.
   (D) compel southern congressmen to attend the emergency session debating a compromise.
   (E) stop abolitionists from sending their literature through the U.S. mail into the South.

25. How did President Grover Cleveland respond to the Pullman Strike in 1894?

    (A) He sent the U.S. military to break the strike that was stopping the U.S. mail service.
    (B) He invited leaders of the Pullman Company and the labor unions to the White House.
    (C) He threatened to take over the trains with the U S. Army in order to restart rail traffic.
    (D) He had Attorney General Richard Olney arrest the labor organizers for racketeering.
    (E) He referred the matter to the Supreme Court, which mediated the dispute with an injunction.

26. All of the following were causes of the Great War (World War I) EXCEPT the

    (A) assassination of the heir to the Austro-Hungarian thrones by a Serbian nationalist.
    (B) sinking of the HMS *Lusitania*, a passenger ship containing American citizens.
    (C) militaristic foreign policy actions of all of the major European powers.
    (D) conflict over imperial holdings on the part of the United Kingdom, France, and Germany.
    (E) unintended consequences of Bismarck's European alliance system.

27. Which of the statements below best expresses the main reason national attention was drawn to the trial of a high school biology teacher named John T. Scopes for violating a state law against teaching the theory of evolution in Tennessee?

    (A) H. L. Mencken, a famous journalist and social commentator, covered the trial for his *American Mercury* magazine.
    (B) Frequent presidential candidate and former Secretary of State William Jennings Bryan was the prosecuting attorney in the case.
    (C) The defense attorney in the case was a professed agnostic in an era of uniformity of religious belief.
    (D) The teacher had also evidenced communist sympathies in his classes during the Second Red Scare.
    (E) The Supreme Court had already declared it was ready to hear the case on appeal as a sign of support for the American Civil Liberties Union if Scopes was found guilty.

28. Despite his charge that there was "creeping socialism" in the United States, what initiative of President Dwight Eisenhower's amounted to a massive public works project on a par with the largest New Deal measures of the Roosevelt administration?

    (A) The instituting of the National Aeronautics and Space Administration
    (B) The formation of the Southeast Asia Treaty Organization
    (C) The passage of the National Defense Education Act
    (D) The passage of the National Interstate and Defense Highways Act
    (E) The instituting of the Department of Health, Education, and Welfare

29. "No, I'm not an American. I'm one of the 22 million black people who are the victims of Americanism. One of the 22 million black people who are the victims of democracy, nothing but disguised hypocrisy. . . . The 22 million victims are waking up."

Which civil rights leader below most likely said these words in 1964?

(A) Martin Luther King Jr.
(B) John Lewis
(C) Malcolm X
(D) Medgar Evers
(E) Jesse Jackson

30. What change contributed to the large migration of the American population to the Sun Belt beginning in the 1960s?

(A) The development of high-speed rail transportation allowing commuters to live in suburbs while working in urban centers
(B) The desegregation of public schools that began in 1954 with the *Brown v. Board of Education* Supreme Court decision
(C) The retirement of the baby boom generation and their desire to escape harsh winters
(D) The collapse of the American steel industry and other manufacturing industries that provided blue collar jobs in the North
(E) The development of air conditioning and more affordable housing to make life in the South more comfortable and practical

31. Which statement below best explains the role of Jesuit missionaries in establishing the culture of Spain's empire in the New World?

(A) They were militant monks who fought alongside the conquistadors in the wars of conquest
(B) They were among the most educated citizens of Spain's colonies who raised the standards of both church and civic institutions
(C) Their study of the indigenous religion of American Indians enriched Roman Catholic theology
(D) They introduced three-sister farming, a cultivation technique combining squash, beans, and corn that improved the diet of the American Indians in their charge
(E) They ruthlessly ferreted out religious dissenters from among the Spanish colonists and thus preserved uniformity of belief and societal unity

32. How was the economy of England's colonies in the North different from the economy of those colonies in the South?

    (A) Northern colonies emphasized manufacturing and trade to such a degree that they were incapable of producing enough food, whereas the South exported surplus food.

    (B) Northern colonies emphasized the cultivation of cash crops, whereas the South remained focused on subsistence-level farming.

    (C) Northern colonies were unable to sustain cash crops like the South and thus had to diversify their economy to include manufacturing, shipping, and timbering.

    (D) Northern colonies required constant financial support from England, whereas southern colonies became self-sustaining by planting tobacco, rice, indigo, and other cash crops.

    (E) Northern colonies avoided urban growth in favor of villages and towns and thus had to rely on the South for professional services like banking and legal counsel.

33. Which statement below best explains the impact of Thomas Paine's work, *Common Sense*, on the sensibilities of Americans during the early American Revolution?

    (A) Although *Common Sense* met with little success, Paine's work, *The Crisis*, galvanized support for the American Revolution during the War for Independence.

    (B) Americans viewed Paine's work merely as a mouthpiece of the Continental Congress and drove the author into exile in France.

    (C) *Common Sense* was viewed as a treasonous work that impacted only the most radical patriots.

    (D) *Common Sense* sold moderately well during the years prior to the War for Independence, but it's scholarly tone and classical references became clear only after the war was won.

    (E) Paine's publishing *Common Sense* when he did marked a turning point in the effort to win bystanders in American society and in the Continental Congress to the patriot cause.

34. What two warnings contained in George Washington's Farewell Address appeared prophetic in later years when events proved that the first president had correctly identified looming dangers?

   (A) That the nation would be shaken by sectionalism and factions, and foreign crises would endanger the country if the United States became involved in them

   (B) That the merchants and bankers in America would threaten democracy, and the Supreme Court would one day be so powerful as to be able to effectively make laws on its own

   (C) That the U.S. Constitution would one day have to address the slavery question, and that the settlement of the slavery question would erupt in civil war

   (D) That the settlement of the West would cost great sacrifices in prolonged war with American Indians, and that European countries would try to take advantage of domestic strife

   (E) That the more populated northern states would eventually reduce southern states' rights, and the southern states would try to leave the union in retaliation

35. Why was Daniel Webster, the antebellum senator from Massachusetts, vilified at home during the debates surrounding the Compromise of 1850?

   (A) His constituents did not approve of his cooperation with slaveholders like John C. Calhoun and Henry Clay.

   (B) His constituents believed he had not done enough to look out for the New England commercial interests they had sent him to Congress to defend.

   (C) His constituents believed his shameless grandstanding in the debates because he wanted to be president reflected poorly on the dignity of Massachusetts.

   (D) His constituents could not stomach compromising with the South at all on the slavery question because Massachusetts was by then largely committed to abolition.

   (E) His constituents believed that his reckless behavior and rhetorical excesses had brought the country to the brink of civil war.

36. Why did the city of Chicago develop into a major component of the late nineteenth-century American economy?

    (A) The first skyscraper was constructed there, which became a model for all other major cities to follow.

    (B) Chicago's location on Lake Michigan and the many railroads that converged there made it a major transportation hub for the steel, beef, and other industries.

    (C) Both Andrew Carnegie and John D. Rockefeller located their corporate headquarters in Chicago because it was near the raw materials from which they made their riches.

    (D) The best financial minds from New York City rebelled against the monopoly Wall Street held on the economy and started their own brokerage firms in Chicago.

    (E) Most immigrants to the United States after the Civil War converged on Chicago because they wanted to leave the dangers of living in eastern cities behind.

37. What design of the Brooklyn Bridge revolutionized civil engineering principles involved in the manufacture of steel bridges?

    (A) The arches supporting the roadway were the first capable of spanning wide areas.

    (B) The pieces of the bridge were assembled with rivets before being set in place by cranes.

    (C) The cables suspending the road surface were made of braided steel wire to increase strength.

    (D) The towers supporting the bridge were built on foundations in the East River.

    (E) The roadway, walkways, and a railroad track all shared the same span for the first time.

38. Which statement below best describes the significance of the Open Door Policy initiated by Secretary of State John Hay in 1899?

    (A) This foreign policy milestone revealed that the United States was a superpower able to project its will on other countries at the dawn of the twentieth century.

    (B) The United States was now an East Asian power with the acquisition of the Philippines, but in regard to China it could only request cooperation from other powers in the region.

    (C) In the conflicts that were erupting in China the United States was the only disinterested power in the region able to mediate among the other nations in order to maintain peace for all.

    (D) As imperialist powers carved up China, the United States was that ancient civilization's only hope for continued autonomy.

    (E) The Open Door Notes circulated among the countries surrounding China clearly signaled that the United States intended to take over territory on the Asian mainland.

39. How did high-level investors practice "pumping and dumping" through the 1920s prior to the stock market crash?

    (A) They purchased a revolving set of stocks and then sold them within a few weeks to produce an artificial level of activity in the market to encourage buyers.
    (B) They sold a particular stock among themselves to create a "hot" stock and then sold their shares after their purchases created a demand.
    (C) They bought controlling shares in corporations and then sold off their stock in the company when the stock price had doubled.
    (D) They bought whole companies and then sold them when their efficient management of those companies had boosted the companies' stock values.
    (E) They bought shares in many companies and then bundled those stocks into holding companies that in turn sold stock to the public.

40. What restrictions were placed on the executive branch by the War Powers Act at the close of the Vietnam War?

    (A) The Congress said the president could not perform surveillance on foreign countries without the consent of the Senate Foreign Relations Committee.
    (B) The Congress banned the use of military force in countries neighboring those countries with whom the United States was at war.
    (C) The Congress restricted the president's National Security Council to the formation of policy in times of peace.
    (D) The Congress restricted the executive branch's ability to conduct "shuttle diplomacy" by sending secret envoys to negotiate peace with enemy nations unless the Senate approved.
    (E) The Congress said the president could send the American military into action for only two months before notifying the Senate of the necessity for such an action.

41. "There were two kinds of Spaniards, one very cruel and pitiless, whose goal was to squeeze the last drop of Indian blood in order to get rich, and one less cruel, who must have felt sorry for the Indians; but in each case they placed their own interests above the health and salvation of those poor people."

    This quotation is an example of the rhetoric behind which of the following ideas or practices associated with the Spanish Empire?

    (A) The Columbian Exchange
    (B) The Spanish Inquisition
    (C) The Black Legend
    (D) The encomienda system
    (E) The mission system

42. The Toleration Act of 1649 in colonial America was mainly designed to settle disputes between which two groups?

    (A) Roman Catholics and Protestants
    (B) American Indians and English colonists on the frontier
    (C) English colonists and the colonists of the Dutch colony of New Amsterdam
    (D) Royal colonial governors and colonial legislatures
    (E) Colonies from the North and colonies from the South

43. Pinckney's Treaty in 1796 was designed to settle conflict between the United States and which country or region and over what issue?

    (A) Canada—the Maine Boundary
    (B) The Old Northwest—American Indian land claims in the wake of border violence
    (C) Spain—free navigation of the Mississippi River and the right of deposit in New Orleans
    (D) Great Britain—debts that Americans had incurred before the American Revolution
    (E) France—merchant ships that had been captured in the Quasi-War on the high seas

44. Which political scandal in American history was associated with the Grant administration?

    (A) The Teapot Dome Scandal
    (B) The Burr Conspiracy
    (C) The Ballinger-Pinchot Affair
    (D) The Credit-Mobilier Scandal
    (E) The Indian Bureau Embezzlement Scandal

45. Which statement below best expresses President Woodrow Wilson's main goal(s) for backing the creation of the Federal Reserve System?

    (A) He determined that a National Bank was an inadequate model for the type of hands-on control he wanted over the economy.
    (B) He wanted to prove once and for all that the executive branch should control the economy rather than the legislative branch.
    (C) He wanted to evenly distribute Federal Reserve Banks around the country to facilitate tighter control over the amount of currency in circulation and thus the value of the currency.
    (D) He wanted to disassociate the presidency from responsibility for reacting to recessions or depressions in the business cycle by creating the Federal Reserve Board.
    (E) He wanted to decentralize the banking industry yet retain a minimum level of involvement with the policies and actions of the Federal Reserve.

46. What rationale described below most compelled the United States to intervene in Cuba after the insurrection began against Spanish rule?

    (A) The United States had strongly desired to take over Cuba since before the Ostend Manifesto.
    (B) Investors in sugar plantations in Cuba insisted that the government protect their assets.
    (C) Admiral Alfred Thayer Mahan had said Cuba was instrumental in protecting a future canal.
    (D) Theodore Roosevelt believed he would be president if he could just become a war hero.
    (E) Cuban-Americans and the popular press urged support of a nearby budding republic.

47. Which principles formed the basis of Woodrow Wilson's Fourteen-Points Address?

    (A) imperialism and militarism
    (B) nationalism and international law
    (C) self-determination and collective security
    (D) arbitration and reciprocal military inspections
    (E) internationalism and humanitarian aid

48. In addition to the National Security Council, the Central Intelligence Agency, and the Joint Chiefs of Staff, what departments in the executive branch were created by the 1947 National Security Act?

    (A) The Department of Energy and the Department of Defense
    (B) The Department of Defense and the Department of the Air Force
    (C) The Department of Veterans Affairs and the Department of the United Nations
    (D) The Department of Housing and Urban Development and the Department of Transportation
    (E) The Department of Federal Security and the Department of International Trade

49. Which of the following federal initiatives were successfully launched by President Lyndon Johnson's Great Society domestic agenda?

    (A) The Peace Corps and the Food Stamp Program
    (B) The Social Security system and the Head Start Program
    (C) The Civil Rights Act and the Voting Rights Act
    (D) The Economic Opportunity Act and National Defense Education Act
    (E) The Upward Bound program and Fair Labor Standards Act

50. How did the Supreme Court decision in *Miranda v. Arizona* alter domestic law enforcement practices beginning in 1966?

    (A)  The practice of profiling based on race, ethnicity, sex, or age was banned.
    (B)  The interrogation of illegal immigrants without a qualified translator present during investigations was banned.
    (C)  The statements made by suspects during interrogation without an attorney present were banned from use during prosecution.
    (D)  The sharing of information among the FBI, the CIA, and state or local law enforcement agencies during investigations or surveillance of suspects was banned.
    (E)  The prosecution of suspects in criminal proceedings above those of misdemeanors without the provision of an attorney at no cost to the defendant was banned.

51. "That loans in times of public danger, especially from foreign war, are found an indispensible resource. . . . And that in a country, which, like this, is possessed of little active wealth, or . . . little monied capital, the necessity for that resource, must, in such emergencies, be proportionally urgent."

    Alexander Hamilton is most likely arguing for which aspect of his financial program in the above quotation?

    (A)  The constitutionality of the Bank of the United States
    (B)  The national debt as an impetus toward nationalism
    (C)  The wisdom of funding bonds issued by the government at par
    (D)  The need for customs duties and excise taxes to pay the national debt
    (E)  The need for the establishment of a Treasury Department in the new American government

52. Which description below best explains the contributions of Sacagawea to the success of the Lewis and Clark expedition?

    (A)  Her services as a guide and translator enabled the Corps of Discovery to travel safely through Shoshone tribal lands.
    (B)  Her having a child that she bore on the journey made encounters with new American Indian tribes realize the intentions of the Corps of Discovery were peaceful.
    (C)  Her extensive knowledge of herbal remedies helped maintain the health of the men of the Corps of Discovery so well that only one member died on the expedition.
    (D)  Her interest in the expedition attracted her husband, Toussaint Charbonneau, to become its chief scout who taught the Corps of Discovery American Indian hunting and survival skills.
    (E)  Her skill as a storyteller and dancer entertained the Corps of Discovery through the long periods in which they were encamped through the rains of the Northwest.

53. The main goal of the delegation sent by the Hartford Convention to the national capital during the War of 1812 was to

(A) reform the federal government's methods of declaring war and of raising an army.

(B) convince the federal government to adopt a new strategy to win the war.

(C) open up negotiations with the British to end the war so trade could recommence.

(D) warn the federal government that New England would secede if the war continued.

(E) initiate impeachment proceedings against President Madison who started the war.

54. Which of Henry Clay's attributes allowed him to become instrumental in negotiating compromises that prevented the onset of the Civil War in his lifetime and why?

(A) He was educated in New England but lived in the South so he understood both sides.

(B) His leadership in the Congress during the War of 1812 and his service in the Blackhawk War made him a respected source on military issues.

(C) His visionary insight into the need for a nationally organized economy and his support for the Bank of the United States earned him the respect of New Englanders even though he was from the Deep South.

(D) He was a Whig but also a slave owner, so he was the only powerful senator to whom major segments of the Congress would all listen.

(E) His service as secretary of state and his organization of support for revolutions in Latin America had won him world fame and thus more respect at home than any other senator.

55. What was the nature of John Slidell's secret mission in Mexico when he was dispatched there by President Polk before the Mexican War?

(A) He was sent to identify elements of Mexican society that would be willing to revolt from Santa Anna.

(B) He was sent to negotiate an attempted purchase of territory from Mexico that would stave off war between the two countries.

(C) He was the representative of the Bank of the United States whom Polk hoped would convince the Mexican government to pay back over $3 million in defaulted loans.

(D) He was sent to scout out the best location for Zachary Taylor to bring his army in order to provoke a response from the Mexican army as a premise Polk could use to start a war.

(E) He was sent to negotiate the release of American citizens who had been arrested in Mexico on the eve of war.

56. Which statement below best states the response of the United States to the Boxer Rebellion in China at the opening of the twentieth century?

   (A) While refusing to participate in the opium trade that had caused such outrage in China, the United States insisted on the safety and freedom of movement of Christian missionaries.
   (B) The United States mounted the China Relief expedition with nearby forces from the Philippines that participated in the Siege of Peking in order to end the fighting.
   (C) The United States referred to its demands in the Open Door Notes and chastised countries for their interference in China's domestic affairs.
   (D) Desiring to carve out spheres of influence for itself, the United States closed off access to selected port cities for its own use during the crisis and beyond.
   (E) Having no territorial aspirations in mainland China, the U.S. military occupied the island of Formosa and awaited developments.

57. Henry Ford's aims in making the Model T automobile are best expressed in which statement?

   (A) Ford attempted to attract a wide range of consumers by changing colors and configurations of this first commercially successful automobile.
   (B) Ford desired to bring about an alteration of American society in increasing the mobility of Americans by providing them an affordable automobile through mass production.
   (C) Ford recognized that this luxury model of his basic car was the only way to make his company profitable through attracting the richest Americans to purchase it.
   (D) Ford sought to give the United States an economic advantage over Germany and other leading industrialized nations by producing mechanically superior automobiles.
   (E) Ford wanted Americans to begin to drive more frequently so he could create a demand for better quality roads in order to increase the business of his construction firm.

58. ". . . the United States may have a rapidly aging population . . . [and] it may have difficulty keeping its position as a major power. Russia may have twice as many men of military age, and twice as many women to propagate the next generation. Other nations encourage reproduction . . . but our country . . . continues to give every advantage and preferment to the unmarried and the childless."

   In what decade of American history was the quote above most likely written?

   (A) The 1920s
   (B) The 1930s
   (C) The 1940s
   (D) The 1950s
   (E) The 1960s

59. Which statement below best characterizes President Richard Nixon's political skills, values, or accomplishments?

   (A) President Nixon was a master of domestic policy but had severe shortcomings in dealing with matters of foreign policy.
   (B) Driven largely by paranoia, President Nixon's administration alienated the nation through his first term in office, and he was reelected to a second term with little to no mandate to govern.
   (C) President Nixon focused excessively on polling data during his administration and moved toward positions based merely on their popularity.
   (D) President Nixon's main goal was restoring order to frightened whites in the South who thought he would use federal power just as Eisenhower and Kennedy had done to impose racial harmony.
   (E) President Nixon employed a blend of liberal, moderate, and conservative positions to achieve a landslide victory in the Election of 1972 before he self-destructed.

60. "They let each of us deliver a short message to our families in front of the TV cameras. I said hello to my wife and told her that I was still alive. I also let her know that I had not received any mail. The whole time I was speaking, I kept glowering at the militants lined up along the back wall."

   The account quoted above is most likely describing an episode during which event?

   (A) The kidnapping of the grandchildren of William Randolph Hearst
   (B) The takeover of the U.S. Embassy in Iran
   (C) The capture of the Marine Corps barracks in Beirut, Lebanon
   (D) The capture of American medical students in Grenada
   (E) The kidnapping of American journalists by al-Qaeda in Pakistan

61. All of the following grievances were listed in the Declaration of Independence among the "repeated usurpations" of King George III EXCEPT

   (A) "He has refused his Assent to Laws, the most wholesome and necessary for the public good."
   (B) "He has kept among us, in times of peace, Standing Armies without the consent of our legislatures."
   (C) "For cutting off our Trade with all parts of the world."
   (D) "For condemning the souls of men to the governance of his church, alone, for the manly firmness of their dissent according to their own consciences."
   (E) "He has plundered our seas, ravaged our Coasts, burnt our towns, and destroyed the Lives of our people."

62. All of the following geographical features were boundaries of the United States as granted under the Treaty of Paris in 1783 EXCEPT the

    (A) shores of the Great Lakes and the St. Lawrence River.
    (B) Mississippi River.
    (C) Atlantic Ocean.
    (D) border with Spanish Florida.
    (E) midway point on Lakes Superior, Huron, Erie, and Ontario.

63. What prompted western farmers in Pennsylvania to take up arms against the United States government in the 1794 climax of the Whiskey Rebellion?

    (A) The laws passed by Congress to limit the manufacture, sale, and consumption of whiskey
    (B) George Washington's practice of patrolling the frontier with a fifteen thousand-man standing army
    (C) Their perception that the federal government was ruining their livelihood through taxation
    (D) The federal government's ignoring of American Indian attacks prompted by whiskey drinking
    (E) The refusal on the part of Congress to establish tariffs to give American distillers fair markets

64. Which statement below best explains how John Jacob Astor came to be among the first rags-to-riches success stories in American history?

    (A) He smuggled the plans of a textile factory out of England by memorizing them, and then he built the first successful water-powered textile mill in American history.
    (B) He established a chain of hotels in major American cities beginning with the Waldorf-Astoria Hotel in New York City.
    (C) He organized the shipment of the first barrels of petroleum in Pennsylvania by creating artificial flood surges in creeks near his oil-drilling locations.
    (D) He organized general stores that outfitted miners for work in the gold fields in California.
    (E) He created a system where mountain men could meet at scheduled gathering times to help them market their furs back east and in Europe.

65. How did Secretary of State John Quincy Adams compel the Spanish to consent to the provisions of the Adams-Onís Treaty in 1819?

    (A) By having the U.S. Navy blockade the outlets of the Rio Grande and the Mississippi Rivers in order to squeeze the Spanish colonial economy

    (B) By organizing British and French support for possible economic sanctions or military action against Spain in Europe

    (C) By pledging to assist the Spanish colonial holdings in South America to revolt from Spanish rule

    (D) By threatening to unleash the wrath of Andrew Jackson whose militia forces were already in Florida putting down attacks by American Indians who were aided there by the Spanish

    (E) By negotiating the preliminaries to a huge transfer of land including Texas and California to the United States in return for American help in Mexico's desire to break free from Spain

66. How did Theodore Roosevelt's (TR's) New Nationalism presidential campaign platform differ from Woodrow Wilson's New Freedom platform for the Election of 1912?

    (A) As a southerner Woodrow Wilson's platform sought to reinstate respect for states' rights, whereas TR's platform retained a healthy distrust of states' rights as a cause of the Civil War.

    (B) TR sought to expand the impact of Progressivism, whereas Woodrow Wilson wanted to limit the power of the federal government by rolling back some Progressive ideas.

    (C) TR's platform pledged to attack bad trusts and merely regulate good trusts, whereas Woodrow Wilson's New Freedom platform viewed all trusts as destructive of the rights of the people.

    (D) As a southerner Woodrow Wilson sought to free southern states from the racial policies of the federal government, whereas TR pushed for more progress for African-Americans' civil rights.

    (E) TR's foreign policy sought to isolate the United States from involvement in world affairs, whereas Woodrow Wilson sought to make the United States an instrument to expand freedom.

Courtesy of the Library of Congress

67. Which statement below best represents the portrayal of the Grant administration by Thomas Nast, the most celebrated political cartoonist in American history?

   (A) President Grant behaved like an ostrich and buried his head in order to avoid dealing with the troubles created by his ineptitude.

   (B) President Grant was being swallowed up by the sheer number of scandals that had erupted during his administration in the Gilded Age.

   (C) President Grant's pledge to get to the bottom of the scandals of his administration was a lie and revealed he was in complicity with the actions of his corrupt subordinates.

   (D) President Grant was surprised by the duplicity of the members of his administration but sincerely sought to prosecute every last one of the troublemakers.

   (E) President Grant discovered that there was no end to the corruption in his own administration and resolved to resign from the presidency if it did not cease.

68. Which statement best describes the results of prohibition, the "Noble Experiment" begun with the ratification of the Eighteenth Amendment and passage of the Volstead Act?

    (A) The widespread animosity toward prohibition created the establishments known as "speakeasies," which sold alcoholic beverages and actually increased consumption.

    (B) The fact that the main supporters of prohibition were young, college-educated women in the Progressive movement led to the younger generations' widespread abstinence from alcohol.

    (C) The illegality of the consumption of alcohol heightened its appeal among young people and contributed to the "flapper" culture, but overall consumption of alcohol dropped considerably.

    (D) The end of the distilling industry ruined thousands of grain farmers and caused them to experience the effect of a great depression a decade before the rest of the nation.

    (E) The animosity toward the manner in which prohibition was enacted caused a widespread grassroots movement to make changes to the U.S. Constitution more difficult to acquire.

69. Herbert Hoover's response to the Great Depression is best characterized by which of the following statements?

    (A) As a conservative Republican, Hoover refused to use the federal government's resources to provide for the welfare of the people.

    (B) Hoover, as a former secretary of commerce, built on his outdated ideas that were inadequate to meet the needs of the present crisis.

    (C) As a self-made millionaire businessman and engineer, Hoover lacked the capacity to sympathize with the masses who were hungry and jobless.

    (D) Hoover resisted resorting to government action to resolve the crisis at first, but then created a bureaucracy designed to help the banking industry that became a model for Franklin D. Roosevelt's New Deal.

    (E) Hoover launched an initiative designed expressly to motivate private corporations, faith-based organizations and churches, and private philanthropists to advance charitable activities.

70. What made the invention of RADAR so important to the success of the Allied Powers in responding to the aggression of the Axis Powers during World War II?

    (A) Allied bombers were able to attack German cities by night using RADAR to guide them and thus avoid accurate antiaircraft fire from the ground.
    (B) Allied forces were able to determine the direction of incoming Axis bombers and direct their limited defensive forces to reduce the success of the enemy.
    (C) Allied forces were able to target their missiles against enemy ships, planes, and even cities by using RADAR.
    (D) Allied RADAR allowed ships to determine the location of submarines in international waters, which made the process of protecting convoys of merchant ships more successful.
    (E) RADAR allowed Allied mechanized units to negotiate mountain passes to prepare for surprise attacks without their lights disclosing their positions.

71. How did the American Indian cultural value of reciprocity affect interactions with Europeans during the colonial era?

    (A) Since American Indian tribes had nothing comparable to the manufactured goods of European explorers and colonists, gift exchanges left native peoples ashamed of their own cultures.
    (B) American Indians' acquiring manufactured goods like rifles and tomahawks destroyed the peace that existed among tribes prior to the arrival of Europeans in the New World.
    (C) Peace was possible between the cultures as long as the supply of furs permitted a medium of exchange for the European items American Indians found desirable.
    (D) Chiefs with strong ties to European powers acquired supremacy over others by using European gifts to create debt burdens that were impossible to reciprocate.
    (E) While gift exchanges allowed Europeans to acquire mutually beneficial relationships with some American Indian tribes, insults and crimes also precipitated reprisals and war.

72. What new approach to fighting the French and Indian War insisted upon by William Pitt allowed not only victory but better relations between England and her American colonies for a time?

    (A) Any American colonists recruited as soldiers in the English army obtained land in the West.
    (B) Pitt decided that the armies fighting this colonial war should use only colonial soldiers.
    (C) American colonies that supported the war were promised land in the Ohio River Valley.
    (D) American companies were given exclusive contracts to supply the British army in America.
    (E) Pitt finally promoted American officers, like George Washington, to the top military ranks.

73. "...that alien-friends are under the jurisdiction and protection of the laws of the state wherein they are; that no power over them has been delegated to the United States, nor prohibited to the individual states distinct from their power over citizens . . . ."

    The quotation above is most likely from which late eighteenth-century document(s)?

    (A) The Land Ordinances of 1785 and 1787
    (B) The Northwest Ordinances of 1787
    (C) The Federalist Papers of 1787 and 1788
    (D) The Alien and Sedition Acts of 1798
    (E) The Kentucky and Virginia Resolutions of 1798 and 1799

74. The 1824 Supreme Court case *Gibbons v. Ogden* was a landmark decision regarding all federal business regulations, but in what industry or economic activity did the case originate?

    (A) Interstate transportation
    (B) Marketing of agricultural products
    (C) The securing of patents associated with the invention of the sewing machine
    (D) The management of employees in textile mills
    (E) The organization of immigrant Irish coal miners

75. What aspect of the construction of the Erie Canal set a precedent for many subsequent infrastructure improvement projects?

   (A) The construction was accomplished primarily with steam power rather than animal power.
   (B) The construction was funded by the state legislature as a means of boosting the economy.
   (C) The construction was the first large federal expenditure for transportation.
   (D) The construction was accomplished exclusively with American engineers.
   (E) The construction was accomplished ahead of schedule by the invention of new equipment.

76. What two aspects of modern American society were created in direct connection to the construction of railroads in the nineteenth century?

   (A) Steam power and the manufacture of iron bridges
   (B) Business trusts and deficit spending
   (C) Time zones and the first large-scale amassing of capital in giant corporations
   (D) The telegraph and the Bessemer process of making steel
   (E) Labor unions and federal regulations about worker safety

77. All of the following components were a part of Henry Clay's American System for the design of a nationally organized economic plan EXCEPT

   (A) the Second Bank of the United States (BUS)
   (B) a high protective tariff
   (C) the extensive use of federal money to enhance infrastructure
   (D) a single national currency
   (E) a federal income tax to fund internal improvements and retirement of the national debt

78. Which of the following was the most important reason(s) that American colonists in Texas sought independence from Mexico in 1836?

   (A) The abolition of slavery once Mexico freed itself from the Spanish Empire
   (B) The atrocities committed by Santa Anna in crushing rebellions in southern Mexico
   (C) The banning of further immigration by Americans into Texas and the end of constitutional government
   (D) The restrictive policies that Santa Anna forced on Texans in that no Mexican land could be purchased by them except for that contained in their original grants
   (E) The forcible closure of all Protestant churches and the exile of all Protestant ministers from Texas

79. The 1892 Homestead Strike at Andrew Carnegie's Homestead Steel Works was sparked by

    (A) Carnegie's insistence that his plants would all be open shops.
    (B) Carnegie's selling of the plant to Henry Clay Frick upon his retirement to Scotland.
    (C) a decline in the steel industry that forced the Carnegie Steel Company to lower wages.
    (D) Henry Clay Frick's lowering wages to break the union at the plant and a subsequent lockout.
    (E) the discovery by the union that Pinkerton Detectives had infiltrated their meetings.

80. Which factor below explains why the First Red Scare occurred in the 1920s?

    (A) Carl Schurz, a radical from Germany, was elected to the Senate after the Seventeenth Amendment allowed direct election of senators for the first time.
    (B) Growing anti-immigrant sentiments in America were coupled with the fear of Bolshevism.
    (C) Julius and Ethel Rosenberg were convicted as communist spies and executed.
    (D) The Ku Klux Klan led a rally in Washington, D.C., that was attended by seventy-five thousand Klansmen.
    (E) The Soviet Union had begun direct radio propaganda broadcasts into the United States.

81. What made the Iroquois unique among the American Indian tribes encountered by the English during the colonial period?

    (A) They lived in settlements that were basically permanent villages.
    (B) They organized their tribal power and family descent through matrilineal connections.
    (C) They were willing to trade and intermarry with the English colonists.
    (D) They sent envoys over the ocean to visit England.
    (E) They had organized their tribes into a military confederation for mutual protection.

82. Which statement below best describes the impact of the Restoration of the British monarchy in 1660 on the British colonies in America?

    (A) This milestone in English history had virtually no impact on England's American colonies.
    (B) The Restoration crushed the hopes of the earliest push toward independence.
    (C) The Restoration ended a period of salutary neglect and for a time brought stringent controls.
    (D) The British Crown in a resurgence of power rescued the colonies from wars with the Dutch.
    (E) The Restoration led to strict enforcement of the already existing Navigation Acts.

83. Which statement best describes the rationale behind the Three-fifth's Compromise that helped unify the Constitutional Convention in order to complete the U.S. Constitution?

    (A) The delegates were operating from the current scientific estimate of the level of human development reached by African slaves by the eighteenth century.
    (B) The southern colonies desired to secure for their slaves at least three-fifths of the rights of white Americans in the formation of the Constitution.
    (C) After almost 170 years of interaction, the southern delegates considered only three out of every five African-Americans capable of participation as citizens of the new republic.
    (D) Northerners did not want southerners to count any number of their African slaves toward increasing their representation in Congress, but three-fifths lowered the South's original request.
    (E) Only 60 percent of the delegates approved of the South's desire to increase their power in the House of Representatives by counting slaves, but it was enough of a majority to win.

84. The goal of the Order of the Cincinnati in the wake of the Revolutionary War was to

    (A) rule the new nation as its nobles by establishing an aristocracy rather than a republic.
    (B) establish a republic just as the Roman war hero Cincinnatus had done for Rome.
    (C) distribute land to every veteran of the war in gratitude for his or her patriotic sacrifices.
    (D) establish a new country on the banks of the Ohio River between the United States and Canada.
    (E) found a historical institution dedicated to keeping alive the patriot spirit that won the war.

85. The five promises made by James K. Polk in his campaign for the presidency in 1844 that he subsequently fulfilled as president included all of the following EXCEPT to

    (A) settle the Oregon dispute with the United Kingdom.
    (B) restore the Bank of the United States that had been killed by President Andrew Jackson.
    (C) lower the tariff.
    (D) acquire California from Mexico.
    (E) leave office after only one term as president.

86. What was contained in the "Mulligan Letters" that hurt James G. Blaine's chances to win the presidency in the Election of 1884 against Grover Cleveland, the only Democrat to become president throughout the Gilded Age?

    (A) Details of his ongoing affair with a mistress named Elizabeth Mulligan
    (B) Testimonials that Blaine had murdered a man named James Mulligan in the Civil War
    (C) Records of money Blaine had received for favors done for businesses while a congressman
    (D) Proof that Blaine had an illegitimate child back in his home state of Maine
    (E) Evidence that Blaine had joined William Walker's expedition to take over Nicaragua in 1856

87. What did the Dupuy de Lôme letter of 1897 and the Zimmermann Telegram of 1917 have in common as causes of American wars?

    (A) They were leaked to newspapers after being intercepted by American intelligence operations.
    (B) They exposed the inner workings and opinions of the U.S. Department of State to the world.
    (C) They caused setbacks in American intervention in foreign affairs by encouraging isolationism.
    (D) They were foreign diplomatic communications that made American presidents look weak.
    (E) They revealed extensive spy networks operating within the United States.

88. Which of the following incidents or policies undermined support for Franklin D. Roosevelt (FDR) and for the New Deal more than any other?

    (A) Widespread boondoggling, or wasteful laziness, discovered in New Deal public works projects
    (B) The banning of African-Americans from Norris, Tennessee, the planned town associated with the first dam constructed by the Tennessee Valley Authority
    (C) The Supreme Court decisions striking down the Agricultural Adjustment Act and the National Recovery Administration as unconstitutional
    (D) The court-packing scheme in which FDR sought to expand the number of justices on the Supreme Court in order to keep the judicial branch from stopping New Deal progress
    (E) The lack of response to help farmers ruined by the impact of the Dust Bowl and the buying up of land by large conglomerates portrayed in *The Grapes of Wrath* by John Steinbeck

89. What role did the Laffer Curve play in the Reagan administration?

(A) The diagram helped Reagan's campaign directors piece together the winning strategies for the Elections of 1980 and 1984.

(B) The diagram illustrated the impact of stagflation on the economy and people of the United States and made Ronald Reagan resolve to end the 1970s recession.

(C) The diagram illustrated how the Soviet Union could not keep up economically with a buildup of American military might and gave Ronald Reagan the resolve to end the Cold War.

(D) The diagram graphically illustrated the plummeting of Reagan's approval ratings after his missteps and scandals of his second term.

(E) The diagram convinced Reagan's advisers that the only way to end the recession and move America forward was to enact significant tax cuts in order to boost the economy.

90. Which of the following statements best explains the significance of the line-item veto temporarily enjoyed by the Clinton administration until it was deemed unconstitutional by the Supreme Court?

(A) During the crisis in the former Yugoslavian region of Europe, the line-item veto allowed President Clinton to continue to cooperate with the North Atlantic Treaty Organization despite the War Powers Act.

(B) Since President Clinton was from the former Confederate state of Arkansas, he was determined to secure a line-item veto like the one the Confederate Constitution had.

(C) The line-item veto was like the Pendleton Act in the Gilded Age; it was the big hope of government reformers who wanted to end excessive federal spending for pet projects.

(D) President Clinton's cooperation with the Republicans' Contract with America provision for a line-item veto proved he was a conservative Democrat.

(E) While President Clinton secured a line-item veto from the Congress, he never used it until the Republican Party regained control of the Congress in 1994.

# Answer Key
## PRACTICE TEST 2

| | | | | | | | |
|---|---|---|---|---|---|---|---|
| 1. | D | 24. | C | 47. | C | 70. | B |
| 2. | C | 25. | A | 48. | B | 71. | E |
| 3. | A | 26. | B | 49. | C | 72. | E |
| 4. | D | 27. | B | 50. | C | 73. | E |
| 5. | B | 28. | D | 51. | C | 74. | A |
| 6. | E | 29. | C | 52. | A | 75. | B |
| 7. | C | 30. | E | 53. | A | 76. | C |
| 8. | B | 31. | B | 54. | D | 77. | E |
| 9. | B | 32. | C | 55. | B | 78. | C |
| 10. | A | 33. | E | 56. | B | 79. | D |
| 11. | D | 34. | A | 57. | B | 80. | B |
| 12. | E | 35. | D | 58. | C | 81. | E |
| 13. | E | 36. | B | 59. | E | 82. | C |
| 14. | B | 37. | C | 60. | B | 83. | D |
| 15. | C | 38. | B | 61. | D | 84. | A |
| 16. | D | 39. | B | 62. | A | 85. | B |
| 17. | A | 40. | E | 63. | C | 86. | C |
| 18. | E | 41. | C | 64. | E | 87. | D |
| 19. | B | 42. | A | 65. | D | 88. | D |
| 20. | D | 43. | C | 66. | C | 89. | E |
| 21. | C | 44. | D | 67. | B | 90. | C |
| 22. | D | 45. | E | 68. | C | | |
| 23. | E | 46. | E | 69. | D | | |

# Test Analysis

**Step 1: Count the number of correct answers.**

Enter the total here: _____

**Step 2: Count the number of incorrect answers.**

Enter the total here: _____

**Step 3: Multiply the number of incorrect answers by .250**

Enter the product here: _____

**Step 4: Subtract the results obtained in Step 3 from the total obtained in Step 1.**

Enter the total here: _____

**Step 5: Round the number obtained in Step 4 to the nearest whole number.**

Raw Score = _____

## Scaled Score Conversion Table

| Raw Score | Scaled Score | Raw Score | Scaled Score | Raw Score | Scaled Score |
|-----------|--------------|-----------|--------------|-----------|--------------|
| 90–79 | 800 | 46–45 | 600 | 8–7 | 400 |
| 78 | 790 | 44–43 | 590 | 6–5 | 390 |
| 77–76 | 780 | 42–41 | 580 | 4–3 | 380 |
| 75 | 770 | 40 | 570 | 2–1 | 370 |
| 74 | 760 | 39–38 | 560 | 0 – –1 | 360 |
| 73–72 | 750 | 37–36 | 550 | –2 – –3 | 350 |
| 71 | 740 | 35–34 | 540 | –4 | 340 |
| 70–69 | 730 | 33–32 | 530 | –5 – –6 | 330 |
| 68 | 720 | 31–30 | 520 | –7 | 320 |
| 67–66 | 710 | 29–28 | 510 | –8 – –9 | 310 |
| 65–64 | 700 | 27 | 500 | –10 | 300 |
| 63 | 690 | 26–25 | 490 | –11 – –12 | 290 |
| 62–61 | 680 | 24–23 | 480 | –13 | 280 |
| 60–59 | 670 | 22–21 | 470 | –14 – –15 | 270 |
| 58–57 | 660 | 20–19 | 460 | –16 – –17 | 260 |
| 56–55 | 650 | 18–17 | 450 | –18 – –19 | 250 |
| 54-53 | 640 | 16–15 | 440 | –20 | 240 |
| 52–51 | 630 | 14–13 | 430 | –21 – –22 | 230 |
| 50–49 | 620 | 12–11 | 420 | | |
| 48–47 | 610 | 10–9 | 410 | | |

# Answer Explanations

1. **D** Both Cortés and Pizarro were indefatigable men of action and staunch Roman Catholics and under the circumstances of the conquest of Latin America responsible for several brutal acts. Answer C is the reverse of the truth. Interestingly, Pizarro began as a pig herder and could not read or write and wound up controlling most of South America before he was assassinated.

2. **C** The Puritans and Presbyterians were more Calvinist than the Anglican Church or its creed in the 39 Articles that Calvin did not write. Nor did he produce the first Bible written in English (that was Wycliffe) or lead churches in Zurich (that was Zwingli). He dedicated his *Institutes of the Christian Religion* to the French king who was not a Protestant and not inclined to listen to Calvin. Answer C reveals that most colonial American Christians did, however, and Calvinism shaped everything Puritans and Presbyterians believed not only about the Bible but about society, politics, economics, and so on.

3. **A** All of the other answers are true, and answer A is not true only because slavery was permitted in the colony. The attempt to produce a silk industry failed when Georgians realized they had planted the wrong kind of mulberry tree all over their colony.

4. **D** None of the answers are true except for answer D in that two of the American envoys were deported. One remained to keep his finger on the pulse of French sentiment, but negotiations broke down because of the insult from France that caused Americans to say what the two said that got them deported (among other harsher words): "Millions for defense but not a penny for tribute!"

5. **B** All of the answers hint at reasons in that there was gold in "them thar hills," but that was not known at the time of the purchase. There were also Apaches and Mormons in the Southwest and even some cotton cultivation farther north in New Mexico, but what was obvious at the time of purchase was the route for the railroad.

6. **E** While answers B, C, and D were accusations hurled at the Knights of Labor, only answer D had some truth to it, but answer D was not Gompers's grievance. The leadership of the Knights was also reluctant to call strikes, so answer A was never true. The problem Gompers saw that made him start the American Federation of Labor was answer E.

7. **C** Answer D was known as the "Ohio Idea," and although answers A, B, and D might have been good ones that were even applicable in Wisconsin, answer C conveys La Follette's practice that became famous as the "Wisconsin Idea" because he did it. The Wisconsin Idea became the bedrock foundation of the Progressive Reform movement and is the model of government that still runs the country.

8. **B** All of the other answers hint at realities becoming apparent to nineteenth-century thinkers of one stripe or another, but Mahan was an imperialist whose ideas launched both imperialism and militarism in the form of modern navies

in the United States, the United Kingdom, and in Germany (among other countries).

9. **B**  Most of the other answers are actually the reverse of various events associated with the Johnson and Nixon administrations' actions in Vietnam. Only answer B reveals the morale-busting interpretation placed on the Tet Offensive by television journalists when the Tet Offensive was actually the most successful episode in the war for killing large numbers of the enemy in one series of engagements. Public opinion about this war was all important, however, and as it swayed, Lyndon Johnson decided not to run for the second term he could have had constitutionally. Answer C is incorrect because atrocities committed against civilians by the Vietcong were nothing new, and the American morale was damaged more when Americans committed atrocities as in the My Lai Massacre.

10. **A**  Even members of the Republican Party were so used to Nixon's assessment that "We're all Keynesians, now," that George H. W. Bush referred to supply-side economics as "voodoo economics." Bush's action was contrary to Reagan's Eleventh Commandment, "Thou shalt not speak ill of any fellow Republican," but Reagan still chose Bush as a running mate.

11. **D**  All of the other answers twist truths from the political science milestones of the colonial American experience. The Mayflower Compact only applied to a tiny shipload of frightened, argumentative settlers, but its symbolic power as a precedent changed the world. The few paragraphs were the closest Englishmen had come by 1620 to writing a constitution. The British monarchy, Parliament, and even the House of Burgesses had all been called into being without a document, and documents like the Magna Carta were only attempts to limit existing governments' powers. The Carolina colony had their constitution written for them by John Locke, and then written constitutions became the norm.

12. **E**  Colonial Americans believed the king of England and his ministers had every right to pass mercantilist laws, even with indirect taxes. The sticking point came with laws like the Stamp Act that were direct taxes. As the eighteenth century went on, however, the economic impact of mercantilism on the colonies expressed in answer E turned many Americans against this economic philosophy.

13. **E**  Mountain men (and probably the women, too) were of such independent natures that they would as a group never have consented to work for the government or a museum. Nor did they build fortifications. Their intermarriage with American Indians did little to brighten native peoples' views of white culture because mountain men were actually adopting much of American Indian culture. The Oregon Trail and other major migration routes were first footpaths and blazed hunting trails.

14. **B**  The other answers are decidedly not true except for answer C, which is more true of the Republican administrations of presidents from the 1920s. Patronage is directly associated with the Gilded Age as the main function of the presidency, hence the name coined by Mark Twain. This reality is why the Gilded Age presidents are also known as the "Forgotten Presidents."

15. **C** Most of the other answers are fabrications except answer D, which is close to the truth. The difference is that the German blockade involved surface ships, whereas the Arabic and Sussex Pledges specifically dealt with the actions of submarines.

16. **D** Answers A and C are not unique to the Roosevelt administration, but answer D was astounding. No modern president has had this steady support from dedicated advisers who weathered criticisms and heated controversies to stick by their chief as much as Franklin D. Roosevelt. Answers B and E are fabrications.

17. **A** Of all the difficulties encountered in fighting the Vietnam War that made it so unpopular with the American people, the most debilitating was this self-imposed and deeply flawed strategic fantasy. After the war, Vietnamese generals revealed how absurd they thought the strategy was because they were used to fighting in jungles and did not value individual citizens' lives.

18. **E** Although all of the answers hint at Cold War realities, the only answer directly tied to the launch of *Sputnik* was the National Defense Education Act described in answer E.

19. **B** Although not the very first attack, the truck bomb that drove into the Marine barracks was certainly the first significant attack and one that altered American foreign policy. Such success encouraged militants to mount more and more attacks including all of the ones referred to in the other answers.

20. **D** Ralph Nader has been a busy man in that he has personally led activist initiatives in all these areas while often running for president. His first important public step, however, was his publication of *Unsafe at Any Speed*, which targeted American cars' lack of safety features and in particular the Chevy Corvair.

21. **C** All of these answers were important turning points in the American economy, but Slater's contribution was his textile mill in Rhode Island.

22. **D** All of these Marshall Court decisions strengthened the power of the federal government, but *Marbury v. Madison* strengthened the power of the Supreme Court with the precedent of judicial review. The Court would not wield this power again, however, until the Dred Scott decision in 1857.

23. **E** Answer E is the reason cities like New York and Boston became largely populated by foreign-born immigrants. The first large migrations of the Irish occurred before the Civil War in 1845, and given the total freedom of movement it is unlikely the Catholic Irish would have wanted to seek out the Scots-Irish Protestants as neighbors. Answer A is untrue because most Irish immigrants of this era arrived in America penniless.

24. **C** Andrew Jackson assumed the power in answer A himself, and answer E explains the concession he made because he controlled the postmaster general. The Force Bill specifically said the president could use the military to enforce federal law; in this case the law was the tariff.

25. **A** Answers B, C, D, and E were all tried at one time or another in the history of the labor movement by various presidents, and even Cleveland tried to break the strike with an injunction (from a lower federal court). When that didn't

work he broke it with military force on the grounds that the mail must get through.

26. **B**   All of the answers are true except for the sinking of the *Lusitania*, which happened after World War I had already begun. The killing of Americans aboard the doomed passenger liner was a cause of American involvement in the war.

27. **B**   Answers D and E are fabrications, whereas answer A was a result of Bryan's being there in Dayton, not the cause of national attention. Clarence Darrow, the defense attorney, was widely known but did not have the celebrity status of William Jennings Bryan. Of course, the merits of the case itself was a pivotal episode in the societal flux of the 1920s.

28. **D**   All of the answers express ideas that would not be foreign to the New Deal, but the Eisenhower highway system is the only one that meets the test of being a massive public works project. The construction of the highway system is and remains one of the most massive public works projects in world history.

29. **C**   In 1964, the only civil rights leader with the temerity to speak in this nearly militant manner was Malcolm X. The other leaders may have had similar sentiments in their hearts, but they tempered their public comments to appeal to American values and morals in a manner short of the "ballot or the bullet" rhetoric of Malcolm X.

30. **E**   All of the answers have or will impact migrations within the United States, but the invention of practical air conditioning systems made living in the Sun Belt desirable to many classes of people, not just the elderly.

31. **B**   American Indians came up with three-sister farming on their own. Monks accompanied conquistadors but as a rule were not warriors. Jesuits did not seek enrichment of Catholic doctrine by studying native religions. Quite the opposite was true, so much so that the Inquisition hinted at in answer E has some ring of truth, but Jesuits' most important role is described in answer B. This result is why the Pope dispatched them to the New World.

32. **C**   No other answer is entirely true is all regards, and answer E is entirely false.

33. **E**   The other answers are nearly all opposites of the truth in that *Common Sense* was a bestselling pamphlet and thus influenced masses of colonial Americans, not just fringe elements. Paine specifically did not write in a scholarly tone or use classical references, and his work encouraged the public to push the Continental Congress toward declaring independence.

34. **A**   Answer A contains the two most famous of Washington's observations that served as prophetic warnings. Washington did not emphasize the slavery issue, although he would soon emancipate all his slaves in his will. Interestingly, Washington did predict the evolution of the Supreme Court into a legislating body, but at the time that was not a looming danger.

35. **D**   All of the answers play upon aspects of Daniel Webster's character or experiences, but only answer D was entirely true. Massachusetts led in reform move-

ments like abolition after the Second Great Awakening just as it had led in the quest for independence after the First Great Awakening.

36. **B**   Answer A was true only after Chicago had become the transportation hub of the West, and answers C, D, and E are fabrications based on truths. In the beginning, geography made almost all of the great cities of the world, and Chicago is no exception.

37. **C**   Answer C is the great technological breakthrough of John and Washington Roebling, the father/son engineering team that created the Brooklyn Bridge. The other answers hint at aspects of the bridge's construction that were not unique.

38. **B**   The Spanish-American War made the United States a world power, but not a superpower. Although answer D is almost true, the involvement of the United States in China was certainly not disinterested. Still, the new world power did not have direct designs to take over territory as Russia and Japan did.

39. **B**   "Pumping and dumping" was a strategy aimed at boosting the price of one type of stock like RCA, not to increase activity in the whole market. Answers C, D, and E describe legitimate business investment practices that still go on today, although pumping and dumping is now illegal (as it was unscrupulous even then, especially because these investors bribed journalists to write positive propaganda stories).

40. **E**   All of the answers hint at diplomatic difficulties associated with the Vietnam War, but the War Powers Act struck at the concept behind the Gulf of Tonkin Resolution that had allowed Lyndon Johnson to escalate the war virtually single-handedly.

41. **C**   All of these issues are related to the Spanish Empire in the New World, but the Black Legend originated in the writings of men like Bartolome de las Casas from which this quote was taken. The Black Legend emphasized the brutality of the Spanish conquest of Latin America and ruthless aspects of its imperial rule. The focus of such an interpretation in recent years has been none other than Christopher Columbus who some consider a villain.

42. **A**   The Acts of Toleration both in England and in colonies like Maryland were aimed at spreading religious toleration between especially Roman Catholics and Protestants. Other religious sects like the Quakers and Unitarians were sometimes wholly left out of the provisions to establish religious peace.

43. **C**   All of the answers hint at diplomatic issues encountered by the new country, but Charles Pinckney's treaty brought peace with Spain.

44. **D**   All of the answers name real political scandals, but the Crédit Mobilier scandalized the Grant administration with members of the president's men as high up as Vice President Schuyler Colfax receiving kickbacks for favors to ward off prosecution of the corrupt leaders of the Union Pacific Railroad.

45. **E**   Andrew Jackson had already determined answer A, and Theodore Roosevelt had already proved answer B. Answer C hints at functions of the Federal

Reserve but as indicated in answer E, Wilson did not want to tighten control. Later presidents did use the Federal Reserve to tighten control, however.

46. **E**  All of the answers are true to a degree except for answer C, although Admiral Mahan would not have necessarily disagreed with its premise. What made Theodore Roosevelt and other Americans incapable of ignoring the pleas of Cuban-Americans, however, was their desire to attain freedom just as the United States had from the British. The desire to take over Cuba evidenced by the Ostend Manifesto had died out with the Civil War.

47. **C**  Answer A is false because these were the principles Wilson directly spoke against. Answer B is a contradiction only coming to light in more recent international debates. Answer C speaks of the thematic principles undergirding Wilson's call for new nations salvaged from old empires, new international commitments to disarmament and world peace, and the League of Nations. Answers D and E address issues that are more associated with the United Nations than Wilson's platform for the League of Nations.

48. **B**  All of the answers mention cabinet positions or proposed cabinet positions, but the two that made it into the executive branch in 1947 were those in answer B. The Department of Defense was made up of previous departments that had responsibilities regarding national security, and the Department of the Air Force's being created reflected the new significance of air power illustrated by World War II. During the war, American pilots mostly flew for an arm of the U.S. Army called the Army Air Corps.

49. **C**  Each of the pairs in the other answers contains a Great Society program and a program begun under other administrations (with which Lyndon Johnson heartily agreed). Only answer C contains two Johnson administration initiatives in that they represent the chief pieces of civil rights legislation passed by Congress at Johnson's prompting. The Civil Rights Act and the Voting Rights Act were for Johnson triumphs of his vision for domestic reform.

50. **C**  Answer C contains the reality that has produced the verb *to mirandize* in the English language that means officers have to read those they arrest certain rights to inform them of their right, among others, not to incriminate themselves. The other answers refer to other landmark cases or issues associated with the evolution of criminal justice.

51. **C**  All of the answers list aspects of Hamilton's financial program, but answer C conveys the idea behind this quote from his "First Report on the Public Credit" that it was essential to fund the war bonds at par in order to expect that bonds could be issued in the future in case of a crisis like another war. Then Hamilton issued more bonds just to fund his launch of the Treasury Department mentioned in answer E.

52. **A**  The other answers are simply imagined fancies except for answer D, which is the opposite of the truth; Sacagawea's husband brought her on the trip. Still, the remarkable exploits of this intrepid woman were instrumental in the success of the Lewis and Clark expedition mainly for the reasons stated in answer A.

53. **A** Although answer D is a hint at the truth in that the Hartford Convention did discuss secession, that fateful doctrine was not a part of their actual proposal. Answer A conveys their most pressing issues because they did not support the War of 1812 being waged against their best trading customer. Their resolutions were moot after they arrived to hear news of the Treaty of Ghent and the heroism of Andrew Jackson and his forces that had defended New Orleans from the third major invasion by the British during the war.

54. **D** Clay was from Kentucky, not the Deep South, but he was a slave owner and a Whig. Answers A, B, and E are fabrications, although he was a War Hawk in 1812 and he did serve as the secretary of state under John Q. Adams. His pivotal role could be summarized by saying he could talk to John C. Calhoun and Daniel Webster, whereas Calhoun and Webster were on opposite poles of the slavery and states' rights issues.

55. **B** All of the answers hint at issues involved in the relationship between Mexico and the United States or the onset of the Mexican War. Slidell's mission, however, was the one effort James K. Polk made to assuage his conscience over his expansionist tendencies in regard to California and Texas.

56. **B** Answer B alone discusses totally accurate events, whereas the other answers merely hint at issues and geographical realities of the troublesome series of events associated with the fall of the Qing Dynasty in China.

57. **B** Answer A represents more of the General Motors approach to the automobile industry, whereas Ford's social engineering goals for American society required a simple, affordable, and durable car to move Americans about their country in order to turn it into a nation of middle-class consumers.

58. **C** This quote could only be written by an American who has gone through the Great Depression and the sacrifices of World War II prior to the baby boom's taking care of the reproduction gap.

59. **E** Answer A is nearly the exact opposite of the truth. Answer B is the Nixon stereotype contradicted by the landslide victory he did receive before he self-destructed in the Watergate scandal. Nixon was a shrewd politician as evidenced by his ability to employ liberal, conservative, and moderate agendas, but he was not known for running around and trying to get ahead of popular breezes through polls. Answer D is the opposite of what Nixon employed as his "southern strategy" to bring the South into the Republican camp.

60. **B** Answer A refers to the kidnapping of one grandchild, Patricia Hearst, who did not have the wife referred to in the document. The Marine barracks were not captured, they were destroyed. No extensive television interaction was involved with the students in Grenada who were taken hostage more precisely by revolutionaries, not militants. Sadly, answer E cannot be true in that it is a reference to Daniel Pearl who did not survive to tell about his experiences as did the hostages in the Iranian Hostage Crisis.

61. **D** Answer D is a fabrication; the other answers are direct quotes from the Declaration of Independence. No reference is made in the Declaration regard-

ing the Anglican Church's being an established church in America because other churches were readily available for dissenters by the time period of the American Revolution.

62. **A**   The only shore of a Great Lake that comes close to serving as a boundary is that of the northern tip of Lake Michigan that thus lies entirely within the United States. The other Great Lakes listed in answer E are shared between Canada and the United States.

63. **C**   Answer C is a reference to Hamilton's excise tax on whiskey and the fact that it hurt frontier farmers because jugs of whiskey were much easier to transport to market than wagons filled with corn. Washington did not patrol the area with fifteen thousand men until the Whiskey Rebellion had already started. Hamilton would of course not want to initiate prohibition because Americans' thirst for whiskey promised to be an excellent source of revenue, hence the taxes.

64. **E**   Answer E explains Astor's start and how he was able to found Astoria, Washington, as a trading post on the Columbia River. He then did build the hotel mentioned in answer B. Answers A, C, and D were the innovative approaches to business success by Samuel Slater, Levi-Strauss, and others.

65. **D**   Answer D reveals that John Quincy Adams had a Big-Stick policy long before Theodore Roosevelt's, and the stick was named Andrew Jackson. General Jackson had led troops in the Creek War and the War of 1812 and he was sent into Florida to settle disputes with the Spanish and with two British spies whom he captured and summarily hanged. The United States did many of the other things alluded to in the other answers, but not in this episode, which clarified the borders of the Louisiana Purchase and allowed the United States to purchase Florida from Spain.

66. **C**   All of the other answers have a part that is false. Wilson was too much of a Hamiltonian to push very hard for states' rights and certainly did not want to roll back any part of Progressivism. What actions Theodore Roosevelt (TR) took for African-Americans' civil rights subjected him to intense criticism so he backed off entirely. Of all things, TR was not an isolationist. Interestingly, the idealism of Wilson's views about trusts, when met with the reality of the difficulty of enforcement, wound up operating exactly as TR's more practical stance had suggested.

67. **B**   All of the other answers are misinterpretations of the cartoon or refer to events that never happened like in answer E; Grant never resolved to resign, although he had virtually surrounded himself with unscrupulous men that today would have forced him to resign and them to go to jail. Still, Grant was surprised by the events and did pledge to get to the bottom of the scandals, but even though he did not sincerely prosecute his own personnel he was never proven to be in complicity with their crimes.

68. **C**   Answer C is the "myth-busting" truth about prohibition, whereas the other answers are only hints about the truth of the context of the "Noble Experiment."

69. **D**   Answer D dispels another myth about the era of the Roaring Twenties and the Great Depression. The other answers are fabrications or expression of the perception of Hoover, but his Reconstruction Finance Corporation could be considered the first New Deal agency.

70. **B**   What appears to be a military question is really a technology question (and a testament to the bravery of British and American pilots who helped win the Battle of Britain with the help of RADAR). The Germans developed the V-1 and V-2 rockets by the end of the war, but they did not even target them with RADAR. RADAR cannot penetrate water to search for submarines, which is why SONAR was invented.

71. **E**   Answer A is a demeaning fabrication. Answer B is a commonly believed myth. Answer C belies the fact that peaceful relations were maintained apart from the fur trade. Answer D is closer to a possible outcome, but answer E was the sad reality.

72. **E**   During the early part of the French and Indian War, British officers like General Braddock scorned American troops and their advice and insisted on fighting according to European standards of military honor (which proved suicidal in Braddock's case). William Pitt wanted to win more than he wanted to honor aristocratic sensibilities, so he promoted men on the basis of merit, including American officers like George Washington, who succeeded in conquering the French in North America.

73. **E**   The lines come from the Kentucky Resolutions (with comparable wording in the Virginia Resolutions) that were passed in response to the Alien and Sedition Acts. Federalists would not have used such logic, and the Land and Northwest Ordinances did not speak of states except in addressing the process on how territories could become one.

74. **A**   *Gibbons v. Ogden* was a case involving steamboat traffic that involved more than one state, thus interstate transportation.

75. **B**   The concept of a state funding a canal was so novel that Dewitt Clinton was derided for proposing the idea that his "Big Ditch" could boost New York's economy and make the $7 million investment pay off. The Erie Canal transformed New York City into a major transportation hub as only the beginning of the expansion of this city's importance to American history. New equipment was invented to help speed production, but no steam shovels were used in its construction (much to the chagrin of man and beast).

76. **C**   Steam power was first applied to steamboats, not steam trains. Deficit spending had begun in America before America could properly be said to have begun. Although the telegraph wires were strung right alongside railroad tracks, all of the other items were more generally developed than with just railroads. Railroads move humans the fastest, however, and the need for time zones to account for the different position of the sun (and thus different times) arose from the desire to avoid collisions by scheduling errors. The size of railroads did necessitate the creation of the first giant corporations, and railroads thus set many important business precedents.

77. **E** All of the other answers were in the head of this economic visionary, but it is quite likely that Henry Clay would have fought a duel with someone over an income tax and killed him. A small income tax was resorted to as an emergency provision during the Civil War, but not until the Sixteenth Amendment of 1913 was such a measure considered constitutional.

78. **C** Answers A and B are true about Santa Anna's government and were distasteful issues to Texans, but answer C lists their main grievances. Answers D and E are plausible fabrications.

79. **D** Although Carnegie preferred an open shop, did sell his company (to J. P. Morgan), and did hire Pinkerton detectives (after the strike broke out), Henry Clay Frick started the showdown by resolving to break the union by lowering wages and provoking a clash.

80. **B** The Bolshevik Revolution in Russia in 1917 did increase fears of especially Russian Jews as potential radicals among immigrants, and a general dislike for immigrants contributed to the Red Scare. Answers C and D were true, but although the Klan did march in Washington, D.C., they were not communists. Julius and Ethel Rosenberg were communists or at least communist spies, but they were executed in the Second Red Scare in the 1950s. The answers that hint about Carl Schurz and the Soviet Union are fabrications built on real events.

81. **E** All of the other answers allude to facts common to several American Indian tribes, but answer E was the unique quality of the Iroquois that were not a tribe but a confederation of six, then later, seven tribes all joined to face the threat of their neighbors to the west, the Huron Indians.

82. **C** There was no push for independence this early, but the Restoration inspired the Navigation Acts, not sought to begin to enforce them. Charles II, but especially his brother who would become James II, decided they should try to run their American colonies as the Spanish ran their New World empire. The arbitrary nature of ending salutary neglect after almost sixty years disturbed England's American colonists, but when they complained, rebelled, and smuggled, the British Crown responded in the worst possible way to maintain control, by ushering in more salutary neglect (until after the French and Indian War).

83. **D** The Three-fifth's Compromise is often misunderstood as a sign of universal racism among the Founding Fathers, but it should be considered in part as a restraint on racism demanded by the North from their countrymen from the South who wanted to count all their slaves without giving any of their slaves the rights they were trying to secure for themselves by boosting their population. That is not to say, however, that white supremacy was not the typical perspective of most colonial- and Early National-period Americans, and the Three-fifth's Compromise was an egregious example of American hypocrisy.

84. **A** This frightening prospect was forestalled almost single-handedly by George Washington who rejected this plan raised by his own veteran officers. The other answers hint at the geographical, social, and historical context of this bizarre episode initiated by men who had heard the Declaration of Independence read aloud to their own troops.

85. **B**  James K. Polk desired so much to be like his hero, Andrew Jackson, that if the Bank of the United States (BUS) was restored for a third time, then Polk would have killed it as Jackson had killed the second BUS. All of the other answers are the campaign promises he made and fulfilled that cause historians to jokingly call the Polk administration the most successful presidency in American history.

86. **C**  The letters emerged during the campaign with the salutation at the bottom saying, "Burn this letter." The letters were not burnt and his own record of his misdeeds undid his chances for the presidency giving Grover Cleveland the singular success of being the only Democrat to attain the presidency in the entire Gilded Age.

87. **D**  The first letter made William McKinley appear weak and compelled him to start the Spanish-American War, and the second letter was made public while Woodrow Wilson seemed increasingly unable to conceive of the necessity of America's fighting and ending World War I. Public opinion took over from the president after the Zimmermann Telegram and the sinking of American merchant vessels. Answer A is incorrect because the Zimmermann Telegram was intercepted by British intelligence operations.

88. **D**  Without question the action that gained for Franklin D. Roosevelt the most detractors, even from within his own Democratic Party, was his willingness to play fast and loose with the U.S. Constitution in a way that was perceived as threatening the balance of powers, which his pack-the-court scheme would likely have done.

89. **E**  The Laffer Curve drawn for President Reagan's advisers could likely be the most significant drawing ever done on a napkin in a restaurant. Although Arthur Laffer said he did not originate the ideas of supply-side economics, his simple illustration was instrumental in the Reagan Revolution.

90. **C**  Although answers D and E hint at truths, neither is entirely accurate. President Clinton positioned himself as a moderate Democrat, and how he used the line-item veto was not as significant as the fact that an American president did have this power for a time. In the same way as the Pendleton Act was not a silver bullet to end political corruption, however, a line-item veto did not prove to be the easy solution for excessive government spending that benefits only regions and locales within the country instead of the entire country, especially after the Supreme Court declared it was unconstitutional.

# Answer Sheet
## PRACTICE TEST 3

| | | | |
|---|---|---|---|
| 1 Ⓐ Ⓑ Ⓒ Ⓓ Ⓔ | 24 Ⓐ Ⓑ Ⓒ Ⓓ Ⓔ | 47 Ⓐ Ⓑ Ⓒ Ⓓ Ⓔ | 70 Ⓐ Ⓑ Ⓒ Ⓓ Ⓔ |
| 2 Ⓐ Ⓑ Ⓒ Ⓓ Ⓔ | 25 Ⓐ Ⓑ Ⓒ Ⓓ Ⓔ | 48 Ⓐ Ⓑ Ⓒ Ⓓ Ⓔ | 71 Ⓐ Ⓑ Ⓒ Ⓓ Ⓔ |
| 3 Ⓐ Ⓑ Ⓒ Ⓓ Ⓔ | 26 Ⓐ Ⓑ Ⓒ Ⓓ Ⓔ | 49 Ⓐ Ⓑ Ⓒ Ⓓ Ⓔ | 72 Ⓐ Ⓑ Ⓒ Ⓓ Ⓔ |
| 4 Ⓐ Ⓑ Ⓒ Ⓓ Ⓔ | 27 Ⓐ Ⓑ Ⓒ Ⓓ Ⓔ | 50 Ⓐ Ⓑ Ⓒ Ⓓ Ⓔ | 73 Ⓐ Ⓑ Ⓒ Ⓓ Ⓔ |
| 5 Ⓐ Ⓑ Ⓒ Ⓓ Ⓔ | 28 Ⓐ Ⓑ Ⓒ Ⓓ Ⓔ | 51 Ⓐ Ⓑ Ⓒ Ⓓ Ⓔ | 74 Ⓐ Ⓑ Ⓒ Ⓓ Ⓔ |
| 6 Ⓐ Ⓑ Ⓒ Ⓓ Ⓔ | 29 Ⓐ Ⓑ Ⓒ Ⓓ Ⓔ | 52 Ⓐ Ⓑ Ⓒ Ⓓ Ⓔ | 75 Ⓐ Ⓑ Ⓒ Ⓓ Ⓔ |
| 7 Ⓐ Ⓑ Ⓒ Ⓓ Ⓔ | 30 Ⓐ Ⓑ Ⓒ Ⓓ Ⓔ | 53 Ⓐ Ⓑ Ⓒ Ⓓ Ⓔ | 76 Ⓐ Ⓑ Ⓒ Ⓓ Ⓔ |
| 8 Ⓐ Ⓑ Ⓒ Ⓓ Ⓔ | 31 Ⓐ Ⓑ Ⓒ Ⓓ Ⓔ | 54 Ⓐ Ⓑ Ⓒ Ⓓ Ⓔ | 77 Ⓐ Ⓑ Ⓒ Ⓓ Ⓔ |
| 9 Ⓐ Ⓑ Ⓒ Ⓓ Ⓔ | 32 Ⓐ Ⓑ Ⓒ Ⓓ Ⓔ | 55 Ⓐ Ⓑ Ⓒ Ⓓ Ⓔ | 78 Ⓐ Ⓑ Ⓒ Ⓓ Ⓔ |
| 10 Ⓐ Ⓑ Ⓒ Ⓓ Ⓔ | 33 Ⓐ Ⓑ Ⓒ Ⓓ Ⓔ | 56 Ⓐ Ⓑ Ⓒ Ⓓ Ⓔ | 79 Ⓐ Ⓑ Ⓒ Ⓓ Ⓔ |
| 11 Ⓐ Ⓑ Ⓒ Ⓓ Ⓔ | 34 Ⓐ Ⓑ Ⓒ Ⓓ Ⓔ | 57 Ⓐ Ⓑ Ⓒ Ⓓ Ⓔ | 80 Ⓐ Ⓑ Ⓒ Ⓓ Ⓔ |
| 12 Ⓐ Ⓑ Ⓒ Ⓓ Ⓔ | 35 Ⓐ Ⓑ Ⓒ Ⓓ Ⓔ | 58 Ⓐ Ⓑ Ⓒ Ⓓ Ⓔ | 81 Ⓐ Ⓑ Ⓒ Ⓓ Ⓔ |
| 13 Ⓐ Ⓑ Ⓒ Ⓓ Ⓔ | 36 Ⓐ Ⓑ Ⓒ Ⓓ Ⓔ | 59 Ⓐ Ⓑ Ⓒ Ⓓ Ⓔ | 82 Ⓐ Ⓑ Ⓒ Ⓓ Ⓔ |
| 14 Ⓐ Ⓑ Ⓒ Ⓓ Ⓔ | 37 Ⓐ Ⓑ Ⓒ Ⓓ Ⓔ | 60 Ⓐ Ⓑ Ⓒ Ⓓ Ⓔ | 83 Ⓐ Ⓑ Ⓒ Ⓓ Ⓔ |
| 15 Ⓐ Ⓑ Ⓒ Ⓓ Ⓔ | 38 Ⓐ Ⓑ Ⓒ Ⓓ Ⓔ | 61 Ⓐ Ⓑ Ⓒ Ⓓ Ⓔ | 84 Ⓐ Ⓑ Ⓒ Ⓓ Ⓔ |
| 16 Ⓐ Ⓑ Ⓒ Ⓓ Ⓔ | 39 Ⓐ Ⓑ Ⓒ Ⓓ Ⓔ | 62 Ⓐ Ⓑ Ⓒ Ⓓ Ⓔ | 85 Ⓐ Ⓑ Ⓒ Ⓓ Ⓔ |
| 17 Ⓐ Ⓑ Ⓒ Ⓓ Ⓔ | 40 Ⓐ Ⓑ Ⓒ Ⓓ Ⓔ | 63 Ⓐ Ⓑ Ⓒ Ⓓ Ⓔ | 86 Ⓐ Ⓑ Ⓒ Ⓓ Ⓔ |
| 18 Ⓐ Ⓑ Ⓒ Ⓓ Ⓔ | 41 Ⓐ Ⓑ Ⓒ Ⓓ Ⓔ | 64 Ⓐ Ⓑ Ⓒ Ⓓ Ⓔ | 87 Ⓐ Ⓑ Ⓒ Ⓓ Ⓔ |
| 19 Ⓐ Ⓑ Ⓒ Ⓓ Ⓔ | 42 Ⓐ Ⓑ Ⓒ Ⓓ Ⓔ | 65 Ⓐ Ⓑ Ⓒ Ⓓ Ⓔ | 88 Ⓐ Ⓑ Ⓒ Ⓓ Ⓔ |
| 20 Ⓐ Ⓑ Ⓒ Ⓓ Ⓔ | 43 Ⓐ Ⓑ Ⓒ Ⓓ Ⓔ | 66 Ⓐ Ⓑ Ⓒ Ⓓ Ⓔ | 89 Ⓐ Ⓑ Ⓒ Ⓓ Ⓔ |
| 21 Ⓐ Ⓑ Ⓒ Ⓓ Ⓔ | 44 Ⓐ Ⓑ Ⓒ Ⓓ Ⓔ | 67 Ⓐ Ⓑ Ⓒ Ⓓ Ⓔ | 90 Ⓐ Ⓑ Ⓒ Ⓓ Ⓔ |
| 22 Ⓐ Ⓑ Ⓒ Ⓓ Ⓔ | 45 Ⓐ Ⓑ Ⓒ Ⓓ Ⓔ | 68 Ⓐ Ⓑ Ⓒ Ⓓ Ⓔ | |
| 23 Ⓐ Ⓑ Ⓒ Ⓓ Ⓔ | 46 Ⓐ Ⓑ Ⓒ Ⓓ Ⓔ | 69 Ⓐ Ⓑ Ⓒ Ⓓ Ⓔ | |

# Practice Test 3

**Directions:** Each of the questions or incomplete statements below is followed by five suggested answers or completions. Select the one that is best in each case and then fill in the corresponding circle on the answer sheet. You can cut the answer sheet along the dotted line to make recording your answers easier. Remember to give yourself only sixty minutes to complete this test in order to prepare for the pace of the real SAT Subject Test in U.S. History.

1. What bearing did the Treaty of Tordesillas have on European exploration and colonization of the New World in 1494?

   (A) The treaty revealed that Portugal and Spain would ally against the English and the French if war erupted over colonization.
   (B) The treaty stated that Portugal would no longer have access to Italian navigators until Spain had caught up in the establishment of trading posts abroad.
   (C) The treaty banned the stationing of fleets of armed naval vessels in the Atlantic Ocean.
   (D) The treaty divided areas of exploration and colonization between Spain and Portugal in such a way as to leave most of the New World for the Spanish.
   (E) The treaty revealed the Pope was going to take a firm hand in controlling exploration and colonization conducted by Christian nations.

2. What made the colony of Maryland unique among all of the original thirteen colonies that eventually became the United States?

   (A) The colonial legislature passed a law allowing any Trinitarian Christian freedom of worship.
   (B) Maryland maintained the longest peaceful relations with American Indians of any colony.
   (C) The colony was founded as a refuge for Roman Catholics being persecuted in England.
   (D) Maryland was the only one of the thirteen colonies whose territory was not contiguous.
   (E) Maryland had by far the most aristocratic society with the most African slaves per capita.

3. Colonial America's trade pattern that originated in England's colonies and was known as the "Triangular Trade" was

   (A) never a single set pattern of trade routes with regular Old World destinations.
   (B) established by the Board of Trade and Plantations and patrolled by the English Navy.
   (C) so successful as to be more lucrative than the annual haul of the Spanish treasure fleet.
   (D) the trade route whereby a wide range of goods manufactured in America were marketed.
   (E) established and operated by Scottish and Dutch middle men who exacted high fees.

4. Which of the following statements best explains the motive of Charles II in establishing the Dominion of New England in 1686 after having been restored to the monarchy over twenty years earlier?

   (A) Charles II needed to find a task for Edmund Andros in order to distract the English people from this popular rival for the throne, so he granted him land in the New World to govern.
   (B) Charles II sought to exact revenge on the Puritans of New England for their complicity in the execution of his father, so he confiscated their colonial charters.
   (C) Charles II needed a firm base of operations with stronger control in order for his brother, James, the duke of York, to stage attacks on the Dutch to take over New Amsterdam.
   (D) Charles II believed he could improve life in the colonies if he could end their squabbling and compel the colonists to unite under one regional government.
   (E) Charles II agreed with his advisers and with his brother that it was time for the English colonies to be run with the same efficiency and productivity as the Spanish colonies.

5. Which statement best describes the value(s) behind the post-Revolution concept of "republican motherhood"?

   (A) American mothers were expected to rear their children with strong attachment to a political party.
   (B) American women were valued for the first time for their childbearing capacities.
   (C) American mothers were responsible for nurturing in their children the values of the American Revolution so that the republic would be perpetuated.
   (D) American parents were expected to instill in their daughters the notion that motherhood was a woman's highest calling in order to boost the population of the fledgling country.
   (E) American schools were tasked with teaching parenting skills in order to provide the best base possible for families' producing of solid citizens for the good of the whole country.

6. "It is evident that the Yearly Meeting [of Philadelphia] does not recognize the institution of Slavery as one that can be upheld where christian [sic] feelings predominate; and that under this conviction its members cannot assist in carrying out such laws as may be enacted to perpetuate its existence. . . ."

The quotation above from 1851 is most likely referring to resistance to what type of laws?

(A) The personal liberty laws
(B) The fugitive slave laws
(C) The black codes
(D) The slave codes
(E) The vagrancy laws for freedmen

7. Which statement below best describes the agreement known as the Compromise of 1877?

(A) The former Confederate states were allowed home rule as long as they submitted to military occupation by the Union Army.
(B) The Ku Klux Klan agreed to cease their militant practices and turn over their weapons as long as the organization's existence as a fraternal order for former Confederates was permitted.
(C) The former Confederate states agreed to peacefully resume status as members of the Union as long as all freed slaves would be counted for purposes of representation in the Congress.
(D) The Republican Party received the presidency as the result of a disputed election in return for an end to military occupation of states that had still not complied with federal Reconstruction.
(E) Former citizens of the Confederacy were restored to full citizenship as long as 10 percent of them in each state took an oath of loyalty to the United States and freed their slaves.

8. Which statement below best identifies the difference that existed between the nineteenth-century political factions known as the Stalwarts and the Mugwumps?

(A) The Stalwarts were Democrats who still supported the values of the Confederacy known as the Lost Cause, whereas the Mugwumps were those willing to submit to federal authority.
(B) The Stalwarts were Republicans who were not opposed to the patronage that existed in the Gilded Age, whereas the Mugwumps were Republicans in favor of civil service reform.
(C) The Stalwarts were Republicans who refused to cooperate with the Democratic Party because of the "bloody shirt," whereas the Mugwumps were willing to support some bipartisan efforts.
(D) The Stalwarts were the Democrats who supported Grover Cleveland for president, whereas the Mugwumps were the political supporters of his Republican challenger, James G. Blaine.
(E) The Stalwarts were the Democrats in New York who supported the patronage of Tammany Hall, whereas the Mugwumps were Democrats who sought to end Boss Tweed's influence.

9. What was the main goal of Harry Truman's program known as the Fair Deal for which he campaigned to win the Election of 1948?

   (A) To provide self-determination for the peoples freed from the Axis after World War II
   (B) To secure civil rights advances for African-Americans who had fought or served in the war
   (C) To create low-cost housing in suburbs for veterans or for the families of those killed
   (D) To provide access to a college education for any man who had served in the military
   (E) To expand all existing domestic programs in order to maintain full employment

10. What was revealed about the Vietnam War by the release of the Pentagon Papers in 1971?

   (A) The strategic flaws that had led to the failure of the United States to achieve its objectives
   (B) The purposefully disproportionate representation of African-Americans in combat roles
   (C) The lack of coordination among the various branches of the military and its consequences
   (D) The failure of the Johnson administration to accurately portray the war and its objectives
   (E) The existence of secret negotiations between the Nixon administration and the enemy

11. Which statement best describes the significance of Samuel de Champlain's contributions to the establishment of New France?

   (A) He explored up the St. Lawrence River and founded the settlements that became both Montreal and Quebec.
   (B) He established the boundary with what would become New Amsterdam by discovering the lake that bears his name.
   (C) He explored the upper length of the Mississippi River watershed and claimed the area for France.
   (D) He established the fur trade with the American Indians of the Great Lakes region that became the basis of the economy of New France.
   (E) He floated down the length of the Mississippi River proving that it flowed into the Gulf of Mexico, and then he founded New Orleans.

12. For what geographical region did England and France originally clash in the battles in 1754 that led to the French and Indian War?

   (A) The province of Quebec
   (B) The upper reaches of New York and Maine
   (C) The Great Lakes region
   (D) The Ohio River Valley
   (E) The Mississippi River delta

13. "There shall be neither Slavery nor involuntary Servitude in the said territory otherwise than in the punishment of crimes. . . . Provided always, That any person escaping into the same, from . . . any one of the original States . . . may be lawfully reclaimed and conveyed to the person claiming his or her labor or service as aforesaid."

This quotation is most likely from which of the following documents?

(A)  The Articles of Confederation
(B)  The Northwest Ordinance
(C)  The original U.S. Constitution
(D)  The Tallmadge Amendment to the application of the Missouri Territory for statehood
(E)  The Lecompton Constitution

14.  What was the main goal of the Missouri Compromise in 1820?

(A)  To find new territory into which southerners could expand the institution of slavery
(B)  To make Missouri enter the Union as a free state despite the support for slavery there
(C)  To keep the balance of free states and slave states in the U.S. Senate to stave off disunion
(D)  To divide the Louisiana Purchase into future slave states and free states
(E)  To ban the spread of slavery in newly established western territories

15.  Which statement below best explains the significance of the Election of 1824 in which John Quincy Adams was elected to the presidency?

(A)  The election was the first for which the candidates' campaigns employed mass marketing strategies to influence voters' decisions.
(B)  The election was the first in which a candidate from the West ran for the presidency.
(C)  The election was the first in which a Democrat ran against a Republican representing the two major modern parties.
(D)  The election was the first in which the provision in the U.S. Constitution for settling an election in which there is no clear electoral winner was tested and managed to keep the peace.
(E)  The election ended the Era of Good Feelings and was the first of what has proven to be a permanent two-party system with some third parties and some peripheral parties on the fringe.

16. What significant role did McGuffey Readers play in the common school movement?

(A) The authorship of the series by a Scots-Irishman smoothed the way for implementing the common school movement in the Appalachian region, which was devoid of public schools.

(B) The widespread use of the readers planted common cultural roots in both the North and the South just prior to the splintering of the nation in the Civil War.

(C) The readers used classical references in the content studied and thus perpetuated the colonial educational foundation for the nation.

(D) The readers taught values along with reading content and thus furthered the character-building agenda of common schools and caused this first attempt at free public education to spread.

(E) The readers were of such high literary quality that cultural tastes were elevated and American society attained a final break with English and other European cultural roots.

17. What was the outcome of the utopian experiment known as Brook Farm?

(A) The leading men of letters who had made Brook Farm famous because of their participation eventually tired of the experience, and the society steadily declined into bankruptcy.

(B) The Shakers who founded the society maintained their vows of celibacy and Brook Farm, while prosperous, disappeared after one generation.

(C) Brook Farm attracted not only utopian-minded Americans but second sons of the aristocracy of Europe, and thus the society became an international bastion of transcendentalism.

(D) Brook Farm prospered until its estate was overrun by Sherman's March to the Sea campaign during the Civil War in which Union soldiers destroyed its buildings and crops.

(E) The utopian nature of the society established at Brook Farm so distanced its inhabitants from their neighbors that the entire community moved west to escape persecution.

18. All of the following were important aspects of "Negro spirituals" during the African-American experience in slavery EXCEPT that the

(A) cadence of the songs called back and forth among field slaves helped to pace their work.

(B) Christian messages of the songs formed a spiritual bond and support among the slaves.

(C) rhythms of the songs were a symbolic connection between African and American culture.

(D) distribution of the songs in hymn books was the first attempt to teach slaves to read.

(E) songs were often used as coded messages notifying slaves of planned escapes.

19. Which statement below best explains the significance of the Monroe Doctrine issued in 1823?

    (A) The policies stated in the Monroe Doctrine affirmed the alliance between the United States and France once Napoleon Bonaparte had been removed from power.

    (B) The Monroe Doctrine committed the U.S. Navy to joint operations with the British Navy to patrol the Atlantic Ocean and to end the menace of the Barbary pirates.

    (C) The Monroe Doctrine was the idea of George Canning, the British foreign minister, and the consent of President Monroe ended all diplomatic conflict between the United States and the United Kingdom.

    (D) The Monroe Doctrine was crafted by Secretary of State John Quincy Adams specifically to establish the independence of the United States in determining its own foreign policy.

    (E) The Monroe Doctrine established the provisions by which England and France could pick up the pieces of Spain's crumbling New World Empire without igniting another war.

20. How did Abraham Lincoln's actions in 1861 in regard to Fort Sumter in Charleston Harbor impact the diplomatic aspects of fighting the Civil War?

    (A) Since Lincoln tried to attack Charleston from Fort Sumter, South Carolinians could claim they were firing in self-defense.

    (B) Since British observers were present on the Confederate side at the opening of hostilities, Lincoln could claim a breach of international law and keep England from joining the war.

    (C) Since Lincoln acted only to supply the fort with food before the Confederate attack, the Union Army could always reflect that the South had started shooting first and would bear the blame.

    (D) Lincoln's decision to commit the fleet of Union ironclads to the battle for Fort Sumter forever altered naval warfare and established the United States as a major sea power for the first time.

    (E) The Union victory at Fort Sumter resulting from Lincoln's decision to start the war there left a symbolic thorn in the side of South Carolina's best port city throughout the rest of the war.

21. Which statement below best explains the significance of the Committees of Correspondence during the American Revolution?

    (A) Correspondents from each colony monitored their neighbors' compliance with boycotts and reported violations to their legislatures in order to maintain economic pressure on England.
    (B) Correspondents from each colony cataloged British actions that were offensive and kept an ongoing record of grievances before the public in newspapers and other periodicals.
    (C) Correspondents pledged to regularly send accounts of British atrocities committed by the illegal standing army back to England where sympathetic editors could publish them.
    (D) Correspondents made regular appeals to authorities in Spain, France, Prussia, and Russia for intervention on the part of these rivals of England on behalf of the American cause.
    (E) Correspondents informed their counterparts in other colonies about the movements and the makeup of British forces in an effort to counterbalance England's military superiority.

22. How did Alexander Hamilton defend his style of interpretation of the U.S. Constitution known as loose construction?

    (A) He said that the Constitution was only intended as a rough guideline for creative thinking about government.
    (B) He said the important principles of proper government could never be written down entirely on a single piece of paper.
    (C) He said that any excesses of interpretation would always be balanced by the two-party system implied in the Constitution and anticipated by the Founding Fathers.
    (D) He said the U.S. Supreme Court would hold government officials accountable for any actions that stepped too far outside the bounds of proper constitutional government.
    (E) He said that necessary and proper conclusions about the duties of the federal government based on the duties specifically stated in the Constitution were also legitimate powers.

23. All of the following are examples of the way President Thomas Jefferson reduced the expenditures of the federal government EXCEPT by

    (A) turning over the services of the Post Office to private companies.
    (B) reducing the size of the navy by replacing frigates with small defensive gunboats.
    (C) firing all of the tax collectors responsible for collecting the excise tax on whiskey.
    (D) curtailing the diplomatic corps to leave ambassadors in only Spain, France, and England.
    (E) reducing the standing army to just over three thousand professional soldiers.

24. Why did the efforts of the American Colonization Society to relocate American slaves back in Africa ultimately fail?

    (A) Shrewd American businessmen realized that once freed, African-Americans would make a ready class of laborers, so they refused to finance the society's activities.
    (B) The eventual head of the organization, Marcus Garvey, was found guilty of racketeering and fraud and deported back to Jamaica whence he came.
    (C) Abraham Lincoln opposed all efforts to deport African-Americans to other countries as a shameful acknowledgment of American racism.
    (D) Most African-Americans raised in the United States had no interest in leaving American society to return to African countries and thus the organization's purpose was flawed.
    (E) The first shiploads of African-Americans going back to Africa were captured upon their arrival by Africans and impressed into force labor, so few others would make the attempt.

25. Which statement best describes how sharecropping differed from slavery?

    (A) Sharecroppers were put to the cultivation of corn unlike slaves in the South who tended cotton fields before the cotton kingdom was destroyed by the Civil War.
    (B) The system of sharecropping permitted only males above the age of fourteen to work for a landowner; whereas slave masters forced whole families to work including the children.
    (C) Both poor whites and African-Americans wound up as sharecroppers after the Civil War, whereas slavery only applied to African-Americans in the height of the cotton kingdom.
    (D) Some African-Americans owned land and hired sharecroppers after the Civil War, whereas in the days of slavery only whites owned slaves.
    (E) Most sharecroppers were able to work their way clear of all debts and eventually owned their own farms, whereas only a small number of African slaves ever attained their freedom this way.

26. "The paupers and the physically incapacitated are an inevitable charge on society. . . . But the weak who constantly arouse the pity of humanitarians . . . are the shiftless, the imprudent, the negligent, the impractical, and the inefficient, or they are the idle, the intemperate, the extravagant, and the vicious."

    The quotation above is most likely an expression of which Gilded Age perspective on wealth?

    (A) The views of philanthropists like John D. Rockefeller and Andrew Mellon
    (B) The policies of the Salvation Army as an expression of the Social Gospel
    (C) The goals of the settlement house movement begun by Jane Addams in Chicago
    (D) The observations of Jacob Riis about immigrants in his book *How the Other Half Lives*
    (E) The tenets of Social Darwinism espoused by Herbert Spencer and William Graham Sumner

27. All of the following were goals of Theodore Roosevelt's domestic program he dubbed the Square Deal in his second term as president EXCEPT

  (A) use of the Sherman Antitrust Act to regulate corporations and break "bad" trusts.
  (B) establishment of the Federal Reserve System to regulate the banking industry.
  (C) passage of the Pure Food and Drug Act to enhance the regulatory power of the government.
  (D) a systematic approach to the conservation of natural resources in national forests and parks.
  (E) a particular emphasis on ridding the meat-packing industry of evils exposed in *The Jungle.*

JUSTICE IN THE WEB.

28. What charge is symbolized in the portrayal of Jay Gould in the 1885 political cartoon above entitled "Justice in the Web" that helped make him "The most hated man in America"?

  (A) The rich are predators preying on the poor.
  (B) To be as rich as Gould men must become loathsome mutants of the human soul.
  (C) Being rich by its very nature is evil and those who attain riches are stealing them.
  (D) Control of cutting-edge communications gave men like Gould unfair leverage in society.
  (E) The rich classes of which Gould was a part are justly entrapped by their own plots.

29. What foreign policy campaign emphasis did Woodrow Wilson use to win reelection in the Election of 1916?

    (A) The United States should lead in the formation of the League of Nations to end all wars.
    (B) The United States should increase patrols by U.S. Navy antisubmarine destroyers.
    (C) The United States should avoid sending Americans to fight in World War I in Europe.
    (D) The United States should take the lead in defending freedom with military intervention.
    (E) The United States should trade with neither the United Kingdom nor Germany to avoid war.

30. Which statement best explains what brought about the end of Joseph McCarthy's campaign to ferret out communists from American government and society?

    (A) Blacklisted Hollywood executives and actors produced a film lampooning McCarthyism.
    (B) Television coverage of McCarthy's hearings turned them into a frivolous media circus.
    (C) Most people found McCarthy's charge that there were communists in the army preposterous.
    (D) Arthur Miller's play *The Crucible* linked McCarthyism to the Salem witch trials.
    (E) Senator McCarthy's claim of communists in the State Department was unsubstantiated.

31. In what way was the 1770 Boston Massacre significantly different from the manner in which it was portrayed by American revolutionary propagandists?

    (A) The number of British soldiers involved in the incident was much lower than reported.
    (B) The size of the Boston mob was much smaller than reported.
    (C) The fact that three British soldiers were killed with clubs by the mob went entirely unreported.
    (D) The fact that the British officer in charge was drunk at the time went unreported.
    (E) The provocations of the mob toward the soldiers who fired in self-defense were unreported.

32. "Now, the fact is, we never have objected to become citizens of the United States and to conform to her laws , . . but we have required the protection and privileges of her laws to accompany that conformity on our part. We have asked this repeatedly and repeatedly has it been denied. . . ."

    The quotation from the early nineteenth-century document above is most likely the plea of what type of individual?

    (A) An escaped slave arguing in court to keep his or her freedom
    (B) An Irish immigrant protesting abuse by the police in Boston
    (C) A Chinese laborer in the California gold rush
    (D) An American Indian chief protesting treatment of his tribe
    (E) A female suffragette giving a speech about women's rights

33. What can be said to have caused the events known collectively as "Bleeding Kansas"?

    (A) The presence of American Indian reservations in the direct path of the first transcontinental railroad
    (B) The competition between northerners and southerners resulting from federal policy regarding the spread of slavery in the territories
    (C) The migration to Kansas of the "Exodusters," or African-Americans trying to escape the dead-end nature of sharecropping by seeking homesteads in the West
    (D) The range wars set in motion by the invention of barbed wire that allowed landowners to protect their land from the ravages of cowboys and their "long drives" taking cattle to market
    (E) The crossover of Confederate troops from Missouri into the new free state of Kansas in an attempt to influence the government's desire to support the Union cause

34. Which statement below best summarizes the "Frontier Thesis" advanced by Frederick Jackson Turner in 1893?

    (A) The frontier, which had always been a democratizing force in American history, was closed.
    (B) The West was the land of opportunity for any enterprising young men desiring advancement.
    (C) Immigration was the key to building a strong society because new laborers were needed.
    (D) The vague borders that existed during the nineteenth century in the West caused unnecessary wars.
    (E) The Anglo-Saxon race was destined to bring civilizing influences to the whole world.

35. How did a "pool" operate as a form of business combination that created monopolistic power over industries in the late nineteenth and early twentieth centuries?

   (A) Large investors combined their stock purchases in holding companies that could then attain controlling interest in the companies in which they wanted to increase profits for themselves.
   (B) A single business magnate would purchase the means of production in an industry from the securing of raw materials to the marketing of the finished products to the public.
   (C) A businessman successful in one aspect of the production of a commodity would gather the majority of companies performing that task in order to exert leverage over other companies.
   (D) Large investment bankers would forge bankrupt companies in their control into larger conglomerates wielding more influence than any one company could on its own.
   (E) Owners of businesses in the same industry would agree among themselves to divide up the markets to avoid competition or agree to operate their factories at less than full capacity.

36. All of the following individuals or organizations contributed to the passage of laws restricting child labor EXCEPT

   (A) Jane Addams and settlement houses advocating for the care of immigrant children.
   (B) Lewis Hine and his series of muckraking photographs of child laborers in dangerous jobs.
   (C) the American Federation of Labor and other labor organizations that said child workers lowered the wages of adults.
   (D) the Supreme Court that declared in a case in 1922 that child labor was unconstitutional.
   (E) the Congress that passed the Fair Labor Standards Act as a federal regulation of child labor.

37. Ida Tarbell published articles from 1903 to 1904 in *McClure's* magazine that attacked which American company for its business practices?

   (A) United States Steel
   (B) The Northern Securities Company
   (C) The General Electric Company
   (D) The Standard Oil Company
   (E) The Western Union Company

38. Which statement below best explains the weakness of the 1914 Clayton Antitrust Act that caused the federal government to fall back on the 1890 Sherman Antitrust Act in prosecutions of business monopolies?

   (A) In cases brought to the Supreme Court under the 1914 law the justices repeatedly declared it unconstitutional because of its lack of distinction between interstate and intrastate commerce.

   (B) The biggest weakness of the 1914 law was that it was supported by Woodrow Wilson whose approval rating plummeted after he failed to bring the United States into World War I.

   (C) The detailed list of business practices that the 1914 law declared illegal was too easy for corporate lawyers to circumvent as opposed to the broad language of the 1890 law.

   (D) The attorneys general under Woodrow Wilson and subsequent presidents believed more in the ideas of New Nationalism than those of New Freedom that motivated the 1914 law.

   (E) The emergency economic measures enacted by the federal government to supply the Allied Powers in Europe directly contradicted the provisions of the 1914 law.

39. Which statement below best describes the political impact of the Dust Bowl on the perception of the American people regarding the New Deal?

   (A) The blow to American agricultural production created by the drought contributed to the apparent success of the Agricultural Adjustment Act's goal to achieve parity in farm prices.

   (B) The suffering created by the Dust Bowl contributed to a nearly successful bid for Republican candidate Alf Landon to unseat Franklin D. Roosevelt in the Election of 1936.

   (C) The dust storms created by the drought diminished support for the New Deal because the management practices suggested by the government led to the disappearance of topsoil.

   (D) The drought's ruining of small farmers led Americans to doubt the New Deal's promises of achieving reform of the economy as large corporations bought up abandoned farms.

   (E) The popularity of the New Deal soared as the Civilian Conservation Corps was formed to give jobs to unemployed young men to work on Midwestern soil reclamation and irrigation efforts.

40. In what way did the death of Emmett Till in 1955 impact the civil rights movement?

    (A)  The photograph of Till's dead face in *Jet* magazine frightened young African-Americans and kept them from joining the civil rights movement.
    (B)  The outcome of the trial of Till's murderers encouraged African-Americans that justice was possible to attain in the courts at last and that lynching would soon cease.
    (C)  Even though Till was killed in Mississippi the fact that he was a fourteen-year-old from the North drew national attention to his case and helped launch a national movement.
    (D)  The convergence of leaders like Martin Luther King Jr. and Malcom X on the scene at the trial of Till's murderers showed that this case was going to become a turning point.
    (E)  The murder of such a young man over such a trivial event as his having spoken to a white woman caused African-American parents to forbid their children from taking action.

41. The Bill of Rights were added as the first ten amendments to the U.S. Constitution for all of the following reasons EXCEPT that they were

    (A)  intended to prevent the types of abuses of justice foisted on the American colonies prior to the American Revolution.
    (B)  concessions to certain states that refused to ratify the Constitution until provisions were made specifically to protect individual rights.
    (C)  a successful attempt on the part of Anti-Federalists to hold in check the growing influence of the Federalist Party in creating a strong central government.
    (D)  agreed upon as the final statement of the meaning of the American Revolution as distilled from all the other founding documents that preceded them.
    (E)  an expression of the liberties cherished by the American people and included a statement clarifying that the government was not the source but the protector of liberty.

42. "3 P.M. Attended the funeral of an Italian as far as the ferry. Hurried back to make his appearance at the funeral of a Hebrew constituent. Went conspicuously to the front both in the Catholic church and the synagogue, and later attended the Hebrew confirmation ceremonies in the synagogue."

The document quoted above is most likely taken from the account of the daily life of which type of individual prevalent during the early years of American urbanization?

(A) A nativist politician from the Know-Nothing Party
(B) A young college woman working in the settlement house movement in Chicago
(C) An Irish police officer responsible for protecting immigrants in New York City
(D) A Pinkerton detective attempting to infiltrate the socialist wing of a labor union
(E) A Tammany Hall politician attempting to turn compassion into votes

43. "Governor of the Philippines, Secretary of War, Governor of Cuba, Acting Secretary of State, President of the United States, and Chief Justice of the Supreme Court"

The list of offices above reads like the résumé of what influential twentieth-century American leader?

(A) William McKinley
(B) Theodore Roosevelt
(C) William Howard Taft
(D) Woodrow Wilson
(E) Herbert Hoover

44. Which statement best defines the concept of "spheres of influence" that made up part of the debate over American imperialism?

(A) They were areas the United States considered as possible countries that could be turned into new democratic republics.
(B) They were regions of the developing world considered as potentially fruitful mission fields for American missionaries' efforts.
(C) They were areas within other countries where the United States sought exclusive economic privileges from the rulers in exchange for economic aid and military protection.
(D) They were seaports in foreign countries that were considered as strategic locations for future American naval bases.
(E) They were islands evenly spaced across the Pacific Ocean that would permit the storage of coal reserves to facilitate the transit of American merchant and naval vessels.

45. The premise behind the formation of the Securities and Exchange Commission (SEC) during the New Deal was that

    (A) the people of America had a right to know the financial health of companies in which they were purchasing stocks, so the stock exchange required publication of quarterly reports.

    (B) the government would end unscrupulous investment practices of banks that caused the crash.

    (C) direct government regulation of the activities on Wall Street would border on socialism, so an indirect approach through self-regulation according to standards set by the industry was best.

    (D) Joseph P. Kennedy was the sharpest of the giant stock traders, so only he could investigate his former associates as the head of the new regulatory agency.

    (E) the Federal Reserve and the SEC could coordinate oversight of the economy and investing.

46. Which statement below best explains why the U.S. Congress supported American involvement in the United Nations, whereas it had rejected involvement in the League of Nations?

    (A) The headquarters of the United Nations would be located on American soil where the United States could exert more influence over its proceedings.

    (B) Even though many other nations could afford to support the foundation and the operations of the United Nations, the United States was the highest bidder and shouldered others aside.

    (C) Because the United States had done so much through World War II to stop aggressor nations, the Congress was convinced the United States would one day be granted a seat on the Security Council.

    (D) New threats that existed after the invention of atomic weapons, among other advances in military technology, created a world where the United States had to join out of self-defense.

    (E) A majority of developing countries that were invited to join the United Nations said there was no point in attempting the goals of the new body without the aid of the United States.

47. What was the result of the involvement of the United States in the Korean War?

    (A) After the Treaty of Beijing was signed, North and South Korea agreed to a cease-fire that left the Korean peninsula divided at the thirty-eighth parallel of latitude.
    (B) The communist forces of the Peoples' Republic of Korea defeated the South Korean military once the North Atlantic Treaty Organization forces pulled out of the war.
    (C) South Korean and North Atlantic Treaty Organization forces defeated the armies of North Korea but left the Communist Party in power as an act of appeasement to the Soviet Union and China.
    (D) The United Nations passed a resolution of formal protest against the U.S. policy of containment and said East Asia was off limits to American intervention.
    (E) Communist aggression was contained and the Korean peninsula remained divided just as it was after World War II but at the cost of over one million Korean lives.

48. How was the 1962 Cuban Missile Crisis resolved?

    (A) The Soviet Union agreed to remove missiles from Cuba and President Kennedy agreed to remove American missiles just outside the border of the Soviet Union in Turkey.
    (B) The United States invaded Cuba with air, sea, and land forces that caused Fidel Castro to turn over the Soviet missiles to inspectors from the United Nations.
    (C) The Soviet Union removed Castro from power in Cuba because of his provocations of the United States and voluntarily removed the missiles aimed at American cities.
    (D) The Soviet Union realized the United States was bent on taking action after a Soviet destroyer moving some of the missiles was sunk by an American submarine, and Khrushchev relented.
    (E) The United Nations intervened with a special meeting of the Security Council where representatives of the Soviet Union and the United States could directly negotiate an answer.

49. Which statement best describes the goals or strategies of Freedom Schools used by civil rights activists in the South during the civil rights movement in the 1960s?

    (A) Consultants hosted the schools in the summers to train high school and college students in the principles of the black power movement.

    (B) African-American students staged walkouts from schools in systems that had not yet complied with the 1954 Supreme Court ruling about segregation in *Brown vs. Board of Education.*

    (C) African-American schoolchildren were given free access to programs designed to encourage appreciation of African-American history, basic academic skills, and voter registration.

    (D) African-American teachers were trained to insert civil rights issues into their regular academic curricula in order to inspire their students to push harder for freedom.

    (E) Workshops were provided by the National Association for the Advancement of Colored People for students like those in Little Rock, Arkansas, and Clinton, Tennessee, who were among the first to attend integrated schools.

50. What was the greatest contribution of Henry Kissinger to keeping the peace between the communist world and the United States during the Cold War?

    (A) He organized the South East Asian Treaty Organization modeled after the North Atlantic Treaty Organization to prevent the spread of communism in that region.

    (B) He helped President Jimmy Carter achieve the successes of the Camp David Accords in order to forge an alliance in the Middle East against communist revolutionary forces there.

    (C) He negotiated the peace settlement that ended the Suez Crisis that threatened to ignite World War III over a conflict among Britain, France, Egypt, and the Soviet Union.

    (D) He recognized the animosity between Chinese communists and Soviet communists and worked to prevent their cooperating with each other in matters of foreign policy.

    (E) He developed a plan for supporting any countries in Europe that were threatened by internal economic collapse or external communist aggression.

51. Which factor contributed to the greater amount of social mobility in colonial American society compared to that of eighteenth-century English society?

    (A) English colonists in America experienced a longer lifespan than their counterparts in England.
    (B) Fewer legal constraints prevailed in America like those that preserved English social classes.
    (C) The limiting of leadership in warfare to aristocrats was not transferred to colonial America.
    (D) New developments in industrial growth in America surpassed those of the English economy.
    (E) The absence of a servant class in colonial America gave a wider range of job opportunities.

52. Which statement best describes the impact of the Half-way Covenant on the society of colonial New England?

    (A) Church membership in New England skyrocketed in the first widespread revival of Protestant Christianity in American history.
    (B) Fewer members of the Congregational churches maintained doctrinal fidelity and as a result society became more democratic but less unified.
    (C) The opening of church membership to American Indians for the first time created more peaceful relations and sparked westward migration.
    (D) As doctrinal distinctions blurred, more and more New Englander Puritans simply returned to the Anglican Church, slowing a desire for political independence because of religious unity.
    (E) As religious devotion became less of a dominant force in society, more New Englanders devoted themselves to hard work in developing a thriving economy.

53. Which series of checks and balances correctly explains constitutional arrangements existing among the three branches of the government under the U.S. Constitution?

    (A) The president can remove incompetent judges; the Congress can remove incompetent presidents; and the Supreme Court can force a gridlocked Congress to pass needed laws.
    (B) The Supreme Court can settle any presidential election in which there is not a clear winner; the president can nullify judicial decisions; and the Congress can remove rogue judges.
    (C) The president can veto legislation by the Congress; Congress can review the nominations of the executive branch; and the Supreme Court can stop enforcement of unconstitutional laws.
    (D) The Supreme Court can refuse to endorse a treaty; the president can refuse to enforce judicial decisions; and the Congress can reverse decisions of the Supreme Court by majority vote.
    (E) The president can close an unruly session of Congress; the Congress can declare a presidential election void; and the Supreme Court can declare a law to be unconstitutional.

54. Why did Jeffersonian Republicans refer to the last nominations of John Adams for judges to fill seats in the federal court system as Midnight Appointments?

    (A) They believed some of the judges appointed by Adams to hold principles about government that were evil.
    (B) President Adams finished writing out the last nomination paperwork at the stroke of midnight during his last night in office.
    (C) They declared the nominations to be invalid because President Adams only got around to working on them at midnight so technically he was no longer president.
    (D) They were celebrating the Jeffersonian Revolution in the Election of 1800 by announcing a campaign to block Adams's last executive proposals from coming to a vote in the Congress.
    (E) They derided the fact that President Adams was trying to prolong Federalist Party influence in government by attempting to install Federalist judges as one of his last acts.

55. The Nullification Crisis over the tariff in the 1830s involved a principle of government most closely associated with which previous law or laws?

    (A) The Judiciary Act of 1789
    (B) The Alien and Sedition Acts of 1798
    (C) The Virginia and Kentucky Resolutions of 1798–1799
    (D) The Embargo Act of 1807
    (E) The Non-Intercourse Act of 1809

56. What was the typical foreign policy position of American presidents toward the United Kingdom after the Treaty of Ghent ended the War of 1812 until after the Treaty of Washington of 1871?

    (A) That the United Kingdom was the natural enemy of the United States and that British foreign policy designs on the Western Hemisphere had to be thwarted
    (B) That the War of 1812 had proved that the United States could dominate the oceans like the United Kingdom once did so the American navy needed constant strengthening
    (C) That after the Treaty of Ghent all of the major differences with the United Kingdom were settled and the two countries should finally be friends and allies in case of trouble
    (D) That any economic agreements with the United Kingdom would inevitably lead to American involvement in the ongoing animosity of the British toward France
    (E) That the United Kingdom was actively conspiring with Mexico to thwart any further American expansion and to look for territory that could be regained in case of a war

57. What was the 1860 proposal known as the Crittenden Compromise that attempted to prevent the outbreak of civil war?

    (A) That the United States purchase or annex Cuba from the Spanish in order to provide more room for the creation of slave states to balance North/South representation in the Senate

    (B) That the U.S. government agree to purchase all the slaves in the South as a way to compensate slave owners for the loss of capital that would come with abolition

    (C) That slaves born after January 1, 1861, would all be emancipated when they reached the age of twenty-five in order to give the South time to adjust their economy in a different way

    (D) That the Missouri Compromise line be reinstated and extended to the Pacific Ocean in order to divide up the West and keep a better balance of slave and free states

    (E) That two presidents be elected, one from the South and one from the North, so that the executive branch would never again fall into the hands of a strictly sectional political party

58. All of the following issues represented foreign policy problems for the United States after the country survived the challenges of the Civil War EXCEPT the

    (A) French were trying to install a puppet government in Mexico in violation of the Monroe Doctrine.

    (B) border between Maine and Canada was disputed in a small conflict known as the Aroostook War.

    (C) Russians were extending their colonies in Alaska and were encroaching on American territory.

    (D) British had provided the Confederacy with ships with which to run the Union blockade during the Civil War and refused to pay damages.

    (E) British disputed a boundary between their territory in South America with Venezuela and threatened the use of force in violation of the Monroe Doctrine.

59. How did the companies building the first transcontinental railroad acquire enough capital in 1862 to finance its construction?

    (A) The prospect of crossing the continent with a railroad attracted so many investors that the companies had only to sell stock to the general public.

    (B) Bonds were issued by the company that were snatched up by foreign and domestic banks enthused by the greatest civil engineering feat of the day.

    (C) The federal government paid the companies a certain amount of money for every mile of railroad constructed as a means of boosting the national economy.

    (D) The corporate leaders of the companies were wealthy enough to pool their resources and build it on their own as long as each segment of the railroad was economically viable.

    (E) The discovery of gold and silver deposits along the way added to the fares immigrants paid the railroad to transport them to homesteads and covered the costs.

60. What effect did the Haymarket Square incident in Chicago have on the Knights of Labor (KOL) in 1886?

   (A) Sympathy for the plight of the KOL demonstrators launched the presidential campaign of the labor union's leader, Terence Powderly.
   (B) The bad press from the incident was what first convinced Samuel Gompers he needed to form the American Federation of Labor and split from the KOL.
   (C) Increased agitation as a result of the incident led both skilled and unskilled workers to unite in KOL solidarity for the first time.
   (D) The labor union immediately disbanded and ceased all operations in an effort to avoid having the stigma of radicalism associated with the KOL to taint the reputation of other labor unions.
   (E) The events orchestrated by anarchists at the KOL demonstration were associated with the KOL, and the labor union's membership went into a steep decline never to recover.

61. All of the following qualities were advantages the Progressive Reform movement had over the Populist movement EXCEPT

   (A) support for Progressivism came from within both major political parties.
   (B) Progressivism appealed to immigrants by recognizing their need for help with assimilation.
   (C) middle-class, well-educated citizens embraced Progressivism.
   (D) Progressivism sought to address the problems of urban industrial workers.
   (E) women took a leading role in Progressivism.

62. The 1896 Supreme Court case *Plessy v. Ferguson* in which the decision sanctioned segregation with the phrase "separate but equal" involved separating the races in what type of setting?

   (A) Restaurants and other dining facilities including bars
   (B) Hotels, inns, and other lodging facilities
   (C) Elementary, secondary, and postsecondary educational facilities
   (D) Transportation facilities including railroads and steamships
   (E) Churches, synagogues, and other worship facilities

63. Which statement best explains how the United States acquired the Hawaiian Islands?

   (A) They were taken from Spain along with the Philippine Islands in the Spanish-American War.
   (B) The United States won the race against the British in populating the islands so the British withdrew.
   (C) Americans helped an indigenous revolution succeed, and then the United States annexed the islands.
   (D) Hawaiians asked for annexation by the United States when pressured by Japanese imperialism.
   (E) American corporations conquered the islands with private armies prior to annexation.

64. What significant theory impacting government revenues did Andrew Mellon pioneer as the secretary of treasury under Warren G. Harding and Calvin Coolidge in the 1920s?

    (A) In times of prosperity such as the Roaring Twenties, the government should issue bonds to store up extra resources for times of greater need.
    (B) The federal government should actively attract foreign investors in American industries to reduce the burden on the federal government for internal improvements.
    (C) When the stock market is experiencing a rapid rise in stock values, the government should directly tax capital gains to benefit from the profits being made by investors.
    (D) Lower federal income taxes and capital gains taxes would allow private investors to boost the American economy by which government revenues will also increase.
    (E) In times of economic growth the federal government should increase taxation in order to distribute wealth among all classes of society.

65. "War is no longer simply a battle between armed forces in the field. It is a struggle in which each side strives to bring to bear against the enemy the coordinated power of every individual and of every material resource at its command. The conflict extends from the soldier in the front line to the citizen in the remotest hamlet in the rear."

    This 1939 assessment of the events leading up to World War II indicates that victory for either side would likely only come through which of the following approaches?

    (A) Performing routine strategic aerial bombing of the enemy's industrial strength
    (B) Being the first power to unlock the technology behind atomic weapons
    (C) Surviving a total war through attrition longer than the enemy could
    (D) Arriving in the enemy's capital city first with sufficient forces to conquer it
    (E) Sustaining air, sea, and ground forces across more of the globe than the enemy

66. Which statement best describes the most significant contribution to the American labor movement by John L. Lewis?

    (A) He restored a belief in the solidarity of skilled and unskilled workers in given industries.
    (B) He was the first major labor leader to repudiate the use of strikes as tools to air grievances.
    (C) He actively rid his national organization of socialists, communists, and other radical elements.
    (D) He embraced the disparate needs of both coal miners and workers in automobile factories.
    (E) He became the leader of the new cabinet position for labor created by Theodore Roosevelt.

67. Which statement best explains how the Cold War ended?

(A) Mikhail Gorbachev single-handedly destroyed communism from within the Soviet Union.
(B) The economic flaws of communism in the Soviet Union undermined their ability to compete.
(C) Leadership in the "free world" inspired new revolutions in Soviet bloc countries.
(D) The development of "Star Wars" defensive technology caused the Soviet Union to surrender.
(E) The United Nations leveraged enough power in the General Assembly to negotiate a peace.

68. All of the following statements about the 1991 Persian Gulf War are true EXCEPT

(A) the United States acted unilaterally to liberate Kuwait after Saddam Hussein invaded.
(B) the main forces attacking Iraqi forces swept through a desert in a flanking maneuver.
(C) the United Nations supported American actions in the Persian Gulf region.
(D) most of Saddam's Republican Guard forces were destroyed from the air.
(E) the war was popular in the United States and boosted the president's approval rating.

69. How was the disputed Election of 2000 between George W. Bush and Al Gore decided?

(A) The election went before the House of Representatives because there was no clear winner.
(B) Overseas ballots of military personnel and other Americans were counted after the fact.
(C) Al Gore conceded the election to avoid delaying the results beyond a constitutional limit.
(D) A recount in Florida, the state in question, was permitted, which cleared up the dispute.
(E) The Supreme Court ruled that recounts were unconstitutional and declared Bush the winner.

70. What did Elisha G. Otis invent that made giant skyscrapers practicable?

(A) The steel I-beams that made construction of multiple stories possible
(B) Threaded steel bars used to reinforce concrete
(C) An enclosed hoist, or elevator
(D) Braided steel cables capable of holding heavy weight at over 200 feet in length
(E) An emergency brake that would activate immediately if a cable snapped

71. What was the Supreme Court's decision regarding Japanese-Americans in the *Korematsu v. United States* case during World War II?

    (A) That Japanese-American males could serve in the American military as noncombatants
    (B) That second-generation Japanese-Americans need not be interned for national security
    (C) That interning the Japanese living in the United States in camps was a reasonable precaution
    (D) That the deportation of Japanese-Americans was unconstitutional and should be stopped
    (E) That interning Japanese-Americans was unconstitutional and they were owed compensation

72. All of the following charges against Anne Hutchinson led to her banishment from the Massachusetts Bay Colony EXCEPT that

    (A) as a woman she was banned from teaching men about spiritual matters.
    (B) she taught about the Bible in her home rather than in church.
    (C) she taught heretical doctrines contrary to Puritan teachings.
    (D) she practiced witchcraft and cursed her neighbors.
    (E) she refused to submit to her earthly spiritual authorities.

73. Which statement correctly identifies Daniel Boone's chief contribution to westward settlement?

    (A) He fought as a scout in the French and Indian War that opened the Ohio River Valley.
    (B) He was Cooper's inspiration for the hero of the popular Leatherstocking Tales.
    (C) He discovered the major gap through the Appalachian Mountains allowing easier passage.
    (D) He befriended American Indian tribes while hunting and trapping in the wilderness.
    (E) He led Tennesseans to volunteer to hold the Alamo in the Texas War for Independence.

74. All of the following were provisions of the 1774 Coercive Acts EXCEPT

    (A) replacing Massachusetts self-government with British martial law.
    (B) closing the port of Boston until damages for the Boston Tea Party were paid.
    (C) allowing British military personnel to be tried in England when accused of crimes.
    (D) requiring the confiscation of all weapons of Americans living in Boston.
    (E) permitting British military officers to take over buildings for housing their troops.

75. What was the result of the 1794 Battle of Fallen Timbers?

    (A) William Henry Harrison personally slew Tecumseh and ended the threat from American Indians to westward settlement inspired by Tecumseh's leadership.

    (B) Several American Indian tribes ceased resisting westward settlement and ceded their land to the American government in the Treaty of Greenville.

    (C) William Henry Harrison was disgraced by his losses in the battle and determined to redeem himself when the War of 1812 broke out so he could become president.

    (D) An amateur American army of frontier militiamen was slaughtered by the coordinated attacks of several American Indian tribes.

    (E) Thomas Jefferson's dream of assimilating American Indians into American society as farmers was dashed because the Cherokee refused to adopt the ways of their conquerors.

76. Why did Thomas Jefferson seek the deal with the French that resulted in the Louisiana Purchase in 1803?

    (A) He hoped to secure New Orleans as an outlet for America's western yeoman farmers.

    (B) He sought to double the size of the country to provide enough land to avoid industrialization.

    (C) He wanted to make the United States stronger to prove that American values were better.

    (D) He wanted to secure a base on the Missouri River from which to resist Spanish aggression.

    (E) He wanted to seek an all-water route across North America to the Pacific Ocean.

77. In which American war did the USS *Constitution* play a decisive role?

    (A) The War of 1812
    (B) The Texas War for Independence
    (C) The Mexican War
    (D) The Civil War
    (E) The Spanish-American War

78. Which statement below best describes Andrew Jackson's views about the spoils system?

    (A) All of the civil servants of the previous presidential administrations should be replaced with his own supporters.

    (B) His supporters should have complete access to him and to the White House while he was president.

    (C) Jobs within the federal bureaucracy did not require skill as much as total loyalty, so key positions of influence should go to people he trusted and whom he nominated to fill them.

    (D) If most of the civil servants in the federal bureaucracy were not left in place, then the country would suffer each time there was rotation in office while the new workers learned their jobs.

    (E) As he was filling his cabinet and other positions in the federal bureaucracy Congress should not have any say in the confirmation process.

79. The common school movement originated from which reform impulse?

    (A) Catholic children should be weaned away from the influence of the Roman Catholic Church by being forced to attend public schools with Protestant overtones in the curriculum.

    (B) Even lower-class children should be taught to discover truth for themselves as they explore what interested them most in the common schools.

    (C) African-American children and children of other races should be trained to end racism by learning to share all things in common while attending public schools.

    (D) Students should be compelled to come to school in a republic so that the country was assured its best chance for survival through the development of better citizens.

    (E) The country would be strengthened if children from various backgrounds shared a common educational experience and thus were trained to love their country and work hard in factories.

80. What impact did the invention of the cotton gin have on the institution of African slavery?

    (A) Plantation owners knew their days as planter aristocrats were numbered as soon as machinery began to be developed to replace their slaves' labor.
    (B) The abolitionist movement attacked slavery all the more because northern ingenuity had proven that slavery was not a productive labor system in the face of modern technologies.
    (C) The demand for slaves went down because the cotton gin eased a labor-intensive stage of cotton production and thus the African slave trade was abolished.
    (D) More and more African slaves were purchased on cotton plantations because what was originally only a tedious family necessity was now a lucrative cash crop.
    (E) The cotton gin had almost no impact for decades on the institution of slavery because its inventor was caught up in lawsuits in order to defend his patent and could not sell any.

81. How did the abolitionism of William Lloyd Garrison differ from that of Frederick Douglass?

    (A) Garrison published an abolitionist newspaper, whereas Douglass put all his efforts into oratory.
    (B) Garrison demanded immediate emancipation, whereas Douglass advocated a gradual approach.
    (C) Garrison's rhetoric appealed to the emotions, whereas Douglass used economic statistics.
    (D) Garrison refused to cooperate with female abolitionists, whereas Douglass worked with them.
    (E) Garrison stopped with the Thirteenth Amendment, whereas Douglass advocated continued agitation.

82. The aspect of the Compromise of 1850 that contributed the most to continued sectional controversy was the

    (A) entrance of California into the Union as a free state thereby giving the North an advantage in the Senate as well as in the House of Representatives.
    (B) expenditure of $10 million to compensate Texas for the loss of territory to the Utah and New Mexico Territories.
    (C) fact that the Utah and New Mexico Territories were open to slavery under popular sovereignty.
    (D) banning of the slave trade in Washington, D.C.
    (E) passage of a stricter Fugitive Slave Law.

83. "The Secretary of War may direct such issues of provisions, clothing, and fuel . . . for the immediate and temporary shelter and supply of destitute and suffering refugees and freedmen."

    What other services did the Freedmen's Bureau provide African-Americans in the South after the Civil War besides those listed in the excerpt from the Congressional authorization of the agency quoted above?

    (A) Passage to the North for those desiring to leave the South
    (B) Monitoring of their treatment by their new employers at jobs in the South
    (C) University education for those who had completed at least ten years of previous schooling
    (D) Relocation to plantations confiscated from former Confederates that were up for purchase
    (E) Passage back to Africa for those desiring to leave the United States

84. What gave John D. Rockefeller his original advantage over his competitors as he entered the oil industry?

    (A) His father gave him his first oil refinery so he was able to operate it at a loss for several years.
    (B) He invented technologically advanced refining equipment that made his plants more efficient.
    (C) He was the first oil man to sell stock to the public to amass enough capital to get ahead.
    (D) He was extremely frugal as a young man and was able to purchase his first refinery with cash.
    (E) He purchased a refinery for a cheap price from a man who had lost a fortune in a family crisis.

85. Why did the Populist Party's influence in American politics end as a result of the Election of 1896?

    (A) Their candidate, former Union General James B. Weaver, turned out to be as corrupt as the Republican candidate, William McKinley, whom he sought to defeat.
    (B) William Jennings Bryan masterfully exposed the flaws in the Populist platform in a series of debates in which the Populist candidate could not compete with Bryan's oratorical skill.
    (C) Word that the Populists planned to run Mary Lease as the first female presidential candidate in American history undermined their support in an era before women could even vote.
    (D) Bryan's moving "Cross of Gold" speech won him the Democratic nomination but also the support of the Populists who did not run a candidate of their own.
    (E) Their candidate's loss of the election on a platform that benefited only farmers proved that the United States was too urbanized for such a candidate to ever win the presidency again.

86. In what way did the principles and activities of Booker T. Washington and W. E. B. Du Bois differ?

    (A) Washington focused more on educating African-Americans to attain economic goals, whereas Du Bois sought to inspire them to attain political goals.
    (B) Washington focused more on the needs of African-Americans in the North, whereas Du Bois dealt most with their needs in the South where he was a professor in Atlanta.
    (C) Washington wanted his students and followers to earn the respect of other Americans by serving in the military, whereas Du Bois said African-Americans should be ashamed to do so.
    (D) Washington advised African-Americans to study the classics of Western Civilization, whereas Du Bois advocated only vocational training for the first generation of freedmen.
    (E) Washington discounted the role of religion in education, whereas Du Bois said all truth should be viewed through the lens of Christianity.

87. What was the cause of Woodrow Wilson's hesitancy to bring the United States into World War I?

    (A) America's tradition of involvement in the affairs of foreign countries had left the nation disillusioned with European conflicts.
    (B) American women who had just received the right to vote had clearly communicated they did not approve of sending their sons to war in Europe.
    (C) Since former president Theodore Roosevelt was such an advocate for American intervention in the war, Wilson avoided it as long as he could so as not to be seen in agreement with Roosevelt.
    (D) Up until 1917 there had been no actual threat to the United States or to American lives.
    (E) After recently overcoming the Panic of 1893 and a more recent recession, Wilson did not believe the United States should threaten trade relationships with either side in the war.

88. Which statement best characterizes Franklin D. Roosevelt's personal contribution to the success of his domestic agenda known as the New Deal?

    (A) He had long been contemplating specific reforms for the role of the federal government in the nation's economy and thus established clear priorities for change.

    (B) He was a master of settling differences between competing political factions and thus garnered bipartisan support for the New Deal.

    (C) He routinely communicated the goals and strategies of the New Deal to the American people and kept up their confidence that the government was taking care of their problems.

    (D) He was trusted by the upper classes because he was one of them and thus inspired the richest Americans to make significant sacrifices in the form of higher income taxes.

    (E) He was able to pick quality advisers and bureaucrats to fill administrative positions in the New Deal who together developed a coherent reform strategy.

89. What was the most significant contribution to African-American civil rights of Ida B. Wells?

    (A) She united the goals of abolitionism and the women's suffrage movement to add renewed strength to both reform movements.

    (B) Her skill as an opera singer broke down barriers for all African-Americans when she was able to perform in auditoriums where they were previously banned even from the audience.

    (C) Her innovative advances in cosmetics encouraged self-respect in African-American women but her company also modeled entrepreneurial skills others could follow.

    (D) She mounted a national campaign against lynching that never secured federal laws against the practice but kept attention on these atrocities committed against African-American men.

    (E) She took up leadership of Mississippi's National Association for the Advancement of Colored People chapters after her husband was assassinated by members of the Ku Klux Klan.

90. All of the following societal factors in the United States after World War II prevented the country from slipping back into the Great Depression EXCEPT the

   (A) profits made by companies supplying the war effort that they could then reinvest in transitioning to the production of consumer goods.
   (B) wage and price controls of President Truman's Fair Deal modeled after those of the National Recovery Administration of Franklin D. Roosevelt's New Deal.
   (C) rapid growth in the American population created by the baby boom that provided an unprecedented demand for consumer goods.
   (D) growth of service industries as the prosperity of the 1950s produced more free time enjoyed by more Americans than ever before.
   (E) continued massive expenditures on the part of the federal government in the interests of national security as the Cold War unfolded.

# Answer Key
## PRACTICE TEST 3

| | | | | | | | |
|---|---|---|---|---|---|---|---|
| 1. | D | 24. | D | 47. | E | 70. | E |
| 2. | C | 25. | C | 48. | A | 71. | C |
| 3. | A | 26. | E | 49. | C | 72. | D |
| 4. | E | 27. | B | 50. | D | 73. | C |
| 5. | C | 28. | D | 51. | B | 74. | D |
| 6. | B | 29. | C | 52. | B | 75. | B |
| 7. | D | 30. | C | 53. | C | 76. | A |
| 8. | B | 31. | E | 54. | E | 77. | A |
| 9. | E | 32. | D | 55. | C | 78. | C |
| 10. | D | 33. | B | 56. | A | 79. | E |
| 11. | A | 34. | A | 57. | D | 80. | D |
| 12. | D | 35. | E | 58. | B | 81. | E |
| 13. | B | 36. | D | 59. | C | 82. | E |
| 14. | C | 37. | D | 60. | E | 83. | B |
| 15. | E | 38. | C | 61. | E | 84. | D |
| 16. | D | 39. | A | 62. | D | 85. | D |
| 17. | A | 40. | C | 63. | C | 86. | A |
| 18. | D | 41. | D | 64. | D | 87. | E |
| 19. | D | 42. | E | 65. | C | 88. | C |
| 20. | C | 43. | C | 66. | A | 89. | D |
| 21. | B | 44. | C | 67. | B | 90. | B |
| 22. | E | 45. | B | 68. | A | | |
| 23. | A | 46. | D | 69. | E | | |

# Test Analysis

**Step 1: Count the number of correct answers.**

Enter the total here: _____

**Step 2: Count the number of incorrect answers.**

Enter the total here: _____

**Step 3: Multiply the number of incorrect answers by .250**

Enter the product here: _____

**Step 4: Subtract the results obtained in Step 3 from the total obtained in Step 1.**

Enter the total here: _____

**Step 5: Round the number obtained in Step 4 to the nearest whole number.**

Raw Score = _____

## Scaled Score Conversion Table

| Raw Score | Scaled Score | Raw Score | Scaled Score | Raw Score | Scaled Score |
|-----------|--------------|-----------|--------------|-----------|--------------|
| 90–79 | 800 | 46–45 | 600 | 8–7 | 400 |
| 78 | 790 | 44–43 | 590 | 6–5 | 390 |
| 77–76 | 780 | 42–41 | 580 | 4–3 | 380 |
| 75 | 770 | 40 | 570 | 2–1 | 370 |
| 74 | 760 | 39–38 | 560 | 0– –1 | 360 |
| 73–72 | 750 | 37–36 | 550 | –2 – –3 | 350 |
| 71 | 740 | 35–34 | 540 | –4 | 340 |
| 70–69 | 730 | 33–32 | 530 | –5 – –6 | 330 |
| 68 | 720 | 31–30 | 520 | –7 | 320 |
| 67–66 | 710 | 29–28 | 510 | –8 – –9 | 310 |
| 65–64 | 700 | 27 | 500 | –10 | 300 |
| 63 | 690 | 26–25 | 490 | –11 – –12 | 290 |
| 62–61 | 680 | 24–23 | 480 | –13 | 280 |
| 60–59 | 670 | 22–21 | 470 | –14 – –15 | 270 |
| 58–57 | 660 | 20–19 | 460 | –16 – –17 | 260 |
| 56–55 | 650 | 18–17 | 450 | –18 – –19 | 250 |
| 54-53 | 640 | 16–15 | 440 | –20 | 240 |
| 52–51 | 630 | 14–13 | 430 | –21 – –22 | 230 |
| 50–49 | 620 | 12–11 | 420 | | |
| 48–47 | 610 | 10–9 | 410 | | |

# Answer Explanations

1. **D** Answer A is incorrect in that although Portugal and Spain might have allied against England and France, the Treaty of Tordesillas was to keep them from going to war against each other. That fact reveals why answer E is also incorrect. The Pope was trying to keep two Roman Catholic countries from fighting; there was no indication he planned to control exploration and colonization. Portugal did not need Italian navigators thanks to Prince Henry the navigator, and no treaty in the fifteenth century could have accomplished answer C. Answer D reveals that although the Portuguese had exclusive access to Africa, the arc drawn by the treaty would only allow them access to Brazil. The rest of the Western Hemisphere was granted to Spain.

2. **C** Answer C is the only answer precisely true of Maryland. Answer A was true of Maryland but was not unique in that several colonies had similar laws. Answer B was true of Pennsylvania. Answer D was true of Massachusetts in that Maine remained a part of the colony and even the state until the Missouri Compromise in 1820. Answer E was true of South Carolina.

3. **A** Answer A explains the truth behind the myth of the shape of the trade routes in the "triangular" trade. Answer B is incorrect in that the Board of Trade and Plantations would have frowned on these routes that bypassed the mother country just as it frowned on the exportation of any manufactured goods from the colonies. Answer D is an antimercantilist premise not tolerated by Great Britain. Nothing quite matched the lucrative nature of the annual Spanish treasure fleet in answer C except over the long haul when Spain's bullion ran out. Scottish and Dutch middle men did operate in, say, the tobacco markets, but they did not control the colonial triangular trade.

4. **E** Charles II was not motivated by rivalry, revenge, or humanitarianism as hinted at in answers A, B, and D, respectively. Nor did he need a base to attack the Dutch because they had already transferred their colony to England in 1664. Answer E indicates the British government's real intention. They wanted Andros to function as a Spanish viceroy did in the Spanish colonies in order to end salutary neglect.

5. **C** Answer A is incorrect in that political parties were not originally valued in the American republic, but answer B is incorrect because women had always been valued for this capacity. The additional new value placed on American women stemmed from the idea expressed in answer C that the republic depended on each citizen's contributions to survive. Answer D could be implied in the notion of "republican motherhood," but the higher calling for women was about much more than boosting population. Answer E is incorrect in that most American children were schooled at home by their mothers, and when schools did become more established they focused more on classical education than practical education.

6. **B** This answer is a close call because black codes (which included vagrancy laws) and slave codes would have been repugnant to many Christians and

others in Philadelphia, but the year is the key. By 1851 all northern ire was focused on the Fugitive Slave Law associated with the Compromise of 1850, and this law was the key legal provision to perpetuate slavery's existence. Personal liberty laws mentioned in answer A were actually passed to protect freedmen and African-Americans who were born free in an era where they could have been captured and either returned to or placed in slavery.

7. **D**  Answer A is entirely a contradiction in terms; the South did not submit to military occupation, and home rule by its very definition would have meant the end of military occupation. The Klan never sought sanction, as suggested in answer B, for its operations, fraternal or militant. Answer C was a tacit understanding associated with Reconstruction, not the Compromise of 1877, which was agreed upon to settle the Election of 1876 in the matter described in answer D for Louisiana, Florida, and South Carolina. Answer E evokes Lincoln's Ten Per Cent Plan that was rejected nearly immediately after his assassination.

8. **B**  Answer B conveys the difference between the Stalwarts, or the Conklingites, and the Mugwumps, the derisive term given to those Republicans in favor of civil service reform by those who needed reforming. Both groups were Republican factions, canceling answers A, D, and E. Answer D is incorrect because nearly all Gilded Age Republicans waved the bloody shirt and shunned bipartisanship.

9. **E**  The Fair Deal took on the macro domestic problem explained in answer E, not specifically any of the others in answers A, B, C, and D. Answer A was more the goal associated with the Truman Doctrine and the Marshall Plan. Answer C was more a function of the private sector and market forces than government action. Answer D is a reference to the G.I. Bill that was only indirectly a part of the Fair Deal. Truman was the first president to take formal actions to advance civil rights for African-Americans, but again, the Fair Deal was focused on the bigger picture.

10. **D**  All of the answers evoke issues associated with the Vietnam War, but even though the Pentagon Papers came out during the Nixon administration they were Daniel Ellsberg's attempt to discredit the whole war by exposing the lies of the Johnson administration. Nixon had his own struggles with telling the truth, and this bipartisan deception on the part of two presidents in a row created the "credibility gap."

11. **A**  While Champlain did discover Lake Champlain, it did not serve as a border between New France and New Amsterdam as suggested in answer B. Answers C, D, and E are all the accomplishments of other explorers, but Samuel de Champlain got the whole enterprise started as noted in answer A.

12. **D**  Answers A, B, and C all named regions fought over during the French and Indian War, but the conflict began when George Washington ran into the French in the Ohio River Valley. The Mississippi River delta was more a theater of the War of 1812 much later.

13. **B**  Because the document bans slavery it can only be associated with the Northwest Ordinance, and the ban in question served as a major precedent evoked by Abraham Lincoln in the 1850s. All of the rest of the documents listed in one

way or another supported slavery or certainly did not ban it. The Tallmadge Amendment wanted to abolish slavery from Missouri but only gradually. The Lecompton Constitution was the pro-slavery (and fraudulent) document that originally tried to organize the Kansas Territory.

14. **C**   Answer B is the opposite of the truth, but answers A, D, and E could all be said to be true of the Missouri Compromise by at least some perspectives. The main goal, however, is expressed in answer C that conveys how Henry Clay tried to keep all those perspectives from destroying the Union. The North already had a population advantage in the House of Representatives; the goal of the compromise was to maintain a balance in the Senate where each state had equal representation regardless of population.

15. **E**   Answers C and D are not true because they are true of other elections (1856 and 1800, respectively). Answers A and B were to a degree true of the Election of 1824 in that Jackson was from the "West," as was Henry Clay, and Jackson was certainly a colorful figure who was "sold" to the American people. Answer E explains the true significance of the election, however, because the two-party system has played a much more significant role than campaigning styles or geographical locations in the history of elections.

16. **D**   Answer A is a fabrication based on a stereotype, and answer B does not address a significant role because common cultural roots existed long before the McGuffey Readers. Both answers C and E are opposite to the actual impact and quality of the Readers. Answer D relates the context of both the Readers and the common school movement in the antebellum era of reform.

17. **A**   Answer A is the ironic truth of this transcendental utopia. Answer B was true of Oneida and other Shaker towns. Answer C was more the dream of Brook Farm that never came to be. Answer D is incorrect in that the Brook Farm was in Massachusetts, not the South. Answer E was truer of the utopian reforms of the Mormons, or the Church of Jesus Christ of Latter-Day Saints.

18. **D**   All of the answers express aspects of the cultural phenomenon wrapped up in the simple elegance of "Negro spirituals" except answer D, which was not true because these songs were not placed in hymn books or in any books until after the Freedman's Bureau and other agencies made efforts to provide literacy to African-Americans after slavery was over. Teaching slaves to read was illegal in the antebellum South, and the style in which these songs were sung was precisely the result of the illiteracy of slaves.

19. **D** Answer D is the truth amid the other answers that hint at realities of the Monroe Doctrine. George Canning did suggest the idea, but there was still diplomatic conflict ahead for the two countries. Adams and Monroe specifically said the New World empire of Spain would not be picked over by England or any other European country. Answers A and B are nearly the exact opposite of the truth. For example, the menace of the Barbary Pirates to American shipping had been ended earlier under Thomas Jefferson.

20. **C**   Answer C related Lincoln's ingenious ploy. All of the other answers are fabrications in that Lincoln did not attack Ft. Sumter at all, let alone with iron-

clads, which did not yet exist, and Ft. Sumter fell. Answer B is a dim reference to the Trent Affair that occurred much later in the war.

21. **B**   All of the other answers hint at issues surrounding the American Revolution that could have used the communication skills of Samuel Adams and others who organized the Committees of Correspondence. Only answer A is close to some of the operations of the Sons of Liberty and other groups searching for "enemies of the people" who cooperated with the British, but the Committees of Correspondence were specifically dedicated to the tasks mentioned in answer B.

22. **E**   All of the answers have been touted by some loose construction supporters at one time or another, except for answer C, which falsely implies the Founding Fathers anticipated a two-party system in American politics, but Hamilton himself simply referred to the implied powers inherent in the elastic clause of the U.S. Constitution. Most of the other rationales exceed Hamilton's position, which actually did stem from a line in the document.

23. **A**   Jefferson did dramatically reduce federal expenditures by taking all of these measures except for answer A, which may eventually happen in the United States but has not yet despite the existence of many successful private shipping companies alongside a Post Office that is struggling financially.

24. **D**   Answer D conveys the reality that the goal of the American Colonization Society was never popular with many of the Americans it tried to serve. Answers A, C, and E are all fabrications, especially because Abraham Lincoln actively supported colonization of South American with African-Americans freed from slavery in the United States. Answer B relates a truth about Marcus Garvey, but he was associated with the much later Back to Africa movement of the 1920s.

25. **C**   All of the other answers are exactly the opposite of the truth regarding sharecropping. Both white Americans and African-Americans fell into sharecropping in the southern economy ruined by the Civil War. Sharecroppers regardless of race cultivated mostly cotton, and the appearance of an incentive in sharecropping led families to put all the children in the fields alongside their parents, whereas under slavery most children started working in the field at the age of eight or nine. Although some African-Americans did own land and "hire" sharecroppers, some African-Americans had also owned slaves in the antebellum South. The nature of sharecropping, however, created a situation where almost no sharecroppers became successful economically until after World War II began, and still the institution of tenant farming died hard.

26. **E**   Although Jacob Riis stereotyped some of his fellow immigrants in *How the Other Half Lives,* his rhetoric never quite took on the biting edge of which the two Social Darwinists mentioned in answer E were capable. Rockefeller and Carnegie may have had Social Darwinian leanings but also did not go on record with such inflammatory diction. Jane Addams, the Salvation Army, and other supporters of the Social Gospel were opposed to such views on those locked in poverty.

27. **B**   Answer B was an initiative of Woodrow Wilson's version of Progressivism. Theodore Roosevelt took on all the others in the Square Deal.

28. **D**   Answers A and C are too general as interpretations, whereas answer B is too metaphorical for the genre of this type of cartoon. Political cartoons of this nature targeted specific people with specific accusations like the one in answer D. Answer E is incorrect in that Gould is portrayed as a spider on a web of telegraph wires ready to catch others, not as entrapped himself. The cartoon criticized Gould's use of the Western Union Telegraph Company he formed that by the 1880s possessed a monopoly of information by being the network to send, among other items, Associated Press stories to member newspapers around the country.

29. **C**   Although all of these policies were either advocated by Wilson or others in regard to the events associated with World War I, in 1916 he was elected because he promised to remain neutral when the electorate of the United States was still largely isolationist. Events after the election as well as Wilson's own change of heart led directly to American involvement by 1917.

30. **C**   Although answers D and E are true and the Second Red Scare did lead to blacklisting of people in Hollywood, neither Arthur Miller's play nor any film directly discredited McCarthy like his televised investigation into the army. During the Cold War most Americans did find the hunt for communists in the army to be preposterous even though McCarthy had the temerity to discredit World War II hero George C. Marshall of Marshall Plan fame for supposedly not doing enough to keep China from becoming communist. Contrary to the media circus of many of today's televised hearings alluded to in answer B, however, the McCarthy hearings were deadly serious affairs put on by this first American politician who understood television's political potential.

31. **E**   Both print coverage and Paul Revere's famous engraving of the Boston Massacre downplayed the size and the ferocity of the Boston mob. The crowd was armed and attacked the British soldiers with rocks, ice chunks, and snowballs while pressing them up against a wall. Some of the mob may have had more lethal weapons, and John Adams actually defended the soldiers to prove American justice could be impartial and got them acquitted of murder on the grounds of self-defense as mentioned in answer E. Answers A and B are the reverse of the truth and answers C and D are fabrications.

32. **D**   Of the groups or individuals listed, only American Indians were pressured culturally, economically, and politically to become citizens of the United States and then denied the full protection of American law as in the incidents known collectively as the "Trail of Tears." Slaves, the Irish, the Chinese, and women all found themselves the victims of discrimination, but these all had to request or fight for citizenship. Thomas Jefferson and other presidents and leaders offered citizenship in the United States to American Indians, but usually the offer meant a repudiation of tribal identities and was motivated by a desire to pacify the indigenous people of North America.

33. **B**   "Bleeding Kansas" is a reference to the antebellum events that are described in answer B and particularly the federal policy of popular sovereignty determining the slavery question as a result of the Kansas-Nebraska Act. Answer A involved bloodshed, but at the time the first transcontinental railroad was

built the territory was open to use by American Indian tribes like the Cheyenne without being placed on reservations. Answer E is a fabrication, but answers C and D reveal that Kansas has had a vibrant history even though these events happened after the Civil War was over.

34. **A**   Answer A conveys the idea of Turner's famous essay, and because the available land was largely taken (closed), answer B was less true even though it is a reference to Horace Greeley's famous "Go West, young man!" Answer C was becoming less popular as the New Immigration was starting, and answer D was more relevant in the early nineteenth century than the late nineteenth century. Answer E, although Turner might have agreed, is more the central idea of the writings of Rudyard Kipling that he called "The white man's burden."

35. **E**   All of the other answers discuss business practices, but only answer E describes a pool that was the loosest form of business combination and operated entirely as a gentlemen's agreement. Answers A and D describe practices of wealthy individuals who operated largely through the buying and selling of stock. Answer B describes vertical combination, whereas answer C describes horizontal combination, both of which were more formal arrangements employed when pools failed.

36. **D**   All of the other answers correctly recount some of the history of the movement to end child labor. Answer D is incorrect because in the 1920s the Supreme Court viewed the first federal anti-child labor laws to be unconstitutional, not child labor itself. Answer C describes how labor unions opposed child labor for less than humanitarian reasons.

37. **D**   Ida Tarbell's father had been put out of the oil-refining business by the rise of Standard Oil of Ohio, John Rockefeller's original company. Ida Tarbell wrote the serialized "history" as a muckraker bent on revenge.

38. **C**   All of the other answers are plausible fabrications involving issues surrounding antitrust legislation of the Wilson era. Answer C explains the reasons Wilson's New Freedom stance on trusts ultimately gave way to Theodore Roosevelt's more practical New Nationalism approach using the "watchdog" method of applying the Sherman Anti-Trust Law to the most egregious offenders.

39. **A**   Answer A shows how Franklin D. Roosevelt's desire to achieve parity in farm prices with the high prices experienced by American farmers during World War I was impossible to achieve by government intervention. The Dust Bowl and the Agricultural Adjustment Act combined did not achieve the goal, but because the natural disaster came during the application of the New Deal's policies they seemed more successful. Answers B, C, and D are the opposite of the truth of the situation, and answer E is irrelevant because the Civilian Conservation Corps (CCC) was founded earlier independently from the Dust Bowl and its effects, even though CCC workers did some of the work described.

40. **C**   Answers A, B, and E are the exact opposite of what happened as a result of this case, which drew national attention and helped launch the civil rights movement as explained in answer C. Answer D is incorrect because the Till case was one of the events like that of the arrest of Rosa Parks in Montgomery,

Alabama, that caused African-Americans to actively participate in civil rights agitation despite the dangers.

41. **D**   All of the other answers reflect the motives and methods of the process that gave rise to the Bill of Rights. As indicated by other amendments and even by the wrangling over what the first ten amendments actually meant as American history unfolded, there has not been and likely never will be an agreed-upon final statement about the meaning of the American Revolution.

42. **E**   The document is actually taken from the account of a day in the life of George Washington Plunkitt, a notorious Tammany Hall grafter. The nativist politician in answer A would likely never be caught dead doing the things described, and although the young woman in answer B might do them, she would not record how she attempted to be prominent at the functions. The Pinkerton detective nor the Irish police officer would either.

43. **C**   This incredible list of key responsibilities belongs to William Howard Taft who is largely unrecognized as a person of such influence. He was the only president to sit on the Supreme Court after his presidency, and of all these offices, chief justice was the one Taft most desired. All of the other presidents listed had colorful careers and key positions in government but none quite like Taft's that included a major office after their presidential administrations ended.

44. **C**   Although answer A is more the perspective on such relationships after World War II, answer C conveys the best overall definition of spheres of influence. Answer B was certainly true for some areas and for some Americans, but answer C was the key in the debate. Answer D was true in some cases but not in all, and answer E is more the definition of coaling stations like Midway Island and Guam, which did not belong to any sovereign nation when American imperialism sought them out for the geographical convenience.

45. **B**   Although answer A was part of the function of the Securities and Exchange Commission's (SEC's) oversight, the premise behind the agency's formation was that banks had caused the stock market crash and thus were largely responsible for the Great Depression as stated in answer B. The SEC was created in the classic sense of a "watchdog" agency in Progressive government. Answer C explains part of the rationale, but the industry's establishing its own standards was more true of the movie industry than the financial industry. There is also some truth to answer D, but it was not the premise behind the formation of the SEC but more an ironic outcome. What truth exists in answer E was not a forethought but more of an afterthought and thus, again, not the premise behind the formation of the SEC.

46. **D**   All of the other answers are fraudulent examples of some of the ironies of the United Nations except A, which was not the reason the Congress chose to be involved and is not necessarily true in regard to the exertion of influence. Answer B is incorrect because no other nation after World War II could afford to finance the United Nations and would have "bid" for the chance. Answer C is untrue in that the United States would never have joined the United Nations were it not guaranteed a permanent seat on the Security Council along with

its World War II allies. Answer E is untrue in that many developing nations take UN and U.S. aid but do not cooperate with either UN or U.S. goals nor recognize UN or U.S. leadership in the world. Of these choices, only the sobering reality of answer D can explain the shift in American involvement from the rejection of the League of Nations to the support of the United Nations.

47. **E** Answer E is the actual outcome. All the rest are twists on the truths of the war that are not beyond imagination in the difficult negotiations of the Cold War. Answer A cannot be true in that no treaty was ever signed to end the Korean War. Answer B was not the case because South Korea remains a free and thriving economy and society in East Asia, and answer C is also not true in that the limited nature of the Korean War did not allow a defeat of communist forces in North Korea. Contrary to answer D, the United Nations supported American involvement in the conflict and thus tacitly supported containment.

48. **A** This close call ended as described in answer A although the withdrawal of American missiles was not publicized and is little remembered. President Kennedy specifically disavowed any intention to perform the act described in answer B, and answer C is incorrect in that Fidel Castro was never removed from power. No actual sinking of Soviet vessels occurred as suggested in answer D as a result of the blockade of Cuba Kennedy did establish. Answer E would have fulfilled the mission of the United Nations but with the Soviet Union and the United States now enemies in the Security Council any such proposals faced the veto power of either side in the Cold War.

49. **C** Answer C conveys the positive message of education and civic involvement the Freedom Schools tried to inculcate in African-American schoolchildren. The Freedom Schools were not a propaganda project for the black power movement as suggested in answer A, nor an activist agency staging demonstrations as in answer B. Answer D was perhaps a spinoff of the Freedom Schools, but not their main goal or strategy. Workshops were provided to prepare students in various locations for their encounters with the public during acts of civil disobedience, but the Freedom Schools were, again, not actively participating in activism.

50. **D** Answers A and C were the doings of the Eisenhower administration without the direct involvement of Kissinger, and answer B was accomplished by Carter himself, again without the direct participation of Kissinger. Answer E was more the responsibility of George C. Marshall in the Truman administration. Answer D reveals that if Kissinger, who worked largely in the Nixon and Ford administrations, did nothing else but recognize the Sino/Soviet dissonance he would have been instrumental in helping the free world survive the Cold War.

51. **B** Answer A was true, especially of New Englanders, but it did not necessarily alter the social class structure. Answer B refers to the fact that primogeniture and other laws designed to preserve the social class structure of England did not transfer to America effectively over time. Answer C did not transfer well either, but it did exist during colonial wars among Americans and did not play a role in social mobility. Answers D and E are false in that the colonial Ameri-

can economy did not experience much industrial growth and the existence of indentured servitude prior to the American Revolution did begin a class structure in America. Part of the revolutionary nature of the American Revolution was the dissolution of a servant class, which did open up new jobs as the nineteenth century began.

52. **B**  Answer A is the opposite of the impact of the Half-way Covenant and was more associated with the First Great Awakening of the 1730s and 1740s. Answer B explains how this compromise in membership vows undermined the whole Puritan movement and made churches operate by congregational vote among members who were no longer believers in Puritan doctrine. Answer C also refers to experiences of the First Great Awakening when Jonathan Edwards and others began active mission work among American Indians after the Half-way Covenant had convinced Edwards that a revival was necessary. Answer D belies the trend among many breakaway groups within Christianity that even amid change they rarely go back to doctrinal roots. Answer E would be true except for the fact that New Englanders under Puritanism were already devoted to hard work in developing a thriving economy, just for different reasons.

53. **C**  Although all of the other answers contain elements of checks and balances that have developed over the years and some that might be convenient even if unconstitutional, only answer C contains three correct statements of constitutional interactions among the three branches of government.

54. **E**  Answers A, C, and D are fabrications, even though answer D is close to the truth in that attempts were made to block the appointments Adams made. Answer B is incorrect in that Adams actually finished the appointments around 9:00 P.M. Answer E is thus the truest explanation for the actions Adams took and the reaction of the Jeffersonian Republicans.

55. **C**  The precedent for the concept of nullification was set in Jefferson's and Madison's reasoning in their reaction to the Alien and Sedition Acts. The resolutions passed by Virginia and Kentucky were acts of nullification, and when South Carolinians nullified what they called the "Tariff of Abominations," they were building on the notion that states should be the primary determiners of the constitutionality of federal laws. The principle of nullification was a chief cause of the threat to the Union during the antebellum period, especially because even South Carolinians viewed the tariff issue as a dry run for federal laws against slavery.

56. **A**  Answer A explains the concept dubbed, "Anglophobia," in that most presidents up through James K. Polk believe the United Kingdom was out to crush the United States, and even subsequent presidents were suspicious of British involvement until the Treaty of Washington settled differences that arose during the American Civil War. From then on through the twenty-first century the two countries have been close allies. Answer B belies the fact that the American navy needed a great deal of strengthening before it could match British might at sea. Answer C was not true until the Treaty of Washington. Answers D and E are fabrications in that answer D was from the past during the period of the question and answer E was from the future but with Germany.

57. **D**  Answer D conveys the basic ideas of Senator John Crittenden's desperate eleventh-hour attempt to stave off the war that the repeal of the Missouri Compromise for the Kansas-Nebraska Act was partly responsible for bringing on. Answer A is a reference to the Ostend Manifesto, which was not a compromise but a cause of the war. Answer B refers to Lincoln's and others' plans for compensation that were laughed to scorn in the North and the South. Answer C is a reference to the Tallmadge Amendment that would have only applied to Missouri if it were accepted, which it was not. Answer E was proposed but never seriously considered.

58. **B**  Answer A refers to Maximilian who was a problem after the Civil War. So were the Russians in answer B until the Alaska Purchase, and the British until the Treaty of Washington produced a settlement. The Venezuela boundary dispute occurred in 1895 so it was after the Civil War, but the Aroostook War happened in the 1830s prior to the war.

59. **C**  Answers A and B are fabrications except for the fact that the transcontinental railroad was the greatest civil engineering feat of its day. The companies only had hope of accomplishing the daunting task because the federal government wanted it done more than they did and was willing to pay for its construction and the most important internal improvement in America to that time. Answers D and E are hints about sources of capital, although answer D is a direct reference to James J. Hill's approach. His Great Northern railroad was the only transcontinental line built without federal assistance.

60. **E**  Answer E is the only completely true answer. Answer A is untrue in that Powderly never ran for president of the United States and that the Knights of Labor (KOL) did not receive much sympathy. Samuel Gompers had already formed the American Federation of Labor for precisely the fact that is the reverse of answer C that skilled and unskilled workers united in the KOL were getting nowhere together. The KOL did not immediately disband as suggested in answer D but instead died a slow death that prolonged the negative (and unfair) stereotype resulting from the Haymarket Square Riot.

61. **E**  All of the answers are true of Progressivism, but although answers A, B, C, and D are exclusively a part of the history of this reform movement, women like Mary Lease also led the Populist revolt. Populism arose from the Patrons of Husbandry, or the Grange, which allowed women to be equal members of the organization. This fact contributed to women's receiving the right to vote in western farming states before they did in other parts of the country.

62. **D**  Although segregation is usually thought of in legal terms in association with education, this case originated with segregated transportation facilities as in answer D.

63. **C**  Answer C conveys how private American citizens like pineapple plantation owners helped depose Queen Liliuokalani of Hawaii, and then the islands were annexed for coaling stations among other reasons. They were not a part of the Spanish Empire, although they were annexed in 1898 along with those territories and islands acquired from Spain after the Spanish-American War. Answer B is a reference to the process of America's acquiring the Oregon Territory, and

answers D and E are fabrications. The Japanese set their sights on Hawaii but not with sufficient zeal to motivate Hawaiians until after they were already Americans. The Dole family helped fight the revolution but not as a corporation wielding private military power.

64. **D** Supply-side economics as described in answer C were not begun in the 1980s but in the 1920s by Andrew Mellon and other advisers in the Harding and Coolidge administrations. The other answers are a mixture of actual ideas that were espoused by Progressives and others along with fabricated ideas.

65. **C** Although answers A, B, and E became apparent strategic goals as World War II progressed, only answer D was thought to be important prior to the war. The document makes no reference to capital cities, however, but does refer to the terrible nature of total warfare that could only be won when the total economic might of a nation was outlasted by the total economic strength of the victor nation or nations.

66. **A** Answer A explains why John L. Lewis was venerated by coal miners and auto workers among others who joined the Congress of Industrial Organizations (CIO) that split off from the American Federation of Labor (AFL; only later to reunite as the AFL-CIO). Lewis did not repudiate strikes as did Terence Powderly of the Knights of Labor but instead routinely called them. He tolerated some level of radicalism within the umbrella of the CIO, but he was not the first secretary of labor and commerce under Roosevelt. He did embrace the needs of coal miners and auto workers that were not necessarily disparate, but his larger significance to the labor movement is conveyed in answer A.

67. **B** Some claim answer A is true, whereas others credit Ronald Reagan, Lech Walesa, Pope John Paul II, and Margaret Thatcher as in answer C, but neither position explains the whole truth. Again, the United Nations proved inadequate to the task suggested in answer E. Answer D was also a factor, but mainly because it exposed to the Soviets and to the free world the reality expressed in answer B. Through the Cold War the Soviet Union spent from one-quarter to one-third of its gross domestic product (GDP) on national defense, whereas the United States spent only 3 to 4 percent of its GDP to keep pace in this potentially deadliest war of attrition in human history.

68. **A** George W. Bush was accused of acting unilaterally (even though the United States had allies in the Iraq War. His father, George H. W. Bush, assembled a vast array of allies to drive Saddam Hussein's forces from neighboring Kuwait in the Persian Gulf War. All of the rest of the answers are true of the Persian Gulf War in contrast to some important aspects of the later war that brought Saddam Hussein to justice.

69. **E** All of the other answers are fabrications based on fine points of law and events surrounding this disputed election. The end result is explained in answer E. Answer C is partly true in that former Vice President Al Gore did at one point concede the election, but then took back his concession and ultimately launched the suit that brought the case before the Supreme Court where only five justices made the final opinion that decided the election.

70. **E**   Skyscrapers as designed by Louis Sullivan needed all of these inventions and innovations, but people were not inclined to get on a hoist for transportation until Elisha Otis demonstrated his brake by personally standing in an elevator and having the rope holding himself up cut. His brake worked. One cannot conceive of skyscrapers passing much higher into the sky than the original ten-story building in Chicago without safe, working elevators in which it was at least theoretically impossible to fall. Otis is often credited with the invention of the elevator when hoists had existed for centuries. The brake made them practical for moving people.

71. **C**   During World War II the Supreme Court upheld the federal government's internment policy. Answer E relates a later Supreme Court's decision in the matter and those interned were compensated slightly for their loss of private property during the war. Answer A belies the fact that some Japanese-Americans entered the American military and were decorated for valor in combat roles. All generations of Japanese-Americans experienced relocation and being interned.

72. **D**   All of the other answers were enough for the Massachusetts Bay authorities to banish Anne Hutchinson from the colony even though she was never charged with practicing witchcraft. Her case and that of Roger Williams revealed that the Puritans had escaped persecution in England but did not intend to practice religious toleration in their colonies.

73. **C**   Daniel Boone's storied career included all of the events listed in answers A, B, C, and D, but the other three events did not compare to the impact of Boone's discovery of the Cumberland Gap as a long hunter in the Appalachian wilderness. The Cumberland Gap became the chief route of the opening of this area to settlement and thus impacted the whole country. Answer E is an accomplishment of Davy Crockett, a frontiersman often confused with Daniel Boone.

74. **D**   All of the other answers contributed to the Coercive Acts being called the Intolerable Acts by American colonists. The British never set out to accomplish the confiscation of all weapons suggested in answer D, but the clash that became known as the battles of Lexington and Concord did erupt when a British military force was sent to confiscate a cache of weapons.

75. **B**   The Treaty of Greenville was the result of the events in answer B that followed the Battle of Fallen Timbers, which was won by Anthony Wayne, not William Henry Harrison, who won the Battle of Tippecanoe. Tecumseh was not killed until much later in the War of 1812. The rest of the answers are fabrications based on the facts that William Henry Harrison did become president after winning the Battle of Tippecanoe, Anthony Wayne was sent to avenge the massacre of militiamen, which came before the Battle of Fallen Timbers, and the Cherokee did adopt American civilization to a large extent.

76. **A**   As much as the other answers were true all or in part regarding the Louisiana Purchase, Jefferson's first priority was to secure New Orleans once Napoleon had wrested control of it from the Spanish. Even though Jefferson was sympathetic to the principles of the French Revolution he could not afford

to have a strong empire take over from a weakening empire in holding the outlet of the Mississippi River. The doubling of the country and the subsequent expeditions by Lewis and Clark and Zebulon Pike were goals established after Jefferson offered $10 million to the French for New Orleans and got the entire Louisiana Purchase for just $15 million.

77. **A**   Although Old Ironsides is still functioning in the U.S. Navy as the oldest commissioned war vessel, her practical use as a combatant ship was only during the War of 1812. The U.S. Navy played no role in the Texas War for Independence but performed admirably in all the wars in answers C, D, and E. By even the Mexican War, however, naval warfare had moved beyond the technology of the USS *Constitution*.

78. **C**   Although answer A conveys the commonly held misconception of Jackson's spoils system, he really once replaced about 20 percent of the civil service job holders. Answer B is a reference to the raucous celebration party the night of Jackson's inauguration, but the event was not a part of his routine administration. Answer C expresses Jackson's true position even though later presidential administrations practiced more extensive patronage. Answer D is the opposite of Jackson's position that the nation should avoid a parasitic civil servant class such as existed during the Era of Good Feelings. Jackson would likely have challenged anyone holding the position in answer E to a duel.

79. **E**   The common school movement was criticized for attempting to improve society by conditioning schoolchildren to the regimented life of factory workers, but it was the first concerted effort to provide public education and answer E expresses these dual goals. The creation of a Catholic school system is evidence that the common schools were Protestant in tone, but answer A was not an official position or design of the curriculum. Common schools sought to help lower-class children as suggested in answer B, but then the answer choice moves toward the educational reforms of John Dewey of Columbia University. Answer C was also not one of the original goals although Massachusetts, the state where Horace Mann launched the common school movement, was the first to provide integrated education. Answer D is incorrect in that the original public schools did not require compulsory attendance.

80. **D**   Answers A, B, and C would be true if other machines had been invented in the antebellum period that could perform all of the other laborious tasks associated with the cultivation of cotton, but because they could not, slaves were in even more demand when the most tedious task of all was made easier with the cotton gin. The cotton gin removed the cotton fibers from the seeds and other matter in cotton bolls, and thus the plantations wanted more cotton produced with slave labor than ever before. Eli Whitney had some patent problems as suggested in answer E, but the manufacturers who made the machines without his consent merely made them more prevalent, increasing their impact. Not until after World War II was progress made in accomplishing the picking of cotton by machine.

81. **E**   One half of each of the other answers is incorrect in that both men published newspapers, both men advocated immediate emancipation, both men

employed emotionally moving and often inflammatory rhetoric, and both men cooperated with female abolitionists. The important contrast occurred after abolition was successful when Garrison considered his work accomplished, whereas Douglass continued to agitate for the advances of African-Americans who remained, he believed, in a state of bondage.

82. **E**   All of the answers reflect aspects of the Compromise of 1850, and some like answers C and D were controversial. The Fugitive Slave Law was a cherished victory for the South, however, that was deeply distasteful to abolitionists and others in the North who resolved to "break it at every hazard." A sort of civil disobedience resulted that involved the Underground Railroad's shepherding of escaped slaves to freedom in Canada. When the South accused the North of breaking the law, the North responded by saying an immoral law was void. The Fugitive Slave Law exposed one of the deepest irreconcilable differences that led to the outbreak of war.

83. **B**   Answers A, C, and E are based on proposals to aid freemen that were of little practical use to them under the circumstances immediately following emancipation or were simply not desirable to freemen. Answer D is close to the proposal of Thaddeus Stevens for "forty acres and a mule" to be given to each African-American family, but the Freedmen's Bureau never had enough land to give or sell to a fraction of the former slaves. Land that had been confiscated from Confederates was slowly given back after pardons and other arrangements. Answer B was a stated goal providing a service to freedmen even though the Freedmen's Bureau's staff was challenged in meeting it.

84. **D**   Although the other answers are plausible ways in which one might get ahead in business, Rockefeller simply followed the path of frugality in answer D and gained an advantage everyone else had to try to overcome by borrowing to obtain, say, the latest refining technology. Although his competitors had to then pay interest on their original capital, Rockefeller made profits that he could reinvest in, among other things, the refineries of failed businessmen. Few recognize or remember that those who became vastly wealthy in the nineteenth century in America almost uniformly began as hardworking and extremely frugal young men. Among the Lions of Capitalism or Robber Barons, depending on one's view, only J. P. Morgan can be said to have inherited a fortune as a start in business.

85. **D**   Answer E was true, but not the real reason the Populist Party made itself obsolete. Answer D explains their fatal error in being wooed into supporting the Democratic candidate who then lost the election. The other answers are plausible fabrications based on issues surrounding the Populist Party, William Jennings Bryan, and the attitude of many in the nation at the time regarding women's participation in politics.

86. **A**   Booker T. Washington's founding of the Tuskegee Institute revealed his interest in elevating African-Americans economically as his number one priority, whereas W. E. B. Du Bois demanded political equality including the vote, which had been largely taken away from African-Americans by the disenfranchising practices of southern states after Reconstruction ended with the Com-

promise of 1877. Answer B is nearly the opposite of the truth, and answer C is a fabrication based on the existence of the famous Tuskegee Airmen in World War II. Answer D is also nearly the opposite of the views of the two men as is answer E. Du Bois ultimately became a Marxist and shunned the importance of religion in changing individuals or the world.

87. **E**  Recent research explains Wilson's hesitancy based on depression associated with the death of his first wife, but the economic reasons expressed in answer E still played the most important role among these choices. Of the other choices, only answer C is close to the truth in that Wilson so despised Theodore Roosevelt (TR) as to be almost capable of making decisions based on choosing the opposite of whatever TR wanted, but no serious case can be made that he acted so childishly. The other answers are incorrect in that America had no tradition of foreign involvement, women did not yet have the right to vote, and German submarines had already proved to be a threat to American lives in the sinking of ships like the *Lusitania.*

88. **C**  Answer C is a reference to many actions on the part of Franklin D. Roosevelt (FDR) but above all was his masterful use of the radio in his famous fireside chats. His communication skills in this regard proved the truth of his statement, "The only thing we have to fear is fear itself." All of the other answers are the exact opposite of the truth in that FDR never established clear priorities for the New Deal, he never inspired bipartisanship, he was not trusted by the members of his class, and although he chose many qualified advisers, they never developed a coherent plan for the New Deal. The power of the New Deal lay in the continual activity of the trial-and-error approach that did inspire Americans that their government was handling the situation largely because FDR told them it was. Their confidence in him was his greatest contribution because it was the key to his power.

89. **D**  Answer D conveys the poignant reality of the contribution of Ida B. Wells. Answer A is a reference to Sojourner Truth. Answer B is a reference to Marian Anderson. Answer C is a reference to the first female African-American millionaire, Madam C. J. Walker. Answer E is a reference to Myrlie Evers-Williams, the widow of assassinated National Association for the Advancement of Colored People leader Medgar Evers.

90. **B**  The nation quickly dispensed with wage and price controls after World War II, a fact that boosted the national economy. The Fair Deal did not propose wage and price controls, and no president seriously did so again until Richard Nixon in the 1970s while facing a deep recession. The other answers relate the circumstances that contributed to a massive expansion of the American economy as opposed to a slip back to a depression. These factors, coupled with the fact that the United States was largely unscathed by World War II while the Axis countries and even the other Allied nations were severely damaged by the war, created a head start for the United States in recovering from the Great Depression and World War II over nearly every other nation on earth.

# Index

## How to Use the CD–ROM

The software is not installed on your computer; it runs directly from the CD–ROM. Barron's CD–ROM includes an "autorun" feature that automatically launches the application when the CD is inserted into the CD–ROM drive. In the unlikely event that the autorun feature is disabled, follow the manual launching instructions below.

**Windows®**

1. Click on the Start button and choose "My Computer."
2. Double–click on the CD–ROM drive, which will be named **SAT_US_History.exe**.
3. Double–click **SAT_US_History.exe** to launch the program.

**Mac®**

1. Double–click the CD–ROM icon.
2. Double–click the **SAT_US_History** icon to start the program.

SYSTEM REQUIREMENTS

(Flash Player 10.2 is recommended)

| **Microsoft® Windows®** | **MAC® OS X** |
|---|---|
| Processor: Intel Pentium 4 2.33GHz, Athlon 64 2800+ or faster processor (or equivalent). | Processor: Intel Core™ Duo 1.33GHz or faster processor. |
| Memory: 128MB of RAM. | Memory: 256MB of RAM. |
| Graphics Memory: 128MB. | Graphics Memory: 128MB. |
| Platforms: | Platforms: |
| Windows 7, Windows Vista®, Windows XP. | Mac OS X 10.5 and higher. |
| 1024 × 768 screen resolution | 1024 × 768 screen resolution |